GPAT

Graduate Pharmacy Aptitude Test

Latest Edition
Practice Kit

25 Tests
15 Sectional Test
10 Mock Test

Based On Real Exam Pattern

✓ Thoroughly Revised and Updated

✓ Detailed Analysis of all MCQs

Title   : GPAT Graduate Pharmacy Aptitude Test

Author Name   : Mr. Rohit Manglik

Published By   : EduGorilla Community Pvt. Ltd.

Publishers Address : 12/651, First Floor Opp. Arvindo Park, Near Jama Masjid,
Indira Nagar, Lucknow, Uttar Pradesh-226016, India

Copyright EduGorilla

Disclaimer EduGorilla

ROHIT MANGLIK
CEO, EduGorilla

Dear Applicants,

People say *"Success comes to those who work hard."* But I've seen people working hard for their exams day in and day out for marginal success. While others succeed in their examinations by putting in just half the work. So are they God Gifted? No! I believe that it's because they work *smart* and not just *hard*. Similarly, for your exams, you should strategize your preparation so as to increase the likelihood of success. Well with EduGorilla get ready to increase your *chances of selection* in your exam by *16x*.

EduGorilla helps you in not only working *hard* but also working in a *smart and strategic* manner. With EduGorilla's preparation package, you get a chance to make your exam preparation easy, and a fun learning path towards selection. Finding the right path to your preparations can be difficult if you don't know in which direction to head. Don't worry, we have you covered! EduGorilla will be your guide to success in your journey. With our Preparation Package, you can prepare strategically and beat the exam in just one attempt.

EduGorilla's Preparation Package includes-

• **Test Series**   • **Books**

Our preparation package is handcrafted as per the latest changes, expert opinions, and students' discretion. Thus, enabling you to get through each stage of the selection process for your exam.

Our Books are designed by the teachers and experts of the respective exam with a combined 150+ years of experience; to provide you with easy, efficient, and effective learning. Our books are smart, in the sense that not only do they give you the answers to the questions but also provide similar questions for practice.

EduGorilla's competent Test Series gives you real-time experience and confidence through which you can clear your offline or online exam in just one attempt. We currently host 83,000+ mock tests for 1,440+ competitive and academic exams.

Thus, EduGorilla misses no chance to assist you in your preparation and covers all stages of the exam, so that you don't have to look anywhere else.

We provide complete preparation packages for defense, banking, teaching, and other National & State-Level exams. Hence, it doesn't matter which exam you aspire to because you will reach your success.

ALL THE BEST !

Let EduGorilla be your Guide to Success.

Rohit Manglik,
Founder and CEO, EduGorilla

INTRODUCTION

EduGorilla focuses on guiding students to succeed in their examinations. With that in mind, our book, titled "GPAT : Graduate Pharmacy Aptitude Test", has been drafted through the collective efforts of our distinguished experts with 150+ years of combined experience. This book consists of questions that are created following the latest changes in the syllabus and exam pattern. We compiled the book on the basis of questions that are most likely to appear in the GPAT. Through EduGorilla's "GPAT : Graduate Pharmacy Aptitude Test" your chances of success will increase 16x.

EduGorilla does this through our Complete Preparation Package. This package consists of well-conceptualized and structured content in the form of questions that are tailor-made according to your needs and will help you practice for exams in a smart way by pinpointing all the necessary information. It also provides hints and solutions, along with a smart answer sheet for your self-evaluation. You can assess your shortcomings and work accordingly on areas that may require more of your attention.

EduGorilla promises to help you succeed in your examination and accomplish your dream goals. We believe in our aspirants and see them at the top of the merit list. And the first step towards the top is to start preparing with us. EduGorilla's "GPAT : Graduate Pharmacy Aptitude Test" includes the following attributes.

➤ Well-Researched Content

➤ Top-Notch Quality

➤ Detailed Answers and Analysis

➤ Smart Answer Sheet

➤ Exam Relevant Questions

Therefore, EduGorilla fortifies your preparation and makes it durable enough to help you stand tall and beat the examination.

GPAT

Scan QR code for Eligibility, Exam Pattern, Syllabus and more.

Book ID: 0506

TABLE OF CONTENTS

Pharmaceutical Chemistry

Q.1 Basicity of organic acids can be determined by:

A. Conductometry

B. Refractometry

C. Non-aqueous titration

D. Complexometry

Q.2 For the detection of amino acids in Thin Layer Chromatography, the best reagent is:

A. Ninhydrin

B. Copper sulphate

C. Iodine

D. Potassium permanganate

Q.3 Which of the following cannot be used as carrier gas in gas chromatography?

A. Hydrogen **B.** Nitrogen

C. Helium **D.** Oxygen

Q.4 Gel chromatography method separates different substances depending on their:

A. Molecular size **B.** Molecular weight

C. Density **D.** Viscosity

Q.5 To explain the column efficiency, two theories i.e., plate and rate theory has been proposed. They are related to:

A. HPLC

B. Gel chromatography

C. Gas liquid chromatography

D. Paper chromatography

Q.6 The D and L isomeric forms can be distinguished by:

A. Polarimetry **B.** Refractometry

C. Potentiometry **D.** Conductometry

Q.7 Sodium vapor lamp used in Polarimeter emit light of wavelength (in Angstrom):

A. 5890 & 5896 **B.** 4368 & 4916

C. 5770 & 5791 **D.** 5461 & 4368

Q.8 Porphyrins can be separated using which stationary phase?

A. Magnesium carbonate

B. Alumina

C. Aluminium silicate

D. Silica gel

Q.9 The composition of sephadex used as stationary phase in gel chromatography is:

A. Starch

B. Polyacrylamide

C. Cross-linked dextran

D. Polyvinyl acetate

Q.10 The principle of separation in ion-exchange chromatography is:

A. Adsorption

B. Partition

C. Reversible exchange of functional groups

D. Chemical reaction

Q.11 Immersion refractometer requires how much sample for determination of refractive index?

A. 2-5 ml **B.** 10-15 ml

C. 40-50 ml **D.** More than 100 ml

Q.12 Glacial acetic acid is an example of:

A. Protogenic solvent

B. Protophillic solvent

C. Amphiprotic solvent

D. Aprotic solvent

Q.13 A drug which prevents uric acid synthesis by inhibiting the enzyme xanthine oxidase is:

A. Aspirin **B.** Allopurinol

C. Colchicine **D.** Probenecid

Q.14 Which of the following is required for crystallization and storage of the hormone insulin?

A. Mn^{++} **B.** Mg^{++} **C.** Ca^{++} **D.** Zn^{++}

Q.15 Oxidation of which substance in the body yields the most calories?

A. Glucose **B.** Glycogen

C. Protein **D.** Lipids

Q.16 Milk is deficient in which vitamins?

A. Vitamin C **B.** Vitamin A

C. Vitamin B **D.** Vitamin K

Q.17 Milk is deficient of which mineral?

A. Phosphorus **B.** Sodium

C. Iron **D.** Potassium

Q.18 The degradative processes are categorized under the heading of:

A. Anabolism **B.** Catabolism

C. Metabolism **D.** None of these

Q.19 The cellular organelles called "suicide bags", are:

A. Lysosomes **B.** Ribosomes

C. Nucleolus **D.** Golgi's bodies

Q.20 Mature erythrocytes do not contain:

A. Glycolytic enzymes

B. HMP shunt enzymes

C. Pyridine nucleotide

D. ATP

Q.21 The aldose sugar is:

A. Glyceraldehyde
B. Ribulose
C. Erythrulose
D. Dihydoxyacetone

Q.22 Two sugars which differ from one another only in configuration around a single carbon atom are termed:
A. Epimers
B. Anomers
C. Optical isomers
D. Stereoisomers

Q.23 Compounds having the same structural formula but differing in spatial configuration are known as:
A. Stereoisomers
B. Anomers
C. Optical isomers
D. Epimers

Q.24 Erythromycin contains:
A. Dimethyl amino sugar
B. Trimethyl amino sugar
C. Sterol and sugar
D. Glycerol and sugar

Q.25 The constituent unit of inulin is:
A. Glucose
B. Fructose
C. Mannose
D. Galactose

Q.26 A positive Benedict's test is not given by:
A. Sucrose
B. Lactose
C. Maltose
D. Glucose

Q.27 A positive Seliwanoff's test is obtained with:
A. Glucose
B. Fructose
C. Lactose
D. Maltose

Q.28 Osazones are not formed with the:
A. Glucose
B. Fructose
C. Sucrose
D. Lactose

Q.29 The specific gravity of urine normally ranges from:
A. 0.900-0.999
B. 1.005-1.030
C. 1.000-1.001
D. 1.101-1.120

Q.30 Specific gravity of urine increases in:
A. Diabetes mellitus
B. Chronic glomerulonephritis
C. Compulsive polydypsia
D. Hypercalcemia

Q.31 Number of stereoisomers of glucose is:
A. 4
B. 8
C. 16
D. 20

Q.32 The highest concentrations of fructose are found in:
A. Aqueous humor
B. Vitreous humor
C. Synovial fluid
D. Seminal fluid

Q.33 During starvation, ketone bodies are used as a fuel by:
A. Erythrocytes
B. Brain
C. Liver
D. All of these

Q.34 Catalytic activity of salivary amylase requires the presence of:
A. Chloride ions
B. Hydride ions
C. Iodide ions
D. All of these

Q.35 Honey contains the hydrolytic product of:
A. Lactose
B. Maltose
C. Inulin
D. Starch

Q.36 Cane sugar (Sucrose) injected into blood:

A. Changed to fructose
B. Changed to glucose
C. Undergoes no significant change
D. Changed to glucose and fructose

Q.37 Pentose production is increased in:
A. HMP shunt
B. Uromic acid pathway
C. EM pathway
D. TCA cycle

Q.38 Glucose tolerance is increased in:
A. Diabetes mellitus
B. Adrenalectomy
C. Acromegaly
D. Thyrotoxicosis

Pharmaceutics

Q.39 Which of the following gelatine concentration is used to determine the viscosity of gelatine used for the preparation of soft gelatine capsules?
A. 62/3%
B. 72/3%
C. 52/3%
D. 63/3%

Q.40 Department of Transport Test (DOT) is performed for which of the following?

[Graduate Pharmacy Aptitude Test, 2011]

A. Aerosols
B. Glass containers
C. Capsules
D. None of these

Q.41 Measurement of particle size in pharmaceutical aerosol is by:
(P) Cascade impactor
(Q) Light scatter decay
(R) K-F method
(S) IR
A. Q, R
B. R, S
C. P, S
D. P, Q

Q.42 According to Drugs and Cosmetics act, List of substances that should be sold by retail only on prescription of registered medical practitioner is given in which of the following Schedule?
A. Schedule 'H'
B. Schedule 'V'
C. Schedule 'X'
D. Schedule 'Q'

Q.43 Identify the correct non-flammable propellant:
A. Dichloro monofluoro methane
B. Trichloro mono fluoro methane
C. Di methyl ether
D. Di fluoro methane

Q.44 The first aerosol insecticide was developed by:
A. Goodhue & Sullivan
B. Goodhue
C. Sullivan
D. Franklin

Q.45 The first pharmaceutical aerosol was developed in the year of:
A. 1945
B. 1956
C. 1949
D. 1960

Q.46 Which drug is formulated as first pharmaceutical aerosol?

A. Epinephrine
C. Chloropromazine
B. Codeine
D. Probenecid

Q.47 The dip tube in an aerosol container is made from one of the following:
A. Polypropylene
B. Glass
C. Al
D. Stainless steel

Q.48 Which one of the following device is used to increase the efficiency of drug delivery via aerosols?
A. Tube spacers
B. Metered valves
C. Actuator
D. Pressure valve

Q.49 To dispense inhalation aerosols, which containers are used?
A. Stainless steel
B. Tin plate
C. Glass
D. Al

Q.50 The valve body/housing in an aerosol bottle valve assembly(BOV), is made from:
A. Nylon
B. Poly ethylene
C. Stainless steel
D. None of these

Q.51 Among the propellants used in aerosols, one of the following is used for topical pharmaceutical aerosols:
A. Tri chloro monofluoro methane
B. Di chloro difluoro methane
C. Di chloro tetrafluoro ethane
D. Propane

Q.52 Which one of the following propellant is used in the aerosol for oral use?
A. Propane
B. Oxygen
C. Trichloro mono fluoro methane
D. Methane

Q.53 The identification of propellants in pharmaceutical aerosols is carried out by:
(P) Gas chromatography
(R) Pycnometer
(Q) Tag open cup apparatus
(S) IR spectrophotometer
A. P, Q
B. P, S
C. Q, R
D. R, S

Q.54 Aerosol packaging container must resist the pressure of:
A. 500 PSIG
B. 140-180 PSIG
C. 40 PSIG
D. 20 PSIG

Q.55 The gasket is made up of:
A. Buratherm N 9544/N
B. Neoprene rubber
C. Both (A) and (B)
D. Non of these

Q.56 Manufacturing of aerosol involves:
A. Gas filling
B. Pressure filling
C. Compressed gas filling
D. All the these

Q.57 The nature of propellant is determined by:
A. R-F method
B. Gas Chromatography
C. UVD
D. None of these

Q.58 A viscosity enhancer in ophthalmic preparation is:
A. Poly vinyl alcohol
B. Povidone
C. Dextran
D. Macrogol

Q.59 The pH of human tears is:
A. 7.6
B. 4.5
C. 7.2
D. 9

Q.60 The ophthalmic solution is sterilized by:
A. Autoclave
B. Hot air oven
C. Membrane filter
D. Bacterial filters

Q.61 Which of the following one is used to adjust the isotonicity?
A. Dextrose
B. Boric acid
C. NaCl
D. All of these

Q.62 The ability of a substance dissolves in a given solvent system is depends on:
A. Nature and intensity of the forces present in the solute.
B. Nature and intensity of the forces present in the solvent.
C. Interactions between solute and solvent.
D. All of these

Q.63 Which of the following substances having poor water solubility?
A. Weak electrolytes
B. Non-polar molecules
C. Both (A) and (B)
D. None of these

Q.64 How co-solvents increase the solubility of poorly soluble drugs?
A. By reducing the interfacial tension between the predominant aqueous solution and hydro-phobic solute.
B. By reducing the interfacial tension between solute and solvent.
C. Both (A) and (B)
D. None of these

Q.65 The solubility of weak electrolytes & non-polar substances can be increased by adding water-miscible solvents. This process is known as:
A. Co-solvency
B. Complexation
C. Both (A) and (B)
D. None of these

Q.66 Which of the following co-solvents are used to increase the solubility of a drug?
A. Ethanol
B. Sorbitol
C. Glycerin
D. All of these

Q.67 Which of the following co-solvent is accepted as a co-solvent in parenteral products, but its use in oral liquids is limited?
A. Glycerol formal
B. Glycerol

C. Dimethyl acetamide   **D.** None of these

Q.68 Due to which factor, dimethyl-acetamide is not been used as a co-solvent in oral liquids?
A. Due to objectionable odor
B. Due to objectionable taste
C. Both (A) and (B)
D. None of these

Q.69 Thiomersal belongs to which category preservative:
A. Acidic
B. Mercurial
C. Neutral
D. Quaternary ammonium compounds

Q.70 Which of the following are widely used and excellent preservatives?
A. Quaternary ammonium compounds
B. Mercurial
C. Both (A) and (B)
D. None of these

Q.71 Benzalkonium chloride is categorized as:
A. Acidic preservative
B. Neutral preservative
C. Mercurial preservative
D. Quaternary ammonium compounds

Q.72 At which concentration, phenol act as a preservative?
A. 0.2-0.5   **B.** 0.5-0.8
C. 0.05-0.1   **D.** None of these

Q.73 Which of the following sugar has bitter taste?
A. Glucose   **B.** Sucrose
C. Saccharine   **D.** None of these

Q.74 Which of the following is a synthetic sweetener?
A. Glucose   **B.** Sucrose
C. Sorbitol   **D.** Aspartame

Q.75 To increase the viscosity of the liquid, which of the following agents are used?
A. PVP
B. Methyl Cellulose
C. Sodium Carboxy Methyl Cellulose
D. All of these

Q.76 Which of the following agents are used as flavoring agents?
A. Menthol   **B.** Chloroform
C. Both (A) and (B)   **D.** None fo these

Pharmacognosy

Q.77 Ginkgo biloba is not useful in:
A. Asthma   **B.** Hepatitis/Diabetes
C. Dementia   **D.** Inflammation

Q.78 Forskolin of Coleus forskohlii is used in treatment of:
A. Diabetes   **B.** Ulcers

C. Hepatitis   **D.** Heart disease

Q.79 Callus culture can be easily initiated from which following tissues of the shoot, roots, etc?
A. Sclerenchymatous   **B.** Collenchymatous
C. Parenchymatous   **D.** Fibrous

Q.80 Swelling Index is used to determine amount of following in the crude drugs:
A. Moisture   **B.** Volatile oils
C. Crude fibres   **D.** Mucilage

Q.81 Salicin on hydrolysis yields:
A. Salicylic acid and glucose
B. Salicyl alcohol and glucose
C. Salicyclic acid and galactose
D. Salicyl alcohol and galactose

Q.82 Vanilla belongs to family:
A. Leguminosae   **B.** Asclepidaceae
C. Orchidaceae   **D.** Polypodiaceae

Q.83 Alizarin is an important chemical constituent of:
A. Madder   **B.** Cascara
C. Rhubarb   **D.** Cochineal

Q.84 Sennosides A and B were first isolated in crystalline form by:
A. Fairbairn   **B.** Lemli   **C.** Stoll   **D.** Tutin

Q.85 Stomata present in Senna are of the following type:
A. Anamocytic   **B.** Anisocytic
C. Paracytic   **D.** Diacytic

Q.86 Trichomes with quadracellular head & sessible stalk are seen in:
A. Digitalis   **B.** Belladona
C. Hyoscyamus   **D.** Vasaka

Pharmacology

Q.87 Which of the following anti-arrhythmic drug is having Iodine?
A. Disopyramide   **B.** Flecainide
C. Amiodarone   **D.** Quinidine

Q.88 Which of the following pairs has an interaction beneficial for routine clinical use?
A. Pseudoephedrine and Aluminium hydroxide gel
B. Tetracycline and milk of magnesia
C. MAO inhibitor and Tyramine
D. Chloramphenicol and Tolbutamide

Q.89 The mechanism of action of rifampicin involve:
A. Inhibition of bacterial DNA directed RNA polymerase
B. Inhibition of mycolic acid synthesis
C. Inhibition of protein synthesis
D. Inhibition of trans peptidase

Q.90 Identify a degenerative disorder characterized by disseminated demyelination of nerve fibers of the brain and spinal cord.

A. Muscular dystrophy   **B.** Multiple sclerosis
C. Myasthenia gravis   **D.** Alzheimer's disease

Q.91 HIV infection can be clinically controlled with:

A. Cydarabine   **B.** Acyclovir
C. Zidovudine   **D.** Amantadine

Q.92 Which of the following drug blocks the sodium channel and dissociates slowly?

A. Quinidine   **B.** Lignocaine
C. Flecainide   **D.** Procainamide

Q.93 Simvastatin belongs to:

A. HMG CoA reductase inhibitor type of antilipidemic agent
B. HMG CoA reductase inhibitor type of anticoagulant agent
C. Fibrate type of anticoagulant agent
D. Fibrate type of antilipidemic agent

Q.94 Which of the following organism is the Source for amphotericin?

A. Streptomyces immodosus
B. Streptomyces nodosus
C. Streptomyces griseus
D. Streptomyces aureofaciens

Q.95 Which of the following drug produces gastric irritation after micronization?

A. Phenobarbital   **B.** Tetracycline
C. Erythromycin   **D.** Nitrofurantoin

Q.96 Adult dose of a drug is 150 mg/kg and the drug is available as tablets of 2 mg strength. Calculate the dosed required for a boy of age 14 yrs and weight of 35 kg?

A. 74.9 mg   **B.** 78 mg   **C.** 82 mg   **D.** 80 mg

Q.97 Which of the following method is used to measure respiratory efficiency of cells in cell culture?

A. Fluroscein Diacetate method
B. Reduction of tetrazolium salts
C. Evan's blue method
D. Calcofluor white method

Q.98 Which of the following Dopaminergic agonist used in the treatment of Parkinsonism?

A. Levodopa   **B.** Carbidopa
C. Mirtazapine   **D.** Ropinirole

Q.99 What is the principle involved in the VDRL test?

A. Agglutination   **B.** Precipitation
C. Flocculation   **D.** Opsonisation

Q.100 Prazosin is a derivative of which of the following?

A. Quinazoline   **B.** Phthalazine
C. Quinoline   **D.** Isoquinoline

Q.101 Bladder toxicity is the side effect of which of the following drug?

A. Vincristine   **B.** Cyclophosphamide
C. 5 -Flouro Uracil   **D.** Doxorubicin

Q.102 Which of the following is a prototype of Sedative?

A. Chloral hydrate   **B.** Chloral
C. Chloroquine   **D.** Chlorpheniramie

Q.103 If the half life for decomposition of a drug is 12 hr, how long will it take for 25 mg of the drug to decompose by 30%? Assume that the drug follows first order kinetics at constant temperature:

A. 6.1 hr   **B.** 8.2 hr   **C.** 7.9 hr   **D.** 5.5 hr

Q.104 In the calculation of total lungs volume capacity, Inspiratory capacity occupy amount of air ________.

A. 1200 ml   **B.** 3600 ml   **C.** 2400 ml   **D.** 4800 ml

Q.105 Which of the following amino acid is present in Captopril?

A. Glycine
B. Cysteine
C. Proline
D. Para Amino benzoic acid

Q.106 Pharmacokinetics is:

A. The study of biological and therapeutic effects of drugs.
B. The study of absorption, distribution, metabolism and excretion of drugs.
C. The study of mechanisms of drug action.
D. The study of methods of new drug development.

Q.107 What does "pharmacokinetics" include?

A. Complications of drug therapy
B. Drug biotransformation in the organism
C. Influence of drugs on metabolism processes
D. Influence of drugs on genes

Q.108 Which statement is correct according to pharmacokinet c?

A. Pharmacological effects of drugs
B. Unwanted effects of drugs
C. Chemical structure of a medicinal agent
D. Distribution of drugs in the organism

Q.109 Marfan syndrome is a kind of:

A. Genetic disorder
B. Viral Infection
C. Degenerative neuromuscular disease
D. Muscular contraction

Q.110 The main mechanism of most drugs absorption in GI tract is:

A. Active transport (carrier-mediated diffusion)
B. Filtration (aqueous diffusion)
C. Endocytosis and exocytosis
D. Passive diffusion (lipid diffusion)

Q.111 What kind of substances can't permeate membranes by passive diffusion?

A. Lipid-soluble
B. Non-ionized substances

C. Hydrophobic substances

D. Hydrophilic substances

Q.112 A hydrophilic medicinal agent has the following property:

A. Low ability to penetrate through the cell membrane lipids.

B. Penetrate through membranes by means of endocytosis.

C. Easy permeation through the blood-brain barrier.

D. High reabsorption in renal tubules.

Q.113 What is implied by "active transport"?

A. Transport of drugs trough a membrane by means of diffusion.

B. Transport without energy consumption.

C. Engulf of drug by a cell membrane with a new vesicle formation.

D. Transport against concentration gradient.

Q.114 What does the term "bioavailability" mean?

A. Plasma protein binding degree of substance.

B. Permeability through the brain-blood barrier.

C. Fraction of an uncharged drug reaching the systemic circulation following any route administration.

D. Amount of a substance in urine relative to the initial doze.

Other Subjects

Q.115 Molarity of a solution is expressed as:

A. The number of moles of a solute present in one litre of the solution.

B. The number of moles of a solute present in 1000 gm of the solvent.

C. The number of gram equivalent of solute present in one litre of solution.

D. The ratio of the number of moles of solute to the total number of moles of solute.

Q.116 Which form of drug shows higher solubility?

A. Stable

B. Metastable

C. Unstable

D. All of these

Q.117 Choose the incorrect option regarding Isomerism:

A. They differ in both physical and chemical properties.

B. They have the different molecular formula.

C. There are two types of Isomerism : Structural and Stereo Isomerism.

D. Geometric and optical isomerism are two types of Stereo Isomerism.

Q.118 Solution of known concentration is known:

A. Standard solution

B. Concentration

C. Solution

D. Concentrated solution

Q.119 Which of following is common compound shared by the TCA cycle and Urea cycle?

A. α – Ketoglutarate

B. Succinyl COA

C. Oxaloacetate

D. Fumarate

Q.120 Restriction enzymes were discovered by:

A. Smith and Nathans

B. Alexander Fleming

C. Berg

D. None of these

Q.121 Who is known as the father of Microbiology?

A. Edwin John Butler

B. Ferdinand Cohn

C. Robert Koch

D. Antoni van Leeuwenhoek

Q.122 Leptomeningitis is an inflammatory process that is localized to the interfacing surfaces of the __________ and the ____________, where __________ flows.

A. Dura, Pia, CSF

B. Arachnoid, Pia, Blood

C. Pia, Arachnoid, CSF

D. Dura, Arachnoid, CSF

Q.123 Which is the major process of absorption for more than 90% of drugs?

A. Facilitated diffusion

B. Active transport

C. Endocytosis

D. Passive diffusion

Q.124 Preparations are avoided during pregnancy is:

A. Vitamin E

B. Vitamin A

C. Folic acid

D. Zinc

Q.125 The __________ is the largest organelles of the cell.

A. Nucleus

B. Mitochondria

C. Golgi Apparatus

D. Ribosomes

// Smart Answer Sheet //

Correct — Percentage of students who answered correctly. **Skipped** — Percentage of students who skipped.

Q.	Ans.	Correct	Skipped	Q.	Ans.	Correct	Skipped	Q.	Ans.	Correct	Skipped	Q.	Ans.	Correct	Skipped	Q.	Ans.	Correct	Skipped	Q.	Ans.	Correct	Skipped
1	A	24.19 %	12.12 %	22	A	30.61 %	19.86 %	43	B	15.63 %	30.17 %	64	A	11.9 %	32.31 %	85	C	22.6 %	31.65 %	106	B	56.01 %	29.4 %
2	A	44.82 %	18.43 %	23	A	58.64 %	9.93 %	44	A	21.01 %	31.6 %	65	A	32.91 %	27.32 %	86	D	12.12 %	30.67 %	107	B	34.56 %	29.29 %
3	D	35.44 %	16.01 %	24	A	25.34 %	19.26 %	45	B	20.35 %	31.87 %	66	D	31.71 %	32.09 %	87	C	23.75 %	29.18 %	108	D	36.26 %	31.21 %
4	A	28.74 %	20.96 %	25	B	19.69 %	19.26 %	46	A	21.5 %	31.98 %	67	C	22.22 %	29.45 %	88	A	12.73 %	30.66 %	109	A	15.25 %	27.98 %
5	C	19.47 %	18.49 %	26	A	21.56 %	20.24 %	47	A	34.23 %	31.76 %	68	C	31.43 %	31.76 %	89	A	31.54 %	29.79 %	110	D	29.79 %	31.32 %
6	A	34.28 %	17.89 %	27	B	31.49 %	12.01 %	48	B	23.7 %	31.7 %	69	B	20.34 %	31.38 %	90	B	16.68 %	31.65 %	111	D	22.0 %	30.93 %
7	A	17.44 %	18.49 %	28	C	22.6 %	20.63 %	49	A	23.04 %	30.39 %	70	A	21.45 %	30.28 %	91	C	26.11 %	30.77 %	112	A	27.32 %	31.26 %
8	A	12.45 %	18.82 %	29	B	29.51 %	14.7 %	50	A	14.54 %	31.76 %	71	D	34.01 %	27.26 %	92	C	9.33 %	30.38 %	113	D	29.73 %	28.75 %
9	C	25.56 %	20.24 %	30	A	35.93 %	18.49 %	51	D	16.62 %	28.14 %	72	A	18.05 %	32.2 %	93	A	30.39 %	31.21 %	114	C	47.56 %	31.21 %
10	C	36.09 %	18.71 %	31	C	33.68 %	17.17 %	52	C	28.03 %	32.15 %	73	C	36.64 %	30.17 %	94	B	17.55 %	31.0 %	115	A	39.0 %	26.22 %
11	B	26.33 %	15.74 %	32	D	30.66 %	15.86 %	53	B	22.0 %	29.51 %	74	D	35.33 %	31.15 %	95	D	12.01 %	31.38 %	116	D	15.91 %	27.81 %
12	C	25.12 %	18.6 %	33	B	20.08 %	13.22 %	54	B	31.32 %	30.67 %	75	D	37.96 %	32.31 %	96	A	15.03 %	30.77 %	117	B	27.87 %	27.09 %
13	B	47.78 %	11.68 %	34	A	14.54 %	20.13 %	55	C	27.37 %	31.98 %	76	C	19.03 %	32.04 %	97	B	10.75 %	29.24 %	118	A	48.55 %	27.97 %
14	D	19.2 %	19.47 %	35	C	26.77 %	16.18 %	56	C	16.62 %	32.15 %	77	B	20.46 %	29.29 %	98	D	9.54 %	30.78 %	119	D	9.93 %	27.15 %
15	A	26.55 %	15.96 %	36	C	20.19 %	16.07 %	57	B	26.17 %	23.14 %	78	D	15.47 %	30.61 %	99	B	14.1 %	28.36 %	120	A	24.14 %	27.64 %
16	A	37.41 %	15.74 %	37	A	36.59 %	20.13 %	58	D	17.61 %	30.17 %	79	B	17.17 %	29.68 %	100	A	14.32 %	31.04 %	121	D	34.28 %	27.71 %
17	C	33.19 %	20.24 %	38	B	13.66 %	19.25 %	59	A	26.77 %	28.63 %	80	D	26.17 %	31.43 %	101	B	15.8 %	29.62 %	122	C	13.6 %	27.92 %
18	B	34.45 %	19.58 %	39	A	15.74 %	28.31 %	60	A	25.29 %	32.14 %	81	B	14.54 %	30.61 %	102	B	9.93 %	29.68 %	123	D	31.93 %	27.7 %
19	A	60.56 %	8.23 %	40	A	21.23 %	31.65 %	61	D	34.83 %	24.74 %	82	C	19.53 %	30.5 %	103	A	13.38 %	31.11 %	124	B	14.32 %	27.86 %
20	C	21.61 %	14.48 %	41	D	21.23 %	30.61 %	62	A	8.01 %	31.7 %	83	A	10.81 %	31.15 %	104	B	16.29 %	31.27 %	125	A	28.96 %	27.54 %
21	A	38.84 %	13.05 %	42	A	42.24 %	32.53 %	63	C	34.5 %	31.6 %	84	C	14.04 %	31.16 %	105	C	17.55 %	27.65 %				

//Hints and Solutions//

1. The basicity of organic acids can be determined by conductometry. Conductometry is the measurement of the electrical conductivity of a solution. The conductance is defined as the current flow through the conductor. In other words, it is defined as the reciprocal of the resistance. The unit for the conductance is Seimens (S) which is the reciprocal of Ohm's (Ω^{-1}).

Hence, the correct option is (A).

2. For the detection of amino acids in Thin Layer Chromatography, the best regent is Ninhydrin. Thin-layer chromatography is an important tool for detecting amino acids by a variety of spray reagents. Among these ninhydrin is the most popular due to its high sensitivity. However, ninhydrin produces the same purple/violet color as most amino acids. Ninhydrin is the most widely used chemical reagent for the detection of latent fingermarks on porous surfaces such as paper and cardboard.

Hence, the correct option is (A).

3. Oxygen cannot be used as a carrier gas in gas chromatography. The combination column is used to separate the argon and oxygen peaks; the oxygen is eliminated due to the catalytic reaction with hydrogen (hydrogen is used as the carrier gas), so only the argon peak is eluted. The concentrations of oxygen and argon can be calculated by comparing the output of both columns.

Hence, the correct option is (D).

4. Gel chromatography separates substances according to their molecular size; large molecules emerge first from the bed, while smaller molecules are retarded. The gel matrices in gel chromatography generally do not cause denaturation, and the procedure is performed under very mild conditions.

Hence, the correct option is (A).

5. Gas-liquid chromatography (often just called gas chromatography) is a powerful tool in analysis. It has all sorts of variations in the way it is done - if you want full details, a Google search on gas chromatography will give you scary amounts of information if you need it! This page just looks in a simple introductory way at how it can be carried out.

Hence, the correct option is (C).

6. The D and L isomeric forms can be distinguished by polarimetry. By swapping the groups at the horizontal and vertical positions, enantiomers can be represented. If CO, R, and N groups are arranged in a clockwise fashion about the chiral center, then it is the D- isomer. If the CO, R, and N groups are arranged in an anticlockwise fashion about the chiral center, then it is the L- isomer.

Hence, the correct option is (A).

7. Sodium vapor lamps used in Polarimeter emit light of a wavelength in 5890 & 5896 Angstrom. A sodium-vapor lamp is a gas-discharge lamp that uses sodium in an excited state to produce light at a characteristic wavelength. The low-pressure sodium arc discharge lamp was first made practical around 1920 owing to the development of a type of glass that could resist the corrosive effects of sodium vapor.

Hence, the correct option is (A).

8. Porphyrins can be separated using the magnesium carbonate stationary phase. The porphyrins are a group of highly colored, naturally occurring pigments containing a tetrapyrrole porphine nucleus (Scheme 2) with substituents at the eight β positions of the pyrroles, and/or the four meso positions between the pyrrole rings.

Hence, the correct option is (A).

9. The composition of sephadex used as stationary phase in gel chromatography is cross-linked dextran. Sephadex is a cross-linked dextran gel used for gel filtration. It was launched by Pharmacia in 1959, after development work by Jerker Porath and Per Flodin. These highly specialized gel filtration and chromatographic media are composed of macroscopic beads synthetically derived from the polysaccharide dextran.

Hence, the correct option is (C).

10. The principle of separation in ion-exchange chromatography is a reversible exchange of functional groups. Ion chromatography (or ion-exchange chromatography) is a chromatography process that separates ions and polar molecules based on their affinity to the ion exchanger. It works on almost any kind of charged molecule including large proteins, small nucleotides, and amino acids.

Hence, the correct option is (C).

11. The immersion refractometer requires a 10-15 ml sample for the determination of the refractive index. A dip or immersion refractometer is designed to allow quick measurement of the refractive index of the liquid directly in the vat, without the need of taking samples. The simplest design is a refractometer that you just immerse partially into the solution to make a measurement.

Hence, the correct option is (B).

12. Glacial acetic acid is an example of an amphiprotic solvent. Solvents act both as protophilic or protogenic, e.g., water, ammonia, ethyl alcohol, etc. Acetic acid that contains a very low amount of water (less than 1%) is called anhydrous (water-free) acetic acid or glacial acetic acid. The reason it's called glacial is that it solidifies into solid acetic acid crystals just cooler than room temperature at 16.7 °C, which is ice.

Hence, the correct option is (C).

13. A drug that prevents uric acid synthesis by inhibiting the enzyme xanthine oxidase is allopurinol. Allopurinol is an inhibitor of xanthine oxidoreductase (XOR) and inhibits the generation of uric acid (UA) as the final product of purine catabolism, as well as the resulting generation of superoxide ($O_2(-)$), in humans.

Hence, the correct option is (B).

14. Zn^{++} is required for crystallization and storage of the hormone insulin. Zinc ions are essential for the formation of hexameric insulin and hormone crystallization. Crystallization of the insulin molecule has always been a key activity since the protein is often administered by subcutaneous injections of crystalline insulin formulations. Over the years, insulin has been crystallized and characterized in a number of crystal systems.

Hence, the correct option is (D).

15. Oxidation of glucose substances in the body yields the most calories. Triacylglycerols are highly concentrated stores of metabolic energy because they are reduced and anhydrous. The yield from the complete oxidation of fatty acids is about 9 kcal g-1 (38 kJ g-1), in contrast with about 4 kcal g-1 (17 kJ g-1) for carbohydrates and proteins.

Hence, the correct option is (A).

16. Milk is deficient in Vitamin C. The vitamin that is not present in milk is Vitamin C . Vitamin C is also known as ascorbic acid (AA) or ascorbate. Of the recognized nutritive factors in milk, vitamin C is probably the most sensitive to destruction, due primarily to its oxidation. Such oxidative changes are greatly accelerated by exposure to air at high temperatures and by the presence of metallic catalysts, particularly copper.

Hence, the correct option is (A).

17. Milk is deficient of iron minerals. Milk is a good source of calcium, magnesium, phosphorus, potassium, selenium, and zinc. Many minerals in milk are associated together in the form of salts, such as calcium phosphate. In milk, approximately 67% of the calcium, 35% of the magnesium, and 44% of the phosphate are salts bound within the casein micelle and the remainder are soluble in the serum phase. The fact that calcium and phosphate are associated as salts bound with the protein does not affect the nutritional availability of either calcium or phosphate.

Hence, the correct option is (C).

18. The degradative processes are categorized under the heading of catabolism. Anabolism is classified as a synthetic process and catabolism as a degradative process. Catabolism is the set of metabolic pathways that breaks down molecules into smaller units that are either oxidized to release energy or used in other anabolic reactions. Catabolism breaks down large molecules (such as polysaccharides, lipids, nucleic acids, and proteins) into smaller units (such as monosaccharides, fatty acids, nucleotides, and amino acids, respectively). Catabolism is the breaking-down aspect of metabolism, whereas anabolism is the building-up aspect.

Hence, the correct option is (B).

19. Lysosomes, which are known as suicide bags, are produced by cellular organelle. They are produced by the Golgi body. They consist of a single membrane surrounding powerful digestive enzymes. Lysosomes are known as the suicidal bag of the cell because it is capable of destroying the cell in which it is present. It contains many hydrolytic enzymes which are responsible for the destruction process.

Hence, the correct option is (A).

20. Mature erythrocytes do not contain pyridine nucleotide. Pyridine nucleotides are small molecules comprised of two mononucleotides, adenosine monophosphate (AMP) and nicotinamide mononucleotide (NMN). They consist of oxidized and reduced nicotinamide adenine dinucleotides in their unphosphorylated (NAD+ or NADH) and phosphorylated (NADP+ or NADPH) forms.

Hence, the correct option is (C).

21. Glyceraldehyde, erythrose, ribose, glucose and galactose are some of the examples of aldose. Aldoses are classified on the basis of the number of carbons present in the main chain. Carbohydrates with three carbons are named trioses. Glyceraldehyde is the only triose having one chiral stereocenter.

Hence, the correct option is (A).

22. Two sugars which differ from one another only in configuration around a single carbon atom are termed Epimers. In organic chemistry, an epimer refers to one of a pair of stereoisomers, which differ in configuration at only one stereogenic center. Any other stereogenic centers in the compounds are the same in each one. The sugars glucose and galactose are epimers.

Hence, the correct option is (A).

23. Compounds having the same structural formula but differing in spatial configuration are known as stereoisomers. Isomers are molecules of the same formula but having a different arrangement of their atoms. When isomers differ only by their spatial configuration rather than by a change in their (bonding) structure, they are referred to as stereoisomers or spatial isomers.

Hence, the correct option is (A).

24. Erythromycn contains a dimethyl-amino sugar. Carbomycin contains the first known 3-amino sugar, 3-amino-D-ribose. The amino sugars are believed to be related to the antibiotic activity of these drugs. Erythromycin is a bacteriostatic antibiotic drug produced by a strain of Saccharopolyspora erythraea (formerly Streptomyces erythraeus) and belongs to the macrolide group of antibiotics which consists of Azithromycin, Clarithromycin, Spiramycin and others. It was originally discovered in 1952.

Hence, the correct option is (A).

25. The constituent unit of inulin is Fructose. Inulins are polymers composed mainly of fructose units (fructans), and typically have a terminal glucose. Fructose is a type of sugar known as a monosaccharide. Like other sugars, fructose provides four calories per gram. Fructose is also known as "fruit sugar" because it primarily occurs naturally in many fruits. It also occurs naturally in other plant foods such as honey, sugar beets, sugar cane and vegetables.

Hence, the correct option is (B).

26. A positive Benedict's test is not given by Sucrose. Sucrose (table sugar) contains two sugars (fructose and glucose) joined by their glycosidic bond in such a way as to prevent the glucose undergoing isomerization to an aldehyde, or fructose to alpha-hydroxy-ketone form. Sucrose is thus a non-reducing sugar which does not react with Benedict's reagent.

Hence, the correct option is (A).

27. A positive Seliwanoff's test is obtained with Fructose. Seliwanoff's test is a compound test that separates aldose and ketose sugars. This test is much like Bial's test. his test depends on the rule that, when heated, ketones are more quickly dried out than aldoses.

Hence, the correct option is (B).

28. Osazones are not formed with sucrose. Osazone formation was developed by Emil Fischer, who used the reaction as a test to identify monosaccharides. The formation of a pair of hydrazone functionalities involves both oxidation and condensation reactions. Sucrose, which is non-reducing, does not form an osazone.

Hence, the correct option is (C).

29. The normal range for urine-specific gravity is 1.005 to 1.030. Normal value ranges may vary slightly among different laboratories. Some labs use different measurements or test different samples. If you drink a lot of water, 1.001 may be normal. If you avoid drinking fluids, levels higher than 1.030 may be normal.

Hence, the correct option is (B).

30. The specific gravity of urine increases in diabetes mellitus. Thus, in uncontrolled diabetic patients, the urine specific gravity might reach 1.045 to 1.050 as a result of the above-mentioned loss of glucose in the urine. Specifically, in a patient with poor glycemic control elevated blood glucose levels should result in an increased urine specific gravity.

Hence, the correct option is (A).

31. The 16 stereoisomers of glucose are in their Fischer projection formulas. Those isomers with their C-5 hydroxyl group on the right are called D-, those with it on the left are L-isomers. Each aldohexose is an enantiomer of one other sugar and a diastereomer of the other 14.

Hence, the correct option is (C).

32. The highest concentrations of fructose are found in Seminal fluid. Listen to pronunciation. (SEH-mih-nul FLOO-id) Fluid from the prostate and other sex glands that helps transport sperm out of the man's body during orgasm. Seminal fluid contains sugar as an energy source for sperm.

Hence, the correct option is (D).

33. During starvation, ketone bodies are used as a fuel by Brain. Ketone bodies are synthesized from the acetyl CoA generated by the oxidation of fatty acids in the liver. Fatty acids themselves are not metabolized by the brain, so that ketone bodies (which do cross the blood-brain barrier) are the fuel of choice during starvation.

Hence, the correct option is (B).

34. Catalytic activity of salivary amylase requires the presence of Chloride ions. For salivary amylase, amongst anions and activators, the presence of chloride and bromide ions is the most effective. Amylase is an enzyme found in the saliva of humans and some other mammals. Furthermore, the structures of the chloride binding site disclose that a basic residue is an important component of the site.

Hence, the correct option is (A).

35. Honey contains the hydrolytic product of Inulin. Inulin is a starchy substance found in a wide variety of fruits, vegetables, and herbs, including wheat, onions, bananas, leeks, artichokes, and asparagus. The inulin that is used in supplements most commonly comes from soaking chicory roots in hot water.

Hence, the correct option is (C).

36. Cane sugar (Sucrose) injected into the blood undergoes no significant change. Sugar comes in many different forms- the one most people think of sucrose, also known as cane or table sugar. Made by processing sugar cane and sugar beets, sucrose consists of glucose bound to fructose in a 1:1 ratio. Another common, maligned form of sugar is high-fructose corn syrup (HFCS), synthesized from corn.

Hence, the correct option is (C).

37. Pentose production is increased in HMP shunt. The HMP shunt is an alternative pathway to glycolysis and is used to produce ribose-5-phosphate and nicotinamide adenine dinucleotide phosphate (NADPH). This pathway occurs in the oxidative and non-oxidative phases, each comprising a series of reactions.

Hence, the correct option is (A).

38. Glucose tolerance is increased in Adrenalectomy. Therefore, adrenalectomy led to a slight but statistical increase in metabolic rate as well as glucose tolerance in the diet-induced mice. Effect of high fat diet and adrenalectomy on glucose tolerance. High fat diet led to impairments in glucose tolerance, which was slightly improved by adrenalectomy.

Hence, the correct option is (B).

39. 62/3% gelatine concentration is used to determine the viscosity of gelatine used for the preparation of soft gelatine capsules. Similar to hard gelatin capsule shells, the basic component of a soft gelatin capsule shell is gelatin. A large number of different gelatin shell formulations are available depending on the nature of the liquid fill matrix. Most commonly, the gelatin is alkali- (or base-) processed (type B) gelatin and it normally constitutes 40% of the wet molten gel mass.

Hence, the correct option is (A).

40. Department of Transport Test (DOT) is performed for aerosols. For aerosol cans for any requirements of dot require approval at. Accessories Jerricans Pails Glass Packaging Metal Packaging Plastic Packaging. For aerosol cans, the carrier must inspect each hire car containing the hazardous material, transfer date otherwise handle hazardous materials during transportation.

Hence, the correct option is (A).

41. Measurement of particle size in pharmaceutical aerosol is by Cascade impactor and Light scatter decay. Aerosols are solid or liquid particles with a radius of 0.001-50 μm suspended in the atmosphere, and most particle radius range from 0.01 to 5 μm. Aerosols play an important role in many atmospheric processes. A cascade impactor measures the reach range of a particulate substance as it moves through an opening with the use of aerosol. Light scatter decay is a technique in physics that can be used to determine the size distribution profile of small particles in suspension or polymers in solution.

Hence, the correct option is (D).

42. According to the Drugs and Cosmetics act, a List of substances that should be sold by retail only on prescription of the registered medical practitioners is given Schedule 'H'. Schedule H is a class of prescription drugs in India appearing as an appendix to the Drugs and Cosmetics Rules, 1945 introduced in 1945. These are drugs that cannot be purchased over the counter without the prescription of a qualified doctor.

Hence, the correct option is (A).

43. Trichloro mono fluoro methane is a correct non-flammable propellant. The presence of greater than 5% water in solutions that contain trichloromonofluoromethane may lead to hydrolysis of the propellant and the formation of traces of hydrochloric acid, which may be irritant to the skin or cause corrosion of metallic canisters.

Hence, the correct option is (B).

44. The first aerosol insecticide was developed by Goodhue & Sullivan. The successful development of mass-produced aerosols occurred in the USA during the late 40s. It was an insecticide called the 'bug bomb' developed by Goodhue & Sullivan. American soldiers used it to fight insect-borne diseases in the Pacific; 50 million units were produced during World War II.

Hence, the correct option is (A).

45. The first pharmaceutical aerosol was developed in the year of 1956. In 1956, Riker Laboratories, Inc., (now 3 M Drug Delivery Systems) introduced the first pressurized metered-dose inhaler (MDI). In many respects, the introduction of the MDI marked the beginning of the modern pharmaceutical aerosol industry.

Hence, the correct option is (B).

46. The drug is formulated as first pharmaceutical aerosol Epinephrine. Epinephrine drug is used to treat severe allergic reactions (anaphylaxis) to insect stings or bites, foods, drugs, and other allergens. Epinephrine auto-injectors may be kept on hand for self-injection by a person with a history of severe allergic reaction.

Hence, the correct option is (A).

47. The dip tube in an aerosol container is made from Polypropylene.

Dip tubes: The dip tubes are made from polyethylene or polypropylene.

The dip tube is used for the following purposes:

- It conveys the liquid from the bottom of the container to the valve at the top.
- It prevents the propellant to come out without dispensing the contents of the package.

Hence, the correct option is (A).

48. Metered valves is used to increase the efficiency of drug delivery via aerosols. Metered-dose inhalers (MDIs), dry powder inhalers (DPIs), and nebulizers are popular modes of aerosol delivery. A spacer is an external device that is attached to an MDI to allow for better drug delivery by enhanced actuation and inhalation coordination.

Hence, the correct option is (B).

49. To dispense inhalation aerosols, Stainless steel containers are used.

- No coating required
- Highly inactive
- Vinyl resins are not used inside coating because of heat sterilized so epoxy is widely used.
- It is very costly it is only its disadvantage.
- It is used for mainly inhalation aerosols.

Hence, the correct option is (A).

50. The valve body /housing in an aerosol bottle valve(BOV) assembly is made from Nylon. The flexible BOV bag film is made from 4 materials (InsidePP, Nylon, Aluminum and PET-Outside). The BOV bag is heat-bonded to the polypropylene valve housing and has a gusseted bottom design for extra drop strength.

Hence, the correct option is (A).

51. Among the propellants used in aerosols, propane is used for topical pharmaceutical aerosols. Hydrocarbon propellants are used in topical pharmaceutical aerosols because of their environmental acceptance, low toxicity, and lack of reactivity. They are useful in three-phase (two-layer) aerosol systems because they are immiscible with water and have a density of less than 1.

Hence, the correct option is (D).

52. Trichloro mono fluoro methane propellant is used in the aerosol for oral use.

Chlorofluorohydrocarbon:- It is mainly used for oral and inhalation preparation. Examples are trichloro mono fluoro methane (Propellant 11), dichlorodifluoromethane (propellant 12), dichloro tetra fluoro methane (propellant 114).

Hence, the correct option is (C).

53. The identification of propellants in pharmaceutical aerosols is carried out by gas chromatography and IR spectrophotometer. Infrared spectroscopy is a versatile method for the determination of fingerprinting and identification of pharmaceutical compounds and functional groups within molecules. It measures energy absorption across the infrared frequency range. Gas, liquid, or solid pharmaceutical samples can be analyzed by infrared spectroscopy. Gas chromatography (GC) is a common type of chromatography used in analytical chemistry for separating and analyzing compounds that can be vaporized without decomposition.

Hence, the correct option is (B).

54. The aerosol packaging container must resist the pressure of 140-180 PSIG. Aerosol containers are generally made of glass, metals (e.g., tin-plated steel, aluminium, and stainless steel), and plastics. The materials of aerosol containers to be selected should be able to withstand high pressure. Thus the aerosol containers must withstand pressure as high as 140 to 180 PSIG (pounds per sq).

Hence, the correct option is (B).

55. The gasket is made up of bure-N and neoprene rubber. Typically used in marine and other outdoor applications, neoprene rubber has the ability to resist moderate levels of sunlight, ozone and other weather elements, as well as greases, fats and oils. Neoprene rubber can also be used in refrigerant applications. This polymer is able to withstand a wide range of temperatures, from negative 31 to 250 degrees Fahrenheit. Buratherm N 9544/N is a soft gasket material with the most up-to-date combination of graphite with reinforcement of para-aramid fiber and reduced fillers. Gasket sheet with highly effective anti-stick coating on both sides.

Hence, the correct option is (C).

56. Manufacturing of aerosol involves compressed gas filling. In the compressed gas filling method, a compressed gas propellant is used. the compressed gas propellant is filled into the aerosol container through a pressure gauge from a large container. Before filling compressed gas propellants, the material is filled inside the aerosol container and assembly is fitted at its place.

Hence, the correct option is (C).

57. The nature of propellant is determined by Gas Chromatography. Propellants used in medicinal and pharmaceutical aerosols require special handling and, in many instances, special test procedures. Gas chromatography is used to determine the identity of the propellant and the composition when a blend of propellants is used.

Hence, the correct option is (B).

58. A viscosity enhancer in ophthalmic preparation is macrogol. Macrogol (or macrogols) is a laxative taken to treat constipation (difficulty pooing). It's also taken to help clear a build-up of hard poo in your bowel, which can happen if you've been constipated for a long time (fecal impaction).

Macrogol, also known as polyethylene glycol (PEG), is used as a medication to treat constipation in children and adults. It is also used to empty the bowels before a colonoscopy. It is taken by mouth. Benefits usually occur within three days. Generally, it is only recommended for up to two weeks.

Hence, the correct option is (D).

59. The pH of human tears is 7.6. The article "Human Tear pH" by Carney and Hill in the May Archives (94:821-824, 1976) concludes, among other things, that tears are more acid in the morning, taken from a yet unopened eye (average pH, 7.25) than later in the day (pH, 7.45; P <. 001).

Hence, the correct option is (A).

60. The ophthalmic solution is sterilized by autoclave. An autoclave is used in medical and laboratory settings to sterilize lab equipment and waste. Autoclave sterilization works by using heat to kill microorganisms such as bacteria and spores. Pressurization allows the steam to reach the high temperatures that are required for sterilization.

Hence, the correct option is (A).

61. Dextrose, boric acid and NaCl are used to adjust the isotonicity.

Dextrose: Solutions that have the same osmotic pressure as that of body fluids are said to be isotonic with the body fluid. Body fluids such as blood and tears have osmotic pressure corresponding to that of 0.9% NaCl or dextrose aqueous solution; thus, a 0.9% Nacl or 5 %, dextrose solution is called as isosmotic or isotonic.

Boric acid: The molecular weight of boric acid is 62, and it is a non-ionizing substance Solution: · By applying formulae for non-ionizing substances; W/V % of boric acid required to make isotonic solution = 0.03% x gram molecular weight = 0.03 x 62

= 1.86

So, 1.86 gms of boric acid is required to make 100ml isotonic.

NaCl: A 0.9% NaCl solution is said to be isotonic when blood cells reside in such a medium, the intracellular and extracellular fluids are in osmotic equilibrium across the cell membrane, and there is no net influx or efflux of water.

Hence, the correct option is (D).

62. The ability of a substance to dissolve in a given solvent system depends on the nature and intensity of the forces present in the solute. Solubility is a property referring to the ability of a given substance, the solute, to dissolve in a solvent. It is measured in terms of the maximum amount of solute dissolved in a solvent at equilibrium.

Hence, the correct option is (A).

63. Weak electrolytes and Non-polar molecules substances are having poor water solubility. Weak acids and weak bases are weak electrolytes. In contrast, strong acids, strong bases, and salts are strong electrolytes. Note a salt may have low solubility in water, yet still be a strong electrolyte because the amount that does dissolve completely ionizes in water. Nonpolar molecules do not dissolve easily in water. They are described as hydrophobic, or water-fearing. When put into polar environments, such as water, nonpolar molecules stick together and form a tight membrane, preventing water from surrounding the molecule.

Hence, the correct option is (C).

64. Co-solvents can increase the solubility of poorly soluble drugs by reducing the interfacial tension between the predominant aqueous solution and hydrophobic solute. This process is known as co-solvency, and the solvents used to increase solubility are known as cosolvent. The Co-solvent system works by reducing the interfacial tension between the aqueous solution and hydrophobic solute. It is also commonly referred to as solvent blending.

Hence, the correct option is (A).

65. The solubility of weak electrolytes & non-polar substances can be increased by adding water-miscible solvents. This process is known as Co-solvency. Weak electrolytes and nonpolar molecules frequently have poor water solubility. Their solubility usually can be increased by the addition of a water-miscible solvent in which the drug has good solubility. This process is known as co-solvency.

Hence, the correct option is (A).

66. Ethanol, sorbitol and glycerin co-solvents are used to increase the solubility of a drug. The advantage of cosolvent technology enhancing drug solubility in a liquid-based formulation includes convenience, removing the need for mixing solvent before administration; safety, avoiding contamination in the dispensing process; inexpensive, no need for expensive pharmaceutical technology for the formulation of the dosage form. The most frequently used low-toxicity cosolvents for parenteral use are propylene glycol, ethanol, glycerin, polyethylene glycol (PEG), dimethyl sulfoxide (DMSO), and dimethylacetamide (DMA).

Hence, the correct option is (D).

67. Dimethyl acetamide co-solvent is accepted as a co-solvent in parenteral products, but its use in oral liquids is limited. Dimethylacetamide is commonly used as a solvent for fibers (e.g., polyacrylonitrile, spandex) or in the adhesive industry. It is also employed in the production of pharmaceuticals and plasticizers as a reaction medium.

Hence, the correct option is (C).

68. Dimethyl-acetamide is not been used as a co-solvent in oral liquids due to some factors these are:

Objectionable odor: "Objectionable odor" means any odor present in the ambient air that, by itself or in combination with other odors, gases, or vapors, is offensive, foul, unpleasant, or repulsive.

Objectionable taste: From a rigorous point of view, therefore, the taste of drinking water can be defined as the sensation that is due to the presence of substances in water that has negligible vapour pressures and negligible odors. It follows that taste tests should be performed only on water samples that are free of odor.

Hence, the correct option is (C).

69. Thiomersal belongs to the mercurial category preservative. Thiomersal, also called thimerosal, is an ethyl mercury derivative used as a preservative to prevent bacterial contamination of multidose vaccine vials after they have been opened. Exposure to low doses of thiomersal has essentially been associated with hypersensitivity reactions. The pharmaceutical corporation Eli Lilly and Company gave thiomersal the trade name Merthiolate.

Hence, the correct option is (B).

70. Quaternary ammonium compounds are widely used and excellent preservatives. Quaternary ammonium compounds (commonly known as quats or QACs) are cationic surfactants (surface active agents) that combine bactericidal and virucidal (generally only enveloped viruses) activity with good detergency and, therefore, cleaning ability.

Hence, the correct option is (A).

71. Benzalkonium chloride is categorized as Quaternary ammonium compounds. Benzalkonium chloride (BZK, BKC, BAK, BAC), also known as alkyl dimethyl benzyl ammonium chloride (ADBAC) and by the trade name Zephiran, is a type of cationic surfactant. It is an organic salt classified as a quaternary ammonium compound.

Hence, the correct option is (D).

72. The phenol act as a preservative at the concentration of 0.2-0.5. M-cresol, a phenol derivative, is frequently utilized as a preservative in numerous antivenom preparations in concentrations that range between 0.15 and 0.35 g% (4, 7, 13). used as antiseptic and disinfectant. In 2-5% of an aqueous solution, phenol is used as an antibacterial and antiviral and antifungal disinfectant. This can be enough to kill the micro bacterium and anthrax spores. They are mainly used as disinfectants of equipment or organic matter.

Hence, the correct option is (A).

73. Saccharine sugar has a bitter taste. Hereby functional expression experiments in human embryonic kidney cells that saccharin and acesulfame K activate two members of the human TAS2R family (hTAS2R43 and hTAS2R44) at concentrations known to stimulate bitter taste. These receptors are expressed in tongue taste papillae. Humans can't break down saccharin, so it leaves your body unchanged. It's around 300–400 times sweeter than regular sugar, so you only need a small amount to get a sweet taste. However, it can have an unpleasant, bitter aftertaste. This is why saccharin is often mixed with other low or zero-calorie sweeteners.

Hence, the correct option is (C).

74. Aspartame is a synthetic sweetener. Aspartame is an artificial sweetener, sold under brand names such as NutraSweet and Equal, that has been in use in the United States since the early 1980s. It is used in many foods and beverages because it is much sweeter than sugar, so much less of it can be used to give the same level of sweetness.

Hence, the correct option is (D).

75. To increase the viscosity of the liquid, PVP, Methyl Cellulose and Sodium Carboxy Methyl Cellulose agents are used. The K value of PVP is actually the characteristic value related to the relative viscosity of PVP aqueous solution, and the viscosity is the physical quantity related to the molecular weight of the polymer, so the K value can be used to characterize the average molecular weight of PVP. Methylcellulose is generally used as a thickening food additive. When methylcellulose is dissolved in a culture medium at a concentration of 3%, it becomes a very viscous solution. We found that this kind of high viscous solution can rapidly form the cell aggregation state which helps to form MCS. Sodium Carboxy Methyl Celluloseserves as a viscosity modifier, thickener, emulsion stabilizer, and water-retention agent (Li et al. 2009). Na-CMC is also used in the production of hydrogels with biomedical applications (drug delivery, tissue engineering) (Ali et al. 2016).

Hence, the correct option is (D).

76. Menthol and Chloroform both agents are used as flavoring agents. menthol, also called peppermint camphor, is terpene alcohol with a strong minty, cooling odor and taste. It is obtained from peppermint oil or is produced synthetically by

hydrogenation of thymol. Flavoring agents are additive substances that give a tablet an additional taste or flavor. In particular, they help in masking unpleasant tastes (e.g., bitter or pungent taste) of drugs/excipients and instead improve the quality of their taste.

Hence, the correct option is (C).

77. Ginkgo biloba is not useful in Hepatitis/Diabetes. Ginkgo might interfere with the management of diabetes. If you have diabetes, monitor your blood sugar closely. Despite widespread use, ginkgo has not been specifically linked to liver injury, either in the form of transient serum enzyme elevations or clinically apparent acute liver injury. Indeed, ginkgo is sometimes used to treat acute or chronic liver injury. Gingko demonstrates some degree of inhibition of cytochrome P450 activity in vitro, but in doses used in humans, it appears to have little effect on drug metabolism. When the liver is inflamed or damaged, its function can be affected. Heavy alcohol use, toxins, some medications, and certain medical conditions can cause hepatitis.

Hence, the correct option is (B).

78. Forskolin of Coleus forskohlii is used in the treatment of heart disease. Forskolin is a herbal supplement that can be used as a natural remedy for treatment in cancer, obesity, glaucoma, allergies and asthma, heart failure, intestinal spasms, painful cramps during your period (dysmenorrhea), irritable bowel syndrome, urinary tract infection, high blood pressure (hypertension), chest pain (angina), difficulty falling asleep (insomnia) and convulsions. Forskolin is available under the following different brand names: coleus forskohlii, colforsin, makandi, maohouqiaoruihua, and pashanabhedi.

Hence, the correct option is (D).

79. Callus culture can be easily initiated from Collenchymatous tissues of the shoot, roots, etc. The collenchymatous tissues are stretched during the elongation of cells to facilitate growth. Due to the presence of collenchyma, the leaves and stems of herbs can bend by wind but do not break.

Note: Collenchyma is a flexible tissue that provides support to the soft and nonwoody parts of the plants.

Hence, the correct option is (B).

80. Swelling Index is used to determine the amount of mucilage in the crude drugs. The swelling index is used to determine the purity of oil or a particular material. For a particular oil, the swelling index is constant. As a result of this is the swelling index is found alternate to the original material then there are some impurities present in that particular material. Mucilage is a thick, gluey substance produced by nearly all plants and some microorganisms. These microorganisms include protists who use it for their locomotion.

Hence, the correct option is (D).

81. Salicin on hydrolysis yields Salicyl alcohol and glucose. The latter can be converted to sialic acid. In 1875, sodium salicylate was first used for the treatment of rheumatic fever and as an antipyretic. Acetylsalicylic acid was synthesized by Hoffman and introduced into medicine in 1899 under the name aspirin, after the demonstration of its anti-inflammatory effects.

Hence, the correct option is (B).

82. Vanilla belongs to the family Orchidaceae. Orchidaceae commonly called the orchid family, is a diverse and widespread family of flowering plants, with blooms that are often colourful and fragrant. Vanilla is a plant. The bean (fruit) is commonly used to make flavoring, but it is also used to make medicine. People take vanilla to treat intestinal gas and fever. They also use it to increase sexual desire (as an aphrodisiac).

Hence, the correct option is (C).

83. Alizarin is an important chemical constituent of madder. Alizarin is the main ingredient for the manufacture of the madder lake pigments known to painters as rose madder and alizarin crimson. A notable use of alizarin in modern times is as a staining agent in biological research because it stains free calcium and certain calcium compounds a red or light purple color.

Hence, the correct option is (A).

84. Sennosides A and B were first isolated in crystalline form by Stoll. Stoll et al. (1941) isolated two active crystalline glycosides, sennoside A and sennoside B. They both hydrolyse to give two molecules of glucose and the aglycones sennidin A and B. They both hydrolyse to give two molecules of glucose and the aglycones sennidin A and B. Sennidin A is dextrorotatory and B is its mesoform formed by intramolecular compensation.

Hence, the correct option is (C).

85. Stomata present in senna are of paracytic type. Anisocytic and paracytic stomata are common in all species. In addition to anisocytic and paracytic types, anomocytic stomata are found in Senna sophera and hexacytic stomata are observed in S.

Hence, the correct option is (C).

86. Trichomes is the term used to refer to tiny outgrowths from the plant epidermis. They are either unicellular or multicellular (epidermal cells), which means that some require a microscope to take a closer look.

Unicellular glandular trichomes:

Sessile trichomes: Without stalk - Piper betel, Vasaka Without stalk - Piper betel, Vasaka.

Hence, the correct option is (D).

87. Amiodarone anti-arrhythmic drug is having Iodine. Amiodarone is a potent antiarrhythmic drug that is used to treat ventricular and supraventricular tachyarrhythmias. It is a benzofuran-derived, iodine-rich compound with some structural similarity to thyroxine (T4). Amiodarone contains approximately 37% iodine by weight.

Hence, the correct option is (C).

88. Pseudoephedrine and Aluminium hydroxide gel has an interaction beneficial for routine clinical use. The absorption rate of pseudoephedrine, measured by its urinary excretion rate, was reliably increased by the aluminum hydroxide gel, probably because the antacid raised the GI pH, thereby increasing the amount of pseudoephedrine available in the nonionized form, which is more readily absorbable.

Hence, the correct option is (A).

89. The mechanism of action of rifampicin involves inhibition of bacterial DNA-directed RNA polymerase.

Mechanism of action: Rifampin is thought to inhibit bacterial DNA-dependent RNA polymerase, which appears to occur as a result of drug binding in the polymerase subunit deep within the DNA/RNA channel, facilitating direct blocking of the elongating RNA. This effect is thought to be concentration-related.

Hence, the correct option is (A).

90. A degenerative disorder characterized by disseminated demyelination of nerve fibers of the brain and spinal cord is multiple sclerosis.

It is an autoimmune inflammatory disease of the brain and spinal cord. In this condition, the coating around nerve fibers is damaged, causing a range of symptoms.

It's normally diagnosed in people between the ages of 20 and 40 and affects almost three times as many women as men.

The most common early symptoms of multiple sclerosis are:

- Fatigue
- Vision problems
- Tingling and numbness
- Vertigo and dizziness
- Muscle weakness and spasms
- Problems with balance and coordination

Hence, the correct option is (B).

91. HIV infection can be clinically controlled with zidovudine. Zidovudine (ZDV), also known as azidothymidine (AZT), is an antiretroviral medication used to prevent and treat HIV/AIDS. It is generally recommended for use with other antiretrovirals. It may be used to prevent mother-to-child spread during birth or after a needlestick injury or other potential exposure.

Hence, the correct option is (C).

92. Flecainide drug blocks the sodium channel and dissociates slowly. Flecainide is used to prevent certain types of life-threatening irregular heartbeats. Flecainide is in a class of medications called antiarrhythmics. It works by slowing electrical signals in the heart to stabilize the heart rhythm. Its use is only recommended in those with dangerous arrhythmias or when significant symptoms cannot be managed with other treatments.

Hence, the correct option is (C).

93. Simvastatin belongs to the drug class known as HMG-CoA reductase inhibitors, also called statins. A class of drugs is a group of medications that work in a similar way. These drugs are often used to treat similar conditions. HMG-CoA reductase is the rate-limiting step in cholesterol synthesis by the liver and inhibition of its activity causes a significant decrease in total and LDL cholesterol levels. The statins also have minor effects on triglyceride or HDL levels.

Hence, the correct option is (A)

94. Streptomyces nodosus organism is the Source for amphotericin. Amphotericin B was isolated from Streptomyces nodosus in 1955 at the Squibb For Medical Research Institute from cultures isolated from the streptomycete obtained from the river bed of Orinoco in that region of Venezuela and came into medical use in 1958.

Hence, the correct option is (B).

95. Nitrofurantoin drug produces gastric irritation after micronization. Nitrofurantoin is used to treat urinary tract infections. Nitrofurantoin is in a class of medications called antibiotics. It works by killing bacteria that cause infection. Antibiotics will not work for colds, flu, or other viral infections. Micronization is the process of reducing a bulk solid material's particle size to the micron or submicron level. Simply put, finer particles increase a material's surface area, which increases bioavailability, especially in poorly soluble materials.

Hence, the correct option is (D).

96. The adult dose of a drug is 150 mg/kg and the drug is available as tablets of 2 mg strength. A boy of age 14 yrs and weight of 35 kg. So, Currently, evidence suggests that a more reliable way to establish how dose relates to bodyweight is through the use of nonlinear relationships, such as, for example, allometric scaling:

$$P_{child} = P_{adults} \times \left(\frac{WT}{70}\right)$$

where P is the parameter of interest, WT the bodyweight of the individual child.

So, by putting the values given we get,

$$P_{child} = 150 \times \left(\frac{35}{70}\right)$$

$$P_{child} = 15 \times 5$$

$$P_{child} = 75$$

Hence, the correct option is (A).

97. The reduction of tetrazolium salts method is used to measure the respiratory efficiency of cells in cell culture. Tetrazolium salt compounds are commonly used to detect viability. There are two basic categories of tetrazolium salts:

- Cationic salts can permeate viable eukaryotic cells through electrostatic interactions with the anionic plasma membrane. Cationic tetrazolium salts include MTT (3-(4,5-dimethyl thiazol-2-yl)-2,5-diphenyltetrazolium bromide).
- Anionic tetrazolium salts require an electron-coupling reagent to permeate live cells.

Hence, the correct option is (B).

98. Ropinirole dopaminergic agonist used in the treatment of Parkinsonism. Ropinirole is a nonergoline dopamine agonist that binds to dopamine D2-receptors; the drug is indicated for use in the symptomatic treatment of early and late Parkinson's disease (PD). Ropinirole is rapidly absorbed after oral administration and undergoes extensive hepatic metabolism to active metabolites.

Hence, the correct option is (D).

99. The principle involved in the VDRL test is precipitation. The basis of the VDRL test is that body produces antibodies when infected, and in this test, the antibody is detected by subjecting the serum to an antigen, which is composed of a colorless alcoholic solution of beef cardiolipin, cholesterol, and lecithin.

Hence, the correct option is (B).

100. Prazosin is a quinazoline derivative with a dual mechanism of antihypertensive activity: direct smooth muscle relaxant effects and peripheral α1-adrenergic receptor inhibition. The efficacy of the drug is similar to that of hydralazine, but prazosin is less likely to cause tolerance.

Hence, the correct option is (A).

101. Bladder toxicity is the side effect of cyclophosphamide drugs. Cyclophosphamide is in a class of medications called alkylating agents. When cyclophosphamide is used to treat cancer, it works by slowing or stopping the growth of cancer cells in your body. When cyclophosphamide is used to treat nephrotic syndrome, it works by suppressing your body's immune system.

Hence, the correct option is (B).

102. Chloral is a prototype of Sedative. CHLORAL HYDRATE (kl or al HI drate) is used for the short-term treatment of insomnia. It may also be used to decrease anxiety or make you sleep before a procedure or test and may be used with painkillers to reduce pain and anxiety after surgery. Sedatives are a type of prescription medication that slows down your brain activity. They're typically used to make you feel more relaxed.

Hence, the correct option is (B).

103. The half-life of a drug is an estimate of the period of time that it takes for the concentration or amount in the body of that drug to be reduced by exactly one-half (50%). The symbol for the half-life is t½. If the half-life for decomposition of a drug is 12 hr it will take 6.1 hr for 25 mg of the drug to decompose by 30%.

Hence, the correct option is (A).

104. In the calculation of total lungs volume capacity, Inspiratory capacity occupies an amount of air 3600 ml. The total lung capacity (TLC) is the volume of gas in the lung at the end of a full inspiration. It is either calculated from:

- TLC = RV+IVC, or
- TLC = FRC+IC;

The latter is the preferred method in body plethysmography. It can also be measured directly by the radiologic technique. The total lung capacity is approximately 5 L. Of this, 1.5 L, the residual volume, remains at the end of forced expiration. The volume of gas, 3.5 L, that can be inhaled from forced expiration to forced inspiration is the vital capacity.

Hence, the correct option is (B).

105. Proline amino acid is present in Captopril. Captopril is a L-proline derivative in which L-proline is substituted on nitrogen with a (2S)-2-methyl-3-sulfanylpropanoyl group. It is used as an anti-hypertensive ACE inhibitor drug. It has a role as an EC 3.4.

15.1 (peptidyl-dipeptidase A) inhibitor and an antihypertensive agent.

Hence, the correct option is (C).

106. Pharmacokinetics is the study of absorption, distribution, metabolism and excretion of drugs. Pharmacokinetics is currently defined as the study of the time course of drug absorption, distribution, metabo- lism, and excretion. Clinical pharmacokinetics is the application of pharmacokinetic principles to the safe and effective therapeutic management of drugs in an individual patient.

Hence, the correct option is (B).

107. Pharmacokinetics include drug biotransformation in the organism. Process of the uptake of drugs by the body, the biotransformation they undergo, the distribution of the drugs and their metabolites in the tissues, and the elimination of the drugs and their metabolites from the body over a period of time.

Hence, the correct option is (B).

108. The distribution of drugs in the organism is the correct statement according to pharmacokinetic. Pharmacokinetics is currently defined as the study of the time course of drug absorption, distribution, metabolism, and excretion. Primary goals of clinical pharmacokinetics include enhancing efficacy and decreasing toxicity of a patient's drug therapy.

Hence, the correct option is (D).

109. Marfan Syndrome is a kind of Genetic disorder.

- Marfan syndrome affects the heart, eyes, blood vessels, and bones.
- People with Marfan syndrome are tall and thin with long arms, legs, fingers, and toes.
- Marfan syndrome is an inherited disorder that affects connective tissue.
- The fibers that support and anchor your organs and other structures in your body.
- Marfan syndrome is caused by a mutation in a gene called FBN1.

Hence, the correct option is (A).

110. The main mechanism of most drugs absorption in GI tract is Passive diffusion (lipid diffusion). The most common mechanism of absorption for drugs is passive diffusion. This process can be explained through the Fick law of diffusion, in which the drug molecule moves according to the concentration gradient from a higher drug concentration to a lower concentration until equilibrium is reached.

Hence, the correct option is (D).

111. Hydrophilic substances can't permeate membranes by passive diffusion. Cellular membranes are often composed of a phospholipid bilayer. In passive diffusion, substances move from an area of higher concentration to an area of lower concentration in a process called diffusion. A physical space in which there is a different concentration of a single substance is said to have a concentration gradient.

Hence, the correct option is (D).

112. A hydrophilic medicinal agent has the low ability to penetrate through the cell membrane lipids. A polar substance or drug mixes well with water, but not with organic solvents and lipids. Dissolves readily in water. Hydrophilic compounds exist in an ionized or polar form and have difficulty crossing biological membranes (except capillary membranes).

Hence, the correct option is (A).

113. During active transport, substances move against the concentration gradient, from an area of low concentration to an area of high concentration. This process is "active" because it requires the use of energy (usually in the form of ATP). It is the opposite of passive transport.

Hence, the correct option is (D).

114. Bioavailability means a fraction of an uncharged drug reaching the systemic circulation following any route administration. Bioavailability refers to the extent and rate at which the active moiety (drug or metabolite) enters systemic circulation, thereby accessing the site of action. The bioavailability of a drug is largely determined by the properties of the dosage form, which depend partly on its design and manufacture.

Hence, the correct option is (C).

115. Molarity of a solution is expressed number of moles of a solute present in one litre of the solution. It is defined as the total number of moles of solute per litre of solution. Molarity is also termed as molar concentration. One molar is the molarity of a solution where one gram of solute is dissolved in a litre of solution. The units of molarity are mol dm^{-3}, mol l^{-1} or one can simply write M.

Hence, the correct option is (A).

116. Stable, Unstable and Metastable are the form of drug that shows higher solubility. Metastable forms are more soluble than the corresponding stable polymorphic forms, but they transform to the more thermodynamically stable form in a relatively short time, and thus it is necessary to monitor the polymorphic transformation during formulation, manufacturing, and storage of dosage forms.

Hence, the correct option is (D).

117. There are three main types of chemical formulas: empirical, molecular and structural. Empirical formulas show the simplest whole-number ratio of atoms in a compound, molecular formulas show the number of each type of atom in a molecule, and structural formulas show how the atoms in a molecule are bonded to each other.

Hence, the correct option is (B).

118. The solution with known concentration is known as the standard solution. Standard solutions are generally used in titration where the unknown concentration of a substance is determined using the solution of substance of known concentration.

Hence, the correct option is (A).

119. Fumarate is an intermediate in the citric acid cycle used by cells to produce energy in the form of adenosine triphosphate (ATP) from food. It is formed by the oxidation of succinate by the enzyme succinate dehydrogenase. Fumarate is also a product of the urea cycle. Aspartate which is regenerated from fumarate is well known. One of the prime precursors of urea, the bicarbonate ion, is also formed from the CO2, which is generated by the TCA cycle. The flux of acetyl CoA through the TCA cycle can indirectly affect the urea cycle by altering the levels of N-acetyl glutamate.

Hence, the correct option is (D).

120. Restriction enzymes were discovered by Smith and Nathans. The Nobel Prize in Physiology or Medicine 1978 was awarded jointly to Werner Arber, Daniel Nathans and Hamilton O. Smith "for the discovery of restriction enzymes and their application to problems of molecular genetics".

Hence, the correct option is (A).

121. Antoni van Leeuwenhoek is known as the father of Microbiology. Antoni van Leeuwenhoek (1632-1723), a cloth trader from Delft, is the founding father of microbiology. He used homemade microscopes to discover the invisible world of micro-organisms. He used homemade microscopes to discover the invisible world of micro-organisms.

Hence, the correct option is (D).

122. Leptomeningitis is an inflammatory process that is localized to the interfacing surfaces of the pia and the arachnoid, where CSF flows. Three layers of membranes known as meninges protect the brain and spinal cord. The delicate inner layer is the pia mater. The middle layer is the arachnoid, a web-like structure filled with fluid that cushions the brain. The tough outer layer is called the dura mater.

Hence, the correct option is (C).

123. Passive diffusion or non-ionic diffusion is considered as the major absorption process for more than 90% of drugs. It is the movement of the drug molecule from a region of higher concentration to a region of lower concentration.

Hence, the correct option is (D).

124. Preparations that are avoided during pregnancy is Vitamin A. It's worth noting that certain foods that are high in vitamin A, such as liver and liver pâté, are on the list of foods to avoid in pregnancy. Some vitamin supplements also contain high levels of vitamin A, such as cod liver oil, so should be avoided during pregnancy.

Hence, the correct option is (B).

125. The nucleus is the largest organelle in a eukaryotic cell and is considered to be the cell's control center. It contains most of the cell's DNA, which makes up chromosomes and is encoded with the genetic instructions for making proteins.

Hence, the correct option is (A).

Pharmaceutical Chemistry

Q.1 Glucose tolerance is decreased in:
A. Diabetes mellitus   **B.** Hypopituitarisme
C. Addison's disease   **D.** Hypothyroidism

Q.2 The specific test for ketohexoses is:
A. Seliwanoff's test   **B.** Osazone test
C. Molisch test   **D.** None of these

Q.3 The tissues with the highest total glycogen content are:
A. Muscle and kidneys   **B.** Kidneys and liver
C. Liver and muscle   **D.** Brain and Liver

Q.4 The Rothera test is not given by:
A. β-hydroxy butyrate   **B.** Bile salts
C. Glucose   **D.** None of these

Q.5 Which one of the following can convert glucose to vitamin C?
A. Albino rats   **B.** Humans
C. Monkeys   **D.** Guinea pigs

Q.6 Which one of the following cannot convert glucose to Vitamin C?
A. Albino rats   **B.** Dogs
C. Monkeys   **D.** Cows

Q.7 Pasteur effect is:
A. Inhibition of glycolysis
B. Oxygen is involved
C. Inhibition of enzyme phosphofructokinase
D. All of these

Q.8 Phenylalanine is the precursor of:
A. L-DOPA   **B.** Histamine
C. Tyrosine   **D.** Throxine

Q.9 Epimers of glucose is:
A. Fructose   **B.** Galactose
C. Ribose   **D.** Deoxyribose

Q.10 Human heart muscle contains:
A. D-Arabinose   **B.** D-Ribose
C. D-Xylose   **D.** L-Xylose

Q.11 Invert sugar is:
A. Lactose
B. Mannose
C. Fructose
D. Hydrolytic product of sucrose

Q.12 Which of the following is not reducing sugar?
A. Lactose   **B.** Maltose   **C.** Sucrose   **D.** Fructose

Q.13 The optically inactive amino acid is:
A. Glycine   **B.** Serine
C. Threonine   **D.** Valine

Q.14 The pH (isoelectric pI) of alanine is:
A. 6.02   **B.** 6.6   **C.** 6.8   **D.** 7.2

Q.15 An amino acid not found in proteins is:
A. β-Alanine   **B.** Proline
C. Lysine   **D.** Histidine

Q.16 A 'suicide enzyme' is:
A. Cycloxygenase   **B.** Lipooxygenase
C. Phospholipase A1   **D.** Cytochrom-C

Q.17 The optimal pH for the enzyme rennin is:
A. 2.0   **B.** 4.0   **C.** 8.0   **D.** 6.0

Q.18 The optimal pH for the enzyme trypsin is:
A. 1.0-2.0   **B.** 2.0-4.0   **C.** 5.2-6.2   **D.** 5.8-6.2

Q.19 The optimal pH for the enzyme chymo-trypsin is:
A. 2.0   **B.** 4.0   **C.** 6.0   **D.** 8.0

Q.20 The main site of urea synthesis in mammals is:
A. Liver   **B.** Skin   **C.** Intestine   **D.** Kidney

Q.21 The number of ATP required for urea synthesis is:
A. 0   **B.** 1   **C.** 2   **D.** 3

Q.22 Control of urea cycle involves the enzyme:
A. Carbamoyl phosphate synthetase
B. Ornithine transcarbamoylase
C. Argininosuccinase
D. Arginase

Q.23 A chemical score of protein zein is:
A. 0   **B.** 57   **C.** 60   **D.** 70

Q.24 The biological value of egg white protein is:
A. 94   **B.** 83   **C.** 85   **D.** 77

Q.25 Net protein utilization of milk protein is:
A. 75%   **B.** 80%   **C.** 86%   **D.** 91%

Q.26 Pulses are deficient in:
A. Lysine   **B.** Threonine
C. Methionine   **D.** Tryptophan

Q.27 Net protein utilization of egg protein is:
A. 75%   **B.** 80%   **C.** 91%   **D.** 72%

Q.28 A trace element deficient in the milk is:
A. Magnesium   **B.** Copper
C. Zinc   **D.** Chloride

Q.29 Milk is deficient in:
A. Vitamin B1   **B.** Vitamin B2

C. Sodium **D.** Potassium

Q.30 Tay-Sachs disease results from inherited deficiency of:
A. Arylsulphatase A **B.** Hexosaminidase A
C. Sphingomyelinase **D.** Ceramidase

Q.31 The largest immunoglobulin is:
A. IgA **B.** IgG **C.** IgM **D.** IgD

Q.32 Allergic reactions are mediated by:
A. IgA **B.** IgG **C.** IgD **D.** IgE

Q.33 An immunoglobulin which can cross the placental barrier is:
A. IgA **B.** IgM
C. IgD **D.** None of these

Q.34 MHC Class II proteins, in conjunction with antigens, are recognised by:
A. Cytotoxic T cells **B.** Helper T cells
C. Suppressor T cells **D.** Memory T cells

Q.35 CD8 is a transmembrane glycoprotein present in:
A. Cytotoxic T cells **B.** Helper T cells
C. Suppressor T cells **D.** Memory T cells

Q.36 CD4 is a transmembrane glycoprotein present in:
A. Cytotoxic T cells **B.** Helper T cells
C. Suppressor T cells **D.** Memory T cells

Q.37 Human immunodeficiency virus destroys:
A. Cytotoxic T cells **B.** Helper T cells
C. B cells **D.** Plasma cells

Q.38 Active immunity can be produced by administration of:
A. Killed bacteria or viruses
B. Live attenuated bacteria or viruses
C. Toxoids
D. All of these

Pharmaceutics

Q.39 Most widely used flavoring agent in food industry:
A. Menthol
B. Chloroform
C. Mono sodium glutamate
D. None of these

Q.40 Which of the following flavor is not responsible for sour taste?
A. Citrus flavors **B.** Liquorice
C. Raspberry **D.** Mint spice

Q.41 The filling method of a pharmaceutical liquid depends on the following factors:
A. Viscosity of the liquid.
B. Surface tension of the liquid.
C. Compatibility with the materials used in the construction of the filling machine.
D. All of these

Q.42 Which of the following methods are generally used in liquid filling?
A. Gravimetric
B. Volumetric
C. Constant level method
D. All of these

Q.43 In the formulation of suspensions, generally, which types of drugs are selected?
A. Hydrophilic **B.** Hydrophobic
C. Both (A) and (B) **D.** None of these

Q.44 In the formulation, to facilitate the wetting of insoluble solids, which of the following agents used?
A. Suspending agents **B.** Wetting agents
C. Flavoring agents **D.** None of these

Q.45 How surfactants will facilitate or aid wetting of hydrophobic materials in liquid?
A. By decreasing the solid-liquid interfacial tension.
B. By increasing the solid-liquid interfacial tension.
C. Both (A) and (B)
D. None of these

Q.46 The stability of suspensions can be evaluated by:
A. Sedimentation volume
B. Degree of flocculation
C. Re-dispersibility
D. All of these

Q.47 To identify the emulsion type, which of the following tests are conducted?
A. Dilution test **B.** Dye test
C. Conductivity test **D.** All of these

Q.48 Stoke's equation is expressed as:
A. $V = 2r^2(d_1 - d_2)g/18\eta$
B. $V = 2r^2(d_1 - d_2)g/9\eta$
C. Both (A) and (B)
D. None of these

Q.49 The temperature at which the inversion occurs depends on emulsifier concentration is known as:
A. Phase temperature
B. Inversion temperature
C. Phase inversion temperature
D. All of these

Q.50 Which of the following mechanical equipment can be used for emulsification?
A. Homogenizers **B.** Mechanical stirrers
C. Ultrasonifiers **D.** All of these

Q.51 Which of the following is not used as an emulsifying agent?
A. Surfactant
B. Hydrophilic colloids
C. Electrolytes
D. Finely divided solids

Q.52 HLB system was developed by:

A. Griffin

B. Stock's

C. Dalla Valle

D. None of these

Q.53 Gum Arabic is a:

A. Anionic polysaccharide

B. Cationic polysaccharide

C. Neutral polysaccharide

D. None of these

Q.54 Which of the following is not a semisolid dosage form?

A. Paste

B. Creams

C. Ointments

D. Suspensions

Q.55 Generally pastes contain:

A. High percentage of insoluble solids

B. Low percentage of insoluble solids

C. Both (A) and (B)

D. None of these

Q.56 Most widely used hydrocarbon in semisolid dosage forms:

A. Petrolatum

B. Mineral oil

C. Both (A) and (B)

D. None of these

Q.57 Which of the following hydrocarbon waxes are employed in the manufacture of creams and ointments?

A. Paraffin wax

B. Ceresin

C. Both (A) and (B)

D. None of these

Q.58 Which of the following is not a vegetable oil?

A. Peanut oil

B. Almond oil

C. Olive oil

D. Petrolatum

Q.59 Which of the following fatty acid used in water removable creams as emulsifier?

A. Palmitic acid

B. Stearic acid

C. Both (A) and (B)

D. None of these

Q.60 Combination of a surfactant with oil-soluble auxiliary emulsifier is known as:

A. Simple emulsifier system

B. Mixed emulsifier system

C. Both (A) and (B)

D. None of these

Q.61 Promulgen means:

A. Anionic emulsifiers composed of fatty alcohols & their ethoxylates

B. Nonionic emulsifiers composed of fatty alcohols & their ethoxylates

C. Cationic emulsifiers composed of fatty alcohols & their ethoxylates

D. All of these

Q.62 Promulgen D contains:

A. Cetyl alcohol & Ceteareth- 20

B. Stearyl alcohol & Ceteareth- 20

C. Both (A) and (B)

D. None of these

Q.63 Promulgen G contains:

A. Cetyl alcohol & Ceteareth- 20

B. Stearyl alcohol & Ceteareth- 20

C. Both (A) and (B)

D. None of these

Q.64 With promulgen D, which type of emulsion generally obtained?

A. Liquid emulsion

B. Thick consistency emulsion

C. Both (A) and (B)

D. None of these

Q.65 With promulgen G, which type of emulsion generally obtained?

A. Liquid emulsion

B. Thick consistency emulsion

C. Both (A) and (B)

D. None of these

Q.66 Which of the following polyols used as humectants in creams?

A. Glycerine

B. Propylene glycol

C. Sorbitol 70%

D. All of these

Q.67 The choice of humectants is based on:

A. Rate of moisture exchange

B. Viscosity and texture of preparation

C. Both (A) and (B)

D. None of these

Q.68 Which of the following is more hygroscopic at low concentration?

A. Sorbitol 70%

B. Glycerine

C. Both (A) and (B)

D. None of these

Q.69 Water number means:

A. Maximum amount of water that can be added to 100 g of a base at given temperature.

B. Maximum amount of water that can be added to 10 g of a base at given temperature.

C. Maximum amount of water tha tcan be added to 5 g of a base at given temperature.

D. All of these

Q.70 Lanolin is which type of base?

A. Hydrocarbon base

B. Absorption base

C. Both (A) and (B)

D. None of these

Q.71 In the preparation of vanishing creams, which types of bases are used generally?

A. Absorption bases

B. Water removable bases

C. Hydrocarbon bases

D. None of these

Q.72 In the preparation of cold creams, which types of bases are used generally?

A. Absorption bases

B. Water removable bases

C. Hydrocarbon bases

D. None of these

Q.73 Water-soluble bases are also known as:
A. Greasy ointment bases
B. Greaseless ointment base
C. Both (A) and (B)
D. None of these

Q.74 In pastes, the concentration of insoluble powder substances is:
A. 20%-50%
B. 50%-100%
C. 50%-75%
D. None of these

Q.75 Jellies are generally:
A. Water-soluble bases
B. Water-insoluble bases
C. Both (A) and (B)
D. None of these

Q.76 As per USP XX, the term "objectionable" means:
A. An organism can cause disease or the presence may interrupt the function of the drug or lead to deterioration of the product.
B. Pathogens if they produce disease or infection, in the newborn or debilitated persons.
C. Organisms or their toxins that are responsible for human disease or infection.
D. None of these

Pharmacognosy

Q.77 Crystal fibres are not present in:
A. Licorice
B. Cinnamon
C. Cascara
D. Senna

Q.78 Stone cells with three side lignin thickening are found in:
A. Rauwolfia
B. Kantakari
C. Cascara
D. Cinnamon

Q.79 Dog senna is obtained from:
A. Cassia auriculata
B. Cassia senna
C. Cassia obovata
D. Cassia occidentalis

Q.80 The outer surface of the bark has silvery grey patches and transversely elongated lenticels are called:
A. Arjun
B. Cascara
C. Cinchona
D. Ceylon cinnamon

Q.81 Rhamnus purshianus is growing in:
A. America
B. Europe
C. India
D. Australia

Q.82 The microscopical study it shows stinecells & crystal fibres is:
A. Cinchona
B. Liquorice
C. Senna
D. Cascara

Q.83 Eugenol is present in:
A. Fennel
B. Clove
C. Cardamom
D. Coriander

Q.84 Rosettes of Calcium oxalate crystals are found in:

A. Senna
B. Rhubarb
C. Cinchona
D. Licorice

Q.85 A spot of alcoholic solution on filter paper shows blue fluorescence in UV light in case of:
A. Indian Rhubarb
B. Chinese Rhubarb
C. Rhapontic Rhubarb
D. Official rhubarb

Q.86 Carminic acid is used as an important colorant and indicator is:
A. A flavonoid glycoside
B. A volatie compound
C. An arthraquinoe o-glycoside
D. An anthraquinone c-glycoside

Pharmacology

Q.87 Which of the following agents is a nonselective beta-receptor agonist?
A. Norepinephrine
B. Terbutaline
C. Isoproterenol
D. Dobutamine

Q.88 The reasons determining bioavailability are:
A. Rheological parameters of blood
B. Amount of a substance obtained orally and quantity of intakes
C. Extent of absorption and hepatic first-pass effect
D. Glomerular filtration rate

Q.89 Pick out the appropriate alimentary route of administration when passage of drugs through liver is minimized:
A. Oral
B. Transdermal
C. Rectal
D. Intraduodenal

Q.90 Which route of drug administration is most likely to lead to the first-pass effect?
A. Sublingual
B. Oral
C. Intravenous
D. Intramuscular

Q.91 What is characteristic of the oral route?
A. Fast onset of effect.
B. Absorption depends on GI tract secretion and motor function.
C. A drug reaches the blood passing the liver.
D. The sterilization of medicinal forms is obligatory.

Q.92 The feature of the sublingual route is:
A. Pretty fast absorption
B. A drug is exposed to gastric secretion
C. A drug is exposed more prominent liver metabolism
D. A drug can be administrated in a variety of doses

Q.93 Find out the parenteral route of medicinal agent administration:
A. Rectal
B. Oral
C. Sublingual
D. Inhalation

Q.94 Parenteral administration:
A. Cannot be used with unconscious patients.

B. Generally results in a less accurate dosage than oral administration.

C. Usually produces a more rapid response than oral administration.

D. Is too slow for emergency use.

Q.95 What is the characteristic of the intramuscular route of drug administration?

A. Only water solutions can be injected

B. Oily solutions can be injected

C. Opportunity of hypertonic solution injections

D. The action develops slower, than at oral administration

Q.96 Correct statements listing characteristics of a particular route of drug administration include all of the following except:

A. Intravenous administration provides a rapid response.

B. Intramuscular administration requires a sterile technique.

C. Inhalation provides slow access to the general circulation.

D. Subcutaneous administration may cause local irritation.

Q.97 Biological barriers include all except:

A. Renal tubules

B. Cell membranes

C. Capillary walls

D. Placenta

Q.98 What is the reason of complicated penetration of some drugs through brain-blood barrier?

[Graduate Pharmacy Aptitude Test, 2013]

A. High lipid solubility of a drug

B. Meningitis

C. Absence of pores in the brain capillary endothelium

D. High endocytosis degree in a brain capillary

Q.99 The volume of distribution (Vd) relates:

A. Single to a daily dose of an administrated drug.

B. An administrated dose to a body weight.

C. An uncharged drug reaching the systemic circulation.

D. The amount of a drug in the body to the concentration of a drug in plasma.

Q.100 For the calculation of the volume of distribution (Vd) one must take into account:

A. Concentration of a substance in plasma

B. Concentration of substance in urine

C. Therapeutical width of drug action

D. A daily dose of drug

Q.101 The term "biotransformation" includes the following:

A. Accumulation of substances in a fat tissue.

B. Binding of substances with plasma proteins.

C. Accumulation of substances in a tissue.

D. Process of physicochemical and biochemical alteration of a drug in the body.

Q.102 Biotransformation of the drugs is to render them:

A. Less ionized

B. More pharmacologically active

C. More lipid soluble

D. Less lipid soluble

Q.103 Find the drug type for which microsomal oxidation is the most prominent:

A. Lipid soluble

B. Water soluble

C. Low molecular weight

D. High molecular weight

Q.104 Find out the correct statement:

A. Microsomal oxidation always results in inactivation of a compound.

B. Microsomal oxidation results in a decrease of compound toxicity.

C. Microsomal oxidation results in an increase of ionization and water solubility of a drug.

D. Microsomal oxidation results in an increase of lipid solubility of a drug thus its excretion from the organism is facilitated.

Q.105 Stimulation of liver microsomal enzymes can:

A. Require the dose increase of some drugs.

B. Require the dose decrease of some drugs.

C. Prolong the duration of the action of a drug.

D. Intensify the unwanted reaction of a drug.

Q.106 Metabolic transformation (phase-1) is:

A. Acetylation and methylation of substances.

B. Transformation of substances due to oxidation, reduction or hydrolysis.

C. Glucuronide formation

D. Binding to plasma proteins

Q.107 Biotransformation of a medicinal substance results in:

A. Faster urinary excretion

B. Slower urinary excretion

C. Easier distribution in organism

D. Higher binding to membranes

Q.108 Conjugation is:

A. Process of drug reduction by special enzymes

B. Process of drug oxidation by special oxidase

C. Coupling of a drug with an endogenous substrate

D. Solubilization in lipids

Q.109 Which of the following processes proceeds in the second phase of biotransformation?

A. Acetylation

B. Reduction

C. Oxidation

D. Hydrolysis

Q.110 Conjugation of a drug includes the following EXCEPT:

A. Glucoronidation

B. Sulfate formation

C. Hydrolysis

D. Methylation

Q.111 In case of liver disorders accompanied by a decline in microsomal enzyme activity the duration of action of some drugs is:

A. Decreased

B. Enlarged

C. Remained unchanged

D. Changed insignificantly

Q.112 Half-life is the time required to:

A. Change the amount of a drug in plasma by half during elimination.

B. Metabolize a half of an introduced drug into the active metabolite.

C. Absorb a half of an introduced drug.

D. Bind a half of an introduced drug to plasma proteins.

Q.113 Half-life (t $\frac{1}{2}$) doesn't depend on:

A. Biotransformation

B. Time of drug absorption

C. Concentration of a drug in plasma

D. Rate of drug elimination

Q.114 Elimination is expressed as follows:

A. Rate of renal tubular reabsorption.

B. Clearance speed of some volume of blood from substance.

C. Time required to decrease the amount of drug in plasma by one-half.

D. Clearance of an organism from a xenobiotic.

Other Subjects

Q.115 Which one of the following is not a colligative property?

A. Osmotic pressure

B. Elevation of boiling point

C. Freezing point

D. Depression in freezing point

Q.116 Andreason pipette utilizes the principle of:

A. Sedimentation   B. Centrifugation

C. Compaction   D. Filtration

Q.117 Isomerism that arises out of the difference in the spatial arrangement of atoms or groups about the doubly bonded carbon atoms is called?

A. Structural Isomerism

B. Stereo Isomerism

C. Geometrical Isomerism

D. Optical Isomerism

Q.118 Phenolphthalein has a pH range of:

A. 6.8-8.4   B. 1.2-2.8   C. 8.3-11.0   D. 4.2-6.3

Q.119 There are about _______ types of specialized cells in the human body.

A. 200   B. 350   C. 450   D. 550

Q.120 Bacteria protect themselves from viruses by fragmenting viral DNA with:

A. Ligase   B. Endonuclease

C. Exonuclease   D. Gyrase

Q.121 Which part of the compound microscope helps in gathering and focusing light rays on the specimen to be viewed?

A. Condenser lens   B. Magnifying lens

C. Objective lens   D. Eyepiece lens

Q.122 Which of the following is true about Pachymeningitis?

A. Inflammation of the Pia

B. Usually a consequence of traumatic brain injury.

C. The arachnoid acts as a barrier to infection.

D. The inflammation is restricted to the outer surface of the brain.

Q.123 What is driving force for passive diffusion?

A. Concentration gradient

B. Electrochemical gradient

C. Charge ecuilibration & Concentration gradient

D. Both (A) and (B)

Q.124 Ototoxicity is a unique side effect of group of diuretics:

A. Loop   B. Thiazide

C. Potassium sparing   D. Osmotic

Q.125 ___________ is the largest organelles of the cytoplasm.

A. Nucleus   B. Mitochondria

C. Golgi Apparatus   D. Ribosomes

// Smart Answer Sheet //

Q.	Ans.	Correct / Skipped	Q.	Ans.	Correct / Skipped	Q.	Ans.	Correct / Skipped	Q.	Ans.	Correct / Skipped	Q.	Ans.	Correct / Skipped	Q.	Ans.	Correct / Skipped
1	A	89.43 % / 10.14 %	22	A	47.34 % / 42.76 %	43	B	76.79 % / 23.09 %	64	B	65.13 % / 31.8 %	85	C	45.58 % / 49.43 %	106	B	78.31 % / 10.37 %
2	A	55.84 % / 31.65 %	23	A	52.4 % / 38.31 %	44	B	88.55 % / 10.62 %	65	A	45.17 % / 50.44 %	86	D	29.98 % / 68.07 %	107	A	52.01 % / 32.6 %
3	C	84.58 % / 11.55 %	24	B	65.4 % / 33.19 %	45	A	68.76 % / 30.24 %	66	D	67.18 % / 31.0 %	87	C	41.12 % / 40.49 %	108	C	66.95 % / 32.04 %
4	A	46.66 % / 40.7 %	25	A	51.58 % / 30.3 %	46	D	60.16 % / 38.16 %	67	C	64.8 % / 32.57 %	88	C	62.2 % / 33.83 %	109	A	45.95 % / 51.98 %
5	A	56.13 % / 30.8 %	26	C	60.9 % / 33.34 %	47	D	48.08 % / 45.98 %	68	A	79.89 % / 14.45 %	89	C	40.97 % / 42.07 %	110	C	61.85 % / 34.11 %
6	C	56.68 % / 35.45 %	27	C	61.69 % / 37.44 %	48	D	47.49 % / 37.35 %	69	A	46.65 % / 33.97 %	90	B	69.61 % / 30.18 %	111	B	58.76 % / 39.48 %
7	D	12.62 % / 67.94 %	28	A	47.69 % / 38.12 %	49	D	17.98 % / 72.23 %	70	D	61.74 % / 31.75 %	91	B	23.0 % / 67.47 %	112	A	79.89 % / 11.35 %
8	C	46.33 % / 44.81 %	29	C	47.67 % / 31.39 %	50	D	67.55 % / 32.32 %	71	B	47.79 % / 38.38 %	92	A	45.98 % / 47.15 %	113	B	69.11 % / 30.19 %
9	B	83.58 % / 15.6 %	30	B	65.74 % / 32.65 %	51	C	89.58 % / 10.07 %	72	A	62.08 % / 30.97 %	93	D	56.09 % / 39.42 %	114	D	55.81 % / 32.44 %
10	C	61.74 % / 32.56 %	31	C	64.47 % / 34.99 %	52	A	62.07 % / 35.48 %	73	B	59.38 % / 37.21 %	94	C	54.7 % / 43.97 %	115	C	78.88 % / 13.81 %
11	D	89.01 % / 10.6 %	32	D	46.39 % / 35.24 %	53	C	60.67 % / 32.35 %	74	A	81.63 % / 10.17 %	95	B	56.11 % / 39.82 %	116	A	57.1 % / 35.26 %
12	C	41.0 % / 31.42 %	33	D	67.88 % / 31.19 %	54	D	56.36 % / 33.95 %	75	A	54.33 % / 34.86 %	96	C	56.56 % / 32.17 %	117	C	57.57 % / 40.48 %
13	A	64.27 % / 31.77 %	34	B	17.99 % / 77.13 %	55	A	40.35 % / 50.49 %	76	A	45.34 % / 43.58 %	97	A	55.88 % / 31.91 %	118	C	88.17 % / 11.31 %
14	A	55.45 % / 31.29 %	35	C	68.9 % / 30.92 %	56	C	82.78 % / 10.03 %	77	B	49.22 % / 46.47 %	98	C	68.99 % / 30.21 %	119	A	68.74 % / 30.76 %
15	A	43.65 % / 41.99 %	36	A	41.29 % / 46.36 %	57	C	59.09 % / 35.14 %	78	B	52.12 % / 36.33 %	99	D	66.35 % / 32.74 %	120	B	69.43 % / 30.46 %
16	A	51.19 % / 31.33 %	37	B	66.0 % / 30.36 %	58	D	63.38 % / 34.35 %	79	C	46.49 % / 48.24 %	100	A	11.21 % / 68.81 %	121	A	44.78 % / 51.43 %
17	B	12.41 % / 76.78 %	38	D	63.27 % / 35.34 %	59	B	63.45 % / 32.08 %	80	B	60.4 % / 33.42 %	101	D	66.79 % / 31.39 %	122	B	58.0 % / 39.75 %
18	C	48.18 % / 42.85 %	39	C	61.17 % / 30.21 %	60	B	89.44 % / 10.54 %	81	A	45.0 % / 52.68 %	102	D	58.97 % / 39.57 %	123	D	46.92 % / 40.96 %
19	D	69.6 % / 30.3 %	40	D	89.93 % / 10.04 %	61	B	52.54 % / 38.23 %	82	B	53.14 % / 37.97 %	103	A	46.77 % / 31.55 %	124	A	46.37 % / 31.53 %
20	A	79.34 % / 18.96 %	41	D	43.55 % / 39.85 %	62	A	60.13 % / 36.13 %	83	B	43.59 % / 39.73 %	104	C	78.4 % / 17.46 %	125	B	69.22 % / 30.23 %
21	D	48.6 % / 41.23 %	42	D	50.85 % / 32.95 %	63	B	47.21 % / 41.7 %	84	B	53.65 % / 36.43 %	105	A	68.62 % / 31.33 %			

//Hints and Solutions//

1. Glucose tolerance is decreased in diabetes mellitus. Glucose tolerance means that blood glucose is raised beyond normal levels, but not high enough to warrant a diabetes diagnosis. With impaired glucose tolerance you face a much greater risk of developing diabetes and cardiovascular disease.

Hence, the correct option is (A).

2. The specific test for ketohexoses is Seliwanoff's test. Seliwanoff's test is a chemical test that distinguishes between aldose and ketose sugars. If the sugar contains a ketone group, it is a ketose. If a sugar contains an aldehyde group, it is an aldose. This test relies on the principle that, when heated, ketoses are more rapidly dehydrated than aldoses. It is named after Theodor Seliwanoff, the chemist that devised the test.

Hence, the correct option is (A).

3. The tissues with the highest total glycogen content are the liver and muscle. The glycogen, white, amorphous, tasteless polysaccharide $(C_6H_{10}O_5)_n$. It is the principal form in which carbohydrate is stored in higher animals, occurring primarily in the liver and muscles.

Hence, the correct option is (C).

4. The Rothera test is not given by β-hydroxybutyrate. The term ketone bodies refer to three intermediate products of fat metabolism, namely acetone (2%), acetoacetic acid (20%) and beta-hydroxybutyrate (78%). Acetoacetic acid and acetone react with an alkaline solution of sodium nitroprusside to form a purple-colored complex. This method can detect above 1-5 mg/dl of acetoacetic acid and 10-20 mg/dl of acetone. Beta-hydroxybutyrate is not detected.

Hence, the correct option is (A).

5. Albino rats can convert glucose to vitamin C. Some tests have indicated that the rat is able to synthesize its own vitamin C. Varying concentrations of ascorbic acid (vitamin C) have been found in the organs of the rat by direct titration with the indophenol indicator (1, 2). The albino rat has an excellent defense against infections (to the extent that experimental surgery is often performed under completely nonsterile conditions), sterile instruments and sterile saline should be used for intraocular grafting.

Hence, the correct option is (A).

6. Monkeys cannot convert glucose to Vitamin C. Most mammals generate vitamin C from d-glucose through gluconic acid in the liver. Humans, other primates cannot synthesize this vitamin because they lack the enzyme l-gluconolactone oxidase. Thus, they must obtain the vitamin from exogenous sources via intestinal absorption.

Hence, the correct option is (C).

7. The finding of Pasteur that glycolysis is linked to respiration and that oxygen consumption inhibits glycolysis has not been fully explored. This is known as the "Pasteur effect." The vital importance of oxygen lies in the conservation of nutrients while the useful energy yield per molecule of glucose is rendered large.

Although we know about the benefits, the mechanism is still obscure. The inhibition of glycolysis in the presence of oxygen is mediated through the changes in the concentrations of metabolites that regulate the activity of phosphofructokinase.

Hence, the correct option is (D).

8. Phenylalanine is a precursor for tyrosine, the monoamine neurotransmitters dopamine, norepinephrine (noradrenaline), and epinephrine (adrenaline), and the skin pigment melanin. It is encoded by the codons UUU and UUC. It is a direct precursor to the neuromodulator phenethylamine, a commonly used dietary supplement.

Hence, the correct option is (C).

9. Epimer of glucose is galactose. Two sugars differing in configuration at a single asymmetric carbon atom are known as epimers. Glucose and mannose are C2 epimers, ribose and xylose are C3 epimers, and gulose and galactose are also C3 epimers.

Hence, the correct option is (B).

10. Human heart muscle contains D-Xylose. The dextrorotary form of xylose, D-xylose, refers usually to the endogenously occurring form of the sugar in living things. The D-xylose absorption test that measures the level of D-xylose, a type of sugar, in a blood or urine sample. This test is done to help diagnose problems that prevent the small intestine from absorbing nutrients in food. D-xylose is normally easily absorbed by the intestines.

Hence, the correct option is (C).

11. Invert sugar is a hydrolytic product of sucrose. Invert sugar, a mixture of glucose (dextrose) and fructose produced from sugar (sucrose) by application of heat and an acid "sugar doctor," such as cream of tartar or citric acid, affects the sweetness, solubility, and amount of crystallization in candy making.

Hence, the correct option is (D).

12. Sucrose is a non-reducing sugar because the monosaccharides' anomeric carbon is involved in glycoside or acetal formation. Sucrose is a naturally occurring sugar found in various amounts in plants like fruits, vegetables and nuts. Sucrose is also produced commercially from sugar cane and sugar beets.

Hence, the correct option is (C).

13. The optically inactive amino acid is Glycine, a building block for protein. The body can make glycine on its own, but it is also consumed in the diet. Glycine is the only chiral amino acid with a single hydrogen atom as its side chain. The absence of asymmetric carbon atoms makes glycine optically inactive that means glycine does not rotate the plane polarised light.

Hence, the correct option is (A).

14. The pH (isoelectric pI) of alanine is 6.02. At a pH lower than 2, both the carboxylate and amine functions are protonated, so the alanine molecule has a net positive charge. At a pH greater than 10, the amine exists as a neutral base and the carboxyl as its conjugate base, so the alanine molecule has a net negative charge. At intermediate pH's the zwitterion concentration increases, and at a characteristic pH, called the isoelectric point (pI), the negatively and positively charged molecular species are present in equal concentration. This behavior is general for simple (difunctional) amino acids. Starting from a fully protonated state, the pKa's of the acidic functions range from 1.8 to 2.4 for -CO_2H, and 8.8 to 9.7 for -$NH_3^{(+)}$. The isoelectric points range from 5.5 to 6.2.

Hence, the correct option is (A).

15. An amino acid not found in proteins is β-Alanine. β-Alanine is a non-proteinogenic amino acid, where the amino group is at the β-position from the carboxylate group (IUPAC name = 3 amino propanoic acid). Beta-alanine is a non-essential amino acid. Unlike most amino acids, it is not used by your body to synthesize proteins. Instead, together with histidine, it produces carnosine.

Hence, the correct option is (A).

16. A 'suicide enzyme' is cycloxygenase. Cyclooxygenase (COX) is a rate-limiting enzyme involved in the conversion of arachidonic acid to prostaglandin H2, which is the precursor of several molecules, including prostaglandins, prostacyclin, and thromboxanes.

Hence, the correct option is (A).

17. The optimal pH for the enzyme rennin is 4. Rennin, also called chymosin, a protein-digesting enzyme that curdles milk by transforming caseinogen into insoluble casein; it is found only in the fourth stomach of cud-chewing animals, such as cows. RENNIN has an optimum pH of 3.4 for the proteolysis of bovine serum albumin[1] and 3.8 for poly-L-glutamic acid[2]. At pH values between 5 and 7 it will coagulate milk and slowly attack casein. It has maximum stability at pH 5.4, while at values above 7 it loses activity rapidly.

Hence, the correct option is (B).

18. The optimal pH for the enzyme trypsin is 5.2-6.2. Trypsin is an enzyme of pancreatic juice secreted by the pancreas. Trypsin works at a basic pH. Every enzyme is pH specific. The change in pH will lead to denaturation or inactivity of enzymes. The pH where the enzyme shows its maximum activity is the optimum pH of the enzyme. Trypsin works at a basic pH of around 7.4 to 8.4. trypsin breaks down the proteins into small polypeptides and a few free amino acids (trypsin can hydrolyze some dipeptides). Trypsin is released in inactive form trypsinogen.

Hence, the correct option is (C).

19. The optimal pH for the enzyme chymo-trypsin is 8.0. The mammalian chymotrypsin has a pH optimum around 8, with two catalytic important pKas of 6.8 and 9.5, corresponding to the active-site histidine and N-terminal leucine, respectively.

Hence, the correct option is (D).

20. The main site of urea synthesis in mammals is the liver. Organisms that cannot easily and safely remove nitrogen as ammonia convert it to a less toxic substance, such as urea, via the urea cycle, which occurs mainly in the liver. Urea produced by the liver is then released into the bloodstream, where it travels to the kidneys and is ultimately excreted in urine.

Hence, the correct option is (A).

21. The number of ATP required for urea synthesis is 3. Urea is produced by hydrolysis of the guanidino group of arginine, along with regeneration of ornithine. Three molecules of ATP are consumed in the synthesis of one urea molecule. Urea is synthesized in the body of many organisms as part of the urea cycle, either from the oxidation of amino acids or from ammonia.

Hence, the correct option is (D).

22. Control of the urea cycle involves the enzyme carbamoyl phosphate synthetase. Human carbamoyl phosphate synthetase (CPS1), a 1500-residue multidomain enzyme, catalyzes the first step of ammonia detoxification to urea requiring N-acetyl-L-glutamate (NAG) as an essential activator to prevent ammonia/amino acids depletion. The urea cycle comprises five enzymes these are carbamyl phosphate synthetase I, ornithine transcarbamylase, arginine-succinate syn- thetase, arginine-succinate lyase, and ar- ginase.

Hence, the correct option is (A).

23. A chemical score of protein zein is 0. Zein is widely used in the food and packaging industry as a coating for candy, nuts, fruits, pills, and other encapsulated foods due to its film-forming property and ability to provide a moisture barrier and has been studied as a potential biomaterial for the development of colloidal delivery systems.

Hence, the correct option is (A).

24. The biological value of egg white protein is 83. Biological value (BV) is a measure of the proportion of absorbed protein from food that becomes incorporated into the proteins of the organism's body. It captures how readily the digested protein can be used in protein synthesis in the cells of the organism. Proteins are the major source of nitrogen in food. BV assumes protein is the only source of nitrogen and measures the amount of nitrogen ingested in relation to the amount which is subsequently excreted.

Hence, the correct option is (B).

25. Net protein utilization of milk protein is 75%. The net protein utilization, or NPU, is the ratio of amino acid mass converted to proteins to the mass of amino acids supplied. This figure is somewhat affected by the salvage of essential amino acids within the body but is profoundly affected by the level of limiting amino acids within a foodstuff.

Hence, the correct option is (A).

26. Pulses are deficient in methionine. In particular, pulses lack methionine and cysteine, substances that are found in cereal-based proteins. These, in turn, lack an essential amino acid, lysine, which is present in legumes.

Hence, the correct option is (C).

27. Net protein utilization of egg protein is 91%. As a value, NPU can range from 0 to 1 (or 100), with a value of 1 (or 100) indicating 100% utilization of dietary nitrogen as protein and a value of 0 an indication that none of the nitrogen supplied was converted to protein.

Certain foodstuffs, such as eggs or milk, rate as 1 on an NPU chart.

Hence, the correct option is (C).

28. A trace element deficient in the milk is magnesium. Magnesium is a cofactor in more than 300 enzyme systems that regulate diverse biochemical reactions in the body, including protein synthesis, muscle and nerve function, blood glucose control, and blood pressure regulation. Trace elements deficiencies represent a common life-threatening health problem in some populations of the world and are responsible for a wide range of clinical disorders. Some groups of individuals, such as children, pregnant women and the elderly, are more prone to develop trace element deficiency.

Hence, the correct option is (A).

29. Milk is deficient in sodium. Milk, yogurt, and many other dairy products are naturally low in salt. When it comes to cheese and butter, look for low- or no-salt options. Cow, nut, or hemp — most kinds of milk and milk alternatives will contribute over 100mg of sodium per cup to your morning drinks and daily meals. Coconut milk, though, often has less than 15mg of sodium per serving and can be found in both canned and carton form.

Hence, the correct option is (C).

30. Tay-Sachs disease results from an inherited deficiency of hexosaminidase A. Tay–Sachs disease is caused by a genetic mutation in the HEXA gene on chromosome 15, which codes for a subunit of the hexosaminidase enzyme known as hexosaminidase A. It is inherited from a person's parents in an autosomal recessive manner.

Hence, the correct option is (B).

31. The largest immunoglobulin is IgM. IgM antibodies are the largest antibody. They are found in blood and lymph fluid and are the first type of antibody made in response to an infection. They also cause other immune system cells to destroy foreign substances. IgM antibodies are about 5% to 10% of all the antibodies in the body.

Hence, the correct option is (C).

32. Allergic reactions are mediated by IgE. Allergic reactions can be grouped into two classes. The most common and best understood is mediated by a class of antibody called immunoglobulin E (IgE). Other reactions are non-IgE mediated and typically cause symptoms to appear more slowly, sometimes several hours after exposure.

Hence, the correct option is (D).

33. An immunoglobulin that can cross the placental barrier is not given here but maybe it is IgG. Placental transfer of maternal IgG antibodies to the fetus is an important mechanism that provides protection to the infant while his/her humoral response is inefficient. IgG is the only antibody class that significantly crosses the human placenta.

Hence, the correct option is (D).

34. MHC Class II proteins, in conjunction with antigens, are recognised by Helper T cells. A type of immune cell that stimulates killer T cells, macrophages, and B cells to make immune responses. A helper T cell is a type of white blood cell and a type of lymphocyte. Also called CD4-positive T lymphocyte.

Hence, the correct option is (B).

35. CD8 is a transmembrane glycoprotein present in Suppressor T cells. CD8 (cluster of differentiation 8) is a transmembrane glycoprotein that serves as a co-receptor for the T-cell receptor (TCR). Along with the TCR, the CD8 co-receptor plays a role in T cells. Suppressor T cells play important roles in the regulation of immune responses and the mediation of dominant immunologic tolerance.

Hence, the correct option is (C).

36. CD4 is a transmembrane glycoprotein present in Cytotoxic T cells. Cytotoxic T cells are effector cells that destroy virus-infected cells, tumor cells, and tissue grafts that exist in the cytosol, or contiguous nuclear compartment. The cells are also known as CD8+ T cells as they express the CD8 glycoprotein at their surfaces and are associated with MHC class I molecules.

Hence, the correct option is (A).

37. The human immunodeficiency virus destroys Helper T cells. HIV destroys CD4 T lymphocytes (helper T cells). Because of this, healthcare professionals measure CD4 levels to monitor HIV progression and AIDS. Helper T cells are crucial for immune system function and activate after encountering antigens from disease-causing microorganisms.

Hence, the correct option is (B).

38. Active immunity can be produced by the administration of killed bacteria or viruses, live attenuated bacteria or viruses, and toxoids. Natural immunity is acquired from exposure to the disease organism through infection with the actual disease. Toxoids are inactivated bacterial/viral toxin elements that are capable of instructing the immune system to develop antibodies to activated toxins.

Hence, the correct option is (D).

39. Most widely used flavoring agent in food industry Mono sodium glutamate. Mono sodium glutamate (MSG) is a flavor enhancer commonly added to Chinese food, canned vegetables, soups and processed meats. The Food and Drug Administration (FDA) has classified MSG as a food ingredient that's "generally recognized as safe," but its use remains controversial.

Hence, the correct option is (C).

40. Mint spice flavor is not responsible for sour taste. Mint or mentha belongs to the Lamiaceae family, which contains around 15 to 20 plant species, including peppermint and spearmint. It is a popular herb that people can use fresh or dried in many dishes and infusions. Manufacturers of toothpaste, gum, candy, and beauty products often use mint oil.

Hence, the correct option is (D).

41. The filling method of a pharmaceutical liquid depends on the viscosity of the liquid, surface tension of the liquid and compatibility with the materials used in the construction of the filling machine. Pharmaceutical filling machines expedite the modern pharmaceutical manufacturing process. Syringe filling equipment is used for large-scale filling and ensures sterility and dispensing of correct volume. Vial filling equipment can fill

hundreds of vials per minute while securing against product loss and inconsistent volume.

Hence, the correct option is (D).

42. The methods that are generally used in liquid filling are gravimetric, volumetric and constant level. Pharmaceutical liquid filling machines expedite the manufacturing of liquid drug suspensions. Used by small and large drug manufacturing firms, liquid filling machines are designed in a variety of formats, from benchtop sizes to larger-scale models.

Hence, the correct option is (D).

43. In the formulation of suspensions, Hydrophobic drugs are selected. The term "hydrophobic drugs" roughly describes a heterogeneous group of molecules that exhibit poor solubility in water but that are typically, but certainly not always, soluble in various organic solvents. Other types of hydrophobic drugs show even a lower aqueous solubility of only a few ng/ml.

Hence, the correct option is (B).

44. In the formulation, to facilitate the wetting of insoluble solids, Wetting agents used. Wetting agent, also called surfactant, chemical substance that increases the spreading and penetrating properties of a liquid by lowering its surface tension-that is, the tendency of its molecules to adhere to each other.

Hence, the correct option is (B).

45. Surfactants will facilitate or aid the wetting of hydrophobic materials in liquid by decreasing the solid-liquid interfacial tension. Surface active agents (surfactants) are commonly used to improve the wetting of aqueous solutions on hydrophobic surfaces. The surfactants, therefore, change the solid-liquid and solid–vapor surface tensions by the same amount, leading to an unchanged contact angle.

Hence, the correct option is (A).

46. The stability of suspensions can be evaluated by sedimentation volume, degree of flocculation and re-dispersibility. Suspension stability can be theoretically estimated prior to the beginning of the formulating process based on the solid phase particle size, liquid phase density, and viscosity. Stokes equation can be used to predict suspension stability in order to save time and resources.

Hence, the correct option is (D).

47. To identify the emulsion type, tests conducted are dye test, dilution test and conductivity test. In a dye test, a small amount of dye soluble in oil is added to the emulsion. The emulsion is shaken well. The aqueous emulsion will not take the colour whereas the oily emulsion will take up the colour of the dye. In the dilution test, the emulsion is diluted either with oil or water. If the emulsion is o/w type and is diluted with water, it will remain stable as water is the dispersion medium. If emulsion o/w type is diluted with oil, the emulsion will break as oil and water are not miscible with each other. Conductivity test is that water is a good conductor of electricity. In the case of o/w emulsion, this test will be positive as water is the continuous phase. If an electrolyte like NaCl is added to the oil in water type emulsion, its conductivity increases greatly.

Hence, the correct option is (D).

48. Stoke's Law states that the force that retards a sphere moving through a viscous fluid is directly proportional to the velocity and the radius of the sphere, and the viscosity of the fluid. Stokes' law is the basis of the falling sphere viscometer, in which the fluid is stationary in a vertical glass tube. A sphere of known size and density is allowed to descend through the liquid. If correctly selected, it reaches terminal velocity, which can be measured by the time it takes to pass two marks on the tube.

Hence, the correct option is (D).

49. The temperature at which the inversion occurs depends on emulsifier concentration is known as Phase inversion temperature. Phase inversion refers to a phenomenon that occurs when agitated oil in water emulsion, reverts to water in oil and vice versa. Emulsification via phase inversion is widely used in the fabrication of cosmetic products, pharmaceutical products (e.g., vesicles for drug delivery), foodstuff and detergents. The emulsification process is strongly affected by the preparation method; a very different droplet size distribution could be achieved, which is strictly linked to the product stability. The phase inversion process leads to the formation of finely dispersed droplets in a continuous phase. In this work, an experimental investigation of phase inversion emulsification to produce stable samples has been performed.

Hence, the correct option is (D).

50. The mechanical equipment that can be used for emulsification are homogenizers, mechanical stirrers and ultrasonifiers. A homogenizer is a piece of laboratory or industrial equipment used for the homogenization of various types of material, such as tissue, plant, food, soil, and many others. While a range of emulsifying mixer designs can be used to produce emulsions, such as stirred vessels/agitators, static mixers and homogenizers, rotor-stator mixers are particularly well suited for emulsifying (especially in the macroemulsion droplet size range).

Hence, the correct option is (D).

51. Electrolytes are not used as emulsifying agents. Examples of emulsifying agents are proteins, gums, natural and synthetic soaps, heavy metal salts of fatty acids, long chain alcohols, lampblack. Here, the electrolyte is not an emulsifying agent and hence is the correct option.

Hence, the correct option is (C).

52. HLB system was developed by Griffin. William C. Griffin of the Atlas Paper Company introduced the HLB system in 1949. Understanding the importance of these hydrophilic-lipophilic proportions, Griffin devised a method to calculate HLB values of nonionic surfactants within a range of 1-20.

Hence, the correct option is (A).

53. Gum Arabic is a branched chain, hetero polysaccharide, slightly acidic or neutral polysaccharide mainly found as a mixed salt of polysaccharidic acids, such as a magnesium and potassium. Gum Arabic contains the l-arabinose, l-rhamnose, and d-glucuronic acid and 1,3-linked β-d-galactopyranosyl units.

Hence, the correct option is (C).

54. Suspensions is not a semisolid dosage form. A suspension is a heterogeneous mixture in which the solute particles do not dissolve, but get suspended throughout the bulk of the solvent, left floating around freely in the medium. A suspension of liquid droplets or fine solid particles in a gas is called an aerosol.

Hence, the correct option is (D).

55. Generally, pastes contain high percentage of insoluble solids. Pastes are semisolid stiff preparations containing a high proportion of finely powdered material. Powders such as zinc oxide, titanium dioxide, starch, kaolin or talc are incorporated in high concentrations into a preferably lipophilic, greasy vehicle.

Hence, the correct option is (A).

56. The most widely used hydrocarbon in semisolid dosage forms are petrolatum and mineral oil. Most often, mineral oil is a liquid by-product of refining crude oil to make gasoline and other petroleum products. This type of mineral oil is a transparent, colorless oil, composed mainly of alkanes and cycloalkanes, related to petroleum jelly. It has a density of around 0.8–0.87 g/cm3 (0.029–0.031 lb/cu in).

Hence, the correct option is (C).

57. Paraffin wax and ceresin hydrocarbon waxes are employed in the manufacture of creams and ointments. Ceresin is a white-to-yellow waxy mixture of hydrocarbons obtained by the purification of ozokerite. It occurs as odorless, tasteless, amorphous (noncrystalline) brittle, waxy cakes or pastilles. Although many natural waxes contain esters, paraffin waxes are hydrocarbon derivatives, mixtures of alkane derivatives usually in a homologous series of chain lengths. These materials represent a significant fraction of crude oil and are refined by vacuum distillation.

Hence, the correct option is (C).

58. Petrolatum is not a vegetable oil. Petrolatum is mineral oil jelly (i.e. petroleum jelly). It is used as a barrier to lock moisture in the skin in a variety of moisturizers and also in hair care products to make your hair shine.

Hence, the correct option is (D).

59. A stearic fatty acid is used in water removable creams as emulsifiers. Stearic acid, also called Octadecanoic Acid, is one of the most common long-chain fatty acids, found in combined form in natural animal and vegetable fats. Pure acid undergoes chemical reactions typical of carboxylic acids. It is a colourless, waxy solid that is almost insoluble in water.

Hence, the correct option is (B).

60. Combination of a surfactant with oil-soluble auxiliary emulsifier is known as Mixed emulsifier system. These mixed emulsifier systems were found to induce long-term emulsion stability against coalescence via a synergistic "two-part" mechanism in which both the surfactant and colloidal particles components have specific functions.

Hence, the correct option is (B).

61. Promulgen means nonionic emulsifier is ethoxylated Cetearyl alcohol compounded with stearyl alcohol. Promulgen D nonionic emulsifier is 100% active and is supplied as a waxy solid. Its excellent stability at pH levels of 3-12 makes it particularly useful in applications such as depilatories. Also, due to its viscosity-building properties, it is recommended for use in hair relaxers and conditioners.

Hence, the correct option is (B).

62. Promulgen D contains Cetyl alcohol & Ceteareth-20. Ceteareth-20 is an oil emulsifier in water. Stable emulsions occur when balanced with low HLB Emulsifiers for body and viscosity. It is used in all emulsion systems including skin care, hair care and basic makeup.

Hence, the correct option is (A).

63. Promulgen G contains Stearyl alcohol & Ceteareth-20. Ceteareth-20 is a glycol ether derived from a blend of natural cetyl and stearyl alcohols (from coconut oil), and Cetearyl Alcohol, emulsified and stabilized and produced from the reduction of plant oils and natural waxes. Stearyl alcohol, $C_{18}H_{38}O$, is a compound produced from stearic acid, a naturally occurring fatty acid. In the pharmaceutical and cosmetics industries, stearyl alcohol can be used as an emulsion stabilizer, fragrance ingredient, surfactant/emulsifying agent, foam booster, and as a viscosity-increasing agent.

Hence, the correct option is (B).

64. With promulgen D, thick consistency emulsion is generally obtained. They can be either o/w or w/o and are generally opaque, thick liquids or soft solids. Emulsions are also the bases used in lotions, as are suspensions. The consistency of emulsions varies from easily pourable liquids to semisolid creams.

Hence, the correct option is (B).

65. With promulgen G, the liquid emulsion is generally obtained. Promulgen G nonionic emulsifier is 100% active and is supplied as a waxy solid. Its excellent stability at pH levels of 3-12 makes it particularly useful in applications such as depilatories. Also, due to its viscosity-building properties, it is recommended for use in hair relaxers and conditioners.

Hence, the correct option is (A).

66. The polyols used as humectants in creams are glycerine, propylene glycol and sorbitol 70%. Sorbitol, a polyol (sugar alcohol), is a bulk sweetener found in numerous food products. In addition to providing sweetness, it is an excellent humectant and texturizing agent. Glycerin is a humectant, a type of moisturizing agent that pulls water into the outer layer of your skin from deeper levels of your skin and the air. Propylene glycol is "generally recognized as safe" by the U.S. Food and Drug Administration (FDA) (FDA 2017).

Hence, the correct option is (D).

67. The choice of humectants is based on the rate of moisture exchange and viscosity and texture of the preparation. In pharmaceuticals and cosmetics, humectants can be used in topical dosage forms to increase the solubility of a chemical compound's active ingredients, increasing the active ingredient's ability to penetrate skin or its activity time.

Hence, the correct option is (C).

68. Sorbitol 70% is more hygroscopic at low concentrations. Sorbitol is a small molecule containing six hydroxyl groups. Sorbitol is not only very hygroscopic but also retains a large amount of water, it is well known that sorbitol can absorb moisture from the atmosphere when the amount of available water is low.

Hence, the correct option is (A).

69. Water number means the maximum amount of water that can be added to 100 g of a base at a given temperature. Ointments have a water number that defines the maximum amount of water that they can contain. They are used as emollients or for the application of active ingredients to the skin for protective, therapeutic, or prophylactic purposes and where a degree of occlusion is desired.

Hence, the correct option is (A).

70. Lanolin is a waxy substance naturally produced as a protective barrier for sheep's wool. It's become a popular ingredient in moisturizers, hair care products, and soaps and is widely promoted as a natural skin care remedy for people who are breastfeeding.

Hence, the correct option is (D).

71. In the preparation of vanishing creams, water removable bases are used. Emulsion or water-removable bases are oil-in-water (o/w) emulsions. As these emulsion bases have an aqueous external phase, they are water wash-able or water removable. They are non/less greasy and occlusive than ole-aginous bases. They can be diluted with water and have a better cosmetic appearance.

Hence, the correct option is (B).

72. In the preparation of cold creams, absorption bases are used. An absorption base is an oleaginous base that contains a w/o emulsifying agent. When water is taken up into the base, it will form a w/o emulsion. Absorption bases typically can incorporate about 50% of their volume in water.

Hence, the correct option is (A).

73. Water-soluble bases are also known as a greaseless ointment base. Water-soluble bases contain only water-soluble ingredients and not fats or other greasy substances hence, they are known as greaseless bases.

- Water-soluble bases consist of water-soluble ingredients such as polyethylene glycol polymer (PEG) which are popularly known as carbowaxes and commercially known as macrogols.
- Example :- Macrogol 200, 300,400 :- viscous liquid
- Macrogol 1500:- greasy semi-solid
- Macrogol 1540,3000,4000:- waxy solids

Hence, the correct option is (B).

74. In pastes, the concentration of insoluble powder substances is 20%-50%. Pastes are a dispersion of high concentrations of insoluble powdered substances (20 to 50%) in a fatty or aqueous base. The fatty bases are less greasy as well as stiffer in consistency than ointment because of the large amount of powdered material present.

Hence, the correct option is (A).

75. Jellies are generally water-soluble bases are called alkalis. Some concentrated solutions may even cause chemical burns. Alkali aqueous solutions are soapy to the touch. It is corrosive. Jellies are usually made by cooking fruit juice with sugar. Jelly should be clear or translucent and firm enough to hold its shape when turned out of the container. Jams are thick, sweet spreads, which will hold their shape but are less firm than jelly. They are made from crushed or chopped fruits and sugar.

Hence, the correct option is (A).

76. As per USP XX, the term "objectionable" means an organism can cause disease or the presence may interrupt the function of the drug or lead to deterioration of the product. Objectionable substances are substances that are unsuitable for discharge into watercourses without treatment. Key Terms and Definitions Objectionable substances are materials that are not fit to be released into rivers and streams without first being treated.

Hence, the correct option is (A).

77. Crystal fibres are not present in cinnamon. Cinnamon are either in single- or double-compound quills, with a size of 1 m length, 0.5 mm thickness, and 6 to 10 mm diameter. The outer surface has yellowish-brown colour having longitudinal lines of pericyclic fibre and scars and holes representing the position of leaves or the lateral shoots. The inner surface is darker than the outer. Cinnamon has a fragrant perfume; taste aromatic and sweet.

Hence, the correct option is (B).

78. Stone cells with three side lignin thickening are found in kantakari. Kantakari is a prickly, prostrate, perennial herb that grows throughout India. It is commonly known as Wild Eggs Plant. The name Kantakari indicates the presence of thorns in its stem. The botanical name of Kantakari is Solanum xanthocarpum and belongs to the family Solanaceae.

Hence, the correct option is (B).

79. Dog senna is obtained from cassia obovata. Dog senna derived from cassia obovata have leaves obovate (ovate with the narrower end at the base) in shape and quite different from the official leaflets. Microscopically identified by the papillose cells of the lower epidermis.

Hence, the correct option is (C).

80. The outer surface of the bark has silvery grey patches and transversely elongated lenticels are called cascara. Cascara bears a somewhat patchy, silvery-grey coat of lichens. Pieces bearing moss are also quite common. Between the patches of lichen may be seen a smooth, dark purplish-brown cork marked with lighter-coloured, transversely elongated lenticels. On scraping the cork, no bright purple inner cork is disclosed (distinction from R. alnus).

Hence, the correct option is (B).

81. Rhamnus purshianus is growing in America. Cascara is a drug of comparatively recent introduction into modern medicine. According to tradition, a cascara, probably R. californica, was known to early Mexican and Spanish priests of California; Rhamnus purshianus, however, was not described until 1805 and its bark was not introduced into medicine until 1877.

Hence, the correct option is (A).

82. The microscopical study shows stinecells & crystal fibres is liquorice. Liquorice consists of subterranean peeled and unpeeled stolons, roots and subterranean stems of Glycyrrhiza glabra Linn, and other species of Glycytrhiza, belonging to family Leguminosae. Liquorice root is in long, straight, nearly cylindrical, unpeeled pieces, several feet in length, varying in thickness from 1/4 inch to about 1 inch, longitudinally wrinkled, externally greyish brown to dark brown, warty; internally tawny yellow; pliable, tough; texture coarsely fibrous; bark rather thick; wood porous, but dense, in narrow wedges; taste sweet, very slightly acrid.

Hence, the correct option is (B).

83. Eugenol is found in a variety of plants including clove buds, cinnamon bark and leaves, tulsi leaves, turmeric, pepper, ginger, oregano, and thyme. In addition, several other aromatic herbs including basil, bay, marjoram, mace, and nutmeg are also claimed to have a significant quantity of eugenol.

The main components were found to be eugenol (76.8%), followed by β-caryophyllene (17.4%), α-humulene (2.1%), and eugenyl acetate (1.2%). Further constituents were found to be in quantities below 0.5%.

Hence, the correct option is (B).

84. Rosettes of Calcium oxalate crystals are found in Rhubarb. Rhubarb consists of the peeled dried rhizomes and roots of Rheum palmatum Linn., belonging to the family Polygonaceae. The leaves of the Turkey Rhubarb are palmate and somewhat rough. The root is thick, of an oval shape, sending off long, tapering branches; externally it is brown, internally a deep yellow colour. The stem is erect, round, hollow, jointed, branched towards the top, from 6 to 10 feet high.

Hence, the correct option is (B).

85. A spot of alcoholic solution on filter paper shows blue fluorescence in UV light in the case of Rhapontic Rhubarb. It is obtained from Rheum rhaponticum. Its odour is sweet. It consists of untrimmed pieces sometimes split longitudinally. The transverse surface shows a radiate structure, with con-centric rings of paler and darker colour and a diffuse ring of star spots. The centre may be hollow. The odour, which is sweetish, differs from that of official rhubarb. Rhapontic rhubarb gives a positive test for anthraquinone derivatives. When the test for the absence of rhapontic rhubarb is applied, it gives a distinct blue fluorescence, which may be further intensified by exposure to ammonia vapour.

Hence, the correct option is (C).

86. Carminic acid is used as an important colorant and indicator is an anthraquinone c-glycoside. Carminic acid, carmine, cochineal extract are produced in Peru, Bolivia, Mexico, Chile, and Spain (Canary Islands), from the dried bodies of female cochineal insects (Dactylopius coccus), primarily grown on Opuntia cacti. The pigments can create red, orange, purple, and pink shades, depending on the formulation. These dyes are allowed by most of the food laws in different countries, such as the Food and Drug Administration (FDA) of the United States, and the European Union, where the food additive identification code is E120 (Müller-Maatsch and Gras 2016). The chemical structure of carminic acid, the main pigment of cochineal, consists of a glucose unit, which is attached to an anthraquinone.

Hence, the correct option is (D).

87. Isoproterenol agent is a nonselective beta-receptor agonist. Isoproterenol is a beta-1 and beta-2 adrenergic receptor agonist indicated primarily for bradydysrhythmias. The administration and subsequent post-administration monitoring of this medication are complex and necessitate an interprofessional approach to its usage. This activity covers isoproterenol, including mechanism of action, pharmacology, adverse event profiles, eligible patient populations, contraindications, monitoring, and highlights the role of the interprofessional team in the management of isoproterenol therapy.

Hence, the correct option is (C).

88. The reason determining bioavailability is the extent of absorption and hepatic first-pass effect. Bioavailability refers to the extent and rate at which the active moiety (drug or metabolite) enters systemic circulation, thereby accessing the site of action. The bioavailability of a drug is largely determined by the properties of the dosage form, which depend partly on its design and manufacture. After a drug is swallowed, it is absorbed by the digestive system and enters the hepatic portal system. It is carried through the portal vein into the liver before it reaches the rest of the body. This first pass through the liver thus may greatly reduce the bioavailability of the drug.

Hence, the correct option is (C).

89. The alimentary route of administration when the passage of drugs through the liver is minimized is rectal. Rectal administration can be used for producing local or systemic effects. It is quite unreliable, however. 75% of drainage of the rectal region bypasses the portal circulation and thus minimizing the first-pass effect. The inferior and middle rectal veins are linked to the systemic circulation whereas the superior rectal vein joins the inferior mesentering vein and from there onto the portal vein. It can be very useful during vomiting and in patients that are unable to take medications by mouth.

Hence, the correct option is (C).

90. The oral route of drug administration is most likely to lead to the first-pass effect. Given by mouth is the most common route of drug administration, however, it is also the one with the most complicated pathway to the target tissues. Most drugs are absorbed in the intestinal tract by passive transfer and usually end up in the portal circulation encountering the liver and a thus high chance of passing the first-pass effect.

Hence, the correct option is (B).

91. Absorption depends on GI tract secretion and motor function is characteristic of the oral route. To be absorbed, a drug given orally must survive encounters with low pH and numerous gastrointestinal (GI) secretions, including potentially degrading enzymes. Peptide drugs (eg, insulin) are particularly susceptible to degradation and are not given orally. Absorption of oral drugs involves transport across membranes of the epithelial cells in the GI tract. Absorption is affected by:

- Differences in luminal pH along the GI tract
- Surface area per luminal volume
- Blood perfusion
- Presence of bile and mucus
- The nature of epithelial membranes

Hence, the correct option is (B).

92. The feature of the sublingual route is pretty fast absorption. One reason for selecting the sublingual route is to avoid drug destruction. Because gastric acid and intestinal and hepatic enzymes are bypassed, sublingual absorption can be more efficient overall for certain drugs than intestinal uptake. The onset of drug effects may also be quicker than with oral ingestion.

Hence, the correct option is (A).

93. The parenteral route of medicinal agent administration is Inhalation. Drugs administered by inhalation through the mouth must be atomized into smaller droplets than those administered by the nasal route so that the drugs can pass through the windpipe (trachea) and into the lungs. How deeply into the lungs they go depends on the size of the droplets. Smaller droplets go deeper, which increases the amount of drugs absorbed. Inside the lungs, they are absorbed into the bloodstream.

Hence, the correct option is (D).

94. Parenteral administration usually produces a more rapid response than oral administration. Parenteral routes of administration include the subcutaneous, intramuscular, and intravenous routes. For these routes to be viable, medication must be water-soluble or in suspension. The intravenous route of administration bypasses the absorption step, resulting in 100% bioavailability.

Hence, the correct option is (C).

95. The characteristic of the intramuscular route of drug administration is that oily solutions can be injected. An intramuscular injection is a technique used to deliver a medication deep into the muscles. This allows the medication to be absorbed into the bloodstream quickly. You may have received an intramuscular injection at a doctor's office the last time you got a vaccine, like the flu shot.

Hence, the correct option is (B).

96. Inhalation provides slow access to the general circulation characteristics of a particular route of drug administration. Drugs administered by inhalation through the mouth must be atomized into smaller droplets than those administered by the nasal route so that the drugs can pass through the windpipe (trachea) and into the lungs.

Hence, the correct option is (C).

97. Biological barriers include cell membranes, capillary walls and placenta except for renal tubules. Overcoming biological barriers including skin, mucosal membranes, blood-brain barrier as well as cell and nuclear membrane constitutes a key hurdle in the field of drug delivery. While these barriers serve the natural protective function in the body, they limit the delivery of drugs into the body. In the kidney, the barrier is located along the renal tubule and sep- arates urine from renal parenchyma.

Hence, the correct option is (A).

98. The absence of pores in the brain capillary endothelium is the reason for the complicated penetration of some drugs through the brain-blood barrier. The blood-brain barrier (BBB) is a crucial immunological feature of the human central nervous system (CNS). Composed of many cell types, the BBB is both a structural and functional roadblock to microorganisms, such as bacteria, fungi, viruses or parasites, that may be circulating in the bloodstream.

Hence, the correct option is (C).

99. The volume of distribution (Vd) relates the amount of a drug in the body to the concentration of a drug in plasma. The volume of distribution (Vd), represents the apparent volume into which the drug is distributed to provide the same concentration as it currently is in blood plasma. It is calculated by the amount of the drug in the body divided by the plasma concentration.

Hence, the correct option is (D).

100. For the calculation of the volume of distribution (Vd) one must take into account the concentration of a substance in plasma. The volume of distribution or better termed apparent volume of distribution (Vd) is another critical PK parameter. Vd is an estimation of drug distribution in the extracellular fluid. Vd can be mathematically defined as:

$$V_{d} = \frac{\text{Amount of drug in body}}{\text{Concentration of drug in blood (plasma)}}$$

Hence, the correct option is (A).

101. The term "biotransformation" includes the process of physicochemical and biochemical alteration of a drug in the body. Biotransformation is the process by which substances that enter the body are changed from hydrophobic to hydrophilic molecules to facilitate elimination from the body. This process usually generates products with few or no toxicological effects

Hence, the correct option is (D).

102. Biotransformation of the drugs is to render them less lipid-soluble. Lipid solubility determines the extent to which a drug partitions between an organic solvent and water. Propranolol, oxprenolol, metoprolol, and timolol are the most lipid-soluble beta-adrenoceptor antagonists, and atenolol, nadolol, and sotalol are the most water-soluble; acebutolol and pindolol are intermediate.

Hence, the correct option is (D).

103. Lipid soluble drug which microsomal oxidation is the most prominent. A substance will become more lipid soluble in a solution with a pH similar to its own pH. A weak base is more lipid-soluble in an alkaline solution. A weak base is more WATER-soluble in an acidic solution. The microsomal ethanol oxidizing system (MEOS) is an alternate pathway of ethanol metabolism that occurs in the smooth endoplasmic reticulum in the oxidation of ethanol to acetaldehyde.

Hence, the correct option is (A).

104. Microsomal oxidation results in an increase of ionization and water solubility of a drug. In this reaction, ethanol is oxidized (losing two hydrogens) and O_2 is reduced (by accepting hydrogen) to form H_2O. This process consumes ATP and dissipates heat, thus leading to the hypothesis that long-term drinkers see an increase in resting energy expenditure.

Hence, the correct option is (C).

105. Stimulation of liver microsomal enzymes can require the dose increase of some drugs. The liver microsomal drug-metabolizing enzyme system consists of two protein components, cytochrome P-450 and NADPH-cytochrome c reductase, and a lipid, phosphatidylcholine. Cytochrome P-450 serves as the binding site for oxygen and substrate while the reductase acts as an electron carrier shuttling electrons from NADPH to cytochrome P-450. The phospholipid facilitates the transfer of electrons from NADPH-cytochrome c reductase to cytochrome P-450 but itself is not an electron carrier.

Hence, the correct option is (A).

106. Metabolic transformation is the transformation of substances due to oxidation, reduction or hydrolysis. Phase I biotransformation reactions introduce or expose functional groups to the drug with the goal of increasing the polarity of the compound. Although Phase I drug metabolism occurs in most tissues, the primary and first-pass site of metabolism occurs during hepatic circulation. Additional metabolism occurs in gastrointestinal epithelial, renal, skin, and lung tissues. Within cells, most phase I enzymes are located in the endoplasmic reticulum and thus are enriched in microsomal preparations.

Hence, the correct option is (B).

107. Biotransformation of a medicinal substance results in faster urinary excretion. Biotransformation of most drugs takes place in hepatic microsomal enzyme systems, though other systems – including plasma, gut, lung or kidney – may be involved. Lipid-soluble drugs are more readily metabolized by hepatic microsomes because of their ease of entry into the cell. The kidneys remove most drugs or their metabolites by renal excretion involving glomerular filtration, active tubular secretion and passive tubular reabsorption. Like all cell membranes, kidney tubular cells are less permeable to the ionized portion of drugs and more permeable to lipid-soluble compounds. Excretion of drugs in other body fluids is relatively unimportant, with the exception of breast milk.

Hence, the correct option is (A).

108. Conjugation is the coupling of a drug with an endogenous substrate. Conjugation reactions usually involve metabolite activation by a high–energy intermediate and have been classified into two general types: type I (e.g., glucuronidation and sulfonation), in which an activated conjugating agent combines with the substrate to yield the conjugated product, and type II.

Hence, the correct option is (C).

109. Acetylation proceeds in the second phase of biotransformation. Phase II reactions involve conjugation by coupling the drug or its metabolites to another molecule, such as glucuronidation, acylation, sulfate, or glycine. The substances that result from metabolism may be inactive, or they may be similar to or different from the original drug in therapeutic activity or toxicity.

Hence, the correct option is (A).

110. Conjugation of a drug includes methylation, sulfate formation and glucuronidation except for hydrolysis.

Mechanism	Involved enzyme	Co-factor	Location
methylation	methyltransferase	S-adenosyl-L-methionine	liver, kidney, lung, CNS
sulphation	sulfotransferases	3'-phosphoadenosine-5'-phosphosulfate	liver, kidney, intestine
acetylation	1. N-acetyltransferases 2. bile acid-CoA:amino acid N-acyltransferases	acetyl coenzyme A	liver, lung, spleen, gastric mucosa, RBCs, lymphocytes
glucuronidation	UDP-glucuronosyltransferases	UDP-glucuronic acid	liver, kidney, intestine, lung, skin, prostate, brain
glutathione conjugation	glutathione S-transferases	glutathione	liver, kidney
glycine conjugation	Two-step process: 3. XM-ligase (forms a xenobiotic acyl-CoA) 4. Glycine N-acyltransferase (forms the	glycine	liver, kidney

	glycine conjugate)		

Hence, the correct option is (C).

111. In the case of liver disorders accompanied by a decline in microsomal enzyme activity, the duration of action of some drugs is enlarged. Duration of drug action depends on several factors are the absolute amount of drug given; the pharmaceutical preparation; the reversibility of drug action; the half-life of the drug; the slope of the concentration-response curve; the activity of metabolites, and the influence of disease on drug elimination.

Hence, the correct option is (B).

112. Half-life is the time required to change the amount of a drug in plasma by half during elimination. The half-life of a drug is the time it takes for the amount of a drug's active substance in your body to reduce by half. This depends on how the body processes and gets rid of the drug. It can vary from a few hours to a few days, or sometimes weeks.

Hence, the correct option is (A).

113. Half-life ($t_{\frac{1}{2}}$) doesn't depend on the time of drug absorption. Half-life elimination is graphically represented with elimination curves that track the amount of a drug in the body over time, typically with time on the independent axis and drug plasma concentration on the dependent axis.

Hence, the correct option is (B).

114. Elimination is expressed as the clearance of an organism from a xenobiotic. Clearance is defined as 'the volume of blood cleared of drug per unit time. Drug elimination rate is defined as 'the amount of drug cleared from the blood per unit time. In first-order kinetics, elimination rate is proportional to dose, while clearance rate remains independent of the dose.

Hence, the correct option is (D).

115. The freezing point is not a colligative property. Colligative properties of solutions are properties that depend upon the concentration of solute molecules or ions, but not upon the identity of the solute. Colligative properties include vapor pressure lowering, boiling point elevation, freezing point depression, and osmotic pressure.

Hence, the correct option is (C).

116. Andreason pipette utilizes the principle of sedimentation. Andreason pipette method is used where the samples are taken in the form of suspension. "Particle size Determination apparatus, (Sedimentation pipette, Anderson) consisting of 500ml. Pipette with three way stopcock, the tip of pipette at the lever of 0 mark at the cylinder.

Hence, the correct option is (A).

117. Isomerism that arises out of the difference in the spatial arrangement of atoms or groups about the doubly bonded carbon atoms is called Geometrical Isomerism. This type of isomerism is found in heteroleptic complexes due to different possible geometrical arrangements of the ligands. When two identical groups occupy adjacent positions, the isomer is called cis and when arranged opposite to one another, the isomer is called trans.

Hence, the correct option is (C).

118. Phenolphthalein has a pH range of 8.3-11.0. Phenolphthalein, ($C_{20}H_{14}O_4$), an organic compound of the phthalein family that is widely employed as an acid-base indicator. As an indicator of a solution's pH, phenolphthalein is colourless below pH 8.5 and attains a pink to deep red hue above pH 9.0.

Hence, the correct option is (C).

119. There are about 200 types of specialized cells in the human body. The cell is the basic unit of life. This makes sense given that every part of our body is made up of them, but not all cells are the same. In fact, our bodies are made up of over 200 types of specialized cells. Being specialized means that even though they are similar, cells differ in size, shape, or function depending on their role in our bodies. In other words, each type of cell is modified to work in the way our bodies need it to. Specialized cells group together to form tissues. Tissues then form organs like the heart, stomach, or skin.

Hence, the correct option is (A).

120. Bacteria protect themselves from viruses by fragmenting viral DNA with an endonuclease. The endonuclease is also known as restriction enzyme which is a protein that is produced by bacterial cells which leaves DNA at specific sites along with the molecule. Endonucleases are enzymes that cleave the phosphodiester bond within a polynucleotide chain.

Hence, the correct option is (B).

121. The condenser lens of the compound microscope helps in gathering and focusing light rays on the specimen to be viewed. A compound microscope contains three separate lens systems. The condenser lens is placed between the light source and the specimen and it gathers and focuses the light rays in the plane of the microscopic field to view the specimen.

Hence, the correct option is (A).

122. Pachymeningitis usually a consequence of traumatic brain injury. Pachymeningitis is a rare illness that can be shown by magnetic resonance imaging (MRI) to be a thickening of the intracranial dura mater when associated with an infectious, malignant, or rheumatic systematic disease.

Hence, the correct option is (B).

123. Concentration gradient and Electrochemical gradient both are driving forces for passive diffusion. A concentration gradient occurs when the concentration of particles is higher in one area than another. In passive transport, particles will diffuse down a concentration gradient, from areas of higher concentration to areas of lower concentration, until they are evenly spaced. Passive transport, which is moving down the electrochemical gradient; and active transport, which is a movement against the electrochemical gradient.

Hence, the correct option is (D).

124. Ototoxicity is a unique side effect of a group of diuretics loop. The most likely mechanism responsible for the potentiation of ototoxicity by loop diuretics is damage to the tight cell junctions in the blood vessels in the stria vascularis resulting in a temporary disruption of the blood-cochlear barrier which increases the permeability of the lateral wall to ototoxic drugs.

Hence, the correct option is (A).

125. Mitochondria is the largest organelles of the cytoplasm. Mitochondria are membrane-bound cell organelles (mitochondrion, singular) that generate most of the chemical energy needed to power the cell's biochemical reactions. Chemical energy produced by the mitochondria is stored in a small molecule called adenosine triphosphate (ATP).

Hence, the correct option is (B).

Pharmaceutical Chemistry

Q.1 Passive immunity can be produced by administration of:

A. Pure antigens

B. Immunoglobulins

C. Toxoids

D. Killed bacteria or viruses

Q.2 An egg is poor in:

A. Essential amino acids

B. Carbohydrates

C. Avidin

D. Biotin

Q.3 Cholesterol is present in all the following except:

A. Milk

B. Fish

C. Egg white

D. Egg yolk

Q.4 Meat is rich in all of the following except:

A. Iron

B. Fluorine

C. Phosphorus

D. Zinc

Q.5 Kwashiorkor occurs when the diet is severely deficient in:

A. Iron

B. Calories

C. Proteins

D. Essential fatty acids

Q.6 During starvation, the first reserve nutrient to be depleted is:

A. Glycogen

B. Proteins

C. Triglycerides

D. Cholesterol

Q.7 Histamine is synthesised in:

A. Brain

B. Mast cells

C. Basophils

D. All of these

Q.8 GABA(gamma-aminobutyric acid) is:

A. Post-synaptic excitatory transmitter

B. Post-synaptic inhibitor transmitter

C. Activator of glia-cell function

D. Inhibitor of glia-cell function

Q.9 The pH of an amino acid depends on:

A. Optical rotation

B. Dissociation constant

C. Diffusion coefficient

D. Chain length

Q.10 Plasma proteins are isolated by:

A. Salting out

B. Electrophoresis

C. Flourimetry

D. Both (A) and (B)

Q.11 NH_3 is detoxified in brain chiefly as:

A. Urea

B. Uric acid

C. Creatinine

D. Glutamine

Q.12 In humans, NH_3 is detoxified in liver as:

A. Creatinine

B. Uric acid

C. Urea

D. Uronic acid

Q.13 Amino acids are insoluble in:

A. Acetic acid

B. Chloroform

C. Ethanol

D. Benzene

Q.14 Which one of the following is not a side effect of using caffeine in excess?

A. Sleeplessness

B. Indigestion

C. Hypersomnia

D. Anxiety syndrome

Q.15 Biuret test is specific for:

A. Two peptide linkage

B. Phenolic group

C. Imidazole ring

D. None of these

Q.16 Dietary fats after absorption appear in the circulation as:

A. HDL

B. VLDL

C. LDL

D. Chylomicron

Q.17 Fucosidosis is characterized by:

A. Muscle spasticity

B. Liver enlargement

C. Skin rash

D. Kidney failure

Q.18 The deficiency of both energy and protein causes:

A. Marasmus

B. Kwashiorkar

C. Diabetes

D. Both (A) and (B)

Q.19 Creatinine EDTA clearance is a test to measure:

A. Renal plasma flow

B. Filtration fraction

C. Glomerular filtration rate

D. Tubular function

Q.20 Glomerular filtration rate can be measured by:

A. Endogenous creatinine clearance

B. Para-aminohippurate test

C. Addis test

D. Mosenthal test

Q.21 De novo synthesis of fatty acids requires all of the following except?

A. Biotin

B. NADH

C. Pantothenic acid

D. ATP

Q.22 Which of the following compounds help in controlling the acid production in the stomach?

A. Histamine

B. Cimetidine

C. Ranitidine

D. Omeprazole

Q.23 Body water is regulated by the hormone:

A. Oxytocin

B. ACTH

C. FSH

D. Epinephrine

Q.24 Normal range of serum albumin is:

A. 2.0-3.6 gm/dl **B.** 2.0-3.6 mg/dl
C. 3.4-5.4 gm/dl **D.** 3.5-5.5 mg/dl

Q.25 The normal range of serum globulin is:
A. 2.0-3.6 mg/dl **B.** 2.0-3.5 gm/dl
C. 3.5-5.5 mg/dl **D.** 3.5-5.5 gm/dl

Q.26 Galactose intolerance can occur in:
A. Haemolytic jaundice
B. Hepatocellular jaundice
C. Obstructive jaundice
D. None of these

Q.27 Inulin clearance is a measure of:
A. Glomerular filtration rate
B. Tubular secretion flow
C. Tubular reabsorption rate
D. Renal plasma flow

Q.28 Phenolsulfonphthalein excretion test is an indicator of:
A. Glomerular filtration
B. Tubular secretion
C. Tubular reabsorption
D. Renal blood low

Q.29 Para-amino hippurate excretion test is an indicator of:
A. Glomerular filtration
B. Tubular secretion
C. Tubular reabsorption
D. Renal plasma flow

Q.30 The renal plasma flow of an average adult man is:
A. 120-130 ml/minute **B.** 325-350 ml/minute
C. 480-52 ml/minute **D.** 560-830 ml/minute

Q.31 All the following are functions of prostaglandins except:
A. Lowering of B.P
B. Introduction of labour
C. Anti-inflammatory
D. Prevention of myocardial infarction

Q.32 Inherited deficiency of enzyme cerebro-sidase produces:
A. Fabry's disease
B. Niemann pick disease
C. Gaucher's disease
D. Tay-sach's disease

Q.33 Which lipoprotein removes cholesterol from the body?
A. HDL **B.** VLDL
C. IDL **D.** Chylomicrons

Q.34 Liposomes are:
A. Lipid bilayered **B.** Water in the middle
C. Carriers of drugs **D.** All of these

Q.35 Bile is produced by:
A. Liver **B.** Gall-bladder
C. Pancreas **D.** Intestine

Q.36 Fats are solids at:

A. 10 °C **B.** 20 °C **C.** 30 °C **D.** 40 °C

Q.37 Amylase present in saliva is:
A. α-Amylase **B.** β-Amylae
C. Y-Amylase **D.** All of these

Q.38 Selwanof's test is positive in:
A. Glucose **B.** Fructose
C. Galactose **D.** Mannose

Pharmaceutics

Q.39 A suppository is generally intended for use in:
A. Rectum **B.** Vagina
C. Urethra **D.** All of these

Q.40 Vaginal suppositories also called as:
A. Pessaries
B. Simple suppositories
C. Bougies
D. None of these

Q.41 "Oleum theobromae" was first recommended by:
A. A. B. Taylor **B.** Griffin
C. Stocks **D.** None of these

Q.42 Weight of rectal suppository for adults is:
A. 1g **B.** 2g
C. 5g **D.** None of these

Q.43 Weight of rectal suppository for children is:
A. 1g **B.** 2g
C. 5g **D.** None of these

Q.44 Plastic containers are generally made from the following material:
A. Polyethylene **B.** Polypropylene
C. Polystyrene **D.** All of these

Q.45 Urethral suppositories also called as:
A. Pessaries **B.** Bougies
C. Both (A) and (B) **D.** None of these

Q.46 Urethral suppositories having which shape:
A. Oviform shape **B.** Torpedo shape
C. Pencil shape **D.** None of these

Q.47 Weight of urethral suppository for males and females respectively:
A. 4 and 2 **B.** 2 and 4 **C.** 4 and 6 **D.** 6 and 4

Q.48 Shape of vaginal suppositories is:
A. Oviform shape **B.** Torpedo shape
C. Pencil shape **D.** None of these

Q.49 Rectal suppositories mainly used for the treatment of:
A. Constipation **B.** Hemorrhoids
C. Both (A) and (B) **D.** None of these

Q.50 The number of milligrams of KOH required neutralizing free acids & saponify the esters contained in 1g of fat is known as:

A. Iodine value
B. Saponification value
C. Water number
D. Acid value

Q.51 The number of grams of iodine that reacts with 100 g of fat is known as:
A. Iodine value
B. Saponification value
C. Water number
D. Acid yalue

Q.52 Due to which factors, petrolatum is most widely used as a hydrocarbon basic in ointments:
A. Its consistency
B. Its neutral characteristics
C. Its ability to spread easily on the skin
D. All of these

Q.53 The number of milligrams of KOH required neutralize the acetic acid used to acetylate 1g of fat is known as:
A. Iodine value
B. Saponification value
C. Hydroxil value
D. Acid value

Q.54 Which of the following method is used to manufacture suppositories?
A. Hand molding
B. Compression molding
C. Pour molding
D. All of these

Q.55 Which of the following is most commonly used suppository base?
A. Cocoa butter
B. PEG 1000
C. PEG + Hexanetriol
D. None of these

Q.56 Cocoa butter available in following forms:
A. α-form
B. β-form
C. γ-form
D. All of these

Q.57 The solidification point of cocoa butter lies between:
A. 12-13 °C
B. 20-30 °C
C. 5-10 °C
D. None of these

Q.58 Which of the following method is simple & oldest method of preparation of suppositories?
A. Pour molding
B. Hand molding
C. Compression molding
D. All of these

Q.59 Most commonly used method for producing suppositories on both a small & large scale is:
A. Hand molding
B. Compression molding
C. Pour molding
D. All of these

Q.60 Which formula can be used to calculate the amount of base that is replaced by active ingredients?
A. 100(G - E) f = +1(G)(X)
B. 100(E-G) f = +100(G)(X)
C. 100(E-G) f = +1(G)(X)
D. 100(E-G) f = +10(G)(X)

Q.61 Rancidity generally results from:
A. Auto-oxidation
B. Decomposition of unsaturated fats
C. Both (A) and (B)
D. None of these

Q.62 Which of the following is not anti-oxidant?
A. BHT
B. BHA
C. Tocopherol
D. Theobroma oil

Q.63 Suppositories are generally evaluated by:
A. Melting range test
B. Breaking test
C. Liquefaction
D. All of these

Q.64 Which of the following materials are used in pharmaceutical packaging?
A. Glass
B. Plastic
C. Metal
D. All of these

Q.65 Which of the following packaging material is used to protect the drug content against light?
A. Plastic containers
B. Amber-colored glass containers
C. Both (A) and (B)
D. None of these

Q.66 Major disadvantages of glass as a packing material are:
A. Fragility
B. Weight
C. Both (A) and (B)
D. None of these

Q.67 Composition of glass is:
A. Sand
B. Soda ash
C. Lime stone & Cullet
D. All of these

Q.68 Soda ash also known as:
A. Pure silica
B. Sodium carbonate
C. Lime stone
D. Calcium carbonate

Q.69 Which of the following one is a broken glass & acts as fusion agent?
A. Cullet
B. Soda ash
C. Lime stone
D. Sand

Q.70 Which of the following methods are used in the production of glass?
A. Blowing
B. Drawing
C. Pressing & casting
D. All of these

Q.71 To produce molten glass, which of the following method is used?
A. Blowing
B. Drawing
C. Pressing
D. Casting

Q.72 To protect the contents of a bottle from the effects of sunlight by UV rays, which glass is used?

A. Amber glass
B. Red glass
C. Both (A) and (B)
D. None of these

Q.73 To evaluate the chemical resistance of glass, which of the following tests are conducted?

A. Powder glass
B. Water attack test
C. Both (A) and (B)
D. None of these

Q.74 Which of the following test is performed on crushed grains, to evaluate the chemical resistance of glass?

A. Powder glass
B. Water attack test
C. Both (A) and (B)
D. None of these

Q.75 Which of the following test is performed on whole container?

A. Powder glass
B. Water attack test
C. Both (A) and (B)
D. None of these

Q.76 Type L glass is also known as:

A. Borosilicate glass
B. Regular soda-lime glass
C. Treated soda-lime glass
D. None of these

Pharmacognosy

Q.77 Reticulate xylem vessels showing no reaction for lignin are found in:

A. Rhubarb
B. Licorice
C. Rauwolfia
D. Ashwagandha

Q.78 Flavonoids dissolve in alkalis gives colour:

A. Blue
B. Green
C. Yellow
D. Red

Q.79 Compound commercially available in tablets and injection as potent coronary vasodilator is:

A. Silymarin
B. Rutin
C. Xanthotoxin
D. Khellin

Q.80 Geraniol is absent in volatile oil of:

A. Dill
B. Rose
C. Geranium
D. Palmarosa

Q.81 Carvone is absent in volatile oil of:

A. Carum carvi
B. Mentha spicata
C. Anethum graveolens
D. Mentha piperata

Q.82 The endosperm of the fruits of Umbelliferae is characterized by the presence of the following types of calcium oxalate crystals:

A. Prisms
B. Microrosettes
C. Clusters
D. Microsphenoids

Q.83 A small secretory canal above vascular bundle is seen in T.S. of:

A. Fennel
B. Coriander
C. Caraway
D. Dill

Q.84 Two lateral ridges are flattened to form wing-like structures in case of:

A. Caraway
B. Dill
C. Coriander
D. Fennel

Q.85 There are only two vittae in each mericarp of:

A. Coriander
B. Caraway
C. Dill
D. Anise

Q.86 There are ten primary ridges which are wavy and inconspicuous on outer surface of:

A. Dill
B. Caraway
C. Fennel
D. Coriander

Pharmacology

Q.87 Indicate the beta-1 selective agonist:

A. Isoproterenol
B. Dobutamine
C. Metaproterenol
D. Epinephrine

Q.88 Pharmacodynamics involves the study of following EXCEPT:

A. Biological and therapeutic effects of drugs
B. Absorption and distribution of drugs
C. Mechanisms of drug action
D. Drug interactions

Q.89 What does "affinity" mean?

A. A measure of how tightly a drug binds to plasma proteins.
B. A measure of how tightly a drug binds to a receptor.
C. A measure of inhibiting potency of a drug.
D. A measure of bioavailability of a drug.

Q.90 Irreversible interaction of an antagonist with a receptor is due to:

A. Ionic bonds
B. Hydrogen bonds
C. Covalent bonds
D. All of these

Q.91 Find the second messenger of G-protein-coupled metabotropic receptor:

A. Adenylyl cyclase
B. Sodium ions
C. Phospholipase C
D. cAMP

Q.92 Which effect may lead to toxic reactions when a drug is taken continuously or repeatedly?

A. Refractoriness
B. Cumulative effect
C. Tolerance
D. Tachyphylaxis

Q.93 What term is used to describe a decrease in responsiveness to a drug which develops in a few minutes?

A. Refractoriness
B. Cumulative effect
C. Tolerance
D. Tachyphylaxis

Q.94 Most local anesthetic agents consist of:

A. Lipophylic group (frequently an aromatic ring)
B. Intermediate chain (commonly including an ester or amide)
C. Amino group
D. All of these

Q.95 Indicate the local anesthetic agent, which has a shorter duration of action:

A. Lidocaine

B. Procaine

C. Bupivacaine

D. Ropivacaine

Q.96 Indicate the drug, which has greater potency of the local anesthetic action:

A. Lidocaine

B. Bupivacaine

C. Procaine

D. Mepivacaine

Q.97 Which one of the following local anesthetics is an ester of benzoic acid?

A. Lidocaine

B. Procaine

C. Ropivacaine

D. Cocaine

Q.98 Local anesthetics are:

A. Weak bases

B. Weak acids

C. Salts

D. None of these

Q.99 Which of the following local anestheties is called a universal anesthetic?

A. Procaine

B. Ropivacaine

C. Lidocaine

D. Bupivacaine

Q.100 Which of the following cholinomimetics activates both muscarinic and nicotinic receptors?

A. Lobeline

B. Pilocarpine

C. Nicotine

D. Bethanechol

Q.101 Indicate cholinesterase reactivator:

A. Pralidoxime

B. Edrophonium

C. Pilocarpine

D. Isoflurophate

Q.102 Which of the following cholinomimetics is most widely used for paralytic ileus and atony of the urinary bladder?

A. Lobeline

B. Neostigmine

C. Pilocarpine

D. Echothiophate

Q.103 Which of the following drugs is both a muscarinic and nicotinic blocker?

A. Atropine

B. Benztropine

C. Hexamethonium

D. Succinylcholine

Q.104 Which of the following agents is a ganglion-blocking drug?

A. Homatropine

B. Hexamethonium

C. Rapacuronium

D. Edrophonium

Q.105 Indicate the skeletal muscle relaxant, which is a depolarizing agent:

A. Vencuronium

B. Scopolamine

C. Succinylcholine

D. Hexamethonium

Q.106 Which of the following drugs is a nondepolarizing muscle relaxant?

A. Pancuronium

B. Succinylcholine

C. Hexamethonium

D. Scopolamine

Q.107 Which of the following drugs is useful in the treatment of Parkinson's disease?

A. Benztropine

B. Edrophonium

C. Succinylcholine

D. Hexamethonium

Q.108 Which of the following drugs has "double-acetylcholine" structure?

A. Rocuronium

B. Carbachol

C. Atracurium

D. Succylcholine

Q.109 Indicate the long-acting neuromuscular blocking agent:

A. Rapacuronium

B. Mivacurium

C. Tubocurarine

D. Rocuronium

Q.110 Which competitive neuromuscular blocking agent could be used in patients with renal failure?

A. Atracurium

B. Succinylcholine

C. Pipecuronium

D. Doxacurium

Q.111 Catecholamine includes following except:

A. Ephedrine

B. Epinephrine

C. Isoprenaline

D. Norepinephrine

Q.112 A relatively pure alfa agonist causes all of the following effects EXCEPT:

A. Increase peripheral arterial resistance

B. Increase venous return

C. Has no effect on blood vessels

D. Reflex bradycardia

Q.113 Which of the following effects is associated with beta- 3 receptor stimulation?

A. Lipolysis

B. Decrease in platelet aggregation

C. Bronchodilation

D. Tachycardia

Q.114 Indicate the alpha-2 selective agonists:

A. Xylometazoline

B. Epinephrine

C. Epinephrine

D. Methoxamine

Other Subjects

Q.115 Which of the following is not a volatile substance?

A. Camphor

B. Petrol

C. Acetone

D. Acetanilide

Q.116 Rate of reaction can be incresed by:

A. Pramotor

B. Enhancer

C. Catalytic poison

D. Catalyst

Q.117 Which among the following defines Meso forms of isomers?

A. Meso form is optically inactive due to external compensation.

B. The molecules of the meso isomers are chiral.

C. It can be separated into optically active enantiometric pairs.

D. It is a single compound.

Q.118 Errors arise due to the individual analyst is responsible for them:

A. Method error

B. Instrumental error

C. Personal error

D. Random error

Q.119 A eukaryotic cell is generally 10 to _____________ μm in diameter.

A. 400   **B.** 300   **C.** 200   **D.** 100

Q.120 Klenow fragment is derived from:

A.   DNA Ligase

B.   DNA Pol-I

C.   DNA Pol-II

D.   Reverse Transcriptase

Q.121 Which microorganism(s) among the following perform photosynthesis by utilizing light?

A. Viruses   **B.** Fungi

C. Cyanobacteria   **D.** None of these

Q.122 In the earliest stages of pulmonary edema all of the following are true except:

A.   Fluid tracks through the interstitium of the thin side of the blood Gas barrier to the perivascular and peribronchial spaces.

B.   There is no increase in lung lymph flow.

C.   Fluid floods the alveoli one by one.

D.   Cuffs of fluid collect around the small arteries and veins.

Q.123 What is the driving force for pore transport?

A.   Hydrostatic pressure

B.   Concentration gradient

C.   Electrochemical gradient

D.   Charge equilibration

Q.124 Antihypertensive therapy should be avoided in type-1 diabetes mellitus:

A.   ACE inhibitors

B.   High dose diuretics

C.   Centrally acting

D.   Calcium channel blockers

Q.125 Plasma membrane consist __________ amount of phospholipids.

A. 53%   **B.** 10%   **C.** 75%   **D.** 100%

// Smart Answer Sheet //

Correct — Percentage of students who answered correctly. **Skipped** — Percentage of students who skipped.

Q.	Ans.	Correct	Skipped	Q.	Ans.	Correct	Skipped	Q.	Ans.	Correct	Skipped	Q.	Ans.	Correct	Skipped	Q.	Ans.	Correct	Skipped	Q.	Ans.	Correct	Skipped
1	B	42.34 %	51.95 %	22	A	63.0 %	35.39 %	43	A	68.02 %	30.67 %	64	D	60.21 %	36.68 %	85	A	52.97 %	34.76 %	106	A	45.97 %	40.09 %
2	B	47.56 %	41.58 %	23	B	14.33 %	76.5 %	44	D	56.21 %	33.78 %	65	B	51.49 %	44.33 %	86	D	69.07 %	30.82 %	107	A	58.54 %	31.78 %
3	C	76.25 %	14.31 %	24	C	68.36 %	31.11 %	45	B	48.28 %	30.86 %	66	C	53.41 %	39.85 %	87	B	42.95 %	38.91 %	108	D	80.57 %	14.1 %
4	B	57.82 %	38.45 %	25	B	41.47 %	41.19 %	46	C	67.2 %	32.56 %	67	D	47.33 %	37.62 %	88	B	61.56 %	32.06 %	109	C	24.97 %	70.25 %
5	C	69.9 %	30.01 %	26	B	65.99 %	32.97 %	47	A	66.98 %	32.19 %	68	B	64.28 %	34.47 %	89	B	44.49 %	33.6 %	110	A	64.03 %	35.85 %
6	A	69.02 %	30.57 %	27	B	63.8 %	34.49 %	48	A	61.82 %	36.42 %	69	A	46.72 %	38.05 %	90	C	77.95 %	12.56 %	111	A	48.58 %	50.2 %
7	D	64.75 %	32.42 %	28	D	47.59 %	30.72 %	49	C	60.75 %	30.1 %	70	D	83.05 %	14.87 %	91	D	65.84 %	33.4 %	112	C	14.21 %	76.7 %
8	B	66.25 %	30.74 %	29	D	50.29 %	42.88 %	50	B	64.39 %	31.45 %	71	A	67.12 %	30.79 %	92	B	55.92 %	35.93 %	113	A	48.59 %	33.42 %
9	B	57.03 %	37.69 %	30	D	47.9 %	32.57 %	51	A	86.58 %	12.94 %	72	A	45.12 %	44.38 %	93	D	43.04 %	44.04 %	114	A	65.25 %	33.8 %
10	D	68.82 %	30.28 %	31	D	31.63 %	68.29 %	52	D	40.76 %	44.06 %	73	C	51.95 %	39.89 %	94	D	62.71 %	36.18 %	115	D	77.74 %	17.6 %
11	D	69.89 %	30.05 %	32	C	47.65 %	33.43 %	53	C	66.68 %	30.91 %	74	A	44.28 %	33.21 %	95	B	88.93 %	10.97 %	116	B	63.47 %	30.71 %
12	C	61.26 %	34.86 %	33	A	57.22 %	31.39 %	54	D	19.79 %	74.3 %	75	B	62.05 %	32.56 %	96	B	60.77 %	34.65 %	117	D	78.74 %	18.83 %
13	D	65.21 %	31.94 %	34	D	59.88 %	36.95 %	55	A	61.62 %	33.06 %	76	A	69.8 %	30.08 %	97	D	63.63 %	34.75 %	118	C	54.37 %	30.98 %
14	C	42.93 %	52.06 %	35	A	89.03 %	10.8 %	56	D	42.82 %	47.54 %	77	A	66.8 %	32.73 %	98	A	47.85 %	42.56 %	119	D	61.2 %	33.75 %
15	A	51.01 %	43.09 %	36	B	58.55 %	40.37 %	57	A	46.25 %	32.35 %	78	C	80.47 %	15.81 %	99	C	48.22 %	51.19 %	120	B	43.83 %	33.71 %
16	D	53.46 %	35.52 %	37	A	84.85 %	12.86 %	58	B	85.15 %	11.64 %	79	D	65.04 %	30.27 %	100	D	47.45 %	35.85 %	121	C	47.12 %	52.72 %
17	A	59.2 %	30.62 %	38	B	67.97 %	30.55 %	59	C	45.15 %	33.22 %	80	A	64.25 %	34.69 %	101	A	14.65 %	84.32 %	122	D	61.64 %	34.72 %
18	D	44.16 %	36.12 %	39	D	65.58 %	32.9 %	60	C	68.86 %	30.07 %	81	D	40.85 %	32.54 %	102	B	62.52 %	30.03 %	123	A	50.64 %	48.42 %
19	C	67.22 %	30.44 %	40	A	45.16 %	47.92 %	61	C	47.5 %	44.27 %	82	B	58.99 %	36.54 %	103	B	60.51 %	38.27 %	124	C	64.81 %	31.45 %
20	A	67.06 %	30.47 %	41	A	67.86 %	32.04 %	62	D	52.38 %	32.03 %	83	C	44.7 %	43.07 %	104	B	54.13 %	36.95 %	125	B	61.31 %	36.23 %
21	D	41.03 %	37.18 %	42	B	46.64 %	30.66 %	63	D	65.63 %	31.65 %	84	B	69.38 %	30.41 %	105	C	50.14 %	40.2 %				

//Hints and Solutions//

1. Passive immunity can be produced by administration of Immunoglobulins. Immunoglobulins, also known as antibodies, are glycoprotein molecules produced by plasma cells (white blood cells). They act as a critical part of the immune response by specifically recognizing and binding to particular antigens, such as bacteria or viruses, and aiding in their destruction.

Hence, the correct option is (B).

2. An egg is poor in carbohydrates. Eggs are a low-carb, low-calorie and low-cost source of protein. One egg provides 6 to 8 grams of protein with only 70 calories. Extremely nutritious, eggs are a complete protein and have a rich supply of key vitamins and minerals.

Hence, the correct option is (B).

3. Cholesterol is present in milk, fish and egg yolk except for egg white. When it comes to egg whites, it's true that there's no cholesterol in the white part of an egg. A whole large egg contains 186 mg of cholesterol, but all of that is found in the yolk or yellow part. For them, eating that many eggs may significantly increase heart disease risk.

Hence, the correct option is (C).

4. Meat is rich in iron, Phosphorus and zinc except for fluorine. Meat is mainly composed of water, protein, and fat. The following vitamins and minerals are abundant in beef:

- **Vitamin B12:** Animal-derived foods, such as meat, are the only good dietary sources of vitamin B12, an essential nutrient that is important for blood formation and your brain and nervous system.

- **Zinc:** Beef is very rich in zinc, a mineral that is important for body growth and maintenance.

- **Selenium:** Meat is generally a rich source of selenium, an essential trace element that serves a variety of functions in your body (12Trusted Source).

- **Iron:** Found in high amounts in beef, meat iron is mostly in the heme form, which is absorbed very efficiently (13Trusted Source).

- **Niacin:** One of the B vitamins, niacin (vitamin B3) has various important functions in your body. Low niacin intake has been associated with an increased risk of heart disease (14Trusted Source).

- **Vitamin B6:** A family of B vitamins, vitamin B6 is important for blood formation and energy metabolism.

- **Phosphorus:** Widely found in foods, phosphorus intake is generally high in the Western diet. It's essential for body growth and maintenance.

Hence, the correct option is (B).

5. Kwashiorkor occurs when the diet is severely deficient in proteins. The main cause of kwashiorkor is not eating enough protein or other essential vitamins and minerals. It's most common in developing countries with a limited food supply, poor hygiene, and a lack of education about the importance of giving babies and children an adequate diet.

Hence, the correct option is (C).

6. During starvation, the first reserve nutrient to be depleted is glycogen. The symptoms of starvation show up in three stages. Phase one and two can show up in anyone that skips meals, diets, and goes through fasting. Phase three is more severe, can be fatal, and results from long-term starvation. In phase 1 when meals are skipped, the body begins to maintain blood sugar levels by producing glycogen in the liver and breaking down stored fat and protein. The liver can provide glycogen for the first few hours. After that, the body begins to break down fat and protein. The body uses Fatty acids as an energy source for muscles but lowers the amount of glucose sent to the brain. Another chemical that comes from fatty acids is glycerol. It can be used as glucose for energy but eventually runs out.

Hence, the correct option is (A).

7. Histamine is synthesized primarily by mast cells, basophils, histaminergic neurons in the basal ganglia of the brain and enterochromaffin-like cells (ECL) in the stomach. Histamine - a chemical found in some of the body's cells - causes many of the symptoms of allergies, such as a runny nose or sneezing. When a person is allergic to a particular substance, such as food or dust, the immune system mistakenly believes that this usually harmless substance is actually harmful to the body.

Hence, the correct option is (D).

8. GABA (gamma-aminobutyric acid) is a post-synaptic inhibitor transmitter. GABA is a small-molecule neurotransmitter synthesized within the presynaptic terminal of GABA-containing neurons. Once synthesized, GABA is packaged in vesicles and stored at the post-synaptic terminal until the arrival of an action potential causes these vesicles to release their contents into the synaptic cleft.

Hence, the correct option is (B).

9. The pH of an amino acid depends on the dissociation constant. The dissociation constant is the ratio of original acid (reactants) to the dissociated ions (products). Ka is the abbreviation for it. Our typical method for determining the dissociation constant is to measure how much is dissociated in water.

Hence, the correct option is (B).

10. Plasma proteins are isolated by salting out and electrophoresis. Nowadays, most coagulation proteins are isolated from plasma using combinations of ion exchange, molecular sieve and affinity chromatographies. Sometimes, e.g. for Vitamin K-dependent factors, specific adsorption properties are utilized. However, at high concentrations of salt, the solubility of the proteins drops sharply and proteins can precipitate out, referred to as "salting out". Lithium-heparin plasma is the most commonly used sample type in many hospitals, but it has been suggested that it is not suitable for protein electrophoresis due to the presence of fibrinogen, which can potentially mask a paraprotein band or be misconstrued as one.

Hence, the correct option is (D).

11. NH_3 is detoxified in brain chiefly as Glutamine. Ammonia in brain is chiefly metabolized ("detoxified") to glutamine in astrocytes due to predominant localization of glutamine synthetase in these cells. While glutamine has long been considered innocuous, a deleterious role more recently has been attributed to this amino acid.

Hence, the correct option is (D).

12. In humans, NH_3 is detoxified in the liver as urea. Ammonia is detoxified in the liver by conversion to urea by the Krebs-Henseleit cycle. Ammonia is also consumed in the conversion of glutamate to glutamine, a reaction that depends upon the activity of glutamine synthetase. Two factors contribute to the hyperammonemia that is seen in cirrhosis.

Hence, the correct option is (C).

13. Amino acids are insoluble in benzene. Amino acids are soluble in polar solvents like H_2O, NaOH and HCl and insoluble in non-polar solvents like benzene, ether, etc. Sidechains which have pure hydrocarbon alkyl groups (alkane branches) or aromatic (benzene rings) are non-polar. Examples include valine, alanine, leucine, isoleucine, phenylalanine.

Hence, the correct option is (D).

14. Caffeine is harmful when used in excess, it causes indigestion, sleeplessness, disturbed functioning of pancreas and kidneys and development of anxiety syndrome. Non-availability causes headache, anxiety and loss of concentration.

Hence, the correct option is (C).

15. Biuret test is specific for two peptide linkage. Biuret test is used for detecting compounds with peptide bonds. A biuret reagent may be used to test the aqueous sample. The test, however, gives positive result to any compound containing two carbonyl groups attached to a nitrogen or carbon atom. Thus, it may not be completely protein-specific.

Hence, the correct option is (A).

16. Dietary fats after absorption appear in the circulation as a chylomicron. Chylomicrons transport lipids absorbed from the intestine to adipose, cardiac, and skeletal muscle tissue, where their triglyceride components are hydrolyzed by the activity of the lipoprotein lipase, allowing the released free fatty acids to be absorbed by the tissues.

Hence, the correct option is (D).

17. Fucosidosis is characterized by muscle spasticity. Fucosidosis is a rare genetic disorder characterized by a deficiency of the enzyme alpha-L-fucosidase, which is required to break down (metabolize) certain complex compounds (e.g., fucose-containing glycolipids or fucose-containing glycoproteins). Fucose is a type of sugar required by the body to perform certain functions (essential sugar). The inability to break down fucose-containing compounds results in their accumulation in various tissues in the body. Fucosidosis results in progressive neurological deterioration, skin abnormalities, growth retardation, skeletal disease and coarsening of facial features.

Hence, the correct option is (A).

18. The deficiency of both energy and protein causes marasmus and kwashiorkar. Nutrient deficiency is the main cause of marasmus. It occurs in children that don't ingest enough protein, calories, carbohydrates, and other important nutrients. This is usually due to poverty and a scarcity of food. Protein-energy undernutrition doesn't occur due to short-term illnesses. It's more likely due to malnutrition over a long period. Two main types of this undernutrition are marasmus and kwashiorkor.

Hence, the correct option is (D).

19. Creatinine EDTA clearance is a test to measure the glomerular filtration rate. Creatinine Clearance (CrCl) versus Glomerular Filtration Rate (GFR) Creatinine clearance (CrCl) is an estimate of Glomerular Filtration Rate (GFR); however, CrCl is slightly higher than true GFR because creatinine is secreted by the proximal tubule (in addition to being filtered by the glomerulus).

Hence, the correct option is (C).

20. Glomerular filtration rate can be measured by endogenous creatinine clearance. The glomerular filtration rate (GFR) describes the volume of fluid filtered from the renal (kidney) glomerular capillaries into the Bowman's capsule per unit time. Creatinine clearance is the volume of blood plasma that is cleared of creatinine per unit time and is a useful measure for approximating the GFR. Creatinine clearance exceeds GFR due to creatinine secretion, which can be blocked by cimetidine. Both GFR and CCr may be accurately calculated by comparative measurements of substances in the blood and urine or estimated by formulas using just a blood test result (eGFR and eCCr).

Hence, the correct option is (A).

21. De novo synthesis of fatty acids requires biotin, NADH and pantothenic acid except for ATP. In humans, biotin is involved in important metabolic pathways such as gluconeogenesis, fatty acid synthesis, and amino acid catabolism by acting a as prosthetic group for pyruvate carboxylase, propionyl-CoA carboxylase, beta-methyl crotinyl-CoA carboxylase, and acetyl-CoA carboxylase. All desaturases require oxygen and ultimately consume NADH even though desaturation is an oxidative process. Two electrons come from NADH + H+ and two from the single bond in the fatty acid chain. Pantothenic acid, in its function as a cofactor for CoA, is necessary for the synthesis of many compounds including fatty acids, cholesterol, steroid hormones, molecules containing isoprenoid units (e.g., vitamins A and D), δ-aminolevulinic acid, and some neurotransmitters and amino acids.

Hence, the correct option is (D).

22. Histamine is the compound that is responsible for the secretion of pepsin and HCl in the stomach. Drugs like cimetidine (Tagamet), ranitidine (Zantac), omeprazole and lansoprazole prevent the interaction of histamine with the stomach wall receptors, resulting in the release of lesser acid.

Hence, the correct option is (A).

23. Body water is regulated by the hormone ACTH. ACTH is a hormone made by the pituitary gland, a small gland at the base of the brain. ACTH controls the production of another hormone called cortisol. Cortisol is made by the adrenal glands, two small glands located above the kidneys. Adrenocorticotropic hormone (ACTH) plays a large role in how your body responds to stress. ACTH is produced in the pituitary gland, its production stimulates the production and release of cortisol from the adrenal gland.

Hence, the correct option is (B).

24. The normal range of serum albumin is 3.4-5.4 gm/dl. If you have a lower albumin level, you may have malnutrition. It can also mean that you have liver disease or an inflammatory disease. Higher albumin levels may be caused by acute infections, burns, and stress from surgery or a heart attack. When a person's levels are found to be lower than the average range, it could indicate conditions, such as Crohn's disease and liver disease.

Hence, the correct option is (C).

25. The normal range of serum globulin is 2.0-3.5 gm/dl. A globulin or mixture of globulins occurring in blood serum and containing most of the antibodies of the blood. Results from a globulin test come in the form of laboratory values. These numbers indicate whether a person has healthy levels of proteins in their blood. Protein globulin levels for adults normally fall between 2.3 and 3.4 grams per deciliter (g/dL). The normal range for total protein is between 6.4 and 8.3 g/dL.

Hence, the correct option is (B).

26. Galactose intolerance can occur in hepatocellular jaundice. It occurs when bilirubin is unable to leave the liver cells and cannot be removed from the body by the kidneys. Hepatocellular jaundice is usually caused by liver failure, liver disease (cirrhosis), hepatitis (inflammation of the liver), or by taking certain types of medication.

Hence, the correct option is (B).

27. Inulin clearance is a measure of tubular secretion flow. The inulin clearance, the procedure by which the filtering capacity of the glomeruli (the main filtering structures of the kidney) is determined by measuring the rate at which inulin, the test substance, is cleared from blood plasma. Tubular secretion is the transfer of materials from peritubular capillaries to the renal tubular lumen; it is the opposite process of reabsorption.

Hence, the correct option is (B).

28. Phenolsulfonphthalein excretion test is an indicator of renal blood low. The phenolsulfonphthalein (PSP [phenol red]) excretion test was developed by Rowntree and Geraghty in 1910 when chemical determinations were generally unavailable, and assessment of renal function was essentially limited to examination of the urine for protein and sediment. Phenolsulfonphthalein is used as a test to help diagnose problems or diseases of the kidneys. This test determines how well your kidneys are working.

Hence, the correct option is (D).

29. Para-amino hippurate excretion test is an indicator of renal plasma flow. Para-amino hippurate (PAH) clearance is a method used in renal physiology to measure renal plasma flow, which is a measure of renal function. PAH is completely removed from the blood that passes through the kidneys (PAH undergoes both glomerular filtration and tubular secretion), and therefore the rate at which the kidneys can clear PAH from the blood reflects total renal plasma flow.

Hence, the correct option is (D).

30. The renal p asma flow of an average adult man is 560-830 ml/minute. In the physiology of the kidney, renal blood flow (RBF) is the volume of blood delivered to the kidneys per unit of time. In humans, the kidneys together receive roughly 25% of cardiac output, amounting to 1.2 - 1.3 L/min in a 70-kg adult male. It passes about 94% to the cortex. RBF is closely related to renal plasma flow (RPF), which is the volume of blood plasma delivered to the kidneys per unit of time.

Hence, the correct option is (D).

31. Lowering of B.P, Introduction of labour and Anti-inflammatory are functions of prostaglandins except for prevention of myocardial infarction. The prostaglandins are a group of lipids made at sites of tissue damage or infection that are involved in dealing with injury and illness. They control processes such as inflammation, blood flow, the formation of blood clots and the induction of labour. Smoking cessation, cholesterol reduction, control of hypertension, maintenance of ideal body weight, and regular exercise all appear to reduce the risk of a first myocardial infarction substantially.

Hence, the correct option is (D).

32. Inherited deficiency of enzyme cerebrosides produces Gaucher's disease. Gaucher disease is a rare, inherited metabolic disorder in which deficiency of the enzyme glucocerebrosidase results in the accumulation of harmful quantities of certain fats (lipids), specifically the glycolipid glucocerebroside, throughout the body especially within the bone marrow, spleen and liver.

Hence, the correct option is (C).

33. HDL lipoprotein removes cholesterol from the body. HDL (high-density lipoprotein), or "good" cholesterol, absorbs cholesterol and carries it back to the liver. The liver then flushes it from the body. High levels of HDL cholesterol can lower your risk for heart disease and stroke.

Hence, the correct option is (A).

34. Liposomes are lipid bilayered, water in the middle and carriers of drugs. A liposome is a tiny bubble (vesicle), made out of the same material as a cell membrane. Liposomes can be filled with drugs and used to deliver drugs for cancer and other diseases. In nature, phospholipids are found in stable membranes composed of two layers (a bilayer).

Hence, the correct option is (D).

35. Bile is produced by the liver. Bile (from Latin bilis), or gall, is a dark-green-to-yellowish-brown fluid produced by the liver of most vertebrates that aids the digestion of lipids in the small intestine. In humans, bile is produced continuously by the liver (liver bile) and stored and concentrated in the gallbladder.

Hence, the correct option is (A).

36. Fats are solids at 20 °C. Saturated fat is solid at room temperature, which is why it is also known as "solid fat." It is mostly in animal foods, such as milk, cheese, and meat. Poultry and fish have less saturated fat than red meat. Saturated fat is also in tropical oils, such as coconut oil, palm oil, and cocoa butter.

Hence, the correct option is (B).

37. Amylase present in the saliva is α-Amylase. α-Amylase is the major digestive enzyme in saliva. It hydrolyses α-1,4 glycosidic linkages in starch. In animals, it is a major digestive enzyme, and its optimum pH is 6.7–7.0. In human physiology, both salivary and pancreatic amylases are α-Amylase.

Hence, the correct option is (A).

38. Selwanof's test is positive in fructose. Fructose and sucrose are two common sugars that give a positive test. Sucrose gives a positive test as it is a disaccharide consisting of fructose and glucose. Generally, 6M HCl is used to run this test. Ketose gets dehydrated faster and hence they give the test faster.

Hence, the correct option is (B).

39. A suppository is generally intended for use in the rectum, vagina and urethra. A suppository is a dosage form used to deliver medications by insertion into a body orifice where it dissolves or melts to exert local or systemic effects. There are three types of suppositories, each to insert into a different section:

- Rectal suppositories into the rectum.
- Vaginal suppositories into the vagina.
- Urethral suppositories into the urethra of a male.

Hence, the correct option is (D).

40. Vaginal suppositories also called as pessaries. A pessary is a prosthetic device that can be inserted into the vagina to support its internal structure. It's often used in the case of urinary incontinence and a vaginal or pelvic organ prolapse. A prolapse occurs when the vagina or another organ in the pelvis slips out of its usual place.

Hence, the correct option is (A).

41. "Oleum theobromae" was first recommended by A. B. Taylor. Oil of theobroma occurs as a yellowish-white solid, having a faint, agreeable odor and a bland chocolate-like taste. It is freely soluble in ether, chloroform and benzene, soluble in absolute alcohol and insoluble in water. Oil of theobroma is used in pharmacy chiefly for the making of suppositories. Also used as a lubricant in massage, and as an application to sore nipples.

Hence, the correct option is (A).

42. Rectal suppositories for adults usually weight about 2 grams while infant rectal suppositories usually weight about 1 gram or about half that of adult suppositories. Vaginal preparations include solutions, powders for solutions, ointments, creams, aerosol foams, suppositories, and tablets.

Hence, the correct option is (B).

43. The weight of rectal suppository for children is 1g. Suppositories are made with clean and non-rancid cocoa butter. The cocoa butter is melted at low heat on the stove. Then herbs or vitamin E or other substances of your choice are added to the melted cocoa butter. These rectal forms were particularly used in some European countries and in Japan where the use of suppositories is more accepted than in other territories like the United States of America or Laos for example.

Hence, the correct option is (A).

44. Plastic containers are generally made from polyethylene, polypropylene and polystyrene. Plastic bottles are made of polymers, which are chemically bonded to create materials such as polyethylene and polystyrene. The different raw materials of plastic bottles include polyethylene terephthalate and high-density polyethylene.

Hence, the correct option is (D).

45. Urethral suppositories, formerly called bougies, vary in their dimensions, depending on the sex of the patient. Suppositories for females are about 5 mm in diameter, 50 mm in length, and 2 g in weight. Suppositories for males are 5 mm in diameter, 125 mm in length, and 4 g in weight.

Hence, the correct option is (B).

46. Urethral inserts, also called bougies, are slender, pencil-shaped suppositories intended for insertion into the male or female urethra. Alprostadil pellets are urethral suppositories used for the treatment of severe erectile dysfunction. They are marketed under the name Muse in the United States of America. Its use has diminished since the development of oral impotence medications.

Hence, the correct option is (C).

47. Weight of urethral suppository for males and females respectively 4 and 2. Urethral suppositories, formerly called bougies, vary in their dimensions, depending on the sex of the patient. Suppositories for females are about 5 mm in diameter, 50 mm in length, and 2 g in weight. Suppositories for males are 5 mm in diameter, 125 mm in length, and 4 g in weight.

Hence, the correct option is (A).

48. The shape of vaginal suppositories is Oviform. Vaginal suppositories or Pessaries weigh about 3- 5gm and are molded in globular or oviform shape or compressed on a tablet press into conical shapes. Vaginal suppositories can help with the treatment of fungal infections and vaginal dryness. Contraceptive suppositories are another type of vaginal suppository that some people used as a form of birth control.

Hence, the correct option is (A).

49. Rectal suppositories are mainly used for the treatment of constipation and hemorrhoids. In 1991, a study on suppository insertion in. The Lancet found that the "torpedo" shape helps the device to travel internally, increasing its efficacy. The findings of this single study have been challenged as there is insufficient evidence on which to base clinical practice.

Hence, the correct option is (C).

50. The number of milligrams of KOH required neutralizing free acids & saponifying the esters contained in 1g of fat is known as saponification value. The saponification value is defined as the amount of potassium hydroxide (KOH) in milligrams required to saponify one gram of fat or oil under the conditions specified (AOCS Method Cd 3–25 and AOCS Method Cd 3c–91).

Hence, the correct option is (B).

51. The number of grams of iodine that reacts with 100 g of fat is known as the Iodine value. Iodine value also called Iodine Number, in chemistry, measure of the degree of unsaturation of an oil, fat, or wax; the amount of iodine, in grams, that is taken up by 100 grams of the oil, fat, or wax.

Hence, the correct option is (A).

52. Due to some factors, petrolatum is most widely used as a hydrocarbon basic in ointments these are its consistency, its neutral characteristics and its ability to spread easily on the skin. While selecting a suitable ointment base, factors such as the action desired, nature of the medicament to be incorporated and the stability of an ointment is to be considered are it should be inert, odourless and smooth and it should be physically and chemically stable.

Hence, the correct option is (D).

53. The number of milligrams of KOH required to neutralize the acetic acid used to acetylate 1g of fat is known as Hydroxil value. In chemistry, the hydroxyl value is defined as the number of milligrams of potassium hydroxide required to neutralize the acetic acid taken upon acetylation of one gram of a chemical substance that contains free hydroxyl groups.

Hence, the correct option is (C).

54. Hand molding, Compression molding and Pour molding methods are used to manufacture suppositories.

(a) Hand Mould Suppositories: This is the oldest and simplest method of preparing suppositories. A skilled person is required for the preparation of suppositories.

(b) Compression mold suppositories (Cold compression):

- Mix theobroma oil and drug.
- The mixture is forced into a mold under pressure, using a wheel-operated press.
- Mould is removed, opened and replaced.

(c) Pour suppositories:

- The drug is dispersed or dissolved in a melted suppository base.
- Pour the mixture into suppository molds and allow cooling in an ice bath.
- Finished suppositories are removed by opening the mold.

Hence, the correct option is (D).

55. The most commonly used suppository bases, especially are cocoa butter, hydrogenated fatty acids of vegetable oils, such as palm kernel oil and cottonseed oil. compounds consisting of glycerides of higher-molecular-weight fatty acids, such as glyceryl monostearate and glyceryl mono palmitate.

Hence, the correct option is (A).

56. Cocoa butter is available in α-form, β-form and γ-form. This application continues to dominate the consumption of cocoa butter. Pharmaceutical companies use cocoa butter's physical properties extensively. As a nontoxic solid at room temperature that melts at body temperature, it is considered an ideal base for medicinal suppositories.

Hence, the correct option is (D).

57. The solidification point of cocoa butter lies between 12-13 °C. Cocoa butter typically has a melting point of around 34–38 °C 93–101 °F, so chocolate is solid at room temperature but readily melts once inside the mouth. Cocoa butter displays polymorphism, having different crystalline forms with different melting points.

Hence, the correct option is (A).

58. Hand molding method is simple & oldest method of preparation of suppositories. A hand mold is a simple mold used for low quantity work. It is used in the injection molding and the printing industry. It is made by a hand injection molding machine. It is a simple machine which contains a barrel, handle, nozzle, mold and heaters.

Hence, the correct option is (B).

59. The most commonly used method for producing suppositories on both a small & large scale is pour molding. It avoids the possibility of sedimentation of the insoluble solids in the suppository base.

Pour Molding: Most commonly used method for production of suppository on both small & large scale. First, the base is melted into a water bath, and then the drugs are either emulsified or suspended in t.

Hence, the correct option is (C).

60. The formula that can be used to calculate the amount of base that is replaced by active ingredients is:

100(E-G) f = + 1(G)(X)

For dry formulations such as wettable powders, granules and dust, the amount of a.i. is expressed as a percentage of the weight.

Hence, the correct option is (C).

61. Rancidity generally results from auto-oxidation and decomposition of unsaturated fats. The condition produced by aerial oxidation of fats and oils in food marked by unpleasant smell and taste is called Rancidity. For Example, Potato Chips when kept in the air for a long time gives an unpleasant smell and bad taste. Rancidity can be retarded by keeping food in Refrigerator.

Hence, the correct option is (C).

62. Theobroma oil is not anti-oxidant. However, the most prominent disadvantage of theobroma oil is its polymorphism. Theobroma oil makes an ideal melting suppository base due to a melting point near human body temperature. In this state, theobroma oil is in its β-crystalline form.

Hence, the correct option is (D).

63. Suppositories are generally evaluated by melting range test, breaking test and liquefaction.

Melting range test: It is a measure of the thermal stability of the suppository. It is the time taken by the entire suppository to melt in a constant temperature water bath. The test is conducted using the tablet disintegration apparatus.

Breaking test: The apparatus used is called the breaking test apparatus. It consists of a double-wall chamber. Through the walls of the chamber, water is pumped. The inner chamber consists of a disc that holds the suppositories.

Liquefaction: Softening time is the time for which the suppository melts completely at a definite temperature. This test measures the softening time of suppositories which indicates the hardness of the base. A liquefaction temperature/time test was done using the fabricated instrument. A big pipette was taken having a narrow opening on one side and a broad opening on another side.

Hence, the correct option is (D).

64. The materials are used in pharmaceutical packaging are:

Glass: It is the most commonly used material for primary packaging. Because glass is chemically inert and inspection of the content in the container is very easy. But the disadvantage of using glass is its delicacy and cost as compared to plastic. The glass is used to manufacture vials, ampoules, dropper bottles, and jar.

Plastic: It is used as the primary as well as secondary packaging of the pharmaceutical product. The plastic used is Ploy ethylene, polyvinyl chloride, polypropylene, and polystyrene. The benefit of using plastic is that it is flexible, low weight and cost-effective. But the drawbacks of using plastics are the low level of inertness compared to glass and permeability to vapor and gas.

Metal: Type of metal used are steel, aluminum, and alloys of aluminum. Metal is mainly used to pack the dosage in gel forms. But metals have the problem also of chemically reactive. So Tin or Tin plated steel is used, because of low reactivity of tin as compared to other metals.

Hence, the correct option is (D).

65. Amber-colored glass containers are used to protect the drug content against the light. Amber glass offers protection against light wavelengths within the 10 nm to 400 nm range. This is the ideal spectrum to protect against UV light radiation, which is why many pharmaceutical and beverage manufacturers choose amber bottles.

Hence, the correct option is (B).

66. The major disadvantages of glass as packing material are weight and fragility. The disadvantages of glass include its weight and vulnerability to fracture from thermal shock (rapid temperature change) and physical shock. In recent years, advances in the science and technology of glass have resulted in lighter, stronger glass containers. Though glass is a strong material, it is also fragile.

Hence, the correct option is (C).

67. The composition of glass is sand, soda ash and limestone & cullet. The exact composition of glass may vary to meet specific applications requirements but the most commonly use type of glass, soda-lime glass, is made of silica sand, soda ash, limestone, dolomite and glass cullets (recycled glass).

Hence, the correct option is (D).

68. Soda ash also known as sodium carbonate (Na_2CO_3), is an alkali chemical refined from the mineral trona or naturally occurring sodium carbonate-bearing brines (both referred to as natural soda ash), the mineral nahcolite (referred to as natural sodium bicarbonate, from which soda ash can be produced), or manufactured.

Hence, the correct option is (B).

69. Cullet is a broken glass & acts as a fusion agent. Broken or waste glass (also called cullet) can partly replace the mineral raw materials. Cullet can consist of process losses as well as recycled glass. Adding a cullet reduces energy use and CO_2 emissions because the melting point of the cullet is lower than that of the mineral raw materials.

Hence, the correct option is (A).

70. The methods are used in the production of glass are blowing, drawing and pressing & casting. Glassblowing was invented by Syrian craftsmen in the area of Sidon, Aleppo, Hama, and Palmyra in the 1st-century bc, where blown vessels for everyday and luxury use were produced commercially and exported to all parts of the Roman Empire. People have used molds for glass casting from ancient to modern times. These molds were most often made of sand, special plaster, metal, or graphite. The graphite and metal molds were expensive to produce and required specialized equipment.

Hence, the correct option is (D).

71. To produce molten glass, the blowing method is used. Glass blowing is a glass forming technique that involves inflating molten glass into a bubble (or parison) with the aid of a blowpipe (or blow tube). A person who blows glass is called a glassblower, glassmith, or gaffer.

Hence, the correct option is (A).

72. To protect the contents of a bottle from the effects of sunlight by UV rays, amber glass is used. Amber glass bottles are the safest choice for products like essential oils, extracts, light-sensitive beauty products, and more. The use of amber glass is still prevalent with some pharmaceuticals, however, nowadays many pharmaceuticals are stored in amber plastic bottles, which can also block most-to-all UV light.

Hence, the correct option is (A).

73. To evaluate the chemical resistance of glass, powder glass and water attack test. Glass containers are classified according to their resistance to chemical attack, a test executed by heating the glass in contact with water for 30 min at 121 degrees C. The USP powdered glass test for glass containers was applied to different kinds of glasses used as containers for parenteral formulations. This is only for treated soda-lime glass containers under the controlled humidity conditions which neutralize the surface alkali and glass will become chemically more resistant. The principle involved is whether the alkali leached or not from the surface of the container.

Hence, the correct option is (C).

74. A powder glass test is performed on crushed grains, to evaluate the chemical resistance of glass. It is done to estimate the amount of alkali leached from the powdered glass which usually happens at elevated temperatures. When the glass is powdered, the leaching of alkali is enhanced, which can be titrated with 0.02N sulphuric acid using methyl red as an indicator.

Hence, the correct option is (A).

75. Water attack test is performed on whole container. Containers are tested by many methods of which commonly used tests for glass are the Crushed glass test, Whole-Container test, Chemical resistance of test, Water Attack Test, etc. Similarly test. Closure materials are tested by Transparency test Penetrability Fragmentation test, Self-seal ability test, Extractive test, etc.

Hence, the correct option is (B).

76. Type L glass is also known as borosilicate glass. Borosilicate glass is a type of glass with the main glass-forming constituents' silica and boron oxide. Borosilicate glasses are known for having very low coefficients of thermal expansion ($\sim 5 \times 10^{-6}$/ °C at 20 °C) making them resistant to thermal shock more so than any other common glass.

Hence, the correct option is (A).

77. Reticulate xylem vessels showing no reaction for lignin are found in rhubarb. The xylem vessel is one of the two cell types of tracheary elements, the other is the tracheid. These two are the water-conducting elements in vascular plants. However, Pteridophytes and most Gymnosperms have only tracheids. Most angiosperms (flowering plants) have both xylem vessels and tracheids but the xylem vessels serve as the major conductive element. Rhubarb consists of the peeled dried rhizomes and roots of Rheum palmatum Linn., belonging to the family Polygonaceae.

Hence, the correct option is (A).

78. Flavonoids generally dissolve in alkalis, giving a yellow solution (phenates) which on addition of acid becomes colourless. The flavonoids are generally yellow compounds and the intensity of their yellow colour increases with the number of OH groups and with increase of the pH of the medium.

Hence, the correct option is (C).

79. Compound commercially available in tablets and injection as a potent coronary vasodilator is a khellin. Khellin has been used to relieve the pain associated with angina pectoris by acting as a selective coronary vasodilator. This can be done either orally or intramuscularly; however, nausea is a major side effect regardless of how the medication is taken.

Hence, the correct option is (D).

80. Geraniol is absent in the volatile oil of dill. Drugs Containing Volatile Oils. Dill consists of the dried ripe fruits of Anethum graveolens Linn., belonging to the family Umbelliferae. DILL. Synonyms. Fructus anethi, Anethum, European dill. Dill fruit and oil of Dill possess stimulant, aromatic, carminative, and stomachic, with considerable medicinal value.

Hence, the correct option is (A).

81. Carvone is absent in volatile oil of mentha piperata. PEPPERMINT (Mentha piperita) is a popular herb that can be used in numerous forms (ie, oil, leaf, leaf extract, and leaf water). Peppermint oil has the most uses, and use data on the oil are considered relevant to the leaf extract formulations as well. This herbal preparation is used in cosmeceuticals, personal hygiene products, foods, and pharmaceutical products for both its flavoring and fragrance properties.

Hence, the correct option is D).

82. The endosperm of the fruits of Umbelliferae is characterized by the presence of the microrosettes calcium oxalate crystals. Calcium oxalate crystal formation in plants appears to play a central role in a variety of important functions, including tissue calcium regulation, protection from herbivory, and metal detoxification. Evidence is mounting to support ascorbic acid as the primary precursor to oxalate biosynthesis.

Hence, the correct option is (B).

83. A small secretory canal above vascular bundle is seen in T.S. of Caraway. A vascular bundle is a part of the transport system in vascular plants. The transport itself happens in the stem, which exists in two forms: xylem and phloem. Both these tissues are present in a vascular bundle, which in addition will include supporting and protective tissues. In addition, there is also a tissue between xylem and phloem which is the cambium.

Hence, the correct option is (C).

84. Two lateral ridges are flattened to form wing-like structures in the case of dill. Dill fruits are oval, compressed, winged with 4 mm in length, about a one-tenth inch wide and 1 mm thick. The fruits are yellowish or slightly brown having three longitudinal ridges on the back and three dark lines or oil cells (vittae) between them and two on the flat surface. The taste of the fruits somewhat resembles caraway (aromatic and characteristic). The seeds are small in size, flat and lighter than caraway and have a pleasant aromatic odour.

Hence, the correct option is (B).

85. There are only two vittae in each mericarp of coriander. Coriander, (Coriandrum sativum), also called cilantro or Chinese parsley, feathery annual plant of the parsley family (Apiaceae), parts of which are used as both an herb and a spice. Native to the Mediterranean and Middle East regions, the plant is widely cultivated in many places worldwide for its culinary uses.

Hence, the correct option is (A).

86. There are ten primary ridges that are wavy and inconspicuous on the outer surface of the coriander. The epidermis of the pericarp, when present, consists of polygonal tabular cells with slightly thickened walls and occasional stomata. Many of these epidermal cells contain small prisms of calcium oxalate. The outer layer of the mesocarp is composed of elongated collenchymatous cells and very reduced vascular bundles.

Hence, the correct option is (D).

87. The beta-1 selective agonist dobutamine is a prescription medicine used to treat the symptoms of cardiac decompensation.

Dobutamine may be used alone or with other medications. Dobutamine belongs to a class of drugs called Inotropic Agents.

Hence, the correct option is (B).

88. Pharmacodynamics involves the study of biological and therapeutic effects of drugs, mechanisms of drug action and drug interactions. But it does not include absorption and distribution of drugs. Pharmacodynamics (PD) is the study of the biochemical and physiologic effects of drugs (especially pharmaceutical drugs). The effects can include those manifested within animals (including humans), microorganisms, or combinations of organisms (for example, infection).

Hence, the correct option is (B).

89. Affinity is a measure of how tightly a drug binds to a receptor. The strength of the binding (interaction) of a ligand and its receptor can be described by affinity. The higher the Kd value, the weaker the binding and the lower the affinity. The opposite occurs when a drug has a low Kd. Potency is a measure of the necessary amount of the drug to produce an effect of a given magnitude.

Hence, the correct option is (B).

90. An irreversible antagonist is a type of antagonist that binds permanently to a receptor, either by forming a covalent bond to the active site, or alternatively just by binding so tightly that the rate of dissociation is effectively zero at relevant time scales.

Hence, the correct option is (C).

91. The second messenger of the G-protein-coupled metabotropic receptor is cAMP. When a ligand binds to a G protein-coupled receptor, a guanine nucleotide-binding protein, or G protein, activates a second messenger cascade which can alter gene transcription, regulate other proteins in the cell, release intracellular Ca^{2+}, or directly affect ion channels on the membrane.

Hence, the correct option is (D).

92. The cumulative effect may lead to toxic reactions when a drug is taken continuously or repeatedly. The process by which blood levels of a drug build up, thereby increasing its therapeutic and toxic effects. Cumulation may result from poor elimination due to slow metabolism, binding the drug to plasma proteins or inhibition of excretion as occurs in sufferers of kidney disease.

Hence, the correct option is (B)

93. Tachyphylaxis is used to describe a decrease in responsiveness to a drug that develops in a few minutes. Tachyphylaxis is a medical term describing an acute, sudden decrease in response to a drug after its administration; i.e. a rapid and short-term onset of drug tolerance. It can occur after an initial dose or after a series of small doses.

Hence, the correct option is (D).

94. A local anesthetic (LA) is a medication that causes the absence of pain sensation. In the context of surgery, a local anesthetic creates an absence of pain in a specific location of the body without a loss of consciousness, as opposed to a general anesthetic. Commonly used amino amides include lidocaine,

mepivacaine, prilocaine, bupivacaine, etidocaine, and ropivacaine and levobupivacaine. Commonly used amino esters include cocaine, procaine, tetracaine, chloroprocaine, and benzocaine.

Hence, the correct option is (D).

95. The local anesthetic agent, which has a shorter duration of action procaine. Procaine and chloroprocaine are the shortest-acting agents (0.25-0.5 hours), followed by lidocaine, mepivacaine, and prilocaine, which have slightly longer durations of action (0.5-1.5 hours).

Hence, the correct option is (B).

96. Bupivacaine has greater potency of the local anesthetic action. Bupivacaine is an anesthetic (numbing medicine) that is used as a local (in only one area) anesthetic. Bupivacaine is given as an epidural injection into the spinal column to produce numbness during labor, surgery, or certain medical procedures. Bupivacaine is also used as an anesthetic for dental procedures.

Hence, the correct option is (B).

97. Cocaine local anesthetics is an ester of benzoic acid. The chemical identification of cocaine as a benzoic acid ester led to the synthesis of numerous compounds which were basically benzoic ester derivates. In 1905, Einhorn reported the synthesis of procaine. Tetracaine, the most potent ester of the benzoic acid series appeared in 1930.

Hence, the correct option is (D).

98. Local anesthetics are basically weak bases whose structure consists of an aromatic half connected to a substituted amine through an ester amide linkage. The pKa values of local anesthetics are close to physiological pH, both protonated and unprotonated forms are present.

Hence, the correct option is (A).

99. Lidocaine local anestheties is called a universal anesthetic. It causes loss of feeling in the skin and surrounding tissues. It is used to prevent and to treat pain from some procedures. This medicine is also used to treat minor burns, scrapes and insect bites.

Hence, the correct option is (C).

100. Acetylcholine and carbachol act on both muscarinic and nicotinic receptors, while methacholine and bethanechol act selectively on muscarinic receptors. Bethanechol is used to treat certain bladder problems such as the inability to urinate or empty the bladder completely due to certain causes (e.g., surgery, bladder muscle problems). It works by helping the bladder muscle to squeeze better, thereby improving your ability to urinate.

Hence, the correct option is (D).

101. Pralidoxime is a cholinesterase reactivator used to treat organophosphate poisoning. If given within 24 hours,after organophosphate exposure, pralidoxime reactivates the enzyme cholinesterase by cleaving the phosphate-ester bond formed between the organophosphate and acetylcholinesterase.

Hence, the correct option is (A).

102. Neostigmine cholinomimetics is most widely used for paralytic ileus and atony of the urinary bladder. Neostigmine is a prescription medicine used to treat the symptoms of Myasthenia Gravis, Reversal of Nondepolarizing Neuromuscular Blockade and Post-Op Distention or Urinary Retention. Neostigmine may be used alone or with other medications.

Hence, the correct option is (B).

103. Benztropinedrugs is both a muscarinic and nicotinic blocker. Benztropine is used along with other medications to treat the symptoms of Parkinson's disease (PD) a disorder of the nervous system that causes difficulties with movement, muscle control, and balance, and tremors caused by other medical problems or medications.

Hence, the correct option is (B).

104. Hexamethonium agent is a ganglion-blocking drug. Hexamethonium was a drug used mainly to treat chronic hypertension and was proposed as a potential drug to treat asthma; however, the non-specificity of its action led to its use being discontinued.

Hence, the correct option is (B).

105. The skeletal muscle relaxant, which is depolarizing agent succinylcholine. The most well-known depolarizing neuromuscular blocking agent is succinylcholine. It is the only such drug used clinically and is considered by many the drug of choice for emergency department RSI, although this is controversial.

Hence, the correct option is (C).

106. Pancuronium drugs are non-depolarizing muscle relaxants. Used as a muscle relaxant during anesthesia and surgical procedures. Pancuronium is a non-depolarising muscle relaxant similar to curare. It acts as a competitive acetylcholine antagonist on neuromuscular junctions, displacing acetylcholine (thus competitive) from its post-synaptic nicotinic acetylcholine receptors.

Hence, the correct option is (A).

107. Benztropine drugs is useful in the treatment of Parkinson's disease. Benztropine is used along with other medications to treat the symptoms of Parkinson's disease (PD; a disorder of the nervous system that causes difficulties with movement, muscle control, and balance) and tremors caused by other medical problems or medications.

Hence, the correct option is (A).

108. Succylcholine drugs has "double-acetylcholine" structure. Succinylcholine is a skeletal muscle relaxant for intravenous (IV) administration indicated as an adjunct to general anesthesia, to facilitate tracheal intubation, and to provide skeletal muscle relaxation during surgery or mechanical ventilation.

Hence, the correct option is (D).

109. The long-acting neuromuscular blocking agent tubocurarine. Tubocurarine chloride is a nondepolarizing neuromuscular blocking agent and is employed intramuscularly or intravenously as a skeletal muscle relaxant to secure muscle relaxation in surgical procedures without deep anesthesia.

Hence, the correct option is (C).

110. Atracurium competitive neuromuscular blocking agent could be used in patients with renal failure. Atracurium is in the neuromuscular-blocker family of medications and is of the non-depolarizing type. It works by blocking the action of acetylcholine on skeletal muscles. The onset of vecuronium, atracurium and mivacurium occurred faster or tended to be faster in patients with end-stage renal failure, but there was no significant difference in onset by rocuronium between the control patients and renal failure patients.

Hence, the correct option is (A).

111. Catecholamine includes epinephrine, isoprenaline, and norepinephrine except for ephedrine. Catecholamines are derived from the amino acid tyrosine, which is derived from dietary sources as well as synthesis from phenylalanine. Included among catecholamines are epinephrine (adrenaline), norepinephrine (noradrenaline), and dopamine.

Hence, the correct option is (A).

112. A relatively pure alfa agonist causes increase peripheral arterial resistance, increase venous return and reflex bradycardia except for it has no effect on blood vessels. Alpha-adrenergic agonists are a class of sympathomimetic agents that selectively stimulates alpha-adrenergic receptors. The alpha-adrenergic receptor has two subclasses α_1 and α_2. Alpha 2 receptors are associated with sympatholytic properties. Alpha-adrenergic agonists have the opposite function of alpha-blockers.

Hence, the correct option is (C).

113. Lipolysis effects is associated with beta-3 receptor stimulation. Lipolysis is the metabolic process through which triacylglycerols (TAGs) break down via hydrolysis into their constituent molecules: glycerol and free fatty acids (FFAs). Fat storage in the body is through adipose TAGs and is utilized for heat, energy, and insulation.

Hence, the correct option is (A).

114. The alpha-2 selective agonist is xylometazoline. Alpha-adrenergic agonists are a class of sympathomimetic agents that selectively stimulates alpha-adrenergic receptors. The alpha-adrenergic receptor has two subclasses α_1 and α_2. Alpha-2 receptors are associated with sympatholytic properties.

Hence, the correct option is (A).

115. Acetanilide is not a volatile substance. Acetanilide is a synthetic organic compound introduced clinically in 1886 as a fever-reducing drug. Its effectiveness in relieving pain was discovered soon thereafter and it was used as an alternative to aspirin for many years in treating such common complaints as headaches, menstrual cramps, and rheumatism.

Hence, the correct option is (D).

116. Rate of reaction can be incresed by enhancers. Enhancer sequences are regulatory DNA sequences that, when bound by specific proteins called transcription factors, enhance the transcription of an associated gene. Additionally, enhancer sequences can be positioned in both forward or reversed sequence orientations and still affect gene transcription.

Hence, the correct option is (B).

117. Meso forms of isomers are single compounds and their molecules are achiral and hence they cannot be separated into pairs. Meso isomer is defined as a compound whose molecule is superimposable on the mirror images in the presence of chiral carbon. Cis [-1,2] dichloro cyclobutane and [2,3] dichlorobutane contain a plane of symmetry.

Hence, the correct option is (D).

118. Errors arise due to the individual analyst is responsible for them the personal error.

Operational and Personal errors: These are due to factors for which the individual analyst is responsible and are not connected with the method or procedure they form part of the personal equation of an observer. An example is the Mechanical loss of materials in various steps of analysis.

Hence, the correct option is (C).

119. Eukaryotic cells are typically larger than prokaryotic cells, ranging from around 10 to 100 µm in diameter. While many eukaryotes consist of multiple cells, there are also single-celled eukaryotes. Eukaryotes are organisms whose cells contain a nucleus and other membrane-bound organelles. There is a wide range of eukaryotic organisms, including all animals, plants, fungi, and protists, as well as most algae. Eukaryotes may be either single-celled or multicellular.

Hence, the correct option is (D).

120. Klenow fragment is derived from DNA Pol-I. DNA Polymerase I, Large (Klenow) Fragment is a proteolytic product of E. coli DNA Polymerase I which retains polymerization and $3' \rightarrow 5'$ exonuclease activity but has lost $5' \rightarrow 3'$ exonuclease activity (1). Klenow retains the polymerization fidelity of the holoenzyme without degrading 5' termini.

Hence, the correct option is (B).

121. Cyanobacteria require light as a source of energy to perform photosynthesis. Fungi and viruses are unable to perform photosynthesis and are heterotrophic. Cyanobacteria are also known as Cyanophyta, are a phylum of Gram-negative bacteria that obtain energy via photosynthesis. Cyanobacteria use photosynthetic pigments, such as carotenoids, phycobilins, and various forms of chlorophyll, which absorb energy from light.

Hence, the correct option is (C).

122. In the earliest stages of pulmonary edema fluid tracks through the interstitium of the thin side of the blood Gas barrier to the perivascular and peribronchial spaces, there is no increase in lung lymph flow and fluid floods the alveoli one by one is true but cuffs of fluid collect around the small arteries and veins are not true. Pulmonary edema is a condition caused by excess fluid in the lungs. This fluid collects in the numerous air sacs in the lungs, making it difficult to breathe. In most cases, heart problems cause pulmonary edema.

Hence, the correct option is (D).

123. The driving force of pore transport is Hydrostatic pressure and Osmotic pressure across the cell membrane. Electrochemical gradient and concentration gradient is the driving force of passive diffusion.

Hence, the correct option is (A).

124. Antihypertensive therapy should be avoided in type-1 diabetes mellitus that is centrally acting. Antihypertensives are a class of drugs that are used to treat hypertension (high blood pressure). Antihypertensive therapy seeks to prevent the complications of high blood pressure, such as stroke and myocardial infarction. The combination of a beta-blocker and a non-dihydropyridine CCB should be avoided because of the risk of bradycardia and heart block. Alternative agents, such as alpha-blockers and hydralazine, may be considered in patients with resistant hypertension.

Hence, the correct option is (C).

125. Plasma membrane consists of 10% amount of phospholipids. Different kinds of cells have different concentrations of proteins, lipids, and carbohydrates in their plasma membranes. Proteins make up about half of a normal human cell's bulk, lipids (of all kinds) make up about 40%, and carbohydrates make up the remaining 10%.

Hence, the correct option is (B).

Pharmaceutical Chemistry

Q.1 Fat-soluble vitamins are:
A. Soluble in alcohol
B. One or more Propene units
C. Stored in liver
D. All of these

Q.2 Deficiency of Vitamin A causes:
A. Xerophthalmia
B. Hypoprothrombinemia
C. Megaloblastic anemia
D. Pernicious anemia

Q.3 An important function of vitamin A is:
A. To act as coenzyme for a few enzymes.
B. To play an integral role in protein synthesis.
C. To prevent hemorrhages.
D. To maintain the integrity of epithelial issue.

Q.4 Retinal is a component of:
A. Iodopsin
B. Rhodopsin
C. Cardiolipin
D. Glycoproteins

Q.5 Vitamin D absorption is increased in:
A. Acid pH of intestine
B. Alkaline pH of intestine
C. Impaired fat absorption
D. Contents of diet

Q.6 A poor source of Vitamin D is:
A. Egg
B. Butter
C. Milk
D. Liver

Q.7 Richest source of Vitamin D is:
A. Fish liver oils
B. Margarine
C. Egg yolk
D. Butter

Q.8 Deficiency of vitamin D causes:
A. Ricket and osteomalacia
B. Tuberculosis of bone
C. Hypthyroidism
D. Skin cancer

Q.9 One international unit (I.U) of vitamin D is defined as the biological activity of:
A. 0.025 µg of cholecalciferol
B. 0.025 µg of 7-dehydrocholecalciferol
C. 0.025 µg of ergosterol
D. 0.025 µg of ergocalciferol

Q.10 The Vitamin B1 deficiency causes:
A. Ricket
B. Nyctalopia
C. Beriberi
D. Pellagra

Q.11 Scurvy is caused due to the deficiency of:
A. Vitamin A
B. Vitamin D
C. Vitamin K
D. Vitamin C

Q.12 Riboflavin deficiency causes:
A. Cheilosis
B. Loss of weight
C. Mental deterioration
D. Dermatitis

Q.13 Pellagra occurs in population dependent on:
A. Wheat
B. Rice
C. Maize
D. Milk

Q.14 Magenta tongue is found in the deficiency of the vitamin B2 or:
A. Riboflavin
B. Thiamin
C. Nicotinic acid
D. Pyridoxine

Q.15 Corneal vascularisation is found in deficiency of the vitamin:
A. B1
B. B2
C. B3
D. B6

Q.16 The pellagra preventive factor is:
A. Riboflavin
B. Pantothenic acid
C. Niacin
D. Pyridoxine

Q.17 What are niacin toxicity symptoms?
A. Rapid heartbeat
B. Abdominal pain
C. Itching
D. All of these

Q.18 Vitamin B6 deficiency may occur during therapy with:
A. Isoniazid
B. Terramycin
C. Sulpha drugs
D. Aspirin

Q.19 A deficiency of vitamin B-12 causes:
A. Beri-Beri
B. Scurvy
C. Pernicious anemia
D. Ricket

Q.20 Factors affecting enzyme activity:
A. Concentration
B. pH
C. Temperature
D. All of these

Q.21 The pH optima for salivary analyse is:
A. 6.6-6.8
B. 2.0-7.5
C. 7.9
D. 8.6

Q.22 The pH optima for pancreatic amylase is:
A. 4.0
B. 7.1
C. 7.9
D. 7.0

Q.23 The ion which activates salivary amylase activity is:
A. Chloride
B. Bicarbonate
C. Sodium
D. Potassium

Q.24 Glucose absorption is promoted by:
A. Vitamin A
B. Thiamine
C. Vitamin C
D. Vitamin K

Q.25 A carbohydrate which cannot be digested in human gut is:

A. Cellulose   **B.** Starch
C. Glycogen   **D.** Maltose

Q.26 The number of ATP molecules generated for each turn of the citric acid cycle is:
A. 8   **B.** 12   **C.** 24   **D.** 38

Q.27 The mitochondrial membrane is freely permeable to:
A. Pyruvate   **B.** Malate
C. Oxaloacetate   **D.** Fumarate

Q.28 The net number of ATP formed per mole of glucose in anaerobic glycolysis is:
A. 1   **B.** 2   **C.** 6   **D.** 8

Q.29 The sites for gluconeogenesis are:
A. Liver and kidney
B. Skin and pancreas
C. Lung and brain
D. Intestine and lens of eye

Q.30 Insulin has no effect on the activity of the enzyme:
A. Glycogen synthetase
B. Fructokinase
C. Pyruvate kinase
D. Pyruvate dehydrogenase

Q.31 In Hunter's syndrome:
A. There is progressive corneal opacity.
B. Keratan sulphate is excreted in the urine.
C. Enzyme defective is arylsulphatase B.
D. Hearing loss is perceptive.

Q.32 An important feature of Von-Gierke's disease is:
A. Muscle cramps
B. Cardiac failure
C. Hypoglycemia
D. Respiratory alkalosis

Q.33 The affected organ in Mc Ardle's syndrome is:
A. Liver   **B.** Kidney
C. Liver and Heart   **D.** Skeletal muscle

Q.34 Refsum's disease is due to deficiency of the enzyme:
A. Phytanate α-oxidase
B. Glucocerebrosidase
C. Ceramide trihexosidase
D. None of these

Q.35 A component of the respiratory chain in mitochondria is:
A. Coenzyme Q
B. Coenzyme A
C. Acetyl coenzyme
D. Coenzyme containing thiamin

Q.36 A pentamer immunoglobulin is:
A. IgG   **B.** IgA   **C.** IgM   **D.** IgE

Q.37 The immunoglobulin which can cross the placenta is:
A. IgA   **B.** IgM   **C.** IgG   **D.** IgD

Q.38 The total iron content of the human body is:
A. 400-500 mg   **B.** 1-2 g
C. 2-3 g   **D.** 4-5 g

Pharmaceutics

Q.39 Which of the following ingredients are present in rubber stopper?
A. Vulcanizing agent   **B.** Softener
C. Antioxidant   **D.** All of these

Q.40 Which of the following packaging systems are identified by the FDA?
A. Blister pack   **B.** Strip pack
C. Bubble pack   **D.** All of these

Q.41 Which of the following packaging is commonly used for packaging tablets & capsules?
A. Blister packaging   **B.** Strip packaging
C. Both (A) and (B)   **D.** None of these

Q.42 Which of the following materials offer moisture barrier properties?
A. Aclar   **B.** Cellophane
C. Polyester   **D.** All of these

Q.43 Which of the following mechanism is responsible for the release of encapsulated core materials?
A. By disrupting the coating by pressure.
B. By offering permeability facilities.
C. By leaching of permanent fluid.
D. All of these

Q.44 Pre-formulation studies mainly focus on:
A. Physical properties of new compound
B. Chemical properties of new compound
C. Physicochemical properties of new compound
D. None of these

Q.45 Which of the following information is helpful in designing the pre-formulation evaluation of a new drug?
A. Structure of a compound
B. Formula & molecular weight of a compound
C. Therapeutic indication of a new compound
D. All of these

Q.46 Which of the following problems commonly encountered in evaluating salt forms are?
A. Poor crystallinity   **B.** Hygroscopicity
C. Instability   **D.** All of these

Q.47 Which of the following salts are generally used in pharmaceutical products?
A. Acetate   **B.** Gluconate
C. Lactate   **D.** All of these

Q.48 Description of the outer appearance of a crystal is known as:
A. Crystal habit   **B.** Internal structure
C. Both (A) and (B)   **D.** None of these

Q.49 Which of the following techniques used to prepare amorphous forms?

A. Rapid precipitation   **B.** Lyophilization
C. Rapid cooling   **D.** All of these

Q.50 Amorphous forms generally having:

A. Low thermodynamic energy & low solubility
B. High thermodynamic energy & high solubility
C. Both (A) and (B)
D. None of these

Q.51 Which of the following compound possess high aqueous solubility?

A. Hydrates   **B.** Anhydrates
C. Both (A) and (B)   **D.** None of these

Q.52 Which of the following properties may change with changing of the internal structure of a solid?

A. Melting point   **B.** Density
C. Optical properties   **D.** All of these

Q.53 Which of the following methods are generally used for studying solid forms?

A. DSC   **B.** XRD
C. TGA   **D.** All of these

Q.54 Which of the following methods generally used to measure heat loss or gain within a sample?

A. DSC   **B.** DTA
C. Both (A) and (B)   **D.** None of these

Q.55 Which of the following co-solvent can be used to increase the solubility of poor soluble drugs?

A. Ethanol   **B.** Propylene glycol
C. Glycerin   **D.** All of these

Q.56 Partition co-efficient generally measures:

A. Drug's lipophilicity
B. Ability of drug to cross cell membrane
C. Both (A) and (B)
D. None of these

Q.57 Dissolution of a drug particle is described by:

A. Stock's equation
B. Noyes-Whitney equation
C. Drag's equation
D. None of these

Q.58 The effect of temperature on drug stability can be described by:

A. Noyes-Whitney equation
B. Stock's equation
C. Arrhenius equation
D. None of these

Q.59 Unequal distribution of color on a tablet refers to:

A. Picking   **B.** Mottling   **C.** Capping   **D.** Sticking

Q.60 Which of the following is responsible for sticking?

A. Excessive moisture   **B.** Low moisture

C. Both (A) and (B)   **D.** None of these

Q.61 If the dose of a drug is inadequate, the nit generally requires the following one, to make up its bulk:

A. Binders   **B.** Disintegrants
C. Lubricants   **D.** Diluents

Q.62 Which of the following mixer is the first high-shear powder blender/mixer?

A. Diosna mixer
B. Plow mixer
C. Littleford lodige mixer
D. Gral mixer

Q.63 The first and most widely used diluents in the tablet formulation is:

A. Dextrose   **B.** Lactose   **C.** MCC   **D.** Starch

Q.64 Anhydrous lactose has the advantage over hydrous lactose:

A. Improved flow
B. Absence of Millard reaction
C. Improved compressibility
D. High microbial load

Q.65 Which of the following is not a commercially available starch product?

A. Sta-Rx 1500   **B.** Celutab
C. Index   **D.** Sugar tab

Q.66 Which of the following is a synthetic adhesive?

A. PVP   **B.** MC   **C.** HPMC   **D.** HPC

Q.67 Which of the following is a water-soluble lubricant?

A. Stearic acid   **B.** Mineral oil
C. PEG   **D.** Magnesium stearate

Q.68 Find out the correct statements regarding a sweetener, saccharin:

(P) It is 500 times sweeter than sucrose, but it is carcinogenic.
(Q) It is 500 times sweeter than sucrose, but it has a bitter taste.
(R) It is sweeter than sucrose but it is safe.
(S) It is sweeter than sucrose, but it is unstable.

A. (P), (S)   **B.** (P), (R)   **C.** (P), (Q)   **D.** (R), (S)

Q.69 Aerosil is used as:

A. Glidant   **B.** Lubricant
C. Antiadherant   **D.** None of these

Q.70 What is the pH of duodenum?

A. 2-3   **B.** 7-8   **C.** 10   **D.** 4-6

Q.71 Tablets, which are placed between cheek and teeth, are known as:

A. Buccal   **B.** Sublingual
C. Lozenges   **D.** Troches

Q.72 Which statement is not correct?

A. Buccal routes avoids first-pass metabolism
B. Parenteral route avoids first-pass metabolism

C. Sublingual route avoids first-pass metabolism
D. Oral route avoids first-pass metabolism

Q.73 Enteric coating is achieved by using:
A. HPMC   B. CMC   C. CAP   D. Povidine

Q.74 The disintegration time for sugar-coated tablets is:
A. 30 minutes   B. 45 minutes
C. 60 minutes   D. 75 minutes

Q.75 Flow rate of granules from the hopper can be improved by adding:
A. Disintegrant   B. Glidant
C. Binder   D. Lubricant

Q.76 Direction: Given below are equipment used in the manufacture of the following products P-T. Match them and find out the correct answer:

(1) Zenasi	(P) Tablet granules
(2) Hepa filter	(Q) Tablet coating
(3) Chilsonator	(R) Emulsion
(4) Accela cota	(S) Injectables
	(T) Capsule

A. (1)-(T), (2)-(S), (3)-(P), (4)-(Q)
B. (1)-(P), (2)-(Q), (3)-(S), (4)-(R)
C. (1)-(T), (2)-(R), (3)-(Q), (4)-(P)
D. (1)-(S), (2)-(R), (3)-(P), (4)-(Q)

Pharmacognosy

Q.77 Drug is dissolved in light petroleum and shaken with dilute copper acetate solution, petroleum layer becomes emarald green in colour; the drug is:
A. Asafoetida   B. Colophony
C. Myrrh   D. Catechu

Q.78 Abietic acid is a major constituent of colophony, it is:
A. Monoterpene   B. Diterpene
C. Sesqiterpene   D. Triterpene

Q.79 Following Pinus species growing in India is used for collection of oleoresin:
A. Pinus palustris   B. Pinus maritima
C. Pinus longifolia   D. Pinus radiata

Q.80 Nutmeg obtained from Myristica fragrans is a:
A. Seed   B. Fruit   C. Arillus   D. Kernel

Q.81 Volatile oil derived from the following Acorus calamus variety is free from beta-asarone:
A. 2n   B. 3n   C. 4n   D. 5n

Q.82 Natural camphor obtained from Cinnamomum camphora is:
A. Levorotatory   B. Dextrorotatory
C. Racemic   D. None of these

Q.83 Pungency of ginger is destroyed by boiling 2% solution of:
A. Sodium carbonate

B. Hydrochloric acid
C. Potassium hydroxide
D. Acetic acid

Q.84 Starch grains found in ginger are:
A. Simple and round
B. Simple and sac shaped
C. Simple and polygonal
D. Compound

Q.85 Removal of water from gingerol yields:
A. Gingerone   B. Gingerdiol
C. Zingiberol   D. Shogaols

Q.86 Coated ginger means, it is:
A. Limed   B. Peeled
C. Unpeeled   D. Peeled and limed

Pharmacology

Q.87 Epinephrine produces all of the following effects except:
A. Positive inotropic and chronotropic actions on the heart (beta receptor).
B. Increase peripheral resistance (alfa receptor).
C. The predominance of alfa effects at low concentration.
D. Skeletal muscle blood vessel dilatation (beta receptor).

Q.88 Epinephrine is used in the treatment of all of the following disorders except:
A. Bronchospasm
B. Anaphylactic shock
C. Cardiac arrhythmias
D. Open-angle glaucoma

Q.89 Norepinephrine produces:
A. Vasoconstriction
B. Vasodilatation
C. Bronchodilation
D. Decresed potassium concentration in the plasma

Q.90 Find out the sympathomimetic, which may cause hypotension, presumably because of a clonidine-like effect:
A. Methoxamine   B. Phenylephrine
C. Xylometazoline   D. Isoproterenol

Q.91 Find out the agent of choice in the emergency therapy of anaphylactic shock:
A. Methoxamine   B. Terbutaline
C. Norepinephrine   D. Epinephrine

Q.92 Non-selective alfa-receptor antagonists are most useful in the treatment of:
A. Asthma
B. Cardiac arrhythmias
C. Pheochromocytoma
D. Chronic hypertension

Q.93 Which of the following drugs is useful in the treatment of pheochromocytoma?
A. Phenylephrine   B. Propranolol

C. Phentolamine   **D.** Epinephrine

Q.94 Find out the adrenoreceptor antagonist agents, which are used for the management of pheochromocytoma:

A. Selective beta-2 receptor antagonists
B. Nonselective beta-receptor antagonists
C. Indirect-acting adrenoreceptor antagonist drugs
D. Alfa-receptor antagonists

Q.95 The principal adverse effects of phentolamine include all of the following except:

A. Diarrhea
B. Bradycardia
C. Arrhythmias
D. Myocardial ischemia

Q.96 Beta-blocking agents have all of the following effects except:

A. Increase plasma concentrations of HDL and decrease VLDL
B. Bronchoconstriction
C. Decrease of aqueous humor production
D. Membrane-stabilizing action

Q.97 Beta-receptor antagonists cause:

A. Stimulation of lipolysis
B. Stimulation of gluconeogenesis
C. Inhibition of glycogenolysis
D. Stimulation of insulin secretion

Q.98 Propranolol has all of the following cardiovascular effects except:

A. It decreases cardiac work and oxygen demand.
B. It reduces blood flow to the brain.
C. It inhibits renin secretion.
D. It increases the atrioventricular nodal refractory period.

Q.99 Find out a beta-receptor antagonist, which has a very long duration of action:

A. Metoprolol   **B.** Propranolol
C. Nadolol   **D.** Pindolol

Q.100 Find out a beta-1 selective receptor antagonist, which has a very long duration of action:

A. Betaxolol   **B.** Sotalol
C. Nadolol   **D.** Metoprolol

Q.101 Characteristics of reserpine include all of the following except:

A. It inhibits the uptake of norepinephrine into vesicles and MAO.
B. It decreases cardiac output, peripheral resistance and inhibits pressor reflexes.
C. It may cause a transient sympathomimetic effect.
D. It depletes stores of catecholamines and serotonin in the brain.

Q.102 Select a hypnotic drug, which is a benzodiazepine derivative:

A. Zolpidem   **B.** Flurazepam
C. Secobarbital   **D.** Phenobarbitone

Q.103 Which of the following barbiturates is an ultra-short-acting drug?

A. Secobarbital   **B.** Amobarbital
C. Thiopental   **D.** Phenobarbital

Q.104 Find out the barbituric acid derivative, which has 4-5 days elimination half-life:

A. Secobarbital   **B.** Thiopental
C. Phenobarbital   **D.** Amobarbital

Q.105 Which of the following hypnotic drugs is more likely to cause cumulative and residual effects?

A. Zolpidem   **B.** Temazepam
C. Phenobarbital   **D.** Triazolam

Q.106 Hepatic microsomal drug-metabolizing enzyme induction leads to:

A. Barbiturate tolerance
B. Cumulative effects
C. Development of physical dependence
D. Hangover effects

Q.107 Barbiturates increase the rate of metabolism of:

A. Anticoagulants
B. Digitalis compounds
C. Glucocorticoids
D. All of these

Q.108 Which of the following agents inhibits hepatic metabolism of hypnotics?

A. Flumasenil   **B.** Cimetidin
C. Phenytoin   **D.** Theophylline

Q.109 Which of the following hypnotic agents is able to interact with both BZ -1 and BZ -2 receptor subtypes?

A. Zaleplon   **B.** Phenobarbital
C. Flurazepam   **D.** Zolpidem

Q.110 Which of the following agents blocks the chloride channel directly?

A. Secobarbital   **B.** Flumazenil
C. Zaleplon   **D.** Picrotoxin

Q.111 Which of the following agents is preferred in the treatment of insomnia?

A. Barbiturates
B. Hypnotic benzodiazepines
C. Ethanol
D. Phenothiazide

Q.112 Find out the main claim for an ideal hypnotic agent:

A. Rapid onset and sufficient duration of action
B. Minor effects on sleep patterns
C. Minimal "hangover" effects
D. All of these

Q.113 Which stage of sleep is responsible for the incidence of dreams?

A. REM sleep   **B.** Slow wave sleep
C. Stage 2NREM sleep   **D.** All of these

Q.114 During slow wave sleep (stage 3 and 4 NREM sleep):

A. Dreams occur

B. The secretion of adrenal steroids is at its highest

C. Somnambulism and nightmares occur

D. The secretion of somatotropin is at its lowest

Other Subjects

Q.115 Which of the following characteristics is not possessed by an ideal solution?

A. Obeys Raoult's law.

B. Volume change on mixing is not equal to zero.

C. There should be no chemical reaction between solute and solvent.

D. Only very dilute solutions behave as ideal solutions.

Q.116 Autocatalysis refers to:

A. When substrate acts as catalyst

B. When product acts as catalyst

C. Both (A) and (B)

D. None of these

Q.117 Which among the following does not exhibit geometric isomerism?

A. 1-hexene   B. 2-hexene   C. 3-hexene   D. 4-hexene

Q.118 Solution of known concentration:

A. Standard solution

B. Concentration

C. Solution

D. Concentrated solution

Q.119 Sub-cellular organelles are _______ in prokaryotic cell.

A. Present   B. Absent

C. Both (A) and (B)   D. None of these

Q.120 Southern blotting is:

A. Attachment of probes to DNA fragments.

B. Transfer of DNA fragments from electrophoretic gel to a nitrocellulose sheet.

C. Comparison of DNA fragments to two sources.

D. Transfer of DNA fragments to electrophoretic gel from cellulose membrane.

Q.121 Which of the following are produced by microorganisms?

A. Alcoholic beverages

B. Fermented dairy products

C. Breads

D. All of these

Q.122 What is the most definitive diagnostic index of meningitis?

A. PMN's in the CSF

B. PMN's in the blood

C. RBC's in the CSF

D. Purulent discharge in the ears

Q.123 Which type of molecules can't pass through pore transport?

A. Low molecular weight molecules

B. Water-soluble drugs

C. Molecules upto 400 dalton's

D. Molecules greater than 400 dalton's

Q.124 Is an example of category X drugs:

A. Diclofenac   B. Ranitidine

C. Lorazepam   D. Paracetamol

Q.125 __________ is known as power house of cell.

A. Lysosomes   B. Mitochondria

C. Nucleus   D. Ribosomes

// Smart Answer Sheet //

Correct — Percentage of students who answered correctly. **Skipped** — Percentage of students who skipped.

Q.	Ans.	Correct	Skipped	Q.	Ans.	Correct	Skipped	Q.	Ans.	Correct	Skipped	Q.	Ans.	Correct	Skipped	Q.	Ans.	Correct	Skipped	Q.	Ans.	Correct	Skipped
1	D	52.47 %	40.01 %	22	D	66.48 %	32.91 %	43	D	63.7 %	34.43 %	64	B	54.42 %	44.22 %	85	D	46.08 %	36.18 %	106	D	64.68 %	32.83 %
2	A	61.62 %	30.6 %	23	A	69.74 %	30.17 %	44	C	41.89 %	52.74 %	65	D	64.56 %	34.08 %	86	A	61.7 %	36.21 %	107	D	18.37 %	74.4 %
3	D	63.93 %	35.04 %	24	B	68.38 %	30.88 %	45	D	52.37 %	31.03 %	66	A	63.31 %	34.7 %	87	C	60.54 %	37.67 %	108	A	64.24 %	33.86 %
4	B	21.59 %	78.17 %	25	A	50.21 %	39.41 %	46	D	25.63 %	68.23 %	67	C	49.09 %	35.42 %	88	C	54.89 %	42.57 %	109	C	63.31 %	31.94 %
5	B	77.96 %	10.96 %	26	B	57.48 %	32.56 %	47	D	59.64 %	32.14 %	68	C	76.02 %	16.69 %	89	A	57.15 %	30.02 %	110	D	47.04 %	46.87 %
6	C	64.86 %	30.42 %	27	B	10.88 %	87.55 %	48	A	68.49 %	30.69 %	69	A	41.69 %	38.07 %	90	C	52.07 %	32.67 %	111	B	45.07 %	53.49 %
7	A	47.22 %	41.64 %	28	B	43.23 %	45.03 %	49	D	53.51 %	38.7 %	70	D	53.85 %	44.25 %	91	D	40.09 %	30.1 %	112	A	59.94 %	31.83 %
8	C	28.58 %	70.02 %	29	A	57.18 %	37.64 %	50	B	82.23 %	10.67 %	71	A	42.16 %	42.76 %	92	C	67.83 %	32.1 %	113	A	60.34 %	32.64 %
9	A	12.89 %	82.9 %	30	B	19.24 %	74.72 %	51	B	44.75 %	33.62 %	72	D	50.19 %	40.48 %	93	C	58.72 %	30.76 %	114	C	15.47 %	78.63 %
10	C	50.56 %	33.22 %	31	D	17.74 %	75.45 %	52	D	28.82 %	68.99 %	73	A	62.7 %	34.56 %	94	D	62.9 %	36.65 %	115	B	61.76 %	33.84 %
11	D	63.13 %	30.7 %	32	C	45.53 %	33.3 %	53	D	66.87 %	31.39 %	74	C	51.73 %	38.1 %	95	B	59.31 %	39.71 %	116	C	85.37 %	11.37 %
12	A	58.51 %	35.56 %	33	D	65.07 %	34.09 %	54	C	65.03 %	32.57 %	75	B	46.15 %	38.66 %	96	A	46.8 %	49.16 %	117	A	50.08 %	48.51 %
13	C	54.19 %	40.63 %	34	A	63.06 %	34.81 %	55	D	40.76 %	57.76 %	76	A	51.15 %	42.27 %	97	C	68.93 %	30.3 %	118	A	77.46 %	14.23 %
14	A	45.48 %	38.92 %	35	A	63.0 %	30.53 %	56	C	47.41 %	47.1 %	77	B	49.53 %	50.34 %	98	B	26.92 %	69.67 %	119	B	63.93 %	31.41 %
15	B	56.56 %	41.39 %	36	C	60.11 %	33.11 %	57	B	45.66 %	46.96 %	78	B	27.23 %	69.08 %	99	C	63.81 %	31.1 %	120	A	54.54 %	31.33 %
16	C	43.92 %	38.24 %	37	C	60.49 %	34.93 %	58	D	56.3 %	35.01 %	79	C	67.86 %	30.58 %	100	A	44.86 %	49.41 %	121	A	68.61 %	30.71 %
17	D	69.63 %	30.2 %	38	D	51.71 %	45.49 %	59	B	41.86 %	45.5 %	80	D	29.9 %	69.27 %	101	A	45.51 %	35.55 %	122	A	63.64 %	31.08 %
18	A	30.29 %	68.1 %	39	D	68.14 %	31.47 %	60	A	65.05 %	32.04 %	81	C	59.69 %	38.47 %	102	B	56.35 %	37.44 %	123	A	81.78 %	17.63 %
19	C	58.74 %	36.25 %	40	D	80.61 %	15.86 %	61	D	22.97 %	74.81 %	82	B	45.98 %	49.21 %	103	C	27.06 %	71.8 %	124	C	10.33 %	79.24 %
20	D	79.19 %	12.77 %	41	A	61.76 %	32.77 %	62	C	46.8 %	42.35 %	83	C	62.87 %	31.75 %	104	C	40.74 %	33.13 %	125	B	89.59 %	10.21 %
21	A	56.67 %	32.92 %	42	D	50.05 %	49.63 %	63	B	27.23 %	70.32 %	84	D	25.07 %	70.68 %	105	C	50.87 %	34.24 %				

//Hints and Solutions//

1. Fat-soluble vitamins are soluble in alcohol, one or more propene units and stored in the liver. Retinol is soluble in fats and oils and practically insoluble in water and glycerol. Vitamin A esters are readily soluble in fats, oils, ether, acetone and chloroform. They are soluble in alcohol but insoluble in water. The liver stores vitamin A, D, E, K and B12. The first four of these are all fat-soluble. All the fat-soluble vitamins contain one or more isoprene units 5 carbon units. They can be stored in the liver and adipose tissue.

Hence, the correct option is (D).

2. Vitamin A deficiency can result from inadequate intake, fat malabsorption, or liver disorders. Deficiency impairs immunity and hematopoiesis and causes rashes and typical ocular effects (eg, xerophthalmia, night blindness). Diagnosis is based on typical ocular findings and low vitamin A levels.

Hence, the correct option is (A).

3. An important function of vitamin A is to maintain the integrity of epithelial issues.

Epithelial cell "integrity": Many epithelial cells appear to require vitamin A for proper differentiation and maintenance. Lack of vitamin A leads to dysfunction of many epithelia-the skins become keratinized and scaly, and mucus secretion is suppressed.

Hence, the correct option is (D).

4. Retinal is a component of rhodopsin. Rhodopsin consists of two components, a protein molecule also called scotopsin and a covalently-bound cofactor called retinal. Thousands of rhodopsin molecules are found in each outer segment disc of the host rod cell. Retinal is produced in the retina from vitamin A, from dietary beta-carotene.

Hence, the correct option is (B).

5. Vitamin D absorption is increased in the alkaline pH of intestine. Avocados, nuts, seeds, full-fat dairy products and eggs are nutritious sources of fat that help boost your vitamin D absorption. Studies indicate that having vitamin D with a large meal or source of fat can significantly increase absorption. Vitamin D is a fat-soluble vitamin, meaning that it does not dissolve in water and is absorbed best in your bloodstream when paired with high-fat foods. For this reason, it's recommended to take vitamin D supplements with a meal to enhance absorption.

Hence, the correct option is (B).

6. A poor source of Vitamin D is milk. Breastfed infants, because human milk is a poor source of vitamin D. If you are breastfeeding, give your infant a supplement of 400 IU of vitamin D every day. Cow's milk, the most commonly consumed type of milk, is naturally a good source of many nutrients, including calcium, phosphorous, and riboflavin. In several countries, cow's milk is fortified with vitamin D. It usually contains about 115–130 IU per cup (237 ml), or about 15–22% of the DV (7, 33).

Hence, the correct option is (C).

7. The richest source of Vitamin D is fish liver oils. Fish oil usually contains some vitamin A and D. It's important to note that the types of omega-3s found in fish oil have greater health benefits than the omega-3s found in some plant sources. Few foods are naturally rich in vitamin D3. The best sources are the flesh of fatty fish and fish liver oils. Smaller amounts are found in egg yolks, cheese, and beef liver.

Hence, the correct option is (A).

8. Deficiency of vitamin D causes hypothyroidism. Hypothyroidism (underactive thyroid) is a condition in which your thyroid gland doesn't produce enough of certain crucial hormones. Hypothyroidism may not cause noticeable symptoms in the early stages. Ginger is rich in essential minerals like potassium and magnesium and helps combat inflammation, one of the primary causes of thyroid issues.

Hence, the correct option is (C).

9. One international unit (I.U) of vitamin D is defined as the biological activity of 0.025 µg of cholecalciferol.

IU (international unit): An international unit (IU) is an internationally accepted amount of a substance. This type of measure is used for the fat-soluble vitamins (such as vitamins A, D and E) and certain hormones, enzymes, and biologicals (such as vaccines).

One microgram is one-millionth of a gram and one-thousandth of a milligram. It is usually abbreviated as mcg or ug. Mcg and ug are the same. The IU is an International Unit, usually used to measure fat-soluble vitamins including Vitamin A, D and E.

Hence, the correct option is (A).

10. Beriberi is a disease caused by a vitamin B-1 deficiency, also known as thiamine deficiency. There are two types of the disease:

Wet beriberi: Wet beriberi affects the heart and circulatory system. In extreme cases, wet beriberi can cause heart failure.

Dry beriberi: The term beriberi is derived from the Sinhalese word meaning "extreme weakness." In the form known as dry beriberi, there is a gradual degeneration of the long nerves, first of the legs and then of the arms, with associated atrophy of muscle and loss of reflexes.

Hence, the correct option is (C).

11. Scurvy is caused due to the deficiency of Vitamin C. Scurvy happens when there is a lack of vitamin C or ascorbic acid. The deficiency leads to symptoms of weakness, anemia, gum disease, and skin problems. This is because vitamin C is needed for making collagen, an important component in connective tissues.

Hence, the correct option is (D).

12. Riboflavin deficiency causes cheilosis. Riboflavin deficiency causes various non-specific skin and mucosal lesions, including maceration of mucosa at the angles of the mouth (angular stomatitis) and surfaces of the lips (cheilosis). Cheilosis is a condition where the corners of the mouth become inflamed, which can lead to cracking and pain at the corners of the mouth. The cracks can split and bleed; they can also make it difficult to yawn, chew, or talk.

Hence, the correct option is (A).

13. Pellagra occurs in populations dependent on maize. Pellagra is encountered in populations that rely on maize as a major food source. Niacin (nicotinic acid and nicotinamide) is converted to nicotinamide adenine dinucleotide (NAD) and NAD phosphate, which are cofactors for more than 200 enzymes.

Hence, the correct option is (C).

14. Magenta tongue is found in the deficiency of vitamin B2 or Riboflavin. The signs and symptoms of riboflavin deficiency (also known as ariboflavinosis) include skin disorders, hyperemia (excess blood) and edema of the mouth and throat, angular stomatitis (lesions at the corners of the mouth), cheilosis (swollen, cracked lips), hair loss, reproductive problems, sore throat, itchy and red. A purplish-red discoloration of the tongue due to vitamin B2 (riboflavin) deficiency. It is also characterized by edema and flattening of the filiform papillae on the dorsum of the tongue.

Hence, the correct option is (A).

15. Corneal vascularisation is found in deficiency of vitamin B2. Corneal neovascularization is characterized by the invasion of new blood vessels into the cornea caused by an imbalance between angiogenic and antiangiogenic factors that preserve corneal transparency as a result of various ocular insults and hypoxic injuries. Its initiation and repair may be used for testing the biological activity of compounds structurally related to riboflavin.

Hence, the correct option is (B).

16. Pellagra is the late stage of severe niacin deficiency. Niacin, or vitamin B-3, is a water-soluble vitamin. In 1926, Goldberger reported that nicotinamide was a preventive factor of pellagra. Pellagra can be divided into primary and secondary forms. Niacin can both prevent and cure pellagra. Now, pellagra is rare in the U.S. because the diet of most people provides sufficient vitamin B-3, partly due to the enrichment of foods with the vitamin.

Hence, the correct option is (C).

17. Niacin overdose is unlikely if you take niacin only in the amount prescribed by your doctor. While it's not possible to overdose on niacin simply by eating too many niacin-rich foods, taking too much over-the-counter or prescription niacin can be dangerous. Niacin toxicity symptoms include:

- Severe skin flushing combined with dizziness
- Rapid heartbeat
- Itching
- Nausea and vomiting
- Abdominal pain
- Diarrhea
- Gout

Hence, the correct option is (D).

18. Vitamin B6 deficiency may occur during therapy with isoniazid. It is possible that vitamin B, deficiency occurs in some patients on isoniazid therapy and not in others because of differences in the amount of vitamin B6 in the food they consume. Isoniazid is used with other medications to treat active tuberculosis (TB) infections. It is also used alone to prevent active TB infections in people who may be infected with the bacteria (people with positive TB skin test). Isoniazid is an antibiotic and works by stopping the growth of bacteria.

Hence, the correct option is (A).

19. A deficiency of vitamin B-12 causes pernicious anemia. Either a lack of vitamin B-12 or a lack of folate causes a type of anemia called megaloblastic anemia (pernicious anemia). With these types of anemia, the red blood cells don't develop normally. Pernicious anemia, which makes it hard for your body to absorb vitamin B-12. Conditions that affect your small intestines, such as Crohn's disease, celiac disease, bacterial growth, or a parasite.

Hence, the correct option is (C).

20. Enzyme activity can be affected by a variety of factors, such as temperature, pH, and concentration. Enzymes work best within specific temperature and pH ranges, and sub-optimal conditions can cause an enzyme to lose its ability to bind to a substrate.

Hence, the correct option is (D).

21. The pH optima for salivary amylase is 6.6-6.8. For salivary amylase action, the optimum temperature and pH are 32oC–37oC (human body temperature) and 6–7 pH respectively. Salivary amylase is most active at 6.8 pH. The effect of the optimum temperature and pH range on the salivary amylase action can be studied using the iodine test. Saliva has a pH normal range of 6.2-7.6 with 6.7 being the average pH. Resting pH of mouth does not fall below 6.3.

Hence, the correct option is (A).

22. The pH optima for pancreatic amylase is 7.0. Purified human pancreatic alpha-amylase (alpha-1,4-glucan 4-glucano-hydrolase, was found to be stable over a wide range of pH values (5.0 to 10.5) with an optimal pH for the enzymatic activity of 7.0. In the digestive systems of humans and many other mammals, an alpha-amylase called ptyalin is produced by the salivary glands, whereas pancreatic amylase is secreted by the pancreas into the small intestine. The optimum pH of alpha-amylase is 6.7–7.0.

Hence, the correct option is (D).

23. The ion which activates salivary amylase activity is chloride. Salivary amylase or ptyalin has one major role to keep bacteria in the mouth in control. They are being activated by chloride ions. Chloride ions are present in the enzymes and act as activators to activate the enzyme so that they can be put into action.

Hence, the correct option is (A).

24. Glucose absorption is promoted by thiamine. The uptake of thiamine is enhanced by thiamine deficiency but can be reduced by the presence of diabetes mellitus. Additionally, thiamine absorption is inhibited by thiamine analogs (such as metronidazole), ethanol, and diuretics (such as amiloride). Thiamine is mostly concentrated in the skeletal muscles.

Hence, the correct option is (B).

25. A carbohydrate that cannot be digested in the human gut is cellulose. Humans are unable to digest cellulose because the appropriate enzymes to breakdown the beta acetal linkages are lacking. Undigestible cellulose is the fiber which aids in the smooth working of the intestinal tract.

Hence, the correct option is (A).

26. The number of ATP molecules generated for each turn of the citric acid cycle is 12. ATP Summary for Citric Acid Cycle (E.T.C = electron transport chain):

Step	ATP produced
7	1
Step 4 (NAD+ to E.T.C.)	3
Step 4 (NAD+ to E.T.C.)	3
Step 4 (NAD+ to E.T.C.)	3
Step 8 (FAD to E.T.C.)	2
NET	**12 ATP**

Hence, the correct option is (B).

27. The mitochondrial membrane is freely permeable to malate. Malate is the ionized form (an ester or a salt) of malic acid. Malic acid is a dicarboxylic acid produced by a living organism, with the chemical formula $C_4H_6O_5$. Apart from the Krebs cycle, malate is also involved in C4 carbon fixation during photosynthesis. It is a source of carbon dioxide in the Calvin cycle. The addition of oxaloacetate to the mitochondrion does not have a net anaplerotic effect, as another citric acid cycle intermediate (malate) is immediately removed from the mitochondrion to be converted into cytosolic oxaloacetate, which is ultimately converted into glucose, in a process that is almost the reverse of glycolysis.

Hence, the correct option is (B).

28. The net number of ATP formed per mole of glucose in anaerobic glycolysis is 2. The anaerobic glycolysis (lactic acid) system is dominant from about 10–30 seconds during a maximal effort. It replenishes very quickly over this period and produces 2 ATP molecules per glucose molecule or about 5% of glucose's energy potential (38 ATP molecules).

Hence, the correct option is (B).

29. The sites for gluconeogenesis are the liver and kidney. In vertebrates, gluconeogenesis occurs mainly in the liver and, to a lesser extent, in the cortex of the kidneys. It is one of two primary mechanisms – the other being degradation of glycogen (glycogenolysis)- used by humans and many other animals to maintain blood sugar levels, avoiding low levels (hypoglycemia).

Hence, the correct option is (A).

30. Insulin has no effect on the activity of the enzyme fructokinase. Fructokinase, the enzyme that initiates the metabolism of fructose, is not inhibited by ADP, so cellular loading with fructose can lead to increased urate generation. Fructose can enter cells via the insulin-independent GLUT5 fructose transporter. In hepatocytes, fructose is phosphorylated to fructose-1-phosphate (F1P) by the enzyme fructokinase. F1P is then hydrolyzed by the enzyme aldolase B to dihydroxyacetone phosphate (DHAP) and glyceraldehyde; the latter is phosphorylated to glyceraldehyde-3-phosphate.

Hence, the correct option is (B).

31. In Hunter's syndrome hearing loss is perceptive. Hunter syndrome is a rare, inherited disorder in which the body does not properly digest (break down) sugar molecules in the body. When these molecules build up in organs and tissues over time, they can cause damage that affects physical and mental development and abilities. Hunter syndrome primarily occurs in boys and is one of about 50 diseases classified as lysosomal storage disorders (LSD). In these disorders, genetic variations disrupt the normal activity of lysosomes in human cells.

Hence, the correct option is (D).

32. An important feature of Von-Gierke's disease is hypoglycemia. Von Gierke disease occurs when the body lacks the protein (enzyme) that releases glucose from glycogen. This causes abnormal amounts of glycogen to build up in certain tissues. When glycogen is not broken down properly, it leads to low blood sugar. Hypoglycemia is a condition in which your blood sugar (glucose) level is lower than normal.

Hence, the correct option is (C).

33. The affected organ in Mc Ardle's syndrome is skeletal muscle. Mc Ardle disease is a genetic disorder that mainly affects skeletal muscles. It occurs due to the deficiency or absence of an enzyme called myophosphorylase, a key substance that the muscles need to break down glycogen into sugar (glucose) for energy. Symptoms include painful muscle cramps, weakness, and fatigue manifested during periods of physical activity.

Hence, the correct option is (D).

34. Refsum's disease is due to deficiency of the enzyme phytanate α-oxidase. The lack of function of the enzyme (phytanoyl-CoA hydroxylase) leads to a build-up of phytanic acid in blood plasma and tissues. The disorder is inherited in an autosomal recessive manner. Refsum disease is an inherited condition that causes vision loss, absence of the sense of smell (anosmia), and a variety of other signs and symptoms. The vision loss associated with Refsum disease is caused by an eye disorder called retinitis pigmentosa.

Hence, the correct option is (A).

35. A component of the respiratory chain in mitochondria is coenzyme Q. The respiratory chain involves four large protein complexes (I–IV) as well as ATP synthase (AS). All of these are embedded in the inner mitochondrial membrane. Coenzyme Q (Q) and cytochrome C (C) are diffusible electron carriers.

Hence, the correct option is (A).

36. A pentamer immunoglobulin is IgM. Soluble immunoglobulin M (IgM) forms a pentamer containing a joining (J) chain polypeptide. While IgM pentamer has various immune functions, it also behaves as a carrier of circulating apoptosis inhibitor of macrophage (AIM; also called CD5L) protein that facilitates repair during different diseases. IgM circulates in serum as a pentamer of disulfide-linked immunoglobulin molecules joined by a single cross-linking peptide (J-chain).

Hence, the correct option is (C).

37. The immunoglobulin which can cross the placenta is IgG. Placental transfer of maternal IgG antibodies to the fetus is an important mechanism that provides protection to the infant while his/her humoral response is inefficient. IgG is the only antibody class that significantly crosses the human placenta.

Hence, the correct option is (C).

38. The total iron content of the human body is 4-5 g. Males of average height have about 4 grams of iron in their body, females about 3.5 grams; children will usually have 3 grams or less. These 3-4 grams are distributed throughout the body in hemoglobin, tissues, muscles, bone marrow, blood proteins, enzymes, ferritin, hemosiderin, and transport in plasma.

Hence, the correct option is (D).

39. Vulcanizing agents, softeners and antioxidants are the ingredients that are present in the rubber stopper. The most common vulcanization agent is sulfur. It forms bridges between individual polymer molecules when heated with rubber. Silicone spray contains the plasticizers needed to restore hardened rubber to its original suppleness. You can also heat rubber to make it more flexible when cold temperatures have caused it to harden. As a kind of ursolic rubber antioxidant, 6PPD has better compatibility with rubbers, seldom blooming, low volatility, low toxicity, with excellent antioxidant, anti-ozone, anti-flex cracks, anti-insolation cracks strong inhibition on copper or manganese and other toxic metals, applicable to all types of synthetic rubber and natural rubber.

Hence, the correct option is (D).

40. Blister pack, strip pack and bubble pack are the packaging systems are identified by the FDA. Blister packs are made through a form-fill-seal method. Strip packs are formed around the tablet at a time when it is dropped to the sealing area between two webs of a heat-sealable flexible film through either a heated reciprocating platen or a heated crimp roller. Bubble Wrap or air bubble packing is a transparent plastic packaging material that is mainly used to pack fragile or easily breakable items.

Hence, the correct option is (D).

41. Blister packaging is commonly used for packaging tablets & capsules. Blister packaging is the most common and widely accepted world-over as the primary pack of tablets or capsules due to its efficacy and safety considerations. Alternative to blister packs is strip packaging or a glass vial with a sealed cap.

Hence, the correct option is (A).

42. Aclar, cellophane and polyester are materials that offer moisture barrier properties. Traditionally, Aclar is used in pharmaceutical, medical, electronics, and military packaging. Aclar has been used to prepare sealed bags for low-oxygen level pest eradication. Cellophane, a thin film of regenerated cellulose, usually transparent, is employed primarily as a packaging material. It was transparent, waterproof, flexible, and strong. Polyethylene terephthalate (PET) is one type of polyester or synthetic fibrous material which has widespread use as a packaging material, especially for bottling gaseous drinks and mineral waters.

Hence, the correct option is (D).

43. The mechanism which are responsible for the release of encapsulated core materials are:

- **By disrupting the coating by pressure:** Coating is a process by which an essentially dry, outer layer of coating material is applied to the surface of a dosage form in order to confer specific benefits over uncoated variety.

- **By offering permeability facilities:** The ability of a drug to pass across a biological membrane is defined as drug permeability. Passive diffusion is the major absorption pathway.

- **By leaching of permanent fluid:** Leaching is the process of a solute becoming detached or extracted from its carrier substance by way of a solvent.

Hence, the correct option is (D).

44. Pre-formulation studies mainly focus on the physicochemical properties of the new compounds. A pre-formulation study is a phase that is initiated once the new molecule is needed. In a broader way, it deals with studies of physical, chemical, analytical, and pharmaceutical properties related to molecules and provides ideas about suitable modifications in molecules to show a better performance.

Hence, the correct option is (C).

45. The information which is helpful in designing the pre-formulation evaluation of a new drug is the structure of a compound, the formula & molecular weight of a compound and the therapeutic indication of a new compound. Among these properties, drug solubility, partition coefficient, dissolution rate, polymorphic forms and stability are plays important role in the pre-formulation study. Polymorphism having crystal and amorphous forms show different chemical-physical and therapeutic descriptions of the drug molecule.

Hence, the correct option is (D).

46. The problems commonly encountered in evaluating salt forms are:

- **Poor crystallinity:** Crystallinity can be defined as the degree of long-range structural order comprising a crystal lattice within a (solid) material. Normally the terms used is single crystalline or polycrystalline. Lower crystalline material means smaller grain size and higher grain density, which may enhance the strength.

- **Hygroscopicity:** Hygroscopicity is the tendency of a solid substance to absorb moisture from the surrounding atmosphere. The process can take on a number of forms. Thus, with a porous solid such as activated carbon, water vapor will be physically adsorbed, both on the external surface and within the pores, to form a condensed layer.

- **Instability:** Without absorption, a drug cannot have a therapeutic effect, so some forms require salt. Many medications need to be water-soluble, too. Therefore, drugs are often chemically made into their salt forms to enhance how the drug dissolves, boost its absorption into your bloodstream, and increase its effectiveness.

Hence, the correct option is (D).

47. Acetate, gluconate and lactate are the salts that are generally used in pharmaceutical products. Over 50% of all drug molecules used in medicine exist as salts, most frequently as hydrochloride, sodium, or sulfate salts. Drugs are often formed as a weak acid or base, but this drug form is not always optimal for dissolution or absorption into your body.

Hence, the correct option is (D).

48. Description of the outer appearance of a crystal is known as crystal habit. Crystal habit, or morphology, is a crucial attribute of powdered materials that affect the ease with which a pharmaceutical formulation can be pressed into a tablet. The crystal habit may lead to change the characteristics of the material like melting point, solubility, dissolution profile, compressibility, flowability, true density, and stability.

Hence, the correct option is (A).

49. Rapid precipitation, lyophilization and rapid cooling are the techniques used to prepare amorphous forms. Precipitation, in chemistry, a process in which a solid is separated from a suspension, sol, or solution. In a suspension such as sand in water, the solid spontaneously precipitates (settles out) on standing. Lyophilization is a water removal process typically used to preserve perishable materials, extend shelf life or make the material more convenient for transport. Rapid cooling using a cool solution (e.g. water, oil) from the solution treatment temperature to obtain a supersaturated solid solution of alloying elements in the host metal.

Hence, the correct option is (D).

50. Amorphous forms generally have high thermodynamic energy & high solubility. Amorphous forms are, by definition, non-crystalline materials which possess no long-range order. Their structure can be thought of as being similar to that of a frozen liquid with the thermal fluctuations present in a liquid frozen out, leaving only "static" structural disorder.

Hence, the correct option is (B).

51. Anhydrates compound possess high aqueous solubility. Anhydrate is the name given to the substance that remains after the water is removed from a hydrate. This is often done by heating the compound, a process that eliminates that water molecules as steam. Ethanoic anhydride can't be said to dissolve in water because it reacts with it to give ethanoic acid. There is no such thing as an aqueous solution of ethanoic anhydride.

Hence, the correct option is (B).

52. The properties which may change with changing of the internal structure of a solid are melting point, density and optical properties. Characteristics such as melting point, boiling point, density, solubility, color, odor, etc. are physical properties. Properties that describe how a substance changes identity to produce a new substance are chemical properties. Among the optical properties, refraction, absorption, reflection, and scattering of light are the most important. The optical appearance properties of a polymer, e.g., its clarity, gloss, dullness, or turbidity, have no (direct) correlation with its chemical structure; they are largely determined by physical factors.

Hence, the correct option is (D).

53. DSC, XRD, TGA methods are used for studying solid forms. Various analytical methods have been employed to characterize and monitor the solid forms of drugs during the various steps of processing and development, including powder X-ray diffraction (PXRD), infrared spectroscopy, scanning electron microscopy (SEM), thermal analysis, and solid-state nuclear magnetic resonance. Differential Scanning Calorimetry (DSC) is a highly sensitive technique to study the thermotropic properties of many different biological macromolecules and extracts. Since its early development, DSC has been applied to the pharmaceutical field with excipient studies and DNA drugs. Thermogravimetric analysis (TGA) is an analytical technique used to determine a material's thermal stability and its fraction of volatile components by monitoring the weight change that occurs as a sample is heated at a constant rate.

Hence, the correct option is (D).

54. DSC and DTA methods are generally used to measure heat loss or gain within a sample.

- DSC is a thermal analysis apparatus measuring how the physical properties of a sample change, along with temperature against time. In other words, the device is a thermal analysis instrument that determines the temperature and heat flow associated with material transitions as a function of time and temperature.

- Differential thermal analysis (DTA) and thermal gravimetric analysis (TGA) measure respectively the temperature difference between a sample and an inert reference sample as a function of temperature, and the weight change of a sample as a function of temperature, while subjected to a controlled heating program.

Hence, the correct option is (C).

55. The co-solvent that can be used to increase the solubility of poor soluble drugs are ethanol, propylene glycol and glycerin. Co-solvent solubilization approach has been used to enhance the solubility of seven antidiabetic drugs: gliclazide, glyburide, glipizide, glimepiride, repaglinide, pioglitazone, and rosiglitazone.

Hence, the correct option is (D).

56. The partition coefficient is the measure of the lipophilicity of a drug and an indication of its ability to cross the cell membrane. It is defined as the ratio between un-ionized drug distributed between the organic and aqueous layers at equilibrium.

Hence, the correct option is (C).

57. The dissolution of a drug particle is described by the Noyes–Whitney equation. The modified Noyes–Whitney equation describes the drug dissolution in which surface area is constant during disintegration.

$$\frac{dC}{dt} = \frac{D}{h} \times A \times (C_s - C)$$

A=surface area of drug-exposed to dissolution medium.
V=volume of the medium.

C_s = Concentration of a saturated solution of the solute in the dissolution medium at the experimental temperature.

Hence, the correct option is (B).

58. The effect of temperature on drug stability can be described by each physical stability of pharmaceutical products and temperature-controlled drug storage may have slightly different storage requirements but all pharmaceuticals need to be properly stored in order to ensure they remain within a specific temperature range.

When a drug is stored in temperatures that are too high or too low, the drug's chemical stability will likely be impacted. That means that the drug may degrade and form impurities. In some cases, improper medicine temperature storage can even alter a drug's physical properties.

Hence, the correct option is (D).

59. Unequal distribution of color on a tablet refers to mottling. 'Mottling' is that the term accustomed describe the associated unequal distribution of color on a pill, with lightweight or dark spots standing to go into the associate otherwise uniform surface. One reason for marking is also a colored drug, whose color differs from the color of excipients used for the granulation of a pill.

Hence, the correct option is (B).

60. Excessive moisture is responsible for sticking. Sticking is one of the major problems associated with tablet manufacturing, and it is due to the inaccurate addition of excipients or errors in the granulation process. Sticking is also called filming. Mostly, tablet sticking occurs when granulated powder sticks to the punch surface causing deformed tablets.

Hence, the correct option is (A).

61. If the dose of a drug is inadequate, the nit generally requires the diluents to make up its bulk. Diluents act as fillers in pharmaceutical tablets to increase weight and improve content uniformity. Natural diluents include starches, hydrolyzed starches, and partially pregelatinized starches. Diluents provide better tablet properties such as improved cohesion or promote flow.

Hence, the correct option is (D).

62. Littleford lodige mixer is the first high-shear powder blender/mixer. A high-shear mixer can be used to create emulsions, suspensions, lyosols (gas dispersed in a liquid), and granular products. It is used in the adhesives, chemical, cosmetic, food, pharmaceutical, and plastics industries for emulsification, homogenization, particle size reduction, and dispersion.

Hence, the correct option is (C).

63. The first and most widely used diluent in the tablet formulation is lactose. Lactose is widely used as an excipient in pharmaceutical manufacturing as a filler or diluent in tablets, capsules and to give bulk to powders. Lactose has no reaction with most drugs, whether it is used in the hydrous or anhydrous form (Lachman et al 1987).

Hence, the correct option is (B).

64. Anhydrous lactose has the advantage over hydrous lactose that the absence of Millard reaction. Maillard reaction produces flavour and aroma during cooking process; and it is used almost everywhere from the baking industry to our day to day life to make food tasty. It is often called a non-enzymatic browning reaction since it takes place in the absence of enzymes.

Hence, the correct option is (B).

65. The sugar tab is not a commercially available starch product. A sugar-coated tablet is coated with sugar to disguise the taste. The hard coating on a sugar-coated tablet is similar to the sweet coatings on some candies. A sugar-coated tablet is coated with sugar to disguise the taste.

Hence, the correct option is (D).

66. PVP is a synthetic adhesive. Synthetic adhesives are based on elastomers, thermoplastics, emulsions, and thermosets. Examples of thermosetting adhesives are: epoxy, polyurethane, cyanoacrylate and acrylic polymers. The first commercially produced synthetic adhesive was Karlsons Klister in the 1920.

Hence, the correct option is (A).

67. PEG is a water-soluble lubricant. MGS is widely used as a lubricant in tablets manufactured at a concentration of 0.25% and 5.0% w/w. The PEG is widely used in a variety of pharmaceutical formulations. PEG is water-soluble and generally regarded as nontoxic and non-irritant material.

Hence, the correct option is (C).

68. The correct statement regarding a sweetener, saccharin is it is 500 times sweeter than sucrose, but it is carcinogenic and it is 500 times sweeter than sucrose, but it has a bitter taste. Saccharin is a non-nutritive or artificial sweetener. It's made in a laboratory by oxidizing the chemicals o-toluene sulfonamide or phthalic anhydride. It looks like white, crystalline powder. Saccharin is commonly used as a sugar substitute because it doesn't contain calories or carbs.

Hence, the correct option is (C).

69. Aerosil is used as a glidant. A glidant is a substance that is added to a powder to improve its flowability. A glidant will only work at a certain range of concentrations. Above a certain concentration, the glidant will in fact function to inhibit flowability. In tablet manufacture, glidants are usually added just prior to compression.

Hence, the correct option is (A).

70. The pH of the duodenum is 4-6. Duodenal contractile activity can help to maintain neutral pH in the duodenum by mixing acid with bicarbonate or by aborally transporting the acid load. The intraluminal pH is rapidly changed from highly acid in the stomach to about pH 6 in the duodenum. The pH gradually increases in the small intestine from pH 6 to about pH 7.4 in the terminal ileum.

Hence, the correct option is (D).

71. Tablets, which are placed between cheek and teeth, are known as buccal. A buccal medicine is a medicine given between the gums and the inner lining of the mouth cheek. This area is called the buccal pouch. Medicine is usually given in the buccal area when it is needed to take effect quickly or when the child is not conscious.

Hence, the correct option is (A).

72. The statement which is not correct is oral route avoids first-pass metabolism. The first pass effect (also known as first-pass metabolism or pre-systemic metabolism) is a phenomenon of drug metabolism whereby the concentration of a drug, specifically when administered orally, is greatly reduced before it reaches the systemic circulation.

Hence, the correct option is (D).

73. Enteric coating is achieved by using HPMC. An enteric coating is a polymer barrier applied to oral medication that prevents its dissolution or disintegration in the gastric environment. Tablets, mini-tablets, pellets and granules (usually filled into capsule shells) are the most common enteric-coated dosage forms. The substances used in enteric coating are hydroxypropyl methylcellulose phthalate (HPMCP), polyvinyl acetate phthalate, diethyl phthalate, and cellulose acetate phthalate. In general, tablets can be coated using either a fluid-bed dryer or air suspension coating.

Hence, the correct option is (A).

74. The disintegration time for sugar-coated tablets is 60 minutes. Sugar-coated tablets comply with the 5.3 disintegration test for tablets and capsules. Operate the apparatus for 60 minutes, unless otherwise specified in the individual monograph, using water, and examine the state of the tablets.

Hence, the correct option is (C).

75. The flow rate of granules from the hopper can be improved by adding glidant. A glidant is a substance that is added to a powder to improve its flowability. A glidant will only work at a certain range of concentrations. Above a certain concentration, the glidant will in fact function to inhibit flowability. In tablet manufacture, glidants are usually added just prior to compression.

Hence, the correct option is (B).

76. The correct match is (1)-(T), (2)-(S), (3)-(P), (4)-(Q). ZENU is a strategic, proprietary blend of safe, effective, scientifically proven, standardized herbal Ayurvedic extracts, creating a superb harmony of beneficial physiological effects on the Nervous System by improving memory, intellect and cognition. It also reduces stress and improves Quality-of-Life. "HEPA" stands for "high-efficiency particulate air" (filter). To be labeled a true HEPA filter, it must be able to trap 99.97 percent of particles that are 0.3 microns. Pharmaceutical products typically contain a blend of active material with additional excipients such as flow agents, disintegrating agents, binders, etc. These are typically fine powders with diverse characteristics is known as chilsonator. For medium to large scale production, the Accelacota range features a unique side vented pan, with patented baffles, a choice of the film application system.

Hence, the correct option is (A).

77. The drug is dissolved in light petroleum and shaken with dilute copper acetate solution, petroleum layer becomes emerald green in colour; the drug is Colophony. Colophony contains resin acids (about 90%), resenes, and fatty acid esters. Of the resin acids, about 90% are isomeric α-, β-, and γ-abietic acids; the other 10% is a mixture of dehydroabietic acid and dehydroabietic acid. Before distillation, the resin contains excess amounts of (+) and (-) pimaric acids.

Hence, the correct option is (B).

78. Abietic acid is a major constituent of colophony, it is a diterpene. Diterpenes are a class of chemical compounds composed of four isoprene units, often with the molecular formula $C_{20}H_{32}$. They are biosynthesized by plants, animals and fungi via the HMG-CoA reductase pathway, with geranylgeranyl pyrophosphate being a primary intermediate. Alcoholic solution of Colophony turns blue litmus to red due to the presence of diterpenic acids.

Hence, the correct option is (B).

79. Pinus species growing in India is used for the collection of oleoresin pinus longifolia. Pine oleoresin is an abundant source of useful terpenes. Oleoresin derivatives can be used by different industries, including pharmaceutical, cosmetic, and food industries, as well as by the chemical industry in the manufacturing of various products, such as paint, varnishes, adhesives, insecticides, and disinfectants.

Hence, the correct option is (C).

80. Nutmeg obtained from Myristica fragrans is a kernel. Nutmeg oil is obtained from the dried kernels of the seeds of Myristica fragrans. It is indigenous to the Moluccas is lands and cultivated in Indonesia, Caribbean islands, India, and other tropical countries. The plant is a dioecious tree. The seed is obtained from the female plants.

Hence, the correct option is (D).

81. Volatile oil derived from 4n of Acorus calamus variety is free from beta-asarone. Calamus leaves and rhizomes contain a volatile oil that gives a characteristic odor and flavor. Major components of the oil are beta-asarone (as much as 75%) and alpha-asarone, saponins, lectins, sesquiterpenoids, lignans, and steroids.

Hence, the correct option is (C).

82. Natural camphor obtained from Cinnamomum camphora is dextrorotatory. Camphor is a chiral substance that in nature occurs in its dextrorotatory form. Camphor (Cinnamomum camphora) is a terpene (organic compound) that's commonly used in creams, ointments, and lotions. Camphor oil is the oil extracted from the wood of camphor trees and processed by steam distillation. It can be used topically to relieve pain, irritation, and itching.

Hence, the correct option is (B).

83. The pungency of ginger is destroyed by boiling a 2% solution of potassium hydroxide. The pungency of gingerol is destroyed by boiling with 2% KOH. Shogaol represents the compounds formed by loss of water from gingerol; it is an artifact of extraction. Starch (Ginger bread)and mucilage. Potassium hydroxide, also known as lye is an inorganic compound with the chemical formula KOH. Also commonly referred to as caustic

potash, it is a potent base that is marketed in several forms including pellets, flakes, and powders. It is used in various chemical, industrial and manufacturing applications.

Hence, the correct option is (C).

84. Starch grains found in ginger are compounds. The starch content of ginger flour was 82%. It had low values for in vitro starch digestibility (45%), dietary fibre (7.36%) and sugars (2.2%). The blue value of ginger starch was found to be 0.1748 g/dL. The AM content of ginger starch (25.5%) was in the normal range (18–30%) found in other starches. The principal components of ginger reported are gingerols, shogaols, and high content of starch (40 to 60 %).

Hence, the correct option is (D).

85. Removal of water from gingerol yields shogaols. Gingerols are the major pungent compounds present in the rhizomes of ginger (Zingiber officinale Roscoe) and are renowned for their contribution to human health and nutrition. Shogaols are important biomarkers used for the quality control of many ginger-containing products, due to their diverse biological activities.

Hence, the correct option is (D).

86. Coated ginger means, it is limed. Ginger can be either 'coated' or 'unscraped' depending on the amount of cork removed. When the rhizome is broken it yields a short fracture with fibrovascular bundle fibers protruding from the broken surface. The rhizome is associated with an agreeable aromatic odor and pungent taste, owing to its use as a spice.

Hence, the correct option is (A).

87. Epinephrine produces positive inotropic and chronotropic actions on the heart (beta receptor), increases peripheral resistance (alfa receptor) and skeletal muscle blood vessel dilatation (beta receptor) but except for the predominance of alfa effects at low concentration. Epinephrine is a sympathomimetic catecholamine that exerts its pharmacologic effects on both alpha and beta-adrenergic receptors using a G protein-linked second messenger system. It has a greater affinity for beta receptors in small doses. However, large doses produce selective action on alpha receptors.

Hence, the correct option is (C).

88. Epinephrine is used in the treatment of bronchospasm, anaphylactic shock and open-angle glaucoma of the disorders except for cardiac arrhythmias. A heart arrhythmia (uh-RITH-me-uh) is an irregular heartbeat. Heart rhythm problems (heart arrhythmias) occur when the electrical signals that coordinate the heart's beats don't work properly. The faulty signaling causes the heart to beat too fast (tachycardia), too slow (bradycardia), or irregularly.

Hence, the correct option is (C).

89. Norepinephrine produces vasoconstriction. Norepinephrine exerts its effects by binding to α- and β-adrenergic receptors (or adrenoceptors, so named for their reaction to the adrenal hormones) in different tissues. In the blood vessels, it triggers vasoconstriction (narrowing of blood vessels), which increases blood pressure.

Hence, the correct option is (A).

90. The sympathomimetic, which may cause hypotension, presumably because of a clonidine-like effect is xylometazoline. A sympathomimetic that directly acts on alpha-adrenergic receptors in arterioles of the nasal mucosa to produce vasoconstriction resulting in decreased blood flow.

Therapeutic Effect: Decreased nasal congestion.

Hence, the correct option is (C).

91. The agent of choice in the emergency therapy of anaphylactic shock is epinephrine. Epinephrine is in a class of medications called alpha- and beta-adrenergic agonists (sympathomimetic agents). It works by relaxing the muscles in the airways and tightening the blood vessels. It has a greater affinity for beta receptors in small doses. However, large doses produce selective action on alpha receptors.

Hence, the correct option is (D).

92. Non-selective alfa-receptor antagonists are most useful in the treatment of pheochromocytoma. Pheochromocytoma is a rare tumor of adrenal gland tissue. It results in the release of too much epinephrine and norepinephrine, hormones that control heart rate, metabolism, and blood pressure. Pheochromocytoma derives its name from phaios (dusky), chroma (color), cytoma (tumor).

Hence, the correct option is (C).

93. Phentolamine drugs are useful in the treatment of pheochromocytoma. Phentolamine belongs to a group of medications called vasodilators. These drugs work by causing blood vessels to expand and allowing more blood to flow through them. Phentolamine Mesylate for Injection, USP is indicated for the prevention or control of hypertensive episodes that may occur in a patient with pheochromocytoma as a result of stress or manipulation during preoperative preparation and surgical excision.

Hence, the correct option is (C).

94. Phenoxybenzamine is a nonselective α-adrenergic receptor antagonist used in patients with pheochromocytoma or paraganglionoma. The drug blunts the effects of catecholamines released from the tumor and is usually administered preoperatively in preparation for pheochromocytoma resection.

Hence, the correct option is (D).

95. The principal adverse effects of phentolamine include diarrhea, arrhythmias and myocardial ischemia but except for bradycardia. Bradycardia (brad-e-KAHR-dee-uh) is a slower than normal heart rate. The hearts of adults at rest usually beat between 60 and 100 times a minute. If you have bradycardia, your heart beats fewer than 60 times a minute.

Hence, the correct option is (B).

96. Beta-blocking agents have bronchoconstriction, a decrease of aqueous humor production and membrane-stabilizing action but except for increased plasma concentrations of HDL and a decrease of VLDL. Beta-blockers, also known as beta-adrenergic blocking agents, are medications that reduce blood pressure.

Beta-blockers work by blocking the effects of the hormone epinephrine, also known as adrenaline. Beta-blockers cause the heart to beat more slowly and with less force, which lowers blood pressure.

Hence, the correct option is (A).

97. Beta-receptor antagonists cause inhibition of glycogenolysis. The inhibitory action of insulin and proinsuiin on basal and glucagon-activated glycogenolysis was studied in cultured rat hepatocytes containing. glycogen. These data point to a direct regulatory role of insulin in the control of hepatic glycogen breakdown even when acting as sole hormone.

Hence, the correct option is (C).

98. Propranolol has properties like it decreases cardiac work and oxygen demand, it inhibits renin secretion and it increases the atrioventricular nodal refractory period cardiovascular effects except for it reduces blood flow to the brain. A stroke is an abrupt interruption of constant blood flow to the brain that causes loss of neurological function. The interruption of blood flow can be caused by a blockage, leading to the more common ischemic stroke, or by bleeding in the brain, leading to the more deadly hemorrhagic stroke.

Hence, the correct option is (B).

99. A beta-receptor antagonist, which has a very long duration of action nadolol. Nadolol is used alone or in combination with other medications to treat high blood pressure. It is also used to prevent angina (chest pain). Nadolol is in a class of medications called beta-blockers. It works by relaxing blood vessels and slowing heart rate to improve blood flow and decrease blood pressure.

Hence, the correct option is (C).

100. A beta-1 selective receptor antagonist, which has a very long duration of action betaxolol. Betaxolol belongs to a class of drugs known as beta-blockers. It works by blocking the action of certain natural chemicals in your body such as epinephrine that affects the heart and blood vessels. This results in a lowering of the heart rate and blood pressure.

Hence, the correct option is (A).

101. The characteristics of reserpine include:

- It decreases cardiac output, peripheral resistance and inhibits pressor reflexes.
- It may cause a transient sympathomimetic effect.
- It depletes stores of catecholamines and serotonin in the brain.

But this is not a characteristic i.e. it inhibits the uptake of norepinephrine into vesicles and MAO. Reserpine is an adrenergic blocking agent used to treat mild to moderate hypertension via the disruption of norepinephrine vesicular storage.

Hence, the correct option is (A).

102. The hypnotic drug, which is a benzodiazepine derivative is flurazepam. Flurazepam is used to treat insomnia (difficulty falling asleep and staying asleep). Flurazepam is in a class of

medications called benzodiazepines. It works by slowing activity in the brain to allow sleep.

Hence, the correct option is (B).

103. Thiopental barbiturates is an ultra-short-acting drug. Ultrashort-acting barbiturates, such as thiopental sodium and thiamylal, are used intravenously to induce unconsciousness smoothly and rapidly in patients about to undergo surgery, after which gaseous anesthetics are used to maintain the unconscious state.

Hence, the correct option is (C).

104. The barbituric acid derivative, which has a 4-5 days elimination half-life is phenobarbital. Phenobarbital is a prescription medicine used to treat and prevent the symptoms of seizures, sedation, hypnotics, Insomnia and Status Epilepticus. Phenobarbital may be used alone or with other medications. Phenobarbital belongs to a class of drugs called Anticonvulsants, Barbiturates.

Hence, the correct option is (C).

105. Phenobarbital hypnotic drugs is more likely to cause cumulative and residual effects. Phenobarbital is a prescription medicine used to treat and prevent the symptoms of seizures, sedation, hypnotics, Insomina and Status Epilepticus. Phenobarbital may be used alone or with other medications. Phenobarbital belongs to a class of drugs called Anticonvulsants, Barbiturates.

Hence, the correct option is (C).

106. Hepatic microsomal drug-metabolizing enzyme induction leads to hangover effects. Drugs that cause hepatic DME induction may increase microsomal enzymes, leading to hypertrophy of hepatocytes in a dose-dependent fashion. However, more recent evidence suggests that drug hepatotoxicity occurs mainly with high-dose (i.e., low-potency) drugs (Lammert et al).

Hence, the correct option is (D).

107. Barbiturates increase the rate of metabolism of anticoagulants, digitalis compounds and glucocorticoids. Barbiturates are drugs that cause relaxation and sleepiness. A barbiturate overdose occurs when someone takes more than the normal or recommended amount of this medicine. This can be done by accident or on purpose. An overdose is life-threatening. At fairly low doses, barbiturates may make you seem drunk or intoxicated.

Hence, the correct option is (D).

108. Flumasenil agents inhibits hepatic metabolism of hypnotics. Flumazenil (also known as flumazepil, code name Ro 15-1788) is a selective $GABA_A$ receptor antagonist administered via injection, otic insertion, or intranasally. Therapeutically, it acts as both an antagonist and antidote to benzodiazepines (particularly in cases of overdose), through competitive inhibition.

Hence, the correct option is (A).

109. Flurazepam hypnotic agents is able to interact with both BZ -1 and BZ -2 receptor subtypes. Flurazepam is used to treat

insomnia (difficulty falling asleep and staying asleep). Flurazepam is in a class of medications called benzodiazepines. It works by slowing activity in the brain to allow sleep.

Hence, the correct option is (C).

110. Picrotoxin agents blocks the chloride channel directly. Picrotoxin, also known as cocculin, is a poisonous crystalline plant compound. Due to its interactions with the inhibitory neurotransmitter GABA, picrotoxin acts as a stimulant and convulsant. It mainly impacts the central nervous system, causing seizures and respiratory paralysis in high enough doses.

Hence, the correct option is (D).

111. Hypnotic benzodiazepines agents are preferred in the treatment of insomnia. Benzodiazepines that have been approved by the FDA for treating chronic insomnia include estazolam, flurazepam (Dalmane), temazepam (Restoril), quazepam (Doral), and triazolam (Halcion). Rapidly acting drugs with shorter half-lives (i.e., estazolam, triazolam, and temazepam) are preferred.

Hence, the correct option is (B).

112. The main claim for an ideal hypnotic agent is that it is a rapid onset and has a sufficient duration of action. An ideal hypnotic should present, among others, the following characteristics:

1. No effect on memory or cognition
2. Rapid absorption
3. Specific binding to the receptor
4. Maintenance of physiological sleep
5. No residual effects
6. Optimal half-life
7. No potential for abuse, tolerance or dependence

Hence, the correct option is (A).

113. The two main stages of sleep are rapid eye movement (REM) and non-REM sleep. Although dreaming can take place during both REM sleep and non-REM sleep, dreams experienced during REM sleep tend to be more vivid. Additionally, REM cycles are typically longer and deeper in the morning (towards the end of sleep).

Hence, the correct option is (A).

114. During slow-wave sleep (stage 3 and 4 NREM sleep) somnambulism and nightmares occur. Enuresis, somnambulism, and nightmares occur in confusional states of arousal, not in "dreaming sleep" Science. Slow-wave sleep (SWS), often referred to as deep sleep, consists of stage three of non-rapid eye movement sleep. Initially, SWS consisted of both stage 3, which has 20–50 percent delta wave activity, and stage 4, which has more than 50 percent delta wave activity.

Hence, the correct option is (C).

115. The characteristic not possessed by an ideal solution is that its volume change on mixing is not equal to zero. The ideal Solutions are those which obey Raoult's Law at all concentrations and Temperatures. Some examples of ideal solution liquid pairs are benzene and toluene, n-heptane and n-hexane, ethyl bromide and ethyl iodide, chlorobenzene and bromobenzene, etc.

Hence, the correct option is (B).

116. Autocatalysis refers to when a substrate acts as a catalyst and when a product acts as a catalyst. In autocatalysis, the reaction is catalyzed by one of its products and that catalyst is called Autocatalyst. One of the simplest examples of this is in the oxidation of a solution of oxalic acid by an acidified solution of potassium manganate (VII) (potassium permanganate). The reaction is very slow at room temperature. A single chemical reaction is said to be autocatalytic if one of the reaction products is also a catalyst for the same or a coupled reaction. Such a reaction is called an autocatalytic reaction.

Hence, the correct option is (C).

117. Alkenes like 1-hexene when flipped from top to bottom they have identical structures and also they have $C=CH_2$ unit which does not exist as cis-trans isomers. 1-hexene does not exhibit geometric isomerism. It cannot form cis-trans isomers because the first carbon carrying the double bond has no substituent attached to it. It only has two attached hydrogen atoms.

Hence, the correct option is (A).

118. The solution with known concentration is known as the standard solution. Standard solutions are generally used in a titration where the unknown concentration of a substance is determined using the solution of substance of known concentration.

Hence, the correct option is (A).

119. Sub-cellular organelles are absent in prokaryotic cell. Prokaryotic cells are surrounded by a plasma membrane, but they have no internal membrane-bound organelles within their cytoplasm. The absence of a nucleus and other membrane-bound organelles differentiates prokaryotes from another class of organisms called eukaryotes.

Hence, the correct option is (B).

120. Southern blotting is the attachment of probes to DNA fragments. Southern blotting is a laboratory technique used to detect a specific DNA sequence in a blood or tissue sample. A restriction enzyme is used to cut a sample of DNA into fragments that are separated using gel electrophoresis. The DNA fragments are transferred out of the gel to the surface of a membrane.

Hence, the correct option is (A).

121. Microorganisms are used in many industries for the production of the food we eat, like fermented dairy products (sour cream, yogurt), as well as fermented foods as pickles, bread and alcoholic beverages. Microorganisms, commonly called microbes, are organisms that are too small to be seen with an unaided eye. To be pharmaceutically relevant, microorganisms would not only constitute health hazards but must be a destructive contaminant of pharmaceutical products.

Hence, the correct option is (A).

122. The PMN's in the CSF's most definitive diagnostic index of meningitis. For a definitive diagnosis of meningitis, you'll need a spinal tap to collect cerebrospinal fluid (CSF). In people with meningitis, the CSF often shows a low sugar (glucose) level along with an increased white blood cell count and increased protein.

Hence, the correct option is (A).

123. Low molecular weight molecules can't pass through pore transport. The molecule (or metabolite) is a low molecular weight organic compound, typically involved in a biological process as a substrate or product. Metabolomics usually studies small molecules within a mass range of 50-1500 daltons (Da).

Hence, the correct option is (A).

124. Lorazepam is an example of a category X drug. Lorazepam, sold under the brand name Ativan among others, is a benzodiazepine medication. It is used to treat anxiety disorders, trouble sleeping, severe agitation, active seizures including status epilepticus, alcohol withdrawal, and chemotherapy-induced nausea and vomiting. It is also used during surgery to interfere with memory formation and to sedate those who are being mechanically ventilated. It is also used, along with other treatments, for acute coronary syndrome due to cocaine use.

Hence, the correct option is (C).

125. Mitochondria is known as the power house of cells. Mitochondria are tiny organelles inside cells that are involved in releasing energy from food. This process is known as cellular respiration. Mitochondria are often called the "powerhouses" or "energy factories" of a cell because they are responsible for making adenosine triphosphate (ATP), the cell's main energy-carrying molecule. Cellular respiration is the process of making ATP using the chemical energy found in glucose and other nutrients.

Hence, the correct option is (B).

Pharmaceutical Chemistry

Q.1 Aldosterone synthesis occurs in:

A. Zona reticularis   **B.** Zona fasciculate

C. Zona glomerulosa   **D.** Chromaffian cells

Q.2 A hormone which cannot cross the blood brain barrier is:

A. Epinephrine   **B.** Aldosterone

C. ACTH   **D.** TSH

Q.3 PKC is activated by:

A. Cyclic AMP

B. Cyclic GMP

C. Diacylglycerol

D. Inositol triphosphate

Q.4 Mental retardation can occur in:

A. Cretinism

B. Juvenile myxoedema

C. Myxoedema

D. Juvenile thyrotoxicosis

Q.5 The most powerful thyroid hormone is:

A. Reverse T3   **B.** DIT

C. T3   **D.** T4

Q.6 Zona glomerulosa of adrenal cortex synthesises:

A. Glucocorticoids

B. Mineralocorticoid

C. Androgens

D. Estrogen and progesterone

Q.7 A nucleoside consists of:

A. Nitrogenous base

B. Purine or pyrimidine base + sugar

C. Purine or pyrimidine base + phosphorous

D. Purine+ pyrimidine base + sugar + phosphorous

Q.8 A nucleotide consists of:

A. A nitrogenous base like choline

B. Purine + pyrimidine base + sugar + phosphorous

C. Purine or pyrimidine base + sugar

D. Purine or pyrimidine base + phosphorous

Q.9 Gout is a metabolic disorder of catabolism of:

A. Pyrimidine   **B.** Purine

C. Alanine   **D.** Phenylalanine

Q.10 Reverse transcriptase is capable of synthesising:

A. RNA to DNA   **B.** DNA to RNA

C. RNA to RNA   **D.** DNA to DNA

Q.11 The p53 gene:

A. A proto-oncogene

B. An oncogen

C. A tumour suppressor gene

D. None of these

Q.12 A Eukaryotic ribosome is made up of subunits:

A. 40S and 60S   **B.** 40S and 50S

C. 40S and 80S   **D.** 60S and 80S

Q.13 In general when an acid and a base are mixed______________.

A. A new acid and a salt are formed.

B. A new base and a salt are formed.

C. No reaction occurs.

D. Salt and water are formed.

Q.14 Hypernatremia may occur in:

A. Diabetes insipidus   **B.** Diuretic medication

C. Heavy sweating   **D.** Kidney disease

Q.15 $CH_3O^- Na^{++} CH_3Cl - CH_3 - O - CH_3 + NaCl$

The above reaction is an example for which of the following?

A. Williamson reaction

B. Clemmenson reaction

C. Wuotz's reaction

D. Reformatsky reaction

Q.16 Which of the following group is detected by using Herzig Meyer method?

A. Alkyl group   **B.** Hydroxy group

C. Alkoxy group   **D.** N-alkyl group

Q.17 Increasing the extent of conjugation of a double-bonded system results in:

A. Hypochromic shift   **B.** Hyperchromic shift

C. Hypsochromic shif   **D.** Bathochromic shift

Q.18 A monochromator is not used in which of the following instrument?

A. Spectroflucrimeter   **B.** UV spectrometer

C. FT-IR spectrometer   **D.** IR spectromete

Q.19 __________ material is used for the preparation of master grafting.

A. Glass   **B.** Iron

C. Teflon   **D.** Aluminum

Q.20 The UV visible region in the electromagnetic spectrum of radiation is:

A. 200-400 nm   **B.** 400-800 nm

C. 200-800 nm   **D.** 300-660 nm

Q.21 Which of the following is not property of base?

A. Bitter taste

B. Turn red litmus blue

C. React with base to form acid

D. Feel slippery on the skin

Q.22 What is Nujol?
A. Hexachlorobutadiene
B. Mineral oil
C. Perfluorokerosene
D. Flurolube

Q.23 IR is useful for understanding of:
A. Drug drug interaction
B. Functional group
C. Physico-chemical propert
D. Conformational Properties

Q.24 In NMR spectrometry the chemical shift (δ) is expressed in:
A. Parts per million
B. Gauss
C. Tesla
D. Herts

Q.25 Tesla is unit used to express:
A. Frequency
B. Pressure
C. Vltage
D. Magnetic Field Strength

Q.26 The number of peak shown by diethyl ether in NMR spectrum are:
A. 4   **B.** 5   **C.** 6   **D.** 7

Q.27 The chemical shift value is:
A. Proportional to field strength.
B. Not proportional to field strength.
C. Ratio of number of protons in each group.
D. Proportional to the total number of protons.

Q.28 _________ is the wave length source in NMR spectrometer.
A. Goniometer
B. Radio frequency oscillator
C. High voltage generator
D. Klystron oscillator

Q.29 A mass spectrum is obtained by plotting graph of:
A. Molecular weight versus peak height.
B. Concentration versus peak height.
C. Concentration versus degree of deflection of ions.
D. Abundance of ions versus their m/e ratio.

Q.30 Removal of single electron from a molecule produce:
A. Fragment ion
B. Molecular ion
C. Metastable ion
D. Rearrangement ion

Q.31 Silica gel used in most of the adsorbent columns contains OH groups. So, it is:
A. Acidic
B. Basic
C. Neutral
D. None of the above

Q.32 One of the units used for expressing pressure is torr and it is equal to:
A. cm of Hg
B. mm of Hg
C. psi
D. gauss

Q.33 Derivatisation techniques in HPLC are intended to enhance:
A. Molecular weight
B. Detactability
C. Reversibility
D. Reproducibility

Q.34 Derivatisation is done in GC:
A. To convert a less polar compound to a more polar compound.
B. To make the compound non-volatile.
C. To convert a polar compound to a less polar compound.
D. To liquefy a solid.

Q.35 The stationary phase used in gel permeation chromatography is:
A. Styrene divinyl benzyl co-polymer
B. Charcoal
C. Alumina
D. Squalene

Q.36 Official methods to analyze of ciprofloxacin is:
A. Potentiometry
B. HPLC
C. Gas chromatography
D. Non aqueous titration

Q.37 In quantitative TLC radioactive material can be studied by:
A. Visual comparison
B. Geiger Counter
C. Densitometer
D. Gravimetry

Q.38 In gel permeation chromatography molecules are separated on the basis of:
A. Size and shape
B. Chemical nature
C. Adsorptive properties
D. Partition coefficient

Pharmaceutics

Q.39 Direction: Match the ingredients according to their purpose in the formulation and find out the correct set:

(1) Film coating	(P) Sodium benzoate
(2) Syrups	(Q) Ethylcellulose
(3) Emulsification	(R) Eudragit
(4) Enteric coating	(S) Sucrose
	(T) Sodium oleate

A. (1)-(P), (2)-(Q), (3)-(R), (4)-(S)
B. (1)-(R), (2)-(S), (3)-(T), (4)-(Q)
C. (1)-(T), (2)-(P), (3)-(S), (4)-(Q)
D. (1)-(R), (2)-(S), (3)-(Q), (4)-(T)

Q.40 Sub coating is given to the tablets:
A. To increase the bulkiness.
B. To avoid deterioration due to microbial attack.
C. To prevent solubility in an acidic medium.
D. To avoid stickiness.

Q.41 The following ingredients are commonly used as coating agents for film coating except:
A. CAP
B. Carnauba wax

C. HEC   **D.** Sodium CMC

Q.42 The courster process can be used to:

A. Coat tablets   **B.** Carnauba wax

C. HEC   **D.** Sodium CMC

Q.43 Which of the following is the first process that must occur before a drug can become available for absorption from a tablet dosage form?

A. Dissolution of the drug in GI fluids

B. Dissolution of the drug in epithelium

C. Ionization of the drug

D. Disintegration of the drug

Q.44 Tablets are placed into coating chamber & hot air is introduced through the bottom of the chamber. Coating solution is applied through anatomizing nozzle from the upper end of the chamber. This technique is called:

A. Sealing before sugar coating

B. Coating by air suspension

C. Spray-pan coating

D. Chamber coating

Q.45 A synthetic sweetening agent which is approximately 200 times sweeter than sucrose & has no taste is:

A. Saccharin   **B.** Aspartame

C. Cyclamate   **D.** Sorbitol

Q.46 Shellac is used the purpose of coating tablets as:

A. Polishing agent

B. Film coating agent

C. Enteric coating agent

D. Sub-coating agent for sugarcoating

Q.47 Dose dumping is a problem in the formulation of:

A. Compressed tab

B. Suppository

C. Soft gelatin capsules

D. Controlled release drug products

Q.48 Find out the equation that gives the rate of drug dissolution from a tablet:

A. Fick's law

B. Henderson-Hasselbatch equation

C. Noyes-Whitney equation

D. Michelis Menton equation

Q.49 Which of the following substance is used as mucoadhesive?

A. Acacia   **B.** Sodium CMC

C. Burnt sugar   **D.** Saccharin

Q.50 In the preparation of multi-layer tablets, one of the following is used for hydrophilic matrix coating:

A. Shellac   **B.** CMC

C. Stearyl alcohol   **D.** Bees wax

Q.51 Reduction in particle size increases absorption because it:

A. Reduces interaction with food molecules.

B. Increases interaction with food molecules.

C. Reduces effective surface area.

D. Increases effective surface area.

Q.52 Diclofenac tablet with CAP has been administered to a patient. Where do you expect the drug to be released?

A. Stomach   **B.** Oral cavity

C. Small intestine   **D.** Liver

Q.53 Which of the following flavour is used in a formulation containing sour taste?

A. Wild cherry   **B.** Vanilla

C. Citrus   **D.** Chocolate

Q.54 Durability of a tablet to combined effects of shock & abrasion is evaluated by using:

A. Hardness tester

B. Disintegration test apparatus

C. Friabilator

D. Screw guace

Q.55 A retardart material that forms a hydrophilic matrix in the formulation of matrix tablets is:

A. HPMC   **B.** CAP

C. Polyethylene   **D.** Carnauba wax

Q.56 A water-soluble substance used as coating material in micro-encapsulation process is:

A. Polyethylene   **B.** Silicone

C. HEC   **D.** Paraffin

Q.57 One of the following is used as a pH dependant controlled release excipient:

A. Carnauba wax

B. HPMCP

C. MC

D. Glyceryl monostearate

Q.58 In the tab et coating process, inadequate spreading of coating solution before drying causes:

A. Orange peel effect   **B.** Sticking effect

C. Blistering effect   **D.** Picking effect

Q.59 Crown thickness of a tablet is measured by:

A. Micrometer   **B.** Pychnometer

C. Hydrometer   **D.** All the above

Q.60 Friabilator is operated at:

A. 100 RPM   **B.** 75 RPM

C. 50 RPM   **D.** 25 RPM

Q.61 Enteric ccated tablet disintegrate in _______ hours in simulated intestinal fluid.

A. 1   **B.** 2   **C.** 3   **D.** 4

Q.62 In dissolution test, flask is maintained at:

A. $37°C \pm 0.5°C$ **B.** $41°C \pm 1°C$

C. $39°C \pm 0.6°C$ **D.** $40°C \pm 1°C$

Q.63 Capping is prevented by using one of the following punches:

A. Flat   **B.** Circular

C. Square   **D.** Rectangular

Q.64 Greenbone is a source of:

A. Type A Gelatin   **B.** Type B Gelatin
C. Both (A) and (B)   **D.** None of these

Q.65 Plating of punch faces are done by:

A. Chromium   **B.** Zinc
C. Iron   **D.** All of the above

Q.66 Sta-Rx-1500 contains _________ % of moisture.

A. 15   **B.** 10   **C.** 18   **D.** 50

Q.67 Acacia and tragacanth are used in the concentration of:

A. 10%-25%   **B.** 60%-70%
C. 40%-50%   **D.** 90%-100%

Q.68 Starch on heating hydrolyze into:

A. Glucose
B. Fructose & Sorbose
C. Fructose & Mannose
D. Dextrin & Glucose

Q.69 The pH of the small intestine is:

A. 1-2   **B.** 3-4   **C.** 6   **D.** 7-8

Q.70 Aqua coat is a:

A. 30% w/v of ethylcellulose dispersion
B. Solution of HPMC
C. 2%w/v of methylcellulose dispersion
D. None of these

Q.71 Lozenges were originally named as:

A. Capsule   **B.** ODT
C. Pastilles   **D.** Sustained axn tab

Q.72 Implantation tab is NMT ________ mm in length.

A. 20   **B.** 100   **C.** 40   **D.** 8

Q.73 Seal coating is done by using:

A. Shellac   **B.** Acacia
C. Gelatin   **D.** None of these

Q.74 Sub coating is done to:

A. Round the edges
B. Increase the bulk of tablet
C. Both (A) and (B)
D. Make water resistant

Q.75 CAP dissolves at pH:

A. Above 6   **B.** Below 6   **C.** 4   **D.** 2

Q.76 Which of the following one is used as an opacifier?

A. TiO$_2$ **B.** Mgo
C. Siliactes   **D.** All of these

Pharmacognosy

Q.77 The drug having very good antiemetic properties is:

A. Fennel   **B.** Ginger
C. Turmeric   **D.** Coriander

Q.78 Cardamom is a following type of fruit:

A. Capsule   **B.** Drupe   **C.** Follicle   **D.** Berry

Q.79 Cardamom belongs to family:

A. Umbelliferae   **B.** Myrtaceae
C. Araceae   **D.** Zingiberaceae

Q.80 Parenchymatous cells of perisperm of cardamom show the following type of small Ca oxalate crystals:

A. Cluster   **B.** Microrosette
C. Prism   **D.** Raphides

Q.81 It is difficult to make fine powder of cardamon due to presence of:

A. Oil cells
B. Sclerenchymatous cells
C. Endosperm cells
D. Perisperm cells

Q.82 Sandalwood oil is obtained from following part of Satalum album:

A. Stem   **B.** Leaf
C. Sapwood   **D.** Heartwood

Q.83 Sandalwood oil is mainly produced in:

A. North India   **B.** South India
C. France   **D.** Australia

Q.84 The surface of the drug is reddish-brown or reddish-yellow in colour and powdery in:

A. Asafoetida   **B.** Benzoin
C. Myrrh   **D.** Guggul

Q.85 Combined umbelliferone test is positive in case of:

A. Bdellium   **B.** Olibanum
C. Asafoetida   **D.** Myrrh

Q.86 The drug consists of fusiform, napiform or irregularly oblong tubercle, 3-5 cm long, dark brown, wrinkled with transverse lenticels is:

A. Ipomoea   **B.** Jalap
C. Black nishodh   **D.** White nishodh

Pharmacology

Q.87 Which of the following opioid receptor types is responsible for euphoria and respiratory depression?

A. Kappa-receptors   **B.** Delta-receptors
C. Mu-receptors   **D.** All of these

Q.88 Mu (µ) receptors are associated with:

A. Analgesia, euphoria, respiratory depression, physical dependence.
B. Spinal analgesia, mydriasis, sedation, physical dependence.
C. Dysphoria, hallucinations, respiratory and vasomotor stimulation.
D. Analgesia, euphoria, respiratory stimulation, physical dependence.

Q.89 All of the hypnotic drugs induce:

A. Increase the duration of REM sleep.

B. Decrease the duration of REM sleep.

C. Do not alter the duration of REM sleep.

D. Increase the duration of slow wave sleep.

Q.90 Which of the following hypnotic drugs causes least suppression of REM sleep?

A. Flumazenil

B. Phenobarbital

C. Flurazepam

D. Secobarbital

Q.91 The mechanism of action of antiseizure drugs is:

A. Enhancement of GABAergic (inhibitory) transmission.

B. Diminution of excitatory (usually glutamatergic C. transmission).

C. Modification of ionic conductance.

D. All of these

Q.92 The drug against myoclonic seizures is:

A. Primidone

B. Carbamazepine

C. Clonazepam

D. Phenytoin

Q.93 The most effective drug for stopping generalized tonic-clonic status epilepticus in adults is:

A. Lamotrigine

B. Ethosuximide

C. Diazepam

D. Zonisamide

Q.94 Find out the appropriate consideration for phenytoin:

A. It blocks sodium channels.

B. It binds to an allosteric regulatory site on the GABA-BZ receptor and prolongs the openings of the Cl channels.

C. It effects on Ca^{2+} currents, reducing the low-threshold (T-type) current.

D. It inhibits GABA-transaminase, which catalyzes the breakdown of GABA.

Q.95 Phenytoin is used in the treatment of:

A. Petit mal epilepsy

B. Grand mal epilepsy

C. Myoclonic seizures

D. All of these

Q.96 Dose-related adverse effect caused by phenytoin is:

A. Physical and psychological dependence

B. Exacerbated grand mal epilepsy

C. Gingival hyperplasia

D. Extrapyramidal symptoms

Q.97 The mechanism of vigabatrin's action is:

A. Direct action on the GABA receptor-chloride channel complex.

B. Inhibition of GABA aminotransferase.

C. NMDA receptor blockade via the glycine binding site.

D. Inhibition of GABA neuronal reuptake from synapses.

Q.98 What is the function of Tiagabine?

A. Blocks neuronal and glial re-uptake of GABA from synapses.

B. Inhibits GABA-T, which catalyzed the breakdown of GABA.

C. Blocks the T-type Ca^{2+} channels.

D. Inhibits glutamate transmission at AMPA/kainate receptors.

Q.99 Find out the drug that induces parkinsonian syndromes:

A. Chlorpromazine

B. Diazepam

C. Triazolam

D. Carbamazepine

Q.100 Which of the following drugs is used in the treatment of Parkinsonian disorders?

A. Phenytoin

B. Selegiline

C. Haloperidol

D. Fluoxetine

Q.101 Find out the agent, which is preferred in the treatment of the drug-induced form of parkinsonism:

A. Levodopa

B. Bromocriptine

C. Benztropine

D. Dopamine

Q.102 Find out a peripheral dopa decarboxylase inhibitor:

A. Tolcapone

B. Clozapine

C. Carbidopa

D. Selegiline

Q.103 The mechanism of carbidopa's action is:

A. Stimulating the synthesis, release, or reuptake of dopamine

B. Inhibition of dopa decarboxylase

C. Stimulating dopamine receptors

D. Selective inhibition of catecol-O-methyltransferase

Q.104 Which of the following vitamins reduces the beneficial effects of levodopa by enhancing its extracerebral metabolism?

A. Pyridoxine

B. Thiamine

C. Tocopherol

D. Riboflavin

Q.105 Which of the following antiparkinsonian drugs has also been used to treat hyperprolactinemia?

A. Benztropine

B. Bromocriptine

C. Amantadine

D. Levodopa

Q.106 Find out a selective inhibitor of monoamine oxidase B:

A. Levodopa

B. Amantadine

C. Tolcapone

D. Selegiline

Q.107 Which of the following statements is correct?

A. MAO-A metabolizes dopamine and MAO-B metabolizes serotonin.

B. MAO-A metabolizes norepinephrine and dopamine and MAO-B metabolizes serotonin.

C. MAO-A metabolizes norepinephrine and serotonin and MAO-B metabolizes dopamine.

D. MAO-A metabolizes dopamine and MAO-B metabolizes norepinephrine and serotonin.

Q.108 Which of the following antiparkinsonian drugs is an antiviral agent used in the prophylaxis of influenza A?

A. Selegiline

B. Sinemet

C. Pergolide

D. Amantadine

Q.109 Which of the following anti-parkinsonism drugs is an anticholinergic agent?

A. Amantadine

B. Selegilin

C. Trihexyphenidyl

D. Bromocriptine

Q.110 Alcohol potentiates is a:

A. SNS depressants

B. Vasodilatators

C. Hypoglycemic agents

D. All of these

Q.111 Which of the following agents is an inhibitor of aldehyde dehydrogenase?

A. Fomepizole

B. Ethanol

C. Disulfiram

D. Naltrexone

Q.112 Find out the drug, which alters brain responses to alcohol:

A. Naltrexone

B. Disulfiram

C. Amphetamine

D. Chlorpromazine

Q.113 Which of the following agents is an opioid antagonist?

A. Amphetamine

B. Naltrexone

C. Morphine

D. Disulfiram

Q.114 Which of the following agents may be used as an antidote for ethylene glycol and methanol poisoning?

A. Disulfiram

B. Fomepizole

C. Naltrexone

D. Amphetamine

Other Subjects

Q.115 The phenomenon of lowering of vapour pressure is defined as:

A. Decrease in vapour pressure of a solvent on the addition of a volatile non-electrolyte solute in it.

B. Decrease in vapour pressure of a solvent on the addition of a non-volatile non-electrolyte solute in it.

C. Decrease in vapour pressure of a solvent on addition of a volatile electrolyte solute in it.

D. Decrease in vapour pressure of a solvent on addition of a non-volatile solute in it.

Q.116 The Free & Blythe method is used to study:

A. Thixotropy

B. Accelerated stability

C. Electrical properties

D. Particle size

Q.117 Which among the following is formed when an alcohol is dehydrated?

A. alkane　　**B.** alkyne　　**C.** alkene　　**D.** aldehyde

Q.118 Acid is a substance which dissociates in water to produce hydrogen ions:

A. Arrhenius theory

B. Lew is theory

C. Bronsted theory

D. Lowry theory

Q.119 __________ is the largest cellular organelle in cell.

A. Golgi apparatus

B. Lysosomes

C. Nucleus

D. Mitochondria

Q.120 ELISA is:

A. Using radiolabelled second antibody.

B. Usage of RBCs.

C. Using complement-mediated cell lysis.

D. Addition of substrate that is converted into a coloured end product.

Q.121 Which of the following are produced by microorganisms?

A. Alcoholic beverages

B. Fermented dairy products

C. Breads

D. All of these

Q.122 __________ are the hallmark of meningitis caused by tuberculosis, viral meningitides, and chronic fungal infections (cryptococcal meningitis).

A. Macrophages

B. Lymphocytes

C. Eosinohpils

D. Monocytes

Q.123 What is mean by carrier?

A. Non polar drug can be transported through carrier mediated transport.

B. Carriers binds reversible & non covalently with solute molecule.

C. It discharges the molecules & destroys itself.

D. Carrier is protein.

Q.124 Has positive evidence of human fetal risk, but the benefits from use in pregnant women may be acceptable despite of risk?

A. Category A

B. Category B

C. Category C

D. Category D

Q.125 __________ bind to amino acid during translation.

A. t-RNA　　**B.** r-RNA　　**C.** m-RNA　　**D.** DNA

// Smart Answer Sheet //

Correct — Percentage of students who answered correctly. **Skipped** — Percentage of students who skipped.

Q.	Ans.	Correct Skipped	Q.	Ans.	Correct Skipped	Q.	Ans.	Correct Skipped	Q.	Ans.	Correct Skipped	Q.	Ans.	Correct Skipped	Q.	Ans.	Correct Skipped
1	C	45.72 % 52.66 %	22	B	48.95 % 46.37 %	43	D	66.71 % 32.89 %	64	B	48.38 % 49.31 %	85	D	47.34 % 39.64 %	106	D	41.67 % 53.75 %
2	A	53.85 % 37.76 %	23	B	88.84 % 10.2 %	44	B	44.66 % 39.17 %	65	A	45.61 % 45.32 %	86	B	16.03 % 68.79 %	107	C	47.03 % 38.0 %
3	C	52.27 % 45.12 %	24	A	61.1 % 32.34 %	45	B	83.94 % 10.08 %	66	B	25.64 % 68.3 %	87	C	41.62 % 37.17 %	108	D	42.98 % 31.12 %
4	A	49.94 % 31.37 %	25	D	85.9 % 11.26 %	46	C	51.9 % 39.14 %	67	A	52.08 % 30.35 %	88	A	41.06 % 45.63 %	109	C	44.61 % 53.2 %
5	C	87.73 % 11.83 %	26	D	21.03 % 67.75 %	47	D	53.76 % 37.0 %	68	D	69.72 % 30.03 %	89	B	47.34 % 40.39 %	110	D	68.6 % 30.9 %
6	A	59.24 % 37.64 %	27	A	65.77 % 32.03 %	48	C	64.51 % 30.53 %	69	D	78.19 % 16.05 %	90	C	42.11 % 51.95 %	111	C	44.24 % 55.63 %
7	B	53.98 % 38.66 %	28	B	68.13 % 30.02 %	49	B	57.93 % 38.41 %	70	B	62.66 % 36.58 %	91	D	13.94 % 67.88 %	112	A	47.68 % 32.1 %
8	B	69.78 % 30.21 %	29	D	59.92 % 32.46 %	50	A	57.06 % 41.1 %	71	C	41.09 % 54.32 %	92	B	67.6 % 30.32 %	113	B	58.05 % 38.57 %
9	B	30.51 % 69.21 %	30	B	85.83 % 11.37 %	51	D	57.93 % 41.96 %	72	C	18.76 % 71.73 %	93	D	41.82 % 37.08 %	114	B	32.57 % 67.15 %
10	A	57.24 % 37.45 %	31	A	60.8 % 31.07 %	52	C	52.0 % 31.58 %	73	A	63.19 % 36.39 %	94	A	54.22 % 43.05 %	115	B	45.45 % 54.11 %
11	C	60.93 % 37.51 %	32	B	67.65 % 31.22 %	53	C	55.37 % 41.46 %	74	C	46.52 % 34.9 %	95	B	62.73 % 31.55 %	116	A	17.18 % 72.25 %
12	A	41.89 % 31.31 %	33	B	43.95 % 51.16 %	54	C	61.06 % 34.85 %	75	A	61.17 % 38.5 %	96	C	59.14 % 39.64 %	117	C	51.12 % 37.97 %
13	D	89.42 % 10.1 %	34	C	47.24 % 36.88 %	55	A	77.82 % 18.22 %	76	A	11.9 % 83.67 %	97	D	58.52 % 30.3 %	118	A	55.75 % 34.11 %
14	A	62.49 % 30.28 %	35	A	23.92 % 70.79 %	56	C	50.17 % 41.62 %	77	B	68.75 % 30.09 %	98	A	64.55 % 32.82 %	119	C	83.32 % 14.11 %
15	A	50.8 % 31.35 %	36	B	60.42 % 38.96 %	57	D	43.62 % 55.75 %	78	A	52.13 % 32.1 %	99	A	58.58 % 33.51 %	120	A	43.01 % 47.3 %
16	D	18.2 % 72.33 %	37	B	43.86 % 36.99 %	58	A	54.7 % 45.27 %	79	D	43.63 % 42.87 %	100	B	57.31 % 35.22 %	121	D	79.0 % 12.54 %
17	D	50.66 % 39.67 %	38	A	66.05 % 32.02 %	59	A	62.47 % 34.57 %	80	B	69.56 % 30.33 %	101	C	63.68 % 30.72 %	122	B	55.48 % 37.96 %
18	C	61.38 % 33.24 %	39	B	21.69 % 67.61 %	60	D	79.88 % 17.88 %	81	D	53.42 % 35.83 %	102	C	50.9 % 44.77 %	123	D	42.12 % 50.07 %
19	D	77.12 % 19.22 %	40	D	62.2 % 37.09 %	61	A	43.76 % 33.54 %	82	D	50.81 % 40.63 %	103	B	57.18 % 40.5 %	124	D	42.85 % 41.46 %
20	C	40.8 % 34.08 %	41	B	57.37 % 42.51 %	62	A	58.36 % 38.03 %	83	B	45.52 % 31.47 %	104	A	62.25 % 33.79 %	125	A	56.33 % 40.92 %
21	C	58.81 % 38.23 %	42	B	80.09 % 19.79 %	63	A	50.23 % 30.96 %	84	A	61.25 % 37.2 %	105	B	27.26 % 68.93 %			

//Hints and Solutions//

1. Aldosterone synthesis occurs in zona glomerulosa. The corticosteroids are synthesized from cholesterol within the zona glomerulosa of the adrenal cortex. Moreover, aldosterone synthase is found within the zona glomerulosa at the outer edge of the adrenal cortex, 11β-hydroxylase is found in the zona glomerulosa.

Hence, the correct option is (C).

2. A hormone that cannot cross the blood-brain barrier is epinephrine. Epinephrine, more commonly known as adrenaline, is a hormone secreted by the medulla of the adrenal glands. Strong emotions such as fear or anger cause epinephrine to be released into the bloodstream, which causes an increase in heart rate, muscle strength, blood pressure, and sugar metabolism.

Hence, the correct option is (A).

3. PKC enzymes in turn are activated by signals such as increases in the concentration of diacylglycerol (DAG) or calcium ions (Ca^{2+}). So, PKC enzymes play important roles in several signal transduction cascades. In biochemistry, the PKC family consists of fifteen isozymes in humans.

Hence, the correct option is (C).

4. Mental retardation can occur in cretinism. Severe iodine deficiency may lead to endemic cretinism, which is characterized by a number of abnormalities, such as mental retardation, neurological abnormalities and hearing disorders. These abnormalities may occur in various combinations, but impaired mental development is always a component.

Hence, the correct option is (A).

5. The most powerful thyroid hormone is T3. One of the most powerful hormones in your body is called Triiodothyronine, also known as T3. T3 specifically supports brain function, heart function, and digestion, and it plays a role in your metabolic rate and bone health.

Hence, the correct option is (C).

6. Zona glomerulosa of the adrenal cortex synthesizes glucocorticoids. The zona glomerulosa cells express a specific enzyme aldosterone synthase (also known as CYP11B2). Situated between the glomerulosa and reticularis, the cells of the zona fasciculata synthesize and secrete glucocorticoids, such as 11-deoxycorticosterone, corticosterone, and cortisol in humans.

Hence, the correct option is (A).

7. A nucleoside consists of purine or pyrimidine base + sugar. Nucleosides consist of a purine or a pyrimidine base and a ribose or a deoxyribose sugar connected via a β-glycosidic linkage. These compounds are associated with structures of RNA (ribose sugars) and DNA (deoxyribose sugars).

Hence, the correct option is (B).

8. A nucleotide consists of purine, pyrimidine base, sugar and phosphorous. A nucleotide is made up of the following Sugar ring, base (adenine, guanine, cytosine, thymine/uracil),

phosphate molecule. The sugar ring is made up of carbon atoms. The bases are nitrogenous.

Hence, the correct option is (B).

9. Gout is a metabolic disorder of catabolism of purine. Gout is an inherited disorder of purine metabolism that causes hyperuricemia in humans, particularly men. The term "gout" in general use refers to a form of arthritis. A purine is an aromatic heterocycle composed of carbon and nitrogen. Purines include adenine and guanine, which participate in DNA and RNA formation. Purines are also constituents of other important biomolecules, such as ATP, GTP, cyclic AMP, NADH, and coenzyme A.

Hence, the correct option is (B).

10. Reverse transcriptase is capable of synthesising RNA to DNA. Reverse transcriptase (RT), also known as RNA-dependent DNA polymerase, is a DNA polymerase enzyme that transcribes single-stranded RNA into DNA. This enzyme is able to synthesize a double helix DNA once the RNA has been reverse transcribed in a first step into a single-strand DNA.

Hence, the correct option is (A).

11. The p53 gene like the Rb gene is a tumor suppressor gene, i.e., its activity stops the formation of tumors. If a person inherits only one functional copy of the p53 gene from their parents, they are predisposed to cancer and usually develop several independent tumors in a variety of tissues in early adulthood. It also plays a critical role in suppressing tumours by inhibiting the division and growth of cells whose DNA has been damaged.

Hence, the correct option is (C).

12. A Eukaryotic ribosome is made up of subunits 40S and 60S. Eukaryotic ribosomes have two unequal subunits, designated small subunit (40S) and large subunit (60S) according to their sedimentation coefficients. Both subunits contain dozens of ribosomal proteins arranged on a scaffold composed of ribosomal RNA.

Hence, the correct option is (A).

13. In general, when an acid and base are mixed salt and water are formed. The reaction of an acid with a base is called a neutralization reaction. The products of this reaction are salt and water. For example, the reaction of hydrochloric acid, HCl, with sodium hydroxide, NaOH, solutions produces a solution of sodium chloride, NaCl, and some additional water molecules.

Hence, the correct option is (D).

14. Hypernatremia may occur in diabetes insipidus. Hypernatremia is usually caused by limited access to water or an impaired thirst mechanism, and less commonly by diabetes insipidus. Manifestations include confusion, neuromuscular excitability, hyperreflexia, seizures, and coma.

Hence, the correct option is (A).

15. The $CH_3O\text{-}Na^{++}CH_3Cl\text{-}CH_3\text{-}O\text{-}CH_3+NaCl$ reaction is an example of the Williamson reaction. The Williamson ether synthesis is an organic reaction, forming an ether from an organohalide and deprotonated alcohol (alkoxide). This reaction

was developed by Alexander Williamson in 1850. The Williamson reaction has a wide range of applications, is commonly used in both laboratory and industrial synthesis, and is still the most straightforward and widely used method of preparing ethers. Williamson synthesis is used to prepare both symmetrical and asymmetrical ethers.

Hence, the correct option is (A).

16. N-alkyl group is detected by using the Herzig Meyer method. The N-alkyl groups are estimated by the Herzig Meyer method in which the alkaloid is heated with hydroiodic acid at 200-300°C under pressure whereby the alkyl groups are converted into alkyl iodide which are estimated as silver iodide by means of alcoholic silver nitrate.

Hence, the correct option is (D).

17. Increasing the extent of conjugation of a double-bonded system results in the bathochromic shift. Also, the molar absorptivity (ε) roughly doubles with each new conjugated double bond. Thus, extending conjugation generally results in bathochromic (to longer wavelength) and hyperchromic (to greater absorbance) shifts in absorption.

Hence, the correct option is (D).

18. A monochromator is not used in the FT-IR spectrometer instrument. Fourier transforms infrared (FT-IR) spectrometer, there is no monochromator to disperse or separate the radiation by wavelength. Instead, a whole single-beam spectrum is generated all at once. The intensities of all of the wavelength elements are analyzed simultaneously.

Hence, the correct option is (C).

19. Aluminum material is used for the preparation of master grafting. The master grafting tool was designed so when pressure is applied to the thumb lever, it gently pushes the tongue out underneath the larvae. Once you release pressure on the lever, the tongue retracts and the larvae are safely placed inside the cell cup. Includes one replacement tongue.

Hence, the correct option is (D).

20. The UV visible region in the electromagnetic spectrum of radiation is 200-800 nm. The wavelength (λ) of light required for electronic transitions is typically in the ultraviolet (200–390 nm) and visible (390–780 nm) region of the electromagnetic radiation spectrum. In UV-V is spectroscopy, the intensity of light (I) that passes through the sample is measured.

Hence, the correct option is (C).

21. To react with a base to form acid is not the property of the base. Bases cannot turn blue litmus to red. Acids can turn Blue litmus to red while bases can turn red litmus to blue. Bases react with acids to form salts i.e. essentially neutralizing them. Bases have a bitter taste while acids have a sour taste. When an acid and a base are placed together, they react to neutralize the acid and base properties, producing a salt. The H(+) cation of the acid combines with the OH(-) anion of the base to form water. The compound formed by the cation of the base and the anion of the acid is called a salt.

Hence, the correct option is (C).

22. Nujol is mineral oil. Mineral oil is any of various colorless, odorless, light mixtures of higher alkanes from a mineral source, particularly a distillate of petroleum, as distinct from usually edible vegetable oils. The name 'mineral oil' by itself is imprecise, having been used for many specific oils over the past few centuries. Mineral oils are complex mixtures of straight and branched-chain paraffinic, naphthenic and aromatic hydrocarbons refined from petroleum crude oils. Mineral oil with a carbon number of 15 to 25 is categorized as light oil and 25 to 50 as heavy oil.

Hence, the correct option is (B).

23. IR is useful for understanding functional groups. IR (infrared) spectroscopy is useful in organic chemistry because it enables you to identify different functional groups. This is because each functional group contains certain bonds, and these bonds always show up in the same places in the IR spectrum.

Hence, the correct option is (B).

24. In NMR spectrometry the chemical shift (δ) is expressed in parts per million. The scale is commonly expressed as parts per million (ppm) which is independent of the spectrometer frequency. The scale is the delta (δ) scale. The range at which most NMR absorptions occur is quite narrow. Almost all 1H absorptions occur downfield within 10 ppm of TMS.

Hence, the correct option is (A).

25. Tesla is a unit used to express magnetic field strength. The tesla (symbol T) is the derived SI unit of magnetic flux density, which represents the strength of a magnetic field. One tesla represents one weber per square meter. The equivalent, and superseded, cgs unit is the gauss (G); one tesla equals exactly 10,000 gausses.

Hence, the correct option is (D).

26. The number of peaks shown by diethyl ether in the NMR spectrum is 7. The NMR spectrum of diethyl ether, however, displays 7 peaks. This multiplicity is due to the phenomenon known as spin coupling and arises because of the interaction of the proton magnetic field with bonding electrons. In essence, each proton can have one of two possible spin orientations in the applied field, so that the magnetic field sensed by adjacent protons can have one of two possible values. The result is that n protons will split adjacent protons into (n + 1) peaks.

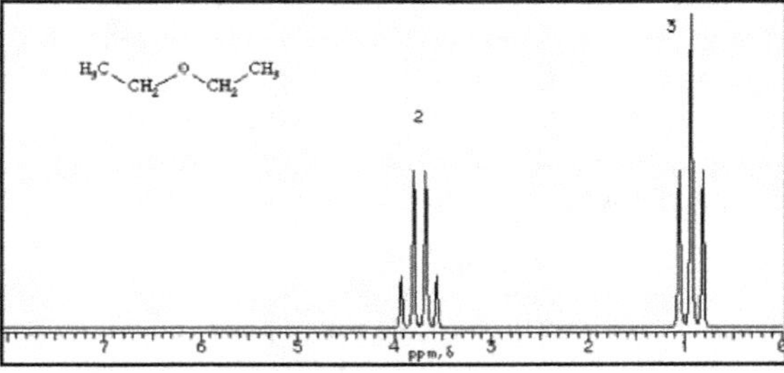

Hence, the correct option is (D).

27. The chemical shift value is proportional to field strength. In nuclear magnetic resonance (NMR) spectroscopy, the chemical shift is the resonant frequency of a nucleus relative to a standard in a magnetic field. Often the position and number of chemical shifts are diagnostic of the structure of a molecule. Chemical shifts are also used to describe signals in other forms of spectroscopy such as photo-emission spectroscopy.

Hence, the correct option is (A).

28. A radiofrequency oscillator is the wavelength source in an NMR spectrometer. An RF oscillator is an electronic oscillator that produces signals that in the radio frequency (often abbreviated to RF) range, which is about 100 kHz to 100 GHz. RF oscillators are known to convert the direct current originating from a power supply into an alternating current signal.

Hence, the correct option is (B).

29. A mass spectrum is obtained by plotting a graph of the abundance of ions versus their m/e ratio. A mass spectrum is an intensity vs. m/z (mass-to-charge ratio) plot representing a chemical analysis. So, the mass spectrum of a sample is a pattern representing the distribution of ions by mass (more correctly: mass-to-charge ratio) in a sample.

Hence, the correct option is (D).

30. Removal of a single electron from a molecule produces a molecular ion. Ionization is the process by which ions are formed by gain or loss of an electron from an atom or molecule. If an atom or molecule gains an electron, it becomes negatively charged (an anion), and if it loses an electron, it becomes positively charged (a cation). Energy may be lost or gained in the formation of an ion.

Hence, the correct option is (B).

31. Silica gel used in most of the adsorbent columns contains OH groups. So, it is acidic. Silica gel is composed of SiO_2 units with high porosity. Silica gel is a three-dimensional polymer composed of four-dimensional silicon dioxide units. It is a porous material. Silica gel is a suitable adsorbent for water, alcohol, phenols, amines, and so on.

Hence, the correct option is (A).

32. One of the units used for expressing pressure is torr and it is equal to mm of Hg. One unit of gas pressure is the millimeter of mercury (mmHg). An equivalent unit to the mm of Hg is called the torr, in honor of the inventor of the barometer, Evangelista Torricelli. The pascal (Pa) is the standard unit of pressure.

Hence, the correct option is (B).

33. Derivatisation techniques in HPLC are intended to enhance detectability. Derivatization, or chemical structure modification, is often used in bioanalysis performed by liquid chromatography technique in order to enhance detectability or to improve the chromatographic performance for the target analytes.

Hence, the correct option is (B).

34. Derivatisation is done in GC to convert a polar compound to less polar compound. The derivatization is typically done to change the analyte properties for better separation and also for enhancing the method sensitivity. In GC/MS, derivatization may improve the capability of compound identification.

Hence, the correct option is (C).

35. The stationary phase used in gel permeation chromatography is styrene divinyl benzyl co-polymer. Gel permeation chromatography (GPC) is a type of size-exclusion chromatography (SEC), that separates analytes on the basis of size, typically in organic solvents. The technique is often used for the analysis of polymers. As a technique, SEC was first developed in 1955 by Lathe and Ruthven. The term gel permeation chromatography can be traced back to J.C. Moore of the Dow Chemical Company who investigated the technique in 1964. The proprietary column technology was licensed to Waters Corporation, which subsequently commercialized this technology in 1964.

Hence, the correct option is (A).

36. The official method to analyze ciprofloxacin is HPLC. Several analytical methods for the quantitative determination of fluoroquinolones in pharmaceutical formulations were reported in the scientific literature as capillary electrophoresis, UV spectrophotometry, titration, and high-performance liquid chromatography (HPLC), which is often used for the quantification of ciprofloxacin in medicines, urine, plasma, animal tissue, and other substances.

Hence, the correct option is (B).

37. In quantitative TLC radioactive material can be studied by the Geiger counter. A Geiger counter (also known as Geiger–Muller counter or Geiger–Muller counter) is an instrument used for detecting and measuring ionizing radiation. It is widely used in applications such as radiation dosimetry, radiological protection, experimental physics, and the nuclear industry.

Hence, the correct option is (B).

38. In gel-permeation chromatography, molecules are separated on the basis of size and shape. Gel-permeation chromatography (GPC) separates molecules according to the difference in their size. This technique is based on the penetration of molecules into the cavities of macroporous support, mostly made from hydrophilic gels of dextran, agarose, or polyacrylamide.

Hence, the correct option is (A).

39. The correct match for the ingredients is (1)-(R), (2)-(S), (3)-(T), (4)-(Q). Drug release from the Eudragit E-coated cores at pH 2.0-5.0 starts after 10-50 min due to the rapid dissolution of the Eudragit E film. Thus, Eudragit E, protected against dissolution in the stomach by an enteric coating, is a suitable coating polymer for drug release in acidic regions such as the inflamed colon. Syrups derived from sucrose fall into three general types: liquid sucrose, invert syrups, and molasses. Sodium oleate is the sodium salt of oleic acid, a monounsaturated fatty acid. This anionic surfactant and emulsifier is a component of commercial soaps. Ethylcellulose, a pH-independent polymer in different percentages from 5 to 35%w/w was applied as barrier coating between the core tablet and enteric coating using pan coating apparatus.

Hence, the correct option is (B).

40. Sub coating is given to the tablets to avoid stickiness. Protects the tablet (or the capsule contents) from stomach acids. Protects the stomach lining from aggressive drugs such as enteric-coated aspirin. Provides a delayed release of the

medication. It involves the application of large quantities of sugar-coatings to the tablet core, significantly increasing the tablet weight by 50–100 %. Subcoating provides the rapid buildup necessary to round up the tablet edge.

Hence, the correct option is (D).

41. The ingredients are commonly used as coating agents for film coating are CAP, HEC and sodium CMC except for carnauba wax. Carnauba wax is used in the pharmaceutical industry for tablet coatings and binding. Carnauba wax comes from the leaves of the Copernicia prunifera palm grown only in Brazil. Carnauba wax is also known as palm wax or Brazil wax. Carnauba wax primarily consists of fatty acid esters.

Hence, the correct option is (B).

42. The courster process can be used to carnauba wax. Carnauba wax, also called Brazil wax or ceara wax, vegetable wax obtained from the fronds of the carnauba palm (Copernicia prunifera) of Brazil. The wax consists primarily of esters of long-chain alcohols and acids. It has a melting point of about 85°C (185°F).

Hence, the correct option is (B).

43. The first process that must occur before a drug can become available for absorption from a tablet dosage form is the disintegration of the drug. Disintegration is the process of breaking down a substance into tiny fragments to improve its solubility in a solvent. The process is used predominantly in the pharmaceutical and chemical industries. Dissolution is also used predominantly in pharmaceutical industries to check how soluble a drug is in the body.

Hence, the correct option is (D).

44. Tablets are placed into the coating chamber & hot air is introduced through the bottom of the chamber. The coating solution is applied through anatomizing nozzle from the upper end of the chamber. This technique is called coating by air suspension. A new method of rapidly coating drug particles of widely varying size and shape is presented. In this process, the drug particles are coated and dried while suspended in an upwardly moving current of air. Solutions and suspensions of coating materials in both water and volatile organic solvents are employed.

Hence, the correct option is (B).

45. A synthetic sweetening agent which is approximately 200 times sweeter than sucrose & has no taste is aspartame. Aspartame is the primary non-nutritive sweetener used in carbonated soft drinks. It is a low-calorie and intense sweetener that is approximately 200 times sweeter than sucrose (table sugar). It is used in a variety of foods and beverages including drinks, energy-reduced diets, and as a tabletop sweetener.

Hence, the correct option is (B).

46. Shellac is used the purpose of coating tablets as enteric coating agent. Shellac is a natural polymer, which is used as enteric coating material in pharmaceutical applications. Shellac coatings effectively masked the unpleasant taste of acetaminophen tablets. Compared to HPMC, again lower coating levels were required to achieve similar effects.

Hence, the correct option is (C).

47. Dose dumping is a problem in the formulation of controlled release drug products. The term controlled release drug product was previously used to describe various types of oral extended-release-rate dosage forms, including sustained-release, sustained-action, prolonged-action, long-action, slow-release, and programmed drug delivery.

Hence, the correct option is (D).

48. The equation that gives the rate of drug dissolution from a tablet is the Noyes-Whitney equation. The dissolution rate of a solid insolvent is written by the Noyes-Whitney equation, as follows:

$$\frac{dM}{dt} = \frac{DS}{h}(C_s - C) = kS(C_s - C)$$

$$\frac{dC}{dt} = \frac{DS}{Vh}(C_s - C)$$

where, C and C_s represent the concentration of the dissolved substance at a given time t and the solubility concentration of the substance, respectively.

Hence, the correct option is (C).

49. PAA and sodium CMC possess excellent mucoadhesive characteristics due to the formation of strong hydrogen bonding interactions with mucin. Polycarbophil (Noveon) and Carbomers (Carbopol), PAA derivatives have been studied extensively as mucoadhesive platforms for drug delivery to the GI tract.

Hence, the correct option is (B).

50. In the preparation of multi-layer tablets, shellac is used for hydrophilic matrix coating. Shellac is a resin secreted by the female lac bug on trees in the forests of India and Thailand. It is processed and sold as dry flakes and dissolved in alcohol to make liquid shellac, which is used as a brush-on colorant, food glaze and wood finish.

Hence, the correct option is (A).

51. Reduction in particle size increases absorption because it increases effective surface area. Smaller particles tend to have higher dissolution rates due to the larger surface area to volume ratio and, therefore, a better chance for faster absorption. It should be noted that particle size has little effect on drugs that are readily water-soluble.

Hence, the correct option is (D).

52. Diclofenac tablet with CAP has been administered to a patient. The drug is to be released in the small intestine. Diclofenac is eliminated following biotransformation to glucoro conjugated and sulphate metabolites which are excreted in the urine, very little drug is eliminated unchanged. The excretion of conjugates may be related to renal function.

Hence, the correct option is (C).

53. The citrus flavour is used in a formulation containing a sour taste. Citrus fruits are both sweet and sour due to the combination of sugar and citric acid. The more acidic a fruit is, meaning bitterness and sugar it contains, the sweeter it tastes.

Oranges, grapefruits, tangerines, and lemons are all a combination of both sweet and sour.

Hence, the correct option is (C).

54. The durability of a tablet to combined effects of shock & abrasion is evaluated by using friabilator. The friability test is closely related to tablet hardness and is designed to evaluate the ability of the tablet to withstand abrasion in packaging, handling and shipping. Tablet friability can be used to measure the efficiency of tableting equipment or as an indicator of formulation suitability as well as routine QC functions. It can also be thought of as measuring "dusting".

Hence, the correct option is (C).

55. A retardant material that forms a hydrophilic matrix in the formulation of matrix tablets is HPMC. Hydroxypropyl methylcellulose (HPMC), a semi-synthetic derivative of cellulose, has its popularity for the formulation of controlled-release (CR) dosage forms as a swellable and hydrophilic polymer (3–5).

Hence, the correct option is (A).

56. A water-soluble substance used as a coating material in the micro-encapsulation process is HEC. Hydroxyethyl cellulose (HEC) is a nonionic, water-soluble polymer. It is a white, free-flowing granular powder and is made by reacting ethylene oxide with alkali-cellulose. In pharmaceuticals, cellulose has been used as an adsorbent, glidant, drug solvent, and suspending agent.

Hence, the correct option is (C).

57. Glyceryl monostearate is used as a pH dependant controlled release excipient. Glyceryl monostearate (GMS) is an effective emulsifier used in the baking industry available in the form of small beads, flakes, or powders. In addition to emulsification, GMS is a thickening agent and a stabilizer. In baking, it is used to improve dough quality and stabilize fat/protein emulsions.

Hence, the correct option is (D).

58. In the tablet coating process, inadequate spreading of coating solution before drying causes the orange peel effect. Inadequate spreading of the coating solution before drying causes a "range-peel" effect on the coating. Orange peel can be the result of poor tablet composition causing it to become soft. It can also be caused by too high a spray pressure combined with a fast spray rate, leading to an uneven coating of the tablet.

Hence, the correct option is (A).

59. The crown thickness of a tablet is measured by a micrometer (sliding caliper scale). This test is necessary for the packaging of tablets as well as drug content uniformly. Micrometer, in full micrometer caliper, is an instrument for making precise linear measurements of dimensions such as diameters, thicknesses, and lengths of solid bodies; it consists of a C-shaped frame with a movable jaw operated by an integral screw.

Hence, the correct option is (A).

60. Friabilator is operated at 25 RPM. Campbell Electronics friabilators FT-20 is designed in accordance with the specifications as laid down in USP and other pharmacopoeia. The standard FT-20 operates at a constant speed of 25 RPM ±1.

Hence, the correct option is (D).

61. Enteric-coated tablets disintegrate in 1 hour in simulated intestinal fluid. Operate the apparatus for 2 hours, unless otherwise specified in the individual monograph (but in any case for not less than 1 hour), and examine the state of the tablets. Enteric-coated penicillamine tablets were tested in vivo in nine weanling pigs divided into three groups:

- A negative control group.
- A test group was dosed with enteric-coated penicillamine tablets.
- A positive control group was dosed with uncoated tablets.

Hence, the correct option is (A).

62. In the dissolution test, the flask is maintained at $37°C \pm 0.5°C$. If the measured percent saturation of total dissolved gases at a given degassing temperature is below the solid line, outgassing will not occur when the temperature of the dissolution media is brought to $37°C$.

Hence, the correct option is (A).

63. Capping is prevented by using flat punches. Since air travels upward during compression and escapes between the upper punch tip and the die, less punch penetration reduces the distance the air must travel to escape and minimizes capping potential. A decrease in main compression force can also reduce capping.

Hence, the correct option is (A).

64. Greenbone is a source of Type B Gelatin. Results Yellow-green bone was encountered in 3 patients during orbital tumor excision or orbital fracture repair procedures. The only common cause was prior use of tetracycline during adolescence. The bone fluoresced with a bright yellow-green color when exposed to 365-nm ultraviolet light.

Hence, the correct option is (B).

65. Plating of punch faces is done by chromium. Punches usually have a longer lifetime than dies if they are made from the same material, that is why manufacturers often choose different steel qualities. D2 and D3 have a high-chromium content of 12 and are additionally carbon-rich over 1.5%. Chromium and carbon together form stable carbide, which increases hardness.

Hence, the correct option is (A).

66. Sta-Rx-1500 contains 10% of moisture. Sta-Rx 1500, a directly compressible starch, was used as the basis for comparison. Evaluated tablet properties included weight and drug content uniformity, hardness and friability as well as disintegration time and dissolution profile. The modified starches exhibited species specificity in terms of the tablet properties.

Hence, the correct option is (B).

67. Acacia and tragacanth are used in concentrations of 10%-25%. Acacia is the dried gummy exudate obtained from the stems and branches of Acacia Senegal or other related species of

Acacia. Tragacanth is a naturally occurring dried gum obtained from Astragalus gummier and other species of Astragalus.

Hence, the correct option is (A).

68. Starch on heating hydrolyzes into dextrin & glucose. The complete hydrolysis of starch yields the sugar d-glucose, or, as it is commonly known, dextrose. The hydrolysis is supposed to proceed by steps, various intermediate products being formed. These have often been enumerated as soluble starch, maltose, and various dextrins.

Hence, the correct option is (D).

69. The pH of the small intestine is 7-8. The pH gradually increases in the small intestine from pH 6 to about pH 7.4 in the terminal ileum. The pH drops to 5.7 in the caecum, but again gradually increases, reaching pH 6.7 in the rectum.

Hence, the correct option is (D).

70. Aqua coat is a solution of HPMC. HPMC is hydrophilic (water-soluble), a biodegradable, and biocompatible polymer having a wide range of applications in drug delivery, dyes and paints, cosmetics, adhesives, coatings, agriculture, and textiles. HPMC forms flexible and transparent films from aqueous solutions.

Hence, the correct option is (B).

71. Lozenges were originally named as pastilles. A throat lozenge (also known as a cough drop, troche, cachou, pastille, or cough sweet) is a small, typically medicated tablet intended to be dissolved slowly in the mouth to temporarily stop coughs, lubricate, and soothe irritated tissues of the throat (usually due to a sore throat or strep throat.)

Hence, the correct option is (C).

72. The implantation tab is NMT 40 mm in length. N-Methyltryptamine (NMT) is a member of the substituted tryptamine chemical class and a natural product that is biosynthesized in the human body from tryptamine by certain N-methyltransferase enzymes, such as in diethylamine N-methyltransferase. It is a common component in human urine.

Hence, the correct option is (C).

73. Seal coating is done by using shellac. Shellac is a polymer used in coating applications to provide various functional properties. It can be used in film coatings to achieve enteric applications, aesthetic and immediate-release properties, taste masking, and seal coating.

Hence, the correct option is (A).

74. Sub-coating is performed to round the edges of the tablet. In this process, there is a significant increase in tablet weight. Generally, lamination process and suspension process methods are used for sub-coating. Sealing is done to ensure that a thin layer of waterproof material, such as cellulose or shellac acid phthalate is deposited on the surface of the tablets. The shellac or cellulose acid phthalate is dissolved in alcohol or acetone & several coats of this are given in the coating pan.

Hence, the correct option is (C).

75. CAP dissolves at pH above 6. For providing delayed absorption of the drug, CAP dissolves at pH above 6, making it a natural enteric polymer for film coatings. Its properties also demonstrate a hygroscopic nature, which makes it susceptible to moisture permeation and solubility in GI fluid.

Hence, the correct option is (A).

76. An opacifier is a substance added to a material in order to make the ensuing system opaque. An example of a chemical opacifier is titanium dioxide (TiO_2), which is used as an opacifier in paints, paper, and plastics. It has a very high refraction index (rutile modification 2.7 and anatase modification 2.55) and optimum refraction is obtained with crystals about 225 nanometers. Impurities in the crystal alter the optical properties. It is also used to opacify ceramic glazes and milk glass; bone ash is also used.

Hence, the correct option is (A).

77. The drug having very good antiemetic properties is Ginger. Ginger is widely used for reducing nausea. Studies have shown ginger to be effective in treating symptoms of nausea and vomiting caused by pregnancy and by chemotherapy. It has relatively few side effects and could be as effective as antiemetic drugs. In relation to its antiemetic properties, ginger (and its constituents) acts peripherally, within the gastrointestinal tract, by increasing the gastric tone and motility due to anticholinergic and antiserotonergic actions. It is also reported to increase gastric emptying.

Hence, the correct option is (B).

78. Cardamom is the type of fruit capsule. Cardamom is the dried fruit of Elettaria cardamomum Maton (Zingiberaceae). It is popularly known as the "queen of spices". There are many varieties, which are classified on the basis of their capsule size and color. Some of the important varieties are Alleppey, Mysore, Malabar, and Mangalore cardamoms. Cardamom is commercially cultivated for its dried fruits (capsules), which is also referred to as cardamom of commerce.

Hence, the correct option is (A).

79. Cardamom belongs to the family Zingiberaceae. Cardamom, also spelled cardamon, spice consisting of whole or ground dried fruits, or seeds, of Elettaria cardamomum, a herbaceous perennial plant of the ginger family (Zingiberaceae). The seeds have a warm, slightly pungent, and highly aromatic flavour somewhat reminiscent of camphor.

Hence, the correct option is (D).

80. Parenchymatous cells of perisperm of cardamom show microrostte type of small Ca oxalate crystals. The endosperm is formed of thick-walled cellulosic cells containing fixed oil and aleurone grains and micro-crystals of calcium oxalate. III Carpophore splits passing at the apex into the raphe of each mericarp and is traversed by a vascular strand of fibers and spiral vessels. Numerous fragments of endosperm with thick-walled polygonal parenchymatous cells containing fixed oil globules and aleurone grains containing microrosette crystals of calcium oxalate.

Hence, the correct option is (B).

81. It is difficult to make a fine powder of cardamon due to the presence of perisperm cells. After double fertilization, the remnants of the nucellus of the ovule in the mature seed is called perisperm. In some angiosperms, the perisperm is a layer of nutritive tissue derived from the nucellus that surrounds the embryo of the seed. It is a diploid food storing tissue. For examples of seeds containing persistent perisperm is black pepper, castor, coffee, cardamom, etc.

Hence, the correct option is (D).

82. Sandalwood oil is an essential oil obtained from the steam distillation of chips and billets cut from the heartwood of various species of sandalwood trees, mainly Santalum album (Indian sandalwood) and Santalum spicatum (Australian sandalwood). Heartwood also called duramen, is the dead, central wood of trees. Its cells usually contain tannins or other substances that make it dark in colour and sometimes aromatic. Heartwood is mechanically strong, resistant to decay, and less easily penetrated by wood-preservative chemicals than other types of wood. One or more layers of living and functional sapwood cells are periodically converted to heartwood.

Hence, the correct option is (D).

83. Sandalwood oil is mainly produced in South India. Satalum album is found in the dry deciduous forests of Deccan Plateau, mostly in the states of Karnataka and Tamil Nadu, The evergreen tree regenerates naturally when conditions are favorable and has been spreading in its distribution.

Hence, the correct option is (B).

84. The surface of the drug is reddish-brown or reddish-yellow in colour and powdery in asafoetida. Asafoetida is a plant that has a bad smell and tastes bitter. It is sometimes called "devil's dung". People use asafoetida resin, a gum-like material, as medicine. Asafoetida resin is produced by solidifying juice that comes out of cuts made in the plant's living roots.

Hence, the correct option is (A).

85. The combined umbelliferone test is positive in the case of Myrrh. myrrh is a sap-like substance (resin) that comes out of cuts in the bark of certain trees. In foods and beverages, myrrh is used as a flavoring component. In manufacturing, myrrh is used as a fragrance, in incense, and as a fixative in cosmetics. It is also used in embalming.

Hence, the correct option is (D).

86. The drug consists of fusiform, napiform or irregularly oblong tubercle, 3-5 cm long, dark brown, wrinkled with transverse lenticels is jalap. The jalap means:

- The dried tuberous root of a Mexican plant (Ipomoea purga synonym Exogonium purga) of the morning-glory family is also a powdered purgative drug prepared from it that contains resinous glycosides.
- The root or derived drug of plants is related to the one supplying jalap.

Hence, the correct option is (B).

87. Mu-receptors are opioid receptor types is responsible for euphoria and respiratory depression. Mu (μ) (agonist morphine)

Mu-receptors are found primarily in the brainstem and medial thalamus. Mu receptors are responsible for supraspinal analgesia, respiratory depression, euphoria, sedation, decreased gastrointestinal motility, and physical dependence.

Hence, the correct option is (C).

88. Mu (μ) (agonist morphine) receptors are found primarily in the brainstem and medial thalamus. Mu receptors are responsible for supraspinal analgesia, respiratory depression, euphoria, sedation, decreased gastrointestinal motility, and physical dependence. The mu receptors are a class of receptors that neuromodulate different physiological functions, but above all, nociception but also stress, temperature, respiration, endocrine activity, gastrointestinal activity, memory, mood, and motivation.

Hence, the correct option is (A).

89. All of the hypnotic drugs induce a decrease in the duration of REM sleep. Hypnotic drugs are intended to induce sedation and promote sleep. As a result, they have deteriorating effects on cognitive performance following intake. Most hypnotics are benzodiazepine receptor agonists which can have effects on memory in addition to their sedative effects.

Hence, the correct option is (B).

90. Flurazepam hypnotic drugs causes least suppression of REM sleep. Flurazepam is used to treat insomnia (difficulty falling asleep and staying asleep). Flurazepam is in a class of medications called benzodiazepines. It works by slowing activity in the brain to allow sleep.

Hence, the correct option is (C).

91. The mechanism of action of antiseizure drugs is the enhancement of GABAergic (inhibitory) transmission, diminution of excitatory (usually glutamatergic C. transmission) and modification of ionic conductance. Benzodiazepines have both antiseizure and anti-anxiety activity. These drugs include diazepam (Valium), lorazepam (Ativan), clonazepam (Klonopin) and Clobazam (Onfi). The danger with using these drugs long-term is their addictive potential. The GABA system can be enhanced by binding directly to GABA-A receptors, by blocking presynaptic GABA uptake, by inhibiting the metabolism of GABA by GABA transaminase, and by increasing the synthesis of GABA.

Hence, the correct option is (D).

92. The drug against myoclonic seizures is carbamazepine. Carbamazepine is a medicine used to treat epilepsy. It can also be taken for nerve pain caused by diabetes (peripheral neuropathy) or if you have a painful condition of the face called trigeminal neuralgia. Carbamazepine is occasionally used to treat bipolar disorder when other medicines have not worked.

Hence, the correct option is (B).

93. The most effective drug for stopping generalized tonic-clonic status epilepticus in adults is zonisamide. Zonisamide is a new generation anticonvulsant that is typically used in combination with other antiepileptic medications for partial-onset seizures. Zonisamide is used in combination with other medications to treat certain types of seizures. Zonisamide is in a

class of medications called anticonvulsants. It works by decreasing abnormal electrical activity in the brain.

Hence, the correct option is (D).

94. Drugs that block sodium channels by blocking from the intracellular side of the channel include local anesthetics i.e. lidocaine. Class I antiarrhythmic agents. Various anticonvulsants are phenytoin, oxcarbazepine (derivative of carbamazepine). Phenytoin (FEN-ih-toe-in) is the generic name (non–brand name) of widely used seizure medicine. Common brand names for this type of medicine include Dilantin, Phenytek, and Epanutin (in the UK), but it is also sold using the name phenytoin or phenytoin sodium.

Hence, the correct option is (A).

95. Phenytoin is used in the treatment of grand mal epilepsy. Phenytoin is a medicine used to treat epilepsy. It can also be used to treat trigeminal neuralgia, a type of nerve pain that affects your face. Phenytoin is available on prescription. It comes as tablets that can be chewed or dissolved in water, capsules, and a liquid that you swallow.

Hence, the correct option is (B).

96. The dose-related adverse effect caused by phenytoin is Gingival hyperplasia. Gingival hyperplasia is an overgrowth of gum tissue around the teeth. There are a number of causes for this condition, but it's often a symptom of poor oral hygiene or a side effect of using certain medications.

Hence, the correct option is (C).

97. The mechanism of vigabatrin's action is the inhibition of GABA neuronal reuptake from synapses. Vigabatrin is an irreversible mechanism-based inhibitor of gamma-aminobutyric acid aminotransferase (GABA-AT), the enzyme responsible for the catabolism of GABA. Inhibition of GABA-AT results in increased levels of GABA in the brain. Vigabatrin is from a group of medicines called anti-epileptics or anticonvulsants.

Hence, the correct option is (D).

98. Tiagabine blocks neuronal and glial re-uptake of GABA from synapses. Tiagabine increases the level of γ-aminobutyric acid (GABA), the major inhibitory neurotransmitter in the central nervous system, by blocking the GABA transporter 1 (GAT-1), and so it is classified as a GABA re-uptake inhibitor (GRI). Tiagabine has shown promise in the treatment of generalized anxiety disorder (GAD), post-traumatic stress disorder, and panic disorder, and as monotherapy or augmentation therapy for patients with anxiety disorders who are partial responders.

Hence, the correct option is (A).

99. Chlorpromazine is the drug that induces parkinsonian syndromes. It was soon recognized that all typical antipsychotics had the potential to cause EPS, including parkinsonism, acute dystonia, akathisia, and TD. Typical antipsychotics include chlorpromazine, promazine, haloperidol, perphenazine, fluphenazine, and pimozide.

Hence, the correct option is (A).

100. Selegiline drugs are used in the treatment of Parkinsonian disorders. Selegiline is used to help control the symptoms of Parkinson's disease (PD: a disorder of the nervous system that causes difficulties with movement, muscle control, and balance) in people who are taking levodopa and carbidopa combination (Sinemet).

Hence, the correct option is (B).

101. Benztropine agent is preferred in the treatment of the drug-induced form of parkinsonism. Benztropine is used along with other medications to treat the symptoms of Parkinson's disease and tremors caused by other medical problems or medications. It is a selective M1 muscarinic acetylcholine receptor antagonist. Benzatropine partially blocks cholinergic activity in the basal ganglia and has also been shown to increase the availability of dopamine by blocking its reuptake and storage in central sites, and as a result, increasing dopaminergic activity.

Hence, the correct option is (C).

102. A peripheral dopa decarboxylase inhibitor is carbidopa. To minimize peripheral metabolism, levodopa is given in combination with a dopa decarboxylase inhibitor that does not cross the blood-brain barrier. The two available inhibitors are carbidopa (combined with levodopa as co-careldopa) and benserazide (combined with levodopa as co-beneldopa).

Hence, the correct option is (C).

103. The mechanism of carbidopa's action is the inhibition of dopa decarboxylase. It works by being converted to dopamine in the brain. Carbidopa is in a class of medications called decarboxylase inhibitors. It works by preventing levodopa from being broken down before it reaches the brain. This allows for a lower dose of levodopa, which causes less nausea and vomiting.

Hence, the correct option is (B).

104. Pyridoxine vitamins reduces the beneficial effects of levodopa by enhancing its extracerebral metabolism. Pharmacologic doses of pyridoxine (vitamin B_6) enhance the extracerebral metabolism of levodopa and may therefore prevent its therapeutic effect unless a peripheral decarboxylase inhibitor is also taken.

Hence, the correct option is (A).

105. Bromocriptine is an antiparkinsonian drug is a dopamine agonist that has been used for the treatment of hyperprolactinemia. Bromocriptine is in a class of medications called dopamine receptor agonists. It treats hyperprolactinemia by decreasing the amount of prolactin in the body. It treats acromegaly by decreasing the amount of growth hormone in the body. It treats Parkinson's disease by stimulating the nerves that control movement.

Hence, the correct option is (B).

106. A selective inhibitor of monoamine oxidase B is selegiline. The amines dopamine (DA) and tyramine show a similar affinity for each enzyme form. Clorgyline is a selective inhibitor of MAO-A while selegiline (I-deprenyl) and rasagiline are relatively selective inhibitors of MAO-B. Selegiline is a selective inhibitor of MAO-B, irreversibly inhibiting it by binding to it covalently. It exerts effects by blocking the breakdown of dopamine, thus increasing its activity.

Hence, the correct option is (D).

107. MAO-A metabolizes norepinephrine and serotonin and MAO-B metabolizes dopamine is the correct statement. Monoamine oxidase A (MAO-A) generally metabolizes tyramine, norepinephrine (NE), serotonin (5-HT), and dopamine (DA) (and other less clinically relevant chemicals). In contrast, monoamine oxidase B (MAO-B) mainly metabolizes dopamine (DA) (and other less clinically relevant chemicals).

Hence, the correct option is (C).

108. Amantadine antiparkinsonian drugs is antiviral agent used in the prophylaxis of influenza A. Amantadine is an antiviral agent with mild antiparkinsonian activity. Amantadine was used in the early 2000s for Influenza A treatment. However, high levels of resistance have emerged recently, initially from Asia and now to North America.

Hence, the correct option is (D).

109. Trihexyphenidyl is an anti-parkinsonism drug is an oral anticholinergic agent used predominantly in the symptomatic therapy of Parkinson disease and movement disorders. Trihexyphenidyl has not been associated with serum enzyme elevations during treatment but has been implicated in rare cases of acute liver injury.

Hence, the correct option is (C).

110. Alcohol potentiates is SNS depressants, vasodilators and hypoglycemic agents. Alcohol works in the brain primarily by increasing the effects of a neurotransmitter called γ-aminobutyric acid, or GABA. This is the major inhibitory neurotransmitter in the brain, and by facilitating its actions, alcohol suppresses the activity of the central nervous system.

Hence, the correct option is (D).

111. Disulfiram agent is an inhibitor of aldehyde dehydrogenase inhibitor that prevents acetaldehyde metabolism and increases circulating acetaldehyde levels to produce symptoms of flushing, dizziness, and vomiting if ethanol is consumed. This aversion therapy can decrease ethanol intake. Disulfiram (Antabuse) is one of several aldehyde dehydrogenase (ALDH) inhibitors that raise the plasma level of acetaldehyde following ethanol ingestion. The usually pleasant reaction to ethanol is thereby changed to an unpleasant one, owing to a number of bodily reactions to acetaldehyde.

Hence, the correct option is (C).

112. Naltrexone drug alters brain responses to alcohol. Naltrexone is pharmacologically effective against alcohol and opioids by blocking the mu-opioid receptor. Endogenous opioids are involved in modulating alcohol and opioids by reinforcing their effects. Vivitrol, the brand name for naltrexone, is a narcotic blocker or what's known as an opioid antagonist. This medication, which is as effective as Suboxone, is a monthly injection.

Hence, the correct option is (A).

113. The two most commonly used centrally acting opioid receptor antagonists are naloxone and naltrexone. Naloxone comes in intravenous, intramuscular, and intranasal formulations and is FDA-approved for the use in an opioid overdose and the reversal of respiratory depression associated with opioid use.

Hence, the correct option is (B).

114. Fomepizole agent is used as an antidote for ethylene glycol and methanol poisoning. Fomepizole, a potent alcohol dehydrogenase (ADH) inhibitor, is an efficient and safe antidote that prevents or reduces toxic EG and methanol metabolism. Although no study has compared its efficacy with ethanol, fomepizole is recommended as a first-line antidote.

Hence, the correct option is (B).

115. The phenomenon of lowering of vapour pressure is defined as the decrease in vapour pressure of a solvent on the addition of a non-volatile non-electrolyte solute in it. Vapor pressure lowering is a colligative property of solutions. The vapor pressure of a pure solvent is greater than the vapor pressure of a solution containing a non-volatile liquid. This lowered vapor pressure leads to boiling point elevation.

Hence, the correct option is (B).

116. The Free & Blythe method is used to study thixotropy. Free and Blythe suggested a similar method in which the fractional life period is plotted against reciprocal temperature, and the time in days required for the drug to decompose to some fraction of its original potency at R.T is obtained. Thixotropy is the property of some non-Newtonian fluids to show a time-dependent change in viscosity. When sheared by mixing, such as simple shaking, the matrix relaxes and forms a solution with the characteristics of a liquid dosage form for ease of use.

Hence, the correct option is (A).

117. The dehydration reaction of alcohols to generate alkene proceeds by heating the alcohols in the presence of a strong acid, such as sulfuric or phosphoric acid, at high temperatures. In an elimination reaction, when protic acids react with alcohol, they lose water molecules to form alkenes. The required range of reaction temperature decreases with increasing substitution of the hydroxy-containing carbon:

- 1° alcohol: 170° - 180°C
- 2° alcohols: 100°– 140 °C
- 3° alcohols: 25°– 80°C

Hence, the correct option is (C).

118. Acid is a substance that dissociates in water to produce hydrogen ions is an Arrhenius theory.

As defined by Arrhenius: An Arrhenius acid is a substance that dissociates in water to form hydrogen ions (H^+). In other words, an acid increases the concentration of H^+ ions in an aqueous solution. In other words, a base increases the concentration of OH^- ions in an aqueous solution.

Hence, the correct option is (A).

119. The nucleus is the largest organelle in a eukaryotic cell and is considered to be the cell's control center. It contains most of the cell's DNA, which makes up chromosomes and is encoded with the genetic instructions for making proteins. The transcription of RNA also takes place in the nucleus.

Hence, the correct option is (C).

120. ELISA stands for enzyme-linked immunoassay. It is a commonly used laboratory test to detect antibodies in the blood. An antibody is a protein produced by the body's immune system when it detects harmful substances, called antigens.

Hence, the correct option is (A).

121. Alcoholic beverages, fermented dairy products and bread are produced by microorganisms. Microorganisms are used in many industries for the production of the food we eat, like fermented dairy products (sour cream, yogurt), as well as fermented foods as pickles, bread and alcoholic beverages.

Hence, the correct option is (D).

122. Lymphocytes are the hallmark of meningitis caused by tuberculosis, viral meningitides, and chronic fungal infections (cryptococcal meningitis). Lymphocytes are white blood cells that are also one of the body's main types of immune cells. They are made in the bone marrow and found in the blood and lymph tissue. The immune system is a complex network of cells known as immune cells that include lymphocytes.

Hence, the correct option is (B).

123. Carrier protein is a type of cell membrane protein involved in facilitated diffusion and active transport of substances out of or into the cell. They are also the proteins that take up glucose molecules and transport them and other molecules (e.g. salts, amino acids, etc.) inside the cell.

Hence, the correct option is (D).

124. Category D: "There is positive evidence of human fetal risk, but the benefits from use in pregnant women may be acceptable despite the risk (e.g. if the drug is needed in a life-threatening situation or for a serious disease for which safer drugs cannot be used or are ineffective.)

Hence, the correct option is (D).

125. t-RNA bind to amino acid during translation. During initiation, the small ribosomal subunit binds to the start of the m-RNA sequence. Then a transfer RNA (t-RNA) molecule carrying the amino acid methionine binds to what is called the start codon of the m-RNA sequence. Transfer ribonucleic acid (t-RNA) is a type of RNA molecule that helps decode a messenger RNA (m-RNA) sequence into a protein. When a t-RNA recognizes and binds to its corresponding codon in the ribosome, the t-RNA transfers the appropriate amino acid to the end of the growing amino acid chain.

Hence, the correct option is (A).

Pharmaceutical Chemistry

Q.1 Thermolabile immiscible liquid can be separated by:

A. Decantation

B. Dilution

C. Counter-counter distribution

D. Capillary centrifugation

Q.2 A widely acceptor detector for pH measurement is:

A. Platinum   **B.** Glass electrode

C. Ag-AgCl detector   **D.** Lanthanum fluoride

Q.3 A glass electrode used in pH measurement is:

A. A glass membrane

B. Ion-selective electrode

C. Metal-metal oxide electrode

D. All of these

Q.4 Conductivity cells are made up of:

A. Two silver rods

B. Two parallel sheets of platinum

C. Glass membrane with Ag/gCl

D. Stainless steel

Q.5 The conductivity of the solution of an electrolyte is:

A. Not temperature dependence

B. Temperature dependence

C. Pressure dependence

D. Volume dependence

Q.6 Ion mobility is denoted by:

A. cm/sec   **B.** mg/sec   **C.** °C/sec   **D.** ml/sec

Q.7 Quantitative analysis by polarography is based on:

A. Electrode potential   **B.** Half-wave potential

C. Migration current   **D.** Limiting current

Q.8 The factor affecting diffusion current in polarography can be denoted by:

A. Ilkovic equation

B. Nernst equation

C. Mark Houwink equation

D. lambert's Law

Q.9 Which one of the following is measured in amperometric titration?

A. Resistance   **B.** Conductance

C. Voltage   **D.** Current

Q.10 In amperometric titration is kept constant when:

A. Resistance   **B.** Voltage applied

C. Current   **D.** Conductance

Q.11 A target material used in the production of X-rays is:

A. Potassium   **B.** Tungsten

C. Aluminium   **D.** Sodium

Q.12 Which one of the following indicator is used in complexometric titration?

A. Crystal violet   **B.** Murexide

C. Eosin   **D.** Methyl orange

Q.13 Aprotic solvents have:

A. Acidic properties   **B.** Basic properties

C. Both (A) and (B)   **D.** None of these

Q.14 The electron transition not observed in UV spectroscopy is:

A. $\sigma \to \sigma^*$ **B.** $n \to \sigma^*$ **C.** $n \to \pi^*$ **D.** $\pi \to \pi^*$

Q.15 Which of the following drugs help in subsiding the effects of allergic reaction?

A. Benadryl   **B.** Dimetapp

C. Seldane   **D.** Nardil

Q.16 What is the unit of specific conductance?

A. Ohm   **B.** Mho

C. Ohm cm^{-1} **D.** Mho m^{-1}

Q.17 How many 1H NMR signals will be given by acetone?

A. One   **B.** Two   **C.** Three   **D.** Six

Q.18 In which order are the various parts of a mass spectrometer found?

A. Ionization chamber - sample - magnet - collector - recorder

B. Sample - ionization chamber - magnet - collector - recorder

C. Sample - magnet - ionization chamber - collector - recorder

D. Ionization chamber-magnet - sample - collector - recorder

Q.19 Which of the following gas is unsuitable for GC as carrier gas?

A. Carbon dioxide   **B.** Helium

C. Nitrogen   **D.** Oxygen

Q.20 To determine the rancidity of Arachis oil __________ method is used.

A. Acid base titration

B. Complexometric titration

C. Redox titration

D. Precipitation titration

Q.21 __________ is the choice for GC separations of halogenated compounds.

A. Electron capture detector

B. Flame ionization detector

C. Thermal conductivity detector

D. Universal detector

Q.22 Attachment of tertiary amino group to the 4ᵗʰ carbon of the butyrophenone makes it:

A. Antidepressant   **B.** Antipsychotic

C. Anticonvulsant   **D.** CNS stimulant

Q.23 Which of the following is prompt acting insulin?

A. Insulin injection

B. Insulin zinc suspension

C. Globin zinc insulin injection

D. Isophane insulin injection

Q.24 Scopolamine is a:

A. 3- α hydroxy tropane

B. 6,7 β - hydroxy tropane

C. 3- β hydroxy tropane

D. 6- β hydroxy tropane

Q.25 Doxorubicin act by:

A. Inhibiting asparaginase

B. Inhibiting topoisomerase-II

C. Inhibiting adenosine deaminase

D. Inhibiting function of microtubule

Q.26 Methotrexate produce their action by:

A. Interfering with purine synthesis

B. Intracellular formation of an amine adduct

C. Forming a conjugate with nucleic acid

D. Inhibit the synthesis of folic acid

Q.27 A metabolites of spironolactone is:

A. Aldosterone   **B.** Cabrenone

C. Corticosterone   **D.** Pregnenolone

Q.28 Peripheral neurotransmitter is:

A. Histamine   **B.** Noradrenalin

C. Hydroxytryptamine   **D.** Prostaglandin

Q.29 The chemical formula of potassium permanganate is:

A. $KMnO_4$ **B.** K_2MnO_4 **C.** KIO_3 **D.** K_2ZnO_2

Q.30 Which is also known as dry ice?

A. Potassium hydroxide

B. Carbon dioxide

C. Calcium Carbonate

D. Calcium oxide

Q.31 Which is used as a disinfectant?

A. Sodium nitrite

B. Selenium nitrite

C. Chlorinated lime

D. Magnesium sulphate

Q.32 The chemical formula of nitrous oxide is:

A. NO_2 **B.** N_2O

C. NO_3 **D.** None of these

Q.33 Chemical name of laughing gas is:

A. Nitrous oxide   **B.** Nitric oxide

C. Silicon oxide   **D.** Calcium oxide

Q.34 The chemical formula of bleaching powder is:

A. $CaOCl_2$ **B.** $CaCO_3$

C. CaO **D.** $Caso_4.2H_2O$

Q.35 What is the chemical name of Rochelle salt?

A. Potassium tartrate

B. Sodium chloride

C. Sodium Potassium tartrate

D. Potassium chloride

Q.36 What is the chemical name of Epsom Salt?

A. Sodium Sulphate

B. Magnesium Sulphate

C. Zinc Sulphate

D. Aluminium Sulphate

Q.37 What is the chemical name of White Precipitate?

A. Silver nitrate   **B.** Silver nitrite

C. Aluminium nitrite   **D.** Aluminium nitrate

Q.38 Which is used as an antacid?

A. Sodium oxide   **B.** Magnesium oxide

C. Calcium oxice   **D.** None of these

Pharmaceutics

Q.39 Empty capsule has moisture content in the range of:

A. 60%   **B.** 12%-15%

C. 50%-70%   **D.** 30%

Q.40 Which treatment is used for solubility of gelatin?

A. Heat   **B.** Formalin   **C.** Water   **D.** Alcohol

Q.41 Which of the following is used to fill powdered dry solid into soft gelatin capsule?

A. Aceo gel   **B.** Rotobil

C. Rotosort   **D.** Rotoweigh

Q.42 Sealing of capsule is achieved by:

A. 100 °C   **B.** 20 °C

C. 37 °C -40 °C   **D.** 70 °C

Q.43 Moisture content is determined by:

A. K-F Method

B. Gas Chromatography

C. Both (A) and (B)

D. None of these

Q.44 Foam stability is measured by:

A. IR Spectroscopy

B. UV Spectroscopy

C. Rotational viscometers

D. All of these

Q.45 Particle size is determined by:

A. Gas Chromatography

B. Cascade impactor

C. Light scatter decay

D. Both (B) and (C)

Q.46 Chewable tablet contains the following base:

A. Mannitol
B. Glucose
C. Lactose
D. None of these

Q.47 Which of the following is not added in lozenges?

A. Sweetener
B. Binder
C. Disintegrant
D. All of these

Q.48 Enteric-coated tablet is disintegrated in:

A. Stomaeh
B. Liver
C. Intestine
D. Mouth

Q.49 Micromeritics is the study of:

A. Big particles
B. Small particles
C. Both (A) and (B)
D. None of these

Q.50 The size and surface area of a particles in ___________.

A. Physical
B. Chemical
C. Pharmacologic properties of products
D. All of these

Q.51 Particle size of product can affect its release from dosage forms administered orally by:

A. Medically
B. Clinically
C. Both (A) and (B)
D. None of these

Q.52 Frequency distribution curve is obtained when:

A. Number of particles is plotted against the mean size range.
B. Mean size range is plotted against the number of particles.
C. Number of particles and the mean size are on x-axis.
D. Both (A) and (B)

Q.53 Methods for determining particle size include:

A. Optical microscopy
B. Sieving
C. Sedimentation
D. All of these

Q.54 Ordinary microscope can measure the particle size between range:

A. 0.2 to 100 m
B. 0.2 to 100 mm
C. 0.2 to 100 um
D. 0.2 to 100 nm

Q.55 The size of particle is measured by microscope with the help of:

A. Eye-piece
B. Micro-meter
C. Eyepiece fitted with a micrometer
D. None of these

Q.56 Sieving method uses a series of standard sieves calibrated by the:

A. National Bureau of standards
B. IUPAC
C. Both (A) and (B)
D. None of these

Q.57 Order of sieves in sieving is:

A. Coarse, moderately coarse, moderately fine, fine, very fine
B. Moderately coarse, coarse, moderately fine, fine, very fine
C. Moderately coarse, coarse, fine, moderately fine, very fine
D. Coarse, moderately coarse, fine, moderately fine, very fine

Q.58 Sieving errors can arise by factors including:

A. Sieve loading & duration
B. Intensity of agitation
C. Both (A) and (B)
D. None of these

Q.59 The particle size in sub sieve range can be found by gravity sedimentation as expressed in:

A. Van't hoff factor
B. Ohm's law
C. Graham's law
D. Stoke's law

Q.60 Andreasen apparatus works under the principle of:

A. Microscopy
B. Sedimentation
C. Sieving
D. All of these

Q.61 Any instrument used for measuring volume of particle is ___________.

A. Andreasen apparatus
B. Coulter counter
C. Fisher sub sieve sizer
D. None of these

Q.62 Granulators are used for:

A. Making particles longitudinal
B. Cuboidal
C. Spherical
D. Elliptical

Q.63 The specific surface is the __________.

A. Surface area per unit volume
B. Surface area per unit weight
C. Both (A) and (B)
D. None of these

Q.64 Methods for determining surface area are:

A. Absorption method
B. Air permeability method
C. Both (A) and (B)
D. None of these

Q.65 The adsorbed layer in adsorption method is monomolecular at:

A. Very low pressure
B. Low pressure
C. High pressure
D. Very high pressure

Q.66 The adsorbed layer in adsorption method is multimolecular at:

A. Very low pressures
B. Low pressures
C. Higher pressures
D. All of these

Q.67 An instrument used to calculate the surface area of particles is:

A. Quantasorb QS-16
B. Quanta-adsorb QD-16
C. Boyton apparatus
D. Quanta-apparatus

Q.68 In adsorption method the particle whose surface area is to be measured is taken as:

A. Adsorbate
B. Adsorbent

C. Both (A) and (B)
D. None of these

Q.69 Particle size of colloids:
A. 1 nm to 0.5 mum
B. 1 mum to 0.5 mm
C. 1 mm to 0.5 m
D. 1 m to 0.5 mm

Q.70 The process which it consisted of at least two phases with one or more disperse phase in a single dispersion medium is called:
A. Disperse phase
B. Dispersion medium
C. Dispersion
D. All of these

Q.71 How many types of dispersion?
A. 1   **B.** 2   **C.** 3   **D.** 4

Q.72 Molecular dispersion ranges from __________.
A. 1 to 500 nm
B. <500 nm
C. <1 nm
D. None of these

Q.73 The increasing trend of diameter is:
A. Molecular dispersion, Colloidal dispersion, Coarse dispersion.
B. Colloidal dispersion, coarse dispersion, molecular dispersion
C. Corse dispersion, molecular dispersion, colloidal dispersion.
D. All of these

Q.74 The dispersion medium in blood is:
A. Platelets   **B.** Serum   **C.** Plasma   **D.** Oxygen

Q.75 The best example of all dispersion is__________.
A. Oxygen
B. Blood
C. Proteins
D. All of these

Q.76 Molecular dispersion easily passes through __________.
A. Electron microscope
B. Ultra filtration
C. Filter paper
D. All of these

Pharmacognosy

Q.77 Ginseng is mainly used as:
A. Diuretics
B. Antiinflammatory
C. Hepatoprotective
D. Adaptogenic

Q.78 Panax ginseng is mainly produced in:
A. Japan   **B.** Korea   **C.** India   **D.** U.S.A.

Q.79 Sarsaparilla is mainly used in treatment of:
A. Skin disease
B. Kidney stone
C. Diabetes
D. Constipation

Q.80 The shape of quillaia bark is:
A. Curved
B. Quilled
C. Flat
D. Recurved

Q.81 Excessive consumption of liquorice leads to:
A. Diarrhea
B. Drowsiness
C. Dryness in mouth
D. Hypertension & hypokalaemic alkalosis

Q.82 Liquorice extract and glycyrrhetinic acid are useful in treatment of:
A. Hypertension
B. Rheumatoid arthritis
C. Dementia
D. Skin disease

Q.83 Flavonoid components of liquorice have following property:
A. Anti-ulcerogenic
B. Sweetening
C. Cardiatonic
D. Livertonic

Q.84 Glycyrrhetinic acid is a following type of saponin:
A. Steroidal
B. a-amyrin
C. Lupeol
D. β-amyrin

Q.85 Fenugreek is widely used in traditional systems of medicine, following activity/ activities are demonstrated:
A. Antidiabetic
B. Antiulcer
C. Cholesterol-lowering
D. All of these

Q.86 Steroidal sapogenin hecogenin is isolated from:
A. Costus speciosus
B. Solanum khasianum
C. Agave sislana
D. Dioscorea tokoro

Pharmacology

Q.87 Find out the opioid receptor type, which is responsible for dysphoria and vasomotor stimulation:
A. Kappa-receptors
B. Delta-receptors
C. Mu-receptors
D. All of these

Q.88 Kappa and delta agonists:
A. Inhibit postsynaptic neurons by opening K^+ channels.
B. Close a voltage-gated Ca^{2+} channel on presynaptic nerve terminals.
C. Inhibit of arachidonate cyclooxygenase in CNS.
D. Both (A) and (B)

Q.89 Which of the following opioid agents is used in the treatment of acute opioid overdose?
A. Pentazocine
B. Methadone
C. Naloxone
D. Remifentanyl

Q.90 Non-narcotic agents cause:
A. Respiratory depression
B. Antipyretic effect
C. Euphoria
D. Physical dependence

Q.91 Correct statements concerning aspirin include all of the following except:
A. It inhibits mainly peripheral COX.
B. It does not have an anti-inflammatory effect.
C. It inhibits platelet aggregation.

D. It stimulates respiration by a direct action on the respiratory center.

Q.92 All of the following are undesirable effects of aspirin except:

A. Gastritis with focal erosions.

B. Tolerance and physical addiction.

C. Bleeding due to a decrease of platelet aggregation.

D. Reversible renal insufficiency.

Q.93 Analgin usefulness is limited by:

A. Agranulocytosis

B. Erosions and gastric bleeding

C. Methemoglobinemia

D. Hearing impairment

Q.94 Methemoglobinemia is possible adverse effect of:

A. Aspirin   **B.** Paracetamol

C. Analgin   **D.** Ketorolac

Q.95 Correct the statements concerning ketorolac include all of the following EXCEPT:

A. It inhibits COX.

B. It is as effective as morphine for a short-term relief from moderate to severe pain.

C. It has a high potential for physical dependence and abuse.

D. It does not produce respiratory depression.

Q.96 Find out the antiseizure drug with an analgesic component of effect:

A. Carbamazepine   **B.** Ethosuximide

C. Phenytoin   **D.** Clonazepam

Q.97 Which of the following non-opioid agents is an antidepressant with analgesic activity?

A. Fluoxetine   **B.** Moclobemide

C. Tranylcypramine   **D.** Amitriptyline

Q.98 Find out the mixed (opioid/non-opioid) agent:

A. Paracetamol   **B.** Tramadol

C. Sodium valproate   **D.** Butorphanol

Q.99 Most antipsychotic drugs:

A. Strongly block postsynaptic D-2 receptor

B. Stimulate postsynaptic D-2 receptor

C. Block NMDA receptor

D. Stimulate 5-HT2 receptor

Q.100 Hyperprolactinemia is caused by blockade of dopamine in:

A. The chemoreceptor trigger zone of the medulla

B. The pituitary

C. The extrapiramidal system

D. The mesolimbic and mesofrontal systems

Q.101 Parkinsonian symptoms and tarditive dyskinesia are caused by blockade dopamine in:

A. The nigrostriatal system.

B. The mesolimbic and mesofrontal systems.

C. The chemoreceptor trigger zone of the medulla.

D. The tuberoinfundibular system.

Q.102 Extrapyramidal reactions can be treated by:

A. Levodopa

B. Benztropine mesylate

C. Bromocriptine

D. Dopamine

Q.103 Lithium carbonate is useful in the treatment of:

A. Petit mal seizures

B. Bipolar disorder

C. Neurosis

D. Trigeminal neuralgia

Q.104 Which of the following agents is related to tricyclic antidepressants?

A. Nefazodon   **B.** Amitriptyline

C. Fluoxetine   **D.** Isocarboxazid

Q.105 Which of the following antidepressants is a selective serotonin reuptake inhibitor?

A. Phenelzine   **B.** Desipramine

C. Maprotiline   **D.** Fluoxetine

Q.106 The therapeutic response to antidepressant drugs is usually over a period of:

A. 2-3 days   **B.** 2-3 weeks

C. 24 hours   **D.** 2-3 month

Q.107 Which of the following tricyclic and heterocyclic agents has the least sedation?

A. Protriptyline   **B.** Trazodone

C. Amitriptyline   **D.** Mitrazapine

Q.108 Anxiolytics are used to treat:

A. Neurosis   **B.** Psychosis

C. Narcolepsy   **D.** Bipolar disorders

Q.109 Find out the mechanism of hypnotic benzodiazepine action:

A. Increasing the duration of the GABA-gated Cl-channel openings

B. Directly activating the chloride channels.

C. Increasing the frequency of Cl-channel opening events.

D. All of these

Q.110 Which of the following anxiolytics has minimal abuse liability?

A. Oxazepam   **B.** Buspirone

C. Flumazenil   **D.** Alprazolam

Q.111 Caffeine does not cause:

A. Inhibition of gastric secretion

B. Hyperglycemia

C. Moderate diuretic action

D. Increase in free fatty acids

Q.112 Therapeutic uses of caffeine include all of the following except:

A. Cardiovascular collapse and respiratory insufficiency

B. Migraine

C. Somnolence

D. Gastric ulceration

Q.113 Respiratory and cardiac analeptics are all of the following agents except:

A. Cordiamine   **B.** Bemegride

C. Caffeine   **D.** Camphor

Q.114 What is the function of Bemegride?

A. Stimulates the medullar respiratory center (central effect).

B. Stimulates hemoreceptors of carotid sinus zone (reflector action).

C. Is a mixed agent (both central and reflector effects).

D. Is a spinal analeptic.

Other Subjects

Q.115 The value of Ebullioscopic constant or boiling point elevation constant depends on:

A. Amount of solute   **B.** Nature of solute

C. Amount of solvent   **D.** Nature of solvent

Q.116 Du Nouy ring method is used for:

A. S.T.Measurment

B. Viscosity determination

C. R.I. calculation

D. HLB calculation

Q.117 A fat on hydrolysis would yield?

A. Glycerol and soap

B. Ethanol and soap

C. Ethanol and glycerol

D. Only soap

Q.118 The colour change is due to ionisation of the acid-base indicators in:

A. Ostwald theory

B. Chromophore theory

C. Quinonoid theory

D. Resonance theory

Q.119 _________ is the major site for purine nucleotide synthesis.

A. Brain   **B.** Liver

C. Adipose Tissue   **D.** Kidney

Q.120 The Golden Rice variety is rich in:

A. Vitamin C

B. Beta-carotene and ferritin

C. Biotin

D. Lysine

Q.121 What is the approximate size of the bacterial cell?

A. 1 mm in diameter

B. 0.5 to 1.0 micrometer in diameter

C. 2 mm in diameter

D. 2 micrometer in diameter

Q.122 Grossly, the brain discloses an exudate of PMN's and fibrin which opacifies the _________, and giving a

_____________ or _____________ appearance, usually over the convexities as well as the base of the brain.

A. Pia, creamy or white

B. Arachnoid, yellow or purulent

C. Arachnoid, creamy or white

D. Dura, Yellow or purulent

Q.123 What is the major difference between facilitated & passive diffusion:

A. Carrier-mediated transport

B. Down hill transport

C. Energy is used

D. Inhibition by metabolic poisons

Q.124 Is indicated in agitation and restlessness in the elderly, despite the high incidence of extrapyramidal side effects?

A. Prochlorperazine   **B.** Clozapine

C. Haloperidol   **D.** Flupentixol

Q.125 In cell division cytoplasmic division is known as:

A. Mitosis   **B.** Telophase

C. Metaphase   **D.** Cytokinesis

// Smart Answer Sheet //

Correct — Percentage of students who answered correctly. **Skipped** — Percentage of students who skipped.

Q.	Ans.	Correct	Skipped	Q.	Ans.	Correct	Skipped	Q.	Ans.	Correct	Skipped
1	A	63.85 %	32.1 %	22	B	48.2 %	42.46 %	43	A	69.41 %	30.41 %
2	B	53.12 %	40.13 %	23	A	55.87 %	34.39 %	44	C	69.68 %	30.29 %
3	A	88.85 %	10.94 %	24	B	64.09 %	34.79 %	45	D	47.3 %	41.35 %
4	B	42.62 %	30.06 %	25	B	19.93 %	72.8 %	46	A	41.99 %	38.43 %
5	B	87.35 %	12.23 %	26	A	69.52 %	30.08 %	47	C	49.5 %	32.07 %
6	A	61.35 %	38.17 %	27	B	57.83 %	38.56 %	48	C	43.65 %	38.6 %
7	B	56.43 %	42.0 %	28	B	57.82 %	37.34 %	49	B	68.06 %	31.39 %
8	A	48.85 %	36.68 %	29	A	88.66 %	10.4 %	50	D	85.86 %	10.23 %
9	D	44.25 %	53.86 %	30	B	62.72 %	32.5 %	51	B	55.21 %	44.14 %
10	B	61.26 %	36.46 %	31	C	67.73 %	32.05 %	52	D	68.67 %	31.2 %
11	B	40.86 %	38.38 %	32	B	80.84 %	13.72 %	53	D	49.32 %	34.46 %
12	B	44.81 %	40.25 %	33	A	86.12 %	10.85 %	54	C	43.37 %	45.23 %
13	D	65.79 %	30.54 %	34	A	54.32 %	32.07 %	55	C	77.01 %	21.48 %
14	A	20.81 %	79.01 %	35	C	46.87 %	50.0 %	56	A	43.96 %	54.25 %
15	D	43.46 %	41.53 %	36	B	45.96 %	34.04 %	57	A	32.93 %	67.01 %
16	D	40.52 %	59.13 %	37	A	52.08 %	39.2 %	58	C	43.67 %	36.81 %
17	A	18.76 %	69.53 %	38	B	53.32 %	35.73 %	59	D	47.82 %	43.72 %
18	B	44.7 %	31.28 %	39	C	46.56 %	30.93 %	60	B	43.12 %	35.4 %
19	A	67.12 %	32.29 %	40	B	41.43 %	52.36 %	61	B	47.23 %	39.25 %
20	C	57.73 %	34.29 %	41	A	41.62 %	37.4 %	62	C	66.43 %	30.23 %
21	A	58.13 %	30.75 %	42	C	45.24 %	34.0 %	63	C	18.59 %	75.4 %

Q.	Ans.	Correct	Skipped	Q.	Ans.	Correct	Skipped	Q.	Ans.	Correct	Skipped
64	D	65.83 %	30.22 %	85	D	80.73 %	18.68 %	106	B	50.49 %	40.45 %
65	B	55.88 %	31.68 %	86	D	11.27 %	81.92 %	107	A	60.81 %	31.43 %
66	C	53.82 %	40.38 %	87	A	62.96 %	36.55 %	108	A	64.39 %	34.86 %
67	A	31.43 %	68.14 %	88	B	17.06 %	81.84 %	109	C	69.6 %	30.2 %
68	B	42.8 %	50.36 %	89	C	46.33 %	40.14 %	110	B	43.77 %	37.26 %
69	A	51.47 %	32.28 %	90	B	78.62 %	17.3 %	111	A	62.73 %	33.82 %
70	C	46.91 %	48.65 %	91	D	24.78 %	72.83 %	112	D	48.76 %	32.28 %
71	C	27.05 %	71.49 %	92	B	62.38 %	35.22 %	113	B	13.16 %	74.65 %
72	C	63.85 %	32.75 %	93	A	40.24 %	58.26 %	114	A	65.7 %	31.62 %
73	A	12.99 %	70.4 %	94	B	56.67 %	39.88 %	115	D	78.54 %	14.24 %
74	C	67.77 %	30.5 %	95	C	32.27 %	67.33 %	116	B	69.45 %	30.26 %
75	B	28.83 %	67.23 %	96	A	51.67 %	41.33 %	117	A	65.52 %	31.9 %
76	D	32.95 %	67.01 %	97	D	62.9 %	34.82 %	118	A	48.67 %	41.74 %
77	D	61.96 %	35.9 %	98	B	51.84 %	33.78 %	119	B	47.3 %	36.77 %
78	B	66.0 %	30.1 %	99	A	64.87 %	30.08 %	120	B	67.57 %	30.71 %
79	A	40.5 %	35.96 %	100	B	48.56 %	46.86 %	121	B	49.75 %	39.05 %
80	C	40.51 %	50.36 %	101	A	63.49 %	33.43 %	122	C	48.89 %	36.77 %
81	D	61.08 %	32.33 %	102	B	53.48 %	43.47 %	123	A	61.51 %	31.15 %
82	B	60.68 %	37.63 %	103	B	50.71 %	45.69 %	124	C	59.44 %	32.1 %
83	A	45.58 %	49.67 %	104	B	41.16 %	36.37 %	125	D	48.02 %	33.68 %
84	D	22.98 %	71.37 %	105	D	49.58 %	31.66 %				

//Hints and Solutions//

1. Thermolabile immiscible liquid can be separated by decantation. Thermolabile refers to a substance that is subject to destruction, decomposition, or change in response to heat. This term is often used to describe biochemical substances. For example, many bacterial exotoxins are thermolabile and can be easily inactivated by the application of moderate heat. Enzymes are also thermolabile and lose their activity when the temperature rises.

Hence, the correct option is (A).

2. A widely acceptor detector for pH measurement is a glass electrode. A glass electrode is a type of ion-selective electrode made of a doped glass membrane that is sensitive to a specific ion. The most common application of ion-selective glass electrodes is for the measurement of pH. The pH electrode is an example of a glass electrode that is sensitive to hydrogen ions.

Hence, the correct option is (B).

3. A glass electrode used in pH measurement is a glass membrane. A glass electrode is a type of ion-selective electrode made of a doped glass membrane that is sensitive to a specific ion. The most common application of ion-selective glass electrodes is for the measurement of pH. The pH electrode is an example of a glass electrode that is sensitive to hydrogen ions. The voltage of the glass electrode, relative to some reference value, is sensitive to changes in the activity of a certain type of ions.

Hence, the correct option is (A).

4. Conductivity cell: Made of pyrex or quartz and are fitted with two platinum electrodes. Should be placed in a vessel containing water to maintain a constant temperature types of conductivity cells are TYPE-A, TYPE-B, & TYPE-C. Platinum parallel sheets each of 1 cm are fixed at a distance of 1 cm.

Hence, the correct option is (B).

5. The conductivity of the solution of an electrolyte is temperature-dependence. The conductivity of electrolytic solutions increases with the increase of temperature because the ions of the electrolytic solution move faster by getting more thermal energy.

Hence, the correct option is (B).

6. Ion mobility is denoted by cm/sec. Ionic mobility in chemistry is the velocity of an ion under a unit potential gradient or field strength. Therefore,

ionic mobility = velocity of the ion/potential gradient or field strength

The velocity of an ion in a solution depends on the nature of the ion, concentration of the solution, temperature, and the applied potential gradient. It is related to the ionic conductance of the solution. From the above formula, unit of ionic mobility in CGS system = cm s^{-1}/volt cm^{-1} = cm^2 s^{-1} volt^{-1}. In the SI system, unit of ionic mobility = metre^2 s^{-1} volt^{-1}. The limiting value of ionic mobility is obtained at infinite dilution when the interionic attraction is totally absent.

Hence, the correct option is (A).

7. Quantitative analysis by polarography is based on the half-wave potential. Qualitative information can also be determined from the half-wave potential of the polarogram (the current vs. potential plot in a polarographic experiment). The value of the half-wave potential is related to the standard potential for the redox reaction being studied.

Half-wave potential ($E_{1/2}$) is a potential at which polarographic wave current is equal to one-half of diffusion current (i_d). Observation of a current peak at a specific half-wave potential, therefore, identifies the chemical species producing the current.

Hence, the correct option is (B).

8. The factor affecting diffusion current in polarography can be denoted by the Ilkovic equation. In polarography with a dropping-mercury electrode, the flow is controlled by the rate of diffusion of the active solution species across the concentration gradient produced by the removal of ions or molecules at the electrode surface. The Ilkovic equation is a mathematical relationship between diffusion current, diffusion coefficient, and active-substance concentration; used for polarographic analysis calculations.

Hence, the correct option is (A).

9. Current is measured in amperometric titration. Amperometric titration refers to a class of titrations in which the equivalence point is determined through the measurement of the electric current produced by the titration reaction. It is a form of quantitative analysis.

Hence, the correct option is (D).

10. In amperometric titration is kept constant when the voltage is applied. In amperometric titrations, the potential applied between the indicator electrode (dropping mercury electrode) and the appropriate depolarizing reference electrode (saturated calomel electrode) is kept constant, and current through the electrolytic cell is then measured on the addition of each increment of titrating.

Hence, the correct option is (B).

11. A target material used in the production of X-rays is tungsten. Most x-ray tube anodes are made of tungsten (the target material). Tungsten has a high atomic number (Z=74) and a high melting point of 3370°C with a correspondingly low rate of evaporation. Most X-ray tubes used for diffraction studies have targets (anodes) made of copper or molybdenum metal. The characteristic wavelengths and excitation potentials for these materials are shown below. Copper radiation is preferred when the crystals are small or when the unit cells are large.

Hence, the correct option is (B).

12. Murexide indicator is used in the complexometric titration.

To carry out metal cation titrations using EDTA, it is almost always necessary to use a complexometric indicator to determine when the endpoint has been reached. Common indicators are organic dyes such as Fast Sulphon Black, Eriochrome Black T, Eriochrome Red B, Patton Reeder, or Murexide.

Hence, the correct option is (B).

13. An aprotic solvent is a solvent that has no O-H or N-H bonds. The "a" means "without", and "protic" refer to protons or hydrogen atoms. The specific meaning of aprotic is that the molecules have no H atoms on O or N. Benzene, carbon tetrachloride, carbon disulphide, etc are examples of aprotic solvents.

Hence, the correct option is (D).

14. The electron transition not observed in UV spectroscopy is $\sigma \to \sigma^*$. The $\sigma \to \sigma^*$ transition requires absorption of a photon with a wavelength that does not fall in the UV-vis range. Thus, only π to π* and n to π* transitions occur in the UV-vis region are observed.

Hence, the correct option is (A).

15. Benadryl, Dimetapp and Seldane are examples or antihistamines which are drugs that interfere with the main actions of histamine, which is a vasodilator and is released during allergic reactions. Nardil is an antidepressant drug.

Hence, the correct option is (D).

16. The unit of specific conductance is Mho m-1. Specific Conductance is the ability of a substance to conduct electricity. It is the reciprocal of specific resistance. Specific conductance is defined as the conducting capacity of a solution of the dissolved electrolyte and the whole solution is being placed between two electrodes are 1 sq. cm and length 1 cm.

Hence, the correct option is (D).

17. 1H NMR signals will be given by acetone is one. The 1H and 13C NMR chemical shifts of 48 industrially preferred solvents in six commonly used deuterated NMR solvents ($CDCl_3$, acetone-d6, DMSO-d6, acetonitrile-d3, methanol-d4, and D_2O) are reported. The solvent that can be used for proton NMR analyses would be chloroform-d, acetone-d6, and deuterium oxide.

Hence, the correct option is (A).

18. Mass spectrometry uses an instrument called a mass spectrometer. The main components of a mass spectrometer are:

- Inlet system (LC, GC, Direct probe, etc.)
- Ion source (EI, CI, ESI, APCI, MALDI, etc.)
- Mass analyzer (Quadrupole, TOF, Ion Trap, Magnetic Sector)
- Detector (Electron Multiplier, Micro Channel Plates MCPs)

The order in which the various parts of a mass spectrometer are found is Sample - ionization chamber - magnet - collector - recorder.

Hence, the correct option is (B).

19. Carbon dioxide gas is unsuitable for GC as carrier gas. The carrier gas in gas chromatography is usually considered to play little part in the analytical process, and its choice is usually determined primarily by the method of detection. That carrier gas may not, and need not, be entirely inert was demonstrated in two separate series of experiments. In one, carbon dioxide was substituted for helium in a gas-solid chromatographic system. In the other, it was substituted for argon in a gas-liquid system.

Hence, the correct option is (A).

20. To determine the rancidity of Arachis oil redox titration method is used. Redox titrimetry is used to analyze a wide range of inorganic analytes. A redox titration (also called an oxidation-reduction titration) can accurately determine the concentration of an unknown analyte by measuring it against a standardized titrant. It is used for the analysis of organic analytes.

Hence, the correct option is (C).

21. Electron capture detector is the choice for GC separations of halogenated compounds. The electron capture detector (ECD) is a selective detector inasmuch that analytes with a high electron affinity, such as halogenated organic compounds, are detected at very low on-column quantities. The Electron Capture Detector, invented by Scientist James Lovelock in 1957, is used to detect molecules and atoms in gas via electron capture ionization, to detect electron-absorbing halogenated compounds.

Hence, the correct option is (A).

22. Attachment of tertiary amino group to the 4th carbon of the butyrophenone makes it antipsychotic. Haloperidol, the most widely used classical antipsychotic drug in this class. Benperidol, the most potent commonly used antipsychotic (200 times more potent than chlorpromazine) Droperidol, Antiemetic for postoperative nausea and vomiting.

Hence, the correct option is (B).

23. Insulin injection is prompt acting insulin. Insulin is a hormone that lowers the level of glucose (a type of sugar) in the blood by helping glucose enter the body's cells. Doctors use this hormone to treat diabetes when the body can't make enough insulin on its own. Rapid-acting insulin also comes in a form that can be inhaled through the mouth. Short-acting insulins take effect and wear off more quickly than long-acting insulins. Short-acting insulin is often used 30 minutes before a meal so that it has time to work.

Hence, the correct option is (A).

24. Scopolamine is a 6,7 β-hydroxy tropane. Tropane is a bicyclic amine that has a pyrrolidine and a piperidine ring sharing a common nitrogen atom and 2 carbon atoms. It is the common structural element of all tropane alkaloids (Lounasmaa and Tamminen, 1993). Any of a large group of alkaloids (as cocaine, atropine, hyoscyamine, and scopolamine) that can be derived from ornithine.

Hence, the correct option is (B).

25. Doxorubicin acts by inhibiting topoisomerase-II. Doxorubicin inhibits topoisomerase II, which overwinds DNA during transcription, thereby preventing the recombination of the DNA double-strand, thus stopping DNA replication[2]. Topoisomerase inhibitors, including doxorubicin, irinotecan and etoposide are often used in the treatment of colorectal, small-cell lung, ovarian and hematological cancers.

Hence, the correct option is (B).

26. Methotrexate produce their action by interfering with purine synthesis. Also, methotrexate indirectly inhibits purine synthesis by blocking the metabolism of folic acid (it is an inhibitor of the dihydrofolate reductase). Allopurinol is a drug that inhibits the enzyme xanthine oxidoreductase and, thus, lowers the level of uric acid in the body.

Hence, the correct option is (A).

27. A metabolites of spironolactone is cabrenone. Canrenone is a diuretic metabolite of spironolactone, the prototypic aldosterone antagonist diuretic. In vivo, spironolactone is metabolized to canrenone, which prolongs the biological effectiveness of spironolactone. Another drug, potassium canrenoate, can also form canrenone as an active metabolite.

Hence, the correct option is (B).

28. A peripheral neurotransmitter is noradrenalin. Primarily using the neurotransmitter acetylcholine (ACh) as a mediator, the parasympathetic system allows the body to function in a "rest and digest" state. Norepinephrine (also called noradrenaline) is a neurotransmitter in both the peripheral and central nervous systems. Norepinephrine produces many effects in the body, the most notable being those associated with the 'fight or flight' response to perceived danger.

Hence, the correct option is (B).

29. The chemical formula of potassium permanganate is $KMnO_4$. Potassium permanganate is a very strong oxidizing agent and can, therefore, be used as an oxidant in a wide spectrum of chemical reactions. It is sometimes called by its common name, Condy's crystals. In its raw state, potassium permanganate is an odourless dark purple or almost black crystal or granular powder.

Hence, the correct option is (A).

30. Dry Ice is the common name for solid carbon dioxide (CO_2). It gets this name because it does not melt into a liquid when heated; instead, it changes directly into a gas (a process known as sublimation). If dry ice is stored in an area without proper ventilation, it may cause people to inhale large amounts of the gas CO_2, which displaces oxygen in the body, the CDC says. This, in turn, can lead to harmful effects, including headache, confusion, disorientation and death.

Hence, the correct option is (B).

31. Chlorinated lime is used as a disinfectant. The definition of chloride of lime is a white powder used for disinfecting which is made by treating slaked lime with chlorine. An example of chloride of lime is a substance used for commercial bleach and in laundering as a disinfectant. Chlorinated lime poisoning occurs when someone swallows chlorinated lime. Do not use it to treat or manage an actual poison exposure.

Hence, the correct option is (C).

32. The chemical formula of nitrous oxide is N_2O. Nitrous oxide is an oxide of nitrogen with a chemical formula N_2O. This organic compound is colourless and non-flammable at room temperature. It is also known as nitrous or laughing gas. Joseph Priestley was the first to identify nitrous oxide in the year 1772. The gas has narcotic effects when inhaled (laughing gas).

Hence, the correct option is (B).

33. The chemical name of laughing gas is nitrous oxide. Nitrous oxide is a safe and effective sedative agent that is mixed with oxygen and inhaled through a small mask that fits over your nose to help you relax. Nitrous oxide sometimes called "laughing gas" is one option your dentist may offer to help make you more comfortable during certain procedures.

Hence, the correct option is (A).

34. The chemical formula of bleaching powder is $CaOCl_2$. It is also called Calcium Oxychloride. It is prepared on dry slaked lime by chlorine gas. Calcium Hypochlorite is an inorganic chemical compound with the chemical formula $CaOCl_2$. They are also called calcium oxychlcride and the common name of $CaOCl_2$ is belching or chlorine powder. It is Regularly used for various day-to-day sanitation purposes. They are also used in water treatment processes.

Hence, the correct option is (A).

35. Sodium potassium tartrate is the chemical name of Rochelle salt. Rochelle salt also called sodium potassium tartrate tetrahydrate, is a crystalline solid having a large piezoelectric effect (electric charge induced on its surfaces by mechanical deformation due to pressure, twisting, or bending), making it useful in sensitive acoustical and vibrational devices.

Hence, the correct option is (C).

36. Magnesium Sulphate is the chemical name of Epsom salt. Magnesium Sulphate, $MgSO_4$, is a colourless crystalline substance formed by the reaction of magnesium hydroxide with sulphur dioxide and air. A hydrated form of magnesium sulphate called kieserite, $MgSO_4 \cdot H_2O$, occurs as a mineral deposit. Synthetically prepared magnesium sulphate is sold as Epsom salt, $MgSO_4 \cdot 7H_2O$.

Hence, the correct option is (B).

37. The chemical name of White Precipitate is silver nitrate. Silver nitrate is an inorganic compound with the chemical formula $AgNO_3$. The silver nitrate, a caustic chemical compound, is important as an antiseptic, in the industrial preparation of other silver salts, and as a reagent in analytical chemistry. Its chemical formula is $AgNO_3$.

Hence, the correct option is (A).

38. Magnesium oxide is used as an antacid. Magnesium oxide may be used for different reasons. Some people use it as an antacid to relieve heartburn, sour stomach, or acid indigestion. Magnesium oxide also may be used as a laxative for short-term, rapid emptying of the bowel (before surgery, for example). As an antacid, magnesium hydroxide suspension neutralizes gastric acid by reacting with hydrochloric acid in the stomach to form magnesium chloride and water. It is practically insoluble in water and does not have any effect until it reacts with the hydrochloric acid in the stomach.

Hence, the correct option is (B).

39. The empty capsule has a moisture content in the range of 50%-70%. Capsules are solid pharmaceutical dosage forms in which the drug or a mixture of drugs is enclosed in a Gelatin Shell or any other suitable material to form various shapes. Capsules generally contain a single dose of active ingredients and are taken orally. Capsules may be printed on the outer surface.

Hence, the correct option is (C).

40. Formalin treatment is used for the solubility of gelatin. Polar solvents like hot water, glycerol, and acetic acid can dissolve gelatin, but it is insoluble in organic solvents like alcohol. Gelatin absorbs 5–10 times its weight in water to form a gel. The gel formed by gelatin can be melted by reheating, and it has an increasing viscosity under stress (thixotropic).

Hence, the correct option is (B).

41. Aceo gel is used to fill powdered dry solid into a soft gelatin capsule. Gelatin and glycerin are used for the preparation of lamellae in a specified ratio. Two plasticized gelatin ribbons are continuously and simultaneously fed with the liquid or paste fill between the rollers of the rotary die mechanism where the capsule is simultaneously filled, shaped, hermetically sealed and cut from the gelatin ribbon.

Hence, the correct option is (A).

42. Sealing of capsule is achieved by 37 °C -40 °C. If locking capsules are not used, a seal can be made by touching the outer edge of the body with a moist towel to soften the gelatin. Alternatively, a cotton swab dipped in warm water can be rubbed around the inner edge of the cap. When the cap is closed on the body, it is slightly twisted to form the seal.

Hence, the correct option is (C).

43. Moisture content is determined by K-F Method. Karl Fischer (KF) titration is a redox reaction that uses the consumption of water during the reaction to measure the amount of water in a sample. It is the reference method for water determination because of its specificity, accuracy and speed of measurement. It takes place in an organic solvent.

Hence, the correct option is (A).

44. Foam stability is measured by Rotational viscometers. Rotational viscometers measure viscosity by immersing a rotating spindle in the fluid to be tested. The amount of power (torque) required to turn the spindle indicates the viscosity of the fluid, and because rotational viscometers do not use gravity to function, their measurements are based on the fluid's internal shear stress.

Hence, the correct option is (C).

45. Particle size is determined by both cascade impactor and light scatter decay. A cascade impactor measures the reach range of a particulate substance as it moves through an opening with the use of aerosol. In addition to measuring the range of substances moved through an opening by aerosol, the impactor can also be used to determine the particle size of the distributed substance. Dynamic light scattering (DLS) is a technique in physics that can be used to determine the size distribution profile of small particles in suspension or polymers in solution.

Hence, the correct option is (D).

46. A chewable tablet contains the mannitol base. Mannitol is a desirable filler in tablets when taste is a factor as in chewable tablets. It is a white, odourless, crystalline powder, or free-flowing granules that is essentially inert and nonhygroscopic. Mannitol also acts as a sweetening agent and is said to be about 70% as sweet as sucrose.

Hence, the correct option is (A).

47. Disintegrant is not added in lozenges. Many chewable tablet products do not contain disintegrants or super-disintegrants, which may lead to prolonged dissolution if they are not chewed. However, disintegration or rapid dissolution is critical to addressing cases in which an individual inadvertently swallows a tablet without chewing it.

Hence, the correct option is (C).

48. An enteric-coated tablet is disintegrated in the intestine. Enteric-coated solid dosage forms serve a special purpose. Enteric-coated tablets are supposed to pass through the stomach intact, disintegrate, and release the drug content for absorption in the intestines.

Hence, the correct option is (C).

49. Micromeritics is the study of small particles. The word micromeritics refers to a discipline of science and technology that deals with studies related to the fundamental as well derived properties of particles. A precise knowledge of the particle's size is of supreme importance in pharmaceutical and materials science.

Hence, the correct option is (B).

50. The size and surface area of particles in physical, chemical and pharmacologic properties of products. Particle size is the physical property of the compound which influences stability, solubility and processability. The unit for the particle size is a micrometer (μm). The surface area is an important physical property that determines the performance characteristics of pharmaceutical powders, ingredients, APIs, and excipients. Gas Adsorption analysis is often used for surface area and porosity measurements within the pharmaceutical industry.

Hence, the correct option is (D).

51. The particle size of the product can affect its release from dosage forms administered orally clinically. Clinically, the particle size of a drug can affect its release from dosage forms that are administered orally, parenterally, rectally and topically. The successful formulation of suspensions, emulsions and tablets; both physical stability and pharmacologic response also depends on the particle size achieved in the product.

Hence, the correct option is (B).

52. Frequency distribution curves are useful when studying colour-difference values. It is generally accepted that tolerance limits can be set at the ±0 (standard deviation) level over the process range for acceptable values. The frequency curve is obtained by joining the points of frequency polygon by a freehand smoothed curve. To plot a frequency curve without using a histogram, we need to plot the frequency of the class against its' class marks and join the points with line segments.

Hence, the correct option is (D).

53. Methods for determining particle size include optical microscopy, sieving and sedimentation.

Sieves: While this is an old technique, it has the advantage of being cheap and particularly useful for the measurement of large particles. In industries such as mining, this can be particularly useful. The main disadvantages associated with this technique include: it is not possible to measure sprays or emulsions and measurement of dry powders is also difficult when particles become small.

Sedimentation: This has been a common method used (historically) in clay and ceramics industries. There are two main problems with this process: the density of the material is needed and so it is not useful for determining particle size of emulsions where the material does not settle or for dense materials where the material settles quickly.

Optical microscopy: In manual optical microscopy, the dispersed particles are viewed by transmission, and the areas of the magnified images are compared with the areas of circles of known sizes inscribed on a graticule. The relative numbers of particles are determined in each of a series of size classes.

Hence, the correct option is (D).

54. The ordinary microscope can measure the particle size between the range of 0.2 to 100 um. The microscope eyepiece is fitted with a micrometer by which the size of the particles can be estimated. The ordinary microscope was used for measuring the particle size in the range of 0.2 to about 100 um.

Hence, the correct option is (C).

55. The size of a particle is measured by a microscope with the help of an eyepiece fitted with a micrometer. The eyepiece, or ocular, magnifies the primary image produced by the objective; the eye can then use the full resolution capability of the objective. The microscope produces a virtual image of the specimen at the point of most distinct vision, generally 250 mm (10 in.) from the eye.

Hence, the correct option is (C).

56. The sieving method uses a series of standard sieves calibrated by the National Bureau of standards. Sieve mesh sizes are based on dimensions of the mesh size opening, or on the number of openings per linear inch. The two major standards governing test sieves and appropriate sizes are ASTM E11 and ISO 565/3310-1, both of which specify parameters for aperture dimensions, mesh size and statistical variations.

Hence, the correct option is (A).

57. Order of sieves in sieving is Coarse, moderately coarse, moderately fine, fine, very fine. The manual sieving method is carried out in places where there is no electricity and is mainly used in, onsite differentiation among large and small particles. The mechanical sieving method is used in laboratories to assure quality and this is the widely used method in present days. In mechanical sieving, the method can be classified into two further groups depending on their sieving movement as horizontal movement sieving method and vertical movement sieving method. The vertical movement sieving method is also known as throw-action sieving and vibratory sieving methods. The dry sieving method is considered mostly and here the testing particles (specimen) are in the dry state. The wet sieving method is considered when the particle that is going to be used is already existing as wet or suspension.

Hence, the correct option is (A).

58. Sieving errors can arise by factors including sieve loading & duration and intensity of agitation. The factors studied included samples size, particle size distribution in the sample and the duration of sieving. The work showed that overloading of the sieves leads to inaccurate results, and that reduction of sample size is a more effective remedy for overloading than the prolongation of sieving time. A measure of the power consumption of the shaft of an agitator used to mix a liquid in a stirred tank.

Hence, the correct option is (C).

59. The particle size in sub sieve range can be found by gravity sedimentation as expressed in Stoke's law. Stokes' Law is a formula for determining the rate of sedimentation. It states that a particle moving through viscous liquid attains a constant velocity or sedimentation rate.

Hence, the correct option is (D).

60. Andreasen apparatus works under the principle of sedimentation. The Andreasen method assumes that particles will sediment at a rate dependent on their size and further assumes the validity of Stoke's Law in this respect. The Andreasen pipette is used to extract precise quantities of suspension ready for analysis.

Hence, the correct option is (B).

61. Any instrument used for measuring the volume of the particle is a coulter counter. The coulter counter is a vital constituent of today's hospital laboratory. Its primary function is the quick and accurate analysis of complete blood counts (often referred to as CBC). The CBC is used to determine the number or proportion of white and red blood cells in the body.

Hence, the correct option is (B).

62. Granulators are used for spherical. Granulators are essentially rotary grinders that are used to grind scrap parts and melt delivery systems (sprues and runners) into feedstock-sized granules for reprocessing. This allows the molder to reduce waste and produce components more cost-effectively.

Hence, the correct option is (C).

63. The specific surface is the surface area per unit volume and surface area per unit weight. Specific surface area (SSA) is a property of solids defined as the total surface area of a material per unit of mass, (with units of m^2/kg or m^2/g) or solid or bulk volume (units of m^2/m^3 or m^{-1}). It is a physical value that can be used to determine the type and properties of a material (e.g. soil or snow).

Hence, the correct option is (C).

64. The most widely used method for surface-area determination is low-temperature gas adsorption, particularly nitrogen and

krypton at liquid-nitrogen temperature. The Brunauer, Emmett and Teller (BET) technique is the most common method for determining the surface area of powders and porous materials.

Hence, the correct option is (D).

65. The adsorbed layer in the adsorption method is monomolecular at low pressure. Initially when the pressure has increased the rate of adsorption increases due to an increase in the gas molecules striking on the surface. Thus, an increase in pressure increases the rate of adsorption linearly.

Hence, the correct option is (B).

66. The adsorbed layer in the adsorption method is multimolecular at higher pressures. Physical absorption forms a multimolecular layer due to diffusion through pores and establishes weak force with solid. Physisorption decreases with an increase in temperature. Chemisorption increases with an increase in temperature. It results in a multimolecular layer.

Hence, the correct option is (C).

67. An instrument used to calculate the surface area of particles is Quantasorb QS-16. P V(P0 – P) P/P004/05/2012 KLE College of Pharmacy, Nipani. 34 Quantasorb QS–16 instrument. The most common method of measuring the specific surface area at present is the volumetric method of N_2 adsorption on the surface of the material under study. The specific surface is calculated by the volume of gas required for the formation of a monolayer of adsorbate molecules on the sample surface.

Hence, the correct option is (A).

68. In the adsorption method, the particle whose surface area is to be measured is taken as an adsorbent. Adsorbents are porous solids that bind liquid or gaseous molecules to their surface. An adsorbent is a solid substance used to collect solute molecules from a liquid or gas.

Hence, the correct option is (B).

69. The particle size of colloids is 1 nm to 0.5 μm. Colloidal particles are small solid particles that are suspended in a fluid phase. This makes them small enough to be suspended in the fluid by thermal motion, provided the buoyancy mismatch between the particles and the fluid is not too large.

Hence, the correct option is (A).

70. The process which consisted of at least two phases with one or more dispersed phases in a single dispersion medium is called dispersion. A dispersion is a system in which distributed particles of one material are dispersed in a continuous phase of another material. The two phases may be in the same or different states of matter. Dispersions are classified in a number of different ways, including how large the particles are in relation to the particles of the continuous phase, whether or not precipitation occurs, and the presence of Brownian motion. In general, dispersions of particles sufficiently large for sedimentation are called suspensions, while those of smaller particles are called colloids and solutions.

Hence, the correct option is (C).

71. There are 3 types of dispersion:

Molecular dispersion: Molecular dispersion is a true solution of a solute phase in a solvent. The dispersed phase (solute) is in form of separate molecules homogeneously distributed throughout the dispersion medium(solvent).

Colloidal dispersion: A colloidal dispersion is composed of solid, liquid or gas particles dispersed in a continuous phase (solid, liquid or gas). Strictly speaking, the term colloidal refers to particles with at least one dimension ranging from 1nm to 1μm.

Coarse dispersion: A pharmaceutical suspension is a coarse dispersion in which insoluble solid particles are dispersed in a liquid medium (usually water or water-based vehicle). Generally, the particles have diameters greater than 0.5μm. The concentration of the dispersed phase may exceed 20%.

Hence, the correct option is (C).

72. Molecular dispersion ranges from <1 nm. Molecular dispersion is a true solution of a solute phase in a solvent. The dispersed phase (solute) is in form of separate molecules homogeneously distributed throughout the dispersion medium(solvent). The molecule size is less than 1 nm ($4*10^{-8}$ inches).

Hence, the correct option is (C).

73. The increasing trend of diameter is Molecular dispersion, Colloidal dispersion, Coarse dispersion. Molecular dispersion is a true solution of a solute phase in a solvent. The dispersed phase (solute) is in form of separate molecules homogeneously distributed throughout the dispersion medium(solvent). The colloidal system is dispersion wherein the internal phase. dispersed particles are distributed uniformly in a dispersion medium. Coarse dispersions are characterized by relatively fast sedimentation of the dispersed phase caused by gravity or other forces.

Hence, the correct option is (A).

74. The dispersion medium in the blood is plasma. In the blood dispersed phase is hormones, Respiratory gases, RBC, WBC, Platelets, proteins and dispersed medium is plasma. Impure blood is purified by kidneys through dialysis. It is an oil-in-water (O/W) type emulsion. It is a liquid in a liquid-type colloid. The dispersion phase is droplets of liquid fat and the dispersion medium is water.

Hence, the correct option is (C).

75. The best example of all dispersion is blood. Blood has the characteristic of both a colloid and a suspension making it a colloidal suspension. In its normal stable state, blood is a suspension, which is a colloid. It mainly consists of red & white blood cells, and lymphocytes suspended in plasma.

Hence, the correct option is (B).

76. Molecular dispersion easily passes through an electron microscope, ultrafiltration and filter paper. Molecular dispersions are dedicated solutions to a solute phase in the solvent. Examples of molecular dispersion are air (consisting of various gasses like nitrogen and oxygen), electrolytes and alloys. The second type of dispersion medium is of the coarse kind. These are heterogeneous dispersed systems.

Hence, the correct option is (D).

77. Ginseng is mainly used as an adaptogenic. Ginseng is an adaptogen. That is, it supports living organisms to maintain optimal homeostasis by exerting effects that counteract physiological changes caused by physical, chemical, or biological stressors.

Hence, the correct option is (D).

78. Panax ginseng is mainly produced in Korea. All ginseng produced in South Korea is Korean ginseng (P. ginseng), while ginseng produced in China includes P. ginseng and South China ginseng (P. noto ginseng). Panax ginseng, ginseng, also known as Asian ginseng, Chinese ginseng, or Korean ginseng, is a species of plant whose root is the original source of ginseng. It is a perennial plant that grows in the mountains of East Asia.

Hence, the correct option is (B).

79. Sarsaparilla is mainly used in the treatment of skin disease. Sarsaparilla is used for treating psoriasis and other skin diseases, rheumatoid arthritis (RA), and kidney disease; for increasing urination to reduce fluid retention; and for increased sweating. Sarsaparilla is also used along with conventional drugs for treating leprosy and for syphilis.

Hence, the correct option is (A).

80. The shape of quillaia bark is flat. Quillaia bark occurs in flat pieces, about 1 m long, 20 cm wide, and 3–10 cm thick. The outer surface is brownish-white, smooth and contains reddish- or blackish-brown patches of rhytidome adhere to the outer surface. The rhytidome is made of dead secondary phloem.

Hence, the correct option is (C).

81. Excessive consumption of liquorice leads to hypertension & hypokalaemic alkalosis. Ingestion of Glycyrrhizic acid, which is the active component in liquorice causes a metabolic syndrome mimicking primary hyperaldosteronism. Chronic intoxication with glycyrrhizic acid may cause hypertension, metabolic alkalosis and hypokalemia with low plasma renin activity.

Hence, the correct option is (D).

82. Liquorice extract and glycyrrhetinic acid are useful in the treatment of rheumatoid arthritis. Liquorice was found to be as effective, if not more so, than Advil (ibuprofen) against the inflammation that causes arthritis, according to a study published in 2014 in Natural Product Communications.

Hence, the correct option is (B).

83. Flavonoid components of liquorice have anti-ulcerogenic property. The antiulcer effect of OS may be due to its cytoprotective effect rather than antisecretory activity. Conclusively, OS was found to possess potent anti-ulcerogenic as well as ulcer-healing properties and could act as a potent therapeutic agent against peptic ulcer disease.

Hence, the correct option is (A).

84. Glycyrrhetinic acid is a β-amyrin type of saponin. Glycyrrhetinic acid, a hydrolytic product of glycyrrhizic acid, is a component of licorice and causes apparent mineralocorticoid excess by inhibition of the enzyme $11-\beta$ hydroxysteroid dehydrogenase \(11-\betaHSD II), which mainly converts cortiscl to the inactive cortisone.

Hence, the correct option is (D).

85. Fenugreek is widely used in the traditional system of medicine, antid abetic, antiulcer and cholesterol-lowering activities are demonstrated. Fenugreek seeds (Trigonella foenum graecum) are high in soluble fibre, which helps lower blood sugar by slowing down digestion and absorption of carbohydrates This suggests they may be effective in treating people with diabetes.

Hence, the correct option is (D).

86. Steroidal sapogenin hecogenin is isolated from Dioscorea tokoro. Diosgenin, a phytosteroid sapogenin, is the product of hydrolysis by acids, strong bases, or enzymes of saponins, extracted from the tubers of Dioscorea wild yam, such as the Kokoro. Steroidal saponins are natural glycosidic compounds of amphiphilic character.

Hence, the correct option is (D).

87. The opioid receptor type, which is responsible for dysphoria and vasomotor stimulation is Kappa-receptors. Zamarripa, C.A., Naylor, J.E., Huskinson, S.L., et al. Kappa opioid agonists reduce oxycodone self-administration in male rhesus monkeys. Psychopharmacology (Berl). Kappa opioid receptors are located on dopamine axon terminals (Svingos et al., 2001), while mu-opioid receptors are not expressed on striatal dopamine axon terminals (Trovero et al., 1990).

Hence, the correct option is (A).

88. Kappa and delta agonists close voltage-gated Ca^{2+} channels on presynaptic nerve terminals. Promising alternatives to MOAs are kappa-opioid agonists (KOAs); these agents have indistinguishable analgesic properties and a reduced side-effect profile. The development of novel KOAs has been limited due to untoward side-effects mediated by centrally-located KORs, including dysphoria, sedation, and hallucinations. Delta-selective agonists have been developed to produce potent analgesic compounds with limited side effects. DPDPE and deltorphin II are considered prototypes, but their delta-selectivity in vivo and the true ability of delta receptors to produce analgesia remain to be demonstrated.

Hence, the correct option is (B).

89. Naloxone opioid agents are used in the treatment of acute opioid overdose. Naloxone is a medicine that rapidly reverses an opioid overdose. It attaches to opioid receptors and reverses and blocks the effects of other opioids. Naloxone is a safe medicine. It only reverses overdoses in people with opioids in their systems.

Hence, the correct option is (C).

90. Non-narcctic agents cause antipyretic effects. Thus narcotic analgesics are usually administered for the relief of severe pain associated with fractures, burns, renal colic, coronary occlusion, etc., while non-narcotic analgesics are generally given for headaches, muscular aches and pains of inflammatory origin. The most common antipyretics in the US are usually ibuprofen and aspirin, which are nonsteroidal anti-inflammatory drugs (NSAIDs) used primarily as analgesics (pain relievers), but which also have antipyretic properties; and paracetamol (acetaminophen), an analgesic with weak anti-inflammatory properties.

Hence, the correct option is (B).

91. The correct statements concerning aspirin include that it inhibits mainly peripheral COX, it does not have an anti-inflámmatory effect and it inhibits platelet aggregation except for it stimulates respiration by a direct action on the respiratory center. Aspirin is non-selective and irreversibly inhibits both forms (but is weakly more selective for COX-1). In ex vivo assays using aggregometry, with sodium arachidonate as an agonist, aspirin inhibits platelet aggregation irreversibly in most people. Aspirin is a unique nonsteroidal anti-inflammatory drug; at high doses (aspirin(high), 1g), it is anti-inflammatory stemming from the inhibition of cyclooxygenase and proinflammatory signaling pathways including NF-kappaB but is cardioprotective at lower doses (aspirin(low), 75 mg).

Hence, the correct option is (D).

92. Gastritis with focal erosions, bleeding due to a decrease of platelet aggregation and reversible renal insufficiency are undesirable effects of aspirin except for tolerance and physical addiction. Aspirin, an acetylated salicylate (acetylsalicylic acid), is classified among the nonsteroidal anti-inflammatory drugs (NSAIDs). These agents reduce the signs and symptoms of inflammation and exhibit a broad range of pharmacologic activities, including analgesic, antipyretic, and antiplatelet properties.

Hence, the correct option is (B).

93. Analgin usefulness is limited by agranulocytosis. Drug-induced agranulocytosis is a life-threatening side effect that usually manifests as a severe form of neutropenia associated with fever or signs of sepsis. It can occur as a problem in the context of therapy with a wide variety of drug classes.

Hence, the correct option is (A).

94. Methemoglobinemia is a possible adverse effect of paracetamol. Methemoglobinemia is a potentially fatal condition, mainly acquired after intoxication by certain drugs. To this date, only three cases associated with paracetamol have been reported.

Hence, the correct option is (B).

95. The correct statements concerning ketorolac include that it inhibits COX, it is as effective as morphine for short-term relief from moderate to severe pain and it does not produce respiratory depression except for it has a high potential for physical dependence and abuse. Ketorolac is used to relieve moderately severe pain, usually after surgery. Ketorolac is in a class of medications called NSAIDs. It works by stopping the body's production of a substance that causes pain, fever, and inflammation.

Hence, the correct option is (C).

96. Carbamazepine is an antiseizure drug with an analgesic component of effect. Carbamazepine is a medicine used to treat epilepsy. It can also be taken for nerve pain caused by diabetes

(peripheral neuropathy) or if you have a painful condition of the face called trigeminal neuralgia. Carbamazepine is occasionally used to treat bipolar disorder when other medicines have not worked.

Hence, the correct option is (A).

97. Amitriptyline is a non-opioid agent is an antidepressant with analgesic activity. Amitriptyline is a type of drug called a tricyclic antidepressant. These drugs were originally developed to treat anxiety and depression, but when taken at a low dose they can reduce or stop the pain. Amitriptyline works by increasing the amount of serotonin your brain makes.

Hence, the correct option is (D).

98. Tramadol is an opioid agent. Tramadol is a centrally-acting μ-opioid receptor agonist and SNRI (serotonin/norepinephrine reuptake-inhibitor) that is structurally related to codeine and morphine. Tramadol binds weakly to κ- and δ-opioid receptors and to the μ-opioid receptor with 6000-fold less affinity than morphine.

Hence, the correct option is (B).

99. Most antipsychotic drugs strongly block postsynaptic D-2 receptors. Unfortunately, when typical antipsychotics are administered, all D2 receptors are blocked, including those in areas of the brain involved in the fine-tuning of motor movement (namely, the basal ganglia and cerebellum).

Hence, the correct option is (A).

100. Hyperprolactinemia is caused by a blockade of dopamine in the pituitary. Dopamine binds to the dopamine D2 receptors on the surface of the lactotroph, which diminish intracellular cyclic AMP (cAMP), consequently decreasing prolactin secretion. Any factor disrupting the delivery of dopamine to the anterior pituitary or disturbing signal transduction may result in hyperprolactinemia.

Hence, the correct option is (B).

101. Parkinsonian symptoms and tarditive dyskinesia are caused by the blockade of dopamine in the nigrostriatal system. However, since levodopa is intermittently taken over the course of a day, the level of dopamine will rise and fall. These dopamine level fluctuations, in combination with the loss of dopaminergic neurons, are thought to cause dyskinesia.

Hence, the correct option is (A).

102. Extrapyramidal reactions can be treated by Benztropine mesylate. Benztropine is FDA-approved as adjunctive therapy for all forms of parkinsonism. It is also used for drug-induced extrapyramidal symptoms and the prevention of dystonic reactions as well as an acute treatment of dystonic reactions.

Hence, the correct option is (B).

103. Lithium carbonate is useful in the treatment of the bipolar disorder. Lithium (Eskalith, Lithobid) is one of the most widely used and studied medications for treating bipolar disorder. Lithium helps reduce the severity and frequency of mania. It may also help relieve or prevent bipolar depression. Studies show that lithium can significantly reduce suicide risk.

Hence, the correct option is (B).

104. Amitriptyline agent is related to tricyclic antidepressants. In addition to antiepileptic drugs, tricyclic antidepressant drugs like amitriptyline are also used as adjunct analgesics in the treatment of neuropathic pain. Amitriptyline was also available under the brand name Endep, but the Food and Drug Administration (FDA) has discontinued these brands. Amitriptyline is still available under its generic name. It belongs to the wider class of drugs called tricyclic antidepressants.

Hence, the correct option is (B).

105. Fluoxetine antidepressant is a selective serotonin reuptake inhibitor. Fluoxetine is a type of antidepressant known as an SSRI (selective serotonin reuptake inhibitor). It is often used to treat depression, and also sometimes obsessive-compulsive disorder and bulimia. Fluoxetine helps many people recover from depression, and it has fewer unwanted effects than older antidepressants.

Hence, the correct option is (D).

106. The therapeutic response to antidepressant drugs is usually over a period of 2-3 weeks. Many antidepressants take between 1 to 3 weeks to start working. It can take even longer before they reach maximum efficacy. Most symptoms associated with depression lack interest in things that were once enjoyable and feelings of hopelessness and sadness will eventually improve with antidepressant treatment.

Hence, the correct option is (B).

107. Protriptyline is a tricyclic and heterocyclic agent that has the least sedation. Protriptyline is used to treat depression. Protriptyline is in a class of medications called tricyclic antidepressants. It works by increasing the amounts of certain natural substances in the brain that help maintains mental balance.

Hence, the correct option is (A).

108. Anxiolytics are used to treat neurosis. Anxiolytics may be used in the neuroses and as adjuncts in other disorders (ex. depression) with a strong anxiety component. Neuroleptics, in very low dosage, are indicated for psychotic anxiety. Dosage, side effects, and duration of treatment must be monitored continuously.

Hence, the correct option is (A).

109. The mechanism of hypnotic benzodiazepine action is increasing the frequency of Cl-channel opening events. Benzodiazepines produce their effects by enhancing the binding of GABA to its receptor. GABA activates the chloride ion channel, allowing chloride ions to enter the neuron. The flow of chloride ions into the neuron hyperpolarizes and inhibits the neuron.

Hence, the correct option is (C).

110. Buspirone anxiolytic has minimal abuse liability. Buspirone differs from typical benzodiazepine anxiolytics in that it does not exert anticonvulsant or muscle relaxant effects. It also lacks the prominent sedative effect that is associated with more typical anxiolytics.

Hence, the correct option is (B).

111. Caffeine does not cause inhibition of gastric secretion. We hypothesized that caffeine evokes effects on GAS by activation of oral and gastric TAS2Rs and demonstrate that caffeine, when administered encapsulated, stimulates GAS, whereas oral administration of a caffeine solution delays GAS in healthy human subjects.

Hence, the correct option is (A).

112. Therapeutic uses of caffeine include cardiovascular collapse and respiratory insufficiency, migraine and somnolence except for gastric ulceration. Caffeine is used to restore mental alertness or wakefulness during fatigue or drowsiness. Caffeine is also found in some headache and migraine medications, in certain dietary supplements used for weight loss, and in many popular energy drinks.

Hence, the correct option is (D).

113. Respiratory and cardiac analeptics are cordiamine, caffeine and camphor except for bemegride. The term analeptics refers to convulsants and respiratory stimulants (i.e. central nervous system stimulants). They comprise a reverse group of agents (for example amphifinazole and doxapram (respiratory stimulants) and strychnine, bicuculline and picrotoxin). Analeptics are mainly experimental drugs.

Hence, the correct option is (B).

114. The function of bemegride is that it stimulates the medullar respiratory center (central effect). Bemegride is a CNS stimulant that is used to induce convulsions in experimental animals. It has also been used as a respiratory stimulant and in the treatment of barbiturate overdose.

Hence, the correct option is (A).

115. The value of the Ebullioscopic constant or boiling point elevation constant depends on the nature of the solvent. Ebullioscopic constant or Molal elevation constant is the elevation in the boiling point produced when one mole of the solute is dissolved in one kilogram of solvent. Its unit is K kg mol^{-1}.

Hence, the correct option is (D).

116. Du Nouy ring method is used for viscosity determination. Du Nouy's method utilizes the interaction of a platinum ring with the surface of the liquid. The ring is submerged below the interface by moving the stage where the liquid container is placed. After immersion, the stage is gradually lowered, and the ring pulls up the meniscus of the liquid.

Hence, the correct option is (B).

117. During the saponification process, fat on hydrolysis will yield glycerol and soap. The process in which a triacylglyceride is reacted with an aqueous hydroxide ion to form a mixture of glycerol and fatty acid salts (soaps). The reaction mechanism follows the nucleophilic carbonyl substitution pathway. Saponification is the hydrolysis of an ester under acidic or basic conditions to form an alcohol and the salt of a carboxylic acid. Saponification is commonly used to refer to the reaction of a metallic alkali (base) with a fat or oil to form soap. Example:

Ethanoic acid reacts with alcohols in the presence of a conc. sulphuric acid to form esters.

Hence, the correct option is (A).

118. The colour change is due to the ionisation of the acid-base indicators in Ostwald theory. The unionised form has a different colour than the ionised form. The ionisation of the indicator is largely affected in acids and bases as it is either a weak acid or a weak base.

Hence, the correct option is (A).

119. The liver is the major site for purine nucleotide synthesis. Purine synthesis occurs in all tissues. The major site of purine synthesis is in the liver and, to a limited extent, in the brain. Substrates:

- Ribose-5-phosphate
- Glycine
- Glutamine
- H_2O
- ATP
- CO_2
- Aspartate

Hence, the correct option is (B).

120. The Golden Rice variety is rich in Beta-carotene and ferritin. It is also known as Oryza sativa. It is developed to produce nutrient-dense staple crops which can reduce malnutrition in developing countries. It has been modified by using a gene from maize and a gene of bacteria that allows biosynthesis of beta-carotene in the rice.

Hence, the correct option is (B).

121. The approximate size of the bacterial cell is 0.5 to 1.0 micrometer in diameter. An average coccus is about 0.5-1.0 micrometer (µm) in diameter. An average-size bacterium such as the rod-shaped Escherichia coli, a normal inhabitant of the intestinal tract of humans and animals is about 2 micrometers (µm; millionths of a metre) long and 0.5 µm in diameter, and the spherical cells of Staphylococcus aureus are up to 1 µm in diameter.

Hence, the correct option is (B).

122. Grossly, the brain discloses an exudate of PMN's and fibrin which opacifies the arachnoid and gives a creamy or white appearance, usually over the convexities as well as the base of the brain. Exudate is a fluid emitted by an organism through pores or a wound, a process known as exuding or exudation. An exudate is any fluid that filters from the circulatory system into lesions or areas of inflammation. It can be a pus-like or clear fluid. When an injury occurs, leaving skin exposed, it leaks out of the blood vessels and into nearby tissues.

Hence, the correct option is (C).

123. The major difference between facilitated & passive diffusion is carrier-mediated transport. Passive diffusion has passive transport of small non-polar molecules across the plasma membrane. Facilitated diffusion has passive transport of glucose and ions into and out of the cell. This is accomplished by a carrier protein, which actually changes shape in the process.

Hence, the correct option is (A).

124. Haloperidol is indicated in agitation and restlessness in the elderly, despite the high incidence of extrapyramidal side effects. Haloperidol is an antipsychotic. The mechanism of action of haloperidol for the treatment of schizophrenia is unclear. However, its efficacy could be mediated through its activity as an antagonist at central dopamine type 2 receptors.

Hence, the correct option is (C).

125. In cell division cytoplasmic division is known as Cytokinesis. The cleavage furrow continues to squeeze the two cells apart until they finally separate in a process called cytokinesis. Cytokinesis occurs at the end of telophase, and some even consider cytokinesis to be a part of telophase. Two new cells are now formed.

Hence, the correct option is (D).

Pharmaceutical Chemistry

Q.1 Anhydrous calcium chloride acts as __________.
A. Dehydrating agent **B.** Drug
C. Oxidant **D.** Mordant

Q.2 Aqua regia is a mixture of __________.
A. HCL and H_2SO_4 **B.** HCL and HNO_3
C. HCL and HBR **D.** HCL and HF

Q.3 During dehydration, the substance that is usually lost by the body is:
A. Sugar **B.** Sodium chloride
C. Calcium phosphate **D.** Potassium chloride

Q.4 Styrene is made up of the elements, hydrogen:
A. Sulphur **B.** Carbon **C.** Oxygen **D.** Nitrogen

Q.5 Sodium bicarbonate is used as __________.
A. An effective antacid
B. Inhalants
C. Calcium accumulation
D. Systemic laxative

Q.6 A gas used for fumigation is:
A. Ethylene **B.** Nitrogen Oxide
C. Sulphur dioxide **D.** Oxygen

Q.7 Alum is commonly used as __________.
A. Anti-infective **B.** Astringent
C. Protective **D.** All of these

Q.8 Dry ice is a solid form of:
A. Carbon dioxide **B.** Oxygen
C. Helum **D.** None of these

Q.9 Iodine is more soluble in __________.
A. Water **B.** Alcohol
C. Chloroform **D.** None of these

Q.10 Zinc chloride is used as:
A. Antibacterial **B.** Astringent
C. Preservative **D.** None of these

Q.11 Which one of these is a major cation in intracellular fluid?
A. Potassium **B.** Sodium
C. Magnesium **D.** Calcium

Q.12 Epsom salt is __________.
A. Sodium sulphinte
B. Magnesium sulphate
C. Potassium Sulphate
D. None of these

Q.13 Baking soda is a common name of:
A. Sodium carbonate
B. Sodium bicarbonate
C. Potassium carbonate
D. Sodium citrate

Q.14 A molecule that has an equal number of positive and negative charges:
A. Isometric **B.** Isoelectric
C. Isobaric **D.** Isotonic

Q.15 A saturated fatty acid with four carbon atoms is known as:
A. Acetic acid **B.** Buytric acid
C. Valeric acid **D.** Propionic acid

Q.16 The citric acid is used in iron limit test:
A. To prevent color due to sulphate.
B. To prevent color due to copper.
C. To prevent color due to chloride.
D. To prevent color due to lead.

Q.17 The barium meal is:
A. Barium chloride **B.** Barium nitrate
C. Barium carbonate **D.** Barium sulphate

Q.18 Which is used as styptic?
A. Zinc oxide **B.** $KMNO_4$
C. Sodium sulphate **D.** Alum

Q.19 Sulpha drugs are titrated by which type of titration?
A. Diazotization titration
B. Redox titration
C. Non-aqueous titration
D. Acid base titration

Q.20 Ciprofloxacin is a:
A. Quinolone **B.** Azole Qunoloine
C. Isoquinoline drug **D.** Quiniclidine drug

Q.21 Calamine is:
A. Basis zinc oxide
B. Basic zinc sulphide
C. Basic zinc carbonate
D. Basic zinc hydroxide

Q.22 Acetylsalicylic acid is:
A. Sulindac **B.** Aspirin
C. Mefenamic acid **D.** Acridine

Q.23 Ocuserts are:
A. Ear preparations **B.** Nasal preparations
C. Oral preparations **D.** Eye preparations

Q.24 The antifungal drug, fluconazole belongs to the class:
A. Pyridine **B.** Azoles
C. Pyrimidines **D.** Acridines

Q.25 Chemically heroin is:
A. 6-Methyl morphine
B. 3,6-Dimethyl morphine
C. 3-Methyl morphine
D. Ethyl morphine

Q.26 Which drug is used for the detection of boric acid?
A. Turmeric
B. Benzoin
C. Myrrh
D. Tolu balsm

Q.27 The chemical name of Plaster of Paris is:
A. Magnesium sulphate
B. Calcium carbonate
C. Magnesium carbonate
D. Calcium sulphate

Q.28 Dimethicone is the other name of:
A. Titanium dioxide
B. Calamine
C. Zinc stearate
D. Polydimethylsiloxane

Q.29 Abrasive agent used in dentifrices:
A. Sodium fluoride
B. Selenium sulphide
C. Zinc sulphate
D. Calcium carbonate

Q.30 An opaque covering agent used in bleaches:
A. Catechol
B. Quinoline
C. Titanium dioxide
D. Hydrogen peroxide

Q.31 What is the chemical formula of Acetic Acid?
A. $CH_3\text{-}(CH_2)_{14}\text{-}COOH$
B. CH_3COOH
C. $CH_3\text{-}(CH_2)_{16}\text{-}COOH$
D. $CH_3\text{-}(CH_2)_2\text{-}COOH$

Q.32 Ringer's injection contains:
A. 10% Fructose and 0.9% sodium chloride.
B. 15% Mannitol and 0.45% sodium chloride.
C. 0.9% Sodium chloride and 0.245% lactic acid.
D. 0.86% Sodium chloride, 0.03% potassium chloride and 0.033% calcium chloride.

Q.33 Calcium gluconate can be assayed by:
A. Acid-base titration
B. Precipitation titration
C. Complexometric titration
D. Redox titration

Q.34 Which one of the following drug is a saline cathartic?
A. Magnesium sulphate
B. Magnesium trisilicate
C. Magnesium carbonate
D. Bismuth subcarbonate

Q.35 Calamine is:
A. Zinc oxide with a small proportion of titanium dioxide.
B. Silicone polymer.
C. Zinc oxide with zince stearate.
D. Zinc oxide with a small proportion of ferric oxide.

Q.36 Which of the compounds listed below contains a free aromatic amino group?
A. Phthalyl sulphathiazole
B. Sulfacetamide
C. Succinlyl sulphathiazole
D. Solapsone

Q.37 Sodium content is determined by:
A. Flame photometer
B. Complexometric method
C. Mass spectroscopic method
D. UV spectroscopic method

Q.38 Radioactivity can be detected by use of:
A. Geiger-Mueller counter
B. X-ray machine
C. Coulter Counter method
D. XRD

Pharmaceutics

Q.39 A disposable syringe made up of:
A. Polypropylene
B. Transparent polystyrene
C. Glass
D. Poly tetra chloro ethylene

Q.40 No diffusion takes place in:
A. Molecular dispersion
B. Colloidal dispersion
C. Coarse dispersion
D. None of these

Q.41 Osmosis cannot formed when particles are in __________.
A. Equilibrium state
B. Random state
C. Both (A) and (B)
D. None of these

Q.42 Microscopic particles can be separated by:
A. Ultra filtration
B. Filtration
C. Dialysis
D. All of these

Q.43 Colloids are:
A. Can't be observed by ordinary microscope.
B. Detected under ultramicroscope.
C. Both (A) and (B)
D. None of these

Q.44 Colloids can pass through:
A. Filter paper
B. Semi-permeable membrane
C. Both (A) and (B)
D. None of these

Q.45 Colloids can't pass through:
A. Filter paper
B. Semi-permeable membrane
C. Both (A) and (B)
D. None of these

Q.46 Diffusion of colloids is:
A. Very slow
B. Slow
C. Fast
D. Very fast

Q.47 Cheese is an example of:
A. Molecular dispersion
B. Colloidal dispersion
C. Coarse dispersion
D. All of these

Q.48 The drug is bound to a resin and released due to changes in pH is:
A. Matrix dissolution
B. Osmotic pump
C. Ion exchange
D. Matrix diffusion

Q.49 An example of colloidal dispersion:
A. Cheese
B. Milk
C. Synthetic polymers
D. All of these

Q.50 Scattering of light from colloidal particles is _____________.
A. Faraday-Tyndall effect
B. Van't hoff factor
C. Van't hoff dispersion
D. None of these

Q.51 Faraday Tyndall effect is observed by _________.
A. Light microscopy
B. Ultramicroscope
C. Radiography
D. None of these

Q.52 Who invented the ultramicroscope?
A. Zsigmonday
B. Faraday
C. Tyndall
D. Ohm

Q.53 As a result of the Tyndall effect, __________.
A. Dark spots
B. Bright spots are formed
C. Both (A) and (B)
D. None of these

Q.54 The process in which dispersed phase is mix in a suitable solvent process is known as:
A. Solvation
B. Dehydration
C. Hydration
D. All of these

Q.55 The instrument which is use to reduce the particle size is called __________.
A. Size reduction
B. Milling
C. Mold
D. All of these

Q.56 The process in which we converted coarse particles into colloidal it is called:
A. Milling
B. Size reduction
C. Size oxidation
D. None of these

Q.57 Any type of chemical compound that possesses two distinct regions that are hydrophilic and hydrophobic portion within same molecule is called:
A. Amphiphilic
B. Electrophyle
C. Both (A) and (B)
D. None of these

Q.58 Amphiphilic are also called:
A. Association colloidal
B. Surface active agents
C. Amphipathics
D. All of these

Q.59 Inter phase is composed of:
A. Water phase
B. Air phase
C. Both (A) and (B)
D. None of these

Q.60 Chemica adsorption is:
A. Reversible
B. Irreversible
C. Mostly reversible
D. Some-times irreversible

Q.61 The large phase is called:
A. Inter phase
B. Bulk phase
C. Both (A) and (B)
D. None of these

Q.62 The point at which bulk phase and air, water inter phase become saturated is called:
A. CMC
B. Bulk phase
C. Inter phase
D. None of these

Q.63 It is an aggregation of surfactant molecules in a colloidal liquid then it is called:
A. CMC
B. Micelles
C. Aggregation number
D. None of these

Q.64 Dispersed phase and dispersion medium of smoke are:
A. Solid and liquid
B. Liquid and liquid
C. Solid and gas
D. Gas and gas

Q.65 The process introduces small, highly charged molecules into the water to destabilize the charges on particles, colloids, or oily materials in suspension is known as:
A. Brownian motion
B. Faraday-Tyndal effect
C. Coagulation
D. Electrophoresis

Q.66 Adsorption is the process of:
A. Repulsion
B. Addition
C. Adhesion
D. None of these

Q.67 Surface on which ions, atoms or molecules accumulate:
A. Adsorbent
B. Adsorbate
C. Specific surface
D. All of these

Q.68 Adsorbate are ions, atoms or molecules:
A. Which allow accumulation on their surface
B. Which accumulate on a specific surface
C. Which don't accumulate
D. Both (A) and (B)

Q.69 If both adsorption & absorption are going side by side then it is:

A. Disorption
B. Desorption
C. Sorption
D. Resorption

Q.70 The reverse of adsorption is called:
A. Disorption
B. Desorption
C. Sorption
D. Resorption

Q.71 Vander-wall adsorption is synonym of:
A. Physical adsorption
B. Chemical adsorption
C. Physisorption
D. Both (A) and (C)

Q.72 Physisorption is affected by:
A. Temperature only
B. Pressure only
C. Temperature and pressure
D. None of these

Q.73 Strong bonding is present in:
A. Chemical adsorption
B. Physical adsorption
C. Vander-wall adsorption
D. Both (A) and (C)

Q.74 Absorption is __________ phenomenon.
A. Bulk
B. Surface
C. Phase difference
D. Bulk & phase

Q.75 Adsorption has:
A. Uniformity
B. Non-uniformity
C. Bulk uniformity
D. None of these

Q.76 Chemical adsorption involves __________ bonding.
A. Hydrogen
B. Ionic
C. Covalent
D. Ionic & covalent

Pharmacognosy

Q.77 Transverse ridges are seen on the outer surface of liquorice:
A. Stolon
B. Rhizome
C. Root
D. Stem

Q.78 Bufadienolides are present in:
A. Digitalis
B. Squill
C. Strophanthus
D. Thevetia

Q.79 Digitalis leaves are dried:
A. Under shade
B. At a temperature of about 60 °C
C. In sunlight
D. At a temperature of about 100 °C

Q.80 The margin of digitalis leaf is:
A. Entire
B. Serrate
C. Lobed
D. Crenate or dentate

Q.81 Prisms of calcium oxalate crystals are present in:
A. Digitalis lanata
B. Digitalis purpurea
C. Digitalis thapsi
D. Digitalis lutea

Q.82 The cardiac glycoside on hydrolysis gives → digitoxigenin + Glucose-acetyl digitoxose(digitoxose)2 the glycoside is:
A. Purpurea glycoside A
B. Lanatoside A
C. Purpurea glycoside C
D. Lanatoside C

Q.83 Leaves of Digitalis lanata are:
A. Petiolate
B. Cordate
C. Ovate-lanceolate
D. Sessile

Q.84 Cardiac glycoside are present in:
A. Rhubarb
B. Calotropis
C. Trigonella
D. Costus

Q.85 Oubain, a cardiac glycoside is present in:
A. Nerium
B. Thevetia
C. Strophanthus
D. Convollaria

Q.86 Deoxy-sugars are generally found attached with:
A. Flavonoids
B. Anthraquinones
C. Cardiac glycosides
D. Biflavonoids

Pharmacology

Q.87 Which of the following abused drugs do not belong to sedative agents?
A. Barbiturates
B. Tranquilizers
C. Cannabinoids
D. Opioids

Q.88 Which of the following agents is related to hallucinogens?
A. Heroin
B. LSD
C. Cocaine
D. Opium

Q.89 Inhaled anesthetics and intravenous agents having general anesthetic properties:
A. Directly activate GABA-A receptors.
B. Facilitate GABA action but have no direct action on GABA-A receptors.
C. Reduce the excitatory glutamatergic neurotransmission.
D. Increase the duration of opening of nicotine-activated potassium channels.

Q.90 Find out the anesthetic, which is an inhibitor of NMDA glutamate receptors:
A. Thiopental
B. Halothane
C. Ketamine
D. Sevoflurane

Q.91 Which of the following general anesthetics belongs to inhalants?
A. Thiopental
B. Desflurane
C. Ketamine
D. Propofol

Q.92 Find out the anesthetic, which is used intravenously:
A. Propofol
B. Halothane
C. Desflurane
D. Nitrous oxide

Q.93 Which of the following inhalants is a gas anesthetic?
A. Halothane
B. Isoflurane
C. Nitrous oxide
D. All of these

Q.94 Which of the following inhaled anesthetics can produce hepatic necrosis?

A. Soveflurane
B. Desflurane
C. Halothane
D. Nitrous oxide

Q.95 Find out the inhaled anesthetic, which may cause nephrotoxicity:

A. Halothane
B. Sevoflurane
C. Nitrous oxide
D. Diethyl ether

Q.96 Gastric acid secretion is under the control of the following agents except:

A. Histamine
B. Acetylcholine
C. Serotonin
D. Gastrin

Q.97 Find out the drug belonging to proton pump inhibitors:

A. Pirenzepine
B. Ranitidine
C. Omeprazole
D. Trimethaphan

Q.98 All of the following agents intensify the secretion of gastric glands except:

A. Pepsin
B. Gastrin
C. Histamine
D. Carbonate mineral waters

Q.99 Find out the mechanism of metoclopramide antiemetic action:

A. H-1 and H-2 receptor blocking effect
B. M-cholinoreceptor stimulating effect
C. D_2 dopamine and 5-HT_3 serotonin receptor blocking effect
D. M-cholinoblocking effect

Q.100 Pernicious anemia is developed due to deficiency of:

A. Erythropoetin
B. Vitamin B12
C. Iron
D. Vitamin B6

Q.101 Find out the drug used for pernicious anemia:

A. Ferrous lactate
B. Cyanocobalamin
C. Iron dextran
D. Ferrous gluconate

Q.102 An adverse effect of oral iron therapy is:

A. Anemia
B. Thrombocytopenia
C. Headache
D. Constipation

Q.103 Find out the drug used as an oral anticoagulant:

A. Heparin
B. Daltreparin
C. Warfarin
D. Enoxaparin

Q.104 Which of the following drugs is fibrinolytic?

A. Ticlopidine
B. Streptokinase
C. Aspirin
D. Warfarin

Q.105 All of the following are recommended at the initial stages of treating patients with heart failure except:

A. Reduced salt intake
B. Verapamil
C. ACE inhibitors
D. Diuretics

Q.106 All of the following agents belong to cardiac glycosides except:

A. Digoxin
B. Strophantin K

C. Amrinone
D. Digitoxin

Q.107 The non-glycoside positive inotropic drug is:

A. Digoxin
B. Strophantin K
C. Dobutamine
D. Digitoxin

Q.108 Aglycone is essential for:

A. Plasma protein binding
B. Half-life
C. Cardiotonic action
D. Metabolism

Q.109 Find out the derivative of the plant Foxglove (Digitalis):

A. Digoxin
B. Strophantin K
C. Dobutamine
D. Amrinone

Q.110 For digitalis-induced arrhythmias the following drug is favoured:

A. Verapamil
B. Amiodarone
C. Lidocaine
D. Propanolol

Q.111 This drug is used in treating supraventricular tachycardias:

A. Digoxin
B. Dobutamine
C. Amrinone
D. Dopamine

Q.112 This drug is associated with Torsades de pointes:

A. Flecainide
B. Sotalol
C. Lidocaine
D. Verapamil

Q.113 This drug has a little or no direct effect on chronotropy and dromotropy at normal doses:

A. Nifedipine
B. Diltiazem
C. Verapamil
D. All of these

Q.114 Find out the adverse reactions characteristic of lidocaine:

A. Agranulocytosis, leucopenia
B. Extrapyramidal disorders
C. Hypotension, paresthesias, convulsions
D. Bronchospasm, dyspepsia

Other Subjects

Q.115 Which of the following is not applicable for Landsberger-Walker method used for determination of molecular weight from boiling point elevation?

A. The solution should be dilute.
B. Air should be passed at low pressure.
C. It is applicable only for non-volatile solutes.
D. The solute should not undergo association or dissociation.

Q.116 SLS has an HLB of:

A. 10
B. 14
C. 40
D. 18

Q.117 Which among the following correctly defines Diastereomer?

A. These have same magnitude but different signs of optical rotation.
B. Nonsuperimposable object mirror relationship.
C. These differ in all physical properties.
D. Separation is very difficult.

Q.118 Substance that can be reversibly oxidized or reduced, having different distinct colour in the individual oxidized and reduced forms:

A. Redox indicators

B. Redox potential

C. Redox number

D. Redox state

Q.119 Nucleus contains __________ the repository of genetic information.

A. Ribosome

B. DNA

C. Cytosol

D. Vacuole

Q.120 The first transgenic cow was called:

A. Dolly

B. Rosie

C. Cumulina

D. Noah

Q.121 The greatest resolution in light microscopy can be obtained with __________.

A. Shortest wavelength of visible light used.

B. Longest wavelength of visible light used.

C. An objective with minimum numerical aperture.

D. Shortest wavelength of visible light used and an objective with the maximum numerical aperture.

Q.122 Which of the following is not a clinical manifestation of Bacterial Meningitis?

A. Head ache

B. Convulsions in adults

C. fever

D. If untreated, coma and death

Q.123 Which type of drug are absorbed by ion pair transport?

A. High lipophilicity

B. Oily droplets

C. Quaternary ammonium compounds

D. All of these

Q.124 __________ is contraindicated during pregnancy due to its Teratogenicity.

A. Folic acid

B. Calcium

C. Retinol

D. Iron

Q.125 __________ tissue cover the body surface and line the internal organs.

A. Muscular

B. Epithelial

C. Nervous

D. Connective

// Smart Answer Sheet //

| Correct | Percentage of students who answered correctly. | | Skipped | Percentage of students who skipped. |

Q.	Ans.	Correct / Skipped	Q.	Ans.	Correct / Skipped	Q.	Ans.	Correct / Skipped	Q.	Ans.	Correct / Skipped	Q.	Ans.	Correct / Skipped	Q.	Ans.	Correct / Skipped
1	A	50.86 % / 47.38 %	22	B	85.22 % / 13.16 %	43	B	62.93 % / 35.37 %	64	C	52.26 % / 35.93 %	85	C	62.27 % / 37.39 %	106	C	58.39 % / 31.13 %
2	B	41.93 % / 41.51 %	23	D	44.41 % / 44.99 %	44	A	82.91 % / 11.24 %	65	C	66.88 % / 32.88 %	86	C	44.31 % / 38.57 %	107	C	53.41 % / 34.16 %
3	B	43.4 % / 55.83 %	24	B	60.38 % / 39.5 %	45	B	57.48 % / 38.93 %	66	C	43.93 % / 49.96 %	87	C	41.18 % / 31.17 %	108	C	69.98 % / 30.02 %
4	B	50.98 % / 42.06 %	25	B	42.67 % / 50.48 %	46	A	54.04 % / 45.82 %	67	A	47.65 % / 42.89 %	88	B	64.05 % / 35.6 %	109	A	52.76 % / 40.87 %
5	A	76.38 % / 12.52 %	26	A	50.95 % / 48.23 %	47	B	69.58 % / 30.29 %	68	B	59.52 % / 38.79 %	89	A	46.87 % / 48.26 %	110	C	52.93 % / 45.82 %
6	C	53.02 % / 35.74 %	27	D	47.41 % / 46.19 %	48	C	40.34 % / 45.66 %	69	C	30.18 % / 68.03 %	90	C	66.33 % / 31.27 %	111	A	42.48 % / 47.32 %
7	B	40.4 % / 44.55 %	28	D	41.96 % / 30.38 %	49	D	69.8 % / 30.17 %	70	B	64.58 % / 32.83 %	91	B	67.11 % / 32.2 %	112	B	57.1 % / 30.6 %
8	A	41.34 % / 51.37 %	29	A	62.32 % / 35.93 %	50	A	54.79 % / 35.68 %	71	D	15.82 % / 83.45 %	92	A	52.43 % / 39.65 %	113	A	57.49 % / 35.44 %
9	B	58.91 % / 38.68 %	30	C	66.9 % / 30.15 %	51	B	57.93 % / 31.61 %	72	C	46.45 % / 50.38 %	93	D	46.55 % / 36.88 %	114	C	48.92 % / 33.21 %
10	C	58.37 % / 33.38 %	31	B	46.6 % / 39.58 %	52	A	61.56 % / 33.18 %	73	A	68.6 % / 31.05 %	94	C	41.5 % / 37.19 %	115	B	52.59 % / 34.48 %
11	A	63.25 % / 30.33 %	32	D	44.91 % / 51.7 %	53	B	58.81 % / 34.22 %	74	A	59.13 % / 37.0 %	95	B	57.26 % / 35.29 %	116	C	56.49 % / 41.5 %
12	B	53.24 % / 34.65 %	33	C	21.69 % / 73.03 %	54	A	61.88 % / 37.59 %	75	B	63.88 % / 35.42 %	96	C	62.85 % / 35.62 %	117	C	49.01 % / 50.89 %
13	B	76.81 % / 11.63 %	34	A	58.8 % / 36.35 %	55	B	64.7 % / 31.66 %	76	B	42.74 % / 33.08 %	97	C	61.32 % / 38.24 %	118	A	49.16 % / 36.13 %
14	B	66.6 % / 31.4 %	35	D	53.38 % / 43.75 %	56	B	53.28 % / 36.04 %	77	B	46.59 % / 39.76 %	98	A	51.04 % / 40.0 %	119	B	66.93 % / 30.73 %
15	B	49.9 % / 37.45 %	36	B	48.33 % / 48.21 %	57	A	66.81 % / 31.02 %	78	A	41.33 % / 39.54 %	99	C	46.49 % / 43.0 %	120	B	58.33 % / 35.71 %
16	B	65.6 % / 30.68 %	37	A	59.85 % / 30.19 %	58	D	68.46 % / 30.03 %	79	B	61.34 % / 35.49 %	100	B	41.54 % / 43.44 %	121	D	78.99 % / 14.47 %
17	D	44.16 % / 31.51 %	38	A	22.59 % / 67.1 %	59	C	50.86 % / 33.57 %	80	D	47.01 % / 41.44 %	101	B	50.69 % / 39.23 %	122	B	51.79 % / 45.17 %
18	D	68.37 % / 31.23 %	39	A	45.1 % / 38.85 %	60	B	77.01 % / 20.89 %	81	C	64.07 % / 35.53 %	102	D	52.46 % / 44.68 %	123	C	46.64 % / 49.89 %
19	A	41.88 % / 39.82 %	40	C	45.67 % / 43.74 %	61	B	48.66 % / 48.24 %	82	A	12.06 % / 75.72 %	103	C	47.22 % / 41.53 %	124	C	54.34 % / 31.61 %
20	A	59.65 % / 37.25 %	41	D	42.51 % / 46.68 %	62	A	40.95 % / 52.93 %	83	C	52.04 % / 40.66 %	104	B	44.79 % / 42.0 %	125	B	89.75 % / 10.03 %
21	A	55.03 % / 42.65 %	42	B	87.77 % / 12.12 %	63	B	40.9 % / 40.01 %	84	B	66.25 % / 30.27 %	105	B	50.22 % / 42.18 %			

//Hints and Solutions//

1. Anhydrous calcium chloride acts as a dehydrating agent. Calcium chloride is strongly hygroscopic (absorbs water from its surroundings), so it removes moisture from the air, making it dryer. Therefore, anhydrous calcium chloride is used as a dehydrating agent.

Hence, the correct option is (A).

2. Aqua regia is a mixture of HCL and HNO. Regal water (royal water) is a mixture of nitric acid and hydrochloric acid, optimally in a molar ratio of 1:3. Aqua regia is a yellow-orange (sometimes red) fuming liquid, so named by alchemists because it can dissolve the noble metals gold and platinum, though not all metals.

Hence, the correct option is (B).

3. During dehydration, the substance that is usually lost by the body is sodium chloride. Dehydration, loss of water from the body; it is almost invariably associated with some loss of salt (sodium chloride) as well. Dehydration means your body loses more fluids than you take in. If it's not treated, it can get worse and become a serious problem.

Hence, the correct option is (B).

4. Styrene is made up of the elements, hydrogen and carbon. Styrene is an organic compound with the chemical formula $C_6H_5CH=CH_2$. This derivative of benzene is a colorless oily liquid, although aged samples can appear yellowish. The compound evaporates easily and has a sweet smell, although high concentrations have a less pleasant odor. Styrene is the precursor to polystyrene and several copolymers.

Hence, the correct option is (B).

5. Sodium bicarbonate is used as an effective antacid. Sodium bicarbonate is an antacid used to relieve heartburn and acid indigestion. Your doctor also may prescribe sodium bicarbonate to make your blood or urine less acidic in certain conditions. Sodium bicarbonate, also known as baking soda, is used to relieve heartburn, sour stomach, or acid indigestion by neutralizing excess stomach acid. When used for this purpose, it is said to belong to the group of medicines called antacids.

Hence, the correct option is (A).

6. A gas used for fumigation is sulphur dioxide. Passive fumigation is the process that is applied weekly. After SO2 application in the room, fans should run at high speed for over 3 hours so that nearly all of the sulphur dioxide is absorbed by the fruit, packaging materials, and room surfaces. Fumigation is the process of gaseous sterilization, which kills microorganisms and prevents microbial growth in the air or on the surface of the wall or floor. For fumigation, use the chemicals or solutions like formaldehyde and potassium permanganate.

Hence, the correct option is (C).

7. Alum is commonly used as astringent. Potassium alum is used in medicine mainly as an astringent (or styptic) and antiseptic. Potassium and ammonium alum are the active ingredients in some antiperspirants and deodorants, acting by inhibiting the growth of the bacteria responsible for body odor.

Hence, the correct option is (B).

8. Dry ice is a solid form of carbon dioxide. Dry ice is actually solid, frozen carbon dioxide, which happens to sublimate, or turn to gas, at a chilly -78.5 °C (-109.3°F). The fog you see is actually a mixture of cold carbon dioxide gas and cold, humid air, created as the dry ice "melts". One of the most common uses for dry ice in the medical field is as a refrigerant. This ice is used to transport body parts, organs, and blood from one medical facility to another. Much colder than regular ice, dry ice is preferred over normal ice when transporting body parts.

Hence, the correct option is (A).

9. Iodine is more soluble in alcohol than in carbon tetrachloride because, in the endothermic process of dissolution, the energy factor opposes the dissolution. Less is the heat of dissolution, i.e., less is the opposing factor, greater is the solubility. Elemental iodine is slightly soluble in water, with one gram dissolving in 3450 ml at 20°C and 1280 ml at 50°C; potassium iodide may be added to increase solubility via the formation of triiodide ions, among other polyiodides.

Hence, the correct option is (B).

10. Zinc chloride is used as a preservative. Zinc chloride is used in dry cells as an electrolyte. Other uses:

- It is used as a condensing agent.
- Disinfecting purposes.
- Dehydrating agent.
- Wood preservative.
- Deodorant.
- Disinfectant.

Hence, the correct option is (C).

11. Potassium is a major cation in intracellular fluid. These electrolytes play an important role in maintaining homeostasis. Potassium is the most abundant exchangeable cation in the body. It exists predominantly in the intracellular fluid at concentrations of 140 to 150 meq/liter and in the extracellular fluid at concentrations of 3.5 to 5 meq/liter.

Hence, the correct option is (A).

12. Epsom salt is also known as magnesium sulphate. It's a chemical compound made up of magnesium, sulphur, and oxygen. It gets its name from the town of Epsom in Surrey, England, where it was originally discovered. Epsom salt is used to relax muscles and relieve pain in the shoulders, neck, back and skull. For example, by relaxing the muscles surrounding the skull, the magnesium in Epsom salt may help release a headache or migraine. Some researchers also think that magnesium is good for reducing inflammation in internal organs.

Hence, the correct option is (B).

13. Baking soda is a common name for sodium bicarbonate. Sodium hydrogen carbonate, commonly known as baking soda or bicarbonate of soda, is a chemical compound with the formula $NaHCO_3$. It is a salt composed of a sodium cation (Na^+) and a

bicarbonate anion (HCO_3). Medikarb is a pharma grade sodium bicarbonate used as an active pharma ingredient or as an excipient in pharmaceutical formulations to execute processes including pH adjustment. It is also widely used as a buffering agent in antacids, dialysis solutions and effervescent tablets.

Hence, the correct option is (B).

14. A molecule that has an equal number of positive and negative charges is isoelectric. The isoelectric point (pI, pH(I), IEP), is the pH at which a molecule carries no net electrical charge or is electrically neutral in the statistical mean. The standard nomenclature to represent the isoelectric point is pH(I). However, pI is also used.

Hence, the correct option is (B).

15. A saturated fatty acid with four carbon atoms is known as butyric acid. Butyric Acid is a saturated short-chain fatty acid with a 4-carbon backbone. Butyric acid is commonly found in esterified form in animal fats and plant oils. Butyric acid is a straight-chain saturated fatty acid that is butane in which one of the terminal methyl groups has been oxidized to a carboxy group.

Hence, the correct option is (B).

16. Citric acid is used in the iron limit test to prevent color due to copper. Iron-free citric acid is used in the limit test for iron. The citric acid acts as a chelating agent bind with iron and forms a soluble complex with the iron. Citric acid also prevents the formation of ferrous hydroxide due to precipitation by ammonia.

Hence, the correct option is (B).

17. The barium meal is barium sulphate. Barium tests are used to examine the digestive tract using a white powder called barium sulphate. This powder can be seen on x-rays. For a barium swallow or barium meal, the barium sulphate powder is mixed with water (and sometimes flavouring) then swallowed. X-rays are taken as you swallow the mixture.

Hence, the correct option is (D).

18. Alum is used as a styptic. A styptic or hemostatic pencil is a short stick of medication, usually anhydrous aluminum sulphate (a type of alum) or titanium dioxide, which is used for staunching blood by causing blood vessels to contract at the site of the wound. An alum is a type of chemical compound, usually a hydrated double sulfate salt of aluminium with the general formula $X\,Al(SO_4)_2 \cdot 12\,H_2O$, where X is a monovalent cation such as potassium or ammonium. By itself, "alum" often refers to potassium alum, with the formula $KAl(SO_4)_2 \cdot 12\,H_2O$. Other alums are named after the monovalent ion, such as sodium alum and ammonium alum.

Hence, the correct option is (D).

19. Sulpha drugs are titrated by diazotization titration. The diazotization titration is nothing but the conversion of the primary aromatic amine to a diazonium compound. In this method, the primary aromatic amine is reacted with the sodium nitrite in an acidic medium to form a diazonium salt. This method is first used in the determination of dyes. It is used determination of alpha drug, sulphanilamide, chlorophenol, procaine, etc.

Hence, the correct option is (A).

20. Ciprofloxacin is a quinolone. Quinolone is a heterocyclic aromatic organic compound with the chemical formula C_9H_7N. It is a colorless hygroscopic liquid with a strong odor. Aged samples, especially if exposed to light, become yellow and later brown. Ciprofloxacin is a quinolone that is quinolin-4(1H)-one bearing cyclopropyl, carboxylic acid, fluoro and piperazine-1-yl substituents at positions 1, 3, 6 and 7, respectively. It has a role as an anti-infective agent, a topoisomerase IV inhibitor, an antibacterial drug, an EC 5.99.

Hence, the correct option is (A).

21. Calamine is basis zinc oxide. Calamine is a combination of zinc oxide and 0.5% ferric oxide (Fe_2O_3). The lotion is produced with additional ingredients such as phenol and calcium hydroxide. The use of calamine lotion dates back as far as 1500 BC.

Hence, the correct option is (A).

22. Acetylsalicylic acid is aspirin. Acetylsalicylic acid (ASA), also known as aspirin, acts by irreversibly inhibiting the platelet cyclooxygenase (COX) enzyme, resulting in inhibition of platelet thromboxane A2 (TXA-2) synthesis. Acetylsalicylic acid (ASA) is a commonly used drug for the treatment of pain and fever due to various causes. Acetylsalicylic acid has both anti-inflammatory and antipyretic effects.

Hence, the correct option is (B).

23. Ocuserts are eye preparations. Ocular inserts (Ocusert) are sterile preparation prolong the residence time of drug with a controlled release manner and negligible or less affected by nasolacrimal drainage. It shows diffusion-controlled release. It consists of a central reservoir of drug enclosed in. specially designed microporous membrane.

Hence, the correct option is (D).

24. The antifungal drug, fluconazole belongs to the class azoles. Fluconazole is used to prevent and treat a variety of fungal and yeast infections. It belongs to a class of drugs called azole antifungals. It works by stopping the growth of certain types of fungus.

Hence, the correct option is (B).

25. Chemically heroin is 3,6-Dimethyl morphine. Heroin is a crude preparation of diamorphine. It is a semisynthetic product obtained by acetylation of morphine, which occurs as a natural product in opium. Opium is the dried latex of certain poppy species (e.g. Papaver somniferum L.). Diamorphine is a narcotic analgesic used in the treatment of severe pain.

Hence, the correct option is (B).

26. Turmeric drug is used for the detection of boric acid. Taken orally, turmeric is used as a treatment for indigestion (dyspepsia), abdominal pain, hemorrhage, diarrhea, flatulence, abdominal bloating, loss of appetite, jaundice, hepatitis, and liver disease, gallbladder complaints, headaches, bronchitis, colds, respiratory infections, fibromyalgia, leprosy, fever.

Hence, the correct option is (A).

27. The chemical name of Plaster of Paris is calcium sulphate. The compound Plaster of Paris is prepared by heating gypsum at 120°C forms a quick-setting paste with water and is used in medicine chiefly in casts and for surgical bandages. The chemical formula for the Plaster of Paris is $(CaSO_4).1/2H_2O$ and is better known as calcium sulphate hemihydrate. Plaster of Paris is a chemical compound consisting of fine white powder, which hardens when exposed to moisture and allowed to dry.

Hence, the correct option is (D).

28. Dimethicone is the other name of polydimethylsiloxane. Polydimethylsiloxane (PDMS), also known as dimethylpolysiloxane or dimethicone, belongs to a group of polymeric organosilicon compounds that are commonly referred to as silicones. PDMS is the most widely used silicon-based organic polymer, as its versatility and properties lead to many applications.

Hence, the correct option is (D).

29. The abrasive agent used in dentifrices is sodium fluoride. Phosphates, carbonates, and silicas are the most common abrasives incorporated in dentifrices. Phosphates give the teeth a clean and white appearance. Dicalcium phosphate dihydrate and calcium pyrophosphates are commonly used. Sodium fluoride (NaF) is an inorganic compound with the formula NaF. It is used in trace amounts in the fluoridation of drinking water, in toothpaste, in metallurgy, and as a flux, and is also used in pesticides and rat poison.

Hence, the correct option is (A).

30. An opaque covering agent used in bleaches is titanium dioxide. Titanium dioxide, also called titania, (TiO_2), is a white, opaque, naturally occurring mineral existing in a number of crystalline forms, the most important of which are rutile and anatase. These naturally occurring oxide forms can be mined and serve as a source for commercial titanium. Titanium dioxide is odourless and absorbent. Its most important function in powder form is as a widely used pigment for lending whiteness and opacity.

Hence, the correct option is (C).

31. Acetic acid, systematically named ethanoic acid, is an acidic, colourless liquid and organic compound with the chemical formula CH_3COOH (also written as CH_3CO_2H, $C_2H_4O_2$, or $HC_2H_3O_2$).

Hence, the correct option is (B).

32. Ringer's injection contains 0.86% Sodium chloride, 0.03% potassium chloride and 0.033% calcium chloride. Lactated Ringer's Injection USP is sterile, non-pyrogenic and contains no bacteriostatic or antimicrobial agents. Each 100 mL of Lactated Ringer's Injection USP contains:

- Sodium Chloride USP 0.6 g
- Sodium Lactate 0.31 g
- Potassium Chloride USP 0.03 g
- Calcium Chloride Dihydrate USP 0.02 g

Hence, the correct option is (D).

33. Calcium gluconate can be assayed by complexometric titration. Calcium gluconate is a medication used to manage hypocalcemia, cardiac arrest, and cardiotoxicity due to hyperkalemia or hypermagnesemia. It is classified as a calcium salt.

Complexometric titration: Classification, metal ion indicators, masking and demasking reagents, estimation of Magnesium sulphate, and calcium gluconate. Complexometric titration is important for metals and their salts, certain anions and indirectly some drugs.

Hence, the correct option is (C).

34. Magnesium sulphate drug is a saline cathartic. Magnesium sulphate, or Epsom salt, is a common osmotic cathartic and is used in 6% isotonic solution. Other magnesium-containing cathartics include magnesium hydroxide (milk of magnesia), magnesium oxide, and magnesium citrate. Saline cathartics or purgatives are agents that quicken and increase evacuation from the bowl. Laxatives are mild cathartics.

Hence, the correct option is (A).

35. Calamine is a zinc oxide with a small proportion of ferric oxide. Calamine is a combination of zinc oxide and 0.5% ferric oxide (Fe_2O_3). The lotion is produced with additional ingredients such as phenol and calcium hydroxide. Calamine is a historic name for an ore of zinc. Zinc carbonate $ZnCO_3$ or smithsonite and. Zinc silicate $Zn_4Si_2O_7(OH)_2·H_2O$ or hemimorphite.

Hence, the correct option is (D).

36. Sulfacetamide compound contains a free aromatic amino group. Sulfacetamide is a sulfonamide that is sulfanilamide acylated on the sulfonamide nitrogen. It has a role as an antimicrobial agent, an anti-infective agent, an EC 2.5 (dihydropteroate synthase) inhibitor and an antibacterial drug. It is a substituted aniline and an N-sulfonylcarboxamide. These are organic compounds containing a benzenesulfonamide moiety with an amine group attached to the benzene ring. The molecular formula is $C_8H_{10}N_2O_3S$. Its scientific name is N-(4-aminophenyl) sulfonylacetamide.

Hence, the correct option is (B).

37. Sodium content is determined by a flame photometer. The calibration curve was done by plotting the emission intensities as a function of Na concentration. Determined the concentration of sodium in the unknown sample by reading the concentration of the sample which corresponds to its emission intensity from the calibration curve. A photoelectric flame photometer is a device used in inorganic chemical analysis to determine the concentration of certain metal ions, among them sodium, potassium, lithium, and calcium.

Hence, the correct option is (A).

38. Radioactivity can be detected by the use of the Geiger-Mueller counter. A variety of handheld and laboratory instruments is available for detecting and measuring radiation. Geiger Counter, with Geiger-Mueller (GM) Tube or Probe a GM tube is a gas-filled device that, when a high voltage is applied, creates an electrical pulse when radiation interacts with the wall or gas in the tube.

A Geiger counter (Geiger-Muller tube) is a device used for the detection and measurement of all types of radiation: alpha, beta and gamma radiation. Basically, it consists of a pair of electrodes surrounded by a gas. The electrodes have a high voltage across them. The gas used is usually Helium or Argon.

Hence, the correct option is (A).

39. A disposable syringe made up of polypropylene. The body and plunger are made from polypropylene, the seal on the plunger is made from polyisoprene (rubber). Plastic syringes are disposable and made from polypropylene or polyethylene. One such application which has been established in India is the use of disposable syringes produced from polypropylene resin by the process of injection moulding. The components include the plunger, main body which is graduated to indicate capacity, gasket, needle holder and the sheath cover for the needle.

Hence, the correct option is (A).

40. No diffusion takes place in coarse dispersion. Coarse dispersions are heterogeneous dispersed systems, in which the dispersed phase particles are larger than 1000 nm. Coarse dispersions are characterized by relatively fast sedimentation of the dispersed phase caused by gravity or other forces. For example, dispersion of oil in water or dispersion of water in oil. The diameters of the globules usually vary from 0.1 to 10 μm, although globule diameters as small as 0.01 μm and as large as 100 μm are possible in some emulsions.

Hence, the correct option is (C).

41. Osmosis cannot be formed when particles are in an equilibrium state. Osmosis is the spontaneous movement of a solvent through a semi-permeable membrane. It occurs when two solutions of different concentrations are separated by such a membrane. The osmosis will continue until both sides of the membrane have the same concentration (same free energy). This is the equilibrium state. Osmosis is a passive form of transport that results in equilibrium.

Hence, the correct option is (D).

42. Microscopic particles can be separated by filtration. Filtration is the first and only sterilization method that eliminates bacteria by separating the microorganisms from the sterilized medium, but unlike other sterilization methods, it doesn't kill or stop the bacteria's ability to reproduce. Microfiltration is a type of filtration physical process where a contaminated fluid is passed through a special pore-sized membrane to separate microorganisms and suspended particles from process liquid.

Hence, the correct option is (B).

43. Colloids are detected under an ultramicroscope. An ultramicroscope has been used for general observation of aerosols and colloids, in studying Brownian motion, in observing ionization tracks in cloud chambers, and in studying biological ultrastructure. An ultramicroscope is a microscope with a system that lights the object in a way that allows viewing of tiny particles via light scattering, and not light reflection or absorption.

Hence, the correct option is (B).

44. Colloids can pass through filter paper. Due to their smaller size, colloidal particles cannot be seen by our naked eyes, they are small enough to easily pass through a filter paper. The size of colloidal particles is less than 100 nm while the size of pores present in an ordinary filter paper is larger than 100 nm.

Hence, the correct option is (A).

45. Colloids can't pass through semi-permeable membranes. A semipermeable membrane allows solvent molecules such as water and very small solute particles to pass through but does not allow the passage of large solute molecules. When a colloidal mixture is placed in a semipermeable membrane, which is then placed in an aqueous solution or pure water, dissolved ions and small molecules are allowed to pass through this membrane. This causes colloidal particles to stay in the membrane because these particles are unable to pass through the small pores of the membrane.

Hence, the correct option is (B).

46. The diffusion of colloids is slow. When the molecules of a solute diffuse through a medium containing large colloidal particles, which absorb the diffusing molecules, the latter are transported in the diffusion flow not as free molecules, but as absorption compounds i.e. solute+colloid.

	Molecular dispersions	Colloidal dispersions	Coarse dispersions
1. Particle size	<1 nm	1 nm to 0.5 μm	>0.5 μm
2. Appearance	Clear, transparent	Opalescent	Frequently opaque
3. Visibility	Invisible in an electron microscope	Visible in an electron microscope	Visible under an optical microscope or the naked eye
4. Separation	Pass through a semi-permeable membrane, filter paper	Pass through filter paper but do not pass through a semi-permeable membrane	Do not pass through normal filter paper and semipermeable membrane
5. Diffusion	Undergo rapid diffusion	Diffuse very slowly	Do not diffuse
6. Sedimentation	No question of settling	Do not settle down	Fast sedimentation of dispersed phase by gravity or other forces

Hence, the correct option is (A).

47. Cheese is an example of colloidal dispersion. The cheese is classified under colloids where solid acts as a dispersion medium and liquid acts as the dispersed phase. The dispersion phase is liquid and the dispersion medium is solid which is known as a Gel. So, cheese is an example of Gel.

Hence, the correct option is (B).

48. The drug s bound to a resin and released due to changes in pH is ion exchange. An ion-exchange resin or ion-exchange polymer is a resin or polymer that acts as a medium for ion exchange. It is an insoluble matrix (or support structure) normally in the form of small (0.25–1.43 mm radius) microbeads, usually white or yellowish, fabricated from an organic polymer substrate.

Hence, the correct option is (C).

49. An example of colloidal dispersion is milk, synthetic polymers and cheese. Even if the dispersed phase is separated from the dispersion medium, they can readily be reconstituted by simply mixing them. Moreover, they are difficult to coagulate due to their stable nature. They are also known as intrinsic colloids. For examples are Starch, rubber, protein, RBC and egg albumin.

Hence, the correct option is (D).

50. The scattering of light from colloidal particles is the Faraday-Tyndall effect. The Tyndall effect is light scattering by particles in a colloid or in a very fine suspension. The individual suspension particles scatter and reflect light, making the beam visible. The Tyndall effect was first described by 19th-century physicist John Tyndall.

Faraday-Tyndall effect: As a light beam passes through a colloidal dispersion, a portion of the light is scattered by the colloidal particles present in the solution leading to a divergence of the light beam. This behavior is called the Faraday-Tyndall effect

Hence, the correct option is (A).

51. Faraday Tyndall effect is observed by ultramicroscope. The ultramicroscope is basically utilized for detecting the matter of particulate size and works on the principle of the Tyndall effect (light scattering). Tyndall effect has been used by zsigmody and Scidentonpf for making an ultramicroscope. Ultramicroscope is a microscope arranged so that light illuminates the object from the side instead of from below. In an ultramicroscope, incident light does not strike the eye of the observer and thus observes the scattering produced by the sol particle against a dark background. An actual image formation is not obtained but the presence of particle can be seen.

Hence, the correct option is (B).

52. In 1902 Richard Zsigmondy introduced an idea that led to the ultramicroscope, which makes it possible to observe very small particles by illuminating the preparation being studied in a direction that is perpendicular to the viewing angle. Richard Zsigmondy received his Nobel Prize one year later, in 1926.

Hence, the correct option is (A).

53. As a result of the Tyndall effect, bright spots are formed. Tyndall effect, also called Tyndall phenomenon, scattering of a beam of light by a medium containing small suspended particles e.g., smoke or dust in a room, which makes visible a light beam entering a window.

Hence, the correct option is (B).

54. The process in which the dispersed phase is mixed in a suitable solvent process is known as solvation. A complex formed of molecule or ion of solute in a solvent is known as a solvation complex. Solvation is the process of rearranging solvent and solute molecules into solvation complexes to distribute solute molecules evenly within the solvent.

Hence, the correct option is (A).

55. The instrument which is used to reduce the particle size is called milling. Milling involves the application of mechanical energy to physically break down coarse particles into finer ones and is regarded as a "top-down" approach in the production of fine particles. Fine drug particulates are especially desired in formulations designed for parenteral, respiratory and transdermal use.

Hence, the correct option is (B).

56. The process in which we converted coarse particles into colloidal is called size reduction. The size reduction is a process of reducing large solid unit masses-vegetables or chemical substances into small unit masses, coarse particles or fine particles. Size reduction is commonly employed in pharmaceutical industries. The size reduction process is also referred to as Comminution and Grinding.

Hence, the correct option is (B).

57. Any type of chemical compound that possesses two distinct regions that are hydrophilic and hydrophobic portion within the same molecule is called amphiphilic. Amphiphiles are a class of compounds comprising a large variety of structures of different natures, including synthetic surfactants and amphiphilic copolymers or peptides.

Hence, the correct option is (A).

58. Amphiphilic are also called association colloidal, surface active agents and amphipathic. Amphiphiles are a special class of surface-active molecules called surfactants. They are called surface-active because they have the unique properties of getting adsorbed at various interfaces(e.g air-water, oil-water, etc) and altering the properties of the interface. Association colloids are microheterogeneous systems in which the particles of the colloidal dispersed phase (micelles) are formed by the agglomeration of molecules or ions of the substance dissolved in the dispersion medium.

Hence, the correct option is (D).

59. Inter phase is composed of water and air phase. HIPE is defined by Dissent as an emulsion in which the total volume fraction of the droplet phases (namely, internal phase) exceeds 74.05%, 48 which is equivalent to the maximum space occupied by monodispersed incompressible spherical particles in a unit cube.

Hence, the correct option is (C).

60. Chemical adsorption is irreversible. Chemisorption involves the formation of new chemical bonds at the contact surface of the adsorbate and adsorbent. It is a reversible process as there is no formation of new chemical bonds. Chemisorption is irreversible. An irreversible adsorption process is defined as a process in which, once adsorbed, a particle can neither diffuse along nor desorb from the surface.

Hence, the correct option is (B).

61. The large phase is called the bulk phase. In adsorption of adsorbate on the adsorbent, the interior of the adsorbent, where the concentration of adsorbate is less as compared to the concentration of adsorbate on the surface is known as the bulk phase.

Hence, the correct option is (B).

62. The point at which the bulk phase and air, water inter phase become saturated is called CMC. The CMC (critical micelle concentration) is the concentration of a surfactant in a bulk phase, above which aggregates of surfactant molecules, so-called micelles, start to form. The CMC is an important characteristic of surfactants. The value of the CMC for a given dispersant in a given medium depends on temperature, pressure, and (sometimes strongly) on the presence and concentration of other surface-active substances and electrolytes. Micelles only form above critical micelle temperature.

Hence, the correct option is (A).

63. It is an aggregation of surfactant molecules in a colloidal liquid then it is called micelles. The molecules that form a micelle hide their water-fearing tails in the middle of the spherical micelle, which is shielded by an outer shield of polar head regions. Micelles can be made of fatty acids, soap molecules and phospholipids. Micelles help the body absorb lipid and fat-soluble vitamins. They help the small intestine to absorb essential lipids and vitamins from the liver and gall bladder. They also carry complex lipids such as lecithin and lipid-soluble vitamins (A, D, E and K) to the small intestine.

Hence, the correct option is (B).

64. The dispersed phase and dispersion medium of smoke are solid and gas. Any colloid consisting of a solid dispersed in a gas is called smoke. Smoke is an example of aerosol where the dispersed phase is Solid and the dispersion medium is gas. Under solid sol, the dispersed phase is gas and the dispersion medium is solid, its example is foam rubber.

Hence, the correct option is (C).

65. The process introduces small, highly charged molecules into the water to destabilize the charges on particles, colloids, or oily materials in suspension is known as coagulation. Coagulation is the chemical water treatment process used to remove solids from water, by manipulating electrostatic charges of particles suspended in water.

Hence, the correct option is (C).

66. Adsorption is the process of adhesion. Adsorption is the adhesion of atoms, ions or molecules from a gas, liquid or dissolved solid to a surface. This process creates a film of the adsorbate on the surface of the adsorbent. This process differs from absorption, in which a fluid (the absorbate) is dissolved by or permeates a liquid or solid (the absorbent). On a molecular level, adsorption is a process where attractive forces associate a solute (adsorbate) to a solid surface (adsorbent).

Hence, the correct option is (C).

67. The surface on which ions, atoms or molecules accumulate is adsorbent. In adsorption, the surfaces on which molecules are bonded are called adsorbents. Adsorbents are used usually in the form of spherical pellets, rods, moldings, or monoliths with a hydrodynamic radius between 0.25 and 5 mm. They must have high abrasion resistance, high thermal stability and small pore diameters, which results in higher exposed surface area and so, a high capacity for adsorption. The adsorbents must also have a distinct pore structure that enables fast transport of the gaseous vapors.

Hence, the correct option is (A).

68. Adsorbate is ions, atoms or molecules which accumulate on a specific surface A substance that is deposited on the surface of another substance. For example, H_2, N_2 and O_2 gases. Adsorbent: Surface of a substance on which adsorbate adsorbs. For example, Charcoal, Silica gel, Alumina.

Hence, the correct option is (B).

69. If both adsorption & absorption are going side by side then it is sorption. Adsorption and absorption mean quite different things. Absorption is where a liquid is soaked up into something like a sponge, cloth or filter paper. The liquid is completely absorbed into the absorbent material. Adsorption refers to individual molecules, atoms or ions gathering on surfaces. Sorption is a physical and chemical process by which a substance (typically a gas or liquid) accumulates within another phase or on the phase boundary of two phases.

Hence, the correct option is (C).

70. The reverse of adsorption is called desorption. Desorption is a phenomenon whereby a substance is released from or through a surface. The process is the opposite of sorption (that is, either adsorption or absorption). When the concentration (or pressure) of substance in the bulk phase is lowered, some of the sorbed substance changes to the bulk state.

Hence, the correct option is (B).

71. Vander-wall adsorption is a synonym of physical adsorption, chemical adsorption and physisorption. If the accumulation of gas on the surface of a solid occurs on account of weak van der Waals' forces, the adsorption is termed physical adsorption or physisorption. So, physisorption can also be called Van der Waals adsorption. Physical adsorption of a gas by a solid is generally reversible.

Hence, the correct option is (D).

72. Physisorption is affected by temperature and pressure.

Effect of temperature: Since physical adsorption is an exothermic process, it occurs more readily at lower temperatures and decreases with an increase in temperature (Le-Chatelier's Principle).

Effect of pressure: In the case of physisorption of gases over solids, the extent of adsorption increases with an increase in pressure as the volume of the gases decreases during adsorption (Le-Chatelier's Principle).

Hence, the correct option is (C).

73. Strong bonding is present in chemical adsorption. Physical adsorption is weak Vander wall force adsorption of molecules on the material while chemical adsorption is a strong chemical bond. Chemical adsorption, also known as chemisorption, on solid materials is achieved by the substantial sharing of electrons between the surface of adsorbent and adsorbate to create a covalent or ionic bond.

Hence, the correct option is (A).

74. Absorption is a bulk phenomenon. Absorption is a phenomenon involving the bulk properties of a solid, liquid or gas. It involves atoms or molecules crossing the surface and entering the volume of the material. As in adsorption, there can be physical and chemical absorption.

Hence, the correct option is (A).

75. Adsorption has non-uniformity. Adsorption of small drug particles on the surface of large excipients has been widely used in the pharmaceutical industry for various purposes, such as improving the content uniformity of low-dose drugs, enhancing the dissolution rate for poorly water-soluble drugs and enhancing some special formulation designs.

Hence, the correct option is (B).

76. Chemical adsorption involves ionic bonding. Ion exchange and adsorption are surface chemical or surface complexation processes leading to the exchange of chemical species between the aqueous solution and the mineral surfaces present in geological porous formations.

Hence, the correct option is (B).

77. Transverse ridges are seen on the outer surface of the liquorice is rhizome. Rhizome, also called creeping rootstalk, horizontal underground plant stem capable of producing the shoot and root systems of a new plant. Rhizomes are used to store starches and proteins and enable plants to perennate (survive an annual unfavourable season) underground.

Hence, the correct option is (B).

78. Bufadienolides are present in digitalis. Cardenolides are produced by plants, whereas bufadienolides are produced by both plants and animals. A bufadienolide-rich plant Scilla Maritima was used by Egyptians to cure heart diseases. Bufadienolides are also the principal bioactive ingredient of a traditional Chinese drug Ch'an Su, containing the skin secretions of toads such as Bufo gargarizans Cantor and Bufo melanostictus Schneider.

Hence, the correct option is (A).

79. Digitalis leaves are dried at a temperature of about 60 °C. Digitalis consists of dried leaves of digitalis purpurea Linn. After collection leaves are dried immediately at a temperature below 60 °C and they contain no more than 5% moisture. After drying leaves are stored in a moisture-proof container.

Hence, the correct option is (B).

80. The margin of the digitalis leaf is crenate or dentate. Taste is distinctly bitter. Length is 10-30 cm and width is 4-10 cm. The shape is may be ovate, lanceolate or petiolate. The margin of leaves is crenate or dentate. Foxglove leaves, digitalis leaves. It is obtained from dried leaves of the digitalis pupurea family

Scrophulariaceae. It is required to contain at least 0.3 % of total cardenolides calculated as Digitoxin.

Hence, the correct option is (D).

81. Prisms of calcium oxalate crystals are present in digitalis thapsi. Digitalis thapsi, which has been called mullein foxglove in the US, is a flowering plant in the genus Digitalis that is endemic to the Iberian Peninsula, where it occurs in eastern Portugal and central and western Spain. It is of commercial importance as an ornamental plant. Hybrids with D. purpurea have proved successful and are fertile.

Hence, the correct option is (C).

82. The cardiac glycoside on hydrolysis gives $\rightarrow$ digitoxigenin + Glucose-acetyl digitoxose(digitoxose)2 the glycoside is purpurea glycoside A. Cardiac glycosides are medicines for treating heart failure and certain irregular heartbeats. They are one of several classes of drugs used to treat the heart and related conditions. Cardiac glycoside overdose occurs when someone takes more than the normal or recommended amount of this medicine.

Hence, the correct option is (A).

83. Leaves of Digitalis lanata are ovate-lanceolate. The lower cauline leaves are 6 to 12 cm (sometimes to 20 cm) long and 1.5 to 3.5 cm wide, the upper cauline leaves are 4 to 10 cm long and lanceolate shaped, usually with entire margins, and with a distinctive mid-rib. The leaves along the stalks are alternate. The lower stem leaves wither by early flowering.

Hence, the correct option is (C).

84. Cardiac glycosides are present in calotropis. Cardiac glycosides are found in several plants, including the leaves of the digitalis (foxglove) plant. This plant is the original source of this medicine. People who eat a large amount of these leaves may develop symptoms of an overdose. Calotropis produces highly poisonous cardiac glycosides and that is why we never see any cattle or goats browsing on this plant. A wide variety of chemical substances that we extract from plants on a commercial scale (nicotine, caffeine, quinine, strychnine, opium, etc.).

Hence, the correct option is (B).

85. Oubain, a cardiac glycoside is present in strophanthus. Ouabain, a cardiac glycoside known also as g-strophanthin, a poisonous glycoside obtained from the fruits of Strophanthus gratus is used widely to block the sodium pump in vitro studies. Strophanthus, which is of the Apocynaceae family, is a flowering plant that grows in tropical Africa, South Africa, southern India, the Philippines, Laos, Vietnam, and South China.

Hence, the correct option is (C).

86. Deoxy-sugars are generally found attached with cardiac glycosides. Cardiac glycosides are medicines for treating heart failure and certain irregular heartbeats. They are one of several classes of drugs used to treat the heart and related conditions. These drugs are a common cause of poisoning.

Hence, the correct option is (C).

87. Cannabinoids abused drugs do not belong to sedative agents. The word cannabinoid refers to every chemical substance,

regardless of structure or origin, that joins the cannabinoid receptors of the body and brain and that have similar effects to those produced by the Cannabis Sativa plant. The two main cannabinoids are delta-9-tetrahydrocannabinol (THC) and cannabidiol (CBD).

Hence, the correct option is (C).

88. LSD agents is related to hallucinogens. LSD, mescaline, psilocybin, and PCP are drugs that cause hallucinations, which can alter a person's perception of reality. LSD, mescaline, and psilocybin cause their effects by initially disrupting the interaction of nerve cells and the neurotransmitter serotonin.

Hence, the correct option is (B).

89. Inhaled anesthetics and intravenous agents have general anesthetic properties which directly activate GABA-A receptors. Of particular importance are drugs that modulate GABA-A receptor complexes, such as benzodiazepines, barbiturates, neuroactive steroids, intravenous and inhalational anesthetics, and ethanol.

Hence, the correct option is (A).

90. Ketamine is the anesthetic, which is an inhibitor of NMDA glutamate receptors. Ketamine is a medication primarily used for induction and maintenance of anesthesia. It induces dissociative anesthesia, a trance-like state providing pain relief, sedation, and amnesia. The distinguishing features of ketamine anesthesia are preserved breathing and airway reflexes stimulated heart function with increased blood pressure and moderate bronchodilation.

Hence, the correct option is (C).

91. Desflurane general anesthetics belongs to inhalants. Inhalation anesthetics (nitrous oxide, halothane, isoflurane, desflurane, sevoflurane, most commonly used agents in practice today) are used for induction and maintenance of general anesthesia in the operating room. This review is a general overview of inhalation anesthetic agents.

Hence, the correct option is (B).

92. Propofol is an intravenous sedative-hypnotic agent that can be used for initiation and maintenance of Monitored Anesthesia Care (MAC) sedation, combined sedation and regional anesthesia, induction of general anesthesia, maintenance of general anesthesia, and intensive care unit (ICU) sedation of intubated.

Hence, the correct option is (A).

93. Nitrous oxide inhalants are gas anesthetics. Inhalation anesthetics (nitrous oxide, halothane, isoflurane, desflurane, sevoflurane, most commonly used agents in practice today) are used for induction and maintenance of general anesthesia in the operating room. This review is a general overview of inhalation anesthetic agents.

Hence, the correct option is (D).

94. Halothane inhaled anesthetics can produce hepatic necrosis. Halothane and other halogenated inhalational anesthetic agents, such as enflurane, isoflurane, sevoflurane, and desflurane, are known to cause severe liver dysfunction. The National Halothane Study, a retrospective analysis, reviewed the incidence and mortality rates of postoperative hepatic necrosis from 1959-1962.

Hence, the correct option is (C).

95. Sevoflurane belongs to the group of medicines known as general anesthetics. Sevoflurane is used to cause general anesthesia (loss of consciousness) before and during surgery. It is inhaled (breathed in). Although sevoflurane can be used by itself, combinations of anesthetics are often used together.

Hence, the correct option is (B).

96. Serotonin s the key hormone that stabilizes our mood, feelings of well-being, and happiness. This hormone impacts your entire body. It enables brain cells and other nervous system cells to communicate with each other. Serotonin also helps with sleeping, eating, and digestion. Gastric acid secretion is under the control of the serotonin agents.

Hence, the correct option is (C).

97. Omeprazole drug belonging to proton pump inhibitors. Omeprazole is a selective and irreversible proton pump inhibitor. It suppresses stomach acid secretion by specific inhibition of the H^+/K^+-ATPase system found at the secretory surface of gastric parietal cells. This enzyme is responsible for the final step in the process of acid secretion; omeprazole blocks acid secretion in response to all stimuli.

Hence, the correct option is (C).

98. Gastrin, histamine and carbonate mineral waters agents intensify the secretion of gastric glands except for pepsin. Pepsin, the proteolytic enzyme of the stomach is normally responsible for less than 20% of the protein digestion occurring in the gastrointestinal tract. It is an endopeptidase enzyme that metabolizes proteins to peptides. It preferentially hydrolyzes peptide linkages where one of the amino acids is aromatic.

Hence, the correct option is (A).

99. The mechanism of metoclopramide antiemetic action D_2 dopamine and 5-HT$_3$ serotonin receptor blocking effect. Metoclopramide causes antiemetic effects by inhibiting dopamine D_2 and serotonin 5-HT$_3$ receptors in the chemoreceptor trigger zone (CTZ) located in the area postrema of the brain.

Hence, the correct option is (C).

100. Pernicious anemia is developed due to a deficiency of vitamin B12. Pernicious anemia is a type of vitamin B12 anemia. The body needs vitamin B12 to make red blood cells. You get this vitamin from eating foods such as meat, poultry, shellfish, eggs, and dairy products.

Hence, the correct option is (B).

101. The drug used for pernicious anemia is cyanocobalamin. Vitamin B12 is available for therapeutic use parenterally as either cyanocobalamin or hydroxocobalamin. Both are equally useful in the treatment of vitamin B12 deficiency, and they are nontoxic (except for rare allergic reactions).

Hence, the correct option is (B).

102. An adverse effect of oral iron therapy is constipation. Gastrointestinal side-effects are the most commonly reported adverse effects associated with oral iron treatment and include nausea, flatulence, abdominal pain, diarrhoea, constipation, and black or tarry stools.

Hence, the correct option is (D).

103. Warfarin continues to be the most widely used oral anticoagulant but the use of the newer oral anticoagulants (dabigatran etexilate, rivaroxaban, edoxaban, and apixaban) is increasing. Warfarin antagonises vitamin K (needed for the synthesis of clotting factors) and takes 2-3 days to exert its full effect.

Hence, the correct option is (C).

104. Streptokinase drugs are fibrinolytic. This drug falls into the category of fibrinolytic, while the others fall into the category of "blood thinners," or anticoagulants. Streptokinase (SK) is a thrombolytic medication and enzyme. As a medication, it is used to break down clots in some cases of myocardial infarction (heart attack), pulmonary embolism, and arterial thromboembolism. The type of heart attack it is used in is an ST-elevation myocardial infarction (STEMI).

Hence, the correct option is (B).

105. Diuretics, ACE inhibitors and reduced salt intake are recommended at the initial stages of treating patients with heart failure except for verapamil. Verapamil is in a class of medications called calcium-channel blockers. It works by relaxing the blood vessels so the heart does not have to pump as hard. It also increases the supply of blood and oxygen to the heart and slows electrical activity in the heart to control the heart rate.

Hence, the correct option is (B).

106. Strophantin K, digoxin and digitoxin agents belong to cardiac glycosides except for amrinone. Amrinone is a phosphodiesterase inhibitor (PDE3), resulting in increased cAMP and cGMP which leads to an increase in the calcium influx like that caused by beta-agonists resulting in an increased inotropic effect.

Hence, the correct option is (C).

107. The non-glycoside positive inotropic drug is dobutamine. Non-glycoside inotropic agents should only be used in patients with acute heart failure with low blood pressure or cardiac output in the presence of signs of hypoperfusion or congestion. Available agents include cAMP-elevating drugs such as dobutamine, dopamine, milrinone, and enoximone.

Hence, the correct option is (C).

108. Aglycone is essential for cardiotonic action. Cardiotonic are drugs used to increase the efficiency and improve the contraction of the heart muscle, which leads to improved blood flow to all tissues of the body. Cardiotonic drugs increase the force of the contraction of the muscle (myocardium) of the heart. This is called a positive inotropic action.

Hence, the correct option is (C).

109. Digitalis A preparation of the dried leaves or seeds of the foxglove (Digitalis), used historically as a heart stimulant. Modern clinically prescribed drugs derived from digitalis include digoxin and digitoxin, both of which belong to a class of drugs known as cardiac glycosides.

Hence, the correct option is (A).

110. For digitalis-induced arrhythmias, the lidocaine drug is favoured. Lidocaine is an antiarrhythmic medication of the class Ib type. This means it works by blocking sodium channels and thus decreasing the rate of contractions of the heart. When injected near nerves, the nerves cannot conduct signals to or from the brain.

Hence, the correct option is (C).

111. Digoxin drug is used in treating supraventricular tachycardias. Digoxin is used to treat heart failure and abnormal heart rhythms (arrhythmias). It helps the heart work better and it helps control your heart rate. Digoxin is a cardiac glycoside used as drug in case of heart problems, including congestive heart failure, atrial fibrillation or flutter, and certain cardiac arrhythmias. It has a very narrow therapeutic window of the medication. Digoxin is a toxic substance with well known cardiotoxic effect.

Hence, the correct option is (A).

112. Sotalol drug is associated with Torsades de pointes. Drugs in a number of drug classes have been associated with torsade. Antiarrhythmic drugs associated with torsade include the following:

Class IA: Quinidine, disopyramide, procainamide.

Class III: Sotalol, amiodarone (rare), ibutilide, dofetilide, almokalant.

Hence, the correct option is (B).

113. Nifedipine drug has little or no direct effect on chronotropy and dromotropy at normal doses. Nifedipine is a medicine used to treat high blood pressure. If you have high blood pressure, taking nifedipine helps to prevent future heart disease, heart attacks and strokes. Nifedipine is also used to prevent chest pain caused by angina. Occasionally, it's used to treat Raynaud's phenomenon and chilblains.

Hence, the correct option is (A).

114. The adverse reactions characteristic of lidocaine is hypotension, paresthesias, convulsions. Adverse drug reactions (ADRs) are rare when lidocaine is used as a local anesthetic and is administered correctly. Most ADRs associated with lidocaine for anesthesia relate to administration technique (resulting in systemic exposure) or pharmacological effects of anesthesia, and allergic reactions only rarely occur. Systemic exposure to excessive quantities of lidocaine mainly results in the central nervous system (CNS) and cardiovascular effects CNS effects usually occur at lower blood plasma concentrations and additional cardiovascular effects present at higher concentrations, though cardiovascular collapse may also occur with low concentrations.

Hence, the correct option is (C).

115. For the Landsberger-Walker method used for the determination of molecular weight from boiling point, elevation air should be passed at low pressure is not applicable. Landsberger has recently described (Bey., IS98, 31, 458) a method adapted for the determination of the molecular weight of substances in solution, in which the external flame is discarded altogether, the solution being kept at its boiling point by the passage through it of the solvent vapour alone so that superheating.

Hence, the correct option is (B).

116. SLS has an HLB of 40. In addition, SLS has a very high HLB value of 40 meaning it is water-soluble and prefers to form o/w emulsions. SLS functions in cleaning products as a surfactant, wetting surfaces, emulsifying or solubilizing oils, and suspending soil so that they can be rinsed away. This ingredient contributes foaming properties to cleaning products. SLS is safe for use in cleaning products.

Hence, the correct option is (C).

117. Diastereomers differ in all physical properties. The rest of the points are related to Enantiomers. Diastereomers are stereoisomers that are not related as objects and mirror images and are not enantiomers. Diastereomers can have different physical properties and reactivity. They have different melting points and boiling points and different densities. They have two or more stereocenters.

Hence, the correct option is (C).

118. A substance that can be reversibly oxidized or reduced, having different distinct colours in the individual oxidized and reduced forms redox indicators. A redox indicator (also called an oxidation-reduction indicator) is an indicator that undergoes a definite color change at a specific electrode potential. The requirement for fast and reversible color change means that the oxidation-reduction equilibrium for an indicator redox system needs to be established very quickly. Therefore, only a few classes of organic redox systems can be used for indicator purposes.

Hence, the correct option is (A).

119. The nucleus contains DNA the repository of genetic information. By housing the cell's genome, the nucleus serves both as the repository of genetic information and as the cell's control center. DNA replication, transcription, and RNA processing all take place within the nucleus, with only the final stage of gene expression (translation) localized to the cytoplasm.

Hence, the correct option is (B).

120. The first transgenic cow was called Rosie and was produced in 1997. It was genetically engineered to produce human protein-enriched milk. This milk contained 2.4gms of human α-lactalbumin per litre of milk. Normal cow milk does not contain this protein. Thus, the milk from the transgenic cow was nutritionally more balanced for human babies than natural cow milk.

Transgenic animals refer to those that have had their genomes modified to possess and express a foreign gene.

Reasons for production of transgenic animals:

1. Study of Physiology & Development -
   - Study of how genes and their regulation affects the physiological functioning of the body.
   - Complex growth factors like insulin can be studied.
2. Study of Diseases -
   - Transgenic animals serve as model organisms for studying human diseases.
   - They help in understanding the disease development process from genes.
   - They are also used for investigating new treatment methods.
   - Transgenic models exist for diseases like cancer, cystic fibrosis, rheumatoid arthritis, and Alzheimer's.
3. Biological Products -
   - Many biological products that are essential for formulating medicines of use are often expensive.
   - These products can be obtained easily from transgenic animals.
   - This can be achieved by just introducing the gene responsible for the desired product into a suitable organism.
   - Example - Alpha-1 antitrypsin is a human protein that is required for emphysema treatment.
4. Vaccine Safety -
   - Transgenic mice can be used to test the safety of vaccines before using for humans.
5. Toxicity Testing -
   - Transgenic animals can be made more sensitive to certain chemicals or drugs.
   - These animals are exposed to toxic substances and their effects are then studied.

- Dolly: It was the first cloned sheep (1996). It was also the first mammal to be cloned.
- Cumulina: It was the first cloned mouse (1997).
- Noah: It was the first cloned gaur (2000), which died with n 2 days. Gaur is an Indian bison that is listed as vulnerable in IUCN Red List.

Hence, the correct option is (B).

121. The greatest resolution in light microscopy can be obtained with the shortest wavelength of visible light used and an objective with the maximum numerical aperture.

The relationship between numerical aperture (NA) and resolution is:

Resolution (d) = wavelength/2(NA)

Thus maximum resolution is obtained with the shortest wavelength of visible light and an objective with the maximum NA.

Hence, the correct option is (D).

122. Convulsions in adults is not a clinical manifestation of Bacterial Meningitis. When meningitis causes brain swelling or pressure, it can disrupt the brain's normal function, causing a seizure. Having seizures during an episode of meningitis does not mean that a person has, or will develop, epilepsy.

Hence, the correct option is (B).

123. Quaternary ammonium compounds of drugs are absorbed by ion pair transport. Ion-Pair Transport is the mechanism where absorption of drugs like quaternary ammonium compounds, sulphonic acids get absorbed. These drugs can get ionize at all pH conditions.

Hence, the correct option is (C).

124. Retinol is contraindicated during pregnancy due to its Teratogenicity. Isotretinoin and its commercially available brands, although effective in the treatment of acne, can cause developmental abnormalities in the fetus (teratogenic effects) and therefore should not be used during pregnancy due to the risk of birth defects.

Hence, the correct option is (C).

125. Epithelial tissue covers the body surface and line the internal organs. Epithelial tissues are widespread throughout the body. They form the covering of all body surfaces, line body cavities, and hollow organs, and are the major tissue in glands. Simple cuboidal epithelium is found in glandular tissue and in the kidney tubules. Simple columnar epithelium lines the stomach and intestines.

Hence, the correct option is (B).

Pharmaceutical Chemistry

Q.1 The recent edition of Pharmacopoeia is:
A. Fourth edition
B. Seventh edition
C. Sixth edition
D. Eighth edition

Q.2 The latest edition of I.P is published in the year:
A. 1955
B. 1965
C. 1986
D. 2018

Q.3 Chemically alum is:
A. Potassium aluminium sulphate
B. Magnesium aluminium Sulphate
C. Potassium magnesium sulphate
D. Aluminium magnesium sulphate

Q.4 pH is usually measured with a:
A. Platinum electrode
B. Mercury electrode
C. Copper electrode
D. Glass electrode

Q.5 All are true about radiation except:
A. Biological
B. Photographic
C. Fluorescent
D. Non-penetrating

Q.6 The best conductor of electricity is:
A. Graphite
B. Coal
C. Coke
D. Diamond

Q.7 NMR spectroscopy is:
A. Diffraction
B. Emission
C. Radiation
D. Absorption

Q.8 Optical activity of organic substances is measured by:
A. Spirometer
B. Polarimeter
C. Photometer
D. Multimeter

Q.9 Aromatic spirit of ammonium is used as:
A. Respiratory stimulant
B. Cardiac stimulant
C. Brain stimulant
D. Spinal stimulant

Q.10 TiO is commonly present in:
A. Vanishing cream
B. Sun screen cream
C. Cold cream
D. Opthalmic cream

Q.11 Iodinated serum albumin is used to determine:
A. Plasma volume
B. Blood volume
C. Both (A) and (B)
D. None of these

Q.12 The native colloidal hydrated aluminum silicate is:
A. Tale
B. Alum
C. Bentonite
D. All of these

Q.13 Chemically Talc is a:
A. Hydrated aluminium silicate
B. Hydrated magnesium silicate
C. Hydrated copper sulphate
D. Hydrated magnesium sulphate

Q.14 The softest mineral is known as:
A. Talc
B. Alum
C. Bentonite
D. All of these

Q.15 Technetium sulphide (Tc-99m) colloidal solution is used to scan:
A. Liver
B. Spleen
C. Brain
D. Both (A) and (B)

Q.16 Sodium chloride hypertonic injection contains:
A. 0.9% W/V
B. 1.6% W/V
C. 0.45% W/V
D. 0.09% W/V

Q.17 Burrow's solution is:
A. Calcium phase sol. strong
B. Ammonium acetate sol. strong
C. Aluminium acetate sol. strong
D. Calcium hydroxide sol. strong

Q.18 The instrument used for measuring the amount of light absorbed by the solution is:
A. Refractometer
B. Polarimeter
C. Spectrophotometer
D. Spirometer

Q.19 A metal ion that donates electrons is:
A. Chelate
B. Ligand
C. Poly ion
D. Complex

Q.20 Titrations involving silver nitrate is known as:
A. Precipitation
B. Acid base
C. Argentometry
D. Complexo metry

Q.21 Drug used for determination of myocardial blood flow is:
A. Ferric chloride solution
B. Potassium chloride injection
C. Rubidium chloride injection
D. Sodium chloride injection

Q.22 Substances used in swimming pools to prevent the growth of algae & snails:
A. Copper sulphate
B. Zinc sulphate
C. Sodium sulphate
D. Ammonium chloride

Q.23 In surgical operations, the CO_2 content is reduced by the use of:
A. Soda-lime
B. Lime
C. Quick lime
D. Slaked lime

Q.24 Chemical formula of sodium phosphate is:
A. NaH_2PO_4
B. Na_3PO_4
C. Na_2HPO_4
D. Na_2SO_4

Q.25 Specific rotation of glucose:
A. 52-53 ° B. 18-19 °
C. 111-112 ° D. 11-12 °

Q.26 Mercury compound used as a preservative:
A. Thiomersal
B. Mercuric Oxide
C. Mercurousted chloride
D. All of these

Q.27 Potassium perchlorate is classified as:
A. Anticonvulsant B. Antithyroid
C. Antidepressant D. Antirheumatic

Q.28 Gold sodium thiomalate is used in:
A. Rheumatoid arthritis
B. Gout
C. Osteoporosis
D. All of these

Q.29 Parasiticide used in the treatment of Leishmaniasis is:
A. Sodium antimony gluconate
B. Potassium antimony tartrate
C. Sodium antimony tartrate
D. All of these

Q.30 Mannitol is used in the assay of:
A. Boric acid B. Copper sulphate
C. Zinc sulphate D. Calcium gluconate

Q.31 H_2O_2 is prepared by adding a paste of barium peroxide in:
A. Nitric acid B. Sulphuric acid
C. Hydrochloric acid D. Sulfurous acid

Q.32 Silicon polymers are synthetically prepared by:
A. Pasteurization B. Decantation
C. Fumigation D. Polymerization

Q.33 Chemically kaolin is:
A. Hydrated aluminium silicate
B. Hydrated magnesium silicate
C. Hydrated silicon dioxide
D. Hydrated ferrous sulphate

Q.34 Antidote for heavy metal poisoning is:
A. Magnesium sulphate
B. Sodium sulphate
C. Copper sulphate
D. Both (A) and (B)

Q.35 Magnesium sulphate BPC is also called as:
A. Gypsum salt B. Epsom salt
C. Glauber's salt D. Plaster of Paris

Q.36 One part of solute is soluble in 1-10 parts of solvent means:
A. Sparingly soluble B. Soluble
C. Slightly soluble D. Freely soluble

Q.37 Saline cathartic used in barium and lead poisoning is:

A. Copper sulphate
B. Magnesium sulphate
C. Ferrous sulphate
D. Sodium sulphate

Q.38 An ingredient in Benedicts and Fehling's reagent is:
A. Copper sulphate
B. Magnesium sulphate
C. Ferrous sulphate
D. Sodium sulphate

Pharmaceutics

Q.39 Water attack test is used to identify the alkalinity in:
A. Type-I Glass B. Type-II Glass
C. Type-III Glass D. All of these

Q.40 As per G.M.P permitted limit of solid contents in water for injection is:
A. 100 ppm B. 1.0 ppm C. 0.1 ppm D. 10 ppm

Q.41 Sterilization temperature for aqueous solution in autoclave (moist heat) is:
A. 72 °C B. 121 °C C. 147 °C D. 160 °C

Q.42 Sterility test for the material meant for surgical suture required incubation for:
A. 7 Days B. 14 Days C. 21 Days D. 28 Days

Q.43 An amphoteric surfactant used in pharmaceutical disperse system is:
A. Bile salt
B. Lecithin
C. Sorbitan monolaurate
D. Sorbitan monostearate

Q.44 An abrasive used in dentifrices is:
A. Dicalcium Phosphate
B. Sodium carboxy methyl cellulose
C. Sodium Lauryl Sulphate
D. Dioctyl Sodium sulfosuccinate

Q.45 The florentine receiver is used to separate the liquids based on:
A. Molecular weight B. Sedimentation rate
C. Density D. Freezing point

Q.46 The official dissolution test apparatus contains cylindrical vessel and the lower edge of the blade is positioned from inside bottom of the vessel at:
A. 18 to 22 mm B. 23 to 27 mm
C. 20 to 24 mm D. 25 to 29 mm

Q.47 As per the Drugs and Cosmetics Act and Rules, the good manufacturing practice is included under schedule:
A. W B. P C. S D. M

Q.48 In multistation punching machine, the upper as well as lower punches are connected by:
A. Cams B. Turrets
C. Wire meshes D. Revolving belts

Q.49 As per the Drugs and Cosmetics Act, the HEPA filters are required to filter the air in the pharmaceutical manufacturing unit. Grade A filter is used for:
A. Aseptic preparation and filling.
B. Background room used for preliminary activities.
C. Filtering liquid preparations.
D. Handling of components after washing.

Q.50 Liposomes are used as carriers for drugs and macromolecules in pharmaceutical formulations. They are:
A. Phospholipids dispersed gently in aqueous medium to obtain multilamellar vesicles.
B. Hydrophilic or lipophilic polymer matrix with a drug reservoir.
C. A shallow compartment moulded from a drug impermeable system and rate controlling polymeric membrane.
D. Microporous membrane made from ethylene/vinyl acetate polymer.

Q.51 What is not the ideal quality of a lipstick?
A. It should be non toxic and non irritating.
B. It should not retard healing of the wound.
C. It should be free from sweating.
D. It should maintain its firmness till it is fully used up.

Q.52 Disadvantages of cachets:
A. Overnight soaking of jelly is required while manufacturing.
B. The shell of cachets are fragile, so the drug can't be compressed in cachets.
C. Fluctuation in temperature may change the consistency.
D. Hygroscopic

Q.53 The most serious type of _______ in the dispensing is an overdose of medication.
A. Contra-indicated drugs
B. Wrong drug
C. Dosage error
D. None of these

Q.54 _______ provide useful information regarding stability of suspension.
A. Electrokinetic's Method
B. Sedimentation Method
C. Micromeritic Method
D. Rheological Method

Q.55 Drawbacks of cocoa butter as a suppository base:
A. Exhibits marked polymorphism
B. Rancidity
C. Stick to mould
D. All of these

Q.56 The ointments used to remove or soften the horny layer of the skin:
A. Hexachloride
B. Parasiticide ointment
C. Protectants
D. Keratolytics

Q.57 Advantages of powder as a dosage form:
A. Each dose can be administered accurately.
B. Convenient for dispersing bulky drug.
C. Immediate therapeutic action is possible.
D. Absorption of the drug faster compare to other route.

Q.58 Advantages of parenteral products:
A. Rapid onset of action.
B. Immediate therapeutic action is possible.
C. Each dose can be administered accurately.
D. All of these

Q.59 The jelly is applied on the electrode to reduce the electrical resistance between the patient's skin and the electrode:
A. Electrocardiography
B. Patch testing
C. Medicated jellies
D. None of these

Q.60 Advantage of cachets:
A. It can be made easily made no complicated machines required.
B. They disintegrate quickly in the stomach.
C. The drug can be easily dispense.
D. All of these

Q.61 _______ are viscous semi-solid emulsions which are meant for external application to the skin or mucous membrane for protective, therapeutic or prophylactic purposes.
A. Ointment
B. Paste
C. Creams
D. Both (A) and (B)

Q.62 What are some of the qualities of good dentifrice?
A. It should be economical.
B. It should be non-toxic.
C. It should be properly sweetened & flavoured.
D. All of these

Q.63 _______ are the solid unit dosage form of drugs.
A. Depilatories
B. Cachets
C. Both (A) and (B)
D. None of these

Q.64 Qualities of an ideal shampoo:
A. It should be non-toxic.
B. It should be capable of removing grease, dirt, and skin debris from the hair and scalp.
C. It should be effective in small amounts.
D. All of these

Q.65 What are some of the examples of Efflorescent powder?
A. Caffeine
B. Ferrous sulphate
C. Ammonium chloride
D. Both (A) and (B)

Q.66 Ointment bases used should possess _______ that should be able to keep the skin moist.
A. Emollient properties
B. Ease of application and removal
C. Non-irritant
D. Adsorption penetration

Q.67 These substances are added to increase the stability or quality of the product:

A. Adjuvants
B. Solubilising agents
C. Preservatives
D. Buffering agents

Q.68 Which of the following ointment bases are of the emulsion type?

A. Cooling ointments
B. W/O emulsions
C. O/W emulsions
D. Oleogels

Q.69 An extraordinary response to a drug which is different from its characteristic pharmacological action is called:

A. Time of administration
B. Accumulation
C. Tachyphylaxis
D. Idiosyncrasy

Q.70 The stability of suspension depends on the particle size of the disperse phase:

A. Sedimentation Method
B. Rheological Method
C. Electrokinetic's Method
D. Micromeritic Method

Q.71 Jellies are clear, sweetened, aromatic, hydroalcoholic liquids prepared for oral use.

A. True
B. False
C. Can't say
D. None of these

Q.72 The reasons causing therapeutic incompatibility are:

A. Error in dosage
B. Wrong dose or dosage form
C. Synergism and Antagonism drug
D. All of these

Q.73 Gum tragacanth , sodium alginate, methyl cellulose are used as:

A. Binders
B. Detergents
C. Abrasives
D. Preservatives

Q.74 ______ are used for counter irritant, rubefacient, soothing or stimulating purposes.

A. Lotions
B. Liniments
C. Both (A) and (B)
D. None of these

Q.75 ______ are used to reduce the sweat formation.

A. Antiperspirants
B. Deodorants
C. Both (A) and (B)
D. None of these

Q.76 Functions of Tartaric acid:

A. Only for neutralization.
B. Sometime added as sweetening agent.
C. The evolved carbon dioxide produce the effervescence.
D. None of these

Pharmacognosy

Q.77 Umbelliferrous fruits are:

A. Drupes
B. Berry
C. Capsule
D. Schizocarps

Q.78 The number of vittae in cremocarp of fennel is:

A. 2
B. 6
C. 10
D. 12

Q.79 Percentage of citral content of lemongrass oil is:

A. 3% to 4%
B. 10% to 12%
C. 50% to 60%
D. 70% to 80%

Q.80 Lemongrass oil is mainly produced from cymbopogon flexuosus in:

A. South India
B. Guafemala
C. West Indies
D. Kenya

Q.81 In India, menthol is mainly produced from oil of:

A. Mentha spicata
B. Mentha arvensis
C. Mentha piperata
D. Mentha viridis

Q.82 Citral is a suitable substance for synthesis of:

A. Vitamin A
B. Vitamin B
C. Vitamin C
D. Vitamin D

Q.83 Percentage of citral in lemon peel oil?

A. 1%
B. 4%
C. 50%
D. 70%

Q.84 The colour shown by thick saction of bitter orange peel is:

A. Red
B. Yellow
C. Dark green
D. Blue

Q.85 Following part of Crocus sativus is called as saffron:

A. Flower
B. Fruit
C. Stigma and upper part of style
D. Anther

Q.86 Proto crocin is a precursor for taste, odour and colour of the saffron, it is:

A. Diterpene glycoside
B. Triterpene glycoside
C. Tetraterpene glycoside
D. Steroidal glycoside

Pharmacology

Q.87 Find out the selective blocker of beta-1 adrenoreceptors:

A. Labetalol
B. Prazosin
C. Atenolol
D. Propranolol

Q.88 This drug is an inhibitor of renin synthesis:

A. Propranolol
B. Enalapril
C. Diazoxide
D. Losartan

Q.89 This drug is a non-peptide angiotensin II receptor antagonist:

A. Clonidine
B. Captopril
C. Losartan
D. Diazoxide

Q.90 All of the following statements regarding verapamil are true except:

A. It blocks L-type calcium channels.
B. It increases heart rate.

C. It relaxes coronary artery smooth muscle.

D. It depresses cardiac contractility.

Q.91 Progesterone is secreted by:

A. Ovarian follicles

B. Corpus luteum

C. Granulosa and theca cells

D. All of these

Q.92 The major natural progestin is:

A. Estradiol

B. Estron

C. Progesterone

D. Estriol

Q.93 Mifepristone (RU-486) is:

A. Antiprogestin

B. Antiandrogen

C. Antiestrogen

D. Androgen

Q.94 Which of the following NSAIDs is a selective COX-2 inhibitor?

A. Piroxicam

B. Indomethacin

C. Celecoxib

D. Diclofenac

Q.95 Which of the following NSAIDs is a nonselective COX inhibitor?

A. Piroxicam

B. Rofecoxib

C. Celecoxib

D. All of these

Q.96 Which of the following drugs is a 5-lipoxygenase (5-LOG) inhibitor?

A. Ibuprofen

B. Zileuton (Zyflo)

C. Metamizole (Analgin)

D. Diclofenac

Q.97 Which of the following drugs is a leucotreine D4 receptor (LTD4) blocker?

A. Ibuprofen

B. Zileuton (Zyflo)

C. Zafirlukast (Accolate)

D. Diclofenac

Q.98 Which of the following drugs is a thromboxane A2 receptor (TXA2) antagonist?

A. Sulotroban

B. Zileuton (Zyflo)

C. Zafirleukast (Accolate)

D. Diclofenac

Q.99 H1 histamine receptor subtype is distributed in:

A. Smooth muscle, endothelium and brain.

B. Gastric mucosa, cardiac muscle, mast cells and brain.

C. Presynaptically in brain, mesenteric plexus and other neurons.

D. All of these

Q.100 H2 histamine receptor subtype is distributed in:

A. Smooth muscle, endothelium and brain.

B. Gastric mucosa, cardiac muscle, mast cells and brain.

C. Presynaptically in brain, mesenteric pléxus and other neurons.

D. All of these

Q.101 Find out for interferon-alpha administration is:

A. Autoimmune diseases

B. Rheumatoid arthritis

C. Organ transplantation

D. Hepatitis C virus infection

Q.102 Find out for interferon alpha administration is:

A. Prophylaxis of sensitization by Rh antigen

B. Rheumatoid arthritis

C. Kaposi's sarcoma

D. Chronic granulomatous disease

Q.103 Immuno-modulating agents are the following except:

A. Cytokines

B. Levamisole

C. BCG (Baci le Calmette-Guerin)

D. Tacrolimus (FK-506)

Q.104 Mechanism of action of levamisole is:

A. Inhibits CD3 receptor

B. Complement-mediated cytolysis of T lymphocytes

C. Substitution for patient's defiecient immunoglobulins

D. Increase the number of T-cells

Q.105 Find out a fat-soluble vitamin:

A. Ascorbic acid

B. Tocopherol

C. Thiamine

D. Riboflavin

Q.106 Which of the following vitamins can be also synthesized from a dietary precursor?

A. Vitamin C

B. Vitamin A

C. Vitamin B1

D. Vitamin B6

Q.107 Which of the following vitamins resembles with hormone?

A. Vitamin K

B. Vitamin A

C. Vitamin D

D. Vitamin E

Q.108 Which of the following vitamins is given along with isoniazid in the treatment of tuberculosis?

A. Nicotinic acid

B. Riboflavin

C. Pyridoxine

D. Ascorbic acid

Q.109 Which of the following vitamins is also known as an anti sterility factor?

A. Vitamin E

B. Vitamin B1

C. Vitamin B6

D. Vitamin K

Q.110 Megadoses of which vitamin are sometimes beneficial viral respiratory infections:

A. Vitamin C

B. Vitamin A

C. Vitamin K

D. Vitamin B12

Q.111 Which of the following antienzymes is a monoamine oxidase (MAO) inhibitor?

A. Physostigmine

B. Selegiline

C. Acetazolamide

D. Disulfiram

Q.112 Which of the following antienzymes is a carbonic anhydrase inhibitor?

A. Physostigmine
B. Selegiline
C. Aminocaproic acid
D. Acetazolamide

Q.113 Which of the following antienzymes is a xantine oxidase inhibitor?

A. Physostigmine
B. Allopurinol
C. Aminocaproic acid
D. Acetazolamide

Q.114 Which of the following antienzymes is an aromatase inhibitor used in cancer therapy?

A. Physostigmine
B. Allopurinol
C. Aminocaproic acid
D. Aminoglutethimide

Other Subjects

Q.115 The unit of cryoscopic constant is:

A. kelvin kg mol $^{-1}$
B. kelvin kg $^{-1}$ mol $^{-1}$
C. kelvin kg mol $^{+1}$
D. kalvin kg $^{-1}$ mol $^{+1}$

Q.116 Particle particle interaction is studied using:

A. Nernst potential
B. Zeta potential
C. Surface potential
D. Log potential

Q.117 The molecular formula C_5H_{12} contains how many isomeric alkanes?

A. 1
B. 2
C. 3
D. 4

Q.118 20 gm NaOH in 500 ml is equal to:

A. 0.1 N
B. 1 M
C. 0.5 M
D. 0.05 N

Q.119 The cellular matrix is collectively referred to as ____________.

A. Ribosome
B. DNA
C. Cytosol
D. Vacuole

Q.120 Plasmids are used as cloning vectors for which of the following reasons?

A. Can be multiplied in culture.
B. Self-replication in bacterial cells.
C. Can be multiplied in laboratories with the help of enzymes.
D. Replicate freely outside bacterial cells.

Q.121 Which of the following is used in electron microscope?

A. Electron beams and magnetic fields
B. light waves
C. Magnetic fields
D. Electron beams

Q.122 The classic signs of meningeal infection include all of the following except:

A. Cervical rigidity
B. Kernig sign
C. Head retraction
D. Murphy's sign

Q.123 What is the other name of cell eating?

A. Transcytosis
B. Pinocytosis
C. Endocytosis
D. Phagocytosis

Q.124 Young's Rule is applicable for calculating dose of children's:

A. Upto 1 year
B. Upto 1 to 2 year
C. Upto 1 to 5 year
D. Upto 1 to 12 years

Q.125 ____________ muscles contraction produce constriction of pupils (Meiosis).

A. Skeletal muscles
B. Spinctor papillae
C. Cardiac muscle
D. Radial muscles

// Smart Answer Sheet //

Correct Percentage of students who answered correctly. **Skipped** Percentage of students who skipped.

Q.	Ans.	Correct	Skipped	Q.	Ans.	Correct	Skipped	Q.	Ans.	Correct	Skipped	Q.	Ans.	Correct	Skipped	Q.	Ans.	Correct	Skipped	Q.	Ans.	Correct	Skipped
1	D	44.65 %	30.34 %	22	A	48.29 %	31.19 %	43	B	62.0 %	30.82 %	64	D	56.22 %	38.61 %	85	C	61.79 %	30.88 %	106	B	84.96 %	12.09 %
2	D	51.36 %	33.51 %	23	A	80.99 %	12.75 %	44	A	52.85 %	30.84 %	65	D	60.68 %	36.67 %	86	C	16.97 %	77.32 %	107	C	67.16 %	32.54 %
3	A	79.28 %	16.95 %	24	B	40.64 %	54.72 %	45	C	65.16 %	32.04 %	66	A	53.82 %	44.62 %	87	C	68.69 %	30.01 %	108	C	49.85 %	44.04 %
4	D	62.82 %	34.03 %	25	A	60.57 %	32.51 %	46	B	65.27 %	32.37 %	67	A	41.57 %	36.84 %	88	A	53.99 %	39.32 %	109	A	51.19 %	36.52 %
5	D	23.77 %	69.25 %	26	A	55.97 %	37.89 %	47	D	52.57 %	31.15 %	68	D	14.32 %	72.08 %	89	B	68.22 %	31.74 %	110	A	46.95 %	30.63 %
6	A	42.64 %	55.69 %	27	B	42.73 %	45.8 %	48	D	61.08 %	36.16 %	69	D	50.77 %	42.8 %	90	B	28.3 %	70.67 %	111	B	43.03 %	49.4 %
7	D	65.35 %	32.73 %	28	A	47.98 %	43.09 %	49	A	45.98 %	50.24 %	70	D	67.04 %	32.32 %	91	B	49.48 %	38.71 %	112	D	68.42 %	31.16 %
8	B	40.88 %	55.26 %	29	D	28.17 %	68.29 %	50	A	58.65 %	32.34 %	71	B	89.23 %	10.4 %	92	C	63.51 %	35.6 %	113	B	47.02 %	49.22 %
9	A	54.6 %	31.55 %	30	A	85.66 %	10.07 %	51	B	59.99 %	39.35 %	72	D	40.09 %	35.0 %	93	A	54.65 %	41.22 %	114	D	49.99 %	32.76 %
10	B	42.74 %	34.42 %	31	B	49.06 %	46.26 %	52	B	63.36 %	36.35 %	73	A	59.96 %	38.31 %	94	C	63.78 %	32.89 %	115	A	45.86 %	35.0 %
11	C	53.24 %	43.34 %	32	D	58.47 %	40.93 %	53	C	45.36 %	34.04 %	74	B	48.98 %	37.68 %	95	A	44.42 %	38.74 %	116	A	65.37 %	30.22 %
12	C	45.79 %	34.41 %	33	A	60.6 %	36.11 %	54	D	66.19 %	32.83 %	75	A	46.69 %	37.88 %	96	B	46.97 %	46.45 %	117	C	85.28 %	13.19 %
13	B	47.35 %	41.45 %	34	A	56.43 %	34.47 %	55	D	46.17 %	37.85 %	76	A	46.48 %	30.94 %	97	C	66.75 %	30.67 %	118	B	62.77 %	37.11 %
14	A	42.99 %	35.19 %	35	B	64.04 %	34.4 %	56	D	57.98 %	40.98 %	77	D	56.24 %	37.03 %	98	A	69.3 %	30.29 %	119	C	48.98 %	37.9 %
15	D	42.36 %	37.99 %	36	D	43.38 %	47.01 %	57	B	68.8 %	30.38 %	78	B	66.96 %	31.13 %	99	A	65.63 %	32.66 %	120	A	65.97 %	30.55 %
16	B	64.14 %	30.34 %	37	B	67.92 %	30.74 %	58	D	55.44 %	34.47 %	79	D	48.15 %	39.76 %	100	B	54.13 %	37.58 %	121	A	61.52 %	36.38 %
17	C	44.33 %	36.63 %	38	A	12.47 %	77.11 %	59	A	69.64 %	30.31 %	80	A	50.78 %	39.58 %	101	D	64.64 %	32.03 %	122	D	44.42 %	45.23 %
18	C	47.54 %	50.33 %	39	B	62.3 %	34.52 %	60	B	61.78 %	36.86 %	81	B	43.22 %	41.08 %	102	C	66.54 %	31.16 %	123	D	60.05 %	39.72 %
19	B	43.61 %	41.37 %	40	D	53.46 %	30.94 %	61	C	59.32 %	39.33 %	82	A	48.54 %	41.41 %	103	D	66.27 %	33.54 %	124	D	50.76 %	45.06 %
20	C	62.06 %	33.25 %	41	B	66.54 %	32.7 %	62	D	41.84 %	38.22 %	83	B	28.7 %	67.03 %	104	D	58.96 %	34.61 %	125	B	63.39 %	36.17 %
21	C	59.91 %	34.59 %	42	B	67.21 %	31.57 %	63	B	43.09 %	43.31 %	84	C	68.0 %	31.93 %	105	B	58.81 %	37.49 %				

//Hints and Solutions//

1. The recent edition of Pharmacopoeia is the eighth edition. The eighth edition of Indian Pharmacopoeia (IP-2018) is published by the Indian Pharmacopoeia Commission (IPC) on behalf of the Ministry of Health and Family Welfare, Government of India in fulfillment of the requirements of the Drugs and Cosmetic Act, 1940 and the Rules there under.

Hence, the correct option is (D).

2. The latest edition of I.P is published in the year 2018. The standards that are in effect since 1 December 2010, are the Indian Pharmacopoeia 2010 (IP 2010). The Pharmacopoeia 2014 was released by Health Minister Ghulam Nabi Azad on 4 November 2013. The Pharmacopoeia 2018 was released by the Secretary, Ministry of Health & Family Welfare, Government of India.

Hence, the correct option is (D).

3. Chemically alum is potassium aluminium sulphate. Alum is an inorganic compound composed of water molecules, aluminium, other metal than aluminium, and sulphates. Alum is a double salt present in the hydrated form. The general chemical formula for alum is $XAl(SO_4)_2 \cdot 12H_2O$.

Hence, the correct option is (A).

4. pH is usually measured with a glass electrode. The liquid inside the glass electrode usually has a pH of 7. Thus, if one measures the electromotive force generated at the electrode membrane, the pH of the sample can be found by calculation. In the glass-electrode method, the known pH of a reference solution is determined by using two electrodes, a glass electrode and a reference electrode, and measuring the voltage (difference in potential) generated between the two electrodes.

Hence, the correct option is (D).

5. Biological, photographic and fluorescent except for non-penetrating. In general, alpha particles have a very limited ability to penetrate other materials. In other words, these particles of ionizing radiation can be blocked by a sheet of paper, skin, or even a few inches of air.

Hence, the correct option is (D).

6. The best conductor of electricity is graphite. In a graphite molecule, one valence electron of each carbon atom remains free. Due to the free electrons in its framework, graphite can perform electricity. Therefore, graphite is said to be a good conductor of electricity.

Hence, the correct option is (A).

7. NMR spectroscopy is absorption. NMR spectroscopy are a form of absorption spectroscopy, but they don't do the same thing. Infrared radiation causes a vibrational transition in a given molecule. Chemists typically use infrared spectroscopy to identify functional groups that are present in the molecules.

Hence, the correct option is (D).

8. The optical activity of organic substances is measured using a polarized source and polarimeter. A polarimeter is a scientific instrument used to measure the angle of rotation caused by passing polarized light through an optically active substance.

This is a tool particularly used in the sugar industry to measure the sugar concentration of syrup, and generally in chemistry to measure the concentration or enantiomeric ratio of chiral molecules in solution.

Hence, the correct option is (B).

9. The aromatic spirit of ammonium is used as a respiratory stimulant. Aromatic ammonia spirit is used to prevent or treat fainting. Fainting may be caused by some kinds of medicine, by an unpleasant or stressful event, or by a serious medical problem, such as heart disease.

Hence, the correct option is (A).

10. TiO is commonly present in sun screen cream. Titanium dioxide (TiO_2) and zinc oxide (ZnO) minerals are frequently employed in sun screens as inorganic physical sun blockers. As TiO_2 is more effective in UVB and ZnO in the UVA range, the combination of these particles assures a broad-band UV protection.

Hence, the correct option is (B).

11. A Iodinated serum albumin is used to determine plasma and blood volume. Iodine (^{125}I) human albumin is used to determine a person's blood volume. For this purpose, a defined amount of radioactivity in form of this drug is injected into a vein, and blood samples are drawn from a different body location after five and fifteen minutes. Iodinated I-131 serum albumin is a radiopharmaceutical agent used for several diagnostic purposes, including the determination of body fluid volumes and the imaging of certain tissues.

Hence, the correct option is (C).

12. The native colloidal hydrated aluminum silicate is bentonite. Bentonite, Native colloidal hydrated aluminum silicate; an absorbent clay found in the western U.S. it is sometimes used to treat diarrhea and skin disorders and was used as a suspending agent in lotions.

Hence, the correct option is (C).

13. Chemically Talc is a hydrated magnesium silicate. Talc, or talcum, is a clay mineral, composed of hydrated magnesium silicate with the chemical formula $Mg_3Si_4O_{10}(OH)_2$. This mineral is used as a thickening agent and lubricant; is an ingredient in ceramics, paint, and roofing material; and is the main ingredient in many cosmetics.

Hence, the correct option is (B).

14. The softest mineral is known as talc. Talc is the softest mineral on the Mohs hardness scale at 1 and can be easily cut and crushed. Talc has perfect cleavage in one direction. This means that it breaks into thin sheets. As a result, it feels greasy to the touch (which is why talc is used as a lubricant). The softness of talc is credited to its physical and chemical properties. Talc is composed of sheet structures with perfect bond cleavages and very weak bond forces between the sheets.

Hence, the correct option is (A).

15. Technetium sulphide (Tc-99m) colloidal solution is used to scan the liver and spleen. Technetium-99m is used to image the skeleton and heart muscle in particular, but also for brain, thyroid, lungs, liver, spleen, kidney, gall bladder, bone marrow, salivary and lachrymal glands, heart blood pool, infection and numerous specialized medical studies. Technetium (Tc-99m) is an isotope commonly used in a number of medical diagnostic imaging scans. Tc-99m is used as a radioactive tracer for nuclear medicine; which is a form of medical imaging that assesses how particular parts of our body are working or functioning.

Hence, the correct option is (D).

16. Sodium chloride hypertonic injection contains 1.6% W/V. These hypertonic sodium chloride solutions are also indicated for the following clinical conditions. Hyponatremia and hypochloremia due to electrolyte and fluid loss were replaced with sodium-free fluids. 3% and 5% Sodium Chloride Injection, USP should be used with great care, if at all, in patients with congestive heart failure, severe renal insufficiency, and in clinical states in which there exists edema with sodium retention.

Hence, the correct option is (B).

17. Burrow's solution is aluminium acetate sol. strong. Burow's has a very short shelf life of 3-6 months. Burow's solution (5% aluminum subacetate) is a liquid made with water and aluminum acetate. This solution relieves the itching and stinging of irritated, inflamed skin and helps stop the growth of bacteria and fungus. Burrow's solution is an aqueous solution of aluminium triacetate.

Hence, the correct option is (C).

18. The instrument used for measuring the amount of light absorbed by the solution is a spectrophotometer. A spectrophotometer is an instrument that measures the number of photons (the intensity of light) absorbed after it passes through the sample solution. Infrared spectroscopy is a versatile method for the determination of pharmaceutical compounds and functional groups within molecules. It measures energy absorption across the infrared frequency range. Gas, liquid, or solid pharmaceutical samples can be analyzed by infrared spectroscopy.

Hence, the correct option is (C).

19. A metal ion that donates electrons is a ligand. Ligands are Lewis bases. They contain at least one pair of electrons to donate to a metal atom/ion. Ligands are also called complexing agents. Metal atoms/ions are Lewis acids-they can accept pairs of electrons from Lewis bases.

Hence, the correct option is (B).

20. Titrations involving silver nitrate are known as argentometry. Argentometry is a type of titration involving the silver(I) ion. Typically, it is used to determine the amount of chloride present in a sample. The sample solution is titrated against a solution of silver nitrate of known concentration. It is a type of precipitation titration which involves the use of silver ion which is taken from its Latin name Argentum. The titrations with silver nitrate are known as argentometric titration.

Hence, the correct option is (C).

21. The drug used for the determination of myocardial blood flow is rubidium chloride injection. Rubidium chloride Rb-82 injection is a sterile nonpyrogenic solution of rubidium Rb 82 chloride. It is indicated for Positron Emission Tomography (PET) imaging of the myocardium under rest or pharmacologic stress conditions to evaluate regional myocardial perfusion in adult patients with suspected or existing coronary artery disease.

Hence, the correct option is (C).

22. Copper su phate substance used in swimming pools to prevent the growth of algae & snails. According to the recommendations of a Journal of Public Health in America, copper sulfate aka bluestone can be used as an algaecide in swimming pools to purify its water by controlling the growth of algae & snails in the pool.

Hence, the correct option is (A).

23. In surgical operations, the CO_2 content is reduced by the use of soda-lime. Soda-lime absorbs carbon dioxide and water vapour and deteriorates rapidly unless kept in airtight containers. Medically, soda-lime is used to absorb carbon dioxide in basal metabolism tests and in rebreathing anesthesia systems. In gas masks, it is an absorbent for toxic gases.

Hence, the correct option is (A).

24. The chemical formula of sodium phosphate is Na_3PO_4. Sodium phosphate is an ionic compound composed of sodium cation and phosphate anion. This is a salt found both in hydrated and anhydrous salts among which anhydrous(water-free) sodium phosphate is more common in nature. The sodium phosphate chemical formula is Na_3PO_4 and it has a molecular weight of 163.94 g/mol.

Hence, the correct option is (B).

25. The specific rotation of glucose 52-53 $^\circ$. In chemistry, specific rotation ($[\alpha]$) is a property of a chiral chemical compound. It is defined as the change in orientation of monochromatic plane-polarized light, per unit distance concentration product, as the light passes through a sample of a compound in solution.

Hence, the correct option is (A).

26. Mercury compound is used as preservative thiomersal. Thimerosal is a mercury-based preservative that has been used for decades in the United States in multi-dose vials (vials containing more than one dose) of medicines and vaccines.

Thiomersal (also know as thimerosal, merthiolate) is an organomercurial derivative of ethylmercury that has been used very widely, and for a very long time, as a preservative in vaccines in their bulk formulations. Its primary purpose has been to prevent microbial growth in the product during storage and use.

Hence, the correct option is (A).

27. Potassium perchlorate is classified as antithyroid. Potassium perchlorate can be used as an antithyroid agent used to treat hyperthyroidism, usually in combination with one other medication. Potassium perchlorate is the inorganic salt with the chemical formula $KClO_4$. Like other perchlorates, this salt is a strong oxidizer although it usually reacts very slowly with organic substances.

Hence, the correct option is (B).

28. Gold sodium thiomalate is used in rheumatoid arthritis. Gold sodium thiomalate is indicated in the treatment of selected cases of active rheumatoid arthritis-both adult and juvenile types. The greatest benefit occurs in the early active stage. It is sometimes also used to treat juvenile rheumatoid arthritis and psoriatic arthritis. Gold appears to work best in the early stages of arthritis but it may be effective in anyone with active joint pain and swelling.

Hence, the correct option is (A).

29. Parasiticide used in the treatment of Leishmaniasis is sodium antimony gluconate, potassium antimony tartrate and sodium antimony tartrate. Sodium stibogluconate has been the drug of choice for the treatment of cutaneous and mucocutaneous leishmaniasis in the United States. This agent is also effective against visceral leishmaniasis and is often the first-line treatment outside the United States. Pentavalent antimonials, including meglumine antimoniate and sodium stibogluconate, have been used for more than half a century in the therapy of the parasitic disease leishmaniasis.

Hence, the correct option is (D).

30. Mannitol is used in the assay of boric acid. Boric acid is a "weak" acid and gives a poor "endpoint". Adding mannitol to the flask changes the weak acid into a stronger acid, which gives a good, clear endpoint in the titration with sodium hydroxide.

Hence, the correct option is (A).

31. H_2O_2 is prepared by adding a paste of barium peroxide in sulphuric acid. Sodium peroxide can be replaced by barium peroxide. In this case, a paste of BaO_2. $8H_2O$ is prepared and added gradually to an ice-cold dilute sulphuric acid. Barium sulphate precipitates out leaving behind a dilute solution of hydrogen peroxide.

Hence, the correct option is (B).

32. Silicon polymers are synthetically prepared by polymerization. Polymerization is a process through which a large number of monomer molecules react together to form a polymer. The macromolecules produced from a polymerization may have a linear or a branched structure. The most simple polymerization reactions involve the formation of polymers from alkenes via free-radical reaction.

Hence, the correct option is (D).

33. Chemically kaolin is hydrated aluminium silicate. Kaolin is a hydrated aluminum silicate with a crystalline structure that allows for a large surface area that adsorbs many times its weight in water. If taken together, the kaolin may adsorb other medications and reduce their systemic absorption.

Hence, the correct option is (A).

34. An antidote for heavy metal poisoning is magnesium sulphate. The main treatment of heavy metal poisoning is the termination of exposure to the metal. Treatment also consists of the use of various chelating agents that cause the toxic (poison) element to bind with the drug and be excreted in the urine.

Magnesium is a naturally occurring mineral that is important for many systems in the body especially the muscles and nerves. Magnesium sulphate also increases water in the intestines. Magnesium sulphate is used as a laxative to relieve occasional constipation.

Hence, the correct option is (A).

35. Magnesium sulphate BPC is also called epsom salt. Magnesium sulphate, sold as Epsom salt, is a mineral compound that's used for different health and medical purposes. It has a role as an anticonvulsant, a cardiovascular drug, a calcium channel blocker, an anaesthetic, a tocolytic agent, an anti-arrhythmia drug, an analgesic and a fertilizer. It is a magnesium salt and a metal sulphate.

Hence, the correct option is (B).

36. One part of solute is soluble in 1-10 parts of solvent means freely soluble. Freely soluble materials are those, which have high solubility. Usually, materials are treated as freely soluble if 1g of the material requires 1 to 10ml of solute to dissolve. In other words, a material will be freely soluble if the amount which can be dissolved in 100ml of solute ranges between 10g and 100g.

Hence, the correct option is (D).

37. Saline cathartic used in barium and lead poisoning is magnesium sulphate. Saline cathartics stimulants act by local irritation on the intestinal tract which increases peristaltic activity. They include phenolphthalein, aloin, cascara extract, rhubarb extract, senna extract, podophyllin, castor oil, bisacodyl, calomel, etc. Examples include magnesium citrate, magnesium sulfate and magnesium hydroxide.

Hence, the correct option is (B).

38. An ingredient in Benedicts and Fehling's reagent is copper sulphate. Benedict's reagent (often called Benedict's qualitative solution or Benedict's solution.) is a chemical reagent and complex mixture of sodium carbonate, sodium citrate, and copper(II) sulphate pentahydrate. It is often used in place of Fehling's solution to detect the presence of reducing sugars.

Hence, the correct option is (A).

39. A water attack test is used to identify the alkalinity in the type-II glass. The principle involved in the water attack test is to determine whether the alkali leached from the surface of a container is within the specified limits or not. Since the inner surface is under test entire container (ampoule) has to be used. This is only for treated soda-lime glass containers under the controlled humidity conditions which neutralize the surface alkali and glass will become chemically more resistant.

Hence, the correct option is (B).

40. As per G.M.P permitted limit of solid contents in water for injection is 10 ppm. Sterile Water for Injection, USP, is sterile, non pyrogenic, distilled water in a single dose container for intravenous administration after the addition of a suitable solute. It may also be used as a dispensing container for diluent use. No antimicrobial or other substance has been added. The pH is 5.5 (5.0 to 7.0).

Hence, the correct option is (D).

41. Sterilization temperature for aqueous solution in autoclave (moist heat) is 121 $^\circ$C. The recommendation for sterilization in an autoclave is 15 minutes at 121 $^\circ$C (200 kPa). The temperature should be used to control and monitor the process; the pressure is mainly used to obtain the required steam temperature.

Hence, the correct option is (B).

42. Sterility test for the material meant for surgical suture required incubation for 14 days. Sterility testing is required to ensure viable contaminating microorganisms are not evident in a product. This testing is conducted by direct inoculation or membrane filtration methods and can be performed in an isolator or cleanroom environment. Sterility testing requires 14 days of long incubation time because there are some bacteria that are very slow-growing like Propionibacterium acne.

Hence, the correct option is (B).

43. An amphoteric surfactant used in pharmaceutical disperse system is lecithin. Lecithin is a mixture of fats that are essential to cells in the human body. In the diet, lecithin is the main source of choline, a nutrient similar to the B vitamins. Lecithin is converted into acetylcholine, a substance that transmits nerve impulses.

Hence, the correct option is (B).

44. An abrasive used in dentifrices are dicalcium phosphate. Dicalcium phosphate is the calcium phosphate with the formula $CaHPO_4$ and its dihydrate. It is also known as dibasic calcium phosphate or calcium mono hydrogen phosphate. Dicalcium phosphate is used as a food additive, it is found in some toothpastes as a polishing agent and is a biomaterial.

Hence, the correct option is (A).

45. The florentine receiver is used to separate the liquids based on density. The liquid runs into the florentine receiver where the water and essential oil phases separate. The essential oils phase separates from water because the oils have a different density than water, and are not water-soluble. There are two main types of florentines in use.

Hence, the correct option is (C).

46. The official dissolution test apparatus contains a cylindrical vessel and the lower edge of the blade is positioned from the inside the bottom of the vessel at 23 to 27 mm. drug dissolution testing is routinely used to provide critical in vitro drug release information for both quality control purposes, i.e., to assess batch-to-batch consistency of solid oral dosage forms such as tablets, and drug development, i.e., to predict in vivo drug release profiles. There are three typical situations where dissolution testing plays a vital role:

- Formulation and optimization decisions during product development, for products where dissolution performance is a critical quality attribute, both the product formulation and the manufacturing process are optimized based on achieving specific dissolution targets.

- Equivalence decisions during generic product development, and also when implementing a post-approval process or formulation changes, the similarity of in vitro dissolution profiles between the reference product and its generic or modified version are one of the key requirements for regulatory approval decisions.

- Product compliance and release decisions during routine manufacturing, dissolution outcomes are very often one of the criteria used to make product release decisions.

Hence, the correct option is (B).

47. As per the Drugs and Cosmetics Act and Rules, good manufacturing practice is included under Schedule M. Schedule M is a part of the Drug and Cosmetic act of 1940. It is GMP for pharmaceuticals that should be followed by pharmaceutical manufacturing units in India.

Hence, the correct option is (D).

48. In a multistation punching machine, the upper, as well as lower punches, are connected by revolving belts. A multistation press is a mechanical device that unlike the single punch tablet press has several tooling stations which rotates to compress granules/powder mixture into tablets of uniform size, shape (depending on the punch design), and uniform weight. It was developed to increase the output of tablets.

Hence, the correct option is (D).

49. As per the Drugs and Cosmetics Act, HEPA filters are required to filter the air in the pharmaceutical manufacturing unit. Grade A filter is used for aseptic preparation and filling. HEPA filters are used as terminal filters for the processing or filtration of air in production spaces. They are mandatory in sterile production, although they are sometimes also used in the manufacture of solid or semisolid dosage forms.

Hence, the correct option is (A).

50. Liposomes are used as carriers for drugs and macromolecules in pharmaceutical formulations. They are phospholipids dispersed gently in an aqueous medium to obtain multilamellar vesicles. Liposomes are a novel drug delivery system (NDDS), they are vesicular structures consisting of bilayers that form spontaneously when phospholipids are dispersed in water.

Hence, the correct option is (A).

51. Lipstick should not retard healing of the wound is not an ideal quality of the lipstick. Lipstick is an almost universal cosmetic since, together with the eyes, the mouth is a leading feature, and it can be attractively coloured and textured. Lipstick has a fatty base that is firm in itself and yet spreads easily when applied.

Hence, the correct option is (B).

52. The shell of cachets are fragile, so the drug can't be compressed in cachets is a disadvantage of cachets. A kind of wafer capsule formerly used by pharmacists for presenting an unpleasant-tasting drug. A solid composed of dry powdered active and/or inert ingredient(s) covered by an edible shell. The shell consists of two concave pieces of wafer made of flour and water.

Hence, the correct option is (B).

53. The most serious type of dosage error in dispensing is an overdose of medication. A drug overdose (overdose or OD) is the ingestion or application of a drug or other substance in quantities greater than are recommended. Typically it is used for cases when a risk to health will potentially result. An overdose may result in a toxic state or death.

Hence, the correct option is (C).

54. The rheological method provides useful information regarding the stability of the suspension. Rheological characterization tools, such as viscometers, allow drug producers to directly affect how a drug is formulated and developed, cutting across parameters and conditions to arrive at product characteristics that can be quantified.

Hence, the correct option is (D).

55. Drawbacks of cocoa butter as a suppository base are exhibit marked polymorphism, rancidity and stick to mould. Cocoa butter, which is still widely used as a suppository base, has several well-known defects, such as slowness to harden if overheated and the assumption of solid forms with low melting points. In tropical countries, a further disadvantage is the proximity of its melting point to average room temperature.

Hence, the correct option is (D).

56. The ointments are used to remove or soften the horny layer of the skin keratolytic. Keratolytics are compounds that break down the outer layers of the skin and can decrease the thickness of psoriatic plaques. This class of compounds includes salicylic acid (2%–10%), urea (20%–40%), and alpha-hydroxy acids (glycolic and lactic acids).

Hence, the correct option is (D).

57. The advantage of powder as a dosage form is that it is convenient for dispersing bulky drugs. Powders have better physicochemical stability and longer shelf life compared to liquid dosage forms. For example, the shelf life of powders for antibiotic syrups is 2 to 3 years, but once reconstituted with water it is 1 to 2 weeks. Powders offer a lot of flexibility in compounding solids.

Hence, the correct option is (B).

58. The advantages of parenteral products are rapid onset of action, immediate therapeutic action is possible and each dose can be administered accurately. Parenteral drug delivery, especially intravenous injection, can gain easy access to the systemic circulation with complete drug absorption and therefore reach the site of drug action rapidly cardiac arrest, asthma and shock.

Hence, the correct option is (D).

59. The jelly is applied to the electrode to reduce the electrical resistance between the patient's skin and the electrode electrocardiography. Electrocardiography, method of graphic tracing (electrocardiogram; ECG or EKG) of the electric current generated by the heart muscle during a heartbeat. An electrocardiogram (ECG) is a medical test that detects cardiac (heart) abnormalities by measuring the electrical activity generated by the heart as it contracts. The machine that records the patient's ECG is called an electrocardiograph.

Hence, the correct option is (A).

60. The advantages of cachets are:

1. Made easily.
2. Disintegrate quickly in the stomach.
3. Drugs can be easily dispensed.
4. A large dose of drug can be swallowed by using cachets.
5. Powders enclosed in cachets & capsules.

Hence, the correct option is (B).

61. Creams are viscous semi-solid emulsions that are meant for external application to the skin or mucous membrane for protective, therapeutic or prophylactic purposes. Creams are semisolid dosage forms containing more than 20% water or volatile components and typically less than 50% hydrocarbons, waxes, or polyols as vehicles. They may also contain one or more drug substances dissolved or dispersed in a suitable cream base.

Hence, the correct option is (C).

62. The qualities of a good dentifrice, toothpaste or tooth powder should have the following qualities:-

1. It should be economical.
2. It should be non-toxic.
3. It should be properly sweetened and flavoured.
4. It should give a fresh and clean sensation.
5. It should be efficient in removing food substances, plaque and other foreign particles.
6. It should clean the teeth.

Hence, the correct option is (D).

63. Cachets are the solid unit dosage form of drugs. Dosage forms (also called unit doses) are pharmaceutical drug products in the form in which they are marketed for use, with a specific mixture of active ingredients and inactive components (excipients), in a particular configuration (such as a capsule shell, for example), and apportioned into a particular dose. For example, two products may both be amoxicillin, but one is in 500 mg capsules and another is in 250 mg chewable tablets.

Hence, the correct option is (B).

64. The qualities of an ideal shampoo are:

1. It should be non-toxic.
2. It should be capable of removing grease, dirt, and skin debris from the hair and scalp.
3. It should be effective in small amounts.
4. It should not form any kind of film on the scalp.
5. It should not support any microbial growth.

Hence, the correct option is (D).

65. Efflorescent powders include caffeine and ferrous sulphate:

Caffeine: Caffeine is a bitter substance that occurs naturally in more than 60 plants including Coffee beans. Tea leaves. Kola nuts, which are used to flavor soft drink colas. Cacao pods, which are used to make chocolate products.

Ferrous sulphate: Ferrous sulphate (or sulphate) is a medicine used to treat and prevent iron deficiency anaemia. Iron helps the body to make healthy red blood cells, which carry oxygen around the body. Some things such as blood loss, pregnancy, or too little iron in your diet can make your iron supply drop too low, leading to anaemia.

Hence, the correct option is (D).

66. Ointment bases used should possess emollient properties that should be able to keep the skin moist. The emollient properties mean soother or softener, an emollient softens dry, rough, flakey skin, making it look and feel better. When the top layer of your skin doesn't contain enough water, it dries out. Emollients are part of a moisturizer that keeps your skin soft and smooth.

Hence, the correct option is (A).

67. Adjuvant substances are added to increase the stability or quality of the product. An adjuvant is an ingredient used in some vaccines that helps create a stronger immune response in people receiving the vaccine. In other words, adjuvants help vaccines work better. Substance or a composition of substances which when used in a vaccine potentiates the immune response to the active substances of the vaccine and/or modulates it towards a desired immune response which cannot be achieved by administration of the active substances alone.

Hence, the correct option is (A).

68. Oleogels ointment bases are of the emulsion type. Oleogels are gels in which the continuous liquid phase is oil. To create a network structure, alternative structuring agents are needed. Often these are small molecular weight molecules. An oleogels is a popular form of cosmetic that allows for oily gel products which become self-emulsifying when in contact with water. They are formed using special oil-gelling and emulsifying ingredients, often based on innovative sucrose chemistry.

Hence, the correct option is (D).

69. An extraordinary response to a drug that is different from its characteristic pharmacological action is called idiosyncrasy. "Drug idiosyncrasy" refers to untoward reactions to drugs that occur in a small fraction of patients and have no obvious relationship to dose or duration of therapy. The liver is a frequent target for toxicity.

Hence, the correct option is (D).

70. The stability of suspension depends on the particle size of the disperse phase is the micromeritic method. The word Micromeritics refers to a discipline of science and technology that deals with studies related to the fundamental as well derived properties of particles. A precise knowledge of the particle's size is of supreme importance in pharmaceutical and materials science.

The size of the particle in a suspension may grow and ultimately leads to the formation of clumps or caking. So, any change in particle size distribution with reference to time gives a stable suspension.

Hence, the correct option is (D).

71. It is false that Jellies are clear, sweetened, aromatic, hydroalcoholic liquids prepared for oral use. Jelly is the firmest type of fruit spread, so it's strong enough to hold its shape when turned out of its container. A fruit jelly should be of a good color, a transparent mass which will quiver, not flow, when taken from the mould, with texture so tender that it may be cut easily with a spoon, and yet so firm that the angles produced by cutting retain their shape.

Hence, the correct option is (B).

72. Therapeutic incompatibility may occur when two or more drugs are administered concurrently. For example, the antibiotics chloramphenicol and penicillin aren't compatible; chloramphenicol reportedly antagonizes penicillin's antibacterial effects. The reasons causing therapeutic incompatibility are:

- Error in dosage.
- The wrong dose or dosage form.
- Synergism and Antagonism drug.

Hence, the correct option is (D).

73. Gum tragacanth, sodium alginate, methylcellulose are used as binders. Gum tragacanth is also used in incense-making as a binder to hold all the powdered herbs together. Its water solubility is ideal for ease of working and an even spread, and it is one of the stronger gums for holding particles in suspension.

Hence, the correct option is (A).

74. Liniments are used for counter-irritant, rubefacient, soothing or stimulating purposes. Liniment is a liquid that you rub into the skin in order to reduce pain or relieve stiffness. Liniments can be rubbed into the skin to relieve aches from arthritis and stiffness in muscles. A liniment is usually in the form of a thin liquid applied to the skin.

Hence, the correct option is (B).

75. Antiperspirants are used to reduce sweat formation. Antiperspirant works by temporarily clogging sweat glands to decrease sweating. It does this by creating a gel on the surface of the skin. It's not absorbed into the skin, but it does contain irritants such as fragrances, alcohol, and other ingredients.

Hence, the correct option is (A).

76. Functions of Tartaric acid for neutralization. Neutralization is a chemical reaction in which acid and a base react quantitatively with each other. In a reaction in water, neutralization results in there being no excess of hydrogen or hydroxide ions present in the solution. The pH of the neutralized solution depends on the acid strength of the reactants.

Hence, the correct option is (A).

77. Umbelliferrous fruits are schizocarps. A schizocarpic fruit is one that develops from a single ovary of a flower. Schizocarps are simple fruits that are generally dry in nature. Schizocarps are a dry compound fruit that splits at maturity into several indehiscent one-seeded carpels.

Hence, the correct option is (D).

78. The number of vittae in the cremocarp of fennel is 6. There are four vittae on the dorsal surface and two vittae on the commissural or the ventral surface. Inner Epidermis or Endocarp shows parquetry arrangement (a group of four to five cells arranged parallelly at acute angles with groups of similar cells in different directions).

Hence, the correct option is (B).

79. The percentage of citral content of lemongrass oil is 70 to 80%. Percentage of oil (citral) varies according to plant species, about 90–98% oil is present in lemon myrtle, 70–80% in litsea cubeba, 65–85% in lemongrass, 30–35% in lemon verbena, 26% in ironbark lemon, 11% in lemon balm, 6–9% in lime, and about 2–5% in lemon and oranges.

Hence, the correct option is (D).

80. Lemongrass oil is mainly produced from cymbopogon flexuosus in south India. Lemon grass is widely cultivated in the states of Kerala, Karnataka, Tamil Nadu in the southern region, parts of Uttar Pradesh and Uttaranchal in the northern region and Assam in the north-eastern region. At present, East Indian lemon grass (C. flexuosus) is mainly cultivated in the western part of India.

Hence, the correct option is (A).

81. In India, menthol is mainly produced from oil of mentha arvensis. Japanese Mint (Mentha arvensis var piperascense) is an aromatic perennial herb, grown as an annual in sub-tropical parts of north India. The over-ground herb (foliage) on distillation yields an essential oil, containing high (75 – 80%) menthol content.

Hence, the correct option is (B).

82. Citral is a suitable substance for the synthesis of vitamin A. Citral is used in the synthesis of vitamin A, lycopene, ionone, and methyl ionone, to mask the smell of smoke. Citral, or 3,7-dimethyl-2,6-octadienal or lemonal, is either a pair or a mixture of terpenoids with the molecular formula $C_{10}H_{16}O$. The two compounds are geometric isomers. The E-isomer is known as geranial or citral A. The Z-isomer is known as neral or citral B.

Hence, the correct option is (A).

83. The percentage of citral in lemon peel oil is 4%. Lemongrass oil contains citral at concentrations of approximately 65-85% w/w, and lemon oil contains citral at a concentration of approximately 2-5% w/w. Lemon oil contains terpenes (about 94% mainly (+)- limonene), sesquiterpenes, aldehydes (citral, about 3.4–3.6%, and citronellal) and esters (about 1% geranyl acetate).

Hence, the correct option is (B).

84. The colour shown by a thick section of bitter orange peel is dark green. They are glossy, dark green on the upper surface, and lighter beneath. The calyx is cup-shaped and the thick, fleshy petals, five in number, are intensely white and curl back.

Hence, the correct option is (C).

85. Stigma and upper part of style of crocus sativus is called as saffron. Saffron is a spice derived from the flower of Crocus sativus, commonly known as the "saffron crocus". The vivid crimson stigma and styles, called threads, are collected and dried for use mainly as a seasoning and colouring agent in food.

Hence, the correct option is (C).

86. Proto crocin is a precursor for the taste, odour and colour of the saffron, it is tetraterpene glycoside. A hypothetical proto crocin of the fresh plant is decomposed on drying into one molecule of crocin and two molecules of picrocrocin. Crocin on hydrolysis yields gentiobiose and crocetin, while picrocrocin yields glucose and safranal.

Hence, the correct option is (C).

87. Atenolol is the selective blocker of beta-1 adrenoreceptors. Beta-1 selective blockers are a subclass of beta-blockers that are commonly used to treat high blood pressure. Drugs in this class include atenolol (Tenormin), metoprolol (Lopressor), nebivolol (Bystolic), and bisoprolol (Zebeta, Monocor).

Hence, the correct option is (C).

88. Propranolol drug is an inhibitor of renin synthesis. Renin-inhibitors are pharmaceutical drugs inhibiting the activity of renin that is responsible for hydrolyzing angiotensinogen to angiotensin I, which in turn reduces the formation of angiotensin II that facilitates blood pressure.

Hence, the correct option is (A).

89. Captopril drug is a non-peptide angiotensin II receptor antagonist. Captopril is in a class of medications called angiotensin-converting enzyme (ACE) inhibitors. It decreases certain chemicals that tighten the blood vessels, so blood flows more smoothly and the heart can pump blood more efficiently. Captopril is indicated in clinically stable patients with asymptomatic left ventricular dysfunction (ejection fraction ≤ 40%) following myocardial infarction to improve survival, delay the onset of symptomatic heart failure, reduce hospitalizations for heart failure.

Hence, the correct option is (B).

90. The statements which are true regarding verapamil are it relaxes coronary artery smooth muscle, depresses cardiac contractility and it blocks L-type calcium channels except for it increases heart rate. Verapamil is a novel antiarrhythmic and antianginal agent which, although introduced in 1962, has only recently gained prominence not only as a significant agent in cardiovascular therapeutics but also as a powerful tool to examine the nature of some of the biophysical phenomena at the membrane of cardiac and other excitable tissues. Verapamil is the prototype of those agents which selectively inhibit membrane transport of calcium, an action that accounts for the drug's peripheral and coronary vasodilator properties, its effect on excitation-contraction coupling.

Hence, the correct option is (B).

91. Progesterone is secreted by the corpus luteum. Progesterone is mainly secreted by the corpus luteum in the ovary during the second half of the menstrual cycle. It plays an important role in the menstrual cycle and in maintaining the early stages of pregnancy.

Hence, the correct option is (B).

92. The major natural progestin is Progesterone. Progesterone (Prometrium, Utrogestan), the natural progestogen in the body and one of the most widely used progestogen medications. Progesterone prepares the endometrium for the potential of pregnancy after ovulation. It triggers the lining to thicken to accept a fertilized egg. It also prohibits the muscle contractions in the uterus that would cause the body to reject an egg.

Hence, the correct option is (C).

93. Mifepristone (RU-486) is antiprogestin. Mifeprex RU486 is a prescription medicine used to treat the symptoms of Cushing Syndrome and pregnancy termination. Mifeprex RU486 may be used alone or with other medications. Mifeprex RU486 belongs to a class of drugs called Antiprogestins; Cortisol Receptor Blockers.

Hence, the correct option is (A).

94. Celecoxib NSAIDs is a selective COX-2 inhibitor. Celebrex (celecoxib) is currently the only brand-name selective COX-2 inhibitor available in the United States; there are also generic versions of celecoxib. In theory, a drug such as celecoxib that selectively inhibited COX-2 might block inflammation, pain, and fever while reducing the side effects (gastric erosions and ulcers) associated with inhibition of COX-1.

Hence, the correct option is (C).

95. Piroxicam NSAIDs is a nonselective COX inhibitor. Piroxicam is used to relieve pain, tenderness, swelling, and stiffness caused by osteoarthritis (arthritis caused by a breakdown of the lining of the joints) and rheumatoid arthritis (arthritis caused by swelling of the lining of the joints). Piroxicam is in a class of medications called NSAIDs.

Hence, the correct option is (A).

96. Zileuton (Zyflo) drug is a 5-lipoxygenase (5-LOG) inhibitor. Zileuton (trade name Zyflo) is an orally active inhibitor of 5-lipoxygenase, and thus inhibits leukotrienes (LTB4, LTC4, LTD4, and LTE4) formation, used for the maintenance treatment of asthma. Zileuton is the only 5-lipoxygenase (5-LOX) inhibitor marketed as a treatment for asthma and is often utilized as a selective tool to evaluate the role of 5-LOX and leukotrienes.

Hence, the correct option is (B).

97. Zafirlukast (Accolate) drugs are leukotriene D4 receptor (LTD4) blockers. Zafirlukast is used to prevent asthma symptoms. Zafirlukast is in a class of medications called leukotriene receptor antagonists (LTRAs). It works by blocking the action of certain natural substances that cause swelling and tightening of the airways. Accolate is a prescription medicine used to treat the symptoms of Asthma. Accolate may be used alone or with other medications. Accolate belongs to a class of drugs called Leukotriene Receptor Antagonists.

Hence, the correct option is (C).

98. Sulotroban drugs is thromboxane A2 receptor (TXA2) antagonist. Sulotroban (S-18886) is a TXA2 receptor antagonist that is reigniting interest in this class of antiplatelet agents (Table 65-2). This oral compound exerts dose-dependent antiplatelet effects with collagen and ADP stimulation that is similar to clopidogrel, although superior to aspirin, under both high and low shear conditions.

Hence, the correct option is (A).

99. H1 histamine receptor subtype is distributed in smooth muscle, endothelium, and brain. The histamine H1 receptors are widely distributed in several tissues, including the brain. The receptor apart from the brain and spinal cord is present in smooth muscles from airways, cardiovascular system endothelial cells, and lymphocytes (Hew et al., 1990).

Hence, the correct option is (A).

100. H2 histamine receptor subtype is distributed in gastric mucosa, cardiac muscle, mast cells, and brain. Both H1 and H2 receptors are widely distributed throughout the animal body in the gastrointestinal, reproductive, respiratory, and cardiovascular systems, nervous systems, and on mast cells and blood leucocytes.

Hence, the correct option is (B).

101. For interferon-alpha administration is hepatitis C virus infection. Alpha interferon is a cytokine produced by the innate immune system in response to environmental exposures including viral infections. Alpha interferon in various formulations has been developed as a therapy for several forms of cancer and viral infections, but its major use has been as therapy for chronic hepatitis C.

Hence, the correct option is (D).

102. For interferon-alpha administration is Kaposi's sarcoma. This medication is used to treat various cancers (e.g., leukemia, melanoma, AIDS-related Kaposi's sarcoma). It is also used to treat virus infections (e.g., chronic hepatitis B, chronic hepatitis C, condylomata acuminata). This medication is the same as a protein that your body naturally produces (interferon).

Hence, the correct option is (C).

103. Immuno-modulating agents are cytokines, levamisole and BCG (Bacille Calmette-Guerin) except for tacrolimus (FK-506). Tacrolimus (FK-506) is an immunosuppressant agent that acts by a variety of different mechanisms which include inhibition of calcineurin. It is used as a therapeutic alternative to cyclosporin and therefore represents a cornerstone of immunosuppressive therapy in organ transplant recipients.

Hence, the correct option is (D).

104. The mechanism of action of levamisole is that it increases the number of T-cells. The mechanism of action of levamisole as an antiparasitic agent appears to be tied to its agnositic activity towards the L-subtype nicotinic acetylcholine receptors in nematode muscles. This agonistic action reduces the capacity of the males to control their reproductive muscles and limits their ability to copulate.

Hence, the correct option is (D).

105. Tocopherol is a fat-soluble vitamin. Vitamin E is a fat-soluble vitamin with several forms, but alpha-tocopherol is the only one used by the human body. Its main role is to act as an antioxidant, scavenging loose electrons so-called "free radicals" that can damage cells.

Hence, the correct option is (B).

106. Vitamin A can also be synthesized from a dietary precursor called beta carotene. The human body converts beta carotene into vitamin A (retinol)-beta carotene is a precursor of vitamin A. We need vitamin A for healthy skin and mucus membranes, our immune system, and good eye health and vision. Vitamin A can be sourced from the food we eat, through beta carotene, for example, or in supplement form.

Hence, the correct option is (B).

107. Vitamin D resembles with hormones. Vitamin D is a hormone the kidneys produce that controls blood calcium concentration and impacts the immune system. It is also known as calcitriol, ergocalciferol, calcidiol and cholecalciferol.

Hence, the correct option is (C).

108. Pyridoxine vitamins are given along with isoniazid in the treatment of tuberculosis. Guidelines for Tuberculosis Preventive Therapy Among HIV Infected Individuals Ministry of Health, South Africa Vitamin B6 (pyridoxine) 25 mg per day should be given concomitantly with isoniazid to prevent the occurrence of peripheral neuropathy. Vitamin B6 plays an important role in the body. It is needed to maintain the health of nerves, skin, and red blood cells. Pyridoxine has been used to prevent or treat a certain nerve disorder (peripheral neuropathy) caused by certain medications (such as isoniazid).

Hence, the correct option is (C).

109. Vitamin E is also known as an anti sterility factor. Vitamin E is also called Tocopherol. It is a reproductive vitamin. It is also called anti-sterility vitamin as its deficiency leads to sterility. Vitamin E was discovered by Evans and Bishop in 1922. Initially, it was denoted as an "anti-sterility factor X" as it is necessary for reproduction in females.

Hence, the correct option is (A).

110. Megadoses of Vitamin C are sometimes beneficial viral respiratory infections. Vitamin C in megadoses administered before or after the appearance of cold and flu symptoms relieved and prevented the symptoms in the test population compared with the control group.

Hence, the correct option is (A).

111. Selegiline anti enzymes is monoamine oxidase (MAO) inhibitor. Selegiline, a selective monoamine oxidase B inhibitor, has been approved for the adjunctive treatment of Parkinson's disease at low doses. At higher doses, oral selegiline is also effective in major depressive disorder (MDD) but loses its selectivity and has the potential for tyramine interactions.

Hence, the correct option is (B).

112. Acetazolamide anti enzymes is a carbonic anhydrase inhibitor. That means this drug works to cause an accumulation of carbonic acid by preventing its breakdown. The result is lower blood pH (i.e., more acidic), given the increased carbonic acid,

which has a reversible reaction into bicarbonate and a hydrogen ion.

Hence, the correct option is (D).

113. Allopurinol anti enzymes is a xantine oxidase inhibitor. Allopurinol was effective in inhibiting xanthine oxidase activity in vivo as measured by the dramatic reduction of uric acid production. Lipid peroxidation, however, was not affected by allopurinol.

Hence, the correct option is (B).

114. Aminoglutethimide anti enzymes is an aromatase inhibitor used in cancer therapy. Aminoglutethimide is an aromatase inhibitor that is successfully used for the endocrine treatment of advanced breast cancer. This drug also stimulates the activity of hepatic mixed-function oxidases, increasing the metabolism of several drugs, including warfarin, digitoxin, antipyrine and theophylline.

Hence, the correct option is (D).

115. The unit of a cryoscopic constant is kelvin kg mol^{-1}. The cryoscopic constant is defined as the molal depression constant Or it may be defined as the depression in freezing point when one mole of non-volatile solute is dissolved in one kilogram of solvent. Its units kelvin kg mol^{-1}.

Hence, the correct option is (A).

116. Particle-particle interaction is studied using Nernst potential. In a biological membrane, the reversal potential (also known as the Nernst potential) of an ion is the membrane potential at which there is no net (overall) flow of that particular ion from one side of the membrane to the other. Equilibrium refers to the fact that the net ion flux at a particular voltage is zero.

Hence, the correct option is (A).

117. The molecular formula C_5H_{12} contains 3 isomeric alkanes.

1. n-pentane
2. 2-ethyl propane
3. 2-methyl butane

To have three isomeric monochlorides, the isomer of the alkane of the molecular formula C_5H_{12} should contain three different types of H-atoms. Therefore, the isomer is n-pentane.

Hence, the correct option is (C).

118. 20 gm NaOH dissolved in 500 ml of the solution has 1M of molarity. 500 ml of a solution contains 20 gm of NaOH (MW = 40). 20% NaOH solution means that 100 grams of solution contain 20 grams of NaOH. It is defined as the ratio of the number of moles of solute in a solution to the volume of the solution.

Hence, the correct option is (B).

119. The cellular matrix is collectively referred to as cytosol. The cytosol, also known as cytoplasmic matrix or groundplasm, is one of the liquids found inside cells (intracellular fluid (ICF)). It is separated into compartments by membranes. For example, the mitochondrial matrix separates the mitochondrion into many compartments.

Hence, the correct option is (C).

120. Plasmids are used as cloning vectors because they can be multiplied in culture. Plasmids come in many different sizes and are used for many different purposes in biotechnology. They first made their mark in the field of recombinant DNA in the 1970s, being used as a tool to insert genes into bacteria to encourage their production of therapeutic proteins such as human insulin.

Hence, the correct option is (A).

121. Electron Microscope uses electron beams and magnetic fields to produce the image, whereas the light microscope uses light waves and glass lenses. In electron microscopy, a much higher resolution is obtained with extremely short wavelength of the electron beam.

Hence, the correct option is (A).

122. The classic signs of meningeal infection include cervical rigidity, kernig sign and head retraction except for murphy's sign. The three classic meningeal signs are Kernig's sign, Brudzinski's sign, and nuchal rigidity noted in each patient prior to lumbar puncture. Murphy's sign is elicited in patients with acute cholecystitis by asking the patient to take in and hold a deep breath while palpating the right subcostal area. If pain occurs on inspiration, when the inflamed gallbladder comes into contact with the examiner's hand, Murphy's sign is positive.

Hence, the correct option is (D).

123. Phagocytosis is the other name of cell eating. Phagocytosis, also known as cell eating, is the absorption of larger particles such as bacteria into the cytosol. Phagocytosis is a special form of endocytosis in which large particles such as microorganisms and dead cells are ingested via large endocytic vesicles called phagosomes. In the gut of animals, for example, the particles of food are broken down extracellularly and their hydrolysis products are imported into cells.

Hence, the correct option is (D).

124. Young's Rule is applicable for calculating a dose of children's up to 1 to 12 years. Young's Rule is an equation used to calculate pediatric medication dosage based on the patient's age and the known recommended adult dose. The definition of Young's Rule is the age of the patient, divided by the age added to twelve, all multiplied by the recommended adult dose.

This formula appears below:

[Age / (Age + 12)] x Recommended Adult Dose = Pediatric Dose

Young's Rule can be applied to quickly approach a situation in which the patient's weight is unknown. Other approaches to pediatric dosing that also use age include Webster's Rule and Fried's Rule.

Hence, the correct option is (D).

125. Spinctor papillae muscles contraction produce constriction of pupils (Meiosis). Causes of miosis. The size of your pupil is controlled by two counteracting muscles-the iris dilator and the iris sphincter. Usually, miosis or pupil contraction is caused by a problem with your iris sphincter muscles or the nerves that control them.

Hence, the correct option is (B).

Pharmaceutical Chemistry

Q.1 Sodium nitrite is used for _______ poisoning.
A. Co
B. Barbiturate
C. Cyanide
D. Alkaloidal

Q.2 A standard titrant in iodometric analysis:
A. Sodium nitrate
B. Sodium thiosulphate
C. Sodium nitrite
D. Copper sulphate

Q.3 Antidote in cyanide poisoning:
A. Sodium citrate
B. Sodium bromide
C. Sodium benzoate
D. Sodium thiosulphate

Q.4 Universal antidote contains:
A. Magnesium oxide
B. Tannic acid
C. Charcoal
D. All of these

Q.5 Solution of potassium chloride is used in poisoning:
A. Opium
B. Digitalis
C. Atropine
D. Alkaloidal

Q.6 Lithium carbonate is used in:
A. Insomnia
B. Schizophrenia
C. Mania
D. Epilepsy

Q.7 Cis-platinum is used as a/an:
A. Antiseptic
B. Antioxidant
C. Antineoplastic agent
D. None of these

Q.8 The basic unit of radio activity is:
A. Becquerel
B. Stable isotope
C. Isotope
D. Marie

Q.9 The colour produced by salicylates with ferric chloride reagent:
A. Violet
B. Pink
C. Red
D. Grange

Q.10 Sodium phosphate (P^{32}) is used in:
A. Leukaemia
B. Purpures
C. Polycythemia vera
D. Luecopenia

Q.11 PM indicators are used in:
A. Complexometric titrations
B. Acid-base titrations
C. Not-aqueous titrations
D. Redox titrations

Q.12 Roentgen(R) is unit of:
A. Absorbed dose
B. Exposure
C. Dose equivalent
D. Adsorbed dose

Q.13 A radio-opaque compound used as diagnostic agent in peptic ulcer is:
A. Zinc sulphate
B. Magnesium sulphate
C. Barium sulphate
D. Potassium sulphate

Q.14 One of the following emissions from the decay of radio nuclides is commonly used in sterilization is:
A. Gamma
B. X-ray
C. Alpha
D. Positron

Q.15 Chemical formula of Plaster of Paris is:
A. $CaSO_4.H_2O$
B. $CaSO_4.1/2\ H_2O$
C. $CaSO_4.2H_2O$
D. $CaSO_4$

Q.16 Calcium salt widely used in dental products is:
A. Calcium lactate
B. Calcium phosphate
C. Calcium sulphate
D. Calcium levulinate

Q.17 The drug used in hypocalcemia is:
A. Magnesium chloride
B. Sodium chloride
C. Ammonium chloride
D. Calcium gluconate

Q.18 Antibacterial calcium preparation is:
A. Calcium phosphate
B. Calcium lactate
C. Calcium mandelate
D. Calcium pantothenate

Q.19 Slaked lime is other name for:
A. Sodium hydroxide
B. Potassium hydroxide
C. Calcium hydroxide
D. Magnesium hydroxide

Q.20 Calcium gluconate injection is stabilized by:
A. Calcium D-saccharate
B. Sodium saccharin
C. Sodium benzoate
D. Sodium metabisulphite

Q.21 The diluent used in tablets is:
A. Calcium lactate
B. Calcium gluconate
C. Calcium chloride
D. Dibasic calcium phosphate

Q.22 Vitamin-B enzyme co-factor is:
A. Calcium phosphate
B. Calcium levulinate

C. Calcium pantothenate

D. Calcium lactate

Q.23 The indicator used in complexometric titration is:

A. Methyl orange **B.** Phenolphthalein

C. Mordant black-T **D.** Phenol red

Q.24 The pH of calcium gluconate injection is adjusted with:

A. Ammonium hydroxide

B. Sodium hydroxide

C. Potassium hydroxide

D. Calcium hydroxide

Q.25 Calcium gluconate is soluble in:

A. Cold water **B.** Boiling water

C. Water **D.** Alcohol

Q.26 Calcium gluconate is assayed by:

[UPSC Drug Inspector, 2019]

A. Acid-base titration

B. Complexometric titration

C. Non-aqueous titration

D. Redox titration

Q.27 Swimming pool disinfectant is:

A. Calcium hypochlorite

B. Calcium phosphate

C. Calcium sulphate

D. Calcium oxide

Q.28 Low calcium in blood causes:

A. Osteoporosity **B.** Hypercalcemia

C. Hyperkalemia **D.** Osteomalacia

Q.29 Calcium gluconate is prepared by boiling gluconic acid solution with:

A. Calcium carbonate **B.** Calcium sulphate

C. Calcium chloride **D.** Calcium oxide

Q.30 Plaster of Paris contains:

A. Copper sulphate

B. Barium sulphate

C. Calcium phosphate

D. Dried calcium sulphate

Q.31 Deficiency of iodine results in:

A. Cretinism **B.** Graves disease

C. Goiter **D.** Wilson's disease

Q.32 All are assayed by complexometric titrations except:

A. Calcium gluconate

B. Magnesium sulphate

C. Zinc sulphate

D. Copper sulphate

Q.33 Non-reducing sugar which does not exhibit mutarotation:

A. Lactose **B.** Glucose **C.** Sucrose **D.** Maltose

Q.34 Potassium perchlorate is used in:

A. Gout **B.** Cretinish

C. Thyrotoxicosis **D.** Goiter

Q.35 The element present in seaweeds is:

A. Iodine **B.** Calcium

C. Zinc **D.** Potassium

Q.36 The indicator used in iodine titration is:

A. Methyl orange of

B. Ferric ammonium sulphate

C. Phenolphthalein

D. Starch mucilage

Q.37 An essential ion necessary for synthesis of thyroid hormone:

A. Fluorine **B.** Iodine **C.** Chorine **D.** Bromine

Q.38 Iodine is soluble in:

A. Concentrated HNO

B. Alcohol

C. Potassium Iodide solution

D. Concentrated H_2SO_2

Pharmaceutics

Q.39 The prescriber indicates on every prescription order whether it may be renewed & if so, how many times. It is important particularly in the prescription containing narcotics & other habit-forming drugs to prevent misuse:

A. Signature

B. Renewal instructions

C. Superscription

D. Name

Q.40 _________ are clear, sweetened and flavored hydro alcoholic liquid preparation intended for oral use.

A. Elixirs **B.** Linctuses

C. Mixture **D.** All of these

Q.41 _________ is black pigmented preparation for application to the eye lashes or eyebrow to beautify the eyes.

A. White Vaseline **B.** Hair Dye

C. Mascara **D.** Both (A) and (B)

Q.42 Precautions needed to be taken in storage of eye drop:

A. If the dropper is separate, always hold it with its tip down.

B. Never used eye drops that have changed color.

C. Use within one month after opening the container.

D. All of these

Q.43 Example of Binders:

A. Magnesium Trisilicate

B. Hydrated alumina

C. Eucalyptus oil

D. Alginate

Q.44 The adult dose of phenobarbitone is 15 mg. What is the dose for a child weighing 40 pounds?

A. 2 mg **B.** 4 mg **C.** 8 mg **D.** 12 mg

Q.45 They contain a high concentration of medicament. And, they are:
A. Paste
B. Ointment
C. Sulphur ointment
D. None of these

Q.46 Properties of ointment base:
A. It should be free from foreign particles.
B. It has sterility.
C. It should be physically and chemically stable.
D. It has large viscosity.

Q.47 What is the displacement value of castor oil?
A. 1.0
B. 4.0
C. 1.5
D. 5.0

Q.48 _______ is used with other suspending agents because of high viscosity of its mucilage.
A. Gum acacia
B. Starch
C. Tragacanth
D. Sodium alginate

Q.49 What are some of the uses of intravenous fluids?
A. To correct electrolyte imbalances.
B. To deliver medications.
C. Used for chemotherapy.
D. All of these

Q.50 Find out an example of indiffusible mixture:
A. Acetyl salicylic acid
B. Calomel
C. Phenacetin
D. All of these

Q.51 Give the metric equivalent of the following 1 pound:
A. 325mg
B. 8ml
C. 450 gm
D. 300ml

Q.52 _______ are viscous, monophasic liquid preparation containing a high concentration of syrup intended to be sipped and swallowed slowly for treatment of cough.
A. Syrup
B. Elixir
C. Linctuses
D. None of these

Q.53 What are some of the parts of the prescription?
A. Subscription
B. Signature
C. Inscription
D. All of these

Q.54 _______ are applied to eyelids in order to produce an attractive moist-looking background to the eyes.
A. Eyeliner
B. Mascara
C. Eye shadow
D. Eyebrow Pencil

Q.55 Latin term "mitte" means the following:
A. Urgent
B. Send
C. Immediate
D. Attention

Q.56 Latin term "talis / tales / talia" means the following:
A. Such
B. Till
C. For
D. All of these

Q.57 Which type of dosage form is useful in hormonal therapy?
A. Tablet
B. Implant
C. Aersol
D. Drops

Q.58 Which liquid preparation is meant for application to the skin without friction?
A. Limniments
B. Lotions

C. Linctuses
D. Both (A) and (B)

Q.59 BID in pharmaceutical terms refers to which of the following?
A. Twice a day
B. Twice
C. Every other day
D. Three times a day

Q.60 Mandl's Paint is also known as:
A. Compound Iodine throat paint
B. Aqueous Iodine solution
C. Strong Iodine solution
D. Lugol's solution

Q.61 Gargles must be _______ before use.
A. Concentrated
B. Warmed
C. Diluted
D. Cooled

Q.62 Elixir contain:
A. 40% glycerol
B. 5-40% alcohol
C. 66.7% sucrose
D. None of these

Q.63 From the below options which will be the most widely used form of dosage?
A. Emulsion
B. Solutions
C. Tablets
D. Powders

Q.64 Bases that are water-washable, non-greasy, can be diluted with water, non-occlusive:
A. Water soluble Bases
B. Water insoluble bases
C. Emulsifiable base
D. Water removable base

Q.65 Methods of granules formation:
A. Spatulation
B. Fusion method
C. Wet method
D. Both (B) and (C)

Q.66 _______ contains one water molecule that acts as binder in fusionmethod for making effervescent granules.
A. Citric Acid
B. Tartaric Acid
C. Benzoic Acid
D. All of these

Q.67 _______ are the finely divided powder meant for introduction into the body cavities.
A. Dusting powder
B. Insufflation
C. Inhalation
D. Medical powder

Q.68 _______ powder must be sterile.
A. Medical Powder
B. Surgical powder
C. Both (A) and (B)
D. None of these

Q.69 Which of the following step in the preparation of powders is very often used?
A. Preparation of wrapping paper
B. Preparation of material
C. Wrapping
D. Double wrapping

Q.70 _______ powders consist of more than one ingredient.
A. Simple
B. Compound
C. Both (A) and (B)
D. None of these

Q.71 Which of the following is substitute for theobroma oil?

A. Hydrogenated oils

B. Emulsified cocoa

C. Polyethylene-Glycol

D. None of these

Q.72 Which of the following is not an example of hydrophilic bases?

A. Soap-glycerin base

B. Emulsified cocoa butter

C. Glycero-gelatin base

D. None of these

Q.73 Which of the following is an example of a synthetic base?

A. Witespol

B. Emulsified cocoa butter

C. Glycero-gelatin base

D. Hydrogenated oils

Q.74 Which of the following is an example of oily bases?

A. Witespol

B. Emulsified cocoa butter

C. Glycero-gelatin base

D. Massupol

Q.75 Which of the following is an example of hydrophilic bases?

A. Hydrogenated oils

B. Emulsified cocoa butter

C. Glycero gelatin base

D. None of these

Q.76 Which of the following is an advantage of suppositories?

A. Need to store at low temp

B. Cost-expensive

C. Drug may be degraded by microbial

D. Can be given to unconscious patient

Pharmacognosy

Q.77 If endosperm is concave on commissural surface, it is called as coelospermons fruit, eg.?

A. Anise

B. Coriander

C. Hemlock

D. Dill

Q.78 It is difficult to make powder of coriander due to presence of:

A. Fixed oil

B. Vittae

C. Endosperm cells

D. Sclerenchymatous cells

Q.79 Bud like odour of green plant is due to trans-tridecene-(2)-al-(1), it is found in:

A. Dill

B. Caraway

C. Coriander

D. Fennel

Q.80 Anethole is sweet odourous constituent of volatile oil of:

A. Rose

B. Sandalwood

C. Lavender

D. Fennel

Q.81 There are 20 to 40 small vittae on dorsal surface of:

A. Cumin

B. Caraway

C. Dill

D. Anise

Q.82 Star Anise fruits belongs to family:

A. Umbelliferae

B. Magnoliaceae

C. Labiatae

D. Myrtaceae

Q.83 Jatamansi is used in:

A. Hepatitis

B. Hysteria

C. Constipation

D. Alzmeir disease

Q.84 Following types of calcium oxalate crystals are found in the hypanthium of clove:

A. Rosettes

B. Acicular

C. Prisms

D. Clusters

Q.85 What is a Eugenol?

A. Limonene

B. Clove oil

C. Sanalene

D. None of these

Q.86 The major chemical constituent of the volatile oil of ocimum sanctum is:

A. Limonene

B. Eugenol

C. Sanalene

D. Menthol

Pharmacology

Q.87 Which of the following drugs used in the treatment of gout has as its primary effect the reduction of uric acid synthesis?

A. Allopurinol

B. Sulfinpyrazone

C. Colchicine

D. Indomethacin

Q.88 All of the following drugs are antibiotics, except:

A. Streptomycin

B. Penicillin

C. Co-trimoxazole

D. Chloramphenicol

Q.89 Which of the following drugs is a gastric acid resistant?

A. Penicillin G

B. Penicillin V

C. Carbenicillin

D. Procain penicillin

Q.90 Which of the following drugs is penicillinase resistant?

A. Oxacillin

B. Amoxacillin

C. Bicillin-5

D. Penicillin G

Q.91 Aminoglycosides have the following unwanted effects:

A. Pancytopenia

B. Hepatotoxicity

C. Ototoxicity, nephrotoxicity

D. Irritation of gastrointestinal mucosa

Q.92 Chloramphenicol has the following unwanted effects:

A. Nephrotox city

B. Pancytopenia

C. Hepatotoxicity

D. Ototoxicity

Q.93 The mechanism of Amphotericin B action is:

A. Inhibition of cell wall synthesis.

B. Inhibition of fungal protein synthesis.

C. Inhibition of DNA synthesis.

D. Alteration of cell membrane permeability.

Q.94 Azoles have an antifungal effect because of:

A. Inhibition of cell wall synthesis

B. Inhibition of fungal protein synthesis

C. Reduction of ergosterol synthesis

D. Inhibition of DNA synthesis

Q.95 Amphotericin B has the following unwanted effects:

A. Psychosis

B. Renal impairment, anemia

C. Hypertension, cardiac arrhythmia

D. Bone marrow toxicity

Q.96 Find out the drug belonging to antibiotics having a polyene structure:

A. Nystatin   **B.** Ketoconazole

C. Griseofulvin   **D.** All of these

Q.97 Mechanism of Izoniazid action is:

A. Inhibition of protein synthesis

B. Inhibition of mycolic acids synthesis

C. Inhibition of RNA synthesis

D. Inhibition of ADP synthesis

Q.98 Mechanism of rifampin action is:

A. Inhibition of mycolic acids synthesis

B. Inhibition of DNA dependent RNA polymerase

C. Inhibition of topoisomerase II

D. Inhibition of cAMP synthesis

Q.99 Mechanism of Cycloserine action is:

A. Inhibition of mycolic acids synthesis.

B. Inhibition of RNA synthesis.

C. Inhibition of cell wall synthesis.

D. Inhibition of pyridoxalphosphate synthesis.

Q.100 Mechanism of Streptomycin action is:

A. Inhibition of cell wall synthesis.

B. Inhibition of protein synthesis.

C. Inhibition of RNA and DNA synthesis.

D. Inhibition of cell membranes permeability.

Q.101 Rifampin has the following unwanted effect:

A. Dizziness, headache

B. Loss of hair

C. Flu-like syndrome, tubular necrosis

D. Hepatotoxicity

Q.102 Isoniazid has following unwanted effect:

A. Cardiotoxicity

B. Hepatotoxicity, peripheral neuropathy

C. Loss of hair

D. Immunotoxicity

Q.103 In the treatment of hypertension which agent is a calcium antagonist?

A. Amlodipine   **B.** Captopril

C. Clonidine   **D.** Minoxidil

Q.104 Mechanism of aminosalicylic acid action is:

A. Inhibition of mycolic acids synthesis

B. Inhibition of folate synthesis

C. Inhibition of DNA dependent RNA polymerase

D. Inhibition of DNA gyrase

Q.105 All of the following agents are the first-line antimycobacterial drugs, except:

A. Rifampin   **B.** Pyrazinamide

C. Isoniazid   **D.** Streptomycin

Q.106 The mechanism of fluoroquinolones action is:

A. Inhibition of phospholipase C

B. Inhibition of DNA gyrase

C. Inhibition of bacterial cell synthesis

D. Alteration of cell membrane permeability

Q.107 What is the mechanism of action of alpha methyl dopa?

A. Increase peripheral vascular resistance.

B. Increase sodium and water retention.

C. Acts centrally to decrease sympathetic activity.

D. Relaxes arterial smooth muscle.

Q.108 All of the following antiviral drugs are the analogs of nucleosides, except:

A. Acyclovir   **B.** Zidovudine

C. Saquinavir   **D.** Didanozine

Q.109 Action mechanism of alkylating agents is:

A. Producing carbonium ions altering protein structure.

B. Producing carbonium ions altering DNA structure.

C. Structural antagonism against purine and pyrimidine.

D. Inhibition of DNA-dependent RNA synthesis.

Q.110 Find out the action mechanism of anticancer drugs belonging to plant alkaloids:

A. Inhibition of DNA-dependent RNA synthesis

B. Cross-linking of DNA

C. Mitotic arrest at a metaphase

D. Nonselective inhibition of aromatases

Q.111 Famotidine act as:

A. H1 Antagonist

B. H2 Antagonist

C. Proton pump inhibitor

D. H2 agonis

Q.112 Find out the selective COX-2 inhibitor is:

A. Ketorolac   **B.** Rofecoxib

C. Indomethacin   **D.** Naproxan

Q.113 Acute migraine is treated with:

A. Prazosin   **B.** Formetrol

C. Sumatriptan   **D.** Dopamine

Q.114 Allopurinol can inhibit the metabolism of:

A. Cisplatin   **B.** Doxorubicin

C. 6-Mercaptopurine   **D.** 5-flurouracil

Other Subjects

Q.115 Van' t Hoff equation for the solution is:

A. pV=n/RT

B. p=Vn/RT

C. pV=nRT

D. p=Vn R/T

Q.116 CMC refers to:

A. Aggregation of surfactant

B. Aggregation of particles

C. Coagulation of particles

D. None of these

Q.117 Identify the chiral molecule among the following:

A. Isopropyl alcohol

B. 2-pentanol

C. 1-bromo 3-butene

D. Isobutyl alcohol

Q.118 In oxidation reduction change in ____________ of reacting element takes place.

A. Volume

B. pH

C. Absorbance

D. Valency

Q.119 ____________ is the programmed cell death or cell suicide.

A. Apoptosis

B. Autotosis

C. Destrosis

D. None of these

Q.120 The first Human hormone product by Recombinant DNA technology is:

A. Insulin

B. Thyroxine

C. Estrogen

D. Progesterone

Q.121 Which among the following are "Spirochetes"?

A. Streptomyces sp

B. Treponema pallidum

C. Spirillum volutans

D. Corynebacterium diphtheriae

Q.122 Which diseased is defined as a neurologic disorder characterized pathologically by the loss of neurons in the Substantia Nigra and clinically by tremors at rest, muscular rigidity, expressionless face, and emotional lability?

A. Bacterial Meningitis

B. Alzheimers Disease

C. Viral Meningitis

D. Parkinsons Disease

Q.123 Who has poorly developed BBB?

A. Infants

B. Adults of age more than 20

C. Aged

D. Children's of puberty

Q.124 Pharmacodynamic drug interactions includes:

A. Changes in gastrointestinal pH.

B. Induction or inhibition of drug transport proteins.

C. Additive or synergistic interactions.

D. Adsorption, chelation and other complexing mechanisms.

Q.125 In ear wax type of secretion produce by ____________ gland.

A. Mammary

B. Thyroid

C. Pituitary

D. Ceruminous

// Smart Answer Sheet //

Correct — Percentage of students who answered correctly. **Skipped** — Percentage of students who skipped.

Q.	Ans.	Correct	Skipped	Q.	Ans.	Correct	Skipped	Q.	Ans.	Correct	Skipped	Q.	Ans.	Correct	Skipped	Q.	Ans.	Correct	Skipped	Q.	Ans.	Correct	Skipped
1	C	48.66 %	48.7 %	22	C	57.45 %	30.19 %	43	D	54.64 %	37.36 %	64	A	56.62 %	38.17 %	85	B	43.52 %	41.29 %	106	B	46.62 %	48.47 %
2	A	40.42 %	48.89 %	23	C	60.47 %	35.53 %	44	B	20.14 %	68.6 %	65	D	44.46 %	51.23 %	86	B	49.54 %	38.86 %	107	C	17.9 %	75.04 %
3	D	42.12 %	34.9 %	24	B	67.87 %	31.56 %	45	A	53.52 %	32.86 %	66	A	63.86 %	34.63 %	87	A	55.59 %	41.97 %	108	B	40.32 %	34.05 %
4	D	57.19 %	41.69 %	25	B	42.95 %	38.28 %	46	C	69.9 %	30.06 %	67	A	56.23 %	40.94 %	88	C	28.5 %	67.68 %	109	B	55.67 %	39.7 %
5	B	54.64 %	36.96 %	26	B	56.39 %	32.67 %	47	A	64.63 %	31.85 %	68	B	62.77 %	35.08 %	89	B	43.09 %	49.31 %	110	C	56.9 %	38.57 %
6	C	51.0 %	47.94 %	27	A	42.07 %	40.05 %	48	B	24.07 %	73.48 %	69	D	49.02 %	35.44 %	90	A	48.61 %	31.18 %	111	B	48.61 %	40.56 %
7	C	68.11 %	31.88 %	28	A	64.06 %	31.75 %	49	D	29.6 %	68.93 %	70	B	53.21 %	31.61 %	91	C	46.78 %	37.68 %	112	B	63.67 %	30.6 %
8	A	49.21 %	46.78 %	29	A	55.69 %	43.76 %	50	D	45.69 %	39.55 %	71	A	63.4 %	34.36 %	92	B	57.36 %	39.83 %	113	C	51.88 %	30.99 %
9	A	44.36 %	31.86 %	30	D	67.8 %	31.67 %	51	C	59.42 %	36.56 %	72	B	55.06 %	30.26 %	93	D	46.41 %	36.52 %	114	C	61.17 %	37.83 %
10	C	22.68 %	69.49 %	31	C	89.82 %	10.09 %	52	C	65.27 %	33.04 %	73	A	58.63 %	40.39 %	94	C	68.7 %	30.58 %	115	C	19.04 %	70.24 %
11	A	50.82 %	37.68 %	32	D	53.58 %	45.8 %	53	D	62.04 %	32.06 %	74	B	53.66 %	31.66 %	95	B	60.97 %	35.91 %	116	D	46.08 %	52.79 %
12	B	47.37 %	32.59 %	33	C	68.6 %	30.46 %	54	C	60.24 %	37.99 %	75	C	58.98 %	32.21 %	96	A	53.98 %	30.07 %	117	D	47.91 %	38.59 %
13	C	40.47 %	36.33 %	34	C	46.02 %	44.38 %	55	B	64.3 %	32.0 %	76	D	45.87 %	47.72 %	97	B	67.4 %	32.13 %	118	D	85.24 %	12.66 %
14	A	20.62 %	69.49 %	35	A	47.2 %	52.16 %	56	A	51.45 %	33.05 %	77	C	51.86 %	39.06 %	98	B	44.11 %	41.2 %	119	A	53.68 %	36.2 %
15	B	59.28 %	33.39 %	36	D	56.65 %	36.65 %	57	B	63.95 %	31.55 %	78	C	42.9 %	40.77 %	99	C	43.03 %	47.75 %	120	A	42.05 %	30.39 %
16	B	53.18 %	41.56 %	37	B	61.37 %	35.99 %	58	B	49.27 %	31.33 %	79	C	66.83 %	32.57 %	100	B	54.98 %	37.2 %	121	B	45.63 %	47.2 %
17	D	67.17 %	32.59 %	38	C	51.88 %	34.26 %	59	A	68.94 %	30.55 %	80	D	60.26 %	34.53 %	101	C	65.53 %	30.42 %	122	D	65.54 %	32.54 %
18	C	49.5 %	40.88 %	39	B	67.51 %	32.24 %	60	A	52.73 %	31.15 %	81	A	47.46 %	45.31 %	102	B	50.81 %	31.59 %	123	A	42.45 %	31.97 %
19	C	82.13 %	16.11 %	40	A	41.69 %	40.27 %	61	C	45.38 %	37.37 %	82	B	54.74 %	41.41 %	103	A	68.43 %	30.49 %	124	C	41.82 %	56.08 %
20	A	46.43 %	52.58 %	41	C	49.38 %	41.42 %	62	B	46.93 %	32.08 %	83	B	40.57 %	47.89 %	104	B	54.87 %	38.87 %	125	D	50.75 %	35.07 %
21	D	47.8 %	47.01 %	42	D	55.37 %	41.99 %	63	C	56.85 %	32.45 %	84	C	59.74 %	38.04 %	105	B	52.92 %	45.19 %				

//Hints and Solutions//

1. Sodium nitrite is used for cyanide poisoning. Sodium nitrite is the most prevalent drug for cyanide poisoning. It takes approximately 12 min to generate approximately 40% of methemoglobin after intravenous administration of the recommended dose (Van Heijst et al., 1987).

Hence, the correct option is (C).

2. A standard titrant in the iodometric analysis is sodium nitrate. Sodium nitrate is a kind of salt that has long been used to preserve foods. Well, you can find it in many foods including bacon, beef jerky, ham, hot dogs, lunch meat, salami, and smoked fish. It creates a distinct flavor, controls lipid oxidation, and acts as an antimicrobial.

Hence, the correct option is (A).

3. An antidote in cyanide poisoning is sodium thiosulphate. Sodium thiosulphate is considered an ineffective antidote for acute cyanide toxicity because of poor intracellular penetration, slow onset of effect, a short half-life, and limited distribution volume, it is often used in conjunction with other rapid-acting antidotes.

Hence, the correct option is (D).

4. Universal antidote contains magnesium oxide, tannic acid, and charcoal:

Magnesium oxide: Magnesium oxide is a supplement that contains magnesium and oxygen ions. It's used to treat a variety of conditions, including heartburn, indigestion, constipation, magnesium deficiency, and other ailments.

Tannic acid: Tannic acid is found in the nutgalls formed by insects on the twigs of certain oak trees. In foods and beverages, tannic acid is used as a flavoring agent. In manufacturing, tannic acid is used in ointments and suppositories; for tanning hides and manufacturing ink; and to kill dust mites on furniture.

Charcoal: Charcoal is a lightweight black carbon residue produced by strongly heating wood (or other animal and plant materials) in minimal oxygen to remove all water and volatile constituents.

Hence, the correct option is (D).

5. Solution of potassium chloride is used in poisoning digitalis. Digitalis is a medicine that is used to treat certain heart conditions. Digitalis toxicity can be a side effect of digitalis therapy. It may occur when you take too much of the drug at one time. It can also occur when levels of the drug build up for other reasons such as other medical problems you have.

Hence, the correct option is (B).

6. Lithium carbonate is used in mania. Lithium (Eskalith, Lithobid) is one of the most widely used and studied medications for treating bipolar disorder. Lithium helps reduce the severity and frequency of mania. It may also help relieve or prevent bipolar depression. Studies show that lithium can significantly reduce suicide risk.

Hence, the correct option is (C).

7. Cis-platinum is used as an antineoplastic agent. Antineoplastic drugs are medications used to treat cancer. Antineoplastic drugs are also called anticancer, chemotherapy, chemo, cytotoxic, or hazardous drugs. These drugs come in many forms. Cisplatin is in the platinum-based antineoplastic family of medications. It works in part by binding to DNA and inhibiting its replication. Cisplatin was discovered in 1845 and licensed for medical use in 1978 and 1979. It is on the World Health Organization's List of Essential Medicines.

Hence, the correct option is (C).

8. The basic unit of radioactivity is becquerel. The unit of radioactive decay is equal to one disintegration per second. The Becquerel is the basic unit of radioactivity used in the international system of radiation units, referred to as the "SI" units.

37 billion (3.7×10^{10}) becquerels = 1 curie (Ci).

Hence, the correct option is (A).

9. The colour produced by salicylates with ferric chloride reagent is violet. Typically, one or two drops of an aqueous 5% by weight solution of ferric chloride in water is added to approximately 1 mL of urine. A dark violet colour indicates the probable presence of salicylate, the major metabolite of ASA. The ferric chloride test was used to compare the salicylic acid, crude aspirin, and purified aspirin. After the addition of the ferric chloride, the salicylic acid solution turned purple, and both the aspirin solutions were yellow.

Hence, the correct option is (A).

10. Sodium phosphate (P^{32}) is used in polycythemia vera. The principal use of sodium phosphate P^{32} is for the treatment of polycythemia vera, and it is effective for the treatment of chronic myelocytic leukemia and chronic lymphocytic leukemia. Sodium Phosphate P^{32} is also used in the palliative treatment of selected patients with multiple areas of skeletal metastases.

Hence, the correct option is (C).

11. PM indicators are used in complexometric titrations. Complexometric indicators are those indicators that are used in complexometric titrations. These indicators undergo a definite color change in presence of specific metal ions. These indicators are also known as PM indicators or metallochromic indicators.

Hence, the correct option is (A).

12. Roentgen(R) is a unit of exposure. The roentgen (symbol R) is a legacy unit of measurement for the exposure of X-rays and gamma rays and is defined as the electric charge freed by such radiation in a specified volume of air divided by the mass of that air (statcoulomb per kilogram).

Hence, the correct option is (B).

13. A radio-opaque compound used as a diagnostic agent in peptic ulcers is barium sulphate. Administered internally ("barium cocktail") as a radio-opaque diagnostic aid. Barium sulphate is a metal sulphate with the formula BaO_4S. Virtually insoluble in water at room temperature, it is mostly used as a component in oil well drilling fluid it occurs naturally as the mineral barite.

Hence, the correct option is (C).

14. The emissions from the decay of radionuclides are commonly used in sterilization is gamma. Gamma irradiation is a physical/chemical means of sterilization because it kills bacteria by breaking down bacterial DNA, inhibiting bacterial division. The energy of gamma rays passes through the equipment, disrupting the pathogens that cause contamination. A radionuclide (radioactive nuclide, radioisotope, or radioactive isotope) is a nuclide that has excess nuclear energy, making it unstable.

Hence, the correct option is (A).

15. The chemical name of Plaster of Paris is calcium sulphate hemihydrate. The chemical formula of Plaster of Paris is $CaSO_4$. $1/2\ H_2O$. When it is mixed with water, crystals of gypsum are produced and set into a hard mass.

Hence, the correct option is (B).

16. Calcium salt widely used in dental products is calcium phosphate. Calcium phosphate (tricalcium phosphate) is a mineral that is used as a supplement in people who do not get enough calcium from food. Calcium phosphate is used to treat calcium deficiencies that may be associated with low blood calcium, a parathyroid disorder, or osteoporosis, and other bone conditions. Although tooth enamel is the hardest substance in your body even stronger than bone it's still susceptible to tooth decay when exposed to acids in the mouth. Because enamel is composed of mainly calcium phosphate, a calcium-rich diet is essential during tooth development.

Hence, the correct option is (B).

17. The drug used in hypocalcemia is calcium gluconate. Calcium gluconate is an over-the-counter and prescription medicine used to treat the symptoms of hypocalcemia (calcium deficiency) and as a calcium supplement. Calcium gluconate may be used alone or with other medications. Calcium gluconate belongs to a class of drugs called antidotes, other; calcium Salts.

Hence, the correct option is (D).

18. Antibacterial calcium preparation is calcium mandelate. Mandelic acid is a 2-hydroxy monocarboxylic acid that is acetic acid in which two of the methyl hydrogens are substituted by phenyl and hydroxyl groups. The structure of calcium mandelate is:

Hence, the correct option is (C).

19. Slaked lime is other name for calcium hydroxide. Calcium hydroxide, also called slaked lime, $Ca(OH)_2$ is obtained by the action of water on calcium oxide. When mixed with water, a small proportion of it dissolves, forming a solution known as limewater, the rest remaining as a suspension called milk of lime.

Hence, the correct option is (C).

20. Calcium gluconate injection is stabilized by calcium D-saccharate. Calcium D-saccharate is the calcium salt of saccharic acid, also known as glucaric acid. Calcium gluconate is used to treat conditions arising from calcium deficiencies such as hypocalcemic tetany, hypocalcemia related to hypoparathyroidism and hypocalcemia due to rapid growth or pregnancy.

Hence, the correct option is (A).

21. The diluent used in tablets is dibasic calcium phosphate. Diluents are added to pharmaceutical tablets or capsules to make the product large enough for swallowing and handling, and more stable. Some calcium phosphate salts can be anhydrous, meaning the water has been removed from the salt form. Dicalcium phosphate (DCP) is an insoluble inorganic diluent. The anhydrous (triclinic crystal) and dihydrate (monoclinic structure) forms of DCP are used in pharmaceutical development (Rowe et al., 2009).

Hence, the correct option is (D).

22. Vitamin-B enzyme co-factor is calcium pantothenate. Calcium pantothenate is the calcium salt of the water-soluble vitamin B5, ubiquitously found in plants and animal tissues with antioxidant property. Pentothenate is a component of coenzyme A (CoA) and a part of the vitamin B2 complex.

Hence, the correct option is (C).

23. The indicator used in complexometric titration is mordant black-T. To carry out metal cation titrations using EDTA, it is almost always necessary to use a complexometric indicator to determine when the endpoint has been reached. Common indicators are organic dyes such as Fast Sulphon Black, Eriochrome Black-T, Eriochrome Red B, Patton Reeder, or Murexide.

Hence, the correct option is (C).

24. The pH of calcium gluconate injection is adjusted with sodium hydroxide. Each mL contains calcium gluconate 94 mg; calcium saccharate (tetrahydrate) 4.5 mg; water for injection q.s. Hydrochloric acid and/or sodium hydroxide may have been added for pH adjustment (6.0 to 8.2).

Hence, the correct option is (B).

25. Calcium gluconate is soluble in boiling water. Calcium gluconate is a mineral supplement and medication. As a medication, it is used by injection into a vein to treat low blood calcium, high blood potassium, and magnesium toxicity. Calcium Gluconate Injection can be diluted with glucose 5% or sodium chloride 0.9%. Dilution into a solution containing bicarbonate, phosphate or sulphate should be avoided.

Hence, the correct option is (B).

26. Calcium gluconate is assayed by complexometric titration. Complexometric titration is the classification, metal ion indicators, masking, and demasking reagents, estimation of Magnesium sulphate, and calcium gluconate. Complexometric titration is important for metals and their salts, certain anions, and indirectly some drugs.

Hence, the correct option is (B).

27. The swimming pool disinfectant is calcium hypochlorite. Calcium hypochlorite is commonly used to sanitize public swimming pools and disinfect drinking water. Generally, the commercial substances are sold with a purity of 65% to 73% with other chemicals present, such as calcium chloride and calcium carbonate, resulting from the manufacturing process.

Hence, the correct option is (A).

28. Low calcium in the blood causes osteoporosity. Osteoporosis is more likely to occur in people who have low calcium intake. A lifelong lack of calcium plays a role in the development of osteoporosis. Low calcium intake contributes to diminished bone density, early bone loss and an increased risk of fractures.

Hence, the correct option is (A).

29. Calcium gluconate is prepared by boiling gluconic acid solution with calcium carbonate. Calcium gluconate is made by mixing gluconic acid with calcium carbonate or calcium hydroxide. Calcium gluconate came into medical use in the 1920s. It is on the World Health Organization's List of Essential Medicines. Calcium gluconate is available as a generic medication.

Hence, the correct option is (A).

30. Plaster of Paris contains dried calcium sulphate. Plaster of Paris, quick-setting gypsum plaster consisting of a fine white powder (calcium sulphate hemihydrate), which hardens when moistened and allowed to dry. Known since ancient times, Plaster of Paris is so-called because of its preparation from the abundant gypsum found near Paris.

Hence, the correct option is (D).

31. Deficiency of iodine results in goiter. Goiter is caused due to adequate iodine, the thyroid progressively enlarges (develops a goiter) as it tries to keep up with demand for thyroid hormone production. Worldwide, iodine deficiency is the most common cause of thyroid enlargement and goiter.

Hence, the correct option is (C).

32. Calcium gluconate, magnesium sulphate and zinc sulphate all are assayed by complexometric titrations except for copper sulphate. Copper sulphate is an inorganic compound that combines copper and sulphate. In its solid, crystal-shaped stone form (known as a pentahydrate) it's known as bluestone or blue vitriol for its blue color. In this form, it's a popular raw material for producing other types of copper salts.

Hence, the correct option is (D).

33. Non-reducing sugar which does not exhibit mutarotation is sucrose. Sucrose does not mutarotate. All sugars, however, do not have this mutarotation property. Sucrose lacks the ketone (>C-0) or free aldehyde (-CHO) groups. As a result, sucrose is incapable of mutarotation.

Hence, the correct option is (C).

34. Potassium perchlorate is used in thyrotoxicosis. Potassium perchlorate acts as a competitive inhibitor of iodine uptake by the thyroid gland and attenuates the production of the thyroid hormone. Thus the use of potassium perchlorate has been extensive for hyperthyroidism during the last 50 years, particularly in the late 1950s and early 1960s.

Potassium perchlorate has not been approved by the US Food and Drug Administration (FDA) for the treatment of thyrotoxicosis. Because potassium perchlorate is a drug that potentially causes aplastic anemia, limits it to patients whose condition cannot be controlled by methimazole alone.

Hence, the correct option is (C).

35. The element present in seaweeds is iodine. The primary mineral components in seaweeds are iodine, calcium, phosphorous, magnesium, iron, sodium, potassium, and chlorine. Added to these are many important trace elements such as zinc, copper, manganese, selenium, molybdenum, and chromium.

Hence, the correct option is (A).

36. The indicator used in iodine titration is starch mucilage. The indicator that is usually chosen for titrations involving iodine (triiodide) is starch. Starch forms a dark blue complex with iodine. The endpoint in iodimetry corresponds to a sudden colour change to blue.

Hence, the correct option is (D).

37. An essential ion necessary for the synthesis of thyroid hormone is iodine. Thyroid hormone synthesis involves the iodination of tyrosyl residues on the precursor protein thyroglobulin. This reaction uses high concentrations of H_2O_2 and oxidized iodine generated by the enzymes thyroid oxidase (ThOX) 1 and 2, and thyroid peroxidase (TPO).

Hence, the correct option is (B).

38. Iodine is soluble in potassium iodide solution. Iodine is a nonpolar compound. The water is a polar solvent. According to the Like dissolves Like a rule, the non-polar iodine molecule cannot be soluble in polar water. Even the KI is also polar but the iodine molecule is soluble in KI. As we all know, when iodine is dissolved in aqueous potassium iodide they generally form a compound that is potassium triiodide. These molecules exist in ionic form, one is cationic and the other is anionic. The K^+ ion is obtained as a cation and the I_3^- ion is obtained as an anion.

Hence, the correct option is (C).

39. The prescriber indicates on every prescription order whether it may be renewed & if so, how many times. It is important particularly in the prescription containing narcotics & other habit-forming drugs to prevent misuse is renewal instructions. The number of times a prescription is to be repeated is written by the physician. It is very important for the case of habit-forming drugs to prevent their misuse.

Hence, the correct option is (B).

40. Elixirs are clear, sweetened, and flavored hydroalcoholic liquid preparation intended for oral use. Elixirs are clear, sweetened, hydroalcoholic solutions that are usually flavored and are suitable for drugs that are insoluble in water alone but soluble in water-alcohol mixtures. Less sweet and less viscous than syrups, elixirs are generally less effective in masking taste.

Hence, the correct option is (A).

41. Mascara is black pigmented preparation for application to the eyelashes or eyebrows to beautify the eyes. Mascara is a cosmetic commonly used to enhance eyelashes. It may darken, thicken, lengthen, and/or define the eyelashes. Normally in one of three forms-liquid, powder, or cream-the modern mascara product has various formulas; however, most contain the same basic components of pigments, oils, waxes, and preservatives. The most common form of mascara is a liquid in a tube with an application brush.

Hence, the correct option is (C).

42. Here are some precautions to follow when using eye drops:

- If the dropper is separate, always hold it with its tip down.
- Never used eye drops that have changed color.
- Use within one month after opening the container.

Eye drops can be used to treat a wide range of eye conditions such as an infection, an allergy, a minor eye injury, to relieve dry or red eyes, for post-operative healing, or in chronic conditions like glaucoma.

Hence, the correct option is (D).

43. An example of binders is alginate. "Alginate" is the term usually used for the salts of alginic acid, but it can also refer to all the derivatives of alginic acid and alginic acid itself; in some publications, the term "algin" is used instead of alginate. The goal of the extraction process is to obtain dry, powdered, sodium alginate.

Hence, the correct option is (D).

44. CLARK'S RULE: Clark's rule is one of three formulas used to calculate dosages for infants and children. Clark's rule is based on the weight of the child. This system is much more accurate than other pediatric methods because the size and bodyweight of children of any age can vary greatly. Clark's rule uses $150 lb$ (70 kg) as the average adult weight and assumes that the child's dose is proportionately less. The adult dose of phenobarbitone is 15 mg. So, the dose for a child weighing 40 pounds is:

$$\text{Pediatric dose} = \frac{\text{Child's weight in pounds}}{150 \text{ pounds}} \times \text{Adult dose}$$

$$\Rightarrow \frac{40}{150} \times 15 \text{ mg}$$

$$= 4 \text{ mg}$$

Hence, the correct option is (B).

45. They contain a high concentration of medicament are paste. The paste is a basic pharmaceutical form. It consists of a fatty base (e.g., petroleum jelly) and at least 25% of a solid substance (e.g., zinc oxide). Pharmaceutical pastes are typically intended for external application to the skin.

Hence, the correct option is (A).

46. The property of the ointment base is that it should be physically and chemically stable. Typical ointment bases comprise petrolatum and mineral oil, or petrolatum and waxy/fatty alcohol combinations, the ratio and grades of these components being selected to give the desired finished product spreadability. The ointment base needs to be heated to above its melting temperature prior to the addition of the other ingredients. Low-shear or mixing speeds are typically used when the ointment base or finished formulation is cold/thick.

Hence, the correct option is (C).

47. The displacement value of castor oil is 1.0. Castor oil is a vegetable oil pressed from castor beans. It is a colorless to very pale yellow liquid with a distinct taste and odor. Its boiling point is 313°C (595°F) and its density is 0.961 g/cm³. It includes a mixture of triglycerides in which about 90% of fatty acids are ricinoleates. Displacement values are important when it comes to reconstituted powders. If a solution were 10mL more than the solution needed, it would dilute the concentration and consequently dilute the dose. For this reason, displacement values play an important role in pharmacy and pharmaceutical calculations.

Hence, the correct option is (A).

48. Starch is used with other suspending agents because of the high viscosity of its mucilage. Mucilages are also used as suspending agents and help to suspend insoluble solid substances in liquid formulations. They prevent immediate sedimentation and caking due to their colloidal character and high viscosity. Their high viscous nature makes mucilage a stabilizer of choice in suspension. starch and arrowroot (Maranta arundinacea) starch as suspending agents in suspension. It was found that the optimal concentration as a suspending agent in paracetamol suspension was in the range of 7-8% for yam starch and 5-6% for arrowroot starch.

Hence, the correct option is (B).

49. Some of the uses of intravenous fluid:

- To correct electrolyte imbalances.
- To deliver medications.
- Used for chemotherapy.
- IV fluids are specially formulated liquids that are injected into a vein to prevent or treat dehydration.
- They are used in people of all ages who are sick, injured, dehydrated from exercise or heat, or undergoing surgery.

Intravenous fluids (usually shortened to 'IV' fluids) are liquids given to replace water, sugar, and salt that you might need if you are ill or having an operation, and can't eat or drink as you would normally. IV fluids are given straight into a vein through a drip.

Hence, the correct option is (D).

50. The common use of indiffusible drugs in mixture form is acetylsalicylic acid, quinine salicylate, calomel, phenacetin, benzoic acid, phenobarbital, etc.

Mixtures containing indiffusible solids: Indiffusible solids are those solids that are not soluble in water and do not remain uniformly distributed in the vehicle for a sufficiently long time. Therefore, to suspend the drug, suspending agents are added.

Hence, the correct option is (D).

51. The pound or pound-mass is a unit of mass used in British imperial and the United States customary systems of measurement. Various definitions have been used; the most common today is the international avoirdupois pound, which is legally defined as exactly 0.45359237 kilograms, and which is divided into 16 avoirdupois ounces. The UK Weights and Measures Act of 1878 first defined the imperial pound in terms of metric units (1lb = 453.59265g), and in 1893 the Mendenhall Order defined the United States pound by describing a kilogram as equivalent to 2.20462 pounds.

Hence, the correct option is (C).

52. Linctuses are viscous, monophasic liquid preparation containing a high concentration of syrup intended to be sipped and swallowed slowly for treatment of cough. A linctus is a medicine in the form of a syrup, taken to relieve coughs and sore throats. Some pharmacists sell codeine in the form of a syrup-like medicine called codeine linctus. A linctus is a medicine in the form of a syrup, taken to relieve coughs and sore throats.

Hence, the correct option is (C).

53. Predating modern legal definitions of a prescription, a prescription traditionally is composed of four parts a

superscription, inscription, subscription, and signature. The superscription section contains the date of the prescription and patient information (name, address, age, etc.).

Hence, the correct option is (D).

54. Eye shadows are applied to eyelids in order to produce an attractive moist-looking background to the eyes. Eye shadow (or eyeshadow) is a cosmetic applied primarily to the eyelids to make the wearer's eyes stand out or look more attractive. Eye shadow can also be applied under the eyes or to brow bones.

Hence, the correct option is (C).

55. Latin term "mitte" means inject, give, send, take. Mitte followed by a numerical amount translates as "send", meaning "give the patient the following amount". Mitte is the first and most central borough of Berlin. Mitte encompasses Berlin's historic core.

Hence, the correct option is (B).

56. Latin term "talis / tales / talia" means such. Healthcare providers sometimes use Latin abbreviations on prescriptions. Understanding these abbreviations can help you avoid a medication error. Some healthcare providers are moving away from Latin abbreviations and using plain language instead.

Hence, the correct option is (A).

57. Implant dosage forms are useful in hormonal therapy. An implant may be defined as a material that is securely placed (inserted or grafted) into the body. Most of the implants are surgically placed inside the body. A drug-containing implant is usually a sterile, solid dosage form prepared by compression or melting for drug delivery at the desired rate over a prolonged period of time.

Hence, the correct option is (B).

58. The lotion is meant for application to the skin without friction. A lotions is a viscous (low to medium viscous) medicated or nonmedicated topical preparation, meant for application to unbroken skin. Lotions are usually applied to external skin with bare hands, a clean cloth, cotton wool, or gauze without friction.

Hence, the correct option is (B).

59. BID (on prescription): BID means twice (two times) a day. It is an abbreviation for "bis in die" which in Latin means twice a day. The abbreviation BID is sometimes written without a period either in lower-case letters as "bid" or in capital letters as "BID".

Hence, the correct option is (A).

60. Mandl's Paint is also known as compound iodine throat paint. It is popularly also known as Mandl's Paint B.P.C 68. It is useful in the treatment of pharyngitis or tonsillitis. It helps to kill germs in situations like sore throats or ulcers. It is composed of 1.25% iodine and 2.5% potassium iodide in peppermint oil and 90% alcohol in glycerine. Glycerine is commonly used as a base because it is viscous. It also adheres to the mucous membrane for a longer period.

Hence, the correct option is (A).

61. Gargles must be diluted before use. Gargles are an aqueous solution used to prevent or treat infection. They are usually available in concentrated form with direction for dilution with warm water for use. They are used to relieve soreness in mild throat infections. The use of gargle is:

- Antiseptic/antibacterial.
- Astringent.
- Relieve soreness in mild throat infection.

Hence, the correct option is (C).

62. The alcoholic contents in the elixir vary from 5% to 40%. In general, they are more stable than the mixture as sufficient alcohol is added to maintain the drug in solution. Most of the elixirs become turbid when moderately diluted by aqueous fluids.

Hence, the correct option is (B).

63. Tablets are the most widely used form of dosage. A tablet is a pharmaceutical oral dosage form (oral solid dosage, or OSD) or solid unit dosage form. It comprises a mixture of active substances and excipients, usually in powder form, pressed or compacted from a powder into a solid dose. Tablets are prepared either by molding or by compression.

Hence, the correct option is (C).

64. Bases that are water-washable, non-greasy, can be diluted with water, non-occlusive is water-soluble bases. Water-soluble bases are called alkalis. They are generally water-soluble. Some concentrated solutions may even cause chemical burns. Alkali aqueous solutions are soapy to the touch. It is corrosive.

Hence, the correct option is (A).

65. Methods of granules formation are the fusion method and the wet method.

Fusion method: The fusion method uses the water of crystallization present in the citric acids which act as binding agent. The powdered mixture is stirred well to obtain a uniform mass and is passed through a sieve to obtain granules and is finally dried in an oven.

Wet method: Wet granulation involves the massing of a mix of dry primary powder particles using a granulating fluid. The fluid contains a solvent that can be removed by drying, and should be non-toxic. (also referred to as a binder or binding agent) which is used to ensure particle adhesion once the granule is dry.

Hence, the correct option is (D).

66. Citric Acid contains one water molecule that acts as a binder in the fusion method for making effervescent granules. Citric acid is an organic compound with the chemical formula $HOC(CO_2H)(CH_2CO_2H)_2$. Usually encountered as a white solid, it is a weak organic acid. It occurs naturally in citrus fruits. In biochemistry, it is an intermediate in the citric acid cycle, which occurs in the metabolism of all aerobic organisms.

Hence, the correct option is (A).

67. Dusting powder is finely divided powder meant for introduction into the body cavities. Dusting powder helps to relieve prickly heat on the back, neck, and shoulder. Helps to treat skin irritation like redness, rashes, and swelling. Prevents fungal infections by keeping the body dry and clean. Improves the symptoms of fungal infections such as itching and skin irritation.

Hence, the correct option is (A).

68. Surgical powder must be sterile. Surgical dusting powders must be sterilized before their use, whereas medical dusting powders must be free from pathogenic microorganisms. Dusting powders are generally prepared by mixing two or more ingredients one of which must be either starch, talc or kaolin as one of the ingredients of the formulation.

Hence, the correct option is (B).

69. The double wrapping step in the preparation of powders is very often used. The powders are mixed by passing through sifters. This process results in an alight fluffy product and is generally not acceptable for the incorporation of potent drugs into a diluent base.

Double-Wrapping: Double-wrapping is essential for volatile or hygroscopic drugs like Menthol, thymol, citric acid, Pepsin, etc.

Hence, the correct option is (D).

70. Compound powders consist of more than one ingredient. In compounding, "powder" refers to a dosage form that exists as fine particles. The formulation may contain only the active drug or may be mixed with other ingredients. Compound powders contain two or more two substances that are mixed together. Then divided into the desired number of individual doses. Then dispensed into each powder paper.

Hence, the correct option is (B).

71. Hydrogenated oils are used as a substitute for theobroma oil. For example, hydrogenated edible oil, coconut oil, hydrogenated pea oil, stearic acids, palm kernel oil, etc. Cocoa butter, also called theobroma oil, is a pale-yellow, edible fat extracted from the cocoa bean. It is used to make chocolate, as well as some ointments, toiletries, and pharmaceuticals.

Hence, the correct option is (A).

72. Emulsified cocoa butter is not an example of hydrophilic bases. Cocoa butter crystallizes at room temperature. To emulsify it, you have to make it liquid by melting the chocolate, for example, in a bain-marie. The idea is to make it hotter than its main melting point, which is around 95°F (35°C). Cocoa butter, which is still widely used as a suppository base, has several well-known defects, such as slowness to harden if overheated and the assumption of solid forms with low melting points.

Hence, the correct option is (B).

73. Witespol is an example of a synthetic base. It is a saturated semi-synthetic triglyceride. The monoglycerides in the structure play an emulsifying role. Thus, the bases acquire the ability to hold water. Witepsol is described according to its chemical structure and physical properties.

Hence, the correct option is (A).

74. Emulsified cocoa butter is an example of oily bases. Fatty bases, also known as oleaginous bases, include synthetic

triglyceride mixtures and theobroma oil. Cocoa butter or theobroma oil is used as a suppository base mainly because, in large measure, it accomplishes the requirements of an ideal base.

Hence, the correct option is (B).

75. The glycerol gelatin base is an example of hydrophilic bases. The hydrophilic class of suppositories includes excipients that dissolve in the presence of water. These include primarily glycerin, gelatin and water-soluble polymers such as PEG. Suppositories based on glycerin are most known for use in the treatment of constipation. This base is dispersed slowly in the body cavity fluids and provides prolonged release and action of drugs.

Hence, the correct option is (C).

76. Can be given to the unconscious patient is an advantage of suppositories. The primary advantages of suppositories over other dosage forms include reduced first-pass metabolism, both topical and systemic effect, accommodates patients who have difficulty swallowing pills, and increased bioavailability of drugs.

Hence, the correct option is (D).

77. If the endosperm is concave on the commissural surface, it is called coelospermons fruit, which is hemlock. Hemlock is a very poisonous plant. In fact, all parts of the plant are toxic. Hemlock is most poisonous during the early stages of growth in the spring, but it is dangerous at all stages of growth. Hemlock is native to Europe and western Asia and was introduced into North America as an ornamental plant.

Hence, the correct option is (C).

78. It is difficult to make powder of coriander due to the presence of endosperm cells. The endosperm is a tissue produced inside the seeds of most of the flowering plants following double fertilization. It is triploid (meaning three chromosome sets per nucleus) in most species, which may be auxin-driven. Some plants, such as orchids, lack endosperm in their seeds.

Hence, the correct option is (C).

79. Bud like odour of green plant is due to trans-tridecene-(2)-al-(1), it is found in coriander. The vitamins, minerals, and antioxidants in coriander provide significant health benefits. Coriander leaves and seeds are full of vitamin K, which plays an important role in helping your blood clot. Vitamin K also helps your bones repair themselves, helping prevent problems like osteoporosis.

Hence, the correct option is (C).

80. Anethole is sweet odourous constituent of volatile oil of fennel. The dominant constituent in essential oils of aniseed and fennel is trans-anethole, which has a sweet herbaceous odour and sweet taste. Fennel (Foeniculum vulgare) is a flowering plant species in the carrot family. It is a hardy, perennial herb with yellow flowers and feathery leaves. It is a highly aromatic and flavorful herb used in cooking and, along with the similar-tasting anise, is one of the primary ingredients of absinthe.

Hence, the correct option is (D).

81. There are 20 to 40 small vittae on the dorsal surface of the cumin. Cumin is a spice made from the seeds of the Cuminum cyminum plant. Many dishes use cumin, especially foods from its native regions of the mediterranean and southwest asia. Cumin lends its distinctive flavor to chili, tamales, and various Indian curries. what's more, cumin has long been used in traditional medicine.

Hence, the correct option is (A).

82. Star Anise fruits belongs to the family magnoliaceae. The Magnoliaceae is a flowering plant family, the magnolia family, in the order Magnoliales. It consists of two subfamilies: Magnolioideae of which Magnolia is the best-known genus, and Liriodendroidae, a monogeneric subfamily, of which Liriodendron (tulip trees) is the only genus.

Hence, the correct option is (B).

83. Jatamansi is used in hysteria. The roots and the rhizomes of N. Jatamansi have been used in various herbal formulations including dietary supplements. This important traditional drug is also used to treat epilepsy, hysteria, syncope, convulsions, and mental weakness.

Hence, the correct option is (B).

84. Prisms types of calcium oxalate crystals are found in the hypanthium of clove. Calcium oxalate crystals, which are found in many organs of plants, have different morphological forms as druses, prism, styloid, raphides and crystal sand. Clove is reddish-brown in colour, with an upper crown and a hypanthium. The hypanthium is sub-cylindrical and tapering at the end. The hypanthium is 10 to 13 mm long, 4 mm wide, and 2 mm thick and has schizolysigenous oil glands and an ovary that is bilocular.

Hence, the correct option is (C).

85. Eugenol, also called clove oil, is an aromatic oil extracted from cloves that are used widely as a flavoring for foods and teas and as an herbal oil used topically to treat toothache and more rarely to be taken orally to treat gastrointestinal and respiratory complaints. Eugenol, a natural substance used as a target molecule for the manufacture of bioactive compounds, was first isolated in 1929 and its commercial production began in 1940 in the United States.

Hence, the correct option is (B).

86. The major chemical constituent of the volatile oil of ocimum sanctum is eugenol. Eugenol, also called clove oil, is an aromatic oil extracted from cloves that are used widely as a flavoring for foods and teas and as an herbal oil used topically to treat toothache and more rarely to be taken orally to treat gastrointestinal and respiratory complaints.

Hence, the correct option is (B)

87. Allopurinol drugs used in the treatment of gout has as its primary effect the reduction of uric acid synthesis. Allopurinol is used to prevent or lower high uric acid levels in the blood. It is also used to prevent or lower excess uric acid levels caused by cancer medicines or in patients with kidney stones. A high uric acid level can cause gout or gouty arthritis (joint pain and inflammation).

Hence, the correct option is (A).

88. Streptomycin, penicillin and chloramphenicol are the antibiotics drug except for co-trimoxazole. Co-trimoxazole is a combination of trimethoprim and sulphamethoxazole and is in a class of medications called sulphonamides. It works by stopping the growth of bacteria. Antibiotics will not kill viruses that can cause colds, flu, or other viral infections.

Hence, the correct option is (C).

89. Penicillin V drugs is gastric acid resistant. The potassium salt of penicillin V has a distinct advantage over penicillin G in resistance to inactivation by gastric acid. It may be given with meals; however, blood levels are slightly higher when the drug is given on an empty stomach.

Hence, the correct option is (B).

90. Oxacillin drugs is penicillinase-resistant. Oxacillin is a penicillinase-resistant β-lactam. It is similar to methicillin, and has replaced methicillin in clinical use. Other related compounds are nafcillin, cloxacillin, dicloxacillin, and flucloxacillin.

Hence, the correct option is (A).

91. Aminoglycosides have unwanted effects which are ototoxicity and nephrotoxicity. Nephrotoxicity and ototoxicity are clinically significant dose-related adverse effects associated with second-line anti-tubercular injectables drugs (aminoglycosides and capreomycin) used during the intensive phase of treatment of multi-drug resistant tuberculosis (MDR-TB) patients.

Hence, the correct option is (C).

92. Chloramphenicol has the pancytopenia unwanted effects. Pancytopenia is a condition in which a person's body has too few red blood cells, white blood cells, and platelets. Each of these blood cell types has a different job in the body:

- Red blood cells carry oxygen throughout your body.
- White blood cells are part of your immune system and help fight off infections.

Hence, the correct option is (B).

93. The mechanism of Amphotericin B action is alteration of cell membrane permeability. Amphotericin B is an example of a "polyene" type of antifungal. Polyenes bind to fungal ergosterol (the primary sterol in fungal cell membranes). This alters cell membrane permeability, and intracellular components leak from the cell.

Hence, the correct option is (D).

94. Azoles have an antifungal effect because of the reduction of ergosterol synthesis. The ergosterol inhibitor class of medications ("conazoles") is used in the management and treatment of fungal infections. These drugs inhibit ergosterol in the cell membrane to help kill fungi. This drug comes in both topical and systemic formulas.

Hence, the correct option is (C).

95. Amphotericin B has renal impairment, anemia effects. Despite this degree of anemia, no elevation of erythropoietin concentrations in urine or serum could be detected. Thus, amphotericin appears to cause anemia by inhibiting erythropoietin production rather than by suppressing bone marrow activity directly.

Hence, the correct option is (B).

96. The drug belonging to antibiotics has a polyene structure is nystatin. The polyene macrolides, including Amphotericin B, 1, and Nystatin, 2, are fungicidal agents. These drugs have worked well for systemic mycoses, but extensive attempts at chemical modification of the drug have been unable to reduce the nephrotoxicity of the polyene macrolides.

Hence, the correct option is (A).

97. Mechanism of Izoniazid action is inhibition of mycolic acids synthesis. The drugs shown to inhibit mycolic acid biosynthesis are isoniazid, ethionamide, isoxyl, thiolactomycin, and triclosan. In addition, pyrazinamide was shown to inhibit fatty acid synthase type I which, in turn, provides precursors for fatty acid elongation to long-chain mycolic acids by fatty acid synthase II.

Hence, the correct option is (B).

98. The mechanism of rifampin action is inhibition of DNA-dependent RNA polymerase. Mechanism of action-Rifampin is thought to inhibit bacterial DNA-dependent RNA polymerase, which appears to occur as a result of drug binding in the polymerase subunit deep within the DNA/RNA channel, facilitating direct blocking of the elongating RNA.

Hence, the correct option is (B).

99. The mechanism of cycloserine action is inhibition of cell wall synthesis. Cycloserine works as an antibiotic by inhibiting cell-wall biosynthesis in bacteria. As a cyclic analogue of D-alanine, cycloserine acts against two crucial enzymes important in the cytosolic stages of peptidoglycan synthesis are alanine racemase (Alr) and D-alanine, D-alanine ligase (Ddl).

Hence, the correct option is (C).

100. The mechanism of Streptomycin action is inhibition of protein synthesis. The mechanism of action of streptomycin is the inhibition of protein synthesis of mycobacteria in the ribosome. Resistance emerges when mutations appear in genes encoding 16S rRNA and protein S12.

Hence, the correct option is (B).

101. Rifampin has unwanted effects these are flu-like syndrome, tubular necrosis. Rifampicin is a polyketide belonging to the chemical class of compounds termed ansamycins, so named because of their heterocyclic structure containing a naphthoquinone core spanned by an aliphatic ansa chain.

Hence, the correct option is (C).

102. Isoniazid has unwanted effects these are hepatotoxicity, peripheral neuropathy. Isoniazid can cause rapid onset of peripheral neuropathy with predominant motor symptoms and should be considered as a possible cause in cases presenting with such symptoms soon after starting the medication. Chronic INH hepatotoxicity results in the induction of hepatocyte apoptosis, with associated disruption of mitochondrial membrane potential and DNA strand breaks. The most likely biochemical mechanism

is that the metabolism of INH produces reactive metabolites that bind and damage cellular macromolecules in the liver.

Hence, the correct option is (B).

103. Calcium antagonists reduce the vascular tone by blocking the release of calcium from the sarcoplasmic reticulum and thus reducing cytosolic calcium ions. The most common side effects are hypotension, flushing and ankle oedema.

Hence, the correct option is (A).

104.

The mechanism of aminosalicylic acid action is inhibition of folate synthesis. It inhibits the onset of bacterial resistance to streptomycin and isoniazid. The mechanism of action has been postulated to be inhibition of folic acid synthesis (but without potentiation with antifolic compounds) and/or inhibition of synthesis of the cell wall component, mycobacteria, thus reducing iron uptake.

Hence, the correct option is (B).

105. Rifampin, isoniazid and streptomycin are the first-line antimycobacterial drugs except for pyrazinamide. Pyrazinamide is used with other medications to treat tuberculosis (TB). It is an antibiotic and works by stopping the growth of bacteria. This antibiotic treats only bacterial infections. It will not work for viral infections (such as common cold, flu).

Hence, the correct option is (B).

106. The mechanism of fluoroquinolone's action is the inhibition of DNA gyrase. Fluoroquinolones act by inhibiting two enzymes involved in bacterial DNA synthesis, both of which are DNA topoisomerases that human cells lack and that are essential for bacterial DNA replication, thereby enabling these agents to be both specific and bactericidal.

Hence, the correct option is (B).

107. Methyldopa is an alpha-adrenergic agonist (selective for α2-adrenergic receptors). Activation of these receptors in the brainstem inhibits sympathetic nervous system output and lowers blood pressure. This is also the mechanism of action of clonidine.

Hence, the correct option is (C).

108. Acyclovir, saquinavir and didanozine antiviral drugs are the analogs of nucleosides, except for zidovudine.

Zidovudine belongs to a class of drugs known as nucleoside reverse transcriptase inhibitors-NRTIs. Zidovudine is used in pregnant women to prevent the passing of the HIV virus to the unborn baby. This medication is also used in newborns born to mothers infected with HIV to prevent infection in newborns.

Hence, the correct option is (B).

109. The action mechanism of alkylating agents is producing carbonium ions altering DNA structure. Most alkylating agents have similar mechanisms of action but differ in their clinical efficacy. These agents act directly on DNA, resulting in its crosslinking and causing DNA strand breaks, leading to abnormal base pairing and inhibiting cell division, eventually resulting in cell death.

Hence, the correct option is (B).

110. The action mechanism of anticancer drugs belonging to plant alkaloids is mitotic arrest at metaphase. Anticancer drugs are traditiona lly classified either by their mechanism of action or by their origir s. Alkylating agents are reactive to DNA and cellular proteins and the primary mode of action is mostly through cross-linking of DNA strands, inhibiting replication of DNA and transcription of RNA.

Hence, the correct option is (C).

111. H2 blockers are a group of medicines that reduce the amount of acid produced by the cells in the lining of the stomach. They are also called 'histamine H2-receptor antagonists' but are comm only called H2 blockers. They include cimetidine, famotidine, nizatidine, and ranitidine, and have various different brand names.

Hence, the correct option is (B).

112.

The selective COX-2 inhibitor is rofecoxib. The COX-2 selective inhibitors, such as rofecoxib and celecoxib, were introduced to decrease the gastrointestinal morbidity and mortality associated with older non-steroidal anti-inflammatory drugs (NSAIDs) which inhibit both the COX-1 and the COX-2 enzymes.

Hence, the correct option is (B).

113. Acute migraine is treated with sumatriptan. Sumatriptan is used to treat the symptoms of migraine headaches (severe, throbbing headaches that sometimes are accompanied by nausea or sensitivity to sound and light). Sumatriptan is in a class of medications called selective serotonin receptor agonists. It works by narrowing blood vessels in the head, stopping pain signals from being sent to the brain, and blocking the release of certain natural substances that cause pain, nausea, and other symptoms of migraine.

Hence, the correct option is (C).

114.

Allopurinol can inhibit the metabolism of 6-Mercaptopurine. Allopurinol inhibits the enzyme xanthine oxidase (XO), which is one of 3 enzymes responsible for inactivating 6-mercaptopurine (the active form of azathioprine). It may also have effects on TPMT activity as one study showed a reduction in methylated metabolites with the combination.

Hence, the correct option is (C).

115. Van' t Hoff equation for the solution is pV=nRT. The Van 't Hoff equation has been widely utilized to explore the changes in state functions in a thermodynamic system. The Van 't Hoff plot, which is derived from this equation, is especially effective in estimating the change in enthalpy and entropy of a chemical reaction.

Hence, the correct option is (C).

116. The CMC (critical micelle concentration) is the concentration of a surfactant in a bulk phase, above which aggregates of surfactant mclecules, so-called micelles, start to form. The CMC is an important characteristic for surfactants.

Hence, the correct option is (D).

117. Isobutyl alcohol is the chiral molecule. Isobutyl alcohol is also called as 2-Butanol. A chiral molecule has non-superimposable mirror images. In a chiral molecule, the carbon atom is attached to four different groups, thus, making it a chiral carbon.

Chirality is the condition for a molecule to be optically active and here isobutyl alcohol is the only compound that is optically active and so, it is the chiral molecule.

Hence, the correct option is (D).

118.

In an oxidation-reduction change in the valency of reacting elements takes place. An atom's increase in oxidation state through a chemical reaction is called oxidation, and it involves a loss of electrons; a decrease in an atom's oxidation state is called reduction, and it involves the gain of electrons.

Hence, the correct option is (D).

119. Apoptosis is programmed cell death or cell suicide. In multicellular organisms, cells that are no longer needed or are a threat to the organism are destroyed by a tightly regulated cell suicide process known as programmed cell death or apoptosis.

Hence, the correct option is (A).

120. The first Human hormone product by Recombinant DNA technology is insulin.

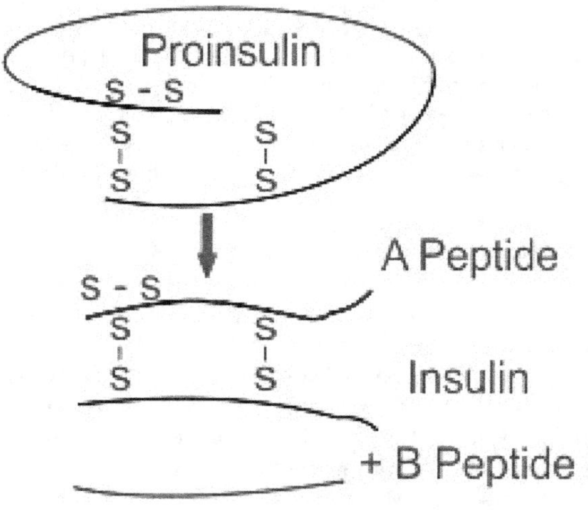

- The first genetically engineered insulin obtained by recombinant DNA technology with the help of E-Coli was developed by the American firm, Eli-Lilly on 5 July 1983.

- Insulin is used for diabetes.

- Insulin consists of two short polypeptide chains: chain A and chain B, that are linked together by disulfide bridges.

- Eli Lilly an American company prepared two DNA sequences corresponding to A and B, chains of human insulin, and introduced them in plasmids of E. coli to produce insulin chains.

- Chains A and B were produced separately, extracted, and combined by creating disulfide bonds to form human insulin.

Therefore the first Human hormone product by Recombinant DNA technology is insulin.

In genetic engineering, we can break the DNA molecule at two desired places with the help of endonuclease. And then insert it in another DNA molecule at the desired place. The new DNA molecule is called recombinant DNA. Genetic engineering can be used to improve the quality of human life.

Hence, the correct option is (A).

121. Spirochetes are flexible and can twist and contort their shape, whereas spirilla are relatively rigid. Treponema pallidum belongs to the spirochetes group and Spirillum volutans belong to the spirilla group. The spirochete, (order Spirochaetales), also spelled spirochaete, is any of a group of spiral-shaped bacteria, some of which are serious pathogens for humans, causing diseases such as syphilis, yaws, Lyme disease, and relapsing fever. Examples of genera of spirochetes include Spirochaeta, Treponema, Borrelia, and Leptospira.

Hence, the correct option is (B).

122. Parkinsons disease is defined as a neurologic disorder characterized pathologically by the loss of neurons in the Substantia Nigra and clinically by tremors at rest, muscular rigidity, expressionless face, and emotional lability.

Parkinson's disease is a brain disorder that leads to shaking, stiffness, and difficulty with walking, balance, and coordination. Parkinson's symptoms usually begin gradually and get worse over time. As the disease progresses, people may have difficulty walking and talking.

Hence, the correct option is (D).

123.

Infants have poorly developed BBB. A newborn usually refers to a baby from birth to about 2 months of age. Infants can be considered children anywhere from birth to 1 year old. Baby can be used to refer to any child from birth to age 4 years old, thus encompassing newborns, infants, and toddlers. Babies do have a blood-brain barrier, but it is possible that some of its components continue to mature after birth.

Hence, the correct option is (A).

124. Pharmacodynamic drug interactions include additive or synergistic interactions. Pharmacodynamic drug-drug interactions (DDIs) occur when the pharmacological effect of one drug is altered by that of another drug in a combination regimen. DDIs often are classified as synergistic, additive, or antagonistic in nature, albeit these terms are frequently misused.

Hence, the correct option is (C).

125. In ear wax type of secretion is produced by the ceruminous gland. The ceruminous glands in the skin of the human external auditory canal are modified apocrine glands, which, together with sebaceous glands, produce the cerumen, the ear wax. Cerumen plays an important role in the protection of the ear canal against physical damage and microbial invasion.

Hence, the correct option is (D).

Pharmaceutical Chemistry

Q.1 Gluconic acid is formed by fermentation of:
A. Fructose   **B.** Ribose
C. Glucose   **D.** Galactose

Q.2 The intravenous iron preparation is:
A. Ferrous sulphate
B. Ferrous fumarate citrate
C. Ferric ammonium
D. Iron dextran

Q.3 Oral liquid preparations of ferrous form are stabilised by:
A. Hypo phosphorus acid
B. Dextrose
C. Sodium meta bisulphite
D. Both (A) and (B)

Q.4 Haematinic is:
A. Ferrous sulphate
B. Sodium sulphate
C. Calcium sulphate
D. Magnesium sulphate

Q.5 Scale preparation of iron is:
A. Ferric ammonium citrate
B. Ferrous fumarate
C. Ferrous sulphate
D. Ferrous gluconate

Q.6 Iron and ammonium citrate is:
A. Electrolyte replenisher
B. Haematinic
C. Antioxidant
D. Preservative

Q.7 Major iron transport protein present in blood plasma is:
A. Ferritin   **B.** Transferrin
C. Hemosiderin   **D.** None of these

Q.8 Taste of ferrous sulphate is:
A. Metallic   **B.** Astringent
C. Saline   **D.** Both (A) and (B)

Q.9 In the assay of ferrous sulphate, it is:
A. Oxidised   **B.** Decomposed
C. Reduced   **D.** Hydrolysed

Q.10 The most commonly used salt of iron is:
A. Ferrous sulphate   **B.** Ferrous carbonate
C. Ferrous iodide   **D.** Fenvous lactate

Q.11 The indicator used in the assay of ferrous sulphate is:
A. Methyl orange   **B.** Phenol red

C. Methyl red   **D.** Ferroin solution

Q.12 Sodium citrate is titrated by:
A. Non-aqueous titration
B. Complexo metric titration
C. Acid-base titration
D. Gravimetric method

Q.13 Hartman's solution is:
A. Compound sodium chloride solution.
B. Compound sodium lactate solution.
C. Dextrose and saline solution.
D. Sodium chloride solution.

Q.14 Systemic alkaliser:
A. Ammonium chloride
B. Sodium citrate
C. Sodium chloride
D. Potassium chloride

Q.15 Which is not an allotropic modification of phosphorous?
A. Pink sulphur   **B.** Red sulphur
C. White sulphur   **D.** Black sulphur

Q.16 Sodium lactate is made by reacting lactic acid with:
A. $NaC_3H_5O_3$ **B.** $NaCl$
C. Na_2SO_4 **D.** NaI

Q.17 Too much potassium is called as:
A. Hypokalemias   **B.** Hyperkalemia
C. Hypercalcemia   **D.** Hypernatremin

Q.18 Oral tehydration therapy is more suitable in treating:
A. Dysentry   **B.** Dehydration
C. Vomming   **D.** None of these

Q.19 BOD (Biochemical oxygen demand) test for:
A. Quantity of air   **B.** Quality of air
C. Quality of water   **D.** Quantity of water

Q.20 Electrolyte replenisher is:
A. Potassium chloride   **B.** Potassium iodide
C. Potassium bromide   **D.** Potassium citrate

Q.21 Substance included in dialysis fluid to maintain osmotic pressure is:
A. Glucose   **B.** Fructose   **C.** Sucrose   **D.** Mannitol

Q.22 The most common electrolyte imbalance is:
A. Hyponatremia   **B.** Hypernatremia
C. Hypercalcemia   **D.** Hypocalcemia

Q.23 Compound sodium chloride injection is known as:
A. Normal saline   **B.** Ringer's injection
C. Harman's solution   **D.** Fowler's solution

Q.24 Nutritional deficiency of calcium leads to:
A. Hypokalemia
B. Hypocalcaemia
C. Hyponautremia
D. Hypercalcemia

Q.25 Calcium lactate is used as:
A. Disinfectant
B. Electrolyte replenisher
C. Antacid
D. Preservative

Q.26 Major cation (+ve) found in the fluid inside of the cells:
A. Sodium
B. Potassium
C. Magnesium
D. Calcium

Q.27 Non-electrolyte is:
A. NaCl
B. KCl
C. $CaCl_2$
D. Dextrose

Q.28 Major cation (+ve) found in fluid outside of the cells:
A. Sodium
B. Potassium
C. Magnesium
D. Calcium

Q.29 All are major extracellular ions except:
A. Calcium
B. Sodium
C. Chloride
D. Potassium

Q.30 Major function of electrolytes are:
A. Maintenance of blood volume
B. Supply of ions
C. Regulation of osmotic aquilibrium
D. All of these

Q.31 Major anion (-ve) found in fluid outside of the cells:
A. Chlorides
B. Bicarbonates
C. Sulphate
D. Carbonate

Q.32 Which of the following commonly available large volume dextrose solution for intravenous use is isotonic?
A. 2.5% W/V
B. 5% W/V
C. 10% W/V
D. 20% W/V

Q.33 Dehydration is caused by:
A. Exercise
B. Diaphoresis
C. Diarrhea & Vomiting
D. All of these

Q.34 Glauber's salt is:
A. Ferrous sulphate
B. Manganesent sulphate
C. Sodium sulphate
D. Magnesium sulphate

Q.35 The drinks commonly sold to public are:
A. Isotonic
B. Hypertonic
C. Hypotonic
D. None of these

Q.36 Sodium benzoate is:
A. Oxidizing agent
B. Reducing agent
C. Preservative
D. Emulsifier

Q.37 Electrolytes commonly exist as solution of:
A. Acids
B. Bases
C. Salts
D. All of these

Q.38 All are major intracellular ions except:
A. Phosphate
B. Potassium
C. Magnesium
D. Chloride

Pharmaceutics

Q.39 Doses of children are calculated by Young's formula, which formula is right?
A. Adult Dose (mg/day) x [Age/(Age+12)]
B. Adult Dose (gm/day) x [Age/(Age+24)]
C. Adult Dose (mg/day) x [Wt in Kg/(Age+12)]
D. Adult Dose (mg/day) x [Wt in Kg/(Age+24)]

Q.40 The schedule of dosing (four times a day, two times a day etc.) is called:
A. Dose inspection
B. Dose regimen
C. Dose calibration
D. All of these

Q.41 Which of the following is not an ideal property of bases?
A. Shall be non-irritant
B. Shall not interfere in release
C. Shall be compatible with drugs
D. None of these

Q.42 Suppository bases __________.
A. Maintain shape
B. Helps in insertion into the body cavity
C. Theobroma oil is example
D. All of these

Q.43 For ideal suspension, the sedimentation volume should be:
A. Zero
B. Equal to one
C. More than one
D. Less than one

Q.44 Cake formation is characteristic feature __________.
A. Flocculated
B. Deflocculated
C. Thixotropic suspension
D. Structured suspension

Q.45 The rate of sedimentation is high in:
A. Flocculated
B. De-flocculated
C. Both (A) and (B)
D. None of these

Q.46 Pharmaceutical suspensions are generally __________.
A. Flocculated
B. De-flocculated
C. Both (A) and (B)
D. None of these

Q.47 Upward creaming is observed in:
A. W/O
B. O/W
C. Micro
D. Both (A) and (B)

Q.48 Creaming is:
A. Reversible
B. Irreversible
C. Difficult to predict
D. Both (A) and (B)

Q.49 The particle size in suspension is:

A. less than 10^3 nm
B. 10^2 nm
C. Greater than 10^3nm
D. 10 nm

Q.50 What is the dispersion of a liquid in another liquid called?
A. Gel
B. Foam
C. Emulsion
D. Aerosol

Q.51 Which of the following statements regarding emulsions is false?
A. Emulsions cannot be separated into their constituent liquids.
B. Emulsions show Brownian motion.
C. Emulsions show Tyndall effect.
D. Emulsions exhibit properties like Electrophoresis and Coagulation.

Q.52 Which of the following is not a method to test the type of emulsion?
A. Microscopic method
B. Conductance method
C. Coagulation method
D. Dye method

Q.53 What is the difference between vanishing cream and cold cream?
A. Both are examples of oil-in-water emulsions.
B. Vanishing cream is an oil-in-water emulsion whereas cold cream is a water-in-oil emulsion.
C. Vanishing cream is a water-in-oil emulsion whereas cold cream is an oil-in-water emulsion.
D. Both are examples of water-in-oil emulsions.

Q.54 Which of the following is not an example of a water-in-oil emulsion?
A. Cod liver oil
B. Butter
C. Cold cream
D. Milk

Q.55 In case of O/W emulsion, creaming takes place at _______.
A. Down side
B. Upside
C. At interface between two phase
D. None of these

Q.56 In case of coalescence _______.
A. Dispersed droplet does not fuse
B. Globules size decrease
C. No of globules increase
D. Dispersed droplets tend to fuse

Q.57 If viscosity of continuous phase increase so creaming _______.
A. No change
B. Increase
C. Decrease
D. None of these

Q.58 In microemulsion, the size of globules are _______.
A. 1 um
B. 0.1 um
C. 0.01 um
D. 10 um

Q.59 In conductivity test, if bulb glows on passing electric current so what would be the type of emulsion?
A. W/O emulsion
B. O/W emulsion

C. Micro emulsion
D. Multiple emulsion

Q.60 In the dye test which is used to identify the type of emulsion in that which dye is used?
A. Scarlet red
B. Scarlet green
C. Crystal violet
D. Methylene blue

Q.61 In the stability of emulsion, which important instability step should be prevented?
A. Breaking
B. Coalescence
C. Flocculation
D. Creaming

Q.62 Oil and Water is an example of an _______.
A. Suspension
B. Emulsion
C. Colloid
D. Solution

Q.63 The tail of a surfactant molecule is oil-loving or known as _______.
A. Hydrophilic
B. Lipophobic
C. Lipophilic
D. Hydrophobic

Q.64 What type of emulsion is a w/o/w emulsion?
A. Primary emulsion
B. Micro-emulsion
C. Multiple-emulsion
D. Monoemulsion

Q.65 In the mixing of thymol and menthol the following type of incompatibility occurs?

[Graduate Pharmacy Aptitude Test, 2010]

A. Chemical incompatibility
B. Therapeutic incompatibility
C. Physical incompatibility
D. Tolerance incompatibility

Q.66 Chemical incompatibility which can be reduced by using dilute solutions or simply changing the order of mixing is called:
A. Tolerated incompatibility
B. Adjusted incompatibility
C. Both (A) and (B)
D. None of these

Q.67 Chemical incompatibility in which change in formulation is needed is called as:
A. Tolerated incompatibility
B. Adjusted incompatibility
C. Both (A) and (B)
D. None of these

Q.68 Immiscibility of oil and water can be overcome by:
A. Formulating an emulsion
B. Formulating suspension
C. Formulating an insufflation
D. Formulating an elixir

Q.69 Strategy to correct eutectic mixture formation is:
A. Dispense ingredients separately.
B. Mix ingredients separately with suitable adsorbent like kaolin and finally mix together.
C. Both (A) and (B)
D. None of these

Q.70 When substances with low melting points such as camphor aretriturated together a liquid mixture is formed the phenomenon iscalled __________.

A. Liquefaction

B. Insolubility

C. Herapath formation

D. Eutectic mixture formation

Q.71 Physical change may almost be __________.

A. Visible

B. Invisible

C. Turbid

D. No change

Q.72 Liquefaction is the example of ________ incompatibility.

A. Immediate

B. Delayed

C. Instantaneous

D. Both (A) and (B)

Q.73 There are _________ types of incompatibilities.

A. 1   **B.** 2   **C.** 3   **D.** 4

Q.74 The date on prescription tells us:

A. Date of writing the prescription

B. Date of presentation of prescription

C. Name of patient

D. Both (A) and (B)

Q.75 Pediatric dose can be calculated by considering child's:

A. Age

B. Body Weight

C. Body Surface area

D. All of these

Q.76 Clark's formula to calculate pediatric dose uses body wt in pounds, which of the following formula is correct representation?

A. Adult Dose (gm/day) x (Child Weight in Lbs /150)

B. Adult Dose (mg/day) x (Child Weight in Lbs /150)

C. Adult Dose (mg/day) x (Child Weight in Lbs /250)

D. Adult Dose (gm/day) x (Child Weight in Lbs /250)

Pharmacognosy

Q.77 In higher doses nutmeg is toxic due to:

A. Myristicin

B. Safrol

C. Borniol

D. Geraniol

Q.78 Mace gives the following colour with alkali or sulphuric acid:

A. Red   **B.** Blue   **C.** Green   **D.** Yellow

Q.79 Valerian is used in:

A. Hysteria

B. Insomnia

C. Palpitation of Heart

D. All of these

Q.80 Indian valerian is considered superior to European because valepotriates are:

A. Two times more

B. Three times more

C. Four times more

D. Six times more

Q.81 Allicin is active up to the following dilution against pathogenic gram-positive and gram-negative bacteria:

A. 1:1000

B. 1:10000

C. 1:100000

D. 1:1000000

Q.82 Garlic is useful in:

A. Diarrhoea

B. Chronic bronchitis

C. Dementia

D. Vertigo

Q.83 Pyrethrum is a contact poison for:

A. Mosquitoes

B. Flies

C. Bugs

D. All of these

Q.84 Cantharicin is used in:

A. Hepatitis

B. Hair tonic preparation

C. Insomnia

D. Constipation

Q.85 Colophony is classified as:

A. Balsam

B. Oleo-gum-resin

C. Acid resin

D. Gum-resin

Q.86 Podophyllum belongs to family:

A. Asclepidaceae

B. Ranunculaceae

C. Compositae

D. Berbeidaceae

Pharmacology

Q.87 The COC-2 inhibitor is not to be given if patient is already taking:

[NEET PG, 2019]

A. Anti-allergic drug

B. Anti hypertensive drug

C. Anxiolytic drug

D. Oral anti-diabetic drug

Q.88 Find out the specific unwanted effect of L-DOPA:

A. Dementia

B. Hypertension

C. Dyskinesia

D. Excitotoxicity

Q.89 Find out the appropriate use of the Imipramine:

A. Insomnia

B. Epilepsy

C. Bedwetting in children

D. Mania

Q.90 An anticholinesterase which is useful in alzheimer's disease:

A. Arecolin

B. Donezepil

C. Isoproterenol

D. Clioquinol

Q.91 Pons is the parts of __________.

A. Brainstem

B. Diencephalon

C. Cerebellum

D. Cerebrum

Q.92 In the middle ear, anvil shaped bone is known as ______________.

A. Incus

B. Malleus

C. Stapes

D. Temporal bone

Q.93 Brain consist ______________ amount of neuron.

A. 1 million

B. 100 billion

C. 1000 billion

D. 10 million

Q.94 According to Rh factor _______________ blood group is know as universal donor.

A. O^{-ve}　　**B.** O^{+ve}　　**C.** AB $^{+ve}$　　**D.** AB^{-ve}

Q.95 In the net filtration pressure, blood colloidal osmotic pressure is ____________.

A. 30 mmHg　　　　**B.** 10 mmHg
C. 55 mmHg　　　　**D.** 15 mmHg

Q.96 ___________ is tidal volume of respiration.

A. 1200 ml　　**B.** 6000 ml　　**C.** 2400 ml　　**D.** 500 ml

Q.97 The pH of semen is ___________.

A. 6-7　　**B.** 4.5-6.9　　**C.** 7.0-7.7　　**D.** 7.2-8.0

Q.98 Aqueous humor is completely replaced about every ___________.

A. 90 minutes　　　　**B.** 15 minutes
C. 10 minutes　　　　**D.** 1 minutes

Q.99 Partial pressure of carbon dioxide in alveoli is _________.

A. 160 mmHg　　　　**B.** 105 mmHg
C. 40 mmHg　　　　**D.** 70 mmHg

Q.100 Blood consist _______________ amount of platelets.

A. 250,000-400,00 mm^3
B. 4000-11000 mm^3
C. 11000 mm^3
D. 250 mm^3

Q.101 ___________ is the area of highest visual activity or resolution.

A. Central fovea　　　　**B.** Blind spot
C. Lens　　　　**D.** Rods receptors

Q.102 ___________ is minute volume of respiration.

A. 1200 ml　　**B.** 6000 ml　　**C.** 2400 ml　　**D.** 500 ml

Q.103 _______________ amount of neutrophils present in normal.

A. 20-25%　　**B.** 60-70%　　**C.** 3-8%　　**D.** 2-4 %

Q.104 The entire nervous system contains ___________ amount of CSF.

A. 80-150 ml　　　　**B.** 1 liter
C. 5-15 ml　　　　**D.** 500 ml

Q.105 Each lacrimal gland produce about _______________ amount per day of lacrimal secration.

A. 10 ml　　**B.** 20 ml　　**C.** 90 ml　　**D.** 1 ml

Q.106 In the ECG, P- wave indicates:

A. Atrial depolarization
B. Ventricle Depolarization
C. Ventricle repolarization
D. Atrial depolarization

Q.107 ___________ muscles contraction produce dilation of pupils.

A. Circulatory muscles　　　　**B.** Spinctor papillae
C. Constrictor papillae　　　　**D.** Iris dilator muscles

Q.108 When the number of sperm falls below ___________ the male is likely to be infertile.

[NEET PG, 2019]

A. 20 million/ml　　　　**B.** 200 million/ml
C. 50-150 million/ml　　　　**D.** 100 million/ml

Q.109 Intraocular tension normally stay about ___________.

A. 10 mmHg　　　　**B.** 36 mmHg
C. 25 mmHg　　　　**D.** 100 mmHg

Q.110 Kidney consist _______________ amounts of juxtamedullary nephrons.

A. 25-30%　　**B.** 15-20%　　**C.** 80-85%　　**D.** 5-10%

Q.111 Drug class causing free water clearance:

A. Diuretic　　　　**B.** Saluretic
C. Uricosuric　　　　**D.** Aquaretic

Q.112 Why is vitamin B6 usually prescribed with isoniazid (INH)?

A. It acts as a cofactor for INH.
B. It prevents some adverse effects of INH therapy.
C. Like INH, it has tuberculostic activity.
D. It prevents metabolism of INH.

Q.113 Which agent is a neurotransmitter used by the sympathetic preganglionic neuron?

A. γ-aminobutyric acid (GABA)
B. Acetylcholine
C. Adrenaline
D. Isoprenaline

Q.114 How can the action of cyclizine be described?

A. 5-HT$_3$ antagonist　　　　**B.** H$_1$ antagonist
C. H$_2$ antagonist　　　　**D.** H$_1$ agonist

Other Subjects

Q.115 When osmotic pressure and temperature are the same then:

A. Equal volume of solutions would contain equal number of moles of the solute.
B. Equal volume of solutions would contain non-equal number of moles of the solute.
C. The non-equal volume of solutions would contain an equal number of moles of the solute.
D. The non-equal volume of solutions would contain a non-equal number of moles of the solute.

Q.116 Kinematic viscosity is:

A. Viscosity/Kinetic energy
B. Viscosity/S.T
C. Viscosity/Density
D. Viscosity/Mol.wt

Q.117 ____________ is not an amphiprotic solvent.

A. Water　　　　**B.** Alcohol
C. Acetic acid　　　　**D.** None of these

Q.118 Carbohydrates are precursors for many _____________ compound.

[NEET PG, 2019]

A. Organic
B. Inorganic
C. Both (A) and (B)
D. None of these

Q.119 The vaccines prepared through recombinant DNA technology are:

A. Third generation vaccines
B. First-generation vaccines
C. Second-generation vaccines
D. None of these

Q.120 Bacteria having clusters of flagella at both poles of cells are known as?

A. Amphitrichous
B. Monotrichous
C. Peritrichous
D. Lophotrichous

Q.121 Hydrocarbons are organic compounds with element ___________.

A. Hydrogen
B. Oxygen
C. Carbon
D. Both (A) and (C)

Q.122 Which of the following is not true of Parkinson's disease?

A. Most commonly occurs in white males.
B. Typically effects those in the 6 th- 8 th decade of their life.
C. Genetic factors do not play a role (except for a rare autosomal dominant disorder).
D. The vast majority of cases are idiopathic.

Q.123 Which of the following has very low perfusion rate?

A. Fat and bone
B. Muscle and skin
C. Lungs and kidneys
D. Liver and heart

Q.124 Which of the following responsibility of the clinical pharmacist is indirect patient care area?

A. Supervision of drug administration techniques.
B. Providing drug information to physicians and nurses.
C. Identify drugs brought into the hospital by patients.
D. Reviewing of each patient's drug administration forms periodically to ensure all doses have been administered.

Q.125 ____________ receptor is useful for color vision.

[NEET PG, 2019]

A. Rod
B. Cone
C. Muscarinic
D. Nicotinic

// Smart Answer Sheet //

Correct — Percentage of students who answered correctly. **Skipped** — Percentage of students who skipped.

Q.	Ans.	Correct	Skipped
1	C	58.14 %	30.03 %
2	D	48.4 %	40.23 %
3	D	55.45 %	36.61 %
4	A	55.22 %	31.39 %
5	A	49.48 %	35.06 %
6	B	78.22 %	20.26 %
7	B	57.8 %	35.39 %
8	A	58.63 %	35.33 %
9	A	68.55 %	31.21 %
10	A	66.98 %	31.03 %
11	D	68.89 %	30.18 %
12	A	52.28 %	46.09 %
13	B	49.05 %	34.13 %
14	B	69.64 %	30.05 %
15	A	56.68 %	31.93 %
16	A	68.72 %	30.94 %
17	B	45.96 %	40.42 %
18	B	68.21 %	30.4 %
19	B	85.52 %	13.24 %
20	A	47.11 %	46.34 %
21	A	52.33 %	42.86 %

Q.	Ans.	Correct	Skipped
22	A	43.11 %	35.94 %
23	B	54.7 %	39.29 %
24	B	66.51 %	32.36 %
25	B	51.07 %	38.76 %
26	B	47.67 %	48.43 %
27	D	44.32 %	39.25 %
28	A	59.27 %	37.85 %
29	D	61.98 %	31.4 %
30	D	69.58 %	30.11 %
31	A	57.54 %	35.46 %
32	B	64.45 %	30.51 %
33	D	54.27 %	34.28 %
34	C	55.56 %	37.48 %
35	A	43.13 %	32.91 %
36	C	69.28 %	30.47 %
37	D	40.77 %	38.44 %
38	D	59.34 %	32.21 %
39	A	57.79 %	30.6 %
40	B	45.03 %	43.47 %
41	D	59.54 %	38.36 %
42	D	43.98 %	35.42 %

Q.	Ans.	Correct	Skipped
43	D	45.02 %	54.46 %
44	B	46.12 %	36.93 %
45	A	67.06 %	31.45 %
46	A	44.71 %	54.24 %
47	B	44.54 %	37.02 %
48	D	47.86 %	42.99 %
49	C	51.35 %	40.21 %
50	C	41.84 %	46.36 %
51	A	66.01 %	30.84 %
52	C	40.23 %	48.02 %
53	B	12.37 %	80.41 %
54	D	87.28 %	10.14 %
55	B	58.81 %	38.74 %
56	D	55.79 %	44.03 %
57	C	44.45 %	35.4 %
58	C	43.86 %	34.08 %
59	B	66.37 %	30.7 %
60	A	46.42 %	30.24 %
61	B	51.59 %	32.63 %
62	B	86.52 %	12.76 %
63	D	56.22 %	40.28 %

Q.	Ans.	Correct	Skipped
64	C	45.78 %	38.49 %
65	C	61.65 %	31.49 %
66	A	45.3 %	41.23 %
67	B	68.3 %	30.37 %
68	A	51.58 %	44.28 %
69	C	29.44 %	67.08 %
70	A	69.36 %	30.3 %
71	A	89.3 %	10.31 %
72	A	64.05 %	31.33 %
73	C	44.7 %	30.34 %
74	D	43.53 %	55.73 %
75	D	52.13 %	37.75 %
76	B	61.97 %	35.53 %
77	A	68.42 %	31.53 %
78	D	47.47 %	48.64 %
79	D	57.54 %	30.43 %
80	B	49.89 %	36.99 %
81	B	66.4 %	31.02 %
82	B	58.09 %	30.08 %
83	D	49.25 %	43.88 %
84	B	68.33 %	31.33 %

Q.	Ans.	Correct	Skipped
85	C	44.19 %	48.67 %
86	D	42.41 %	32.83 %
87	B	50.26 %	47.3 %
88	C	63.68 %	31.49 %
89	C	60.85 %	37.26 %
90	B	49.96 %	40.58 %
91	A	69.9 %	30.09 %
92	A	82.53 %	10.3 %
93	B	69.94 %	30.01 %
94	A	62.14 %	32.95 %
95	A	20.77 %	76.43 %
96	A	56.49 %	40.5 %
97	D	51.83 %	39.56 %
98	A	59.05 %	35.94 %
99	C	15.8 %	73.58 %
100	A	51.76 %	36.64 %
101	A	63.94 %	31.03 %
102	B	58.92 %	33.17 %
103	B	49.32 %	31.11 %
104	A	50.75 %	45.84 %
105	D	66.51 %	30.11 %

Q.	Ans.	Correct	Skipped
106	A	63.91 %	30.88 %
107	D	43.85 %	56.03 %
108	A	24.07 %	69.34 %
109	A	45.1 %	46.34 %
110	A	63.42 %	32.31 %
111	D	65.09 %	33.79 %
112	B	48.12 %	30.98 %
113	B	54.83 %	37.69 %
114	B	14.52 %	84.39 %
115	A	40.38 %	54.15 %
116	A	58.39 %	30.31 %
117	D	47.68 %	32.77 %
118	A	41.46 %	35.38 %
119	C	69.37 %	30.08 %
120	A	62.19 %	34.86 %
121	D	56.64 %	34.29 %
122	A	43.56 %	49.55 %
123	A	46.19 %	33.48 %
124	D	61.97 %	36.13 %
125	B	41.38 %	53.76 %

//Hints and Solutions//

1. Gluconic acid is formed by fermentation of glucose. Gluconic acid is presently produced commercially either by employing the fungus Aspergillus niger or the bacterium, Acetobacter suboxydans through a submerged fermentation process, in which gluconic acid, sodium and calcium gluconate and glucose oxidase are produced.

Hence, the correct option is (C).

2. The intravenous iron preparation is iron dextran. In 1999 and 2001, two new intravenous iron preparations (ferric gluconate and iron sucrose) were introduced into the market as safer alternatives to iron dextran. Iron dextran is an iron replacement product that is used to treat iron deficiency, such as anemia (not enough iron in the blood) or blood loss in patients with certain conditions (eg, hemophilia, gastrointestinal bleeding).

Hence, the correct option is (D).

3. Oral liquid preparations of ferrous form are stabilised by hypo phosphorus acid and dextrose. In 1934, Husa and Klotz developed a formula for a stable ferrous iodide syrup in which hypophosphorous acid was used to prevent the liberation of iodine, and dextrose rather than sucrose was used to give the properties of a syrup. Later it was found that some of the dextrose crystallized at refrigerator temperatures. The preparation was also considered lacking in sweetness. Research reported in the present paper shows that the disadvantages may be overcome by reducing the proportion of dextrose and adding sodium benzoate as a preservative and saccharin sodium as a sweetening agent. The resulting product shows excellent stability except for the appearance of a barely perceptible precipitate after six months.

Hence, the correct option is (D).

4. Haematinic is ferrous sulphate. Ferrous sulfate (or sulphate) is a medicine used to treat and prevent iron deficiency anaemia. Iron helps the body to make healthy red blood cells, which carry oxygen around the body. Some things such as blood loss, pregnancy or too little iron in your diet can make your iron supply drop too low, leading to anaemia.

Hence, the correct option is (A).

5. Scale preparation of iron is ferric ammonium citrate (iron (III) ammonium citrate, is a complex salt of an undetermined structure composed of 16.5 to18.5 percent iron, approximately 9 percent ammonia, and 65 percent citric acid and occurs as reddish-brown or garnet red scales or granules or as a brownish-yellowish powder.

Hence, the correct option is (A).

6. Iron and ammonium citrate is haematinic. Ammonium Citrate is a white powdery material with a slight ammonia odor. It is used in pharmaceuticals and rust-proofing compounds, and in chemical analysis. A complex salt of indefinite composition that contains varying amounts of iron, that is obtained as red crystals or a brownish-yellow powder or as green crystals or powder, and that was formerly used in medicine for treating iron-deficiency anemia.

7. The major iron transport protein present in blood plasma is transferrin. Greater than 95% of the iron in plasma is bound to its circulating transport protein transferrin, which delivers most of its iron to erythrocyte precursors i.e. erythroid progenitor cells of the bone marrow that differentiate into mature RBCs.

Hence, the correct option is (B).

8. The taste of ferrous sulphate is metallic and astringent. Ferrous sulphate exhibited a metallic taste and metallic aftertaste and copper sulphate exhibited a more pronounced metallic aftertaste. The primary hazard is the threat to the environment. Immediate steps should be taken to limit its spread to the environment. Used for water or sewage treatment, as a fertilizer ingredient.

Hence, the correct option is (A).

9. In the assay of ferrous sulphate, it is oxidised. Oxidation is the loss of electrons from a substance. It is also the gain of oxygen by a substance. Potassium permanganate ($KMnO_4$) is used as an oxidising agent to oxidise ferrous sulphate. In the presence of dil H_2SO_4 ferrous sulfate is oxidized to ferric sulfate. As soon as the oxidation of ferrous sulfate is completed the addition of a drop of $KMnO_4$ produces permanent pink color which indicates the endpoint. No indicator is required as $KMnO_4$ is a self-indicator.

Hence, the correct option is (A).

10. The most commonly used salt of iron is ferrous sulphate. Oral ferrous iron salts are the most economical and effective medication for the treatment of iron deficiency anemia. Of the various iron salts available, ferrous sulphate is the one most commonly used.

Hence, the correct option is (A).

11. The indicator used in the assay of ferrous sulphate is ferroin solution. It is a popular redox indicator for visualizing oscillatory belousov–zhabotinsky reactions. Ferroin is suitable as a redox indicator, as the color change is reversible, very pronounced, and rapid, and the ferroin solution is stable up to 60°C. It is the main indicator used in cerimetry.

Hence, the correct option is (D).

12. Sodium citrate is titrated by non-aqueous titration. Non-aqueous titration refers to a type of titration in which the analyte substance is dissolved in a solvent that does not contain water. Proton donation with other weak acids and bases dissolved in it. Sodium citrate is assayed by titrating a solution of the salt in glacial acetic acid with standard acetous perchloric acid, the end-point being detected potentiometrically.

Hence, the correct option is (A).

13. Hartman's solution is a compound sodium lactate solution. Ringer's lactate solution (RL), also known as sodium lactate solution and Hartmann's solution, is a mixture of sodium chloride, sodium lactate, potassium chloride, and calcium chloride in water. It is used for replacing fluids and electrolytes in those who have low blood volume or low blood pressure.

Hence, the correct option is (B).

14. Sodium citrate is absorbed and metabolized to sodium bicarbonate, thus acting as a systemic alkalizer. The effects are essentially those of chlorides before absorption and those of bicarbonates subsequently. Oxidation is virtually complete so that less than 5% of sodium citrate is excreted in the urine unchanged.

Hence, the correct option is (B).

15. Pink sulphur is not an allotropic modification of phosphorous. Roll sulphur is not the allotropic form of sulphur. Monoclinic sulphur, Plastic sulphur and Rhombic sulphur are the allotropic forms of sulphur. Phosphorus exists in a few allotropic structures. Of these, the three principle structures are white phosphorus, black phosphorus, and red phosphorus. However, another form of phosphorus that is violet phosphorus also exists.

Hence, the correct option is (A).

16. Sodium lactate is the sodium salt of lactic acid and has a mild saline taste. It is produced by fermentation of a sugar source, such as corn or beets, and then, by neutralizing the resulting lactic acid to create a compound having the formula $NaC_3H_5O_3$. Sodium lactate, chemical formula $CH_3CHOHCOONa$, molecular weight 112.06, pure sodium lactate is a colorless or almost colorless transparent liquid and can be mixed with water, ethanol, and glycerol.

Hence, the correct option is (A).

17. Too much potassium is called as hyperkalemia. High potassium (called "hyperkalemia") is a medical problem in which you have too much potassium in your blood. Your body needs potassium. It is an important nutrient that is found in many of the foods you eat. Potassium helps your nerves and muscles, including your heart, work the right way.

Hence, the correct option is (B).

18. Oral tehydration therapy is more suitable in treating dehydration. ORT is suitable for people who are not dehydrated and those who show signs and symptoms of mild to moderate dehydration. People who have severe dehydration should seek professional medical help immediately and receive intravenous rehydration as soon as possible to rapidly replenish fluid volume in the body.

Hence, the correct option is (B).

19. BOD (Biochemical oxygen demand) test for the quality of air. Biochemical oxygen demand, or BOD, measures the amount of oxygen consumed by microorganisms in decomposing organic matter in stream water. BOD also measures the chemical oxidation of inorganic matter (i.e., the extraction of oxygen from water via chemical reaction).

Hence, the correct option is (B).

20. Electrolyte replenisher is potassium chloride. Potassium chloride (KCl, or potassium salt) is a metal halide salt composed of potassium and chlorine. It is odorless and has a white or colorless vitreous crystal appearance. In oral rehydration therapy, electrolyte drinks containing sodium and potassium salts replenish the body's water and electrolyte concentrations after dehydration caused by exercise, excessive alcohol consumption, diaphoresis (heavy sweating), diarrhea, vomiting, intoxication or starvation.

Hence, the correct option is (A).

21. The substance included in dialysis fluid to maintain osmotic pressure is glucose. Dialysis fluid consists of purified water, glucose, and electrolytes. The concentration of electrolytes (besides potassium and the buffer substance) closely resembles that which occurs naturally in the blood.

Hence, the correct option is (A).

22. The most common electrolyte imbalance is hyponatremia. Hyponatremia, or low sodium, is the most commonly seen type of electrolyte imbalance. Treatment of electrolyte imbalance depends on the specific electrolyte involved and whether the levels are too high or too low.

Hence, the correct option is (A).

23. Compound sodium chloride injection is known as ringer's injection. Ringer's Injection, USP is a sterile, nonpyrogenic solution for fluid and electrolyte replenishment in single-dose containers for intravenous administration. It contains no antimicrobial agents. The pH may have been adjusted with sodium hydroxide.

Hence, the correct option is (B).

24. Nutritional deficiency of calcium leads to hypocalcaemia. Hypocalcemia, also known as a calcium deficiency disease, occurs when the blood has low levels of calcium. A long-term calcium deficiency can lead to dental changes, cataracts, alterations in the brain, and osteoporosis, which causes the bones to become brittle. A calcium deficiency may cause no early symptoms.

Hence, the correct option is (B).

25. The calcium lactate is used as an electrolyte replenisher. A sterile solution of calcium chloride, potassium chloride, sodium chloride, and sodium lactate in water, given intravenously as a systemic alkalizer and as a fluid and electrolyte replenisher.

Hence, the correct option is (B).

26. The major cation (+ve) is found in the fluid inside of the cells is potassium. These substances are located in the extracellular and intracellular fluids. Within the extracellular fluid, the major cation is sodium and the major anion is chloride. The major cation in the intracellular fluid is potassium.

Hence, the correct option is (B).

27. Non-electrolyte is dextrose. Dextrose is not an electrolyte because it does not conduct electricity when it is dissolved in water. Glucose (sugar) readily dissolves in water, but because it does not dissociate into ions in solution, it is considered a non-electrolyte; solutions containing glucose do not, therefore, conduct electricity "non-electrolyte".

Hence, the correct option is (D).

28. Major cation (+ve) is found in fluid outside of the cells is sodium. Within the extracellular fluid, the major cation is sodium and the major anion is chloride. The major cation in the intracellular fluid is potassium. These electrolytes play an important role in maintaining homeostasis.

Hence, the correct option is (A).

29. All are major extracellular ions except for potassium. Within the extracellular fluid, the major cation is sodium and the major anion is chloride. The major cation in the intracellular fluid is potassium. The levels of electrolytes in your body can become too low or too high. The main electrolytes include sodium, chloride, potassium, calcium and magnesium. These five nutritional elements are minerals, and when minerals dissolve in water they separate into positive and negative ions.

Hence, the correct option is (D).

30. The major function of electrolytes is the maintenance of blood volume, supply of ions and regulation of osmotic equilibrium. Body fluid contains electrolytes, chemicals which, when they dissolve in water, produce charged ions. These ions enable the flow of electrical signals through the body. Electrolytes play an important role in the body; they regulate the osmotic pressure in cells and help maintain the function of muscle and nerve cells.

Hence, the correct option is (D).

31. Major anion (-ve) found in fluid outside of the cells chlorides. These substances are located in the extracellular and intracellular fluids. Within the extracellular fluid, the major cation is sodium and the major anion is chloride. The major cation in the intracellular fluid is potassium. These electrolytes play an important role in maintaining homeostasis.

Hence, the correct option is (A).

32. 5% W/V commonly available large volume dextrose solution for intravenous use is isotonic. D5W (dextrose 5% in water) is a crystalloid isotonic IV fluid with a serum osmolality of 252 mOsm/L. D5W is initially an isotonic solution and provides free water when dextrose is metabolized (making it a hypotonic solution), expanding the ECF and the ICF.

Hence, the correct option is (B).

33. Dehydration is caused by exercise, diaphoresis and diarrhea & vomiting. The most likely group to experience severe diarrhea and vomiting, infants and children are especially vulnerable to dehydration.

Sometimes dehydration occurs for simple reasons: You don't drink enough because you're sick or busy, or because you lack access to safe drinking water when you're traveling, hiking or camping.

Other dehydration causes include:

Diarrhea & vomiting: Severe, acute diarrhea that is, diarrhea that comes on suddenly and violently can cause a tremendous loss of water and electrolytes in a short amount of time. If you have vomiting along with diarrhea, you lose even more fluids and minerals.

Fever: In general, the higher your fever, the more dehydrated you may become. The problem worsens if you have a fever in addition to diarrhea and vomiting.

Excessive sweating: You lose water when you sweat. If you do vigorous activity and don't replace fluids as you go along, you can become dehydrated. Hot, humid weather increases the amount you sweat and the amount of fluid you lose.

Increased urination: This may be due to undiagnosed or uncontrolled diabetes. Certain medications, such as diuretics and some blood pressure medications, also can lead to dehydration, generally because they cause you to urinate more.

Hence, the correct option is (D).

34. Glauber's salt is sodium sulphate. Glauber's salt is the decahydrate form of sodium sulphate. It is also known as mirabilite. The chemical formula of Glauber's salt can be written as Na_2SO_4. Glauber's salt is known to be a vitreous mineral with a white or colourless appearance that is formed as an evaporite from brines containing sodium sulphate.

Hence, the correct option is (C).

35. The drinks commonly sold to the public are isotonic. For large volume replacement, isotonic or nearly isotonic solutions are used. Sodium chloride (0.9%) solution or Ringer's solution (not lactated Ringer's) is a good base solution. Potassium chloride should be added to either solution at a rate of 20 to 40 mEq/L.

A solution that has the same salt concentration as cells and blood. Isotonic solutions are commonly used as intravenously infused fluids in hospitalized patients.

Hence, the correct option is (A).

36. Sodium benzoate is a preservative. As a food additive, sodium benzoate has the E number E211. It is bacteriostatic and fungistatic under acidic conditions. Sodium benzoate is the sodium salt of benzoic acid, widely used as a food preservative and pickling agent. A white crystalline chemical with the formula C_6H_5COONa. Sodium benzoate is used as a preservative in soft drinks to increase the acidity flavor and as a preservative to extend the shelf life.

Hence, the correct option is (C).

37. Electrolytes commonly exist as solution of acids, bases, and salts. The most familiar electrolytes are acids, bases, and salts, which ionize when dissolved in such solvents as water or alcohol. Many salts, such as sodium chloride, behave as electrolytes when melted in the absence of any solvent; and some, such as silver iodide, are electrolytes even in the solid-state.

Hence, the correct option is (D).

38. Phosphate, potassium and magnesium are major intracellular ions except for chloride. Chloride is the major extracellular anion; Cl^- ions are almost completely absorbed from the GI tract. As the most abundant cation in intracellular fluid, potassium plays an important role in a variety of cell functions.

Hence, the correct option is (D).

39. Young's Rule is an equation used to calculate pediatric medication dosage based on the patient's age and the known recommended adult dose. The definition of Young's Rule is the age of the patient, divided by the age added to twelve, all multiplied by the recommended adult dose. This formula appears below:

[Age / (Age + 12)] x Recommended Adult Dose = Pediatric Dose

Young's Rule can be applied to quickly approach a situation in which the patient's weight is unknown. Other approaches to pediatric dosing that also use age include Webster's Rule and Fried's Rule. If the weight of the patient is known, Clark's Rule or the Body Surface Area rule can be implemented.

Hence, the correct option is (A).

40. The schedule of dosing (four times a day, two times a day, etc.) is called a dose regimen. A dosage regimen is defined as the manner in which a drug is taken. For successful therapy, the design of an optimal multiple dosage regimen is necessary. A multiple dosage regimen is defined as the manner in which the drug is administered in suitable doses by suitable route, with sufficient frequency that ensures maintenance of plasma concentrated within the therapeutic window for the entire period of therapy. In designing a dosage regimen. All kinetic parameters of the drug remain constant during the course of therapy once the Dosage regimen is established.

Hence, the correct option is (B).

41. Bases cannot turn blue litmus to red. Acids can turn blue litmus to red while bases can turn red litmus to blue. Bases react with acids to form salts i.e. essentially neutralizing them. Bases have a bitter taste while acids have a sour taste. It should melt at body temperature or disperse in the body fluids. It should be non-toxic and non-irritating to mucous membranes. It should be stable on storage. It should not bind or otherwise interfere with the release or absorption of drug substances.

Hence, the correct option is (D).

42. Suppository bases are in maintain shape, helps in insertion into the body cavity and theobroma oil is an example. Cocoa butter or theobroma oil is used as a suppository base mainly because, in large measure, it accomplishes the requirements of an ideal base. Cocoa butter, also called theobroma oil, is a pale-yellow, edible fat extracted from the cocoa bean. It is used to make chocolate, as well as some ointments, toiletries, and pharmaceuticals.

Hence, the correct option is (D).

43. For ideal suspension, the sedimentation volume should be less than one. Sedimentation volume (F) or height (H) for flocculated suspensions: Sedimentation volume is a ratio of the ultimate volume of sediment (Vu) to the original volume of sediment (VO) before settling. The qualities of ideal suspension are:

- It should settle slowly and should be readily re-dispersed on gentle shaking of the container.
- The particle size of the suspension remains fairly constant throughout its long period of undisturbed standing.
- The suspension should pour readily and evenly from its container.

Hence, the correct option is (D).

44. Cake formation is a characteristic feature of deflocculated. A deflocculated suspension is a suspension in which no flocculation has taken place. So, there are no floccules or other aggregates. Here, single colloid particles act as individual particles. The rate of sedimentation is slow since smaller particles are settling rather than large floccules.

Hence, the correct option is (B).

45. The rate of sedimentation is high in flocculated. Flocculation refers to the formation of a loose aggregation of discrete particles held together in a network-like structure by physical adsorption of macromolecules when the longer-range van der walls forces of attraction exceed the shorter-range forces of repulsion. Such a suspension is called flocculated suspension.

Hence, the correct option is (A).

46. Pharmaceutical suspensions are generally flocculated. A pharmaceutical suspension is a coarse dispersion of insoluble solid particles in a liquid medium. The particle diameter in a suspension is usually greater than 0.5 μm. Suspensions are an important class of pharmaceutical dosage forms. Most stable pharmaceutical suspensions are flocculated.

Hence, the correct option is (A).

47. Upward creaming is observed in O/W. Upward creaming, is due to the dispersed phase being less dense than the continuous phase. This is normally observed in O/W emulsions. Creaming is the upward movement of dispersed droplets of emulsion relative to the continuous phase (due to the density difference between two phases). Creaming is the concentration of globules at the top or bottom of the emulsion.

Hence, the correct option is (B).

48. Creaming is reversible and irreversible. Creaming is a reversible process, whereas breaking is irreversible. When breaking occurs, simple mixing fails to resus-pend the globules in a stable emulsified form, since the film surrounding the particles has been destroyed and the oil tends to coalesce.

Hence, the correct option is (D).

49. The particle size in suspension is greater than 10^3nm. Suspensions having particle sizes greater than about 1micron in diameter are called as coarse suspensions. A suspension is defined as a homogenous mixture of particles with a diameter greater than 1000 nm such that the particles are visible to naked eyes. In this type of mixture, all the components are completely mixed and all the particles can be seen under a microscope. A suspension is a heterogeneous mixture containing solid particles that are sufficiently large for sedimentation.

Hence, the correct option is (C).

50. The dispersion of a liquid in another liquid is called emulsion. The emulsion is the term used for explaining the dispersion of one liquid in another liquid. The emulsion is a type of liquid-liquid colloidal system. An emulsion is a mixture of two immiscible liquids or partially miscible liquids.

Hence, the correct option is (C).

51. Emulsions can be separated into their constituent liquids by boiling, freezing, centrifuging, electrostatic precipitation by the addition of large amounts of electrolytes to precipitate out the dispersed phase or by the chemical destruction of the emulsifier.

Hence, the correct option is (A).

52. The coagulation method is not a method to test the type of emulsion. Coagulation is a process of aggregating together the

colloidal particles so as to change them into large-sized particles which ultimately settle as a precipitate. When an electrolyte is added to the colloidal solution, the particles of the sol take up the ion which is oppositely charged, and thus get neutralised.

Hence, the correct option is (C).

53. Vanishing cream is an oil-in-water emulsion, that is, oil is the dispersed phase and water is the dispersion medium. Cold cream is a water-in-oil emulsion, that is, water is the dispersed phase and oil is the dispersion medium. Cold cream is an emulsion of water in a larger amount of oil, unlike the oil in water emulsion of vanishing cream, so-called because it seems to disappear when applied on the skin. The name "cold cream" derives from the cooling feeling that the cream leaves on the skin.

Hence, the correct option is (B).

54. In an emulsion of water-in-oil (w/o), water is the dispersed phase and oil is the dispersion medium. Cod liver oil, butter and cold cream are all examples of the water-in-oil type of emulsions.

When an emulsion is "oil-in-water," oil is the dispersed phase that is distributed into the continuous phase, water. In a water-in-oil emulsion, the roles are switched. Milk is an example of an oil-in-water emulsion, while butter is water-in-oil.

Hence, the correct option is (D).

55. In the case of O/W emulsion, creaming takes place at the upside. Upward creaming, is due to the dispersed phase being less dense than the. continuous phase. This is normally observed in o/w emulsions. The velocity of sedimentation becomes negative. Creaming is the concentration of globules at the top or bottom of the emulsion. Droplets larger than 1 mm may settle preferentially to the top or the bottom under gravitational forces.

Hence, the correct option is (B).

56. In the case of coalescence dispersed droplets tend to fuse. Coalescence of emulsions is an irreversible process by which two or more droplets merge during contact to form a single daughter droplet. The driving force for emulsion coalescence is the thinning and disruption of the liquid film between the droplets.

Hence, the correct option is (D).

57. If the viscosity of the continuous phase increase so creaming decreases.

Modifying viscosity of the continuous phase: Creaming or gravitational separation can be retarded by increasing the viscosity of the medium surrounding emulsion droplets. Regarding W/O emulsions, a network of aggregated fat crystals in the oil phase can stabilize water droplets against gravitational separation.

Hence, the correct option is (C).

58. In microemulsion, the size of globules is 0.01 um. Microemulsions have been extensively explored as drug delivery systems; these (globule size <100 nm) are a clear, thermodynamically stable, isotropic mixture of oil and water, which is stabilized by an interfacial film of surfactant and cosurfactant molecules.

Hence, the correct option is (C).

59. In the conductivity test, if the bulb glows on passing electric current so it would be the O/W type of emulsion. When current is passed to an emulsion connected to a voltage bulb, the bulbs glow if it is an O/W emulsion since water is a good conductor of electricity. When the bulb does not glow, it is a W/O emulsion because oil is a non-conductor of electricity.

Hence, the correct option is (B).

60. In the dye test, scarlet red is used to identify the type of emulsion in that which dye is used. If the scattered globules appear red and continuous phase colorless, then it is w/o type. Similarly, if an oil-soluble dye (Scarlet red C or Sudan III) is added to an emulsion and the continuous phase appears red, then it is w/o emulsion.

Hence, the correct option is (A).

61. In the stability of the emulsion, the coalescence instability step should be prevented. Coalescence is the process where droplets come into contact and merge, creating larger droplets. With time, this reduces the average droplet size and consequently, reduces the stability of the emulsion.

Hence, the correct option is (B).

62. Oil and Water is an example of an emulsion. Two liquids can form different types of emulsions. As an example, oil and water can form, first, an oil-in-water emulsion, in which the oil is the dispersed phase, and water is the continuous phase. Second, they can form a water-in-oil emulsion, in which water is the dispersed phase and oil is the continuous phase.

Hence, the correct option is (B).

63. The tail of a surfactant molecule is oil-loving or known as hydrophobic. A surfactant molecule possesses both a polar "water-loving" headgroup attached to a non-polar "water-hating" (or "oil-loving") tail. Due to their dual nature, they are associated with many useful interfacial phenomena, and as such are key components for many diverse industrial products and processes.

Hence, the correct option is (D).

64. Multiple model emulsions are also used in the studies of the release rates, stability, rheological characteristics, and other properties of emulsions. Multiple emulsions are emulsions where the disperse phase is itself an emulsion containing drops of another phase. This results in a w/o/w multiple emulsion.

Hence, the correct option is (C).

65. In the mixing of thymol and menthol, physical incompatibility occurs. When two or more than two substances are combined together, a physical change takes place and an unacceptable product is formed. Interaction between two or more substances may lead to a change in color, odor, taste, viscosity and morphology. It is also called as pharmaceutical incompatibility.

Hence, the correct option is (C).

66. Chemical incompatibility which can be reduced by using dilute solutions or simply changing the order of mixing is called tolerated incompatibility. In this type of incompatibility, the chemical interactions can be changing the order of mixing the

solutions in dilute forms, without or by changing the order of mixing.

Hence, the correct option is (A).

67. Chemical incompatibility in which change in formulation is needed is called as adjusted incompatibility. Adjusted incompatibility has chemical interaction can be prevented by the addition or substitution of one of the reacting ingredients of a prescription with another of equal therapeutic value.

Hence, the correct option is (B).

68. The immiscibility of oil and water can be overcome by formulating an emulsion. The process of formation of an emulsion is termed emulsification. Emulsified systems range from lotions of relatively low viscosity to ointments and creams, which are semisolid in nature. Pharmaceutical emulsions are used for the administration of nutrients, drugs, and diagnostic agents.

Hence, the correct option is (A).

69. The strategy to correct eutectic mixture formation is to dispense ingredients separately and mix ingredients separately with suitable adsorbents like kaolin and finally mix them together. A eutectic mixture is defined as a mixture of two or more components that usually do not interact to form a new chemical compound but, at certain ratios, inhibit the crystallization process of one another resulting in a system having a lower melting point than either of the components.

Hence, the correct option is (C).

70. When substances with low melting points such as camphor are triturated together a liquid mixture is formed the phenomenon is called liquefaction. Liquefaction is a phenomenon in which the strength and stiffness of soil are reduced by earthquake shaking or other rapid loading. Liquefaction occurs in saturated soils, that is, soils in which the space between individual particles is completely filled with water.

Hence, the correct option is (A).

71. Physical change may almost be visible. Any change that occurs without altering the chemical composition of a substance is a physical change. Physical changes can include changing the color, shape, state of matter, or volume of a substance.

Hence, the correct option is (A).

72. Liquefaction is an example of immediate incompatibility. If the chemical reaction takes place, immediately after combining the prescription ingredients, they are called immediate incompatibilities. So, they should be dispensed only after correction.

Hence, the correct option is (A).

73. There are 3 types of incompatibilities. It includes:

Physical incompatibilities: When two or more than two substances are combined together, a physical change takes place and an unacceptable product is formed. Interaction between two or more substances may lead to a change in color, odor, taste, viscosity and morphology. It is also called as pharmaceutical incompatibility.

Chemical incompatibilities: Reaction between two or more substances which lead to change in chemical properties of the pharmaceutical dosage form. As a result of this, a toxic or inactive or product may be formed.

Therapeutic incompatibilities: It is the modification of the therapeutic effect of one drug by the prior concomitant administration of another. It may be as a result of prescribing certain drugs to a patient with the intention to produce a specific degree of pharmacological action, but have restore or intensity of the action produced in the different room that intended by the prescriber.

Hence, the correct option is (C).

74. The date on the prescription tells us the date of writing the prescription and the date of presentation of the prescription. The inscription of the date on the prescription is not only important for the patient but the prescriber and the pharmacist as well. On a prescription label, this information is usually written after the refill information.

Hence, the correct option is (D).

75. The pediatric dose can be calculated by considering the child's age, body weight and body surface area. Although pediatric doses for biotherapeutics are often based on patients' body weight (mg/kg) or body surface area (mg/m2), linear body size dose adjustment is highly empirical. Growth and maturity are also important factors that affect the absorption, distribution, metabolism and excretion (ADME) of biologics in pediatrics. The complexity of the factors involved in pediatric pharmacokinetics lends to the reconsideration of body size-based dose adjustment.

Hence, the correct option is (D).

76. Clark's formula to calculate pediatric dose uses body wt in pounds the formula is represented as:

Adult Dose (mg/day) x (Child Weight in Lbs /150)

Clark's rule equation is defined as the weight of the patient in pounds divided by the average standard weight of 150 pounds (68 kg) multiplied by the adult dose of a drug equals the pediatric medication dose.

Hence, the correct option is (B).

77. In higher doses, nutmeg is toxic due to myristicin. The chemical responsible for the "high" caused by nutmeg is known as myristicin. Myristicin is a compound found naturally in the essential oils of certain plants, such as parsley, dill, and nutmeg.

Hence, the correct option is (A).

78. Mace gives yellow colour with alkali or sulphuric acid. Fruit is a pendulous, globose drupe, consisting of a pericarp with light yellow colour with the mace arillus covering the hard endocarp. The arillus is stripped off and form a mace. The arillus when fresh is a brilliant scarlet and when dry becomes more horny, brittle, and yellowish-brown in colour.

Hence, the correct option is (D).

79. Valerian has been used medicinally since the times of early Greece and Rome. Historically, valerian was used to treat insomnia, migraine, fatigue, and stomach cramps, hysteria, heart

palpitation. Today, valerian is promoted for insomnia, anxiety, depression, premenstrual syndrome (PMS), menopause symptoms, and headaches.

Hence, the correct option is (D).

80. Indian valerian is considered superior to European because valepotriates are three times more. Valerian is a common ingredient in products sold as mild relaxants and the relief of nervous tension and insomnia. Valerian preparations have been associated with few side effects.

Hence, the correct option is (B).

81. Allicin is active up to 1:10000 dilution against pathogenic gram-positive and gram-negative bacteria. Allicin is an organosulfur compound obtained from garlic, a species in the family Alliaceae. It was first isolated and studied in the laboratory by Chester J. Cavallito and John Hays Bailey in 1944. When fresh garlic is chopped or crushed, the enzyme alliinase converts alliin into allicin, which is responsible for the aroma of fresh garlic. The allicin generated is unstable and quickly changes into a series of other sulfur-containing compounds such as diallyl disulfide. Allicin is part of a defense mechanism against attacks by pests on the garlic plant.

Hence, the correct option is (B).

82. Garlic is useful in chronic bronchitis. Garlic is believed to have a number of healing properties. Results of a 2016 study show that garlic effectively inhibited the growth of infectious bronchitis virus. This finding suggests garlic can be used as a natural remedy for bronchitis.

Hence, the correct option is (B).

83. Pyrethrum is a contact poison for mosquitoes, flies and bugs. Pyrethrum was a genus of several Old World plants now classified as Chrysanthemum or Tanacetum (e.g., C. coccineum) which are cultivated as ornamentals for their showy flower heads. Pyrethrum continues to be used as a common name for plants formerly included in the genus Pyrethrum. Pyrethrum is also the name of a natural insecticide made from the dried flower heads of Chrysanthemum cinerariifolium and Chrysanthemum coccineum. Its active ingredient is pyrethrins.

Hence, the correct option is (D).

84. Cantharidin is used in hair tonic preparation. Cantharidin is a substance that comes from the green blister beetle. It is sometimes used to treat warts if salicylic acid or freezing with liquid nitrogen (cryotherapy) has not been useful. Cantharidin is a vesicant, which means it causes the skin to blister.

Hence, the correct option is (B).

85. Colophony is classified as acid resin. Colophony is an unhomogeneous mixture of resin acids like abietic acid and neutral substances. The effects of exposure to colophony are classified into bronchial asthma and contact dermatitis. Colophony fumes cause bronchial asthma by its nonspecific irritation.

Hence, the correct option is (C).

86. Podophyllum belongs to the family berbeidaceae. Podophyllum is an herbaceous perennial plant in the family Berberidaceae, described as a genus by Linnaeus in 1753. In the past, several species were included in the genus, but all but one have been transferred to other genera (Dysosma and Sinopodophyllum). The one remaining species is Podophyllum peltatum, with common names mayapple, American mandrake, wild mandrake, and ground lemon. It is widespread across most of the eastern United States and southeastern canada.

Hence, the correct option is (D).

87. The COC-2 inhibitor is not to be given if patient is already taking anti hypertensive drug. Examples include drugs such as losartan, candesartan, and telmesartan. These are substances that act on the central nervous system to induce blood vessel dilation and, in turn, blood pressure. Drugs in this class include methyldopa and clonidine. Methyldopa is suitable for pregnant women with hypertension.

Hence, the correct option is (B).

88. Dyskinesia is the specific unwanted effect of L-DOPA. Dyskinesias are involuntary, erratic, writhing movements of the face, arms, legs, or trunk. They are often fluid and dance-like, but they may also cause rapid jerking or slow and extended muscle spasms. They are not a symptom of Parkinson's itself. Rather, they are a complication from some Parkinson's medications.

Hence, the correct option is (C).

89. The appropriate use of Imipramine is bedwetting in children. Imipramine generally is not used to treat bed-wetting in children younger than 6 to 7 years of age. Success rates have been found to be higher in older children. As with all drugs used to treat bed-wetting if the drug is stopped, bed-wetting is likely to reoccur.

Hence, the correct option is (C).

90. An anticholinesterase that is useful in Alzheimer's disease is donezepil. Donepezil is a synthetic noncovalent reversible inhibitor of acetylcholinesterase (AChE) for the treatment of mild to moderate dementia associated with Alzheimer's disease.

Hence, the correct option is (B).

91. Pons is the parts of the brainstem. Pons, portion of the brainstem lying above the medulla oblongata and below the cerebellum and the cavity of the fourth ventricle. The pons is a broad horseshoe-shaped mass of transverse nerve fibres that connect the medulla with the cerebellum.

Hence, the correct option is (A).

92. In the middle ear, anvil-shaped bone is known as the incus. The incus or anvil is a bone in the middle ear. The anvil-shaped small bone is one of three ossicles in the middle ear. The incus receives vibrations from the malleus, to which it is connected laterally, and transmits these to the stapes medially.

Hence, the correct option is (A).

93. Brain consist of 100 billion amount of neuron. We found that on average the human brain has 86 billion neurons. And not one that we looked at so far has 100 billion. Even though it may sound like a small difference the 14 billion neurons amount to

pretty much the number of neurons that a baboon brain has or almost half the number of neurons in the gorilla brain.

Hence, the correct option is (B).

94. According to the Rh factor, the O^-ve blood group is known as the universal donor. For emergency transfusions, blood group type O^-ve blood is the variety of blood that has the lowest risk of causing serious reactions for most people who receive it. Because of this, it's sometimes called the universal blood donor type.

Hence, the correct option is (A).

95. In the net filtration pressure, blood colloidal osmotic pressure is 30mmHg. NET FILTRATION PRESSURE (NFP) is the total pressure that promotes filtration. To calculate NFP, we subtract the forces that oppose filtration from the GBHP. Glomerular filtration occurs when glomerular (blood) hydrostatic pressure exceeds the hydrostatic pressure of the glomerular capsule and the blood colloid osmotic pressure. The sum of all of the influences, both osmotic and hydrostatic, results in a net filtration pressure (NFP). Glomerular hydrostatic pressure is typically about 55 mmHg pushing fluid into the glomerular capsule. This outward pressure is countered by a typical capsular hydrostatic pressure of about 15 mmHg and a blood colloid osmotic pressure of 30 mmHg.

Hence, the correct option is (A).

96. 1200 ml is the tidal volume of respiration. Tidal volume is the amount of air that moves in or out of the lungs with each respiratory cycle. It measures around 500 ml in an average healthy adult male and approximately 400 ml in a healthy female. It is a vital clinical parameter that allows for proper ventilation to take place. The volume of air remaining in the lungs even after a forcible expiration. This averages 1100 ml to 1200 ml.

Hence, the correct option is (A).

97. The World Health Organization laboratory manual, last revised in 1992, states that the normal pH of semen ranges from 7.2 to 8.0. This implies an adjustment compared with the previous version (WHO, 1987) in which the upper limit was 7.8, whereas in the WHO clinical manual (1993) the normal range of values is still stated to be in the range of 7.2-7.8.

Hence, the correct option is (D).

98. Aqueous humor is completely replaced about every 90 minutes. As the fluid bathes the anterior lens, iris, and corneal endothelium, its composition is altered as a result of the exchange of nutrients, cellular waste products, and other substances within these structures. The entire volume of the aqueous humor is replaced every 90 to 100 minutes.

Hence, the correct option is (A).

99. The partial pressure of carbon dioxide in alveoli is 40 mmHg. $PaCO_2$ is the partial pressure of carbon dioxide in alveoli (in normal physiological conditions around 40 to 45 mmHg). RQ is the respiratory quotient. The value of the RQ can vary depending upon the type of diet and metabolic state.

Hence, the correct option is (C).

100. Blood consist of 250,000-400,00 mm³ amount of platelets. The number of platelets varies across individuals. The normal physiologic range is 200,000 to 500,000 per microliter of blood. Since they contain receptors for thrombopoietin (the protein that facilitates the maturation of megakaryocytes and release of platelets), a higher number of platelets binds more of the protein.

Hence, the correct option is (A).

101. The central fovea is the area of highest visual activity or resolution. At the posterior pole of the eye lateral to the blind spot, there is a yellowish pigmented spot called macula lutea with a central pit called the fovea. The fovea is a thinned-out portion of the retina where only the cones are densely packed. It is the point where the visual acuity (resolution) is the greatest.

Hence, the correct option is (A).

102. 6000 ml is the minute volume of respiration. Minute ventilation is the tidal volume times the respiratory rate, usually,

=500 ml × 12 breaths/min

= 6000 ml/min

Increasing respiratory rate or tidal volume will increase minute ventilation. Dead space refers to airway volumes not participating in gas exchange.

Hence, the correct option is (B).

103. 60-70% amount of neutrophils present in normal. A 70% Relative Neutrophil Count may seem within normal limits. However, if the total WBC is 30,000, the absolute value (70% x 30,000) of 21,000 would be an abnormally high count. A neutrophil's count is between 2,500 and 7,000.

Hence, the correct option is (B).

104. The entire nervous system contains 80-150 ml amount of CSF. There is about 125–150 mL of CSF at any one time. This CSF circulates within the ventricular system of the brain. The ventricles are a series of cavities filled with CSF. The CSF volume, estimated to be about 150 ml in adults, is distributed between 125 ml in cranial and spinal subarachnoid spaces and 25 ml in the ventricles, but with marked interindividual variations.

Hence, the correct option is (A).

105. Each lacrimal gland produce about 1 ml amount per day of lacrimal secration. Normal tear fluid represents the basal level, and from 0.75 to 1.1 mL of this fluid is secreted by the lacrimal glands per day and drains through the nasolacrimal ducts.

Hence, the correct option is (D).

106. In the ECG, P- wave indicates atrial depolarization. The P wave indicates atrial depolarization. The P wave occurs when the sinus node, also known as the sinoatrial node, creates an action potential that depolarizes the atria. The P wave should be upright in lead II if the action potential is originating from the SA node.

Hence, the correct option is (A).

107. Iris dilator muscles contraction produces dilation of pupils. The iris dilator muscle has fibers arranged radially from the sphincter to the ciliary border, receives sympathetic innervation, and functions to cause dilation of the pupil

(mydriasis). In bright light, the circular muscles contract whilst the radial muscles relax.

Hence, the correct option is (D).

108. When the number of sperm falls below 20 million/ml the male is likely to be infertile. Sperm counts below 10 million per milliliter of ejaculate are considered poor; counts of 20 million or more may be acceptable if motility and morphology are normal. A complete lack of sperm occurs in about 10% to 15% of men who are infertile. A hormone imbalance or blockage of sperm movement can cause a lack of sperm. In some cases of infertility, a man produces less sperm than normal.

Hence, the correct option is (A).

109. Intraocular tension normally stay about 10 mmHg. The normal range for intraocular pressure is about 10-20 mmHg. The current consensus among ophthalmologists and optometrists define normal intraocular pressure as that between 10 mmHg and 20 mmHg. The average value of intraocular pressure is 15.5 mmHg with fluctuations of about 2.75 mmHg.

Hence, the correct option is (A).

110. The kidney consists of 25-30% amounts of juxtamedullary nephrons. The kidneys contain two types of nephrons, superficial cortical nephrons (70-80%) and juxtamedullary nephrons (20-30%). These names refer to the location of the glomerular capsule, which is either in the outer cortex of the kidney or near the corticomedullary border.

Hence, the correct option is (A).

111. Drug class causing free water clearance aquaretic. An aquaretic causes the excretion of water without electrolyte loss. Aquaretics are not strictly speaking diuretics, but are sometimes classified as such. Aquaresis is preferable to diuresis in the treatment of hyponatremia. A number of herbal medicines are classified as aquaretics, for example common horsetail or common nettle leaves.

Synthetic aquaretics are vasopressin receptor antagonists, such conivaptan, tolvaptan, demeclocycline and OPC-31260, as well as lithium.

Hence, the correct option is (D).

112. Vitamin B6 is usually prescribed with isoniazid (INH) because it prevents some adverse effects of INH therapy. Peripheral neuropathy occurs in less than 0.2% of people taking INH at conventional doses. It is more likely in the presence of other conditions associated with neuropathy such as diabetes, HIV, renal failure, and alcoholism. Pyridoxine (vitamin B6) supplementation is recommended only in such conditions or to prevent neuropathy in pregnant or breastfeeding women.

Hence, the correct option is (B).

113. Acetylcholine agent is a neurotransmitter used by the sympathetic preganglionic neuron. Acetylcholine (ACh) is a neurotransmitter that functions in both the PNS and the CNS. The ANS (sympathetic and parasympathetic) uses acetylcholine to generate a nerve impulse. In PNS, ACh mainly acts on the muscular system by activating muscle contraction after being released in the neuromuscular junction. Both the parasympathetic and sympathetic preganglionic neurons use acetylcholine as a neurotransmitter.

Hence, the correct option is (B).

114. The action of cyclizine is described by an H_1 antagonist. Cyclizine is a histamine H_1 and muscarinic M_1 receptor antagonist. It is used in the prevention of nausea, vomiting and dizziness associated with motion sickness. The exact mechanism by which cyclizine can prevent or suppress both nausea and vomiting from various causes is unknown. Cyclizine increases lower oesophageal sphincter tone and reduces the sensitivity of the labyrinthine apparatus. It may inhibit the part of the midbrain known collectively as the emetic centre.

Hence, the correct option is (B).

115. When osmotic pressure and temperature are the same then an equal volume of solutions would contain an equal number of moles of the solute. From the Van't Hoff equation, the osmotic pressure is directly proportional to the system temperature, which is an indispensable factor for the FO process.

Hence, the correct option is (A).

116. Kinematic viscosity is viscosity/kinetic energy. The kinematic viscosity is defined as the absolute viscosity of a liquid divided by its density at the same temperature. Like friction between moving solids, viscosity transforms the kinetic energy of (macroscopic) motion into heat energy.

Hence, the correct option is (A).

117. Amphiprotic solvents have both protophilic and protogenic properties. Examples are acetic acid and alcohol. Water is an amphiprotic solvent as it can accept protons as well as give protons. In chemistry and physical sciences, a substance is described as amphiprotic if it can both donate or accept a proton, thus acting either like an acid or a base according to Brønsted-Lowry theory of acids and bases where acids are proton donors and bases are proton acceptors.

Hence, the correct option is (D).

118. Carbohydrates are precursors for many organic compounds. Gluconeogenesis is the formation of carbohydrates from noncarbohydrate precursors, the most important of which are pyruvate, lactate, and alanine. Invertebrates, gluconeogenesis in the liver and kidney provides glucose for use by the brain, muscle, and erythrocytes. The carbohydrate-binding sites of lectins are usually composed of amino acids from a single polypeptide chain with certain exceptions, such as wheat germ agglutinin (WGA) where amino acids from different polypeptide chains are involved in ligand binding.

Hence, the correct option is (A).

119. The vaccines produced by recombinant DNA technology are called second-generation vaccines. These vaccines do not contain the whole organism instead, they contain a part of the organism. Examples of second-generation vaccines are the Hepatitis B virus, Herpes virus, pneumonia vaccine, etc.

Hence, the correct option is (C).

120. Bacteria having clusters of flagella at both poles of cells are known as amphitrichous. In amphitrichous, flagella occur either singly or in clusters at both cell poles. Lophotrichous refers to a cluster of polar flagella, peritrichous is surrounded by lateral flagella and monotrichous is for a single polar flagellum.

Hence, the correct option is (A).

121. Hydrocarbons are organic compounds with elements hydrogen and carbon. A hydrocarbon is any of a class of organic chemicals made up of only the elements carbon and hydrogen. The carbon atoms join together to form the framework of the compound, and the hydrogen atoms attach to them in many different configurations.

Hence, the correct option is (D).

122. Parkinson's disease is primarily associated with the gradual loss of cells in the substantia nigra of the brain. This area is responsible for the production of dopamine. Dopamine is a chemical messenger that transmits signals between two regions of the brain to coordinate activity. But it does not commonly occur in white males.

Hence, the correct option is (A).

123. Fat and bone has a very low perfusion rate. A high perfusion rate is seen in the organs such as lungs, kidneys, adrenals, liver, heart, brain. The moderate perfusion rate is in muscles and skin. The least perfusion rate is in fat and bones.

Hence, the correct option is (A).

124. Reviewing each patient's drug administration forms periodically to ensure all doses have been administered is the responsibility of the clinical pharmacist in the indirect patient care area. Clinical pharmacists are responsible and accountable for medication therapy and patient outcomes. They are a primary source of scientifically valid information on the safe, appropriate, and cost-effective use of medications.

Hence, the correct option is (D).

125. Cone receptor is useful for color vision. Cone cells, or cones, are photoreceptor cells in the retinas of vertebrate eyes including the human eye. They respond differently to light of different wavelengths and are thus responsible for color vision, and function best in relatively bright light, as opposed to rod cells, which work better in dim light.

Hence, the correct option is (B).

Q.1 Sodium bromide is used as:

A. Oxidising agent   **B.** Hypnotic

C. Sedative   **D.** Both (B) and (C)

Q.2 Metabolic acidosis is usually treated by:

A. Sodium bicarbonate   **B.** Sodium lactate

C. Sodium citrate   **D.** All of these

Q.3 An anticoagulant extensively used is:

A. Sodium sulphate   **B.** Sodium benzoate

C. Potassium citrate   **D.** Sodium citrate

Q.4 Burow's solution contains:

A. Aluminum phosphate

B. Aluminum sulphate

C. Aluminum chloride

D. Aluminum acetate

Q.5 Tartar emetic is:

A. Copper sulphate

B. Zink sulphate

C. Antimony sodium tartrate

D. Potassium iodide

Q.6 Unit for the rate of decay of radioactivity is:

A. Becquerel   **B.** Roentgen

C. Both (A) and (B)   **D.** None of these

Q.7 An antiprotozoal drugs to treat leishmaniasis is:

A. Antimony tartrate

B. Potassium tartrate

C. Antimony potassium tartrate

D. All of these

Q.8 A drug used in the treatment of schistosomiasis (Kala-azar):

A. Antimony potassium tartrate

B. Potassium tartrate

C. Antimony tartrate

D. All of these

Q.9 Systemic acidifier is:

A. Potassium citrate

B. Sodium bicarbonate

C. Ammonium chloride

D. Sodium citrate

Q.10 Room temperature indicates:

A. 15-25°C   **B.** -15°C   **C.** 8-15°C   **D.** 2-8°C

Q.11 The acid used in the assay of copper sulphate:

A. Oxalic acid   **B.** Acetic acid

C. Sulphuric acid   **D.** Citric acid

Q.12 Saline expectorants is:

A. Ammonium chloride

B. Potassium chloride

C. Sodium iodide

D. All of these

Q.13 The indicator used in the assay of ammonium chloride is:

A. Phenolphthalein   **B.** Methyl red

C. Phenol rec   **D.** Storch mucilage

Q.14 Solid gas widely used in refrigeration is:

A. NO_2 **B.** CO_2 **C.** O_2 **D.** H_2O

Q.15 Which cf the following is used as a respiratory stimulant or CNS stimulant?

A. Doxapram   **B.** NO

C. N_2O **D.** None of these

Q.16 An inert gas used to prevent oxidation of parenteral products is:

A. Hydrogen   **B.** Helium

C. Nitrogen   **D.** Sulphur

Q.17 Which cf the following gas is used for supporting respiration during anesthesia?

A. Oxygen   **B.** Carbon dioxide

C. Nitrous oxide   **D.** All of these

Q.18 The use of dilute ammonia solution (10%W/V):

A. Respiratory stimulant

B. Rubefacient

C. Both (A) and (B)

D. None of these

Q.19 Nitrogen oxide is obtained by heating ammonium nitrate to about:

A. 140°C   **B.** 170°C   **C.** 180°C   **D.** 160°C

Q.20 Substance used in cryoscopy surgery to remove tumors:

A. Liquid nitrogen   **B.** Nitrogen oxide

C. Carbon dioxide   **D.** Sulphur dioxide

Q.21 As per the Drugs and Cosmetics Act and Rules, the Good Manufacturing Practice is included under Schedule:

A. W   **B.** P   **C.** S   **D.** M

Q.22 Which cf the following is not antimicrobial?

A. Antiseptics   **B.** Antibacterial drugs

C. Anesthetics   **D.** Disinfectants

Q.23 Liquid generally used in manufacture of tooth pastes:

A. Glycerin, Water   **B.** Propylene glycol

C. Sorbitol solution   **D.** All of these

Q.24 Laughing gas is:

A. Oxygen   **B.** Nitrous oxide

C. Carbondioxide   **D.** Methane

Q.25 Maddrell's salt is:

A. Glycerin, Water   **B.** Propylene glycol
C. Sorbitol solution   **D.** All of these

Q.26 Which of the following compounds does not inhibit the enzymes which catalyse the degradation of noradrenaline?

A. Citalopram   **B.** Terfenadine
C. Iproniazid   **D.** Phenelzine

Q.27 Removal of tartar from teeth:

A. Scaling   **B.** Filling
C. Bonding   **D.** Bleaching

Q.28 A certain antibiotic X is effective only against a few types of harmful microbes and cells. X is an antibiotic:

A. broad-spectrum   **B.** narrow-spectrum
C. limited-spectrum   **D.** All of these

Q.29 Tooth powders & pastes contain:

A. Calcium levulinate
B. Dibasic calcium phosphate
C. Calcium gluconate
D. Calcium lactate

Q.30 The bleaching agent in dental practice is:

A. Zinc chlonde   **B.** Zinc peroxide
C. Zinc sulphate   **D.** Zinc oxide

Q.31 Dentifrice is a material used for cleansing of:

A. Eye   **B.** Nose   **C.** Teeth   **D.** Eur

Q.32 Dental caries prophylactic:

A. Sodium fluoride
B. Stannous fluoride
C. Sodium metaphosphate
D. Both (A) and (B)

Q.33 An antirusting agent for surgical instrument:

A. Sodium metaphosphate
B. Strontium chloride
C. Calcium phosphate
D. Calcium carborate

Q.34 The best cementing material in dental practice is:

A. Calcium oxide   **B.** Zinc oxide
C. Titanium dioxide   **D.** Ferric oxide

Q.35 Specialist corrects the improper position of teeth is:

A. Endodontist   **B.** Orthodontist
C. Peridontist   **D.** Prosthodontist

Q.36 A chemical present in toothpaste to relieve dental hypersensitivity is:

A. Calcium carbonate   **B.** Calcium phosphate
C. Stannous fluoride   **D.** Strontium chloride

Q.37 Most dental products are:

A. Nonprescription products (OTC)
B. Prescription products
C. Restricted products
D. None of these

Q.38 The permanent filling materials for dental cavities are:

A. Gold   **B.** Silver
C. Both (A) and (B)   **D.** None of these

// Smart Answer Sheet //

Correct Percentage of students who answered correctly. **Skipped** Percentage of students who skipped.

Q.	Ans.	Correct / Skipped	Q.	Ans.	Correct / Skipped	Q.	Ans.	Correct / Skipped	Q.	Ans.	Correct / Skipped	Q.	Ans.	Correct / Skipped	Q.	Ans.	Correct / Skipped
1	D	53.0 % / 30.66 %	8	A	60.89 % / 38.36 %	15	A	40.96 % / 54.85 %	22	C	68.49 % / 30.38 %	29	B	56.23 % / 38.34 %	36	D	22.68 % / 70.27 %
2	D	67.44 % / 30.65 %	9	C	41.88 % / 36.35 %	16	C	55.4 % / 33.24 %	23	D	44.16 % / 38.48 %	30	B	60.08 % / 39.16 %	37	A	48.96 % / 32.93 %
3	D	47.42 % / 35.45 %	10	A	83.27 % / 14.55 %	17	D	18.13 % / 67.75 %	24	B	81.28 % / 16.04 %	31	C	58.64 % / 35.6 %	38	C	87.88 % / 11.06 %
4	D	65.91 % / 30.87 %	11	B	68.76 % / 30.68 %	18	C	61.4 % / 34.06 %	25	A	65.3 % / 31.0 %	32	D	48.87 % / 38.97 %			
5	C	57.92 % / 35.47 %	12	D	65.97 % / 32.35 %	19	D	57.54 % / 30.92 %	26	B	63.31 % / 33.92 %	33	A	49.27 % / 46.84 %			
6	A	79.31 % / 13.19 %	13	A	49.74 % / 45.51 %	20	A	54.2 % / 38.15 %	27	A	63.9 % / 35.25 %	34	B	45.09 % / 53.47 %			
7	C	55.74 % / 43.63 %	14	B	59.2 % / 34.88 %	21	D	23.46 % / 71.36 %	28	A	45.27 % / 50.71 %	35	B	57.1 % / 33.22 %			

//Hints and Solutions//

1. Sodium bromide, also known as Sedoneural, can be used as a hypnotic, as an anticonvulsant, and as a sedative. In the field of medicine, it is widely used as an anticonvulsant and a sedative. In the late 19th and early 20th centuries.

Hence, the correct option is (D).

2. Metabolic acidosis is usually treated by sodium bicarbonate, sodium lactate and sodium citrate. Sodium bicarbonate is clearly effective in raising the arterial pH in critically ill patients with lactic acidosis. Sodium citrate can be used if sodium bicarbonate is not effective or not well tolerated. Citrate is converted to bicarbonate in the body and helps to correct the acid buildup in the blood. In addition, citrate helps to prevent calcium deposits in the kidney. Sodium (found in sodium bicarbonate, sodium citrate or other sodium salts) can increase calcium levels in the blood and urine.

Hence, the correct option is (D).

3. An anticoagulant extensively used is sodium citrate. Sodium citrate has been used as an anticoagulant to stabilize blood and blood products for over 100 years, presumably by sequestering Ca(++) ions in vitro. Anticoagulation of blood without chelation can be achieved by inhibition of the contact pathway by corn trypsin inhibitor (CTI).

Hence, the correct option is (D).

4. Burow's solution contains aluminum acetate. Solutions for the ear are commonly marketed as Burow's solution. This is a mixture of 13 percent aluminum acetate. Burow's solution (5% aluminum subacetate) is a liquid made with water and aluminum acetate. This solution relieves the itching and stinging of irritated, inflamed skin and helps stop the growth of bacteria and fungus.

Hence, the correct option is (D).

5. Tartar emetic is antimony sodium tartrate. Antimony potassium tartrate, also known as potassium antimonyl tartrate, potassium antimontarterate, or emetic tartar, has the formula $K_2Sb_2(C_4H_2O_6)_2$. Properties are:

1. Transparent odorless crystals efflorescing on exposure to air.
2. White powder.
3. Sweetish metallic taste.
4. At 100 °C losses all its water.
5. Soluble in water and glycerol.
6. Insoluble in alcohol.
7. An aqueous solution is slightly acidic.

Hence, the correct option is (C).

6. Unit for the rate of decay of radioactivity is becquerel. Becquerel (Bq) is one of three units of measurement used to indicate radioactivity or how many atoms in the material decay or disintegrate in a specific amount of time. A Bq represents the rate of decay equal to one disintegration per second.

Hence, the correct option is (A).

7. An antiprotozoal drug to treat leishmaniasis is antimony potassium tartrate. Antiprotozoal drugs are a class of medication used to treat infections caused by protozoa, which are single-cell organisms that belong to the type of parasites. Antimony potassium tartrate, also known as potassium antimonyl tartrate, potassium antimontarterate, or emetic tartar, has the formula $K_2Sb_2(C_4H_2O_6)_2$. The compound has long been known as a powerful emetic and was used in the treatment of schistosomiasis and leishmaniasis. It is used as a resolving agent.

Hence, the correct option is (C).

8. A drug used in the treatment of schistosomiasis (Kala-azar) is antimony potassium tartrate. Antimony potassium tartrate, also known as potassium antimonyl tartrate, potassium antimontartrate, or emetic tartar, has the formula $K_2Sb_2(C_4H_2O_6)_2$. The compound has long been known as a powerful emetic and was used in the treatment of schistosomiasis and leishmaniasis. It is used as a resolving agent.

Hence, the correct option is (A).

9. A systemic acidifier is ammonium chloride. The ammonium chloride that is used as a treatment for severe metabolic alkalosis is a systemic acidifier. Ammonium chloride is primarily used in fertilizers as a source of nitrogen. Fluxes such as ammonium chloride are used to prepare metal for tin coating, galvanizing, or soldering.

Hence, the correct option is (C).

10. Room temperature: Store at 15°-25°C (59°-77°F). It means "room temperature" or normal storage conditions, which means storage in a dry, clean, well-ventilated area at room temperatures between 15° to 25°C (59°-77°F) or up to 30°C, depending on climatic conditions.

Hence, the correct option is (A).

11. The acid used in the assay of copper sulphate is acetic acid. The assay is done on the basis of the oxidation-reduction reaction of iodine/thiosulphate. A solution of copper sulphate is first treated with potassium iodide and acetic acid. Cuprous iodide (CuI) is formed with iodine and the liberated iodine is titrated with 0.1 N sodium thiosulphate.

Hence, the correct option is (B).

12. Saline expectorants are ammonium chloride, potassium chloride and sodium iodide. Expectorants are drugs that enhance the secretion of the sputum by the air passages so that it is easier to remove the phlegm through coughing. They are used in cough mixtures for this purpose they act either by increasing the bronchiole secretion or by making it less viscous (mucolytic agents). Drugs such as ipecacuanha in small doses act as stimulant expectorants. For example, inorganic saline expectorants are ammonium salts (ammonium chloride), iodides (potassium iodide/sodium iodide), citrates and antimony potassium tartrate.

Hence, the correct option is (D).

13. The indicator used in the assay of ammonium chloride is phenolphthalein. A strong acid- strong base titration is

performed using a phenolphthalein indicator. Phenolphthalein is chosen because it changes color in a pH range between 8.3–10. It will appear pink in basic solutions and clear in acidic solutions. Phenolphthalein indicator gives pink colour when added to a base. Thus, the colour of test tube B will turn pink. Sodium sulphate and ammonium chloride are both salts and are neither basic or acidic in nature and therefore, do not turn pink on the addition of phenolphthalein.

Hence, the correct option is (A).

14. Solid gas widely used in refrigeration is CO_2. Solid carbon dioxide is also called as dry ice and is commonly used for refrigeration because of its properties. It exhibits a property called as sublimation. In this process a solid changes to a gaseous state when exposed to a particular temperature. CO_2 has high energy content at higher temperatures, and when this heat can be reclaimed for heating sanitary water or similar application, the efficiency of the total system becomes very high. From an environmental perspective, CO_2 is a very attractive refrigerant with zero ODP and a GWP of 1.

Hence, the correct option is (B).

15. Doxapram is a respiratory stimulant and an analeptic (CNS stimulant) that is used to treat drug-induced ventilatory depression and apnoea in newborn animals and humans. At low doses, doxapram increases ventilation primarily through action on the carotid bodies and higher doses may increase ventilation through direct stimulation of respiratory neurons in the CNS.

Hence, the correct option is (A).

16. An inert gas used to prevent the oxidation of parenteral products is nitrogen. Nitrogen gas is used to replace a hazardous or undesirable atmosphere with an inert dry atmosphere. Nitrogen gas reduces the presence of oxygen that may provide the catalyst for combustion or negatively affect product quality. Molecular nitrogen is a colorless, odorless, tasteless, and inert gas at normal temperatures and pressures.

Hence, the correct option is (C).

17. Oxygen, Nitrous oxide and Carbon dioxide gases are used for supporting respiration during anesthesia. The medical gases commonly used for anesthesia and critical care are oxygen, nitrous oxide, medical air, entonox, carbon dioxide and heliox. Oxygen is breathed during the induction of anesthesia, and an increased concentration of oxygen O_2 is given during the surgery to reduce the risk of hypoxemia. However, oxygen is rapidly adsorbed behind closed airways, causing lung collapse (atelectasis) and shunt.

Hence, the correct option is (D).

18. The use of dilute ammonia solution (10%W/V) is a respiratory stimulant, rubefacient and vasoconstrictor. 10% ammonia water as a reflex respiratory stimulant.

MEDICATION (VET): Externally on bites & stings. As rubefacient on bruises, sprains; inhalant; internally as an antacid & carminative.

Ammonium Hydroxide, 10 %(W/V) NH3 Solution, (U.S.P. Test Solution) is a solution of ammonia in water. Aqueous ammonia, as it's otherwise known is used as a complexant and base in qualitative inorganic analysis. It becomes a deep blue color with copper solutions.

Hence, the correct option is (C).

19. Nitrogen oxide is obtained by heating ammonium nitrate to about 160°C. To start the reaction, ammonium nitrate must come into contact with an open flame or other ignition sources. Once a reaction is sparked, ammonium nitrate explodes violently. The explosive force occurs when solid ammonium nitrate decomposes very rapidly into two gases, nitrous oxide and water vapor.

Hence, the correct option is (D).

20. The substance used in cryoscopy surgery to remove tumors is liquid nitrogen. Cryosurgery is a type of surgery that involves the use of extreme cold to destroy abnormal tissues, such as tumors. The surgery most often involves the use of liquid nitrogen, although carbon dioxide and argon may also be used. Cryotherapy is a procedure that uses extreme cold (liquid nitrogen) to destroy tissue. It's often used to treat skin lesions, which are skin growths or patches that don't look like the skin around them.

Hence, the correct option is (A).

21. As per the Drugs and Cosmetics Act and Rules, the Good Manufacturing Practice is included under Schedule M. Schedule M is a part of the Drug and Cosmetic act 1940. It is GMP for pharmaceuticals that should be followed by pharmaceutical manufacturing units in India. Schedule M is having the details about company premises, quality control system, quality control laboratories, GMP in production, cleaning of equipment, housekeeping, cross-contamination and other related topics.

Hence, the correct option is (D).

22. Antimicrobials are substances that are used to prevent and treat infections due to various microorganisms like fungi, viruses, bacteria or parasites. They can be used for curing diseases and avoiding them. Anesthetics are drugs that produce an insensitivity to pain.

Hence, the correct option is (C).

23. The liquid generally used in the manufacture of tooth pastes are glycerin, water, propylene glycol and sorbitol solution. Toothpaste generally contains the following components:

1. Water (20–40%).

2. Abrasives (50%) include aluminum hydroxide, calcium hydrogen phosphates, calcium carbonate, silica and hydroxyapatite.

3. Fluoride (usually 1450 ppm) is mainly in the form of sodium fluoride. Stannous fluoride and sodium mono fluorophosphate have also been used.

4. Detergents, mainly sodium lauryl sulfate (SLS) with concentration ranges of 0.5–2%.

5. Antibacterial agents such as triclosan or zinc chloride.

6. Flavourants include spearmint, peppermint, and wintergreen.

7. Remineralizers in some toothpaste containing hydroxyapatite nanoparticles and calcium phosphate.

8. Humectants include glycerol, xylitol, sorbitol, polyethylene glycol, and propylene glycol.

9. Antisensitivity agents in sensitive toothpaste containing strontium chloride and potassium nitrate or arginine.

10. Anticalculus agents such as sodium polyphosphate or zinc citrate.

Hence, the correct option is (D).

24. Laughing gas is nitrous oxide. Nitrous oxide, commonly known as laughing gas or happy gas, is a colorless, non-flammable gas. This gas is used in medical and dental procedures as a sedative. It helps to relieve anxiety before the procedure and allows the patient to relax. Nitrous oxide is also called laughing gas or happy gas due to its intoxicating effects when inhaled.

Hence, the correct option is (B).

25. Maddrell's salt is glycerine and water. Maddrell's salt is also known as Sodium hexametaphosphate (SHMP). Sodium hexametaphosphate (SHMP) is a salt of composition Na6[(PO3)6]. Sodium hexametaphosphate of commerce is typically a mixture of metaphosphates (empirical formula: NaPO3), of which the hexamer is one, and is usually the compound referred to by this name. Such a mixture is more correctly termed sodium poly metaphosphate. They are white solids that dissolve in water.

Hence, the correct option is (A).

26. Terfenadine compounds do not inhibit the enzymes which catalyse the degradation of noradrenaline. Low levels of noradrenaline in the body reduce the signal-sending activity of neurons and lead to depression. Citalopram, iproniazid and phenelzine are antidepressants that inhibit the catalysis of the degradation of noradrenaline and help treat depression.

Hence, the correct option is (B).

27. Removal of tartar from teeth is called scaling. Scaling is when your dentist removes all the plaque and tartar (hardened plaque) above and below the gum line, making sure to clean all the way down to the bottom of the pocket. Your dentist will then begin root planning, smoothing out your teeth roots to help your gums reattach to your teeth.

Hence, the correct option is (A).

28. Antibiotics are classified based on the range of microbes that are affected by them. Broad-spectrum antibiotics affect Gram-positive as well as Gram-negative bacteria. Narrow spectrum is used only against either Gram-positive or Gram-negative bacteria, whereas limited spectrum antibiotics kill or inhibit only one particular organism.

Hence, the correct option is (A).

29. Tooth powders & pastes contain dibasic calcium phosphate. Toothpaste that contains calcium phosphate, stannous fluoride or similar forms of fluoride can help remineralize tooth enamel as long as there is enough left to build on. When applied directly to your teeth, it can help condition, protect and rebuild your teeth's surface. MI Paste uses calcium and phosphate to replenish these minerals in your teeth and strengthen them.

Hence, the correct option is (B).

30. The bleaching agent in dental practice is zinc peroxide. Both tooth-whitening options use peroxide-based bleaching agents. At-home systems contain from 3% to 20% peroxide (carbamide or hydrogen peroxides). In-office systems contain from 15% to 43% peroxide. Generally, the longer you keep a stronger solution on your teeth, the whiter your teeth become.

Hence, the correct option is (B).

31. Dentifrice is a material used for the cleansing of teeth. Dentifrices, including toothpowder and toothpaste, are agents used along with a toothbrush to clean and polish natural teeth. They are supplied in paste, powder, gel, or liquid form. Dentifrices are designed to be used with toothbrushes to remove dental stains, to introduce a fresh, pleasant and clean feeling, and to deliver active agents into the oral cavity.

Hence, the correct option is (C).

32. Dental caries prophylactic that are sodium fluoride and stannous fluoride. Stannous fluoride is the active ingredient in Crest Pro-Health and Crest Gum toothpaste, and protects against plaque/ gingivitis, tooth sensitivity and cavities, making it the only fluoride source that fights all three. Sodium fluoride varnish is used to prevent caries development, arrest early enamel and even soft dentine caries through the promotion of remineralization of carious tooth substance. It is also used to treat tooth hypersensitivity.

Hence, the correct option is (D).

33. An antirusting agent for a surgical instrument is sodium metaphosphate. Sodium Metaphosphate is the general term for any polyphosphate salt with four or more phosphate units. No reproductive or developmental toxicity was seen in studies using rats exposed to Sodium Hexametaphosphate or Sodium Trimetaphosphate. Sodium metaphosphate is a type of dental product used to produce effect on teeth and in the dental cavity.

Hence, the correct option is (A).

34. The best cementing material in dental practice is zinc oxide. Because of their poor mechanical properties, the conventional zinc oxide-eugenol cement is mainly used as temporary fixing contents and filling materials, for gingival dressings and together with filling materials as impression materials. Zinc oxide-eugenol cement (IRM) is a low-strength base used as a temporary cement filling in the event that the patient will return at a later date for a semi-permanent restoration. The powder is mainly zinc oxide and the liquid is eugenol with olive oil as a plasticizer.

Hence, the correct option is (B).

35. Specialist corrects the improper position of teeth as an orthodontist. An orthodontist is a special kind of dentist that corrects misaligned teeth for an optimal smile and bite. In other words, orthodontists are responsible for helping patients achieve their best smiles. Orthodontics is a specialty within dentistry that focuses on correcting bites, occlusion, and the straightness of teeth.

Hence, the correct option is (B).

36. A chemical present in toothpaste to relieve dental hypersensitivity is strontium chloride. Strontium Chloride has:
1) Molecular formula: $SrCl_2. 6H_2O$
2) Molecular weight: 267 gm
3)Preparation:
It is prepared by treating HCl with strontium oxide.
$$SrO + 2HCl \rightarrow SrCl_2 + H_2O$$

4) Properties:

- Greyish–white powder.
- Odourless and tasteless.
- It is insoluble in water.

5) Use:

- To relieve dental hypersensitivity (reduce the sensitivity of teeth to heat and cold).
- Strontium can replace in bone formation and has been used to hasten bone remineralization in diseases. Eg. osteoporosis.

6) Storage: It Should be stored in a well-closed air-tight container.

Hence, the correct option is (D).

37. Most dental products are nonprescription products (OTC). Over-the-counter medicine is also known as OTC or nonprescription medicine. All these terms refer to medicine that you can buy without a prescription. They are safe and effective when you follow the directions on the label and as directed by your health care professional. Nonprescription or OTC drugs are medicines the FDA determines are safe and effective for use without a doctor's prescription. The American Dental Association (ADA) also recommends that you provide specific and personalized recommendations of over-the-counter (OTC) products for home care.

Hence, the correct option is (A).

38. The permanent filling materials for dental cavities are gold and silver. Teeth can be filled with gold; porcelain; silver amalgam (which consists of mercury mixed with silver, tin, zinc, and copper); or tooth-colored, plastic, and materials called composite resin fillings. Teeth can be filled with gold; porcelain; silver amalgam (which consists of mercury mixed with silver, tin, zinc, and copper); or tooth-colored, plastic, and materials called composite resin fillings.

Hence, the correct option is (C).

Q.1 The dentin desensitizer used in tooth preparation is:

A. Stannous fluoride

B. Strontium chloride

C. Sodium fluoride

D. Dicalcium phosphate

Q.2 Dental products include mainly:

A. Anticaries agent

B. Cleaning agent

C. Polishing agent

D. All of these

Q.3 Graham's salt is also known as:

A. Sodium polymetaphosphate

B. Sodium thiosulphate

C. Sodium meta sulphate

D. Sodium chloride

Q.4 Buffer used in adrenaline injection:

A. Boric acid

B. Sodium bicarbonate

C. Sodium hydroxide

D. $Na_2S_2O_5$

Q.5 Poisoned is chemically:

A. Poly pyrrolidane

B. Iodine + Potassium iodide

C. Polyvinylpyrrolidone

D. Iodine

Q.6 Borax is chemically:

A. Sodium metaborate

B. Boric acid

C. Sodium borate

D. None of these

Q.7 Solution used to clean septic sockets and root canals:

A. H_2O_2 Solution

B. $KMnO_4$ Solution

C. NaCl Solution

D. Mg $(OH)_2$ Solution

Q.8 Betadine is:

A. Povidone-Iodine 5%

B. Lugol's solution

C. Mandl's paint

D. Iodine tincture

Q.9 "Fine particles" is a physicochemical parameter prescribed in I.P for:

A. Bentonite

B. Barium sulphate

C. Light kaolin

D. Plaster of Paris

Q.10 Sulphur is used internally as a:

A. Scabicide

B. Cathartic

C. Antiseborrhoeic

D. Keratolytic

Q.11 EDTA is:

A. Ethylene diamine tetraacetic acid

B. Ethylene dibromotrimethyl acete acid

C. Ethylene dichloro tetraacetic acid

D. Ethylenediamine trichloroacetic acid

Q.12 Lugol's solution is:

A. Aqueous solution of iodine

B. Strong solution of iodine

C. Weak solution of iodine

D. Both (A) and (B)

Q.13 Silver nitrate is stored in:

A. Dry white bottles

B. Lead-free white bottles

C. Amber coloured bottles

D. Neutral glass bottles

Q.14 Chemically, Primaquine is:

A. 8--[4-amino-1-methylbuty1 amino]-6 methoxy quinoline

B. 8-[4-amino-1-ethy1butylamino]-6-methoxy quinolinei

C. 8-[2-amino-1-methybutylamino]-6methoxy quinoline

D. 8-[2-amino -1-ethy1butyl 1amino]-6-ethoxy quinoline

Q.15 A parameter prescribed in I.P for bentonite is:

A. Bulkiness

B. Swelling power

C. Solubility

D. None of these

Q.16 Indicator used in assay of iodine is:

A. Phenolphthalein

B. Ferric alum

C. Methyl orange

D. Starch mucilage

Q.17 Opacity agent is:

A. Titanium dioxide

B. Silicon dioxide

C. Magnesium oxide

D. Zinc oxide

Q.18 Starting material for Ibuprofen is:

A. P-Isorporpoy Ibenezene

B. P-Isobutyl benzene

C. P-Isobutyl acetophenone

D. P-Isopropyl acetophenone

Q.19 Anti-caking agent for hygroscopic powder & granules is:

A. Kaolin

B. Magnesium oxide

C. Colloidal silicon dioxide

D. Titanium dioxide

Q.20 Boric acid is freely soluble in:

A. Water

B. Alcohol

C. Glycerin

D. All of these

Q.21 French chalk is:

A. Bentonite

B. Light kaolin

C. Purified talc

D. Heavy kaolin

Q.22 White precipitate is:

A. Mercuric oxide

B. Mercurous chloride

C. Yellow mercuric oxide

D. Ammoniated mercury

Q.23 Aluminium Sulphate is used in dusting powders as an:

A. Antiseptic　　　　**B.** Astringent

C. Antiperspirant　　**D.** All of these

Q.24 Antifungal drug is:

A. Zinc state　　　　**B.** Zinc undecylenate

C. Zinc oxide　　　　**D.** Zinc sulphate

Q.25 A drug commonly used in shampoo for treating dandruff:

A. Zinc sulphido　　　**B.** Selenium sulphide

C. Sulphur　　　　　**D.** Sodium sulphide

Q.26 Scabicide is:

A. Sulphur containing medicine

B. Yellow mercuric oxide

C. Ammoniated mercury

D. None of these

Q.27 Chlorinated lime is prepared by the action of chlorine gas on:

A. Slaked lime　　　　**B.** Quick lime

C. Lime water　　　　**D.** Lime

Q.28 Surgical solution of chlorinated soda is:

A. Lysol　　　　　　**B.** Eusol

C. Dakin's solution　　**D.** Lugol's solution

Q.29 A chemical compound that affects human metabolism and provides cure from diseases is called:

A. poison　**B.** medicine　**C.** enzyme　**D.** hormone

Q.30 Use of calomel is:

A. Cathartic　　　　**B.** Antifungal

C. Antiperspirant　　**D.** Diuretic

Q.31 A weak solution of iodine is also known as:

A. Aqueous solution of iodine

B. Tincture of iodine

C. Lugol's solution

D. All of these

Q.32 A chemical used in eye infection is:

A. Sodium citrate　　**B.** Silver nitrate

C. Sodium chloride　　**D.** Sodium nitrate

Q.33 The indicator used in silver nitrate assay is:

A. Phenolphthalein

B. Methyl orange

C. Methyl red

D. Ferric ammonium sulphate solution

Q.34 Antidote for calcium channel blockers poisoning is:

A. Sodium bicarbonate injection

B. Sodium chloride injection

C. Calcium chloride injection

D. Sodium nitrite

Q.35 The chemical formula of talc is:

A. $MgSi_4O_{10}(OH)_2$　　**B.** $Mg_3Si_4O_{10}(OH)_2$

C. $Mg_3Si_4O_{10}(OH)$　　**D.** $Mg_3SiO_{10}(OH)_2$

Q.36 Which of the following chemicals is used as gargle?

A. Zink sulphate　　　**B.** Iodine solution

C. Diluted $KMnO_4$　　**D.** $AgNO_3$

Q.37 Potassium permanganate assayed by titration it with standard:

A. Hypo　　　　　　**B.** Oxalic acid

C. Sodium hydrogen　　**D.** None of these

Q.38 Antioxidant used as blocking agent in sterile product is:

[Graduate Pharmacy Aptitude Test, 2017]

A. Vitamin C

B. EDTA

C. Ascorbic acid esters

D. Sodium metabisulphite

// Smart Answer Sheet //

| Correct | Percentage of students who answered correctly. | Skipped | Percentage of students who skipped. |

Q.	Ans.	Correct / Skipped	Q.	Ans.	Correct / Skipped	Q.	Ans.	Correct / Skipped	Q.	Ans.	Correct / Skipped	Q.	Ans.	Correct / Skipped	Q.	Ans.	Correct / Skipped
1	B	64.56 % / 34.06 %	8	A	44.69 % / 53.84 %	15	B	66.7 % / 31.12 %	22	D	31.54 % / 67.87 %	29	B	56.71 % / 32.79 %	36	C	49.52 % / 34.51 %
2	D	31.66 % / 67.09 %	9	C	49.51 % / 38.32 %	16	D	27.96 % / 71.17 %	23	B	44.25 % / 32.44 %	30	A	47.69 % / 37.01 %	37	B	28.4 % / 70.88 %
3	A	62.75 % / 36.24 %	10	B	65.81 % / 31.76 %	17	A	54.34 % / 42.2 %	24	B	53.17 % / 31.59 %	31	B	45.7 % / 53.55 %	38	C	44.68 % / 45.36 %
4	A	64.74 % / 31.0 %	11	A	49.77 % / 48.44 %	18	C	62.85 % / 32.33 %	25	B	47.82 % / 34.38 %	32	B	30.17 % / 68.25 %			
5	C	42.59 % / 53.13 %	12	D	48.58 % / 41.44 %	19	C	67.8 % / 31.6 %	26	A	16.01 % / 67.16 %	33	D	54.28 % / 39.78 %			
6	C	58.23 % / 39.82 %	13	C	79.96 % / 19.35 %	20	D	84.86 % / 10.17 %	27	A	88.75 % / 10.17 %	34	C	10.39 % / 76.19 %			
7	A	57.59 % / 32.18 %	14	A	25.93 % / 72.39 %	21	C	56.37 % / 42.06 %	28	C	68.3 % / 31.22 %	35	B	55.52 % / 43.19 %			

//Hints and Solutions//

1. The dentin desensitizer used in tooth preparation is strontium chloride. Although there is limited clinical evidence that dentifrices containing strontium chloride or potassium nitrate alone, as the major desensitizing agent, has an effect on reducing DH, no clinical studies have shown the effectiveness of a dentifrice containing both strontium chloride and potassium nitrate in silica.

Hence, the correct option is (B).

2. Dental products include mainly anticaries, cleaning and polishing agent.

Anticaries agents: Dental caries or tooth decay is caused by acids produced by the action of microorganisms on carbohydrates. Example-Ammoniated toothpaste, urea ammonia-containing powders, antibiotic-containing mixtures.

Cleaning agents or dentifrices: A dentifrice is a substance used with a toothbrush for the purpose of cleaning the surface of teeth. It is available in the form of pastes and powders. Many dentifrices contain flavours and soap or detergent. Example-Calcium carbonate, Calcium phosphate dibasic and tribasic, Sodium metaphosphate.

Polishing agents: Polishing is achieved by abrasive action (polishing and cleaning the hard surface) of dentifrices. It provides whiteness to the teeth. Example- sodium metaphosphate.

Hence, the correct option is (D).

3. Graham's salt is also known as sodium polyphosphate. Calgon or Graham's Salt is a white powdery substance comprising sodium and metaphosphates. Calgon (amorphous sodium polyphosphate) is sodium hexametaphosphate with the chemical formula Na(PO3)6 of which the hexamer is one, and is usually the compound referred to by this name. Such a mixture is more correctly termed sodium polymetaphosphate. They are white solids that dissolve in water.

Hence, the correct option is (A).

4. The buffer used in adrenaline injection is boric acid. Adrenaline injection strong APF 13 contains boric acid as the adjusting substance. The rapid oxidation of L-adrenaline in aqueous solutions to strongly colored, pharmacologically inactive adrenochrome and adrenolotin6 necessitated the use of auxiliary compounds in the injectable formulations. Several studies addressed the potential drug-stabilizing effects of sodium metabisulfite, EDTA, ascorbic acid, boric acid, acetylcysteine, and other substances,7,9 as well as optimized conditions of the preparation and packaging of the adrenaline solutions.

Hence, the correct option is (A).

5. Poisoned is chemically polyvinylpyrrolidone. Polyvinylpyrrolidone (PVP), commonly called polyvidone or povidone, is a water-soluble polymer made from the monomer N-vinylpyrrolidone [87,88]. Dry PVP is a light flaky hygroscopic powder and readily absorbs up to 40% of water by its weight. It deemed that the probability of sensitizing through oral intake of PVP alone is extremely low. Moreover, FSCJ concluded that PVP is of no concern for genotoxicity, acute toxicity, repeated dose toxicity, carcinogenicity and reproductive and developmental toxicity, on the basis of the available toxicological data.

Hence, the correct option is (C).

6. Borax is chemically sodium borate. Borax is a natural mineral with a chemical formula $Na_2B_4O_7.10H_2O$. Borax also is known as sodium borate, sodium tetraborate, or disodium tetraborate. It is one of the most important boron compounds. The International Union of Pure and Applied Chemistry (IUPAC) name for borax is sodium tetraborate decahydrate.

Hence, the correct option is (C).

7. The solution used to clean septic sockets and root canals is H_2O_2 solution. The dentist will also recommend an at-home care regimen, including:

- Take pain medicine and antibiotics as directed.
- Applying a cold pack to the outside of the jaw.
- Carefully rinsing the dry socket (typically with saltwater).

Hydrogen peroxide (H_2O_2) has been used as an endodontic irrigant for years, mainly in concentrations ranging between 3% and 5%. It is active against bacteria, viruses, and yeasts. Hydroxy free radicals ($•OH$) destroy proteins and DNA. The tissue-dissolving capacity of H_2O_2 is clearly lower than that of NaOCl. The surgical site can be cleaned with a cotton swab, moistened with a mouth rinse or 3% hydrogen peroxide.

Hence, the correct option is (A).

8. The betadine is povidone-iodine 5%. Betadine 5% sterile ophthalmic prep solution contains 5% povidone-iodine (0.5% available iodine) as a sterile dark brown solution stabilized by glycerin. Inactive Ingredients: purified water, citric acid, glycerin, nonoxynol-9, sodium chloride, sodium hydroxide, and dibasic sodium phosphate.

Hence, the correct option is (A).

9. "Fine particles" is a physicochemical parameter prescribed in I.P for light kaolin. Kaolin is a layered silicate mineral. Kaolin is used in ceramics, medicine, coated paper, as a food additive, in toothpaste, as a light diffusing material in white incandescent light bulbs, and in cosmetics. Until the early 1990s, it was the active substance of anti-diarrhea medicine Kaopectate.

Hence, the correct option is (C).

10. Sulphur is used internally as a cathartic. Catharsis can be an effect of pesticide poisonings, such as with elemental sulphur. Cathartics such as sorbitol, magnesium citrate, magnesium sulphate, or sodium sulphate were previously used as a form of gastrointestinal decontamination following poisoning via ingestion. Cathartics are substances that loosen stools and increase bowel movements. They are used to treat and/or prevent constipation.

Hence, the correct option is (B).

11. EDTA is ethylene diamine tetraacetic acid. Ethylenediaminetetraacetic acid (EDTA) is an amino polycarboxylic acid with the formula $[CH_2N(CH_2CO_2H)_2]_2$. This white, water-soluble solid is widely used to bind to iron and calcium ions. It binds these ions as a hexadentate ("six-toothed") chelating agent. EDTA is produced as several salts, notably disodium EDTA, sodium calcium edetate, and tetrasodium EDTA.

Hence, the correct option is (A).

12. Lugol's iodine, also known as aqueous iodine and strong iodine solution, is a solution of potassium iodide with iodine in water. It is a medication and disinfectant used for a number of purposes. A solution composed of iodine and potassium iodide, which can be used as a reagent and antiseptic, with potential use in cancer diagnosis. The iodine in Lugol's solution selectively binds to alpha-1,4 glucans found in polysaccharides, such as glycogen. It is a medication and disinfectant used for a number of purposes. A small amount may also be used for emergency disinfection of drinking water.

Hence, the correct option is (D).

13. Silver nitrate is stored in amber coloured bottles. In the presence of light silver nitrate decompose to form silver. So, to prevent decomposition it is kept in dark coloured bottles. Silver nitrate $AgNO_3$ is a liquid that precipitates out whenever exposed to light. that's why a dark bottle is used to block out the light so that liquid Will remain as liquid. So, it is used to protect the liquid.

Hence, the correct option is (C).

14. Chemically, Primaquine is 8--[4-amino-1-methylbuty1 amino]-6 methoxy quinoline. Primaquine is an N-substituted diamine that is pentane-1,4-diamine substituted by a 6-methoxyquinolin-8-yl group at the N(4) position. It is a drug used in the treatment of malaria and Pneumocystis pneumonia. It has a role as an antimalarial. It is an aminoquinoline, an N-substituted diamine and an aromatic ether.

Hence, the correct option is (A).

15. A parameter prescribed in I.P for bentonite is swelling power. Bentonite is insoluble and does not swell in organic solvents. Bentonite swelling power is determined by various experimental procedures such as loading difference and conditions of wetting. Sometimes the property may vary on the water content, the chemical composition which can be called as grades of bentonite.

Hence, the correct option is (B).

16. An indicator used in the assay of iodine is starch mucilage. Starch is a viable indicator in the titration process because it turns deep dark blue when iodine is present in a solution. When starch is heated in water, decomposition occurs and beta-amylose is produced. Vitamin C converts iodine to iodide, so the starch mixture won't turn blue until all the vitamin C is used up.

Hence, the correct option is (D).

17. The opacity agent is titanium dioxide. TiO_2 is also an effective opacifier in powder form, where it is employed as a pigment to provide whiteness and opacity to products such as paints, coatings, plastics, papers, inks, foods, medicines (i.e. pills and tablets), and most toothpaste; in 2019 it was present in two-thirds of toothpaste on the French market. In paint, it is often referred to offhandedly as "brilliant white", "the perfect white", "the whitest white", or other similar terms. Opacity is improved by optimal sizing of the titanium dioxide particles.

Hence, the correct option is (A).

18. Starting material for Ibuprofen is P-Isobutyl acetophenone. Ibuprofen is a commonly used nonsteroidal anti-inflammatory (NSAID) drug that is available both by prescription and over-the-counter. Ibuprofen is considered to be among the safest NSAIDs and is generally well tolerated but can, nevertheless, rarely cause clinically apparent and serious acute liver injury.

Hence, the correct option is (C).

19. An anti-caking agent for hygroscopic powder & granules is colloidal silicon dioxide. An anticaking agent is an additive placed in powdered or granulated materials, such as table salt or confectioneries, to prevent the formation of lumps (caking) and to ease packaging, transport, flowability, and consumption. Some anticaking agents function by absorbing excess moisture or by coating particles and making them water-repellent. Calcium silicate $(CaSiO_3)$, a commonly used anti-caking agent, added to e.g. table salt, absorbs both water and oil. An anticaking agent in salt is denoted in the ingredients, for example, as "anti-caking agent (554)", which is sodium aluminosilicate.

Hence, the correct option is (C).

20. Boric acid is freely soluble in glycerin water and alcohol. This product is soluble in water (40 mg/ml), yielding a clear, colorless solution. Powdered boric acid may dissolve more slowly in water than a crystalline product, but with gentle warming, it will dissolve to give a clear solution. Boric acid has also been reported to be soluble in alcohol (1 part in 16) and in 85% glycerol solution (1 part in 4).

Hence, the correct option is (D).

21. French chalk is purified talc. French Chalk is also known as Magnesium silicate, talc or talcum powder. It is used as a filler and for its slippery and soapy effects. Most tailor's chalk, or French chalk, is talc, as is the chalk often used for welding or metalworking. Talc is also used as a food additive or in pharmaceutical products as a glidant. French Chalk mainly consists of refined silica and magnesium oxides. It is used for marking textiles and materials for laser cutting procedures. French Chalk is also called Talcum Powder.

Hence, the correct option is (C).

22. The white precipitate is ammoniated mercury. A heavy white odorless amorphous compound NH_2HgCl was obtained by treating a solution of mercuric chloride with an excess of ammonia and used in the external treatment of skin diseases and to destroy lice called also white precipitate. Ammoniated mercury is used to treat impetigo, psoriasis, minor skin infections, and other skin disorders.

Hence, the correct option is (D).

23. Aluminium Sulphate is used in dusting powders as an astringent. Hydrated grades as Alum are high volume commercial chemicals. Sizing paper, lakes, alums, dyeing mordant, agent in fire fighting foams, cloth fireproofing, white leather tannage, pH control in the paper industry, waterproofing agent for concrete, deodorizer and decolouriser in petroleum refining, sewage precipitating agent and for water purification.

Medical use: Astringent, treatment of jellyfish stings.

Hence, the correct option is (B).

24. The antifungal drug is zinc undecylenate. Salts of undecylenate are found in topical over-the-counter or mixture products as antifungal agents. Zinc undecylenate is an example of a topical antifungal agent that treats skin infections such as athlete's foot and relieves itching, burning, and irritation associated with the skin condition.

Hence, the correct option is (B).

25. A drug commonly used in shampoo for treating dandruff is selenium sulphide. Selenium sulphide is a chemical compound that is often used to treat dandruff. It's an antifungal that also helps with dandruff scratching, flaking, scaling, and dry skin on the scalp. Seborrhea and tinea versicolor, a fungal infection of the skin, are also treated with selenium sulphide.

Hence, the correct option is (B).

26. Scabicide is sulphur.

Scabicide: A medication used to treat scabies. Although they were the most effective treatment, medications such as the lindane solution Kwell contain benzene and are no longer recommended for use.

Background: Many therapeutic modalities for scabies were available, topical sulfur ointment is a cost-effective and safe therapeutic agent. It is often applied to the whole body for three successive days.

Other topical treatments include crotamiton (Croatan, Eurax) cream or lotion, lindane (not usually used as a first-line treatment due to risk of seizures), sulphur ointment, and benzyl benzoate.

Hence, the correct option is (A).

27. Chlorinated lime is prepared by the action of chlorine gas on slaked lime. Chlorinated lime is a chemical that was first made by passing chlorine gas over slaked lime [Ca(OH$_2$)] to form a chemical with the formula CaOCl$_2$. It is used for bleaching and is commonly referred to as bleaching powder.

Hence, the correct option is (A).

28. A surgical solution of chlorinated soda is Dakin's solution. In recent years surgical solution of chlorinated soda (Dakin's solution) has been used to irrigate the pericardial cavity in the treatment of purulent pericarditis. Dakin's solution is a dilute solution of sodium hypochlorite (0.4% to 0.5%) and other stabilizing ingredients, traditionally used as an antiseptic, e.g. to cleanse wounds in order to prevent infection.[The preparation was for a time called also Carrel–Dakin solution or Carrel–Dakin fluid.

Hence, the correct option is (C).

29. The chemical compounds which interact with specific targets and initiate a biological response in the body are called drugs. When the response is therapeutic and useful, they are called medicines and when it is harmful, they are called poisons. Enzymes are the preferred markers in various disease states such as myocardial infarction, jaundice, pancreatitis, cancer, neurodegenerative disorders, etc. Hormones are chemical substances that act like messenger molecules in the body.

Hence, the correct option is (B).

30. The use of calomel is cathartic. calomel (Hg$_2$Cl$_2$), also called mercurous chloride or mercury(I) chloride, is a very heavy, soft, white, odourless, and tasteless halide mineral formed by the alteration of other mercury minerals, such as cinnabar or amalgams. Once the most popular cathartics, calomel has been used in medicine since the 16th century.

Hence, the correct option is (A).

31. A weak solution of iodine is also known as a tincture of iodine. A tincture of iodine, iodine tincture, or weak iodine solution is an antiseptic. It is usually 2 to 7% elemental iodine, along with potassium iodide or sodium iodide, dissolved in a mixture of ethanol and water. Tincture solutions are characterized by the presence of alcohol. A tincture of iodine, iodine tincture, or weak iodine solution is an antiseptic. It is usually 2 to 7% elemental iodine, along with potassium iodide or sodium iodide, dissolved in a mixture of ethanol and water. Tincture solutions are characterized by the presence of alcohol.

Hence, the correct option is (B).

32. A chemical used in eye infection is silver nitrate. Another change is that silver nitrate is no longer used because it is extremely irritating to the eye and can cause severe pain, chemical pink eye (eye irritation), and temporary vision problems (Standler, 2006). The use of silver nitrate as prophylaxis for neonatal ophthalmia was instituted in the late 1800s to prevent the devastating effects of neonatal ocular infection with Neisseria gonorrhoeae.

Hence, the correct option is (B).

33. The indicator used in silver nitrate assay is ferric ammonium sulphate solution. Ferric ammonium sulphate is the choicest indicator since the endpoint is visibly detected by a deep red colour (ferric thiocyanate) due to the interaction of Fe^{2+} ions with a trace of SCN$^-$ ion. Pharmaceutical substances essentially containing halides may be estimated by direct titration with silver nitrate solution as a titrant. Estimation of excess silver nitrate solution by carrying out residual titration with standard ammonium thiocyanate solution, employing ferric ammonium sulphate as an indicator.

Hence, the correct option is (D).

34. An antidote for calcium channel blockers poisoning is calcium chloride injection. Calcium channel blockers (CCB) are used extensively for the treatment of hypertension, angina pectoris, tachyarrhythmias and migraine prophylaxis. It should be emphasized that there is no single, predictable "antidote" for CCB poisoning. Generally, therapy should be directed at the likely mechanism of toxicity. Calcium infusion provides a direct antidote and may be helpful; however, the response to calcium is also often inadequate.

Hence, the correct option is (C).

35. Talc is a hydrous silicate mineral composed of magnesium (Mg), silicon and oxygen (SiO_2, silica), and water. Its chemical formula is $Mg_3Si_4O_{10}(OH)_2$. Talc is relatively pure in composition but can contain small amounts of aluminum, iron, manganese, and titanium. Talc can be white, apple green, dark green, or brown, depending on its composition. Talc is the softest mineral, having a Mohs hardness of 1, compared to a diamond with a hardness of 10.

Hence, the correct option is (B).

36. Diluted $KMnO_4$ chemical is used as a gargle. Potassium permanganate functions as an oxidising agent. Through this mechanism results in disinfection, astringent effects, and decreased smell. Potassium permanganate is used as a medication for a number of skin conditions. This includes fungal infections of the foot, impetigo, pemphigus, superficial wounds, dermatitis, and tropical ulcers. For tropical ulcers, it is used together with procaine benzylpenicillin.

Hence, the correct option is (C).

37. Potassium permanganate assayed by titration with standard oxalic acid. The titration of potassium permanganate ($KMnO_4$) against oxalic acid ($C_2H_2O_4$) is an example of redox titration. In close proximity to the endpoint, the action of the indicator is analogous to the other types of visual colour titrations in oxidation-reduction (redox) titrations. We get the strength of potassium permanganate by titrating it against the standard solution of 0.1M oxalic acid. Oxalic acid is oxidised to carbon dioxide by $KMnO_4$, which itself gets reduced to $MnSO_4$. Oxalic acid reacts with potassium permanganate in the following way:

The chemical reaction at room temperature is given below:

Reduction Half reaction:

$$2KMnO_4 + 3H_2SO_4 \rightarrow K_2SO_4 + 2MnSO_4 + 3H_2O + 5[O]$$

Oxidation Half reaction:

$$5(COOH)_2 + 5[O] \rightarrow 5H_2O + 10CO_2\uparrow$$

The overall reaction that takes place in the process is:

Overall reaction:

$$2KMnO_4 + 3H_2SO_4 + 5(COOH)_2 \rightarrow K_2SO_4 + 2MnSO_4 + 8H_2O + 10CO_2\uparrow$$

Hence, the correct option is (B).

38. Antioxidant used as a blocking agent in a sterile product is ascorbic acid esters. It is a mild reducing agent and antioxidant. It is oxidized with the loss of one electron to form a radical cation and then with the loss of a second electron to form dehydroascorbic acid. It typically reacts with oxidants of the reactive oxygen species, such as the hydroxyl radical. Salts of sulfur dioxide, including bisulfite, metabisulfite, and sulfite, are the most common antioxidants used in aqueous parenteral. These antioxidants maintain product stability by being

preferentially oxidized and gradually consumed over the shelf life of the product.

Hence, the correct option is (C).

Q.1 Hydrogen peroxide liberates:

A. Oxygen   **B.** Molecular oxygen

C. Ozone   **D.** Atomic oxygen

Q.2 Calcium hydroxide is commonly known as:

A. Quick lime   **B.** Slaked lime

C. Lime water   **D.** Lime

Q.3 A powerful astringent is:

A. Aluminium hydroxide

B. Alum

C. Aluminium sulphate

D. Aluminium chloride

Q.4 Precipitated sulphur is soluble in:

A. Water

B. Carbon tetrachloride

C. Chloroform

D. Carbon disulphide

Q.5 Calamine is used as topical protectant in:

A. Urticaria   **B.** Eczema

C. Sunburns   **D.** All of these

Q.6 Lime water test is used for detection of:

A. Oxygen   **B.** Carbon dioxide

C. Hydrogen   **D.** Nitrogen

Q.7 The formula of alum is:

A. $K_2SO_4 (FeSO_4). 24H_2O$

B. $K_2SO_4 (Fe_2SO_4)_3. 24H_2O$

C. $KAl(SO_4)_2 \cdot 12H_2O$

D. $K_2SO_4 (NH_4SO_4)_3. 24H_2O$

Q.8 Zinc stearate is used as a/an:

A. Astringent   **B.** Antimicrobial agent

C. Lubricant   **D.** All of these

Q.9 Potassium permanganate on oxidation liberates:

A. Atomic oxygen   **B.** Molecular oxygen

C. Ozone   **D.** None of these

Q.10 Glycerin in calamine solution acts as:

A. Protective   **B.** Humectant

C. Antiseptic   **D.** Solublising agent

Q.11 The chemical formula of titanium dioxide:

A. TiO_2 **B.** SiO_2 **C.** BiO_2 **D.** ClO_2

Q.12 Sodium phosphate is used as a diagnostic agent in:

A. Renography   **B.** Thyroid cancer

C. Leukemia   **D.** Liver function

Q.13 Zinc oxide with small portion of ferric oxide is:

A. Calamine   **B.** Calomel

C. Caramel   **D.** Calcium oxide

Q.14 Bentonite is used as:

A. Oxidizing agent   **B.** Suspending agent

C. Preservative   **D.** Starch mucilage

Q.15 An agent that prevents infection by the destruction of pathogenic micro-organisms and applied to an inanimate object is:

A. Antiseptic   **B.** Bacteriostatic

C. Disinfectant   **D.** Bacteriocide

Q.16 Determination of viscosity is by:

A. Ostwald method   **B.** Gutzeit method

C. Karl-Fisher method   **D.** All of these

Q.17 Sweetening agent included in antacid preparation is:

A. Sorbitol   **B.** Sucrose

C. Saccharin   **D.** All of these

Q.18 4-(2-Hydroxy -3-Isopropyl amino propyl phenacetamide) is a chemical name for:

A. Atenolol   **B.** Labetalol

C. Metoprolol   **D.** Acubetol

Q.19 Cream of tartar is:

A. Sodium phosphate

B. Dried sodium phosphate

C. Sodium potassium tartrate

D. Potassium bitartrate

Q.20 Mercurous chloride is:

A. Calomel   **B.** Calamine

C. Caramel   **D.** Chalk

Q.21 Most antidiarrheal products contain an:

A. Antibacterial

B. Antispasmodic

C. Adsorbent-protective

D. All of these

Q.22 All are saline purgatives except:

A. Sodium sulphate

B. Sodium phosphate

C. Magnesium sulphate

D. $Al(OH)_3$ gel

Q.23 Antiflatulent used in antacid preparation is:

A. Dimethicone   **B.** Simethicone

C. Talc   **D.** Both (A) and (B)

Q.24 Light kaolin I.P is prepared from heavy kaolin by:

A. Grinding   **B.** Elutriation

C. Decantation   **D.** Distillation

Q.25 Bismuth sub-salicylate mainly acts as:

| A. Antidiarrheal | B. Antiflatulent | A. Hyperacidity | B. Peptic ulcer |
| C. Antiemetic | D. Astringent | C. Achlorhydria | D. Hyper chlorhydria |

Q.26 Magnesium trisilicate is a compound of magnesium oxide and ________.
A. Simethicone
B. Dimethicone
C. Silicon dioxide
D. Aluminium hydroxide

Q.27 Use of aluminium glycinate is an:
A. Astringent
C. Antacid
B. Antiseptic
D. None of these

Q.28 Heavy kaolin is used in the preparation of:
A. Dentifrices
C. Dusting powders
B. Poultice
D. All of these

Q.29 Captopril contains which of the following acid residue?
A. Proline
C. Valine
B. Leucine
D. Isoleucine

Q.30 Antidote for cyanide poisoning is:
A. Sodium sulphate
C. Sodium nitrite
B. Potassium nitrite
D. Sodium fluoride

Q.31 A preparation containing aluminium magnesium carbonate hydroxide hydrate is:
A. Aluminium glycinate
B. Hydrotalcite
C. Magaldrate
D. Dimethicone

Q.32 A saline purgative is:
A. Magnesium chloride
B. Sodium chloride
C. Ammonium chloride
D. Magnesium sulphate

Q.33 Filter aid is:
A. Sodium sulphate
C. Light kaolin
B. Sodium phosphate
D. Calcium carbonate

Q.34 The drug that used as both laxative & antacid:
A. Magnesium Sulphate
B. Magnesium chloride
C. Magnesium hydroxide
D. Sodium sulphate

Q.35 Antacid should be given:
A. After meals
C. Between meals
B. Before meals
D. All of these

Q.36 Atropine contains:
A. One asymmetric carbon
B. Three asymmetric carbon
C. Two hydroxymethyls carbone
D. Two hydroxyl groups

Q.37 Dilute HCl is used to treat:

Q.38 An adsorbent used in bacterial toxoids:
A. Sodium aluminium phosphate
B. Light kaolin
C. Aluminium chloride
D. Aluminium oxide

// Smart Answer Sheet //

| Correct | Percentage of students who answered correctly. | Skipped | Percentage of students who skipped. |

Q.	Ans.	Correct / Skipped	Q.	Ans.	Correct / Skipped	Q.	Ans.	Correct / Skipped	Q.	Ans.	Correct / Skipped	Q.	Ans.	Correct / Skipped	Q.	Ans.	Correct / Skipped
1	D	59.89 % / 32.86 %	8	D	54.01 % / 41.28 %	15	C	61.9 % / 30.97 %	22	D	44.36 % / 51.75 %	29	A	14.19 % / 79.19 %	36	B	59.12 % / 38.87 %
2	B	60.66 % / 36.96 %	9	A	10.67 % / 83.14 %	16	A	42.23 % / 35.99 %	23	D	68.94 % / 30.06 %	30	C	68.46 % / 30.33 %	37	C	61.54 % / 32.5 %
3	B	43.98 % / 47.73 %	10	B	60.41 % / 31.75 %	17	D	62.04 % / 35.62 %	24	B	56.04 % / 36.64 %	31	B	32.05 % / 67.48 %	38	A	64.6 % / 34.68 %
4	D	52.55 % / 30.28 %	11	A	83.34 % / 11.53 %	18	A	18.47 % / 67.76 %	25	A	67.49 % / 31.62 %	32	D	54.35 % / 39.24 %			
5	D	19.1 % / 75.06 %	12	C	63.32 % / 35.11 %	19	D	46.02 % / 35.64 %	26	C	66.97 % / 31.74 %	33	C	61.26 % / 35.32 %			
6	B	82.88 % / 16.21 %	13	A	58.7 % / 30.29 %	20	A	52.38 % / 34.12 %	27	C	55.47 % / 40.87 %	34	C	50.16 % / 46.39 %			
7	C	48.44 % / 50.12 %	14	B	51.61 % / 30.66 %	21	D	50.83 % / 41.65 %	28	C	67.16 % / 31.41 %	35	A	84.61 % / 13.43 %			

//Hints and Solutions//

1. Hydrogen peroxide liberates atomic oxygen. Hydrogen peroxide decomposes into water and oxygen upon heating or in the presence of numerous substances, particularly salts of such metals as iron, copper, manganese, nickel, or chromium. It combines with many compounds to form crystalline solids useful as mild oxidizing agents; the best-known of these is sodium perborate ($NaBO_2 \cdot H_2O_2 \cdot 3H_2O$ or $NaBO_3 \cdot 4H_2O$), used in laundry detergents and chlorine-free bleach products.

Hence, the correct option is (D).

2. Calcium hydroxide is commonly known as slaked lime. Calcium hydroxide, also called slaked lime, $Ca(OH)_2$, is obtained by the action of water on calcium oxide. When mixed with water, a small proportion of it dissolves, forming a solution known as limewater, the rest remaining as a suspension called milk of lime.

Hence, the correct option is (B).

3. A powerful astringent is an alum. An alum block is a mineral block made of potassium alum, a compound that has antiseptic and astringent properties. The antiseptic properties of the alum block offer protection against disease-causing microorganisms, while the astringent properties help reduce inflammation and bleeding. Some common astringents are an alum, acacia, sage, yarrow, witch hazel, bayberry, distilled vinegar, very cold water, and rubbing alcohol.

Hence, the correct option is (B).

4. Precipitated sulphur is soluble in carbon disulphide. Carbon disulphide is a non-polar solvent. We know sulphur and most of its compounds are nonpolar. According to the like dissolve like the rule, sulphur is soluble in carbon disulphide. While some nonpolar solvents like toluene can partially dissolve it, the most effective chemical for dissolving sulphur is carbon disulphide. While the actual dissolving process is simple, carbon disulphide is extremely hazardous due to its flammable and chemical toxicity, and extreme care must be exercised when using it.

Hence, the correct option is (D).

5. Calamine is used as a topical protectant in urticaria, eczema and sunburns. Calamine also dries oozing or weeping from minor skin irritation. Calamine topical (for the skin) is used to treat itching and skin irritation caused by chickenpox, insect bites or stings, measles, eczema, sunburn, poison ivy, and other minor skin conditions. Topical analgesic and skin protectant. Calamine plus itch reliever. Antihistamines like Benadryl and Claritin (calamine lotion) are often effective in relieving the symptoms of urticaria.

Hence, the correct option is (D).

6. A lime water test is used for the detection of carbon dioxide. Limewater is a solution of calcium hydroxide. If carbon dioxide is bubbled through limewater, the limewater turns milky or cloudy white. Using lime water is a fun and easy way to test for the presence of carbon dioxide. The exhaled carbon dioxide is used to produce a precipitate of calcium carbonate with lime water.

Hence, the correct option is (B).

7. The formula of alum is $KAl(SO_4)_2 \cdot 12H_2O$. Alum is an inorganic compound composed of water molecules, aluminium, other metal than aluminium, and sulphates. Alum is a double salt present in the hydrated form. The general chemical formula for alum is $XAl(SO_4)_2 \cdot 12H_2O$. These compounds are sweet in taste. They generally crystallize in the regular octahedral form. The alum crystals get liquified when heated. Alums generally exist in the form of a white and transparent crystalline form.

Hence, the correct option is (C).

8. Zinc stearate is used as a/an astringent, antimicrobial agent and lubricant. In cosmetics, zinc stearate is a lubricant and thickening agent used to improve texture. It is an "activator" for accelerated rubber sulphur vulcanization. Zinc stearate has antiseptic, astringent and topical protective properties. Zinc is used as an antimicrobial, it has been added to mouth rinses and toothpaste to control dental plaque, inhibit calculus formation and reduce halitosis.

Hence, the correct option is (D).

9. Potassium permanganate on oxidation liberates atomic oxygen. Solid potassium permanganate decomposes when heated:

$$2\ KMnO_4 \rightarrow K_2MnO_4 + MnO_2(s) + O_2$$

Here, the oxidation state of manganese changes as the potassium permanganate (oxidation state +7) decomposes to potassium manganate (oxidation state +6) and manganese dioxide (oxidation state +4). Oxygen gas is also liberated.

Hence, the correct option is (A).

10. Glycerin in calamine solution acts as humectant. A humectant is a hygroscopic substance used to keep things moist. In pharmaceuticals and cosmetics, humectants can be used in topical dosage forms to increase the solubility of a chemical compound's active ingredients, increasing the active ingredients' ability to penetrate skin or its activity time. Glycerin is a humectant, a type of moisturizing agent that pulls water into the outer layer of your skin from deeper levels of your skin and the air.

Hence, the correct option is (B).

11. The chemical formula of titanium dioxide TiO_2. Titanium dioxide is a titanium oxide with the formula TiO_2. A naturally occurring oxide sourced from ilmenite, rutile and anatase, it has a wide range of applications. It has a role as a food colouring. Titanium dioxide, also known as titanium(IV) oxide or titania, is the naturally occurring oxide of titanium.

Hence, the correct option is (A).

12. Sodium phosphate is used as a diagnostic agent in leukemia. The principal use of Sodium phosphate P32 is for the treatment of polycythemia vera, and it is effective for the treatment of chronic myelocytic leukemia and chronic lymphocytic leukemia. Sodium phosphate P 32 is also used in the palliative treatment of selected patients with multiple areas of skeletal metastases.

Hence, the correct option is (C).

13. Zinc oxide with a small portion of ferric oxide is calamine. Calamine is a combination of zinc oxide and 0.5% ferric oxide (Fe_2O_3). Calamine lotion is a topical medication that people use to treat itchy skin, sometimes called pruritus. Calamine lotion contains the active ingredient zinc oxide that has both mild antiseptic and pore tightening, or astringent, properties. It may help treat acne.

Hence, the correct option is (A).

14. Bentonite:

1. Bentonite is an absorbent natural smectite clay. It has a colloidal structure in water. Each smectite particle is composed of thousands of submicroscopic platelets stacked in a sandwich fashion with a layer of water between each. A single platelet is 1 nm thick and up to several 100 nm across.

2. It is stable at pH > 6.

3. Most often, bentonite suspensions are thixotropic (shear thinning), although rare cases of rheopectic (shear-thickening) behavior have also been reported. At higher concentrations, bentonite suspensions begin to take on the characteristics of a gel (a fluid with minimum yield strength required to make it move).

4. Bentonite is used as a **suspending and rheological agent**.

Hence, the correct option is (B).

15. An agent that prevents infection by the destruction of pathogenic micro-organisms and is applied to an inanimate object is a disinfectant. Commercially available 3% hydrogen peroxide is a stable and effective disinfectant when used on inanimate surfaces. A germicide is an agent that can kill microorganisms, particularly pathogenic organisms ("germs"). The term germicide includes both antiseptics and disinfectants. Antiseptics are germicides applied to living tissue and skin; disinfectants are antimicrobials applied only to inanimate objects.

Hence, the correct option is (C).

16. Determination of viscosity is by the Ostwald method. Ostwald viscometer is used to determine the viscosity of a Newtonian fluid. When the liquid flow by gravity time required for the liquid to pass between two marks A and B through the capillary tube is determined. The method of determining viscosity with this instrument consists of measuring the time for a known volume of the liquid (the volume contained between marks A and B) to flow through the capillary under the influence of gravity. Ostwald viscometers named after the German chemist Wilhelm Ostwald (1853-1932).

Hence, the correct option is (A).

17. The sweetening agent included in antacid preparation is sorbitol, sucrose and saccharin. Sweetening agents are employed in liquid formulations designed for oral administration specifically to increase the palatability of the therapeutic agent. The main sweetening agents employed in oral preparations are sucrose, liquid glucose, glycerol, sorbitol, saccharin sodium and aspartame. The use of artificial sweetening agents in formulations is increasing and, in many formulations, saccharin sodium is used either as the sole sweetening agent or in combination with sugars or sorbitol to reduce the sugar concentration in the formulation.

Hence, the correct option is (D).

18. 4-(2-Hydroxy -3-Isopropyl amino propyl phenacetamide) is a chemical name for is atenolol. Atenolol is an ethanolamine compound having a (4-carbamoyl-methyl phenoxy)methyl group at the 1-position and an N-isopropyl substituent. It has a role as a beta-adrenergic antagonist, an anti-arrhythmia drug, an antihypertensive agent, a sympatholytic agent, a xenobiotic and an environmental contaminant.

Hence, the correct option is (A).

19. The cream of tartar is potassium bitartrate, also known as potassium hydrogen tartrate, which has a chemical formula of $KC_4H_5O_6$. A cream of tartar is an odorless white crystalline powder. A cream of tartar is the potassium acid salt of tartaric acid, otherwise known as potassium acid tartrate or potassium bitartrate. It's a powdery form of "tartaric acid" so it's an acidic substance simi ar to lemon or vinegar.

Hence, the correct option is (D).

20. Mercurous chloride is calomel. Calomel (Hg_2Cl_2), also called mercurous chloride or mercury(I) chloride, is a very heavy, soft, white, odourless, and tasteless halide mineral formed by the alteration of other mercury minerals, such as cinnabar or amalgams. Once the most popular cathartics, calomel has been used in medicine since the 16th century.

Hence, the correct option is (A).

21. Most antidiarrheal products contain an antibacterial, antispasmodic and adsorbent-protective. The substances which protect the mucosal linings of GIT are called adsorbents & protective. subnitrate milk of Bismuth. These are chemically inert substances that are used in the treatment of mild diarrhea or dysentery of GIT because of their ability to adsorb gases, toxins and bacteria. An antidiarrheal is a drug that is used to slow down or stop loose stools (diarrhea). Over-the-counter antidiarrheal medications are found in most drug stores or pharmacies or they can be prescribed by a physician. Antidiarrheals are used for acute, non-life-threatening situations, such as viral gastroenteritis.

Hence, the correct option is (D).

22. Sodium sulphate, sodium phosphate and magnesium sulphate are all saline purgatives except for $Al(OH)_3$ gel. These are drugs when given orally retained in GIT, increase the intestinal bulk by drawing water from circulation by osmosis. They act as a mechanical stimulus, producing increased peristaltic movement causing diarrhoea. They are also called as saline purgatives or osmotic laxatives. Aluminium hydroxide gel is an aqueous suspension of hydrated aluminium oxide together with varying amounts of basic aluminium carbonate. It contains aluminium oxide, glycerin, sucrose or saccharin as a sweetening agent, peppermint oil as a flavouring agent and sodium benzoate as a preservative.

Hence, the correct option is (D).

23. Antiflatulents used in antacid preparation are dimethicone and simethicone. Simeticone or (simethicone) is a type of medicine called an antiflatulent. It is used to treat wind (flatulence). It is a mixture of silica gel and dimethicone (or dimethicone, a type of silicone) and is known as "activated dimethicone". It can help with trapped wind and bloating as well as colic in babies. Dimethicone is a common additive to antacids, although its value in the treatment of reflux oesophagitis is unproven.

Hence, the correct option is (D).

24. Light kaolin I.P is prepared from heavy kaolin by elutriation. Light Kaolin is a native hydrated aluminium silicate, freed from most of its impurities by elutriation and dried. It contains a suitable dispersing agent. Elutriation is a process for separating particles based on their size, shape and density, using a stream of gas or liquid flowing in a direction opposite to the direction of sedimentation.

Hence, the correct option is (B).

25. Bismuth sub-salicylate mainly acts as an antidiarrheal. Bismuth sub-salicylate is an antidiarrheal and anti-inflammatory agent used for symptomatic treatment of nausea, indigestion, upset stomach, diarrhea, and other temporary discomforts of the stomach and gastrointestinal tract. Exhibiting antibacterial and gastroprotective properties, bismuth sub-salicylate is an insoluble salt of salicylic acid linked to trivalent bismuth cation.

Hence, the correct option is (A).

26. Magnesium trisilicate is a compound of magnesium oxide and silicon dioxide. Magnesium trisilicate is an inorganic compound that is used as a food additive. The additive is frequently used by fast-food chains to absorb fatty acids and extract impurities formed while frying edible oils. The chemical formula of magnesium trisilicate is $Mg_2O_8Si_3$.

Hence, the correct option is (C).

27. The use of aluminium glycinate is an antacid. Aluminium glycinate is a medication indicated to treat heartburn, indigestion, acid reflux, ulcers, and gas. Aluminium glycinate (or dihydroxy aluminium amino acetate) is an antacid. It tends to concentrate in the brain, liver, thyroid and lungs. The elderly and those with kidney damage are especially at risk of accumulating aluminium. Aluminium can be toxic if it is present in tissues in excessive amounts.

Hence, the correct option is (C).

28. Heavy kaolin is used in the preparation of dusting powders. When applied topically, it serves as an emollient and drying agent. When ingested, it acts as an adsorbent to bind GI toxins and control diarrhea. Kaolin has been added to dusting powders and is used as a tablet excipient.

Hence, the correct option is (C).

29. Captopril contains proline acid residue. Captopril, 1-[(2S)-3-mercapto-2-methylpropionyl]-l-proline, is synthesized by direct acylation of l-proline with 3-acetylthio-2-methylpropionic acid chloride, which is synthesized from 3-acetylthio-2-methylpropionic acid, which is in turn synthesized by reacting methacrylic and thioacetic acid. 1-(3-Acetylthio-2-d-methylpropanoyl)-l-proline is formed by reacting l-proline with 3-

acetylthio-2-methylpropionic acid chloride, and it undergoes further ammonolysis with ammonia, to give the desired captopril.

Hence, the correct option is (A).

30. An antidote for cyanide poisoning is sodium nitrite. Sodium nitrite induces methemoglobin in red blood cells, which combines with cyanide, thus releasing cytochrome oxidase enzyme. The combination of sodium thiosulfate and sodium nitrite has been used in the United States since the 1930s as the primary antidote for cyanide intoxication.

Hence, the correct option is (C).

31. A preparation containing aluminium magnesium carbonate hydroxide hydrate is hydrotalcite. Hydrotalcite, a magnesium–aluminium hydroxycarbonate, is a naturally occurring mineral of chemical composition $Mg_6Al_2(OH)_{16}CO_3 .4H_2O$ exhibiting a layered crystal structure, which is comprised of positively charged hydroxide layers and interlayers composed of carbonate anions and water molecules.

Hence, the correct option is (B).

32. A saline purgative is magnesium sulphate. Saline purgatives are salts containing highly charged ions that do not readily cross cell membranes and therefore remain inside the lumen, or passageway, of the bowel. By retaining water through osmotic forces, saline purgatives increase the volume of the contents of the bowel, stretching the colon and producing a normal stimulus for contraction of the muscle, which leads to defecation. Some commonly used salts are magnesium sulphate (Epsom salts), magnesium hydroxide (milk of magnesia), sodium sulphate (Glauber salt), and potassium sodium tartrate (Rochelle salt or Seidlitz powder).

Hence, the correct option is (D).

33. The filter aid is light kaolin. Efficient filtration of fine kaolin particles plays a crucial role in processing raw kaolin into a marketable product. Oftentimes, filtration is the rate-controlling step of the whole process. As a consequence, plant production is dependent, to a great extent, on the rates being achieved in filtration.

Hence, the correct option is (C).

34. The drug that is used as both laxative & antacid is magnesium hydroxide. Magnesium hydroxide is in a class of medications called saline laxatives. It works by causing water to be retained with the stool. This increases the number of bowel movements and softens the stool so it is easier to pass. Aluminum Hydroxide, Magnesium Hydroxide are antacids used together to relieve heartburn, acid indigestion, and upset stomach.

Hence, the correct option is (C).

35. Antacid should be given after meals. It's best to take antacids with food or soon after eating because this is when you're most likely to get indigestion or heartburn. The effect of the medicine may also last longer if taken with food. This allows you up to three hours of relief. When ingested on an empty stomach, an antacid leaves your stomach too quickly and can only neutralize acid for 30 to 60 minutes.

Hence, the correct option is (A).

36. Atropine contains three asymmetric carbon. Atropine, a tropane alkaloid, is an enantiomeric mixture of d-hyoscyamine and l-hyoscyamine, with most of its physiological effects due to l-hyoscyamine. Its pharmacological effects are due to binding to muscarinic acetylcholine receptors. It is an antimuscarinic agent.

Hence, the correct option is (B).

37. Dilute HCl is used to treat achlorhydria. Achlorhydria is a condition in which the stomach does not produce hydrochloric acid, one of the components of gastric acid. Hydrochloric acid plays an integral role in the digestion of food and protects the body from pathogens ingested with food or water.

Hence, the correct option is (C).

38. An adsorbent used in bacterial toxoids is sodium aluminium phosphate. Toxoid, bacterial poison (toxin) that is no longer active but retains the property of combining with or stimulating the formation of antibodies. In many bacterial diseases, the bacteria itself remains sequestered in one part of the body but produces a poison (exotoxin) that causes the disease manifestations. Sodium aluminum phosphate is an ingredient commonly found in baking powders and processed cheeses. In baking powders, bakers use it as an acid that provides the baked goods' chemical reaction needed to rise. Sodium aluminum phosphate reacts with heat and the other leavening ingredients to allow baked goods to rise.

Hence, the correct option is (A).

Q.1 Polymers of ethylene oxide are ________.

A. Spans
B. Macrogols
C. Tweens
D. Polawax

Q.2 The drug is compressed into tablets with slowly soluble polymer is called:

A. Matrix dissolution
B. Ion exchange
C. Matrix diffusion
D. Osmotic pump

Q.3 Which of the following is not a semisolid dosage form?

A. Paste
B. Creams
C. Ointments
D. Suspensions

Q.4 Most nasal solutions are mildly buffered at pH between:

A. Less than 4.0
B. 5.5-7.5
C. Above 8.0
D. 7.5-8

Q.5 Method suitable for preparation of spirits:

A. Chemical reaction
B. Distillation
C. Simple solution
D. All of the above

Q.6 Mucilage is described best as which of the following systems?

A. Sol **B.** Gel **C.** Magma **D.** Milk

Q.7 Oily liquid preparations, intended for external application with rubbing is:

A. Liniments
B. Paints
C. Lotions
D. Pastes

Q.8 Medical soft soap is also known as:

A. Hard soap
B. Green soap tincture
C. Sodium lauryl sulphate
D. Sodium stearate

Q.9 Water-soluble bases are also known as:

A. Greasy ointment bases
B. Greaseless ointment bases
C. Both (A) and (B)
D. None of these

Q.10 Cetyl esters wax approximates the composition of:

A. Bees wax
B. Spermaceti
C. Lanolin
D. Carnauba wax

Q.11 Vaginal suppositories are also called:

A. Paraffin
B. Mineral oil
C. Petrolatum
D. Liquid petrolatum

Q.12 Camphorated Tincture Opium is ________.

A. Paregoric
B. Tr. Opium
C. Camphor spirit
D. None of these

Q.13 An example of a water-soluble ointment base:

A. Polyethylene glycol ointment
B. Cold cream
C. Hydrophilic petrolatum
D. Hydrophilic ointment

Q.14 The healing agent used in hand cream is:

A. Soft paraffin
B. Bees wax
C. Hard paraffin
D. Urea

Q.15 The solidification point of cocoa butter lies between:

A. 12–13ºC
B. 20–30ºC
C. 5–10ºC
D. None of these

Q.16 Bloom strength is used to check the quality of:

[Graduate Pharmacy Aptitude Test, 2010]

A. Lactose
B. Gelatin
C. Hardness of tablets
D. Ampoules

Q.17 The purity of water can be assessed by determining one of the following properties instrumentally:

A. Viscosity
B. pH
C. Conductivity
D. Refractivity

Q.18 Who is the father of medicine?

A. Ebers
B. Hippocrates
C. Egyptian
D. Pontus

Q.19 The first edition of IP was published in ________.

A. 1965 **B.** 1975 **C.** 1946 **D.** 1985

Q.20 The "Pharmacy Act" came into force in ________.

A. 1947 **B.** 1948 **C.** 1949 **D.** 1950

Q.21 Biologically active products are dried using:

A. Drum dryer
B. Tray dryer
C. Fluidized bed dryer
D. Freeze dryer

Q.22 What is USP?

A. The United States Pharmacology
B. The United States Pharmacy
C. The United States Pharmacopoeia
D. The United States Pharmaceuticals

Q.23 Drugs converted to suitable form are known as ____________.

A. Excipient
B. Source of drug
C. Dosage form
D. API

Q.24 Every dosage form is a combination of drug and different kind of non-drug components called ________.

A. Additives
B. Non-Additives
C. New chemical entity
D. All of these

Q.25 Simple syrup is a saturated solution of ________.

A. Sucrose **B.** Fructose
C. Dextrose **D.** None of these

Q.26 When two or more drugs are used in combination to increase the pharmacological action, the phenomenon is known as _____________.
A. Synergism **B.** Tolerance
C. Potentiation **D.** Idiosyncrasy

Q.27 When the action of the drug is opposed by the other drug, the phenomenon is known as:
A. Antagonism **B.** Analgesics
C. Addition **D.** Antioxidant

Q.28 Is the state of psychic and physical drug dependence?
A. Habituation **B.** Addiction
C. Anxiety **D.** Tolerance

Q.29 Acute tolerance is also known as ____________.
A. Addiction **B.** Idiosyncrasy
C. Tachyphylaxis **D.** Habituation

Q.30 A genetically determined abnormal or unusual response to a drug is _________.
A. Idiosyncrasy
B. Tolerance
C. Genetic polymorphism
D. Salicylism

Q.31 Powders used for external use are _________.
A. Dusting powder
B. Bulk powder
C. Divided powder
D. Effervescent powder

Q.32 Bulk powders are _________.
A. Potent **B.** Non-Potent
C. Both (A) and (B) **D.** None of these

Q.33 Powders are more stable than ____________.
A. Syrup **B.** Tablet **C.** Capsule **D.** Elixirs

Q.34 The component present in solution in small quantity is known as _________.
A. Solvent **B.** Solution **C.** Solute **D.** Liquid

Q.35 The component present in solution in large quantity is known as _________.
A. Solvent **B.** Solution **C.** Solute **D.** Liquid

Q.36 Throat paints are liquid preparations:
A. Viscous **B.** Non viscous
C. Solid **D.** Gas

Q.37 A separator that has no moving parts is:
A. Bag filter **B.** Cyclone separator
C. Dor thickener **D.** Basket centrifuge

Q.38 The syrup is in nature:
A. Aqueous **B.** Non aqueous
C. Gas **D.** Solid

// Smart Answer Sheet //

Correct	Percentage of students who answered correctly.	Skipped	Percentage of students who skipped.

Q.	Ans.	Correct / Skipped	Q.	Ans.	Correct / Skipped	Q.	Ans.	Correct / Skipped	Q.	Ans.	Correct / Skipped	Q.	Ans.	Correct / Skipped	Q.	Ans.	Correct / Skipped
1	B	54.13 % / 41.12 %	8	B	55.68 % / 34.25 %	15	A	46.37 % / 51.02 %	22	C	46.17 % / 52.64 %	29	C	48.33 % / 34.91 %	36	A	60.44 % / 34.95 %
2	A	46.01 % / 44.62 %	9	B	58.86 % / 38.32 %	16	B	68.83 % / 30.15 %	23	C	81.77 % / 10.46 %	30	A	49.32 % / 46.95 %	37	B	49.17 % / 39.84 %
3	A	64.51 % / 30.54 %	10	B	26.41 % / 70.49 %	17	C	61.6 % / 35.23 %	24	A	44.81 % / 45.64 %	31	A	64.08 % / 35.73 %	38	A	77.64 % / 13.44 %
4	B	47.18 % / 38.04 %	11	A	57.71 % / 35.8 %	18	B	42.81 % / 42.48 %	25	A	66.92 % / 30.85 %	32	B	57.19 % / 39.02 %			
5	A	84.25 % / 10.71 %	12	A	28.23 % / 69.57 %	19	C	44.79 % / 51.78 %	26	A	60.52 % / 36.44 %	33	A	59.79 % / 34.68 %			
6	B	59.62 % / 32.33 %	13	A	88.26 % / 11.47 %	20	B	68.32 % / 30.04 %	27	A	61.66 % / 34.37 %	34	C	80.21 % / 18.3 %			
7	A	60.24 % / 38.95 %	14	D	52.56 % / 41.69 %	21	D	41.28 % / 35.4 %	28	B	51.17 % / 33.73 %	35	A	85.03 % / 10.89 %			

//Hints and Solutions//

1. Polymers of ethylene oxide are macrogols. Macrogol 20000R (A high molecular weight compound of polyethylene glycol with a diepoxide). Polyethylene oxide is a nonionic homopolymer of ethylene oxide. Polyethylene oxide is an excellent bioadhesive polymer and is employed as a binder. Moreover, this polymer controls the release of components in tablet formulations. Macrogol (or macrogols) is a laxative taken to treat constipation (difficulty pooing). It's also taken to help clear a build-up of hard poo in your bowel, which can happen if you've been constipated for a long time (fecal impaction).

Hence, the correct option is (B).

2. The drug is compressed into tablets with a slowly soluble polymer is called matrix dissolution. In a homogeneous matrix system, the drug is either dissolved or dispersed in a homogeneous matrix, mostly a polymer. Once the matrix system is immersed in a dissolution medium the drug, present at the surface of the matrix, will dissolve in the dissolution medium.

Hence, the correct option is (A).

3. Pastes are not a semisolid dosage form. Particle size and size distribution play an important part in manufacturing processes (such as blending, flow property, and tablet compression) of solid dosage forms (tablet and capsule) as does physical stability in the manufacture of semisolid dosage forms (ointment, cream, and suspension). In solid dosage form with less soluble drugs, particle size is a major consideration for bioavailability.

Hence, the correct option is (A).

4. Most nasal solutions are mildly buffered at a pH between 5.5-7.5. Commercial 0.9% saline solution for infusion has a pH of around 5.5. There are many reasons for this acidity, some of them still obscure. It is also true that infusion of normal saline can lead to metabolic acidaemia, yet the link between the acidity of saline solution and the acidaemia it can engender is not straightforward.

Hence, the correct option is (B).

5. A method suitable for the preparation of spirits is a chemical reaction. Spirit is Ethyl Alcohol or ethanol. It can be prepared by the fermentation of sugar (e.g., from molasses), which requires an enzyme catalyst that is present in yeast; or it can be prepared by the fermentation of starch (e.g., from corn, rice, rye, or potatoes), which requires, in addition to the yeast enzyme, an enzyme present in an extract of malt.

Hence, the correct option is (A).

6. Mucilage is described best as a gel system.

Mucilage:

- A gelatinous substance of various plants (such as legumes or seaweeds) that contains protein and polysaccharides and is similar to plant gums.
- An aqueous usually viscid solution (as of gum) is used especially as an adhesive.

Hence, the correct option is (B).

7. Oily liquid preparations, intended for external application with rubbing is liniments.

Liniment:

1. Liquid or semisolid preparation.
2. Meant for application to skin with friction & Rubbing of the skin.
3. May contain alcohol or oily solution or emulsion.
4. Liniment should not be applied to broken skin or broken skin.
5. Liniment should be dispersed in colored fluted Bottles in order to distinguish it from preparation meant for internal use.
6. External use only; shake well before use & not to be applied to open wound and broken skin.
7. Example: Terpintine liniment.

Hence, the correct option is (A).

8. Medical soft soap is also known as green soap tincture. Tincture of green soap is a mild liquid soap that contains isopropyl alcohol and glycerin, but no animal ingredients, dye or fillers. Technical Tincture of Green Soap is used for skin cleansing, cleaning of medical utensils prior to sterilization, and pre-scrub sanitation.

Hence, the correct option is (B).

9. Water-soluble bases are also known as greaseless ointment bases. Water-soluble bases contain only water-soluble ingredients and not fats or other greasy substances so, they are known as greaseless bases. This group of so-called "greaseless ointment bases" comprises water-soluble constituents. Polyethylene Glycol Ointment is the only Pharmacopeial preparation in this group.

Hence, the correct option is (B).

10. Cetyl esters wax approximates the composition of spermaceti. Spermaceti (from Greek sperma meaning "seed", and ceti, the genitive form of "whale") is a waxy substance found in the head cavities of the sperm whale (and, in smaller quantities, in the oils of other whales). Spermaceti is created in the spermaceti organ inside the whale's head. This organ may contain as much as 1,900 litres (500 US gal) of spermaceti.

Hence, the correct option is (B).

11. Vaginal suppositories are also called paraffin. Paraffin is a petroleum product is used to increase the consistency of an ointment. Liquid paraffin is primarily used as a pediatric laxative in medicine and is a popular treatment for constipation and encopresis. Because of its ease of titration, the drug is convenient to synthesize.

Hence, the correct option is (A).

12. Camphorated Tr. opium is paregoric. This medication is used to treat diarrhea. It helps to decrease how often you have bowel movements. It works by slowing the movement of the intestines. Paregoric belongs to a class of drugs known as opioid pain relievers, but this medication acts mainly to slow the gut. The abbreviation "DTO," traditionally used to refer to Deodorized

Tincture of Opium, is sometimes also erroneously employed to abbreviate "diluted tincture of opium." Diluted tincture of opium, also known as Camphorated Tincture of Opium (Paregoric) is a 1:25 mixture of opium tincture to water prescribed to treat withdrawal symptoms in newborns whose mothers were using opioids while pregnant.

Hence, the correct option is (A).

13. An example of water-soluble ointment base polyethylene glycol ointment. A water-soluble ointment containing polyethylene glycol. Suitable for the treatment of minor cuts, wounds, abrasions, scalds, and other skin irritations. Polyethylene glycol, referred to as PEG, is used as an inactive ingredient as a solvent, plasticizer, surfactant, ointments, and suppository base, and tablet and capsule lubricant. PEG has low toxicity with systemic absorption of less than 0.5%.

Hence, the correct option is (A).

14. The healing agent used in hand cream is urea. The use of urea as a healing agent goes back thousands of years. Urea was the first organic compound to be synthesised in a laboratory from inorganic materials, and urea preparations were used in the late 19th and early 20th century for the topical treatment of infections. The reduction in the water content of the epidermis changes the properties of the skin barrier, favouring the penetration of irritants, as well as reducing the itching threshold and predisposing the skin to infections.

Hence, the correct option is (D).

15. The solidification point of cocoa butter lies between 12–13oC. Melting the cocoa butter in chocolate and then allowing it to solidify without tempering leads to the formation of unstable polymorphic forms of cocoa butter. This can easily happen when chocolate bars are allowed to melt in a hot room and leads to the formation of white patches on the surface of the chocolate called fat bloom or chocolate bloom. Cocoa butter and other confectionery fats do not behave alike in molding.

Hence, the correct option is (A).

16. Bloom strength is used to check the quality of gelatin. Bloom is a test to measure the strength of a gel or gelatin. The number of grams is called the Bloom value, and most gelatins are between 30 and 300 g Bloom. The higher a Bloom value, the higher the melting and gelling points of a gel, and the shorter its gelling times. This method is most often used on soft gels.

Hence, the correct option is (B).

17. The purity of water can be assessed by determining conductivity instrumentally. The reason that the conductivity of water is important is that it can tell you how much-dissolved substances, chemicals, and minerals are present in the water. Higher amounts of these impurities will lead to higher conductivity. Conductivity measures water's ability to conduct electricity due to the presence or absence of certain ions.

Hence, the correct option is (C).

18. Hippocrates is considered to be the father of modern medicine because in his books, which are more than 70. He described in a scientific manner, many diseases and their treatment after detailed observation. He lived about 2400 years ago. Hippocrates is credited with being the man who invented medicine. He was a Greek physician who wrote the Hippocratic Corpus, a collection of seventy medical works.

Hence, the correct option is (B).

19. The first edition of IP was published in 1946. The actual process of publishing the first Pharmacopoeia started in the year 1944 under the chairmanship of Col. R. N. Chopra. The I. P. list was first published in the year 1946 and was put forth for approval. The titles are suffixed with the respective years of publication, e.g. IP 1996.

Hence, the correct option is (C).

20. The "Pharmacy Act" came into force in 1948. 4th March 1948 an act to regulate the profession of pharmacy. Whereas it is expedient to make better provision for the regulation of the profession and practice of pharmacy and for that purpose to constitute Pharmacy Councils. The act Pharmacy Collaborative is operational learning and acting collaborative between colleges/schools of pharmacy and clinically integrated networks of community-based pharmacies.

Hence, the correct option is (B).

21. Biologically active products are dried using a freeze dryer. Freeze-drying, also known as lyophilization or cryodesiccation, is a low-temperature dehydration process that involves freezing the product, lowering pressure, then removing the ice by sublimation. This is in contrast to dehydration by most conventional methods that evaporate water using heat.

Hence, the correct option is (D).

22. The United States Pharmacopeia (USP) and National Formulary (NF) are the official standards for all prescription and over-the-counter medicines, dietary supplements, excipients and other healthcare products manufactured and sold in the United States. Spectrum Chemical is the leading manufacturer and offers the widest selection of certified USP chemicals, USP test solutions, USP volumetric solutions and USP Reagents.

Hence, the correct option is (C).

23. Drugs converted to suitable forms are known as dosage forms. Dosage forms (also called unit doses) are pharmaceutical drug products in the form in which they are marketed for use, with a specific mixture of active ingredients and inactive components (excipients), in a particular configuration (such as a capsule shell, for example), and apportioned into a particular dose.

Hence, the correct option is (C).

24. Every dosage form is a combination of drugs and different kinds of non-drug components called additives. The additives are being used in each and every formulation, but due to the lack of awareness as well as regulations regarding the additives, patients, being the end consumers, may have to suffer serious side effects. A few countries like the United States, China, Japan, and India have put efforts into developing the regulations for the additives along with FDA but still their implementation during the manufacturing process of additives as well as formulations is still in doubt. All the additives should be manufactured, tested, stored, and utilized according to the specific guidelines.

Hence, the correct option is (A).

25. Simple syrup is a saturated solution of sucrose. A syrup is a concentrated or nearly saturated solution of sucrose in water. A simple syrup contains only sucrose and purified water (e.g. Syrup USP). Syrup, USP contains 850 gm sucrose and 450 ml of water in each liter of syrup. Although very concentrated, the solution is not saturated.

Hence, the correct option is (A).

26. When two or more drugs are used in combination to increase pharmacological action, the phenomenon is known as synergism. Two or more drugs that individually produce overtly similar effects will sometimes display greatly enhanced effects when given in combination. When the combined effect is greater than that predicted by their individual potencies, the combination is said to be synergistic.

Hence, the correct option is (A).

27. When the action of the drug is opposed by the other drug, the phenomenon is known as antagonism. An interaction between two or more drugs that have opposite effects on the body. Drug antagonism may block or reduce the effectiveness of one or more of the drugs. Antagonists cause no opioid effect and block full agonist opioids. Examples are naltrexone and naloxone.

Hence, the correct option is (A).

28. Addiction is the state of psychic and physical drug dependence. Dependence means that when a person stops using a drug, their body goes through "withdrawal" a group of physical and mental symptoms that can range from mild (if the drug is caffeine) to life-threatening (such as alcohol or opioids, including heroin and prescription pain relievers). Addiction is defined as a chronic, relapsing disorder characterized by compulsive drug seeking, continued use despite harmful consequences, and long-lasting changes in the brain. It is considered both a complex brain disorder and a mental illness. Addiction is the most severe form of a full spectrum of substance use disorders and is a medical illness caused by repeated misuse of a substance or substances.

Hence, the correct option is (B).

29. Acute tolerance is also known as tachyphylaxis. The term tachyphylaxis is used to describe desensitization that occurs very rapidly, sometimes with the initial dose. The term tolerance is conventionally used to describe a more gradual loss of response to a drug that occurs over days or weeks. Tachyphylaxis is a medical term describing an acute, sudden decrease in response to a drug after its administration; i.e. a rapid and short-term onset of drug tolerance. It can occur after an initial dose or after a series of small doses.

Hence, the correct option is (C).

30. A genetically determined abnormal or unusual response to a drug is idiosyncrasy. Idiosyncratic adverse drug reactions are unpredictable and thought to have an underlying genetic etiology. Idiosyncrasy is an unusual feature of a person which denotes a non-immunological hypersensitivity to a substance.

Hence, the correct option is (A).

31. Powders used for external use are dusting powder. An example of dusting powder is what people living in humid climates use to keep their skin from being shiny and sticky. A fine powder, such as talcum powder, is used on the skin. Any fine, light powder used as an insecticide, medicine, toiletry, etc., or used to prevent sticking.

Hence, the correct option is (A).

32. Bulk powders are non-potent. Bulk powders are non-potent and can be dosed with acceptable accuracy and safety using measuring devices such as the teaspoon, cup, or insufflator. This practically limits the use of orally administered bulk powders to antacids, dietary supplements, laxatives, and a few analgesics. Many bulk powders are used topically. Bulk powders refer to a mixture of all the materials (usually non-potent drugs), packed into properly designed bulk containers, such as a tight, wide-mouthed glass or plastic bottle, and are intended for either internal or external administration.

Hence, the correct option is (B).

33. Powders are more stable than syrup. Powders have better physicochemical stability and longer shelf life compared to liquid dosage forms. For example, the shelf life of powders for antibiotic syrups is 2 to 3 years, but once reconstituted with water it is 1 to 2 weeks. Powders are not well suited for dispensing hygroscopic or deliquescent drugs.

Hence, the correct option is (A).

34. The component present in solution in small quantity is known as solute. The solute is that component of the solution, which is present in a smaller amount by weight in the solution. A dilute solution is one that has a relatively small amount of dissolved solute. The component of a two-component solution that is present in a smaller quantity is called the solute.

Hence, the correct option is (C).

35. The component present in solution in large quantity is known as a solvent. A solvent is a component in a solution that is present in the largest amount. In a NaCl solution (salt-water), the solvent is water. A solution is a homogeneous mixture of two or more substances. The substance that is present in the largest amount is called the solvent.

Hence, the correct option is (A).

36. Throat paints are liquid preparations viscous.

Throat paints: Viscous liquid preparations used for mouth and throat infections. Glycerin is commonly used as a base it adheres to mucous membrane for a long period and it possesses a sweet taste. Nasal drops; solutions of drugs that are instilled into the nose with a dropper.

Hence, the correct option is (A).

37. A separator that has no moving parts is a cyclone separator. Cyclone separators or simply cyclones are separation devices (dry scrubbers) that use the principle of inertia to remove particulate matter from flue gases. Cyclone separators are one of many air pollution control devices known as pre-cleaners since they generally remove larger pieces of particulate matter.

Hence, the correct option is (B).

38. The syrup is aqueous in nature. A syrup is a concentrated or nearly saturated solution of sucrose in water. A simple syrup contains only sucrose and purified water (e.g. Syrup USP). Syrups containing pleasantly flavored substances are known as flavoring syrups (e.g. Cherry Syrup, Acacia Syrup, etc.).

Hence, the correct option is (A).

Q.1 Which is the correct english translation of "Inter cibos"?
A. After meals
B. Before meals
C. During milk
D. Between meals

Q.2 Which is the correct english translation of "Omni nocte"?
A. Day night
B. Night and morning
C. Every night
D. During meals

Q.3 Which type of containers are used for suppositories?
A. Aluminium foils
B. Plastic tubes
C. Vials
D. Ampoules

Q.4 Which type of containers are used for single-dose parenteral?
A. Glass bottles
B. Plastic tubes
C. Vials
D. Ampoules

Q.5 One microliter means __________ liter.
A. 0.001
B. 0.0000001
C. 0.00001
D. 0.001

Q.6 __________ is the condition when a usually large dose is required to produce an effect that has been produced by the normal doses.
A. Idiosyncrasy
B. Tolerance
C. Hypersensitivity
D. Addiction

Q.7 __________ is a branch of medicine which deals with doses of drug.
A. Pharmacology
B. Pharcotherapeutics
C. Posology
D. None of these

Q.8 Mixing olive oil to water is a __________.
A. Therapeutic Incompatiblity
B. Physical Incompatibility
C. Chemical Incompathtibility
D. None of these

Q.9 The combination of drug enhance the therapeutic effect is called ____________.
A. Anatgpmistic effect
B. Cmtraimdicated effect
C. Synergistic effect
D. None of these

Q.10 Given the following are the types of chemical incompatibilities except __________.
A. Alkaloidal salts with an alkaline substance.
B. Soluble salicylates with ferric salts.
C. Prescribing imporoper dose of drug.
D. Incompatibilities causing evolution of gas.

Q.11 One milligram means __________ microgram.
A. 100
B. 10000
C. 10
D. 1000

Q.12 Given the following which are the methods of preparation of effervescent granules?
A. Cold method
B. Wet method
C. Heat method
D. None of these

Q.13 __________ substances absorb the moisture from the atmosphere and turn into liquid form.
A. Hygroscopic
B. Hydrophilic
C. Deliquescent
D. Both (A) and (C)

Q.14 __________ is a power used to clean the teeth with the help of tooth brush.
A. Talcum powder
B. Dusting powder
C. Detergent
D. Dentifrices

Q.15 __________ are unit solid dosage forms of drugs in which the drug is enclosed in a tasteless sheet.
A. Tablet
B. Pills
C. Capsules
D. Cachets

Q.16 __________ is the condition when a patient continues to be under psychic and physical dependence on drug.
A. Antagonism
B. Synergism
C. Addiction
D. None of these

Q.17 __________ is the condition when a patient continues to be under emotional and physiological dependence rather than compulsion.
A. Antagonism
B. Synergism
C. Accumulation
D. Habituation

Q.18 Following are the disadvantages of liquid dosage form except:
A. More chance of microbial contamination
B. Poor stability of medicament
C. Chance of variation in the doses
D. Not suitable of hygroscopic substances

Q.19 Externally used powders for body cavities are called __________.
A. Detergent
B. Dusting powder
C. Talcum powder
D. Insufflations

Q.20 Lipstick renders lips:
A. Swollen
B. Tasty
C. Antiseptic
D. Colored

Q.21 The basic requirement for effervescent granules is __________.
A. Citric acid
B. Tartaric acid
C. Sodium bicarbonate
D. All of these

Q.22 Which drugs are not suitable for dispensing in the form of powders?
A. Hygroscopic drugs
B. Deliquescent drugs
C. Hydrophilic drugs
D. Both (A) and (B)

Q.23 Which instructions are required on the labels of the power for dusting powders?
A. "For internal use only"
B. "For external use only"
C. "Shake well berfore use"
D. None of these

Q.24 ___________ is the technique that enhances the solubility of a poorly drug in water by adding water-miscible solvent.
A. Complexation
B. Chemical modification
C. Cosolvency
D. Hydrotrophy

Q.25 Which preparations are used for throat infections?
A. Throat paints
B. Gargles
C. Douches
D. Both (A) and (B)

Q.26 Generally ______ and _______ are given in the form of drops.
A. Vitamins, steroids
B. Steroids, enzymes
C. Vitamins, antibiotics
D. Antibiotics, steroids

Q.27 Which alcoholic and oily preparation intended for use with friction?
A. Lotions
B. Linctuses
C. Liniments
D. Collodions

Q.28 Given the following are biphasic liquid dosage form except:
A. Liniments
B. Aerosols
C. Douches
D. None of these

Q.29 Given the following are monophasic liquid dosage forms except:
A. Droughts
B. Tinctures
C. Spirits
D. Enemas

Q.30 Given the following are the examples of natural hydrocolloids except:
A. Colloidal silica
B. Bentonite
C. Methylcellulose
D. Gum

Q.31 Given the following are the examples of surfactants excepts:
A. Sodium lauryl sulphate
B. Dioctyl sodium sulphosuccinate
C. Sodium carboxymethyl cellulose
D. Cetyl trimethyl ammonium bromide

Q.32 _______ are high molecular weight substances used to increase the viscosity of aqueous system.
A. Emulsifying agents
B. Surfactant
C. Suspending agents
D. Hydrocolloids

Q.33 Following kinds of flavor are used for developing a salty taste in the preparation except:
A. Butterscotch
B. Apricot

C. Vanilla
D. Berry

Q.34 Given the following which are used to increase the viscosity of liquid preparation?
A. Polyvinylpyrrolidone
B. Alginates
C. Benzalkonium chloride
D. Both (A) and (B)

Q.35 Given the following which preservative are suitable for aqueous preparation?
A. Parahydroxy benzoic acid esters
B. Benzoic acid
C. Sorbic acid
D. All of these

Q.36 Given the following are the ideal properties for suspension:
A. It should be pharmaceutically elegant.
B. It should be physically and chemically inter.
C. The sediment must be redispersed upon gentle shaking of the container.
D. All of these

Q.37 If you want to give your pharmaceutical preparation brown colour following flavours are used:
A. Chocolate
B. Honey
C. Pistachio
D. Caramel

Q.38 Which vehicle is very good for throat paints?
A. Propylene glycol
B. Sorbitol
C. Glycerol
D. Poly ethylene glycol

// Smart Answer Sheet //

Correct Percentage of students who answered correctly.　　**Skipped** Percentage of students who skipped.

Q.	Ans.	Correct / Skipped	Q.	Ans.	Correct / Skipped	Q.	Ans.	Correct / Skipped	Q.	Ans.	Correct / Skipped	Q.	Ans.	Correct / Skipped	Q.	Ans.	Correct / Skipped
1	D	40.03 % / 55.13 %	8	B	55.22 % / 37.4 %	15	D	59.66 % / 30.38 %	22	D	57.62 % / 33.12 %	29	D	57.71 % / 34.19 %	36	D	43.65 % / 47.17 %
2	C	42.36 % / 56.77 %	9	C	55.03 % / 42.03 %	16	C	50.97 % / 45.4 %	23	B	51.64 % / 44.47 %	30	C	13.96 % / 82.61 %	37	C	46.8 % / 34.85 %
3	B	78.74 % / 14.41 %	10	C	64.31 % / 31.71 %	17	D	40.06 % / 33.87 %	24	C	62.35 % / 32.84 %	31	C	25.56 % / 67.23 %	38	C	40.56 % / 58.21 %
4	D	47.94 % / 42.41 %	11	D	89.56 % / 10.36 %	18	D	50.38 % / 30.3 %	25	D	80.88 % / 11.9 %	32	D	55.79 % / 43.67 %			
5	C	53.77 % / 33.75 %	12	B	54.73 % / 39.41 %	19	D	44.35 % / 54.86 %	26	C	56.48 % / 39.08 %	33	D	45.27 % / 49.69 %			
6	B	54.0 % / 32.86 %	13	D	51.6 % / 37.1 %	20	D	51.72 % / 47.6 %	27	B	68.73 % / 30.77 %	34	D	53.82 % / 40.2 %			
7	C	52.08 % / 46.81 %	14	D	43.83 % / 30.85 %	21	D	53.91 % / 44.27 %	28	D	68.97 % / 30.49 %	35	D	17.47 % / 67.79 %			

//Hints and Solutions//

1. The correct english translation of "Inter cibos" is between meals. Inter cibos is a Latin word. A drug-food interaction occurs when your food and medicine interfere with one another. Interactions can happen with both prescription and over-the-counter medicines. These include antacids, vitamins, and iron pills. Not all medicines are affected by food.

Term or Phrase	Abbreviation	Meaning
Anti cibos	a.c.	Before meals,
Ante cibum	-	Before food
Post cibos.	p.c.	After meals,
Post cibum	i.c.	After food
Inter cibos	-	Between meals,
Inter cibum	-	Between food

Hence, the correct option is (D).

2. The correct english translation of "Omni nocte" is every night. Omni nocte is a Latin term or a phrase. Drugs can also change the way the body uses food. Food can prevent medicine from working the way it should and can cause medicinal side effects to become better or worse and/or cause new side effects to occur.

Term or Phrase	Abbreviation	Meaning
Prima luce	prim. luc	Early in the morning
Primo mane	prim. m	Early in the morning
Mane	m.	In the morning
Omni mane	o.m.	Every morning
Jentaculum	jentac	Breakfast
Meridie	-	Noon
Prandium	prand	Dinner
Vespere	vesp.	In the evening
Nocte	n.	At night
Inter noctem	inter. noct	During the night
Omni nocte	o.n.	Every night
Hora decubitus	h.d.	At bedtime
Hora somni	h.s.	At bed time
Nocte et mane	n. et m.	Night and morning
Nocte maneque	n.m.	Night and morning
Hac nocte	hac noct.	To night
Cras vespere	cras vesp.	Tomorrow evening
Mane sequenti	m.seq.	The following morning

Hence, the correct option is (C).

3. Plastic tubes containers are used for suppositories. Suppositories are alternatively prepared and stored in disposable plastic shell containers that are often connected in strip form for individual dispensing by a patient. These plastic shells are commonly made of relatively soft plastic such as polystyrene. A container is a device that holds the drug and may be in direct contact with the product.

Hence, the correct option is (B).

4. Ampoules containers are used for single-dose parenteral. An ampoule (also ampul and ampule) is a small sealed vial that is used to contain and preserve a sample, usually a solid or liquid.

Ampoules are usually made of glass. Modern ampoules are most commonly used to contain pharmaceuticals and chemicals that must be protected from air and contaminants. They are hermetically sealed by melting the thin top with an open flame and usually opened by snapping off the neck. The space above the chemical may be filled with an inert gas before sealing. The walls of glass ampoules are usually sufficiently strong to be brought into a glovebox without any difficulty.

Hence, the correct option is (D).

5. One microliter means 0.00001 liters. A microliter is a unit of capacity equal to one-millionth of a liter. A measure of volume for a liquid, using the metric system. Although the liter is not an SI unit, it is accepted by the CGPM (the standards body that defines the SI) for use with the SI.

Hence, the correct option is (C).

6. Tolerance is the condition when a usually large dose is required to produce an effect that has been produced by the normal doses. Drug tolerance is indicative of drug use but is not necessarily associated with drug dependence or addiction. The process of tolerance development is reversible (e.g., through a drug holiday) and can involve both physiological factors and psychological factors. Drug tolerance should not be confused with drug tolerability, which refers to the degree to which overt adverse effects of a drug can be tolerated by a patient.

Hence, the correct option is (B).

7. Posology is a branch of medicine which deals with doses of drugs. So posology is a branch of medical science which deals with the dose & quantity of drugs that can be administered to a patient to get the desired action. In this, there are many factors that influence the doses. The pharmaceutics of many drugs changes with age.

Hence, the correct option is (C).

8. Mixing olive oil to water is a physical incompatibility. Physical Incompatibility is:

- A visible physical change takes place.
- An unacceptable, non-uniform, unpalatable product is formed.
- Difficult to measure an accurate dose.
- Result of insolubility & immiscibility, precipitation, liquefaction. Adsorption and complexation of solid materials.
- Can be corrected by applying pharmaceutical skills.

Hence, the correct option is (B).

9. The combination of drugs that enhance the therapeutic effect is called a synergistic effect.

Synergism:-

- Aspirin & Paracetamol increases analgesic activity.
- Penicillin & streptomycin increase the antibacterial activity.

Rx:

- Amphetamine Sulphate 20 mg.
- Ephedrine Sulphate 100 mg.
- Simple syrup up to 100 ml.

Make a mixture.

Overcome:-

1. Both are sympathomimetic drugs that cause additive effects. So of individual drugs dose should be reduced to avoid therapeutic incompatibility.

2. Otherwise, the prescription should be referred back to the

3. prescriber for necessary correction.

Hence, the correct option is (C).

10. Alkaloidal salts with an alkaline substance, soluble salicylates with ferric salts and incompatibilities cause the evolution of gas except for prescribing an imporoper dose of the drug.

Chemical Incompatibilities:

1. Chemical Incompatibilities are usually a result of chemical interaction taking place among the ingredients of a prescription.

2. Such interactions may take place immediately upon compounding when these are termed as immediate incompatibilities and are evident as effervescence, precipitation or colour change.

3. More often the interaction is not evident immediately on compounding but take place over a period of time. Such interactions are termed delayed incompatibilities.

Hence, the correct option is (C).

11. One milligram means 1000 micrograms. On the other hand, the milligram is the long form of the abbreviation "mg." One mg is equal to 1000 micrograms. This means that a milligram is 1000 times bigger than a microgram. Moreover, a milligram is a thousandth of gram.

Hence, the correct option is (D).

12. The wet method is the method of preparation of effervescent granules. Effervescent granules are prepared by the wet method, the fusion method or dry method, hot-melt extrusion method, in which the fusion method is the most important method for the formulation of effervescent granules. Effervescent ibuprofen granules were formulated by the wet granulation method. Croscarmellose sodium, powder of banana and other ingredients were used in the formulation of effervescent granules.

Hence, the correct option is (B).

13. Hygroscopic and Deliquescent substances absorb the moisture from the atmosphere and turn into liquid form. Most deliquescent substances are salts. Examples include sodium hydroxide, potassium hydroxide, ammonium chloride, gold(III) chloride, sodium nitrate, and calcium chloride. Deliquescent substances are solids that absorb moisture from the atmosphere until they dissolve in the absorbed water and form solutions.

Hence, the correct option is (D).

14. Dentifrices is a power used to clean the teeth with the help of a toothbrush. Dentifrices, including toothpowder and toothpaste, are agents used along with a toothbrush to clean and polish natural teeth. They are supplied in paste, powder, gel, or liquid form. Dentifrices are designed to be used with toothbrushes to remove dental stains, to introduce a fresh, pleasant and clean feeling, and to deliver active agents into the oral cavity.

Hence, the correct option is (D).

15. Cachets are unit solid dosage forms of drugs in which the drug is enclosed in a tasteless sheet. A kind of wafer capsule formerly used by pharmacists for presenting an unpleasant-tasting drug. Cachets are oral preparation consisting of dry powder enclosed in a shell of rice paper (wafer capsule) formerly used by pharmacists for presenting unpalatable drugs.

Hence, the correct option is (D).

16. Addiction is the condition when a patient continues to be under psychic and physical dependence on drugs. Drug addiction, also called substance use disorder, is a disease that affects a person's brain and behavior and leads to an inability to control the use of a legal or illegal drug or medication. Substances such as alcohol, marijuana and nicotine also are considered drugs.

Hence, the correct option is (C).

17. Habituation is the condition when a patient continues to be under emotional and physiological dependence rather than compulsion. Habituation is defined as a condition resulting from the repeated consumption of a drug because of overpowering desire, the development of psychic dependence, with detrimental effects to the individual. "Habituation" is the term used to refer to psychological dependence on a drug.

Hence, the correct option is (D).

18. Disadvantages of liquid dosage forms are:

1. Liquid dosage forms are usually more susceptible to chemical degradation when compared to solid dosage forms.

2. They are bulky and therefore inconvenient to transport and store.

3. Accidental breakage of the container results in loss of whole dosage form.

4. The shelf-life of a liquid dosage form is often much shorter than that of the corresponding solid preparation due to low stability.

5. The solution often provides suitable media for microbial growth and may, therefore, require the incorporation of a preservative.

6. Liquid dosage forms e.g., vaccines may require special storage conditions

7. The taste of a drug that is usually unpleasant is always more prominent when in solution than in a solid form.

8. There is a higher chance of dose variability since the delivery of the dose depends upon the patient measuring the proper volume. This can be a significant issue for vision-impaired patients, patients with

arthritis, or patients unable to read the numbers on an oral dosing syringe or medicine cup.

Not suitable for hygroscopic substances is not a disadvantage of liquid dosage form.

Hence, the correct option is (D).

19. Externally used powders for body cavities are called insufflations. Insufflations are extremely fine powders to be introduced into body cavities. To administer an insufflation, the powder is placed in the insufflator, and when the bulb is squeezed, the air current carries the fine particles through the nozzle to the region for which the medication is intended.

Hence, the correct option is (D).

20. Lipstick renders lips colored. The earliest known use of colored cosmetics was in Mesopotamia 5000 years ago, where precious and semi-precious gems were ground and applied to lips and eyelids. In Ancient Egypt, much of the population used cosmetics both for beauty enhancement but also to protect themselves from the sun and desert wind. Lipsticks became part of their daily routine, except for the poor who could not afford cosmetics.

Hence, the correct option is (D).

21. The basic requirement for effervescent granules is citric acid, tartaric acid and sodium bicarbonate.

Effervescent granules: Effervescent granules are the specially prepared solid dosage form of medicament, meant for internal use. They contain a medicament mixed with citric acid, tartaric acid and sodium bicarbonate. Sometimes saccharin or sucrose may be added as a sweetening agent.

Hence, the correct option is (D).

22. Hygroscopic drugs and deliquescent drugs are not suitable for dispensing in the form of powders. Dispensing of powders involving Special Problems. A number of problems arise while dispensing a powder containing volatile substances, hygroscopic and deliquescent powders, eutectic mixtures, efflorescent powders, liquids, explosive substances and potent drugs. So special considerations are done while dispensing such powders.

Hygroscopic and deliquescent powders: The powders which absorb moisture from the atmosphere are called hygroscopic powders. But certain powders absorb moisture to such a great extent that they go into solution and are called deliquescent powders. Examples of such substances include ammonium chloride, iron and ammonium citrate, pepsin, phenobarbitone, sodium bromide, sodium iodide, potassium citrate, zinc chloride, etc.

Hence, the correct option is (D).

23. "For external use only" instruction is required on the labels of the power for dusting powders. They are meant for external application to the skin generally applied in a very fine state of subdivision to avoid local irritation.

Dusting Powders: These are used for external application on the skin & generally applied in a very fine state to avoid local irritation. - Therefore, dusting powder should be passed through sieve no. 80 or 120 to enhance their effectiveness.

Hence, the correct option is (B).

24. Cosolvency is the technique that enhances the solubility of a poorly drug in water by adding water-miscible solvent. A co-solvent system is one in which a water-miscible or partially miscible organic solvent is mixed with water to form a modified aqueous solution. And the phenomenon is called cosolvency. Co-solvents have some degree of hydrogen bond donating and or hydrogen bond accepting ability as well as small hydrocarbon regions.

Hence, the correct option is (C).

25. Throat paints and gargles preparations are used for throat infections. Throat paints are solution or dispersion of one or more active agents. Throat paints are viscous liquid preparations used for mouth and throat infections. Glycerin is commonly used as a base because being viscous it adheres to mucous membrane for a long period. Glycerin prolongs the action of medicaments. If you gargle, you wash your mouth and throat by filling your mouth with a liquid, tipping your head back and using your throat to blow bubbles through the liquid, and finally spitting it out.

Hence, the correct option is (D).

26. Generally, vitamins and antibiotics are given in the form of drops. This combination medication is used to temporarily relieve symptoms caused by the common cold, flu, allergies, or other breathing illnesses (such as sinusitis, bronchitis). Drops may be swallowed directly, added to a small amount of liquid, or mixed with a small amount of food such as applesauce.

Hence, the correct option is (C).

27. Linctuses alcoholic and oily preparation intended for use with friction. f- Linctuses are viscous, liquid oral preparations that are usually prescribed for the relief of cough. It contains a high proportion of syrup and glycerol which have a demulcent effect on the membranes of the throat. The dose volume is small (5ml) and, to prolong the demulcent action, they should be taken undiluted.

Hence, the correct option is (B).

28. Liniments and douches are biphasic liquid dosage forms except for aerosols.

Types Of Biphasic Liquid:

There are two types of biphasic liquid:

- **SUSPENSION:** Suspensions are categorized into applications, Enemas, Lotion, Inhalation, Aerosols, Eye Drop.
- **EMULSION:** Emulsions are categorized into an application, Liniment, Lotion.

Hence, the correct option is (D).

29. Droughts, tinctures and spirits are monophasic liquid dosage forms except for enemas.

Monophasic Liquids:

1. As the word, ' MONOPHASIC' suggests that system contains only one phase no matter the components might be a minimum of 2 or more than.

2. One phase is the solvent and the other one is the solute. Solute might be one or more than one.

3. This is the simplest form of presenting medication for rapid absorption of the drug.

4. They are dispensed for various purposes.

Hence, the correct option is (D).

30. Colloidal silica, bentonite and gum are examples of natural hydrocolloids except for methylcellulose. Natural hydrocolloids are derived from plant (pectin, carrageenan, cellulose gum, locust bean gum), animal (gelatin), or microbial (xanthan gum, gellan gum) sources. Some chemical manufacturers have combined science with nature to generate semisynthetic hydrocolloids. Methylcellulose is not a naturally occurring element. This chemical compound is derived from treating vegetable cellulose with a chemical agent to create a tasteless, colorless powder. This powder is commonly used as a binding or thickening agent in many foods like ice creams, bread, cakes and chocolate.

Hence, the correct option is (C).

31. Sodium lauryl sulphate, dioctyl sodium sulphosuccinate and cetyl trimethyl ammonium bromide are examples of surfactants except for sodium carboxymethyl cellulose. Sodium stearate is a good example of a surfactant. It is the most common surfactant in soap. Another common surfactant is 4-(5-dodecyl)benzene sulphonate. Other examples include docusate (dioctyl sodium sulfosuccinate), alkyl ether phosphates, benzalkonium chloride (BAC), and perfluoro octanesulphonate (PFOS).

Hence, the correct option is (C).

32. Hydrocolloids are high molecular weight substances used to increase the viscosity of an aqueous system. Hydrocolloids are polysaccharides of high molecular weight extracted from plants and seaweeds or produced by microbial synthesis. They are typically used as rheology control and suspending agents to provide many attractive features to liquid oral pharmaceutical formulations.

Hence, the correct option is (D).

33. Butterscotch, apricot and vanilla kinds of flavor are used for developing a salty taste in the preparation except for berry. Products and their preferred flavors:

1. Cough syrup- anise, raspberry, mint, licorice.

2. Liver preparation- Apricot, raspberry, Strawberry.

3. Protien hydrolysate- Honey, butterscotch, pineapple, banana.

4. Antacid- Mint menthol, ginger.

5. VitaminA- Caramel, butterscotch, orange.

6. Laxative- Vanilla, strawberry.

7. Papain pepsin- cardamom, pineapple.

Hence, the correct option is (D).

34. Polyvinylpyrrolidone and alginates are used to increase the viscosity of liquid preparation. Polyvinylpyrrolidone, also known

as povidone or PVP, is used in pharmaceutics as a synthetic polymer vehicle for dispersing and suspending drugs. Povidone formulations are widely used in pharmaceutics due to their ability to dissolve in both water and oil solvents. Sodium Alginate (E401) is extracted from brown seaweed. It is also used as a stabilizer, thickener and emulsifier for food products such as ice cream, yogurt, cream, and cheese. It is a cold gelling agent that needs no heat to gel.

Hence, the correct option is (D).

35. Parahydroxy benzoic acid esters, benzoic acid and sorbic acid preservatives are suitable for aqueous preparation. Parabens are a class of widely used preservatives in cosmetic and pharmaceutica products. Chemically, they are a series of parahydroxybenzoates or esters of parahydroxybenzoic acid (also known as 4-hydroxybenzoic acid). Parabens are effective preservatives in many types of formulas. These compounds, and their salts, are used primarily for their bactericidal and fungicidal properties. They are found in shampoos, commercial moisturizers, shaving gels, personal lubricants, topical/parenteral pharmaceuticals, suntan products, makeup, and toothpaste. They are also used as food preservatives.

Hence, the correct option is (D).

36. The ideal properties for suspension are:

1. It should be pharmaceutically elegant.

2. It should be physically and chemically inter.

3. The sediment must be redispersed upon gentle shaking of the container.

4. It should settle slowly and should be readily re-dispersed on gentle shaking of the container.

5. The particle size of the suspension remains fairly constant throughout its long period of undisturbed standing.

6. The suspension should pour readily and evenly from its container.

7. It should be free from large particles which spoil its appearance, give a gritty taste to oral preparations and also causes irritation to sensitive tissues when applied externally.

Hence, the correct option is (D).

37. If you want to give your pharmaceutical preparation brown colour pistachio flavours are used. The pistachio (Pistacia vera), a member of the cashew family, is a small tree originating from Central Asia and the Middle East. The tree produces seeds that are widely consumed as food. Pistacia vera often is confused with other species in the genus Pistacia that are also known as pistachio. These other species can be distinguished by their geographic distributions (in the wild) and their seeds which are much smaller and have a softshell.

Hence, the correct option is (C).

38. Glycerin is used as a vehicle in preparation to get a prolonged contact of medicament to the infected surfaces because of its high viscosity. Peppermint oil is used to flavor the throat paint and to keep it in sol little alcohol is added. Glycerol ($C_3H_8O_3$), also known as glycerin and glycerine, is an odorless, colorless, oily, viscous liquid that has a sweet taste.

Hence, the correct option is (C).

Q.1 Given the following antioxidants are used for the aqueous system:

A. Sodium thiosulphate

B. Sodium disulfite

C. Butylated hydroxyanisole (BHA)

D. All of these

Q.2 Given the following antioxidants are used for oily system except:

A. Ascorbyl palmitate   **B.** Propyl gallate

C. Ascorbic acid   **D.** Lecithin

Q.3 Given the following are the synthetic hydrocolloids:

A. Carbopols

B. Polyol

C. Hydroxpropyl cellulose

D. Both (A) and (B)

Q.4 Given the following are the anionic emulsifying agent except:

A. Sorbitan monooleate

B. Sodium oleate

C. Triethanolamine oleate

D. Both (A) and (B)

Q.5 __________ are the substance which reduce the interfacial tension between the two immiscible liquids.

A. Suspending agents   **B.** Solubilizing agent

C. Emulsifying agent   **D.** None of these

Q.6 Which is the labeling requirement for suspension?

A. For external use only

B. Shake well before use

C. For internal use only

D. None of these

Q.7 Which parameters are used for evaluation of suspension?

A. Determination of rate of sedimentation

B. Determination of viscosity

C. Determination of Zeta potential

D. All of these

Q.8 In flocculated suspension the rate of sedimentation:

A. Slow   **B.** High

C. Absent   **D.** Intermediate

Q.9 The rate of sedimentation is expressed by:

A. Newton law   **B.** Dalton law

C. Raults law   **D.** Stock's law

Q.10 Preparation used for the eye are called __________.

A. Parenteral Preparation

B. Ophthalmic Preparation

C. Topical Preparation

D. None of these

Q.11 Hydrous wool fat is also known as ______.

A. Lignin   **B.** Lipoplysaccharide

C. Lanolin   **D.** None of these

Q.12 HLM value of Tween 80 is:

A. 20   **B.** 18   **C.** 8   **D.** 15

Q.13 The synonym of aqueous iodine solutions is:

A. Benedict solution   **B.** Lysol solution

C. Lugol solution   **D.** None of these

Q.14 Saccharine is __________ times sweeter than sucrose.

A. 200   **B.** 250   **C.** 450   **D.** 300

Q.15 HLB value range for detergent is:

A. 1-3   **B.** 3-6   **C.** 15-20   **D.** 13-15

Q.16 Which part of the prescription is represented by symbol Rx?

A. Date   **B.** Subscription

C. Inscription   **D.** Superscription

Q.17 Given the following are the parts of prescription except:

A. Date   **B.** Subscription

C. Inscription   **D.** Compounding

Q.18 ______ are commonly used preservative for ophthalmic products.

A. Suspending agent   **B.** Thickening agent

C. Surfactant   **D.** Emulsifying agent

Q.19 __________ are commonly used preservatives for ophthalmic products.

A. Benzyl konium chloride

B. Benzoyl chloride

C. Benzoic acid

D. Mercurial

Q.20 The membrane filter having pore size __________ is the best filtration medium to remove any foreign particles.

A. 0.6 μm   **B.** 0.8 μm   **C.** 0.3 μm   **D.** 0.2 μm

Q.21 An eye can tolerate ______ to ______ % w/v solution of sodium chloride.

A. 0.6, 2.8   **B.** 0.6, 2.5

C. 0.6, 2.0   **D.** None of these

Q.22 Antiperspirants are used to reduce:

A. Pain   **B.** Fever

C. Body odor   **D.** Tension

Q.23 BHT stands for:

A. Butylated hydrated trioxide

B. Butylated hydroxytoluene

C. Butylene hydroxide toluene

D. Butylated hydroxyl terpene

Q.24 What is used as opacifying agent in face powder?

A. Zinc oxide   **B.** Magnesium oxide
C. Aluminum oxide   **D.** Titanium dioxide

Q.25 Given the following are the liquid dosage forms except:

A. Eye drops   **B.** Nasal drops
C. Pills   **D.** Ear drops

Q.26 Which part of the prescription contains directions of the prescerber of the pharmacist?

A. Date   **B.** Subscription
C. Inscription   **D.** Supercription

Q.27 Which part of the prescription contains names and quantities of the prescription?

A. Date   **B.** Subscription
C. Inscription   **D.** Superscription

Q.28 Given the followings are emulsifying agent except:

A. Lanolin   **B.** Tragacanth
C. Polysorbate60   **D.** Sodium oleate

Q.29 HLB value of sodium lauryl sulphate is:

A. 20   **B.** 30   **C.** 40   **D.** 23

Q.30 Which methods are used for the preparation of emulsion on small scale?

A. Dry gum method   **B.** Wet gum method
C. Bottle method   **D.** All of these

Q.31 Given the followings are absorption bases except:

A. Wool fat   **B.** Hydrous wool fat
C. Wool alcohol   **D.** Petrolatum

Q.32 Poultices are also known as:

A. Catalysis   **B.** Counter irirtant
C. Cataplasm   **D.** Catalog

Q.33 "The quantity of the drug which displace one part of the base" is called:

A. Saponification value
B. Acid value
C. Displacement value
D. Rencidity

Q.34 O/W type of emulsion are preferred for:

A. External use   **B.** Internal use
C. Topical use   **D.** None of these

Q.35 Ointments are prepared by following methods except:

A. Trituration method
B. Fusion method
C. Chemical reaction method
D. Bottle method

Q.36 In which test ampoules are dipped in 1% solution of methylene blue in vaccum chamber:

A. Pyrogen test   **B.** Leakage test
C. Clarity test   **D.** Sterility test

Q.37 Given the following test for identification of emulsion except:

A. Dilution test   **B.** Conductivity test
C. Fluorescence test   **D.** Clarity test

Q.38 Given the following emulsifying agents are obtained from animal sources except:

A. Wool fat   **B.** Gelatin   **C.** Pectin   **D.** Egg yolk

// Smart Answer Sheet //

Correct — Percentage of students who answered correctly.   **Skipped** — Percentage of students who skipped.

Q.	Ans.	Correct / Skipped	Q.	Ans.	Correct / Skipped	Q.	Ans.	Correct / Skipped	Q.	Ans.	Correct / Skipped	Q.	Ans.	Correct / Skipped	Q.	Ans.	Correct / Skipped
1	D	44.73 % / 38.49 %	8	B	40.07 % / 47.02 %	15	D	27.19 % / 72.58 %	22	C	54.67 % / 34.11 %	29	C	48.05 % / 48.05 %	36	B	67.97 % / 31.15 %
2	C	53.32 % / 33.01 %	9	D	45.82 % / 43.19 %	16	D	43.19 % / 41.25 %	23	B	85.46 % / 10.77 %	30	D	49.88 % / 43.56 %	37	D	40.59 % / 50.56 %
3	D	46.22 % / 38.42 %	10	B	40.33 % / 37.97 %	17	D	32.65 % / 67.09 %	24	D	40.99 % / 46.74 %	31	D	56.72 % / 30.19 %	38	C	69.3 % / 30.6 %
4	A	83.59 % / 13.36 %	11	C	66.03 % / 30.32 %	18	B	41.53 % / 36.14 %	25	C	59.0 % / 40.67 %	32	C	50.29 % / 44.38 %			
5	B	60.81 % / 35.4 %	12	D	25.82 % / 71.99 %	19	D	56.75 % / 38.57 %	26	B	56.92 % / 30.73 %	33	C	47.04 % / 45.59 %			
6	B	66.74 % / 30.95 %	13	C	50.01 % / 41.82 %	20	B	62.11 % / 33.98 %	27	C	50.73 % / 42.82 %	34	B	62.69 % / 31.6 %			
7	D	47.83 % / 32.41 %	14	C	67.89 % / 30.18 %	21	C	40.78 % / 51.11 %	28	A	32.3 % / 67.12 %	35	D	26.09 % / 68.08 %			

//Hints and Solutions//

1. Sodium thiosulphate, sodium bisulfite and butylated hydroxyanisole (BHA) antioxidants are used for the aqueous system. Sodium bisulfite (SB) is an inorganic compound commonly used as an antioxidant in pharmaceutical formulations. The addition of sulfur to sodium sulfite produces sodium thiosulfate, a salt that contains an S–S bond. Its antioxidant properties are due to the presence of a reduced sulfur atom, but it also forms strong complexes with iron, copper, and other metal ions. Butylated hydroxyanisole (BHA) is an antioxidant consisting of a mixture of two isomeric organic compounds, 2-tert-butyl-4-hydroxyanisole and 3-tert-butyl-4-hydroxyanisole.

Hence, the correct option is (D).

2. Ascorbyl palmitate, propyl gallate and lecithin antioxidants are used for oily systems except for ascorbic acid. Ascorbyl palmitate has milder effects on the skin than ascorbic acid. However, it is still beneficial for aiding in collagen production, mitigating hyperpigmentation, and improving skin texture. Ascorbyl palmitate ($C_{22}H_{38}O_7$) is a fat-soluble form of vitamin C (antioxidant) used in some pharmaceutical products, such as suppositories.

Hence, the correct option is (C).

3. Carbopols and polyols are synthetic hydrocolloids. Common synthetic hydrocolloids are acrylic acid polymers, also known as carbomers. Natural hydrocolloids are derived from plant (pectin, carrageenan, cellulose gum, locust bean gum), animal (gelatin), or microbial (xanthan gum, gellan gum) sources. Nowadays the main indication for polyols as pharmaceutical active is the reduction of brain swelling and acute kidney failure. Here, polyols act as osmotic diuretics and remove excess water from the body.

Hence, the correct option is (D).

4. Sodium oleate and triethanolamine oleate are the anionic emulsifying agent except for sorbitan monooleate. Their appearance may vary from an amber-colored oily, viscous liquid, to a light cream color, to tan beads or flakes or a hard, waxy solid with a slight odor They are also used as surfactants or emulsifying agents in the preparation of emulsions, creams, and ointments for pharmaceutical and cosmetic use.

Hence, the correct option is (A).

5. Solubilizing agents are substances that reduce the interfacial tension between the two immiscible liquids. A solubilizing agent acts as a surfactant and increases the solubility of one agent in another. A substance that would not normally dissolve in a particular solution is able to dissolve with the use of a solubilizing agent. The polyoxyethylene-based surfactants were found to be more suitable as solubilizing agents than the sugar surfactants due to better solubilization capacities combined with lower hemolytic activities.

Hence, the correct option is (B).

6. Shake well before use is the labeling requirement for suspension. When the medicine is at rest for a long period of time then the heavier particles settle at the bottom. On shaking the bottle, the heavier particles get properly dispersed into the solution which will add to the medicinal properties of the medicine. The important thing to remember is that you have to shake a suspension before giving each dose so that the medicine particles are evenly distributed throughout the liquid. Elixirs are typically more concentrated, so remember to always read the dosage instructions on the bottle before giving your child any medication.

Hence, the correct option is (B).

7. The prepared suspension was evaluated by studying different parameters like pH, sedimentation volume, re-dispersibility, Flow rate (F), viscosity, degree of flocculation, the effect of temperature, etc. the zeta potential of the formulated suspensions was determined using a Zeta Plus. (Brook haven Instruments Corporation, USA). Approximately 1mL of suspension was transferred into a plastic cuvette using a pipette and diluted with distilled water. The Brookhaven zeta potential software was used for the measurement. Parameters set to a temperature of 250°C and refractive index(1.33). The zeta potential of the formulations was determined on days 0,7, 14,21and day 28 post formulation.

Hence, the correct option is (D).

8. In flocculated suspension the rate of sedimentation is high. Because the particles are closer together in a concentrated suspension, flocculation is more marked in an ionized solvent, and the effective size of the small particles is increased. The ratio of the sedimentation volume in case of flocculated suspension to the sedimentation volume in case of deflocculated suspension is called. For a flocculated suspension, the degree of flocculation is observed to be one. The sedimentation volume is also 1.

Hence, the correct option is (B).

9. The rate of sedimentation is expressed by Stock's law. Stcoks' Law is a formula for determining the rate of sedimentation. It states that a particle moving through viscous liquid attains a constant velocity or sedimentation rate. Grain starts to move on a planned sand bed when the combined lift and drag forces produced by the fluid exceed the gravitational and cohesive forces of the sediment grain. The cohesive forces are applied by finer-grained sediments only.

Hence, the correct option is (D).

10. The preparation used for the eye is called ophthalmic preparation. Ophthalmic preparations are specialized dosage forms designed to be instilled onto the external surface of the eye (topical), administered inside the eye (intraocular) or adjacent to it (periocular, e.g., juxtascleral or subtenon), or used in conjunction with an ophthalmic device. Ophthalmic anti-infectives are anti-infectives contained in a product formulated especially to be instilled or applied in the eye or eyes. Ophthalmic anti-infectives include eyedrops, gels or ointments.

Hence, the correct option is (B).

11. Hydrous wool fat is also known as lanolin. Lanolin (hydrous wool fat containing 25 to 30% of water) contains primarily esters of C18-C26 alcohols and fatty acids, sterols (cholesterol) and terpene alcohols. It is chemically wax rather than fat. Lanolin has already been included in Annex II of Council Regulation (EEC) No

2377/90. Lanolin is also known as wool fat, wool grease or wool wax. It is secreted by the sebaceous glands of wool-bearing animals. It is obtained by the sheep which has been raised specifically for wool.

Hence, the correct option is (C).

12. HLM value of Tween 80 is 15. In early drug development, drug-drug interaction (DDI) risk is routinely assessed using human liver microsomes (HLM). Non-specific binding of drugs to HLM can affect the determination of accurate enzyme parameters (Km, Ki, KI). A novel in vitro model consisting of HLM bound to magnetizable beads (HLM-beads). The HLM-beads enable rapid separation of HLM from incubation media by applying a magnetic field. Here, HLM-beads were further characterized and evaluated as a tool to assess the HLM non-specific binding of small molecules.

Hence, the correct option is (D).

13. The synonym of aqueous iodine solutions is the lugol solution. Lugol's iodine, also known as aqueous iodine and strong iodine solution, is a solution of potassium iodide with iodine in water. It is a medication and disinfectant used for a number of purposes. A solution composed of iodine and potassium iodide, which can be used as a reagent and antiseptic, with potential use in cancer diagnosis. The iodine in Lugol's solution selectively binds to alpha-1,4 glucans found in polysaccharides, such as glycogen.

Hence, the correct option is (C).

14. Saccharine is 450 times sweeter than sucrose. Saccharin is approved for use in food as a non-nutritive sweetener. Saccharin is about 300–500 times as sweet as sucrose, depending upon its concentration and the type of food medium in which it is used. Compared with sucrose, it has a slow onset of sweetness that increases to a maximum and then persists.

Hence, the correct option is (C).

15. HLB value range for detergent is 13-15. Oils used in the formulation of emulsions require a certain HLB value to be formulated as W/O emulsion or O/W emulsion. For the same oil, the required HLB value for the O/W emulsion is higher than the required HLB value for the W/O emulsion. The calculated HLB values from both methods can be used to predict the surfactant properties of a surfactant molecule, where a value from 1 to 3 indicates an antifoaming agent; a value from 3 to 6 indicates a W/O emulsifier; a value from 7 to 9 indicates a wetting agent; a value from 8 to 12 indicates an O/W emulsifier; a value from 13 to 16 is typical of detergents; a value of 15–20 indicates a hydrotrope.

Hence, the correct option is (D).

16. Superscription is represented by the symbol Rx. The symbol "Rx" is usually said to stand for the Latin word "recipe" meaning "to take." It is customarily part of the superscription (heading) of a prescription. The superscription is typically found on the outer-facing address leaf and was, therefore, one of the most 'public' parts of a letter, especially during transit between writer and addressee. The superscription could ostensibly be read by anyone along the way before it even reached its recipient.

Hence, the correct option is (D).

17. Subscription, date and inscription are the parts of prescription except for compounding. Predating modern legal definitions of a prescription, a prescription traditionally is composed of four parts: a superscription, inscription, subscription, and signature. Each prescription is dated and some jurisdictions may place a time limit on the prescription. Drug compounding is often regarded as the process of combining, mixing, or altering ingredients to create a medication tailored to the needs of an individual patient. Compounding includes the combining of two or more drugs. Compounded drugs are not FDA-approved.

Hence, the correct option is (D).

18. Thickening agents have commonly used preservatives for ophthalmic products. Dextran is a polysaccharide obtained by fermenting sucrose and is used as a thickening agent and a stabilizer for eye drops. In the preparation of ophthalmic solutions, a suitable grade of methylcellulose or other thickening agent is frequently added to increase the viscosity and thereby aid in maintaining the drug in contact with the tissues to enhance therapeutic effectiveness.

Hence, the correct option is (B).

19. Mercurials have commonly used preservatives for ophthalmic products. Mercurial compounds are incompatible with aluminium. They are strongly absorbed by rubber. They loss potency in polythene containers.

Organic Mercurials:

When Benzalkonium chloride could not be used in a particular formulation, one of the following organic mercurial's is used:

1. Phenyl mercuric nitrate: 0.002-0.004%.
2. Phenyl mercuric acetate: 0.005-0.02%.
3. Thimerosal: 0.01-0.02%.

Alcohol Substitutes:

- Chlorobutanol(0.5%).
- Effective only at pH 5-6.
- Phenyl ethanol (0.5%).
- Methyl & Propyl Paraben: They are used in combination, with methyl paraben (0.03-0.1%) and propyl paraben (0.01-0.02%).

Hence, the correct option is (D).

20. The membrane filter has a pore size of 0.8 μm is the best filtration medium to remove any foreign particles. MCE membranes are manufactured to comply with the ASTM and the Standard Methods for the Examination of Water and Wastewater. MCE 0.80 μm filters meet NIOSH requirements for air sampling applications. Membrane filter (pore size, 0.22-0.45 micro m; thickness, 150 micro m) passing-through activity of Pseudomonas aeruginosa and other bacterial species with indigenous infiltration ability.

Hence, the correct option is (B).

21. An eye can tolerate 0.6 to 2.0 % w/v solution of sodium chloride. Products with all these characteristics are supposed to be ideal ophthalmic products:

1. They must be sterile to prevent serious eye infections.

2. They should be free from foreign particulate matter since they cause irritation and discomfort to the eye.

3. **They should be iso-osmotic with lachrymal secretion. An eye can tolerate 0.6 to 2.0% w/v solution of sodium chloride.**

4. They should have a pH of tear fluid. pH may slightly vary but it should not cause discomfort, pain and irritation to the eye.

5. They should have optimum viscosity (25-50cps) to increase the contact time of the preparation in the age.

6. They should contain proper preservatives for the growth of microorganisms.

Hence, the correct option is (C).

22. Antiperspirants are used to reduce body odor. Antiperspirants and deodorants work in different ways to reduce body odor. Antiperspirants reduce sweat, and deodorants increase skin acidity, which odor-causing bacteria don't like. While there are rumors linking antiperspirants to cancer, research suggests that antiperspirants don't cause cancer.

Hence, the correct option is (C).

23. BHT stands for Butylated hydroxytoluene. Butylated hydroxytoluene (BHT), also known as dibutyl hydroxy toluene, is a lipophilic organic compound, chemically a derivative of phenol, that is useful for its antioxidant properties. The safety of BHT has been assessed by the Cosmetic Ingredient Review (CIR) Expert Panel. The Expert Panel reviewed the available data and concluded that BHT was safe for use in cosmetics and skincare products.

Hence, the correct option is (B).

24. Titanium dioxide is used as opacifying agent in face powder. Titanium dioxide is odourless and absorbent. Its most important function in powder form is as a widely used pigment for lending whiteness and opacity. Titanium dioxide has been used as a bleaching and opacifying agent in porcelain enamels, giving them brightness, hardness, and acid resistance.

Hence, the correct option is (D).

25. Eye drops, nasal drops and ear drops are the liquid dosage forms except for pills.

Liquids meant for body cavity: Gargles, throat paints, mouthwashes, eye drops, eye lotions, ear drops, nasal drops, sprays and inhalations.

Liquid state forms are meant for internal, parental or external use. They are available in monophasic and biphasic forms. Monophasic liquid dosage forms order soma pills are the true or colloidal solution.

Hence, the correct option is (C).

26. The subscription part of the prescription contains directions of the prescerber of the pharmacist. This part of the prescription consists of directions to the pharmacist for preparing the prescription. These may include the dosage form to be prepared and the number of doses to be dispensed.

Hence, the correct option is (B).

27. The inscription part of the prescription contains names and quantities of the prescription. The body of the prescription, or inscription, contains the name and amount or strength of the drug to be dispensed, or the name and strength of each ingredient to be compounded.

Hence, the correct option is (C).

28. Tragacanth, polysorbate60 and sodium oleate are emulsifying agents except for lanolin. Gum tragacanth is one of the most widely used natural emulsifiers and thickeners available to the food, drug, and allied industries. Polysorbates are a class of emulsifiers used in some pharmaceuticals and food preparation. They are often used in cosmetics to solubilize essential oils into water-based products. Sodium Oleate is a major component of soap as an emulsifying agent. Sodium Oleate is used in medicines. It is used in the treatment of cholelithiasis. In various oil-based cosmetics. Sodium Oleate is used as a cleansing agent, emulsifying agent, surfactant, thickening or gelling agent and viscosity controlling agent. Lanolin has long been used in the skincare and cosmetics industry as an effective emollient, commonly used in body creams and lotions to lock in much-needed moisture and prevent water loss. But lanolin also has a bad rep for irritating sensitive skin and causes allergic reactions.

Hence, the correct option is (A).

29. HLB value of sodium lauryl sulphate is 40. Since sodium lauryl sulphate is more soluble in water than oil, water is the continuous phase while oil is the internal phase. In addition, sodium lauryl sulphate has a very high HLB value of 40 meaning it is water-soluble and prefers to form o/w emulsions.

Hence, the correct option is (C).

30. In the small-scale extemporaneous preparation of emulsions, three methods may be used. They are the Continental or dry gum method, the English or wet gum method, and the bottle or Forbes bottle method. In the first method, the emulsifying agent (usually acacia) is mixed with the oil before the addition of water, that is, dry gum. In the second method, the emulsifying agent is added to the water (in which it is soluble) to form mucilage, and then the oil is slowly incorporated to form the emulsion, that is, wet gum. The bottle method is reserved for volatile oils or less viscous oils and is a variation of the dry gum method.

Hence, the correct option is (D).

31. Wool fat, hydrous wool fat and wool alcohol are absorption bases except for petrolatum. An absorption base is an oleaginous base that contains a w/o emulsifying agent. When water is taken up into the base, it will form a w/o emulsion. Absorption bases typically can incorporate about 50% of their volume in water. Incorporating insoluble drugs into these bases can be done mechanically or by fusion. Petrolatum Ointment Base is a cholesterolized absorbent ointment base that can be used as a skin protectant or as a compounding vehicle.

Hence, the correct option is (D).

32. A poultice, also called a cataplasm, is a paste made of herbs, plants, and other substances with healing properties. The paste is spread on a warm, moist cloth and applied to the body to relieve inflammation and promote healing.

Hence, the correct option is (C).

33. "The quantity of the drug which displace one part of the base" is called displacement value. Displacement value can be defined as the volume of drug that displaces 1 gram of suppository base. The most commonly used suppository base is Coca Butter or Theobroma oil. Traditionally suppositories are prepared using suppositories molds which can generally hold 1 gram or 2 grams of the base.

Hence, the correct option is (C).

34. O/W type of emulsion is preferred for internal use. They are preferred for formulations meant for external use like creams. They are preferred for formulations meant for internal use as the bitter taste of oils can be masked. There are two basic types of emulsions, that is, oil in water (O/W) and water in oil (W/O). In addition to these two types, a relatively complex emulsion, called multiple emulsions can also be formulated.

Hence, the correct option is (B).

35. Ointments are prepared by trituration method, chemical reaction method and fusion method except for bottle method.

Trituration Method: Trituration Method Widely used method For extemporaneous preparation of ointments. When the base is soft and medicament is solid insoluble Small amount of liquid to incorporate in the base Advantage Involves mixing as well as size reduction procedure:

- Reduce the solid medicament to a fine powder.
- The medicament is mixed with a small amount of base on an ointment slab with a stainless steel spatula until a homogeneous product is formed.
- Add remaining quantities of the base with uniform mixing.
- Incorporate any liquid ingredient if present (mortar and pestle to be used in case of a large quantity of liquid).

Fusion method: Suitable when ointment base contains the number of solid ingredients of different melting points. Procedure:

- Ointment bases are melted in decreasing order of their melting point.
- The highest melting point should be melted first, the low melting point next.
- This avoids overheating of substances of low melting point.
- Incorporate medicament slowly into the melted mass.
- Stir thoroughly until mass cools down and a homogeneous product is formed.

- Liquid ingredients or aqueous substances should be heated to the same temperature as the melted bases before addition.

Chemical reaction method: Chemical reaction method preparation of some ointment involves chemical reactions:

- Iodine ointment (iodine free form).
- Iodine ointment (iodine combined form with ointment base).
- Ointments containing free iodine.
- Iodine is slightly soluble in fats and vegetable oils.

Bottle method: This method is a variation of the dry gum method. One part powdered acacia (or other gum) is placed in a dry bottle and four parts oil are added. The bottle is capped and thoroughly shaken. To this, the required volume of water is added all at once, and the mixture is shaken thoroughly until the primary emulsion forms.

Hence, the correct option is (D).

36. Leakage test is performed in the vacuum chamber. The ampoules are dipped in a 1% solution of methylene blue in vacuum chamber and vacuum is applied. When vacuum is released, the colored solution will entered the ampoules with defective sealing. The presence of dye in ampoules, confirm the leakage and hence rejected.

Hence, the correct option is (B).

37. Dilution test, conductivity test and a fluorescence test are the test for identification of emulsion except for clarity test. Clarity testing is carried out to check the particulate matter in the sample. In this test, transparent particles or white particles were observed against the black background and the black or dark particles were observed against the white background.

Hence, the correct option is (D).

38. Wool fat, gelatin and egg yolk emulsifying agents are obtained from animal sources except for pectin. Pectin is extracted from apples and citrus fruits. Soluble pectin is capable of forming a gel once the correct concentrations of acid and sugar are reached. This is helpful to thicken syrups, such as those used to make jams and jellies.

Hence, the correct option is (C).

Q.1 Active constitute of podophyllum is useful in treatment of:

A. Blood pressure   **B.** Blood sugar

C. Carcinoma   **D.** Hypercholestremia

Q.2 Resin content of Indian podophyllum is:

A. 1-2%   **B.** 2-4%   **C.** 4-8%   **D.** 6-12%

Q.3 With sulphuric acid, Curcuma shows the following colour?

A. Red   **B.** Blue   **C.** Yellow   **D.** Green

Q.4 Boric acid gives following colour with turmeric paper:

A. Blue   **B.** Green   **C.** Red   **D.** Yellow

Q.5 Following alkaloid is useful as bioavailability enhancer:

A. Vasicine   **B.** Piperine   **C.** Nicotine   **D.** Lobeline

Q.6 Shape of Arjuna bark is:

A. Curved   **B.** Flat

C. Recurved   **D.** Quilled

Q.7 Cyanogenetic glycosides do not give the following test positive:

A. Grignard   **B.** Kellerkilliani

C. Borntrager   **D.** Baljet

Q.8 Gentian is used as:

A. Cardiac tonic   **B.** Sweetening agent

C. Laxative   **D.** Bitter tonic

Q.9 Chirayta is an important ingredient of:

A. Trikatu Churna   **B.** Hingvastak Churna

C. Sudarshan Churna   **D.** Sitopaladi Churna

Q.10 Picrorrhiza belongs to family:

A. Ranunculacene   **B.** Scrophulariaceae

C. Gentianaceae   **D.** Combrataceae

// Smart Answer Sheet //

| Correct | | Percentage of students who answered correctly. | | Skipped | | Percentage of students who skipped. |

Q.	Ans.	Correct / Skipped	Q.	Ans.	Correct / Skipped	Q.	Ans.	Correct / Skipped	Q.	Ans.	Correct / Skipped	Q.	Ans.	Correct / Skipped	Q.	Ans.	Correct / Skipped
1	C	50.3 % / 44.6 %	3	A	11.73 % / 68.98 %	5	B	44.8 % / 37.12 %	7	A	18.52 % / 73.98 %	9	B	20.83 % / 77.61 %			
2	D	21.19 % / 72.82 %	4	C	66.35 % / 32.27 %	6	B	63.87 % / 34.84 %	8	D	50.69 % / 35.98 %	10	B	66.61 % / 30.55 %			

//Hints and Solutions//

1. Active constitute of podophyllum is useful in the treatment of carcinoma. Carcinoma is a type of cancer that starts in cells that make up the skin or the tissue lining organs, such as the liver or kidneys. Like other types of cancer, carcinomas are abnormal cells that divide without control. Epi-steganangin and steganoate-B also have cytotoxic properties against 11 different human tumor cell lines, and burseran from Bursera microphylla (Burseraceae) displays antitumor properties against human epidermoid carcinoma of the nasopharynx cell culture.

Hence, the correct option is (C).

2. The resin content of Indian podophyllum is 8-16%. The amount of podophyllin or resin present in American podophyllum is 2-8% and in Indian podophyllum, it is about 6-12%. In roots, C18 compounds derivetives also active chemical constituents. Other chemical constituents are podophyllotoxin(0.25%), beta-peltatin(0.33%) and alpha-peltatin(0.25%).

Hence, the correct option is (D).

3. With sulphuric acid, Curcuma shows red colour. Turmeric is the dried rhizome of Curcuma longa Linn. (syn.C.domestica Valeton)., belonging to the family Zingiberaceae. Chemical tests are:

1. Turmeric powder on treatment with concentrated sulphuric acid forms red colour.

2. On addition of alkali solution to Turmeric powder red to violet colour is produced.

3. With acetic anhydride and concentrated sulphuric acid, Turmeric gives violet colour. Under UV light this colour is seen as an intense red fluorescence.

4. A paper containing Turmeric extract produces a green colour with borax solution.

5. On the addition of boric acid, a reddish-brown colour is formed which, on the addition of alkalies, changes to greenish-blue.

Hence, the correct option is (A).

4. Boric acid gives a red colour with turmeric paper. In addition to boric acid, a reddish-brown colour is formed which, on the addition of alkalies, changes to greenish-blue. Turmeric is used as aromatic, anti-inflammatory, stomachic, uretic, anodyne for biliary calculus, stimulant, tonic, carminative, blood purifier, antiperiodic, alterative, spice, colouring agent for ointments and a common household remedy for cold and cough. Externally, it is used in the form of a cream to improve complexion.

Hence, the correct option is (C).

5. Piperine alkaloid is useful as a bioavailability enhancer. It has been confirmed that piperine acts as an efficient bioavailability enhancer for different nutrients and trace elements and exhibits potential anti-microbial, anti-oxidant, anti-inflammatory, anti-cancer, anti-depressant, anti-apoptotic, anti-pyretic and analgesic activities.

Hence, the correct option is (B).

6. The shape of Arjuna bark is flat. Its bark is thick, grey to pinkish green, smooth, thin, coming off in irregular sheets. Leaves are usually sub-opposite, 10–15 cm long, and 4–7 cm broad; the base is rounded or heart-shaped, often unequal sided; veins are reticulate. Arjuna bark is used as a diuretic and astringent. The diuretic properties can be attributed to the triterpenoids present in fruits. It causes a decrease in blood pressure and heart rate. It is used in the treatment of various heart diseases in indigenous systems of medicines.

Hence, the correct option is (B).

7. Cyanogenetic glycosides do not give Grignard test positive.

1) Keller-Killiani test: Add 0.4 ml of glacial acetic acid and a few drops of 5% ferric chloride solution to a little drug extract. Further, add 0.5 ml of concentrated sulfuric acid. The formation of blue color in the acetic acid layer confirmed the test.

2) Glycosides (Liebermann's Test): 2ml extract + 2ml $CHCl_3$ + 2ml CH_3COOH Violet to Blue to Green coloration 2 Anthraquinones (Borntrager's Test) 3ml extract + 3ml Benzene + 5ml NH_3 (10%) Pink, Violet or Red coloration in ammonical layer.

- CHEMICAL IDENTIFICATION: 8 Coumarins 2ml extract + 3ml NaOH (10%) Yellow coloration 9 Saponins (Foam Test) (a)5ml extract + 5ml H_2O + heat (b) 5ml extract + Olive oil (few drops) Froth appears Emulsion forms.

3) Baljet test: To a section of digitalis, add sodium picrate solution it shows yellow to orange color.

Hence, the correct option is (A).

8. Gentian is used as a bitter tonic. Gentian root is known for its bitter taste. It's particularly used in traditional settings as a digestive tonic to stimulate stomach, liver, and gallbladder function. In fact, the name gentian comes from the ancient Illyrian king Gentius, who identified that the herb could be used as a tonic.

Hence, the correct option is (D).

9. Chirayta is an important ingredient of hingvastak churna. Indian Gentian, Indian Balmony, Chirayta, Ophelia chirata, Swertia chirayita. Hingvashtak churna is an ayurvedic formulation that is a combination of several significant ingredients. As the name suggest hing (asafetida) is the major ingredient of this formulation. Hing is known as old Indian culinary ingredient which is enriched with various healthy properties. This formulation is known to treat the problems of digestion.

Hence, the correct option is (B).

10. Picrorhiza belongs to the family scrophulariaceae. It is used heavily as a substitute for Picrorhiza kurroa and is considered non-threatened under CITES. It is similar to P. kurrooa but has left up to 6cm long and stems which are decumbent. Flowers of this plant are 1.5 cm long, deep blue-purple with exserted styles and stamens.

Hence, the correct option is (B).

Q.1 Picrorrhiza is very useful in:

A. Bronchitis **B.** Kidney stone

C. Hyperacidity **D.** Jaundice

Q.2 Kalmegh belongs to family:

A. Acanthaceae **B.** Gentianaceae

C. Scrophulariaceae **D.** Ranumculaceae

Q.3 Andrographolide is the active constituent of:

A. Gentian **B.** Picrorrhiza

C. Chirata **D.** Kalmegh

Q.4 Psoralea corylifolia is useful in:

A. Hepatitits **B.** Diabetes

C. Leucoderma **D.** Leprosy

Q.5 Rutin is used in capillary fragilities, it has following vitamin-like action:

A. B **B.** P **C.** E **D.** A

Q.6 On hydrolysis gaultherin gives:

A. Monotropitoside **B.** Acetyl salicylate

C. Propylsalicylate **D.** Methyl salicylate

Q.7 The word alkaloid was first coined by W.Meissner in the year:

A. 1805 **B.** 1819 **C.** 1854 **D.** 1925

Q.8 Van Urk reagent gives purple colour with:

A. Tropane alkaloids **B.** Cinchona alkaloids

C. Ipecac alkaloids **D.** Ergot alkaloids

Q.9 Vitali-Morin reagent gives bright purple colour with:

A. Tropane alkaloids **B.** Ergot alkaloids

C. Cinchona alkaloids **D.** Ipecac alkaloids

Q.10 Following one is a liquid alkaloid:

A. Berberine **B.** Nicotine

C. Ergotamine **D.** Quinine

// Smart Answer Sheet //

| Correct | | Percentage of students who answered correctly. | | Skipped | | Percentage of students who skipped. |

| Q. | Ans. | Correct | Q. | Ans. | Correct | Q. | Ans. | Correct | Q. | Ans. | Correct | Q. | Ans. | Correct | Q. | Ans. | Correct |
		Skipped			Skipped			Skipped			Skipped			Skipped			Skipped
1	D	42.88 %	3	D	58.95 %	5	B	60.45 %	7	B	53.0 %	9	A	53.77 %			
		55.41 %			37.78 %			31.12 %			32.21 %			34.97 %			
2	A	56.83 %	4	C	56.78 %	6	D	57.2 %	8	D	19.57 %	10	B	48.14 %			
		40.71 %			31.91 %			41.46 %			76.38 %			30.8 %			

//Hints and Solutions//

1. Picrorrhiza is very useful in jaundice. Picrorhiza is used for yellowed skin (jaundice), sudden liver infections caused by a virus (acute viral hepatitis), fever, allergy, and asthma. It is also used to treat skin conditions including eczema and vitiligo, a disorder that causes white patches on the skin.

Hence, the correct option is (D).

2. Kalmegh belongs to the family acanthaceae. Acanthaceae is a family (the acanthus family) of dicotyledonous flowering plants containing almost 250 genera and about 2500 species. Most are tropical herbs, shrubs, or twining vines; some are epiphytes. Only a few species are distributed in temperate regions. Kalmegh consists of leaves or the entire aerial part of Andrographis paniculata Nees., belonging to the family acanthaceae.

Hence, the correct option is (A).

3. Andrographolide is the active constituent of kalmegh. Kalmegh, which is widely used in Indian medicine as a bitter tonic, for snakebite, and for the treatment of hepatitis. Andrographolide is a diterpenoid lactone obtained from A. Paniculata Nees. (Kalmegh), which is widely used in Indian medicine as a bitter tonic, for snakebite, and for the treatment of hepatitis.

Hence, the correct option is (D).

4. Psoralea corylifolia is useful in leucoderma. The plant has been used for centuries in leukoderma, psoriasis, vitiligo, asthma, ulcers, kidney disorders, and as an aphrodisiac and an anti-inflammatory. It is reported to contain essential oil, coumarins, alkaloids, flavonoids, and terpenoids.

Hence, the correct option is (C).

5. Rutin is used in capillary fragilities, it has P vitamin-like action. Rutin is a plant pigment that is found in certain fruits and vegetables. Buckwheat, Japanese pagoda tree, and Eucalyptus are sources of rutin.

Rutin is also found in lime tree flowers, elderflowers, hawthorn, rue, St. John's Wort, Ginkgo, apples, and other fruits and vegetables. Rutin might have antioxidant and anti-inflammatory effects. It might also offer some protection against cancer and other diseases. Rutin is commonly used for autism, aging skin, airway infections caused by exercise, and many other purposes, but there is no good scientific evidence to support any of these uses.

Hence, the correct option is (B).

6. On hydrolysis gaultherin gives methyl salicylate. Methyl salicylate is a benzoate ester that is the methyl ester of salicylic acid. It has a role as a flavouring agent, a metabolite and an insect attractant. It is a benzoate ester and a member of salicylates. It forms a colorless to yellow or reddish liquid and exhibits a characteristic odor and taste of wintergreen.

Hence, the correct option is (D).

7. The word alkaloid was first coined by W.Meissner in the year 1819. The word "alkaloid" was first coined by the German chemist Carl F. W. Meissner in 1819, derived from the Arabic name al-qali, which is associated to the plant from which soda was first sequestered (Croteau et al., 2000).

Hence, the correct option is (B).

8. Van Urk reagent gives purple colour with ergot alkaloids. Ergot is a fungal disease very common and widely observed on a good number of the wild as well as cultivated grasses, and is produced by different species of Claviceps. This particular disease is usually characterized by the formation of hard and seedlike 'ergots' in place of the normal seeds. However, these specific structures are frequently termed as sclerotia, which represent the 'resting stage' of the fungus

The generic name, 'Claviceps', usually refers to the club-like nature of the sclerotium*, whereas purpurea signifies its purple colour. As these sclerotia are elongated and somewhat pointed in shape and appearance, hence the common name of spurred rye has been assigned to the drug.

Hence, the correct option is (D).

9. Vitali-Morin reagent gives bright purple colour with tropane alkaloids.

Vitali-Morin reaction: Alkaloid/atropine+ drop of H_2SO_4, evaporate to dryness and add 0.3 ml of 3% solution of KOH in methyl alcohol, which produces bright purple colour indicates the presence of atropine.

Hence, the correct option is (A).

10. Oxygen-free alkaloids, such as nicotine or coniine, are typically volatile, colorless, oily liquids. Some alkaloids are colored, like berberine (yellow) and sanguinarine (orange). Most alkaloids are weak bases, but some, such as theobromine and theophylline, are amphoteric.

Hence, the correct option is (B).

Q.1 Lobeline is useful as:

A. Diuretic

B. Purgative

C. Respiratory stimulant

D. Liver tonic

Q.2 Leaves of Lobelia nicotianaefolia have following shape:

A. Ovate

B. Obovate

C. Oblong-lanceolate

D. Cordate

Q.3 Following types of abundant calcium oxalate crystals are found in Belladonna?

A. Cluster

B. Prisms

C. Acicular

D. Microsphenoidal

Q.4 Cuticle found on epidermis of Belladonna leaves is:

A. Smooth

B. Striated

C. Thick

D. None of these

Q.5 Hyoscyamine has following type of activity:

A. Parasympatholytic

B. Sympatholytic

C. Cholinergic

D. Spasmogenic

Q.6 Choose the drugs which contain alkaloids derived from ornithine:

A. Hellebori rhizome

B. Henbane leaf

C. Cocae leaf

D. Ribis nigri leaf

Q.7 Which of the following reactions are specific for alkaloids?

A. Vitali-reaction

B. Borntrager-reaction

C. Kedde-reaction

D. Liebermann-Burchard-reaction

Q.8 Which of the following reactions are specific for cardiac glycosides?

A. Kedde-reaction

B. Murexid-reaction

C. Borntrager-reaction

D. Vitali-reaction

Q.9 Which of the following reactions are specifically linked to the presence of the $\alpha, \beta -$ unsaturated- γ-lactone?

A. Liebermann-Burchard reaction

B. Kedde-reaction

C. Keller-Kiliani-reaction

D. Xanthydrol-reaction

Q.10 Find out the lysine-derived alkaloids from the following list:

A. Coniine

B. Pilocarpine

C. Strychnine

D. Tropine

// Smart Answer Sheet //

| Correct | | Percentage of students who answered correctly. | | Skipped | | Percentage of students who skipped. |

Q.	Ans.	Correct	Q.	Ans.	Correct	Q.	Ans.	Correct	Q.	Ans.	Correct	Q.	Ans.	Correct	Q.	Ans.	Correct
		Skipped			Skipped			Skipped			Skipped			Skipped			Skipped
1	C	44.2 %	3	D	28.57 %	5	A	45.23 %	7	C	47.05 %	9	D	68.98 %			
		1.53 %			4.99 %			1.65 %			1.7 %			1.8 %			
2	A	56.24 %	4	B	59.35 %	6	D	45.51 %	8	C	69.0 %	10	C	62.66 %			
		1.37 %			1.75 %			1.37 %			1.03 %			1.78 %			

//Hints and Solutions//

1. Lobeline is useful as a respiratory stimulant. It has been used as an emetic, antidepressant, respiratory stimulant, aid to smoking cessation, and treatment for metamfetamine abuse. Lobeline has peripheral effects similar to those of nicotine, whereas its central activity may be different.

Hence, the correct option is (C).

2. Leaves of Lobelia nicotianaefolia have ovate shape. Lobelia nicotianifolia is a species of flowering plant with a distribution primarily across India and Sri Lanka. It is commonly called wild tobacco, because the leaves resemble tobacco leaves. It is a poisonous plant.

Hence, the correct option is (A).

3. Microsphenoidal types of abundant calcium oxalate crystals are found in Belladonna. A transverse section of the leaf of A. belladonna has a bifacial structure. The epidermal cells have wavy walls and a striated cuticle. Anisocytic type and some of the anomocytic type stomata arc are present on both surfaces but are most common on the lower. Hairs are most numerous on young leaves, uni-seriate, two- to four-celled clothing hairs; or with a uni-cellular glandular head. Some hair has a short: pedicel and a multicellular glandular head. Certain of the cells of the spongy mesophyll are filled with micro-sphenoidal (sandy) crystals of calcium oxalate. The midrib is convex above and shows the usual bi-collateral vascular bundle. A zone of collenchyma is present in the epidermis near the midrib.

Hence, the correct option is (D).

4. Cuticle found on epidermis of Belladonna leaves is striated. Belladonna has a bifacial structure. The epidermal cells have wavy walls and a striated cuticle. Anisocytic type and some of the anomocytic type stomata arc are present on both surfaces but are most common on the lower. Hairs are most numerous on young leaves, uni-seriate, two- to four-celled clothing hairs; or with a uni-cellular glandular head.

Hence, the correct option is (B).

5. A parasympatholytic agent is a substance or activity that reduces the activity of the parasympathetic nervous system. (The parasympathetic nervous system is often colloquially described as the "Feed and Breed" or "Rest and Digest" portion of the autonomic nervous system. The parasympathetic nervous system becomes strongly engaged during or after a meal and during times when the body is at rest.)

Hence, the correct option is (A).

6. Ribis nigri leaf is a drug that contains alkaloids derived from ornithine. Ornithine is a non-proteinogenic amino acid that plays a role in the urea cycle. Ornithine is abnormally accumulated in the body in ornithine transcarbamylase deficiency. The radical is ornithyl. Witches prepared mixtures of extracts of henbane (Hyoscyamus niger), deadly nightshade (Atropa belladonna) and mandrake root, to be applied on the skin or on the genitals.

Hence, the correct option is (D).

7. Kedde-reaction is specific for alkaloids. A solution of glycosides is treated with a small amount of Kedde reagent (Mix equal volumes of a 2% solution of 3, 5 di-nitrobenzoic acid in menthol and a 7.5% aqueous solution of KOH). Development of a blue or violet colour that faded out in1 to 2 hrs shows it presence of cardenolides.

Hence, the correct option is (C).

8. Borntrager-reaction is specific for cardiac glycosides. The Borntrager test is used for the identification and determination of anthraquinones or glycosides.

Modified Borntrager's test: The C-Glycoside of Anthraquinone requires more drastic conditions for hydrolysis and thus a modification of the above test is to use ferric chloride and hydrochloric acid to affect oxidative hydrolysis.

Hence, the correct option is (C).

9. Xanthydrol-reaction is specifically linked to the presence of the $\alpha, \beta -$ unsaturated- γ-lactone. Xanthydrol is an organic chemical compound. Its formula is $C_{13}H_{10}O_2$. Its total molecular weight is 198.221 g/mol. Xanthydrol is used to test the levels of urea in the bloodstream

Hence, the correct option is (D).

10. Strychnine lysine-derived alkaloids. Lysine are belonging to so-called "true alkaloids" because their nitrogen atoms originate from an amino acid, and in general, the carbon skeleton of the particular amino acid precursor is also largely retained intact in the alkaloid structure.

Hence, the correct option is (C).

Q.1 Mechanism of action of clindamycin is inhibition of:

A. Protein synthesis

B. DNA gyrase

C. Lysosomal enzyme

D. Cell wall synthesis

Q.2 Mechanism of action of tetracycline:

A. Prevents binding of m-RAN to RAN

B. Misreading of m-RNA

C. Transcription of DNA to RNA inhibited

D. Bind to 30-S ribosome

Q.3 Most serious adverse effect of penicillin is:

A. Skin rashes

B. Jarish hexheimer reaction

C. Anaphylaxis

D. Convulsion

Q.4 The genetically determined unwanted reactivity to chemical or drug is called:

A. Intolerance

B. Drug allergy

C. Poisoning

D. Idiosyncrasy

Q.5 Amyl nitrate is used as an antidote for:

A. Cobalt poisoning

B. Dapsone poisoning

C. Cyanide poisoning

D. Barbiturates poisoning

Q.6 Side effect of zidovudine in AIDS patients is:

A. Megaloblastic anemia

B. Peripheral neuropathy

C. Bone marrow suppression

D. Pancreatitis

Q.7 Which of the following drugs is not an antifungal agent?

A. Ciclopiroxolmine

B. Ketoconazole

C. Undecylenic acid

D. Clofazimine

Q.8 The most effective drug against M. Leprae is:

A. Dapsone

B. Rifampicin

C. Clofazamine

D. Prothionamide

Q.9 The following can be used as a second-line anti TB drug:

A. Kanamycin

B. Cycloserine

C. Streptomycin

D. All of these

Q.10 Digitalis toxicity produces the following change in ECG mainly:

A. Absence of T-wave

B. ST depression

C. Prolonged PR Interval

D. Absence of QRS complex

Q.11 Barbiturates are derivative of:

A. Urea

B. Ethylalshol

C. Opium

D. Oxazepam

Q.12 Antidepressant is:

A. Chlorpropamide

B. Imipramine

C. Fluphenazine

D. Both (A) and (B)

Q.13 False statement regarding Clozapine:

A. Used in resistant schizophrenia

B. Can cause agranulocytosis

C. Decrease on & off effect

D. Has the maximum extrapyramidal effect

Q.14 Which drug should be given along with Levodopa?

A. Carbidopa

B. Benserazide

C. MAO inhibitors

D. Both (A) and (B)

Q.15 Tinnitus is a most common side effect of:

A. Metformin

B. Reserpine

C. Aspirin

D. Quinune

Q.16 Lithium carbonate is used for:

A. Seizures

B. Bipolar mood disorder

C. Psychosis

D. Depression

Q.17 HDL is increased by:

A. Lovstain

B. Nicotinic acid

C. Clofiberate

D. Gemfibrozil

Q.18 Antidote for heparin is:

A. Protamine

B. EDTA

C. Sodium bicarbonate

D. Des frrioxamine

Q.19 Loop diuretic act by:

A. Inhibition of Na+Cl-symport

B. Inhibition of Na+K+2C1-cotrasport

C. Inhibition of Na+-K+ATP

D. Inhibition of H+-K+ATP

Q.20 K+ channel opener is:

A. Verapamil

B. Sodium nitropruside

C. Minoxidil

D. Amrinone

Q.21 All of following are example of Calcium channel blockers expect:

A. Nifedipine

B. Diltiazem

C. Pirenzepine

D. Verapamil

Q.22 Which diurectic act on late distal tubule & collecting duct?

A. Spironolactone

B. Chlorothiazide

C. Furosemide

D. Aceteazolamine

Q.23 Vasopressin is used to treat:

A. Doctorate medicine
B. Congestive heart failure
C. Diabetes Insipidus
D. Hypertension

Q.24 Muscarinic (M_2) receptors are present in:

A. Exocrine gland
B. Visceral smooth muscle
C. Heart
D. Gastric glands

Q.25 The most common side effect of insulin is:

A. Allergy
B. Hypoglycemia
C. Edema
D. Swelling at junction site

Q.26 Therapeutic index of a drug is an indicator of:

A. Potency   B. Safety   C. Toxicity   D. Efficacy

Q.27 A substrate having affinity and intrinsic activity is:

A. Agonist   B. Inverse agonist
C. Antagoint   D. Partial antagonist

Q.28 A false neurotransmitter is:

A. Epinephrine   B. B-methyldopa
C. Acetylcoline   D. Dopamine

// Smart Answer Sheet //

Correct — Percentage of students who answered correctly. **Skipped** — Percentage of students who skipped.

Q.	Ans.	Correct / Skipped	Q.	Ans.	Correct / Skipped	Q.	Ans.	Correct / Skipped	Q.	Ans.	Correct / Skipped	Q.	Ans.	Correct / Skipped	Q.	Ans.	Correct / Skipped
1	B	51.03 % / 36.62 %	6	A	44.72 % / 35.48 %	11	A	51.66 % / 43.23 %	16	B	55.59 % / 38.69 %	21	C	27.57 % / 68.35 %	26	B	68.75 % / 30.76 %
2	D	66.58 % / 31.22 %	7	D	62.38 % / 31.56 %	12	B	42.03 % / 55.2 %	17	B	51.96 % / 40.71 %	22	A	43.22 % / 42.93 %	27	A	43.02 % / 52.0 %
3	C	55.71 % / 36.83 %	8	B	57.78 % / 37.68 %	13	D	55.55 % / 37.04 %	18	A	48.54 % / 47.75 %	23	C	40.17 % / 45.44 %	28	B	44.04 % / 39.08 %
4	D	45.27 % / 38.21 %	9	D	61.79 % / 35.04 %	14	D	43.81 % / 38.54 %	19	B	21.65 % / 68.98 %	24	C	54.58 % / 34.99 %			
5	C	42.66 % / 36.54 %	10	A	49.07 % / 39.84 %	15	D	60.48 % / 34.59 %	20	C	56.14 % / 36.94 %	25	B	52.69 % / 46.46 %			

//Hints and Solutions//

1. The mechanism of action of clindamycin is inhibition of DNA gyrase. DNA gyrase is an essential bacterial enzyme that catalyzes the ATP-dependent negative super-coiling of double-stranded closed-circular DNA. Gyrase belongs to a class of enzymes known as topoisomerases that are involved in the control of topological transitions of DNA.

Hence, the correct option is (B).

2. Mechanism of action of tetracycline bind to the 30-S ribosome. Tetracyclines inhibit protein synthesis through reversible binding to bacterial 30-S ribosomal subunits, which prevent binding of new incoming amino acids (aminoacyl-tRNA) and thus interfere with peptide growth

Hence, the correct option is (D).

3. The most serious adverse effect of penicillin is anaphylaxis. Penicillin is prescribed for treating various bacterial infections. Common signs and symptoms of penicillin allergy include hives, rash, and itching. Severe reactions include anaphylaxis, a life-threatening condition that affects multiple body systems.

Hence, the correct option is (C).

4. Idiosyncrasy: Genetically determined abnormal reactivity to a chemical. Certain Bizarre drug effects due to peculiarities of an individual for which no definite genotype has been described are also included. "Drug idiosyncrasy" refers to untoward reactions to drugs that occur in a small fraction of patients and have no obvious relationship to dose or duration of therapy. The liver is a frequent target for toxicity.

Hence, the correct option is (D).

5. Amyl nitrate is used as an antidote for cyanide poisoning. Amyl nitrite is employed medically to treat heart diseases as well as angina. Amyl nitrite is sometimes used as an antidote for cyanide poisoning.

Hence, the correct option is (C).

6. A side effect of zidovudine in AIDS patients is megaloblastic anemia. Several studies showed that human immune deficiency/HIV infection is frequently associated with hematologic abnormalities. The use of antiretroviral treatment (ART) regimen containing zidovudine (AZT) is associated with hematological toxicity to varying degrees of cytopenias particularly megaloblastic anemia.

Hence, the correct option is (A).

7. Clofazimine drugs are not antifungal agents. Clofazimine is a drug used to treat leprosy. It can slow down growth and weakly kill mycobacterium leprae, the bacterium that causes leprosy. It is used in combination with rifampicin and dapsone for the treatment of the many forms of leprosy.

Hence, the correct option is (D).

8. The most effective drug against M. Leprae is rifampicin. Rifampicin is the only strongly bactericidal anti-leprosy drug that makes the patient non-infectious within days of initiation of treatment. The drug is also effective against dapsone-resistant organisms.

Hence, the correct option is (B).

9. Kanamycin, Capreomycin and Amikacin are injectable second-line anti TB drug. Bedaquiline and Delamanid are new drugs. Ethambutol, Pyrazinamide, Thioamides, Cycloserine, Para-aminosalicylic acid, Streptomycin, and Clofazimine are possibly effective. Kanamycin, Capreomycin and Amikacin are injectable second-line anti TB drug.

Hence, the correct option is (D).

10. Digitalis toxicity produces the absence of T-wave in ECG mainly. When interpreting electrocardiogram (ECG) findings in patients receiving digitalis, one must distinguish between normal and toxic effects. Normal ECG changes with therapeutic levels of digitalis include the following:

- T-wave changes (often the earliest sign), ranging from flattening to inversion or peaking of the terminal portion of the T wave.
- Shortening of the Q-T interval.
- Increased U-wave amplitude.

Hence, the correct option is (A).

11. Barbiturates are derivative of urea. Barbiturates are derivatives of barbituric acid (malonyl urea), which is formed from malonic acid and urea. Barbital was first synthesized in 1903, and phenobarbital became available in 1912. Barbiturates act by depressing the central nervous system, particularly on certain portions of the brain, though they tend to depress the functioning of all the body's tissues. Most of them exert a sedative effect in small doses and a hypnotic effect in larger doses. The barbiturates have largely been replaced as sedatives by benzodiazepines and other minor tranquilizers, which have fewer unfavorable side effects and less abuse potential.

Hence, the correct option is (A).

12. Antidepressant is imipramine. Imipramine is in a class of medications called tricyclic antidepressants. It treats depression by increasing the amounts of certain natural substances in the brain that are needed to maintain mental balance.

Hence, the correct option is (B).

13. Clozapine has the maximum extrapyramidal effect. Some people may develop muscle-related side effects while taking clozapine. The technical terms for these are "extrapyramidal symptoms" (EPS) and "tardive dyskinesia" (TD). Symptoms of EPS include restlessness, tremor, and stiffness.

Hence, the correct option is (D).

14. Levodopa is almost always given in combination with the drug carbidopa, which prevents nausea that can be caused by levodopa alone. Carbidopa is also a levodopa enhancer. The combination of levodopa and benserazide is an anti-Parkinsonian agent [3,2]. Levodopa itself is the metabolic precursor of dopamine. In Parkinson's disease, dopamine is depleted to a large degree in the striatum, pallidum, and substantia nigra in the central nervous system (CNS)[3,2].

Hence, the correct option is (D).

15. Tinnitus is the most common side effect of quinune. Tinnitus is usually caused by an underlying condition, such as age-related hearing loss, an ear injury, or a problem with the circulatory system. For many people, tinnitus improves with treatment of the underlying cause or with other treatments that reduce or mask the noise, making tinnitus less noticeable.

Hence, the correct option is (D).

16. Lithium carbonate is used for bipolar mood disorder. Lithium (Eskalith, Lithobid) is one of the most widely used and studied medications for treating bipolar disorder. Lithium helps reduce the severity and frequency of mania. It may also help relieve or prevent bipolar depression. Studies show that lithium can significantly reduce suicide risk.

Hence, the correct option is (B).

17. HDL is increased by nicotinic acid. Nicotinic acid, or niacin, has been the most widely used medication to raise HDL-C levels, increasing HDL-C by 16 to 25 %. The Coronary Drug Project was the first randomized controlled trial to assess the efficacy of niacin.

Hence, the correct option is (B).

18. An antidote for heparin is protamine. Despite the low therapeutic index, protamine is the only registered antidote of heparins. The toxicology of protamine depends on a complex interaction of the high molecular weight, a cationic peptide with the surfaces of the vasculature and blood cells.

Hence, the correct option is (A).

19. Loop diuretic act by inhibition of Na+K+2C1-cotrasport. Loop diuretics bind reversibly to a chloride channel receptor site in the ascending limb of the loop of Henle, inhibiting the reabsorption of filtered sodium and chloride. This reduces the hypertonicity of the renal medulla, inhibiting water reabsorption by the collecting ducts.

Hence, the correct option is (B).

20. K+ channel opener is minoxidil. Minoxidil is a potassium channel opener that hyperpolarizes cell membranes, causing vascular muscle dilation and a consequent increase in blood flow. It is approved for both men and women for the treatment of androgenetic alopecia as a topical solution and topical foam.

Hence, the correct option is (C).

21. Calcium channel blockers are available in short-acting and long-acting forms. Short-acting medications work quickly, but their effects last only a few hours. Long-acting medications are slowly released to provide a longer-lasting effect. Examples of **calcium channel blockers** include:

- Amlodipine (Norvasc)
- **Diltiazem (Cardizem, Tiazac, others)**
- Felodipine
- Isradipine
- Nicardipine
- **Nifedipine (Procardia)**

- Nisoldipine (Sular)
- **Verapamil (Calan SR, Verelan)**

Sometimes, a doctor might prescribe a calcium channel blocker with other high blood pressure medications or with cholesterol-lowering drugs such as statins.

Pirenzepine: Pirenzepine belongs to a group of medications called antispasmodics/anticholinergics. These medications are used to relieve cramps or spasms of the stomach, intestines, and bladder. Pirenzepine is used to treat duodenal or stomach ulcers or intestine problems.

Hence, the correct option is (C).

22. Spironolactone diurectic act on late distal tubule & collecting duct. Potassium-Retaining Diuretics (e.g., Spironolactone, Amiloride, Eplerenone) spironolactone is an aldosterone receptor antagonist that acts in the renal distal tubule and collecting ducts, decreasing the reabsorption of sodium and water and decreasing the excretion of potassium.

Hence, the correct option is (A).

23. Vasopressin is used to treat D.I (Diabetes insipidus). Vasopressin injection is used to control frequent urination, increased thirst, and loss of water caused by diabetes insipidus. This is a condition that causes the body to lose too much water and become dehydrated.

Hence, the correct option is (C).

24. The M_2 muscarinic receptors are located in the heart, where they act to slow the heart rate down to normal sinus rhythm after negative stimulatory actions of the parasympathetic nervous system, by slowing the speed of depolarization.

Hence, the correct option is (C).

25. The most common side effect of insulin is hypoglycemia. Hypoglycemia is the most common and serious side effect of insulin, occurring in approximately 16% of type 1 and 10% of type II diabetic patients (the incidence varies greatly depending on the populations studied, types of insulin therapy, etc).

Hence, the correct option is (B).

26. The therapeutic index of a drug is an indicator of safety. The therapeutic index (TI; also referred to as therapeutic ratio) is a quantitative measurement of the relative safety of a drug. It is a comparison of the amount of a therapeutic agent that causes the therapeutic effect to the amount that causes toxicity.

Hence, the correct option is (B).

27. A substrate having affinity and intrinsic activity is an agonist. Agonists are drugs with both affinity (they bind to the target receptor) and intrinsic efficacy (they change receptor activity to produce a response). Antagonists have affinity but zero intrinsic efficacy; therefore they bind to the target receptor but do not produce a response.

Hence, the correct option is (A).

28. A false neurotransmitter is B-methyldopa. Methyldopa is taken up into sympathetic nerve terminals and metabolized to α-methylnorepinephrine, which is a selective α2 receptor agonist. α-methylnorepinephrine is taken up into presynaptic vesicles and released in place of norepinephrine. As a result, methyldopa is often referred to as a "false neurotransmitter".

Hence, the correct option is (B).

Q.1 Vincristine and vinblastine act by:
- **A.** Binding with the protein tubulin & arrest at metaphase
- **B.** Indhibiting the protein synthesis
- **C.** Inhibting the enzyme synthesis
- **D.** Both (A) and (B)

Q.2 Nimesulide is banned in pediatric formulation because:
- **A.** CNS depression
- **B.** Liver damage
- **C.** CNS side effect
- **D.** Physical dependance

Q.3 Dapsone is used primarily for the treatment of:
- **A.** Malaria
- **B.** Tubereulosis
- **C.** Thorat infection
- **D.** Leprosy

Q.4 Which of the given agents acts by inhibiting xanthine oxidase?
- **A.** Methotrexate
- **B.** Azathioprine
- **C.** Allopurinol
- **D.** Cyclophosphamide

Q.5 Anti-herps antiviral drug is ___________.
- **A.** Acyclovir
- **B.** Amantadine
- **C.** Zidovudine
- **D.** Didanosine

Q.6 Ganciclovir is most effective against which viral infection:
- **A.** Herpes simplex I
- **B.** Herpes simplex II
- **C.** Vericella zoster
- **D.** Cyomegalo virus

Q.7 Quinidine exerts its action on heart by inhibiting:
- **A.** Na+ channel
- **B.** K+ channel
- **C.** Cl- channel
- **D.** Ca+2 channel

Q.8 Which malaria is deadly?
- **A.** Plasmodium falciparum
- **B.** Plasmodium vivax
- **C.** Plasmodium ovale
- **D.** Plasmodium malaria

Q.9 Which of the following is the function of nitric oxide?
- **A.** Vasodilation
- **B.** Platelet inhibition
- **C.** Immune regulation
- **D.** All of these

Q.10 The dose of oral digoxin in an adult mg per kg weight is:
- **A.** 0.06 to 0.08
- **B.** 0.05 to 0.1
- **C.** 0.75 to 1.5
- **D.** 1.0 to 2.0

Q.11 Morphine cause:
- **A.** Simulaton of CTZ zone of medulla
- **B.** Stimulate respiratory center of medulla
- **C.** Depresses CTZ zone of medulla
- **D.** None of these

Q.12 Herps infection is treated with:
- **A.** Ritonavir
- **B.** Acyclovir
- **C.** Dadinosine
- **D.** Amantadine

Q.13 Aspirin has all properties except:
- **A.** Brings down elevated temperature
- **B.** Prevents platelet aggregation
- **C.** Brings down normal temperature
- **D.** Used in rheumatoid arthritis

Q.14 Dinzoxide is a:
- **A.** Myocardial deprassant
- **B.** Centrally acting agent
- **C.** Antihypertensive acting directly on blood vessels
- **D.** Adrenergic blocking arthritis

Q.15 In the function of heart, systolic arterial blood pressure in the arteries at the time of cardiac systole shows:
- **A.** Maximum blood pressure
- **B.** Minimum blood pressure
- **C.** Moderate blood pressure
- **D.** Differential blood pressure

Q.16 Which is an antimetabolite?
- **A.** Chlorambucil
- **B.** Methotrexate
- **C.** Etoposide
- **D.** Vinblastine

Q.17 Idiosyncrasy is:
- **A.** A genetically determined abnormal reaction to drugs.
- **B.** A characteristic toxic effect at therapeutic dose.
- **C.** An attired physiological state produced by repeated drug use.
- **D.** An immunologically mediated reaction.

Q.18 Which is a prodrug?
- **A.** Paracetamo
- **B.** Enalapril maleate
- **C.** Sulphamethoxazole
- **D.** Trimethorprim

Q.19 A substance having affinity but no intrinsic activity is:
- **A.** Againts
- **B.** Partial agonist
- **C.** Antagonist
- **D.** Physioloical antagonist

Q.20 What is a desflurane?
- **A.** Is non-irritant to the airways.
- **B.** Is more/less potent than Sevoflurane.
- **C.** Has a higher molecular weight than isoflurane and enflurane.
- **D.** Is a chlorinated methyl ethyl ether.

Q.21 Penicillanse resistant penicillin is:
- **A.** Methicillin
- **B.** Oxacillin
- **C.** Cloxacillin
- **D.** All of these

Q.22 Chloroquine is used in the treatment of:
- **A.** Stomatitis
- **B.** Malaria

C. Urticaria   **D.** Bronchitis

Q.23 In reversing neuromuscular blockade, which of the following combinations is best matched with respect to time of onset?

A.   Atropine & Neostigmine
B.   Atropine & Glycopyrrolate
C.   Atropine & Edrophonium
D.   Atropine & Physostigmine

Q.24 Toxicology science deals with:

A.   Poisons
B.   For deterction of posion ingested
C.   Diagnosis and treatment of poison
D.   All of these

Q.25 Which of the following may cause the gingival hyperplasia?

A. Minoxidil   **B.** Phenytoin
C. Reserpine   **D.** Warfarin

Q.26 The following is a competitive type of enzyme inhibitor:

A. Acetazolamide   **B.** Disulfiram
C. Physostigmine   **D.** Theophylline

Q.27 Drug transport mechanism includes:

A. Active transport   **B.** Liquid solubility
C. Passive transport   **D.** All of these

Q.28 What we do after using Inhalers?

A.   Clean and dry
B.   Keep as such
C.   May be placed anywhere
D.   Put in the pocket

// Smart Answer Sheet //

Correct — Percentage of students who answered correctly.   **Skipped** — Percentage of students who skipped.

Q.	Ans.	Correct / Skipped	Q.	Ans.	Correct / Skipped	Q.	Ans.	Correct / Skipped	Q.	Ans.	Correct / Skipped	Q.	Ans.	Correct / Skipped	Q.	Ans.	Correct / Skipped
1	A	47.46 % / 40.1 %	6	D	47.74 % / 49.73 %	11	A	68.69 % / 30.94 %	16	B	66.67 % / 31.87 %	21	D	45.71 % / 54.07 %	26	C	56.08 % / 42.14 %
2	B	68.94 % / 30.73 %	7	A	66.5 % / 30.48 %	12	B	48.7 % / 32.34 %	17	A	53.88 % / 35.71 %	22	B	56.8 % / 33.48 %	27	D	66.62 % / 30.69 %
3	D	58.32 % / 40.37 %	8	A	52.01 % / 37.05 %	13	C	51.55 % / 32.85 %	18	B	42.31 % / 47.81 %	23	C	56.5 % / 30.89 %	28	A	61.08 % / 34.88 %
4	C	64.91 % / 34.59 %	9	D	48.43 % / 37.98 %	14	C	42.06 % / 34.18 %	19	C	65.18 % / 32.89 %	24	D	65.9 % / 32.25 %			
5	A	41.46 % / 49.04 %	10	B	57.42 % / 32.18 %	15	A	52.54 % / 33.74 %	20	B	45.74 % / 32.21 %	25	B	42.98 % / 45.3 %			

//Hints and Solutions//

1. Vincristine and vinblastine act by binding with the protein tubulin & arrest at metaphase. The mechanism of vincristine is the inhibition of microtubule dynamics that would cause mitotic arrest and eventual cell death. Unlike the taxanes, which bind poorly to soluble tubulin, vincristine can bind both soluble and microtubule-associated tubulin. Both vincristine and vinblastine bind to the microtubular proteins of the mitotic spindle and prevent cell division during the anaphase of mitosis.

Hence, the correct option is (A).

2. Nimesulide is banned in pediatric formulation because of liver damage. Nimesulide causes liver failure. The government has banned the pediatric use of the common fever and pain drug nimesulide for its adverse effects on the liver, in a much-delayed move. The clinical presentation may vary from abnormal liver enzyme levels with no symptoms to fatal hepatic failure. Therefore, monitoring liver enzymes after initiating therapy with nimesulide seems prudent.

Hence, the correct option is (B).

3. Dapsone is used primarily for the treatment of leprosy. Dapsone is used to treat leprosy (Hansen's disease) and to help control dermatitis herpetiformis, a skin problem. When it is used to treat leprosy, dapsone may be given with one or more other medicines. Dapsone may also be used for other conditions as determined by your doctor.

Hence, the correct option is (D).

4. Allopurinol agents act by inhibiting xanthine oxidase. Allopurinol is a xanthine oxidase (XO) inhibitor that prevents the conversion of hypoxanthine and xanthine to uric acid. It has been widely used since 1963 to treat patients with both symptomatic and asymptomatic hyperuricemia.

Hence, the correct option is (C).

5. Anti-herps antiviral drug is acyclovir. Acyclovir is the antiviral most commonly used to treat herpes simplex virus (HSV) infections. Other oral medications include famciclovir, which is a prodrug that is converted to penciclovir, and valacyclovir, which is a prodrug that is converted to acyclovir.

Hence, the correct option is (A).

6. Ganciclovir is most effective against which viral infection cyomegalo virus. These are particularly important in patients with AIDS or iatrogenic immunosuppression. Ganciclovir is a virostatic agent that prevents viral DNA replication: it is effective in CMV retinitis, colitis and pneumonitis.

Hence, the correct option is (D).

7. Quinidine exerts its action on the heart by inhibiting the Na+ channel. Like all other class I antiarrhythmic agents, quinidine primarily works by blocking the fast inward sodium current (I_{Na}). Quinidine's effect on I_{Na} is known as a use-dependent block. This means at higher heart rates, the block increases, while at lower heart rates, the block decreases.

Hence, the correct option is (A).

8. Plasmodium falciparum malaria is deadly. Plasmodium falciparum is the type of malaria that is most likely to result in severe infections and if not promptly treated, may lead to death. Although malaria can be a deadly disease, illness and death from malaria can usually be prevented. It is responsible for around 50% of all malaria cases. P. falciparum is therefore regarded as the deadliest parasite in humans.

Hence, the correct option is (A).

9. Vasodilation, platelet inhibition and immune regulation are the function of nitric oxide. Nitric oxide is produced by nearly every type of cell in the human body and is one of the most important molecules for blood vessel health. It's a vasodilator, meaning it relaxes the inner muscles of your blood vessels, causing the vessels to widen. In this way, nitric oxide increases blood flow and lowers blood pressure.

Hence, the correct option is (D).

10. The dose of oral digoxin in an adult mg per kg weight is 0.05 to 0.1. Miglitol, also an alpha-glucosidase inhibitor, may impair the oral absorption of digoxin and lead to subtherapeutic serum digoxin concentrations in some patients. In healthy volunteers, coadministration of miglitol 50 mg or 100 mg with digoxin reduced the average plasma concentrations of digoxin by 19% and 28%, respectively. However, in diabetic patients under treatment with digoxin, plasma digoxin concentrations were not altered when coadministered with miglitol. The mechanism of the interaction is not well understood. The manufacturer of digoxin recommends measuring digoxin concentrations prior to initiating acarbose or miglitol. Continue monitoring during concomitant treatment and increase the digoxin dose by 20-40% as necessary. Some experts have recommended that these agents be administered 6 hours after an oral digoxin dose to ensure time for adequate digoxin absorption.

Hence, the correct option is (B).

11. Morphine causes stimulation of the CTZ zone of the medulla. Labyrinth stimulation leads to impulses passing along the vestibular nerve to the central nervous system, where it activates the CTZ to produce emesis. The chemoreceptor trigger zone (CTZ) for emesis, also commonly known as the area postrema (AP), is located within the dorsal surface of the medulla oblongata, on the floor of the fourth ventricle of the brain.

Hence, the correct option is (A).

12. Herps infection is treated with acyclovir. Antiviral medications, such as acyclovir, famciclovir, and valacyclovir, are the most effective medications available for people infected with HSV. These can help to reduce the severity and frequency of symptoms, but cannot cure the infection.

Hence, the correct option is (B).

13. Aspirin has brought down the elevated temperature, prevents platelet aggregation and is used in rheumatoid arthritis except for bringing down the normal temperature. Aspirin is an orally administered non-steroidal anti-inflammatory agent. Acetylsalicylic acid binds to and acetylates serine residues in cyclooxygenases, resulting in decreased synthesis of prostaglandin, platelet aggregation, and inflammation. This agent exhibits analgesic, antipyretic, and anticoagulant properties.

Hence, the correct option is (C).

14. Dinzoxide is antihypertensive acting directly on blood vessels. Diazoxide is an antihypertensive which also acts to keep the K-ATP channel in the "open" state, permitting beta-cell membrane stability and reducing excursions in insulin secretion. Diazoxide is the only medicinal product licensed by the Food and Drug Administration in the United States for the treatment of CHI.

Hence, the correct option is (C).

15. In the function of the heart, systolic arterial blood pressure in the arteries at the time of cardiac systole shows maximum blood pressure. During systole, arterial blood pressure reaches its peak (systolic blood pressure), normally about 90 to 120 mm of mercury in humans. In an electrocardiogram (ECG, or EKG), the beginning of ventricular systole is marked by the deflections of the QRS complex.

Hence, the correct option is (A).

16. Methotrexate is an antimetabolite. Methotrexate is an anti-cancer ("antineoplastic" or "cytotoxic") chemotherapy drug. This medication is classified as an "antimetabolite."Methotrexate is an antimetabolite of the antifolate type. It is thought to affect cancer and rheumatoid arthritis by two different pathways. For cancer, methotrexate competitively inhibits dihydrofolate reductase (DHFR), an enzyme that participates in the tetrahydrofolate synthesis.

Hence, the correct option is (B).

17. Idiosyncrasy is a genetically determined abnormal reaction to drugs. Idiosyncrasy is an imprecise term that has been defined as a genetically determined abnormal response to a drug, but not all idiosyncratic reactions have a pharmacogenetic cause. The term may become obsolete as specific mechanisms of ADRs become known.

Hence, the correct option is (A).

18. Enalapril maleate is a prodrug which when administered orally is hydrolyzed to release the active converting enzyme inhibitor enalaprilat. Enalapril maleate is 60% absorbed and 40% bioavailable as enalaprilat. Both compounds undergo renal excretion without further metabolism. Enalapril is a medicine used to reduce high blood pressure and to prevent or treat heart failure. If you have high blood pressure, taking enalapril will help prevent a future heart attack or stroke.

Hence, the correct option is (B).

19. A substance having affinity but no intrinsic activity is antagonist. Antagonists exhibit affinity for the receptor but do not have intrinsic activity at the receptor. An antagonist that binds to the receptor in a reversible mass-action manner is referred to as a competitive antagonist.

Hence, the correct option is (C).

20. Desflurane is less potent than Sevoflurane (MAC of 6.0). Sevoflurane has a blood gas partition coefficient of 0.65, which is slightly greater than desflurane. The major advantage over desflurane is the better scent. It is considered to be less airway irritation in LMA anesthesia with smooth induction and recovery.

Hence, the correct option is (B).

21. Penicillinase-resistant penicillins: oxacillin, cloxacillin, dicloxacillin, methicillin, and nafcillin. Aminopenicillins: ampicillin and amoxicillin.

Carboxypenicillins: carbenicillin and ticarcillin. Ureidopenicillins: azlocillin, mezlocillin, and pipercillin.

Hence, the correct option is (D).

22. Chloroquine is used to prevent and treat malaria. It is also used to treat liver infections caused by protozoa (extraintestinal amebiasis). Chloroquine is a member of the drug class 4-aminoquinoline. As an antimalarial, it works against the asexual form of the malaria parasite in the stage of its life cycle within the red blood cell.

Hence, the correct option is (B).

23. In reversing neuromuscular blockade, Atropine & Edrophonium is best matched with respect to time of onset. Edrophonium chloride antagonizes the effect of nondepolarizing neuromuscular blocking agents primarily by inhibiting or inactivating acetylcholinesterase. By inactivating the acetylcholinesterase enzyme, acetylcholine is not hydrolyzed as rapidly by acetylcholinesterase and is thereby allowed to accumulate.

Hence, the correct option is (C).

24. Toxicology science deals with poisons, for the detection of poison ingested and the diagnosis and treatment of poison. Toxicology is the study of the adverse effects of chemicals (including drugs) on living systems and the means to prevent or ameliorate such effects. In addition to therapeutic agents, toxicologists examine many environmental agents and chemical compounds that are synthesized by humans or that originate in nature.

Hence, the correct option is (D).

25. Phenytoin may cause gingival hyperplasia. Phenytoin is an anti-epileptic drug, also called an anticonvulsant. Phenytoin works by slowing down impulses in the brain that cause seizures. Phenytoin is used to control seizures. It does not treat all types of seizures, and your doctor will determine if it is the right medicine for you.

Hence, the correct option is (B).

26. Physostigmine is a competitive type of enzyme inhibitor. The inhibition of cholinesterase by physostigmine is competitive. A single molecule of physostigmine or acetylcholine combines with one center of cholinesterase n = 1 and the mechanism n = 2 has been excluded. Combination of physostigmine with cholinesterase is slow at all but large concentrations of inhibitor.

Hence, the correct option is (C).

27. The drug transport mechanism includes active transport, liquid solubility and passive transport. The five groups of drug transports are as follows: Organic ion transporter superfamily.

1. ATP-dependent transporter superfamily.

2. Peptide transporter family.

3. Organic anion transporting polypeptide family originated from the liver.

4. Amino acid-polyamine-choline transporter superfamily.

Hence, the correct option is (D).

28. Inhalers after use clean and dry. If wet or not cleaned, the consistency of the medication can be altered, changing the dose of medication inhaled. If the device is not cleaned, the medicine can build up and clog the device, preventing it from spraying properly. A dry powdered inhaler (DPI) is an asthma treatment option for older kids and teens. Using a dry powdered inhaler allows the medicine to get deep into the lungs. Unlike other inhalers which deliver a puff of medicine, these inhalers hold the medicine as a dry powder.

Hence, the correct option is (A).

Q.1 Amoebiasis is a disease caused by:

A.   House fly

B.   Entamoeba histolytica

C.   Mosquitos

D.   Typhosa salmomella

Q.2 Tablet Nitroglycerin is given through sublingual route in case of:

A.   Hypertension

B.   Hypotension

C.   Angina pectoris

D.   Rheumatic heart disease

Q.3 Pharmacogenetics, the branch of pharmacology deals with:

A. Drugs metabolism   **B.** Genetic variation

C. Tolerance of drug   **D.** None of these

Q.4 Sodium cromoglycate act by:

A.   Broncho relaxation

B.   Anti histaminic action

C.   Mast cell stabilization

D.   By preventing antigen antobody reaction

Q.5 The term bradycardia means:

A. Heart beats slowly   **B.** Heart beats normal

C. Heart beats rapidly   **D.** Murmur

Q.6 The objectives of clinical testing of a new drug are:

A.   To determine efficacy and safety.

B.   To assess optimal conditions for use of drug.

C.   Method of use and route of administration.

D.   All of these

Q.7 Morphine is contraindicated in head injury because:

A.   It increase intracranial pressure

B.   Causes respiratory depression

C.   Mental clouding

D.   All of these

Q.8 First pass effect is seen with which route of administration:

A. Oral route   **B.** Sub lingual

C. Intra muscular   **D.** Intra venous

Q.9 The toxic effect of insulin are:

A.   Cause hypoglycaemia

B.   Loss of consciousness and com

C.   Increase in body weight

D.   All of these

Q.10 In case of Diabetes mellitus,the aim of treatment is:

A.   To correct metabolic disorder (disturbance).

B.   To correct body weight.

C.   To control symptoms with diet, exercise, and drugs.

D.   All of these

Q.11 Antipyretics are drugs (medicine) used:

A.   To lower elevated body temperature.

B.   To lower raised blood pressure.

C.   To relive pain abdomen.

D.   To proudce symptomatic relief from ough.

Q.12 An abnormal condition of the heart, tachycardia is defined as:

A. Normal heartbeat   **B.** Heartbeat rapid

C. Heartbeat slow   **D.** Heartbeat not heard

Q.13 Advantages of injection are:

A.   Rapid response of drug.

B.   Route can be used in unconsciond patients.

C.   Less dose required as compared to oral route.

D.   All of these

Q.14 The effect of drug given through sublingual route is:

A.   Onset action is quick

B.   Overdose can be avoided by spitting tablet

C.   Drug is not destroyed by stomach enzymes

D.   All of these

Q.15 A clinica thermometer is used to measure:

A.   Boiling point of water

B.   Body temperature in human being

C.   Freezing point of water

D.   None of these

Q.16 First pass metabolism occurs in:

A. Liver   **B.** In lungs

C. Intestinal walls   **D.** All of these

Q.17 Doctors always measure blood pressure on arms and not any other part of the body, because:

A.   Patient feel no pain.

B.   Patient feels no shy with naked arms.

C.   Left brachial artery on the arm is perfect point as it is near the heart.

D.   All of these

Q.18 Why does a bread piece taste sweet when it is chewed?

A.   The starch in the bread is converted into maltose, a disaccharide by the action of ptyalin.

B.   Because sugar is added in the bread.

C.   Yeast adced for fermentation makes bread sweet.

D.   Bread becomes sweet during baking.

Q.19 A highly ionised drug:

A.   Is excreted mainly by kindeys.

B.   Crosses the placental barrier easily.

C.   Is well absorbed from the intestine.

D.   Is highly protein bound.

Q.20 Use of sunlight in the treatment of disease is called as:

A. Heliotherapy
B. Hydrotherapy
C. Placebo therapy
D. Radio therapy

Q.21 While administrating of drugs to a female patient which factor is to be kept in mind?

A. Lactation
B. Pregnancy
C. Menstruation
D. All of these

Q.22 Eye drops should be instilled:

A. Into the lower eyelid pouch.
B. Below upper eyelid.
C. Instill drops by closing eyelids.
D. On outer side of eyelids.

Q.23 Amanita muscaria (fly Amanita) is a fungal muscarinic agonist, which is most often associated with which side effect?

A. Tachycardia
B. Bradycardia
C. Euphoria
D. Sedation

Q.24 A patient having obesity requires dose:

A. Normal size
B. Large
C. Reduced
D. None of these

Q.25 The drug out of following is not used in acute asthma:

A. Salbutamol
B. Ipra tropium
C. Hydro cortisone
D. Tinidazole

Q.26 Drug containing two sulfhydryl groups in a molecule is:

A. BAL
B. Endta
C. Penicillamine
D. None of these

Q.27 The name of anticoagulant heparin is named as:

A. It was obtained from liver.
B. It is strongest organic acid present in the body.
C. Do not prevent clotting.
D. Both (A) and (B)

Q.28 A drug addict was caught hold by a narcotic drug addiction department. He was found to have jet black tongue teeth. The individual is likely drug addiction of:

A. Diazepam
B. Charas (Cannabis)
C. Cocaine
D. Heroin

// Smart Answer Sheet //

| Correct | Percentage of students who answered correctly. | Skipped | Percentage of students who skipped. |

Q.	Ans.	Correct / Skipped	Q.	Ans.	Correct / Skipped	Q.	Ans.	Correct / Skipped	Q.	Ans.	Correct / Skipped	Q.	Ans.	Correct / Skipped	Q.	Ans.	Correct / Skipped
1	B	53.56 % / 36.59 %	6	D	62.27 % / 34.64 %	11	A	41.58 % / 46.79 %	16	D	64.78 % / 33.25 %	21	D	40.66 % / 53.05 %	26	A	65.9 % / 32.81 %
2	C	48.03 % / 51.06 %	7	D	58.89 % / 37.19 %	12	B	55.33 % / 32.65 %	17	C	22.18 % / 70.51 %	22	A	43.97 % / 37.95 %	27	D	18.2 % / 69.54 %
3	B	56.86 % / 37.61 %	8	A	59.58 % / 31.27 %	13	D	30.08 % / 68.42 %	18	A	51.22 % / 35.9 %	23	D	32.53 % / 67.26 %	28	C	56.16 % / 37.93 %
4	C	64.44 % / 30.47 %	9	D	65.02 % / 31.28 %	14	A	58.12 % / 30.36 %	19	D	61.85 % / 35.17 %	24	B	62.67 % / 34.37 %			
5	A	61.38 % / 33.34 %	10	D	80.38 % / 17.71 %	15	B	85.93 % / 12.13 %	20	A	65.11 % / 33.94 %	25	D	51.67 % / 47.88 %			

//Hints and Solutions//

1. Amoebiasis is a parasitic infection of the intestines caused by the protozoan entamoeba histolytica, or entamoeba histolytica. The symptoms of amoebiasis include loose stool, abdominal cramping, and stomach pain. However, most people with amoebiasis won't experience significant symptoms. It is often transmitted through contaminated food or water. There may be no symptoms or the severity may range from mild diarrhea to dysentery, an inflammation of the intestine.

Hence, the correct option is (B).

2. Tablet Nitroglycerin is given through a sublingual route in the case of angina pectoris. Glyceryl trinitrate (or nitroglycerin) undergoes extensive hepatic pre-systemic metabolism when given orally, and is therefore usually given by the sublingual route, by which it is well absorbed and rapidly taken up into the circulation.

Hence, the correct option is (C).

3. Pharmacogenetics, the branch of pharmacology deals with genetic variation. Pharmacogenomics is the branch of pharmacology that deals with the influence of genetic variation on drug response in patients by correlating gene expression or single-nucleotide polymorphisms with a drug's efficacy or toxicity.

Hence, the correct option is (B).

4. Sodium cromoglycate act by mast cell stabilization. A chromone complex that acts by inhibiting the release of chemical mediators from sensitized mast cells. It is used in the prophylactic treatment of both allergic and exercise-induced asthma, but does not affect an established asthmatic attack.

Hence, the correct option is (C).

5. The term bradycardia means heart beats slowly. Bradycardia (brad-e-KAHR-dee-uh) is a slower than normal heart rate. The hearts of adults at rest usually beat between 60 and 100 times a minute. If you have bradycardia, your heart beats fewer than 60 times a minute

Hence, the correct option is (A).

6. The objectives of clinical testing of a new drug are to determine efficacy and safety, to assess optimal conditions for use of drug and method of use and route of administration. The main purpose of phase 1 clinical trials is to demonstrate that patients tolerate well the new drug under investigation. The toxicity data (adverse effects) derived from these studies are used to characterize the safety profile of the new medicinal product.

Hence, the correct option is (D).

7. Morphine is contraindicated in head injury because it increases intracranial pressure, causes respiratory depression and mental clouding. The results support the hypothesis that the increase in intracranial pressure produced by morphine is the result of an increase in arterial carbon dioxide tension, with its consequent rise in cerebral blood flow, secondary to a decrease in pulmonary ventilation.

Hence, the correct option is (D).

8. The first pass effect is seen with the oral route of administration. The first-pass metabolism or the first-pass effect or pre-systemic metabolism is the phenomenon that occurs whenever the drug is administered orally, enters the liver, and suffers extensive biotransformation to such an extent that the bioavailability is drastically reduced, thus showing subtherapeutic action.

Hence, the correct option is (A).

9. The toxic effect of insulin is cause hypoglycaemia, loss of consciousness and com and increase in body weight. To correct this problem, you might take insulin or other drugs to lower blood sugar levels. But too much insulin or other diabetes medications may cause your blood sugar level to drop too low, causing hypoglycemia.

Hence, the correct option is (D).

10. In case of Diabetes mellitus,the aim of treatment is to correct metabolic disorder (disturbance), to o correct body weight and to control symptoms with diet, exercise, and drugs. The goal of diabetes management is to keep blood glucose levels as close to normal as safely possible. Since diabetes may greatly increase risk for heart disease and peripheral artery disease, measures to control blood pressure and cholesterol levels are an essential part of diabetes treatment as well.

People with diabetes must take responsibility for their day-to-day care. This includes monitoring blood glucose levels, dietary management, maintaining physical activity, keeping weight and stress under control, monitoring oral medications and, if required, insulin use via injections or pump.

Hence, the correct option is (D).

11. Antipyretics are drugs (medicines) used to lower elevated body temperature. Drugs that are used to reduce body temperature in fever. An analgesic drug used alone or in combination with opioids for pain management, and as an antipyretic agent. A salicylate used to treat pain, fever, inflammation, migraines, and reducing the risk of major adverse cardiovascular events.

Hence, the correct option is (A).

12. An abnormal condition of the heart, tachycardia is defined as heartbeat rapid. In tachycardia, an abnormal electrical impulse starting in the upper or lower chambers of the heart causes the heart to beat faster. Tachycardia is the medical term for a heart rate over 100 beats per minute. There are many heart rhythm disorders (arrhythmias) that can cause tachycardia.

Hence, the correct option is (B).

13. The advantages of injection are:

1. Rapid and uniform absorption of the drug, especially those of the aqueous solutions.

2. Rapid onset of the action compared to that of the oral and the subcutaneous routes.

3. IM injection bypasses the first-pass metabolism.

4. It also avoids the gastric factors governing the drug absorption.

5. Has efficacy and potency comparable to that of the intravenous drug delivery system.

6. Highly efficacious in emergency scenarios such as acute psychosis and status epilepticus.

7. Depot injections allow slow, sustained, and prolonged action.

8. A large volume of the drug can be administered compared to that of the subcutaneous route.

Hence, the correct option is (D).

14. The effect of drug given through sublingual route is onset action is quick. Because of the high permeability and the rich blood supply, the sublingual route is capable of producing a rapid onset of action which makes it an appropriate route for drugs with short delivery period and in frequent dosing regimen. The onset of action also appears comparable with that of oral drugs. The second possible use for SL administration in dentistry is in management of postoperative pain.

Hence, the correct option is (A).

15. A clinical thermometer is used to measure body temperature in human beings. A medical thermometer (also called a clinical thermometer) is used for measuring human or animal body temperature. The tip of the thermometer is inserted into the mouth under the tongue (oral or sub-lingual temperature), under the armpit (axillary temperature), into the rectum via the anus (rectal temperature), into the ear (tympanic temperature), or on the forehead (temporal temperature).

Hence, the correct option is (B).

16. First pass metabolism occurs in the liver and intestinal walls. The first-pass effect can occur in the gastrointestinal tract, the liver, and the lung. Although the liver is the main drug-metabolizing organ in the body, the gut wall can play an important role in the first-pass metabolism of certain drugs. For example, first pass metabolism occurs in the gut for benzylpenicillin and insulin and in the liver for propranolol, lignocaine, chloromethiasole and GTN.

Hence, the correct option is (D).

17. Doctors always measure blood pressure on arms and not any other part of the body, because left brachial artery on the arm is perfect point as it is near the heart. Blood pressure readings between the two arms can be different, and that disparity can sometimes be a warning sign of heart trouble down the road. When taking your blood pressure for the first time, it makes sense to measure the blood pressure in both arms, because it's sometimes high on only one side. The values that are higher are always the ones used for assessing blood pressure. After that it is enough to measure the blood pressure only in the arm that produced the higher reading. A person is considered to have high blood pressure if the systolic value is over 140 mmHg, the diastolic value is over 90 mmHg, or if both are higher than these readings.

Hence, the correct option is (C).

18. A bread piece taste sweet when it is chewed because of the starch in the bread is converted into maltose, a disaccharide by the action of ptyalin. Saliva of mouth contains salivary amylase an enzyme which converts starch into maltose and breaks it into a simpler form which gives a sweet taste. An amylase is an enzyme that catalyses the hydrolysis of starch into sugars. Amylase is present in the saliva of humans and some other mammals, where it begins the chemical process of digestion. So, when a piece of bread is chewed long enough, it begins to taste sweet because the amylase breaks down starches to disaccharides.

Hence, the correct option is (A).

19. A highly ionised drug is highly protein bound. Highly ionized drugs are lipid insoluble. So, they are poorly absorbed by the intestine. They cannot cross the placental barrier easily. And since they are not reabsorbed in the renal tubules, they are excreted in urine. The lower F/M blood concentration ratios of highly protein-bound drugs (e.g. bupivacaine) have been attributed to their more restricted placental transfer compared with less protein-bound drugs (e.g. lidocaine).

Hence, the correct option is (D).

20. Use of sunlight in the treatment of disease is called as heliotherapy. Banana leaf bath (BLB) [a type of heliotherapy (sunbath)] is being used in various diseases like skin diseases, obesity and other metabolic disorders in many naturopathy hospitals in India. However, its precise physiology is less understood. Thus, this study was conducted to evaluate the effect of BLB on heart rate variability (HRV) in healthy individuals. Sunlight (ultraviolet light) is extremely beneficial. Outdoor 4-week heliotherapy promotes significant clearance of symptoms in 84% of subjects.

Hence, the correct option is (A).

21. While administrating of drugs to a female patient lactation, pregnancy and menstruation is to be kept in mind. The most common teratogenic effects are neural tube defects, congenital heart abnormalities, cleft lip or palate, and fetal stillbirth. Conversely, adverse fetal effects result in dysfunction of an organ or tissue after that organ or tissue has been formed. As a pharmacist, being asked to give advice about medication use during pregnancy or lactation can be daunting.

Hence, the correct option is (D).

22. Eye drops should be instilled into the lower eyelid pouch. Eye drop instillation is a instillation of prescribed occular preparation into the eyes. This is a clean procedure where both eyes may require treatment, each eye must be treated separately. Gently pull down the lower eyelid and ask the patient to look upward. Instill prescribed number of drops into center of lower fornix · If additional eye drop ordered wait for 5 minutes between each medication. Be careful that the dropper or ointment tube does not touch the eye.

Hence, the correct option is (A).

23. Amanita muscaria (fly Amanita) is a fungal muscarinic agonist, is most often associated with sedation side effect. Within this genus there are a number of poisonous relatives including the panther (Amanita pantherina), the death cap (Amanita phalloides) and the delightfully termed destroying angel (Amanita verna). Fly agaric has a long history of use as a sedative material and the main psychoactive compounds within these species are thought to be analogues of the neurotransmitter gamma-aminobutyric acid (GABA) and glutamic acid, notably muscimol and ibotenic acid, respectively.

Hence, the correct option is (D).

24. A patient having obesity requires large dose. Some drugs have a licensed dichotomised dose based on total body weight. The maximum daily dose of carvedilol is 50 mg in patients weighing less than 85 kg and 100 mg for patients weighing 85 kg or more. Consequently a patient weighing 86 kg would receive twice the dose of a patient weighing 84 kg. Dichotomised dose strategies can result in under-and overdosing and should be used with caution in patients with obesity. Apixaban, ribavirin and prasugrel have similar dosing recommendations.

Hence, the correct option is (B).

25. The Tinidazole drug is not used in acute asthma. Tinidazole is used to treat infections caused by protozoa (eg, trichomoniasis, giardiasis, and amebiasis). It is also used to treat adult women with vaginal infections (bacterial vaginosis). Tinidazole belongs to the group of medicines called antiprotozoals. Tinidazole is a drug used against protozoan infections. It is widely known throughout Europe and the developing world as a treatment for a variety of anaerobic amoebic and bacterial infections.nitroimidazole antibiotic class.

Hence, the correct option is (D).

26. Drug containing two sulfhydryl groups in a molecule is BAL. Dimercaprol, also called British anti-Lewisite (BAL), is a medication used to treat acute poisoning by arsenic, mercury, gold, and lead. BAL (British anti-lewisite; dimercaprol; 2,3-dimercaptopropanol) is a dithiol chelating agent that is used in the treatment of poisoning by the heavy metals arsenic, mercury, lead, and gold.

Hence, the correct option is (A).

27. The name of anticoagulant heparin is named as it was obtained from liver and it is strongest organic acid present in the body. The heparins are a group of anticoagulants that consist of unfractionated heparin, low molecular weight heparins, and heparinoids. Heparin cofactor I1 (HCII) is produced by the liver. Although a heparin cofactor, it requires 10- fold as much heparin to enhance its ability to inhibit thrombin than is needed by ATIII.

Hence, the correct option is (D).

28. A drug addict was caught hold by a narcotic drug addiction department. He was found to have jet black tongue teeth. The individual is likely drug addiction of cocaine. Cocaine (benzoylmethyl ecgonine) is the psychoactive alkaloid of the coca plant (Erythroxylon coca). Cocaine is the only naturally occurring local anaesthetic. Unlike amphetamines, which structurally resemble dopamine and noradrenaline, cocaine has a similar structure to other synthetic local anaesthetics.

Hence, the correct option is (C).

Q.1 Vapour pressure decreases with:

A. Increase in concentration of the solution.

B. Decrease in solute particles in the solution.

C. Decrease in boiling point.

D. Increase in freezing point.

Q.2 The flocculated suspension follows:

A. Plastic flow
B. Pseudoplastic flow
C. Dialetent flow
D. Newtonian flow

Q.3 The simplest member of organic compounds is:

A. Methanol
B. Methane
C. Formaldehyde
D. Formic acid

Q.4 _________ is not type of co-precipitation.

A. Surface adsorption

B. Occlusion

C. Crystallization

D. Mechanical entrapment

Q.5 Monosaccharides is based on which of the following functional group:

A. Phenol
B. Alcohol
C. Ketoses
D. None of these

Q.6 Which is a genetically modified crop?

A. Bt-cotton
B. Bt-brinjal
C. Golden rice
D. All of these

Q.7 The respiratory chain of bacteria is associated with the

___________.

A. Cytoplasmic membrane

B. Cell wall

C. Cytoplasm

D. Mitochondrial membrane

Q.8 What type of infection resulting in injury (gross loss of pigmentation) to the substantia nigra occured during the infuenza pandemic of 19161920 which lead to the clinical expression of "postencephalitic parkinsonism"?

A. Bacterial meningitis

B. Acute hepatitis

C. Von Economo Encephalitis

D. Sinusitis

Q.9 Blood testis barrier is located at:

A. Capillary endothelium

B. Sertoli sertoli cell junction

C. Fetal blood vessels

D. None of these

Q.10 Which of the following responsibility of community pharmacist is in dispensing area?

A. Reviews all doses missed, reschedule the doses as necessary & signs all drugs not given notices.

B. Supervision of drug administration.

C. Ensures that establishes policies & procedures are followed.

D. Reviewing of each patient's drug administration forms periodically to ensureall doses have been administered.

Q.11 _________ muscles contraction produce dilation of pupils (Mydriasis).

A. Circulatory muscles
B. Spinctor papillae
C. Constrictor papillae
D. Radial muscles

// Smart Answer Sheet //

Correct Percentage of students who answered correctly. **Skipped** Percentage of students who skipped.

Q.	Ans.	Correct / Skipped	Q.	Ans.	Correct / Skipped	Q.	Ans.	Correct / Skipped	Q.	Ans.	Correct / Skipped	Q.	Ans.	Correct / Skipped	Q.	Ans.	Correct / Skipped
1	A	41.64 % / 36.06 %	3	B	42.44 % / 36.56 %	5	C	51.08 % / 46.14 %	7	A	54.13 % / 35.55 %	9	C	53.56 % / 43.2 %	11	D	53.2 % / 40.68 %
2	D	47.07 % / 31.34 %	4	D	65.03 % / 32.85 %	6	D	14.19 % / 70.21 %	8	C	49.04 % / 40.94 %	10	B	65.99 % / 30.41 %			

//Hints and Solutions//

1. Vapour pressure decreases with an increase in the concentration of the solution. Vapor pressure is a colligative property, so the vapor pressure of solutions is directly proportional to the amount of solute present in a solution. When a solute is present in a solvent, the vapor pressure is lowered because fewer solvent molecules are present at the top of the solution. The vapor pressure of a liquid can be measured in a variety of ways.

Hence, the correct option is (A).

2. The flocculated suspension follows newtonian flow. In Newtonian flow, viscosity is a constant of the motion (barring changes due to pressure and temperature) that is unambiguously determined from viscometer measurement. Newton's law of flow states that the application of stress on a liquid leads to flow in direct proportion to the amount of stress applied. The higher the viscosity of a liquid, the greater the shearing stress required to produce a certain rate of shear.

Hence, the correct option is (D).

3. The simplest member of organic compounds is methane. Methane is the simplest member of the alkane family and indeed the simplest of organic compounds, as all other compounds are derived by altering this compound. The simplest Organic compounds are made up of only Carbon and Hydrogen atoms only. Compounds of Carbon and Hydrogen only are called Hydrocarbons. The simplest hydrocarbon is methane, CH_4. This is the simplest member of a series of hydrocarbons.

Hence, the correct option is (B).

4. Mechanical entrapment is not a type of co-precipitation. Mechanical entrapment occurs when crystals lie close together during growth. Here, several crystals grow together and in so doing trap a portion of the solution in a tiny pocket. coprecipitation (CPT) or co-precipitation is the carrying down by a precipitate of substances normally soluble under the conditions employed. Analogously, in medicine, coprecipitation is specifically the precipitation of an unbound "antigen along with an antigen-antibody complex". Coprecipitation is an important topic in chemical analysis, where it can be undesirable, but can also be usefully exploited.

Hence, the correct option is (D).

5. Monosaccharides is based on the ketoses functional group. Monosaccharides are also classified as aldoses or ketoses. Those monosaccharides that contain an aldehyde functional group are called aldoses; those containing a ketone functional group on the second carbon atom are ketoses.

Hence, the correct option is (C).

6. Bt-cotton, bt-brinjal and golden rice are genetically modified crops. Bacillus thurin-giensis (Bt) crops are plants genetically engineered (modified) to contain the endospore (or crystal) toxins of the bacterium, Bt to be resistant to certain insect pests. Golden rice is a genetically modified, biofortified crop. Biofortification increases the nutritional value of crops. Golden rice is genetically modified to produce beta-carotene, which is not normally present in rice.

Hence, the correct option is (D).

7. The respiratory chain of bacteria is associated with the cytoplasmic membrane and that of eukaryotes is present in the mitochondrial membrane. The electron transport chain is also called the Cytochrome oxidase system or as the Respiratory chain. The components of the chain include FMN, Fe–S centers, coenzyme Q, and a series of cytochromes (b, c1, c, and aa3). The bacterial cytoplasmic membrane is a fluid phospholipid bilayer that encloses the bacterial cytoplasm. The cytoplasmic membrane is semipermeable and determines what molecules enter and leave the bacterial cell.

Hence, the correct option is (A).

8. Von Economo Encephalitis infection resulting in injury (gross loss of pigmentation) to the substantia nigra occurred during the influenza pandemic of 19161920 which lead to the clinical expression of "postencephalitic parkinsonism". Postencephalitic parkinsonism (PEP) is currently perceived as having a very close etiologic relat onship with encephalitis lethargica (von Economo's disease [EL]), with PEP developing immediately after the acute phase of EL or at some time later.

Hence, the correct option is (C).

9. The blood-testis barrier is located at fetal blood vessels. The blood-testis barrier, one of the tightest tissue barriers in the mammalian body, divides the seminiferous epithelium into 2 compartments, basal and adluminal. The blood-testis barrier is different from most other tissue barriers in that it is not only comprised of tight junctions. Instead, tight junctions coexist and cofunction with ectoplasmic specializations, desmosomes, and gap junctions to create a unique microenvironment for the completion of meiosis and the subsequent development of spermatids into spermatozoa via spermiogenesis.

Hence, the correct option is (C).

10. The responsibility of the community pharmacist is in dispensing area is the supervision of drug administration. Pharmacists who work in this field are responsible for dispensing medications, quality testing, formulating and re-formulating dosage forms, monitoring and reporting drug safety, and preparing budges for medications.

Hence, the correct option is (B).

11. Radial muscles contraction produce dilation of pupils (Mydriasis). Sympathetic stimulation of the adrenergic receptors causes the contraction of the radial muscle and subsequent dilation of the pupil. Conversely, parasympathetic stimulation causes contraction of the circular muscle and constriction of the pupil. The mechanism of mydriasis depends on the agent being used.

Hence, the correct option is (D).

Q.1 Positive deviation from Raoult's law is observed when:

A. Inter molecular forces of attraction between the two liquids is greater than that be tween individual liquids.

B. Inter molecular forces of attraction between the two liquids is smaller than that between individual liquids.

C. Force of attraction between two liquids is greater than that between individual liquids.

D. The force of attraction between two liquids is smaller than that between individual liquid.

Q.2 Colloidal particles have size from:

A. 0.5 micron to 10 micron

B. 1 nm to 0.5 micron

C. 10 micron to 100 micron

D. 0.1 nm to 1 nm

Q.3 Ethylene is obtained by electrolyzing __________.

A. Potassium formate　　　**B.** Potassium succinate

C. Potassium acetate　　　**D.** Potassium fumarate

Q.4 Oxidation-Reduction titration is also known as:

A. Complexometric titration

B. Gravimetric titration

C. Redox titration

D. Gasometric titration

Q.5 The carbohydrate that is taken as a reference for writing the configuration of others:

A. Dihydroxyacetone　　　**B.** Glyceraldehyde

C. D-Erythrose　　　　　　**D.** D-Xylose

Q.6 PCR technique was invented by:

A. Karry Mullis　　　　　**B.** Boyer

C. Sanger　　　　　　　　**D.** Cohn

Q.7 Glycolysis can occur in __________.

A. Anaerobic cells　　　　**B.** Aerobic cells

C. Both (A) and (B)　　　**D.** None of these

Q.8 Microscopically, what are the changes seen in Parkinson's disease?

A. Loss of pigmentation in the substantia nigra.

B. Residual atrophic nerve cells are seen known as "Hewey Bodies".

C. Pigmented neurons are scarce with small extracellular deposits of melanin, from necrotic neurons.

D. Loss of pigmentation in the locus ceruleus.

Q.9 Which of the following has a very high perfusion rate?

A. Fat and skin　　　　　**B.** Muscle and skin

C. Liver and heart　　　　**D.** All of these

Q.10 Which of the following is verbal communication skill for effective patient counselling?

A. Language　　　　　　　**B.** Proximity

C. Facial expression　　　　　**D.** Eye contact

Q.11 The process of quickly obtaining an out-of-stock medication in an urgent situation is called _________.

A. Emergency drug procurement

B. Bulk compounding log

C. Code cart

D. Final fllter

// Smart Answer Sheet //

| Correct | | Percentage of students who answered correctly. | | Skipped | | Percentage of students who skipped. |

Q.	Ans.	Correct / Skipped	Q.	Ans.	Correct / Skipped	Q.	Ans.	Correct / Skipped	Q.	Ans.	Correct / Skipped	Q.	Ans.	Correct / Skipped	Q.	Ans.	Correct / Skipped
1	D	54.77 % / 36.24 %	3	B	67.04 % / 31.49 %	5	B	52.12 % / 34.13 %	7	C	84.28 % / 13.77 %	9	C	66.29 % / 30.93 %	11	A	48.95 % / 39.65 %
2	D	58.1 % / 31.65 %	4	C	88.56 % / 10.92 %	6	A	67.28 % / 31.36 %	8	C	52.21 % / 36.76 %	10	A	65.48 % / 34.19 %			

//Hints and Solutions//

1. Positive deviation from Raoult's law is observed when the force of attraction between two liquids is smaller than that between individual liquid. Positive deviation from Raoult's law is seen when the observed vapor pressure is greater than expected vapor pressure and it occurs when the A-B attractions are weaker than the average of the intermolecular attractions in the pure constituents of the mixture.

Hence, the correct option is (D).

2. Colloidal particles have sizes from 0.1 nm to 1 nm. A colloid is typically a two-phase system consisting of a continuous phase (the dispersion medium) and dispersed phase (the particles or emulsion droplets). The particle size of the dispersed phase typically ranges from 0.1 nm to 1 nm.

Hence, the correct option is (D).

3. Ethane is obtained by electrolyzing potassium succinate. Potassium succinate undergoes decarboxylation and forms carbon dioxide CO_2 and alkene (ethylene- C_2H_4) at the cathode and potassium hydroxide and hydrogen gas form at the anode. By electrolyzing potassium succinate (the process is generally called Kolbe's electrolysis), ethylene is obtained.

$$K_2C_4H_4O_4 + 2H_2O \xrightarrow{electrolysis} C_2H_4 + 2CO_2 + 2KOH + H_2$$

Hence, the correct option is (B).

4. Oxidation-Reduction titration is also known as redox titration. As with acid-base titrations, a redox titration (also called an oxidation-reduction titration) can accurately determine the concentration of an unknown analyte by measuring it against a standardized titrant.

Hence, the correct option is (C).

5. The carbohydrate that is taken as a reference for writing the configuration of others is glyceraldehyde. A convention of nomenclature, devised in 1906, states that the form of glyceraldehyde whose asymmetrical carbon atom has a hydroxyl group projecting to the right is designated as of the d-configuration; that form, whose asymmetrical carbon atom has a hydroxyl group projecting to the left, is designated as.

Hence, the correct option is (B).

6. PCR technique was invented by Karry Mullis. Clearly, PCR is enormously important for both the scientist and the non-scientist alike. The technique was developed by Kary Mullis in the 1980s, and he received the 1993 Nobel Prize in chemistry as a result. PCR (polymerase chain reaction) is a method used in molecular biology to make millions of physical copies of a specific DNA sequence, for example, a gene. It has several key ingredients: a DNA template to copy, short DNA sequences called "primers", and a master mix containing the rest of the necessary molecules.

Hence, the correct option is (A).

7. Glycolysis does not require the presence of oxygen and therefore can occur in both aerobic and anaerobic cells. In anaerobic cells glucose is degraded into fermentation products and in aerobic cells glucose is degraded into carbon dioxide and water.

Hence, the correct option is (C).

8. Microscopically, the changes seen in Parkinson's disease are pigmented neurons are scarce with small extracellular deposits of melanin, from necrotic neurons. Parkinson's disease (PD) is a neurodegenerative disorder that affects predominately dopamine-producing ("dopaminergic") neurons in a specific area of the brain called substantia nigra. Parkinson's disease is primarily associated with the gradual loss of cells in the substantia nigra of the brain. This area is responsible for the production of dopamine. Dopamine is a chemical messenger that transmits signals between two regions of the brain to coordinate activity.

Hence, the correct option is (C).

9. The liver and heart have a very high perfusion rate. A high perfusion rate is seen in the organs such as lungs, kidneys, adrenals, liver, heart, brain. Moderate perfusion rate is in muscles and skin. Perfusion is measured as the rate at which blood is delivered to tissue, or volume of blood per unit time (blood flow) per unit tissue mass. The normal perfusion index (PI) ranges from 0.02% to 20% showing weak to strong pulse strength.

Hence, the correct option is (C).

10. Language is verbal communication skill for effective patient counselling. Effective communicators draw people out through the frequent use of open-ended questions. Appropriate nonverbal cues are also critical for effective communication. Facial expressions, body posture, gestures, tone of voice and use of eye contact are all forms of nonverbal communication.

Hence, the correct option is (A).

11. The process of quickly obtaining an out-of-stock medication in an urgent situation is called emergency drug procurement. Procurement is defined as a process of acquiring supplies through purchases from the manufacturers, their agents like distributors or from private or public suppliers. Purchasing of medicines starts with the framing of buying policies and ends with receiving, stocking, and payment. Emergency drugs are those which are classified under this category because they are needed immediately, like in the case of cardiac arrest and hypersensitivity.

Hence, the correct option is (A).

Q.1 If a solute is in an associated state then van't Hoff factor is:

A. i = 1   **B.** i > 1   **C.** i = 0   **D.** i < 1

Q.2 The Brownian motion refers to:

A. Zig-zag motion of particles
B. Criss cross motion of particles
C. Settelment of particles
D. All of these

Q.3 The hydrocarbon in which all the 4 valencies of carbon are fully occupied is called as __________.

A. Alkene   **B.** Alkyne
C. Alkane   **D.** Cycloalkane

Q.4 Potentiometry is type of __________ method.

A. Qualitative   **B.** Chromatographic
C. Classical   **D.** Electrochemical

Q.5 If two monosaccharide differ in configuration around a single carbon atom, they are known as:

A. Diclomers   **B.** Bimers
C. Epimers   **D.** None of these

Q.6 The first transgenic plant to be produced is:

A. Brinjal   **B.** Tobacco   **C.** Rice   **D.** Cotton

Q.7 Which of the following enzyme removes the RNA primer with its 5'-nuclease activity?

A. DNA polymerase III
B. RNA polymerase
C. DNA polymerase I
D. DNA polymerase II

Q.8 Blood from GI tract enters the liver through __________.

A. Hepatic vein   **B.** Hepatic artery
C. Portal artery   **D.** Portal vein

Q.9 Which one of the following bond is not generally bind in our body?

A. Hydrogen bond   **B.** Hydrophobic bond
C. Ionic bonds   **D.** Covalent bonds

Q.10 The most specific & sensitive method for assessment of compliance can be used to detect potent therapeutic agent in body fluids is:

A. Drug analysis
B. Interrogation
C. Urine marker
D. Residual Tablet counting

Q.11 In the middle ear, hammer shaped bone is known as __________.

A. Incus   **B.** Malleus
C. Stapes   **D.** Temporal bone

// Smart Answer Sheet //

Correct — Percentage of students who answered correctly.　　**Skipped** — Percentage of students who skipped.

Q.	Ans.	Correct / Skipped	Q.	Ans.	Correct / Skipped	Q.	Ans.	Correct / Skipped	Q.	Ans.	Correct / Skipped	Q.	Ans.	Correct / Skipped	Q.	Ans.	Correct / Skipped
1	D	63.07 % / 31.7 %	3	C	89.14 % / 10.8 %	5	C	68.52 % / 31.41 %	7	C	58.87 % / 36.66 %	9	D	53.06 % / 31.09 %	11	B	80.79 % / 14.17 %
2	A	43.28 % / 37.51 %	4	D	49.16 % / 41.56 %	6	B	65.94 % / 32.24 %	8	D	49.79 % / 43.71 %	10	A	46.05 % / 45.67 %			

//Hints and Solutions//

1. The van't Hoff factor for a solute that associates in solution is i<1 for the association. Since the solute undergoes association, so, the value of the observed colligative property will be less than the calculated one. So, van't Hoff factor will be less than 1. The van't Hoff factor offers insight into the effect of solutes on the colligative properties of solutions. It is denoted by the symbol 'i'. The van't Hoff factor can be defined as the ratio of the concentration of particles formed when a substance is dissolved to the concentration of the substance by mass.

Hence, the correct option is (D).

2. Brownian motion referes to zig-zag motion of particles. This random or zig-zag motion of the colloidal particles in sol is called Brownian motion or Brownian movement. The phenomenon of Brownian motion was observed by Robert Brown in the form of random zig-zag motion of pollen grains suspended in water. This kind of movement is found in all colloidal systems.

Hence, the correct option is (A).

3. The hydrocarbon in which all the 4 valencies of carbon are fully occupied is called alkane. Alkanes, the saturated hydrocarbons are those in which the carbon atoms are bonded covalently to each other (fully occupied). Each carbon atom is tetrahedrally surrounded by H-atoms.

Hence, the correct option is (C).

4. Potentiometry is a type of electrochemical method. In food analysis, the most common electrochemical methods are potentiometric and voltametric. In potentiometric methods, the potential between a reference and an indicator electrode is measured, which corresponds to the analyte activity.

Hence, the correct option is (D).

5. If two monosaccharides differ in configuration around a single carbon atom, they are known as epimers. One of a pair of stereoisomers that differ from a single stereocenter's absolute configuration. If there is only one stereocenter in the molecule, so the epimers are enantiomers. If there are two or more stereocenters in the molecule, so the epimers are diastereomers.

Hence, the correct option is (C).

6. The first transgenic plant to be produced is tobacco. Transgenic crops are disease resistant, pest resistant, environmental change-resistant and etc. The world's first genetically modified crop is the tobacco plant, which was produced in 1982; this plant was antibiotic-resistant. Tobacco is widely used as a model plant system in transgenic research for several reasons: its molecular genetics is well understood, its genomic mapping is almost complete, genetic transformation can be readily achieved, tobacco plants survive well in vitro and under greenhouse conditions, and tobacco produces large.

Hence, the correct option is (B).

7. Escherichia coli DNA polymerase I, the first DNA polymerase to be discovered and also the first to be studied structurally, serves as an important prototype for this family of enzymes. The bacterial DNA polymerase I enzymes are multifunctional, with three distinct enzymatic activities located on three separate structural domains. In addition to the polymerase activity, there is a 3'–5' exonuclease that serves to proofread polymerase errors, and a structure-specific 5' nuclease capable of removing a DNA strand ahead of the site of polymerase addition during synthesis on double-stranded DNA.

Hence, the correct option is (C).

8. Blood from the GI tract enters the liver through the portal vein. There are 2 distinct sources that supply blood to the liver oxygenated blood flows into the liver through the hepatic artery, nutrient-rich blood flows into the liver from the intestines through the hepatic portal vein.

Hence, the correct option is (D).

9. The covalent bond is not generally bound in our body. Covalent bonds are strong bonds. Drugs always bind through weak chemical bonds such as that of the hydrogen bond, hydrophobic bond, ionic bond, and van der Waal's forces. Covalent drugs block protein function by forming a specific bond between the ligand and target protein. A covalent mechanism of action can provide many pharmacological advantages over a reversible mechanism of action; these advantages include enhanced potency, selectivity and prolonged duration of action.

Hence, the correct option is (D).

10. The most specific & sensitive method for assessment of compliance that can be used to detect potent therapeutic agents in body fluids is drug analysis. Based on our review, the best methods for point-of-care drug testing are handheld infrared spectroscopy, Raman spectroscopy, and ion mobility spectrometry; mass spectrometry is the current gold standard in forensic drug analysis.

Hence, the correct option is (A).

11. In the middle ear, hammer-shaped bone is known as malleus. The malleus, or hammer, is a hammer-shaped small bone or ossicle of the middle ear. It connects with the incus and is attached to the inner surface of the eardrum. The word is Latin for 'hammer' or 'mallet'.

Hence, the correct option is (B).

// Notes //

// Notes //